ILLUSTRATIONS

OF

BIBLICAL LITERATURE,

EXHIBITING

THE HISTORY AND FATE

OF

THE SACRED WRITINGS,

FROM THE

EARLIEST PERIOD TO THE PRESENT CENTURY;

INCLUDING

BIOGRAPHICAL NOTICES OF TRANSLATORS, AND OTHER EMINENT BIBLICAL SCHOLARS.

BY REV. JAMES TOWNLEY, D. D

VOLUME I.

New-York:
PUBLISHED BY CARLTON & PHILLIPS,
200 MULBERRY-STREET.
1856.

MEMOIR OF THE AUTHOR.

In offering the present work to the American reader, the editor has thought a brief notice of the author would not be out of place. The following is taken from a Memoir published in the Wesleyan Methodist Magazine:—

James Townley was born of respectable parents in Manchester, May 11th, 1774. His father, Mr. Thomas Townley, was in extensive business. His mother, a very sensible woman, was a regular attendant at the services of the established Church, and an occasional hearer at the evening services in the Methodist chapel.

The care of his education was intrusted for some years to the late Rev. David Simpson, of Macclesfield: after his death he was continued at the school of his curate, where he was instructed in some departments of classical literature, and passed through the usual routine of an English education.

In his twenty-second year Mr. Townley was received on probation as a travelling preacher by the Wesleyan Methodist conference. From this time till the year 1832, when by a failure of health he was compelled to retire, a period of six-and-thirty years, he continued, with uniform consistency and increasing honour, to fulfil his duties as a minister, and to occupy some of the most important offices of the connection to which he belonged.

In addition to the advantages of education, Mr. Townley had received the impulse arising from early literary associations. While in Manchester he had become a member of a Philological Society, originated by the late Dr. Adam Clarke; and, in common with many other young men, was urged, by the example and exhortations of that celebrated scholar, to great diligence in the pursuit of knowledge, the fruits of which were seen throughout his future course. His first publication of note was a volume of "Biblical Anecdotes," which appeared in the year 1814. He had been desired by his children to preach them a sermon on the history of the Holy Scriptures, and on the early translations of them into different languages. As he found that they and others were delighted with the facts he had collected and arranged for their information, he yielded to the further request of his family, and prepared the volume already mentioned.

The work which next proceeded from his pen was one which procured to him considerable celebrity in the literary and religious world

Appearing about seven years after the publication of his "Biblical Anecdotes," it affords striking evidence that he continued his diligent researches into ecclesiastical history and sacred criticism with unabated ardour. It was entitled, "Illustrations of Biblical Literature, exhibiting the History and Fate of the Sacred Writings, from the earliest period to the present century, including notices of translators and other eminent Biblical scholars."

It was no small tribute to its worth, that a review of it, for the Methodist Magazine, was written by one of the most accomplished Biblical scholars of the age. He thus describes it:—"These volumes present a connected view of the history of Biblical translations from the earliest date to the present century, and are enriched by most copious and interesting biographical notices of the most eminent scholars and critics, and such occasional sketches of the history of the manners and superstitions of the darker ages, as may illustrate the advantages to be derived from a more general dissemination of the inspired writings."

On his visit to Ireland, as president of the conference, in the year 1830, he was congratulated by several members of the Dublin University, and the highest encomiums were pronounced on his performance.

The next contribution of Dr. Townley to the literature of his country was a translation into English of the "*More Nevochim* of Maimonides; or, Reasons for the Law of Moses," with prefatory dissertations and appended notes, displaying considerable acquaintance with Jewish learning, and the results of much patient research.

Doctor Townley's last publication was an "Introduction to the critical Study of the Old and New Testaments," imbodying much of that correct and interesting information which his peculiar taste and reading had rendered familiar to him. This volume has been very widely circulated, and is much admired. It is fully worthy of the piety and talents of its author. The book of God was his favourite study, and the productions of his pen chiefly tended to aid those who love to follow him in tracing its interesting history, and are desirous to understand its sacred contents.

At the conference held in Sheffield, July and August, 1829, Dr. Townley was elected to the chair; and thus received the highest honour Methodism confers, and the most decided proof of the confidence and love of his brethren in the ministry.

His sufferings terminated Dec. 12th, 1833, when he died in great peace, and in the full triumph of faith, in the sixtieth year of his age.

The present work was, upon its first appearance, favourably reviewed in several of the best periodicals in Great Britain.

New-York, September, 1842. GEORGE PECK.

PREFACE.

"THE BIBLE," said the immortal Locke, "has GOD for its author; truth, without any mixture of error, for its matter; and salvation for its end." These views are cordially adopted by the author of the following volumes, to whom it has long appeared as an indubitable fact, that mankind are indebted to revelation for all true knowledge of God and divine things. No modification of inert, divisible, and senseless matter, can suggest the idea of one infinite, indivisible, self-existent Spirit, the Creator, and Preserver, and Governor of all things:—the wisest heathen philosophers have acknowledged themselves indebted to tradition for their purest and most sublime notions of the Deity:—and the great sages of antiquity sought information from Eastern sources, by travel or inquiry.

Impressed with these sentiments, the study of the invaluable records of wisdom and grace has formed one of the most interesting and delightful occupations of the present writer; and the more diligently and critically he has examined them, the more fully he has been convinced of their divine origin and inspiration. To trace the successive history, and various fate, of these divine writings, from the promulgation of the law, on Sinai, to the present eventful period, has, for several years, employed the hours which he could spare from the laborious engagements of ministerial duty. The present work is the result of some of those inquiries, and will, it is hoped, supply a desideratum in sacred literature, by offering to the reader a more comprehensive view of the progress of Biblical translations, and of the literary and ecclesiastical history of the Holy Scriptures, than has hitherto been presented to the public.

Numerous bibliographical and historical works, of various merit and popularity, have been published, in which the different versions of the Scriptures, the multiplied editions of them, and their general history, have been expressly considered, or incidentally noticed; but so far as the author is acquainted with them, they are more limited in their objects than the present work. Lewis, Newcome, Johnson, Cruttwell, Gray, and Todd, confine their inquiries to the English translations: Crowe's "Elenchus Scriptorum," a small, but valuable work, now become extremely rare, is in a great measure superseded by more recent publications: the "Bibliotheca Sacra" of Le Long, and of his editors Boerner and Masch, is indispensable to the bibliographer and Biblical student, but is chiefly, though not entirely, restricted to bibliographical notices, and the catalogue of the works of writers on Biblical subjects: the excellent works of De Bure, Clement, Panzer, Dibdin, Peignot, and other similar writers, only notice Biblical publications as connected with bibliography: Adler's "Bibliotheca Biblica," though professedly a catalogue of the editions of the Scriptures in the king of Wurtemberg's library, is interspersed with very brief, but important notes, relative to the editions in that collection: Father Simon's Critical Histories, and other works, are the productions of an original and daring genius, exhibiting extraordinary research, and critical ability; and notwithstanding his occasional aberrations, and the publication of more modern compilations, will always claim the attention of the Biblical student: the works of Korthold, Hottinger, and Sixtus Senensis, though comparatively antiquated, have still their value: Michaelis's "Introduction to the New Testament," translated from the German by Bishop Marsh, and accompanied with his notes, will be duly appreciated by every scholar desirous of a critical acquaintance with the sacred writings, though only those versions and MSS. are noticed in it which serve to illustrate the original text: and Bishop Marsh's controversial treatise, entitled "A History of the Translations which have been made of the Scriptures, from the earliest to the present Age," notwithstanding its brevity, will not detract from the high character of its distinguished author: Thomson and Orme's "Historical Sketch of the Translation and Circulation of the Scriptures," designed to illustrate the principles and importance of Bible societies, comprises, within a small compass, much valuable information, and is highly creditable to the learned secretaries of the Perthshire Bible Society: Horne's "Introduction to the Critical Study of the Bible;" Bishop Marsh's "Course of Lectures on Divinity;" Hamilton's "Introduction to the Hebrew Scriptures;" Whitaker's "Historical and Critical Inquiry into the Interpretation of the Hebrew Scriptures;" and other similar works, though discovering extensive learning, and exceedingly valuable for the purposes of sacred criticism, are too cursory in their observations upon the different versions, to preclude the necessity of a more extensive view of Biblical translations: Archbishop Usher's rare and erudite "Historia Dogmatica de Scripturis et Sacris Vernaculis," published after his decease, with additions, by Dr. Henry Wharton, displays an astonishing acquaintance with ecclesiastical writers of every age and country, and is intended to show that it was the universal practice of the ancient Christians to read and circulate the Holy Scriptures in the vernacular tongues, and consequently consists, almost wholly, of extracts and references: Walch's "Bibliotheca Theologica," though exceedingly important as a work of reference to the theological student, affording a most extensive catalogue of works on divinity and ecclesiastical history, gives little more than the dates, and the names of editors of select editions of the Bible in the original text, or vernacular translations: Dr. Adam Clarke's "General Preface," and "Introduction to the Gospels and Acts of the Apostles," prefixed to his commentary, display the profound learning, and sound judgment, of that eminent Oriental scholar and divine; and will be found particularly useful, the former for the list of the most celebrated Jewish and Christian commentators, and the critical judgment of their respective merits, the latter for the account it contains of the origin of the various readings, the most important Greek MSS., and the ancient versions; they do not, however, preclude the necessity of a more detailed and general history of sacred literature: Calmet's notices of versions, given in his "Dictionnaire de la Bible," are comparatively meagre and incomplete: Butler's "Horæ Biblicæ" is an inestimable little work, comprising a compendious and elegant view of Biblical literature, but principally restricted to the original texts and ancient versions: and finally, the various *Prolegomena* of Walton, Mill, Houbigant, and others, though profoundly learned, are only intended to assist the theologian in his critical inquiries, and therefore cannot supersede the attempt of a work less critical, but more comprehensive and historical.

In 1813, the author published a small volume entitled

"Biblical Anecdotes," which met with a favourable reception, and was noticed in some of the literary journals with peculiar candour and liberality; another edition being called for, the writer conceived he could not more properly mark his grateful sense of the public approbation, than by endeavouring to render his work more perfect, and thereby, as he hoped, more useful to the Biblical scholar, and more worthy of general perusal. This he has attempted in the present "Illustrations," which, from its embracing a range and variety of information inconsistent with the size and object of his former publication, may be considered as a new work, and to which he has, therefore, prefixed a title more appropriate to the diversified nature of the subjects it embraces.

In this work it has been the wish of the writer to present his readers with a connected view of the history of Biblical translations, and of the state of sacred literature, from the earliest date to the commencement of the present century, with "biographical notices of eminent Biblical scholars and critics," and such occasional sketches of the history of the manners and superstitions of the darker ages, as may illustrate the advantages derivable from a more general dissemination of the inspired writings. In such a work, various imperfections will, doubtless, be discovered by many excellent scholars, whose profound learning, and extensive acquaintance with every part of sacred literature and criticism, would have qualified them for undertaking a similar work with peculiar success; the author, nevertheless, is assured, that those who are best able to appreciate the difficulties of the work will be the first to apologize for its defects, and to render justice to its merits. He is, however, free to confess, that had he contemplated the obstacles which presented themselves to the accomplishment of his design, he should scarcely have ventured to undertake it. With hardly a ray to guide him through the untravelled paths of the dark ages of ignorance and superstition, he has turned over many a ponderous tome, hoping to meet with information suited to his subject, and been utterly disappointed. The scantiness of biographical history, the diversity of dates, and the discordant opinions of bibliographers, increased his labour: hours, and sometimes days, have been spent in procuring a biographical notice, fixing a date, ascertaining the author of a version, or reconciling the apparent contradictions of historical details, and, in some cases, without effect. If, after all, his work prove serviceable to the interests of the Christian religion, to which he is infinitely indebted for invaluable consolations and hopes, and receive the approbation of the almighty Head of the church, the author will be more than remunerated for his labours.

It is with feelings of grateful pleasure that the writer acknowledges the aid afforded him by several gentlemen of literary eminence and piety; to several of whom he is personally unknown.

The Rev. Dr. Ebenezer Henderson, with characteristic kindness, not only permitted him to abridge the account of Icelandic versions, given in the appendix to his "Iceland, or the Journal of a Residence in that Island," but, on learning the nature of this work, unsolicitedly requested the committee of the British and Foreign Bible Society to place in his hands a most valuable *Manuscript History of Danish Versions*, written by himself, and presented to the library of that institution;—a request most liberally and promptly granted.

The Rev. W. A. Thomson of Perth, one of the authors

of the excellent "Historical Sketch of the Translation and Circulation of the Scriptures," favoured him with several important communications: and by his friendly and successful application obtained a biographical account of the late pious and Rev. James Stuart, the translator of the Gaelic New Testament, and "Notices," &c., relative to the editions and translations of the Gaelic Scriptures, from Dr. Stuart, of Luss, the translator of the Gaelic Old Testament, and the modest and learned emulator of his father's virtues and studies.

The Rev. John Hughes, the valuable author of "Horæ Britannicæ, or Studies in Ancient British History," supplied nearly the whole account of the editions of the Welsh Bible, and of the translators and editors of that version.

The Rev. Dr. Adam Clarke; the Rev. Thomas Hartwell Horne; W. Yates, Esq., of Manchester; Mr. Jonathan Crowther, jun., of Frodsham; and Mr. T. J. Wood, of Bury, Lancashire, have likewise lent occasional aid, by valuable communications, or friendly counsel, or the loan of rare and expensive books.

The author also records, with peculiar gratification, the prompt and liberal replies to his inquiries, with which he was favoured by the Rev. Dr. Milner, a Catholic prelate of distinguished eminence and learning; and the Rev. C. Plowden, the venerable superior of the Catholic seminary at Stoneyhurst; both of whom, but more especially the latter, manifested a generous solicitude to procure him the information he desired.

But notwithstanding the kindness of his friends, the author must necessarily have been greatly restricted in his opportunities of consulting the works requisite for the completion of his design, but for the advantages afforded by the collegiate library of his native place;

a library which is, in the fullest sense, *public*, and which presents every facility of access and assistance to the student in the prosecution of his inquiries.

In the selection of references to the works consulted, the author has sometimes been influenced by the authority of the works themselves, and, at others, by their being more accessible to the junior student, who may be desirous of pursuing the subject more extensively; but in no case has he referred to a work at the foot of the page, which he has not either personally examined, or acknowledged the authority to which he was indebted. To have increased the number of references would have been easy, but it was deemed unnecessary.

The work is now presented to the public, not without hope that the same indulgent candour which encouraged the minor publication of the writer will be exercised toward the present volumes; and that the severity of criticism will be superseded by the plaudit of approval.

J. TOWNLEY.

Salford, Manchester, March 14*th*, 1821.

ILLUSTRATIONS

OF

BIBLICAL LITERATURE

PART I.

FROM THE GIVING OF THE LAW TO THE BIRTH OF CHRIST.

CHAPTER I.

Introductory Remarks—Giving of the Law—Origin of Alphabetical Characters—Eulogium on Moses—Samaritan Pentateuch—Materials used in Writing—Ancient Manuscripts.

A DIVINE REVELATION is indispensably necessary to man, to instruct him in the nature and perfections of the Deity; to acquaint him with the history of his own creation; to explain to him his moral duties, and to inform him of his future destiny: for without a revelation, the most vigorous mind, the most cultivated understanding must be incapable of apprehending the Infinite, of discovering the origin of man, or of deducing with certainty the acts of devotion and morality most acceptable to Him who "dwelleth in the light which no man can approach unto," 1 Tim. vi, 16.

During the early ages of the world, the extraordinary longevity of mankind rendered a *written* revelation unnecessary. Tradition was sufficient to transmit, with accuracy, the truths which were revealed to the patriarchal families. Adam and Noah were connected together by Methuselah, who lived to see them both; Shem might converse with Noah and Abraham, as Isaac did with Joseph, with whom Amram the father of Moses was contemporary. But, after the years of the life of man had been abridged to threescore and ten, the rapid succession of human generations required another mode of revelation, to prevent the obliteration of the records of the world, and to guard against the corruption of the divine precepts by the frequency of oral communication.*

* Clarke's Bibliographical Miscellany, vol. i, pp. 4–6.

The infinitely wise and gracious God condescended to the necessities of man, and favoured him with a revelation suited to the brevity of his life. The first instance of this kind of revelation was that of the *two tables of stone*, on which the DECALOGUE, or ten commandments, was written with the finger of God. Exod. xxxi, 18.

To this period the origin of writing has been referred by many learned men, and Moses has been considered as instructed in the knowledge of alphabetical characters, by divine revelation. Clemens Alexandrinus informs us, (Stromat, lib. i,) that Eupolemus states it as a correct opinion, "that Moses was the first sophist, or wise-man; and that he first delivered grammar or letters to the Jews, from whom they were received by the Phenicians, and from the Phenicians by the Greeks." And Augustin (De Civit. Dei, lib. xviii, ch. xxxix,) asserts, that "the Hebrew letters began from the law given by Moses." The same opinion has been defended by several modern writers of eminent learning and ability, especially by Gale in "The Court of the Gentiles," pt. i, b. i, ch. x. Hartley in his "Observations on Man," pt. i, ch. iii, prop. 83. The learned author of "Conjectural Observations on the Origin and Progress of Alphabetic Writing;" Winder in his "History of Knowledge," vol. ii, ch. i–iv. Clarke (Dr. A.) in "Remarks on the Origin of Language," inserted in his "Bibliographical Miscellany," vol. i, and "Succession of Sacred Literature," vol. i; and Horne in his "Introduction to the Study of Bibliography," vol. i, pt. i, ch. ii, sec. 1. This opinion has been vigorously opposed by numerous and erudite writers, among whom Astle ranks foremost, for his elaborate defence of the *human* invention of alphabetical characters in his celebrated work on the "Origin and Progress of Writing." The arguments of Mr. Astle were, however, powerfully combated by an able critic in the Monthly Review, (Old Series,) vol. lxxi, p. 271, *et seq.*

The invention of an ALPHABET, or of a limited number of arbitrary signs, which by their varied position should express all the variety of human sentiment and language, seems to be a discovery, of so sublime and complicated a nature, that if not absolutely beyond the possibility of the mental energy of man to elicit, it must necessarily demand the lapse of ages to complete its development, and to advance it to perfection. For the ideas of all the *elements* of language, or the very *beginnings* of every simple unarticulated sound from which these are produced, as lines are generated by the fluxion of a point, "must have previously existed in the mind of the first inventor of a complete alphabet, or it would have been impossible to determine what number of *elemental characters* were requisite, to express the seeming infinite variety of complex sounds in every language upon earth, even in the most ordinary conversation."* But when, it may be inquired, was such a process actually contemplated; what were the various stages of its advancement toward perfection; and at what period was it completed?

It is true the advocates of the mere human origin of letters, refer us to the Egyptian and Mexican hieroglyphics as to the rudiments of alphabets, and assure us that necessity, convenience, or chance would produce abbreviated marks, and ultimately the alphabetic character and system; but in no instance do they show us a nation carrying hieroglyphic signs to their completion in an alphabet. The Egyptians and Mexicans never appear to have deduced letters from the symbolic figures which they were accustomed to describe, but to have continued the use of them with unvaried similarity, through the whole period of their history. The Greeks and other nations, on the contrary, who made use of alphabetical characters, never spoke of them as derived from hieroglyphical delineations, but as the invention of particular persons, or as communicated to them by their gods.

The earliest account we have of the use of alphabetical characters is among the Jews, a people certainly not remarkable for their inventive genius, however venerable in other respects; and the most ancient records in existence are those of Moses, their great legislator. Prior to his day we have no certain proofs of the practice of writing, and the most zealous supporters of the antemosaic origin of letters, can only offer plausible conjectures; but from the period of the giving of the law, the graphic art was in constant use among the Jews wherever dispersed by conquest, persecution, or traffic. It is therefore not an improbable hypothesis, that the knowledge of alphabetical characters was one of the benefits conferred upon the Israelites by the Divine Being, by the instrumentality of Moses, to whom, at least the rudiments were divinely revealed.

The advantages resulting from a knowledge of what has sometimes been called *epistolic* writing, to distinguish it from *symboli-*

* Conjectural Observations on the Origin and Progress of Alphabetic Writing, p. 41. Lond. 1772. 8vo.

The able mathematician Tacquet (*Arithmetical Theor.*, p. 517) calculates that the various combinations of the twenty-four letters of the alphabet, without any repetition, will amount to 620,448,401,733,239,439,360,000.—See Astle on the *Origin and Progress of Writing*, ch. ii, p. 20. Lond. 1803. fol.

cal, or *hieroglyphical*, are so immense, and its practice so peculiarly adapted to the state of the Jewish nation at the time of the Mosaic legislation, as to confirm the opinion that God communicated the knowledge of letters to Moses. "The usefulness of alphabetical characters," says a learned author, "cannot be sufficiently estimated. Without *writing*, the histories of ancient times had never reached us; and the necessary intercourses of friendship and business must have been greatly retarded in general, and in many cases wholly obstructed. Without it, those *living oracles* which teach the science of salvation, and make known the God of truth, could never have existed. When God, therefore, purposed to give a revelation of himself to mankind, is it not reasonable to suppose, that he graciously taught them the use of alphabetical characters, that these divine and interesting records might be handed down from generation to generation?"*

Of the insufficiency of hieroglyphic symbols to preserve and transmit the treasures of wisdom and science to posterity, there is demonstrative proof in the instance of Egypt. "We have remaining at this day," observes Michaelis, "an immense number of Egyptian hieroglyphics, partly on stones, walls, and obelisks, and partly too on copper plates, which have been submitted to all the literary world: but out of them all, no mortal has hitherto elicited one rational sentence, of the length of a single line; although from the work of *Horapollo*, we know many particulars relative to the meaning of the individual characters. The key having been once lost, it is seemingly impossible ever to find it again. The ancient learning of Egypt, which might include many things of supreme importance to mankind, could never have thus irrecoverably perished, had alphabetical characters been inscribed on these monuments. For such characters may always be deciphered; and it is a very singular phenomenon, that, when correct plates of the Palmyrene inscriptions, which several learned men had before attempted unsuccessfully to decipher, were published in "Wood's Ruins of Palmyra," explanations were at once given by two literati, unknown to each other, namely, Mr. Swinton and the Abbé Barthelemy. But the Egyptian hieroglyphics, of which there are extant, not a hundred, but a thousand times as many, as of the Palmyrene monuments, will, I fear, remain undeciphered till the day of judgment."†

* Clarke's Bibliographical Miscellany, vol. i, p. 6. Lond. 1806. 8vo.

† Michaelis' Commentaries on the Laws of Moses, translated by Alex. Smith, D. D., vol. iv, art. 250, p. 58. Lond. 1814. 8vo.

The stones upon which the Egyptians inscribed their hieroglyphic figures, were regarded as objects of idolatrous veneration by the ignorant multitude; and Jablonski (*Pantheon Egypti*, vol. v) has shown, that the Egyptian god *Thoth*, denominated by other nations *Hermes*, or *Mercury*, and who was usually accounted the inventor of all sciences, meant nothing more than stones with hieroglyphic symbols engraven upon them. The symbolic writing of the Egyptians may, therefore, be reasonably supposed to have been one source of the idolatrous worship with which the Israelites were infected at the time of their coming out of Egypt; for even as late as the time of Ezekiel we find an imitation of this species of idolatry common among the Jews, and described in chap. viii, 8--11, of his prophecy.* To stop the progress of this idolatrous attachment to hieroglyphical monuments, the adoption of alphabetic characters was a wise and salutary measure, and from its congeniality with the inhibitory precepts of the Mosaic law, may, with considerable probability, be supposed to have had the same origin, and to have been revealed to the Jewish legislator at the same time.

At what period in the life of Moses the revelation of alphabetic characters was made to him, if we consider them of divine origin, is not possible to decide. The author of "Conjectural Observations on the Origin and Progress of Alphabetic Writing" (pp. 13, 42) supposes it to have occurred upon the first arrival of the Israelites before Horeb, immediately after the first defeat of the Amalekites. Exod. xvii. Dr. A. Clarke, Hartley, Winder, and others fix the time at the giving of the law at Sinai; for "as there is no evidence whatever," say they, "that there was any writing in existence before the giving of the law; and as then, God is said to have written the decalogue with his own finger, Exod. xxxi, 18; and as after this time *writing* is always mentioned, when a suitable occasion offers," that may justly be regarded as the date of the revelation of letters to Moses.

To this latter opinion it has been objected that "alphabetic writing must have been in use before the giving of the law at Sinai, since Moses had been directed before that time to write an account of the battle with Amalek *in a book*, and also to write the names of the children of Israel upon the high priest's breast-plate, like the engravings of a signet." To which it has been replied, "that both these may refer to a picture-writing, or to some improvement of it, whereby entire words were denoted, without being resolved

* Michaelis' Commentaries on the Laws of Moses, translated by Alex. Smith, D. D., vol. iv, pp. 55, 56, 59. Conject. Obser., p. 51.

into their simple sounds. The first might also be a prophetic intimation to Moses, however, not understood by him when it was given, that he should be soon enabled to write in a much more complete manner than he or his enemies, the Egyptians, could at present."* To which may be added, that as the engraving on signets was probably symbolical, the injunction might merely refer to the mode of engraving *in relievo*, or embossing the characters.

It has also been urged against this hypothesis, that the precept by which the Israelites were enjoined to write the words of the law upon the door posts and gates of their houses, (Deut. xi, 20,) presents the idea of a people already well acquainted with the art of writing. To this it is replied, that even if this or any other similar injunction be taken literally, and not, as is more probable, figuratively, for the attention demanded by the divine laws, it must necessarily refer to a period somewhat future, the original copy of the law being laid up in the ark, from which transcripts must be subsequently made. The precept itself evidently refers to the time of their residence in the land of promise, and not to that of their wandering in the desert and living in tents. There would therefore be ample opportunity for certain scribes to learn the art of alphabetic writing, and to acquire a facility in transcription, so that if the great mass of the people had not become acquainted with alphabetic characters before their entrance into Canaan, they might easily be furnished by the scribes with copies of the very small portions of the law, to be enclosed in the *Mezuzoth*, and affixed to their door-posts, or worn in their *phylacteries*. It is even possible, that the rabbinical legends, respecting the explanations of the law, or Mishna given, secretly by Moses, first to Aaron, then to his sons, and afterward to the seventy elders, might originate in the information communicated by the Jewish legislator to certain persons selected for the purpose, and designated to the office of transcription, and graphic instruction.

But whatever may be our opinion as to the precise period of the discovery to Moses, it must be acknowledged, that "if the knowledge of alphabetic writing was not originally communicated by Moses to the Israelites, by whom it was imparted to the nations around them, such is the confusion of historic evidence upon the subject, that we are altogether at a loss to fix even the date of this astonishing, if not divine discovery,—a discovery which, after Providence thought proper to contract the term of human life within

* Hartley's Observations on Man, vol. i, p. 314. See also Winder's Hist. of Knowledge, vol. ii, ch. iv, pp. 32–55.

the narrow boundary of seventy years, became *necessary* to advance the progress of science, as well to enlighten and prepare men's minds for the reception of revealed truths, which had been so generally perverted, as in order to prevent such a perversion of them for the future."

"The supposition that *letters*, properly so called, were not first taught by Moses, leaves us utterly ignorant of the first inventor of them; and all that we are able to trace out from history concerning their invention, amounts to little more than some few plausible *conjectures* in what country they were earliest propagated, while the author of them is entirely unknown: and these conjectures are supported, rather upon our knowledge of what relative height the arts and sciences had attained in some nations above others, than upon any credit that is due to the authority of the most ancient writers in this particular; since whoever shall take the trouble of inquiring into their several pretensions, will find the accounts they have left us to be not only different from each other, but, for the most part, inconsistent in themselves."*

The Hebrew, the Samaritan, the Syriac, to which we may add the Greek alphabets, not to mention any other, seem to have but one author, their respective letters following each other in the same, or nearly the same order, having the same numeral as well as vocal powers, and being called by similar names. Of these, the *Samaritan*† is generally allowed to be the oldest; and the ancient characters of it to be those originally in use among the Hebrews. In it the decalogue probably was inscribed on the tables of stone, and the sacred Name engraven or embossed upon the golden plate of the mitre of the high priest. Exod. xxviii, 36. Profane writers usually distinguished it by calling it *Phenician;* and from it are derived by far the greater part of the alphabets now used in different parts of the globe. By the Jews it was continued in use till the time of Ezra; when the Chaldee or present Hebrew character was adopted, and the former relinquished to the Samaritans, in order, as it is said, to render the separation between them and the Jews more complete.‡

In the early ages certain alphabetic letters had a *numerical* value affixed to them, and were generally used as the signs of numbers, as is occasionally the practice at present. Numerical

* Conjectural Observations, pp. 4, 5.

† See Plate 1.

‡ Walton in Bib. Polyg. Proleg. ii, iii. Hugo, De prima Scrib. Orig., cap. 3, p. 16, ed. Trozii, 1738, 8vo. Astle's Origin and Progress of Writing, ch. iv, p. 51. Lond. 1803. fol. Hamilton's Int. to Heb. Scrip., ch. ii, pp. 32, 38. Conject. Ob. *pass.*

characters are of later date ; and those which have for some centuries prevailed in Europe are certainly Indian. By the Indians they were communicated to the Arabs, from whom they were introduced into Europe by the Moors.*

Nearly contemporaneous with the decalogue was the promulgation of the *ceremonial law ;* which was transcribed by Moses, and, with the other portions of the Pentateuch, delivered to the Israelites before his death, about 1450 years prior to the Christian era; and about 500 preceding the age of Homer, the first and most celebrated of the Greek poets.

The character of the inspired legislator and his writings is admirably appreciated, in the following just and spirited eulogium by a learned commentator :—

" Moses was in every respect a great man ; for every virtue that constitutes genuine nobility was concentred in his mind, and fully displayed in his conduct. He ever conducted himself as a man conscious of his own integrity, and of the guidance and protection of God, under whose orders he constantly acted. He therefore betrays no confusion in his views, nor indecision in his measures : he was ever without anxiety, because he was conscious of the rectitude of his motives, and that the cause which he espoused was the cause of God ; and that *his* power and faithfulness were pledged for his support. His courage and fortitude were unshaken and unconquerable, because his reliance was unremittingly fixed on the unchangeableness of JEHOVAH. He left Egypt, having an eye "to the recompence of reward" in another world ; and never lost sight of this grand object : he was therefore neither discouraged by difficulties, nor elated by prosperity. He, who in Egypt refused to be called the son of Pharaoh's daughter, thereby renouncing the claim he might have had on the Egyptian throne, was never likely to be influenced by *secular* views in the government of the miserable multitudes which he led out of that country. His renunciation of the court of Pharaoh and its advantages, was the amplest proof that he neither sought nor expected honour or emolument in the wilderness, among a people who had scarcely any thing but what they received by immediate miracle from the hand of God."

" His WORKS, we may justly say, have been a kind of *text-book* to almost every writer on *geology*, *geography*, *chronology*, *astronomy*, *natural history*, *ethics*, *jurisprudence*, *political economy*, *theology*, *poetry*, and *criticism*, from his time to the present day. Books, to which the choicest writers and philosophers in pagan

* Astle's Origin and Progress of Writing, ch. vii, p. 186.

antiquity, have been deeply indebted; and which were the text-books to all the prophets;—books from which the flimsy writers against divine revelation have derived their natural religion and all their moral excellence;—books written in all the energy and purity of the incomparable language in which they are composed; and finally, books, which for importance of matter, variety of information, dignity of sentiment, accuracy of facts, impartiality, simplicity, and sublimity of narration, tending to improve and ennoble the intellect, and ameliorate the physical and moral condition of man, have never been equalled, and can only be paralleled by the gospel of the Son of God!"*

The five books of Moses are probably found most perfect in what is called the *Samaritan Pentateuch*, from being written in that character. Several copies of it have at different times been obtained at Nablous and other places in the East, from the descendants of the Cuthites, and others who colonized Samaria, and embraced the Mosaic ritual, after the captivity and dispersion of the ten tribes. 2 Kings, xvii.

Eusebius and Jerome refer to the Samaritan Pentateuch; but from their time, no European appears to have seen it till the beginning of the seventeenth century, when Pietro Della Valle, during his travels, obtained not only a copy of the Samaritan Pentateuch itself, but also a translation of it into the Samaritan language. The latter he took with him to Rome: the former he sent to Harlæus de Sancy, ambassador of France at Constantinople, and afterward bishop of St. Malo, who presented it in 1620 to the library of the Oratory at Paris. Johannes Morinus, a priest, and one of the fathers of that religious house, gave a short account of this Pentateuch in the preface to his edition of the Septuagint, which was printed at Paris in 1628; and defended it also in another work published in 1631; and under his inspection the Samaritan Pentateuch, with its translation into the Samaritan language, was printed in the sixth volume of the Paris Polyglott, in 1632.†

The Samaritan Pentateuch was afterward reprinted by Bishop Walton in the London Polyglott, and collated with other copies, procured from the East by Archbishop Usher, who expended considerable sums annually in the purchase of manuscripts. The person principally employed by the archbishop to purchase Ori-

* Dr. Clarke's Commentary on Deuteronomy.

† Marsh's Course of Lectures on Divinity, sec. 10, p. 86, sec. 9, p. 93, pt. ii. Cambridge, 1810.

ental manuscripts was Mr. Thomas Davis, an English merchant at Aleppo; who, though not a learned man, exerted himself in the most handsome manner to fulfil the orders of his great correspondent, as the following extracts from his letters sufficiently prove.*

"The five books of Moses in the Samaritan character, I have found by meer accident, with the rest of the Old Testament joyned with them; but the mischief is there wants two or three leaves of the beginning of Genesis; and as many in the Psalms."

"I sent a messenger on purpose to Mount Libanus and Tripoly, for the Old Testament in the Syriack tongue, but he returned without it, and brought word that there I might have one after two months. The reason why they sent it not was, they wanted parchment to copy one of the books, and so not being perfect, did not send it. But I pray understand that by the *Syriack* tongue here they mean the *Caldean*. Therefore if your lordship mean and desire to have the Old Testament in *Caldean*, I beseech you to write me, by the first over land, that I may provide it by the next ship; and if your lordship will have me send it at adventures, though it cost dear, (as it will cost £10,) I will do my best endeavour to send it by the first conveyance. *Aleppo, Aug.* 29, 1624."

"I perceive that my letter,—together with the five books of Moses in the Samaritan character,—came in safety to your hands, being very glad it proves so acceptable to your lordship. However, I find myself to have been abused by a Jew, who pretends to have knowledge in that tongue, affirming to me, that it contained all the Old Testament. How they read those books I have inquired, having no better means, of him, who I perceive knows no more, if so much, than their alphabet; and to hear him read the first two verses of Genesis, I could not, because another of those books is not here to be had. The name of God, *Jehovah*, is pronounced by them, as saith he, YEHUEH. And the fift, eight, and sixteen of these letters of their alphabet are pronounced HEI, CHEI, EI; the CH of the eight letter must be pronounced deep in the throat, CHEI."

"I sent to Damascus to see if I could procure the Grammar, Chronicles, and Calender which your lordship desires, but could not obtain any of them, there being but one poor man of the Samaritan race left in Damascus, who is not able to satisfy me in any thing you desire; only he said there were certain books in their language pawned to a great *spahee* of that city, but what they contained the poor fellow knew not. The spahee would not part with

* Parr's Life of Archbishop Usher, p. 35. Lond., 1686, fol.

them under 200 dollars, which is £60 sterling: so I durst not venture upon them, being ignorant of their worth. *Aleppo, 16th of January*, 1625."

In 1670, the Rev. Robert Huntington, afterward bishop of Rapho, in Ireland, was appointed chaplain to the English merchants at Aleppo, at the recommendation of the great Orientalist, Dr. Pocock. He sailed the same year for Smyrna, and from thence proceeded to Aleppo.

Among his friends and correspondents he numbered most of the learned Oriental scholars of the age, who, on a variety of occasions, acknowledged their obligations to him for the valuable MSS. he procured for them, and the very great readiness he discovered to obtain satisfactory answers to their various inquiries. At his request Dr. Pocock translated the principal parts of the English Liturgy into Arabic. This work, as well as the Arabic translations of the Catechism, and of Grotius on the Truth of the Christian Religion, by the same author, and the Turkish Catechism, by Mr. Seaman, he was active in distributing among the Christians, and others in the Turkish dominions.*

During eleven years' residence and travels in the East, he collected, and transmitted to England, many rare and curious manuscripts. Among these were three Greek MSS. of the gospels; one of which he had obtained at Cairo; another of them from a monastery in the Desert of Nitria; and the third at Jerusalem. These, with several other Coptic and Arabico-Coptic MSS. he sent to Dr. Thomas Marshall, the editor of the Anglo-Saxon, and Mœso-Gothic versions of the gospels. In his own possession also was a Greek MS. of the gospels; and another of the Acts, the epistles of St. Paul, the seven catholic, or general epistles, and the Revelation. Both these manuscripts were afterward collated by Dr. Mill, and supposed to be 500 years old.†

But Dr. Huntington is most generally known as the person who engaged the Samaritans at Sichem or Nablous, to send a copy of their Pentateuch, accompanied with a letter explanatory of their tenets and rites, to their *supposed* brethren in England. In this letter expressions were used which conveyed the idea of dissimulation having been practised by Dr. H. in order to obtain the Samaritan Pentateuch. "We give you notice," say they, "you that are our brethren, children of Israel, that R. Huntington, an uncircumcised

* Twell's Life of Dr. Pocock, prefixed to Theological Works, vol. i, *pas.*

† Huntingtoni Epistolæ, à T. Smith, p. 17. Marsh's Michaelis, vol. ii, p. 1, cap. viii, pp. 267, 268.

man, is arrived here from Europe, and has acquainted us, that you are a great people, composed of men pure and holy like ourselves, and that you have sent him to desire of us a copy of the law; to whom we would not give credit, till he had written before us some characters of the holy language, in order to assure you that we have the same Mosaic religion that you profess, and if we had not been willing to oblige you, we should not have sent a copy of the law by the hands of the uncircumcised, for that is a reproach to us. Nevertheless we have committed it to him with two other little books, that we might not absolutely deny your request."*

This charge he repels, in a letter addressed to the celebrated Job Ludolf, in which he communicates so much information respecting the modern Samaritans, that I shall present the readeı with an extract from it. It is dated the "last day of March,' 1690.

"The Samaritans, or rather the remains of the Cuthites, are so few in number, that they are by far the smallest sect in these parts. Even in Sichem, (now Neapolis or Nablous,) the seat of the prefect of that region, and the richest emporium of Palestine, there are scarcely more than twenty families. Pietro Della Valle testifies, that formerly they flourished at Damascus, where they are now become extinct; and though they once inhabited Cairo in considerable numbers, as their letter to Scaliger proves, and their brethren at Sichem still boast of those who reside in Egypt, I could find only one poor old Samaritan and his wife living at Cairo."

"They have but one synagogue, and that nothing more than a small, square, filthy, obscure chamber. In it are kept two copies of the law, written on parchment, and probably about 500 years old. They have also a form of prayer, the book of Joshua, or rather a chronicle under that name; not indeed that which has been praised by Scaliger, which I have never seen, but a brief one from the creation of the world to the time of Mohammed, whom they call the *cursed*. This word, however, they write in the Samaritan character, that the believers in the Alcoran may not understand it. They also possess a shorter and larger commentary on the law. These are in Arabic;—but in their quotations from the law, and in writing the names of their high priests, they make use of the Samaritan characters."

"As to the very ancient copy of the law, of which they boast so

* Fleury's Manners of the Israelites, edited by Adam Clarke, LL.D. pt. iv, ch. viii, pp. 356, 360, 8vo., 3rd. edit., Lond., 1809.

much in all their epistles, as if it had been written by Abisha, the son of Phineas, the son of Eleazar, the son of Aaron, the high priest, the report is altogether erroneous and false. For when I passed through Sichem the second time, I inquired strictly into it; but when I had nearly finished unrolling the book, which they professed to be it, and which was one of those I have already mentioned as being kept in their synagogue, they began to despair of supporting their assertion; but affirmed that those words had formerly existed in their copy, but had been erased by some sacrilegious unknown hand."

"It is true, as has been told you, that many of them are secretaries to the bashaw, or collectors of the customs; an office which they exercise in Joppa, and it is said at Gaza, similar to the Copts in Egypt, and the Jews in the other parts of the Ottoman empire. These are as well clothed as their circumstances will allow, especially the chief collector, Merchib ben Jacob."

"At the time I transacted the business of the tax usually demanded from the Franks,* but from which we were exempted by an order from the vizier of Damascus, I made inquiries of Merchib ben Jacob, and four or five others who were present, respecting their nation, laws, rites, and customs. This solicitude on my part led them in return to ask, whether any Hebrews resided in the country from which I came? I answered in the affirmative, believing them to mean Jews. They then handed me a piece of paper with Samaritan characters upon it; which, when I read, led them instantly to exclaim, 'Ah! doubtless they are our brethren!' I assured them they were usually called Jews; but they still continued to affirm, 'They are indeed Israelites and Hebrews, and our dearest brethren!' For they glory in appropriating to themselves the name of Israelites and Hebrews; hating the Jews, and even their very name, with the most inveterate hatred."

"It cannot therefore be said with truth, that I persuaded them that they had brethren living in England; for I expressly assured them to the contrary. But from their extreme desire to have it so, they were unwilling to believe me, neither could they conjecture how it was possible for me to have learned the Samaritan letters, except from Samaritans themselves. In particular, I never told them that many of them lived among us, nor that they had sent me to Sichem for a copy of their law. This, indeed, I told them, that in order to know who or what those *Hebrews* were, of whom I had

* A name which the Turks, Arabs, Greeks, &c., give to all the people of the western parts of Europe.

spoken, it would be well for them to write out a sufficiently ample history of their religion, especially wherein they differed from the Jews; and at the same time to send them a copy of their law; and in consequence of my speaking thus, one of them, who carried a copy suspended round his neck, took it out of his bosom, and presented it to me. It was written in small characters, and the writing in many places considerably faded."*

This Samaritan Pentateuch was afterward presented by the Rev. Mr. Huntington to Archbishop Marsh. It is Cod. 65 in Kennicott's Collection. The 33rd and 34th chapters of Deuteronomy are supplied in this manuscript, which is in the duodecimo form, by Merchib ben Jacob, before mentioned. It is also probable, that the letter sent by the Samaritans at Sichem, to their *supposed* brethren in England, is still preserved, since Dr. A. Clarke† informs us, that in the year 1790 he met with an epistle in Marsh's library, St. Patrick's, Dublin, neatly written upon paper, in a very legible Samaritan character, directed "To the Congregation of the Children of Israel, the Samaritans, dwelling in the City England."

The latest account of the ancient manuscript examined by Dr. Huntington, is in a letter from Mr. John Usgate to Mr. Swinton, dated from Acre, and received at Oxford in August, 1734. In this letter Mr. Usgate tells him, that he had been at Naplose the preceding February; that several families of the Samaritans then resided there; that they had still their old MS. of the Pentateuch, some passages of which were so effaced as to be scarce legible; and that he had made proposals, and hoped soon to agree with them for the purchase of it; of which he would send Mr. Swinton notice. No such notice was received; the purchase being probably prevented by the unfortunate death of Mr. Usgate, who was afterward cut to pieces by a party of Persians. So that this curious MS. seems to remain still at Nablous.‡ Some curious observations relative to the situation and practices of the Samaritans in the East, at so late a period as 1808, may be found in the Jewish Expositor, vol. i, published in 1816.

An edition of the *Hebræo Samaritan Pentateuch*, with various readings, was published in the Hebrew character, in 1790, in an octavo volume, by the late Dr. Blaney, Hebrew professor at Oxford.

* Huntingtoni Epistolæ. Ep. xxxiii, pp. 47–50.

† Fleury's Manners of the Israelites, pt. 4, ch. 8. p. 363.

‡ Kennicott's Dissert., vol. ii, p. 541.

There also exists an Arabic version of the Samaritan Pentateuch, written in the Samaritan character; but it has never been printed. Some critics have supposed that there was also another version of the Samaritan Pentateuch in Greek; but as no copy of such a version can be found, the fact has been doubted.*

In some parts of the Pentateuch, *transpositions* appear to have taken place, by which the chronological order is interrupted; these have occasioned a discussion respecting the *materials* upon which the autograph of Moses, and the early transcripts of the law, were written. Father Simon, and Dr. A. Clarke suppose, that by being inscribed upon leaves, or portions of bark or papyrus, the facts or transactions which were entered upon them were very liable to be deranged, especially as the separate pieces of Oriental writing are not paged like our printed books, nor have any catch-words or signatures to connect the series.† But Dr. Kennicott conjectures, that many of the first manuscripts were upon skins sewed together; and that these transpositions were occasioned by the skins being separated from each other, and afterward misplaced; and adduces a singular instance of the kind, in a roll preserved in the Bodleian library, at Oxford.‡

Mr. Whiston and M. Toinard have attempted to prove similar transpositions in the New Testament, from the same cause; but have been successfully combated by the Rev. Jeremiah Jones, in his "Vindication of the former part of St. Matthew's Gospel," ch. xiv.§ The following remarks on the different substances upon which ancient writings have been inscribed, and the various modes by which they have been engraved or written, may serve not only to elucidate this subject, but to illustrate many parts of the sacred volumes.

The first writing of which we have any certain knowledge, was, as already observed, that of the decalogue, delivered to Moses on Mount Sinai. This was inscribed on *tables* or *slabs of stone;* which were written or graven on both their sides; hence some rabbins suppose that the letters were cut *through* the tables, so that they might be read on both sides, though on one side they would appear reversed. This could not have been done, if the

* Walton in Bib. Polyg. Proleg., vol. xi, pp. 21, 22. Kennicott's Dissert., vol. ii, pp 540, 541.

† Simon. Hist. Crit. du V. T. L. i, ch. v. Clarke's Com. Numbers ix, 1.

‡ Kennicott's Dissert., vol. ii, pp, 342, 571.

§ Jones' New and Full Method of settling the Canonical Authority of the N. T., vol. iii, Oxford, 1798.

letters were the same with those called *Hebrew* now in common use, because the *close* letters, such as ס *samech* and ם *final mem*, could not be cut through without falling out; but if this ancient character were the same with the Samaritan, this *thorough* cutting might have been quite practicable, as there is not one *close* letter in the whole Samaritan alphabet.*

On the entrance of the Israelites into the land of Canaan, the law was commanded to be engraved on stones, that a genuine exemplar of it might be transmitted even to the latest generation. Deut. xxvii, 1–8. Some suppose, that the writing was to be in *relievo*, and that the spaces between the letters were filled up by the mortar or cement. "This," says Dr. A. Clarke, (comment. *in loc.*,) "is quite a possible case, as the Eastern inscriptions are frequently done in this way. There now is before me a large slab of basal tes, two feet long, by sixteen inches wide, on which there is an inscription in Persian, Arabic, and Tamool: in the two former, the letters are all raised, the surface of the stone being *dug out;* but the Tamool is indented: a kind of reddish paint had been smeared over the letters, to make them more apparent. Two Arabic marbles in the University of Oxford have the inscriptions in *relievo*, like those on the slab of basalt in my possession." We also find in some burial grounds grave stones thus cut in *relievo*. There is one of this kind on the north side of the church yard at Northwich in Cheshire. Michaelis, however, objects to this opinion, and maintains that the law was engraved on these stones *en creux*, or cut into the stones themselves; but his observations are so novel and ingenious, that I shall give them in his own words:— "Moses," says he, "commanded that the stones should be coated over with lime; but this command would have been quite absurd, had his meaning only been, that the laws should be cut through this coating; for after this unnecessary trouble, they could by no means have been thus perpetuated with such certainty, nor have nearly so long resisted the effects of wind and weather, as if at once en graven in the stones themselves. Kennicott, in his Second Disser tation on the printed Hebrew Text, p. 77, supposes that they might have been cut out in black marble, with the letters raised, and the hollow intervals, between the black letters, filled up with a body of white lime, to render them more distinct and conspicuous. But even this would not have been a good plan for eternizing them; because lime cannot long withstand the weather, and

* Clarke's (Dr. A.) commentary on Exodus xxxii, 15.

whenever it began to fall off in any particular place, the raised characters would, by a variety of accidents, to which writing deeply engraved is not liable, soon be injured, and become illegible. No one that wishes to write any thing in stone, that shall descend to the most remote periods of time, will ever think of giving a preference to characters thus in relief. And, besides, Moses, if this was his meaning, has expressed himself very indistinctly; for he says not a word of the colour of stone, on which, however, the whole idea turns."

"I rather suppose, therefore, that Moses acted in this matter with the same view to future ages as is related of Sostratus, the architect of the Pharos, who, while he cut the name of the king of Egypt in the outer coat of lime, took care to engrave his own name secretly in the stone below, in order that it might come to light in after times, when the plaster with the king's name should have fallen off. In like manner, Moses, in my opinion, commanded that his laws should be cut in the stones themselves, and these coated with a thick crust of lime, that the engraving might continue for many ages secure from all the injuries of the weather and atmosphere; and then, when by the decay of its covering it should, after hundreds or thousands of years, first come to light, serve to show to the latest posterity whether they had suffered any change. It is by no means impossible that these stones, if again discovered, might be found still to contain the whole engraved perfectly legible. Probably, however, this discovery, highly desirable though it would be, both to literature and religion, being in the present state of things, and particularly of the Mosaic law, now so long abrogated, not indispensably necessary, is reserved for some future age of the world."*

Similar practices were afterward adopted by other nations; and hard substances, such as stones and metals, were generally made use of for edicts, and matters of public notoriety; hence the celebrated *Laws of the Twelve Tables* among the Romans were so called from being written or engraved on twelve slabs, or tablets of brass, or ivory, or oak; and hung up for public inspection. The laws penal, civil, and ceremonial, among the Greeks, were engraven on triangular tables of brass, which were called *Cyrbes*. Trithemius asserts, that the public monuments of France were anciently inscribed on *silver*.† The Rev. Dr. Claudius Buchanan,

* Michaelis' Commentaries on the Laws of Moses, translated by Alex. Smith, D. D., vol. i, pp. 556–558. Lond. 1814. 8vo.

† Hugo, De prima Scrib. Orig., p. 87.

in 1807, found the Jews in India in possession of several tablets of brass, containing grants of privileges made to their ancestors.* In the *Asiatic Researches*, particularly in vol. ix, art. 10, various notices may be found of ancient grants and inscriptions upon tablets or plates of brass: Gibbon also (Decline and Fall of the Rom. Emp., vol. viii, ch. xliv, pp. 5, 6) remarks, that in the year 1444 seven or eight tables of *brass* were dug up between Cortona and Gubio; part of them inscribed with the Etruscan character; the rest representing the primitive state of the Pelasgic letters and language. And Capt. Percival relates, that when Raja Singa, king of Candy, sent an embassy to the Dutch governor of Pulicat in 1636, the letter with which the ambassador was charged was written in Arabic, on tablets of *gold*. Mountfaucon (Journey through Italy, p. 287) says, that in the palace of Strozzi, at Rome, he saw a book made of *marble*, the leaves of which were cut to a wonderful thinness, so that turning them over, you might see all the several kinds of marble. The ancient Chaldeans stamped or engraved their astronomical observations upon *bricks*; and within a few years considerable quantities of such bricks have been dug up in the vicinity of Hilleh, the real or supposed site of the ancient Babel. Several fac similes of the inscriptions on these bricks are given in the Classical Journal, No. v, p. 127. Diogenes Laertius tells us concerning the Greek philosopher, Cleanthes, that "being poor, and wanting money to buy paper, he was accustomed to write the lectures and discourses of his master Zeno on small *shells*, or bones of oxen. The Koran of Mohammed was recorded at first, by his disciples, on palm-leaves, and the shoulder bones of mutton; and kept in a domestic chest, by one of his wives." (Gibbon, Decline and Fall of Rom. Emp., vol. ix, ch. l, p. 258.)

According to Pliny, (lib. ix, ch. xi,) one of the most ancient methods of writing was, upon the *leaves of the palm-tree*, and afterward, upon the *inner bark of trees*. This mode of writing is still common in the East. In Tanjore, and other parts of India, the palmyra-leaf is used, on which they engrave with an iron style or pen; and so expert are the natives, that they can write fluently what is spoken deliberately. They do not look much at their ollas, or leaves, while writing, the fibre of the leaf serving to guide the pen. The aptitude of the Christian Hindoos, to copy the sermons they hear, is particularly noticed by the Rev. Dr. C. Buchanan, in his "Christian Researches," p. 66, where he observes, that "while the Rev. Dr. John delivered an animated discourse in the

* Percival's Account of Ceylon, ch. i, p. 3.

Tamul tongue, many persons had their ollas in their hands, writing the sermon in Tamul short-hand." Dr. Francis Buchanan, in a valuable essay "On the Religion and Literature of the Burmas," informs us, that "in their more elegant books, the Burmas write on sheets of ivory, or on very fine white palmyra-leaves. The ivory is stained black, and the margins are ornamented with gilding, while the characters are enamelled or gilded. On the palmyra-leaves the characters are in general of black enamel; and the ends of the leaves and margins are painted with flowers in various bright colours. In their more common books, the Burmas, with an iron style, engrave their writing on palmyra-leaves. A hole through both ends of each leaf serves to connect the whole into a volume, by means of two strings, which also pass through the two wooden boards, that serve for binding. In the finer binding of these kinds of books, the boards are lacquered, the edges of the leaves cut smooth and gilded, and the title is written on the upper board; the two cords are, by a knot or jewel, secured at a little distance from the boards, so as to prevent the book from falling to pieces, but sufficiently distant to admit of the upper leaves being turned back, while the lower ones are read. The more elegant books are in general wrapped up in silk cloth, and bound round by a garter, in which the Burmas have the art to weave the title of the book."*

A beautifully written Indian manuscript now lies before me. The characters are minute and neatly executed. They have been written or engraved so as to enter into the substance of the leaf. The ink is black. The whole is composed of seven distinct portions of leaf, each portion being sixteen and a quarter inches in length and one and a quarter in breadth, the lines running parallel to each other from end to end of the leaf. Two holes are made in each leaf about six inches asunder. A string passed through the holes at each end secures the whole; but the leaves being written on both sides must be untied before they can be read.

The Ceylonese sometimes make use of the palm-leaf, and sometimes of a kind of paper, made of bark, but most generally employ the leaf of the talipot-tree. From these leaves, which are of immense size, they cut out slips, from a foot to a foot and a half long, and about a couple of inches broad. These slips are smoothed, and all excrescences pared off with a knife, and are then, without any other preparation, ready to be used. A fine pointed steel pencil, like a bodkin, and set in a wooden or ivory handle, is em-

* Asiatic Researches, vol. vi, p, 306. Lond. 8vo.

ployed to write or rather to engrave their letters, on these talipot slips, which are very thick and tough; and in order to render the writing distinct and permanent, they rub them over with oil mixed with pulverized charcoal. They afterward string several slips together, by a piece of twine passed through them, and attach them to a board in the same way as we file newspapers. In those letters or despatches which were sent by the king of Candy to the Dutch government, the writing was enclosed in leaves of beaten gold, in the shape of a cocoa-tree leaf. This was rolled up in a cover richly ornamented, and almost hid in a profusion of pearls and other precious stones. The whole was enclosed in a box of silver or ivory, which was sealed with the king's great seal.*

Diodorus Siculus (lib. ii, p. 84) affirms, that the Persians of old wrote all their records on *skins;* and Herodotus, who flourished more than five hundred and fifty years before the Christian era, informs us, (lib. v,) that sheep skins and goat skins were made use of in writing by the ancient Ionians. Mr. Yeates even thinks it exceedingly probable that the very autograph of the law, written by the hand of Moses, was upon prepared skins.† In Exodus xxvi, 14, we read that *rams' skins, dyed red,* made part of the covering for the tabernacle; and it is a singular circumstance, that in the year 1806, Dr. Claudius Buchanan obtained from one of the synagogues of the Black Jews,‡ in the interior of Malayala in India, a very ancient manuscript roll, containing the major part of the Hebrew Scriptures, written upon *goats' skins,* mostly *dyed red;* and the Cabul Jews, who travel annually into the interior of China, remarked, that in some synagogues the law is still found written on a roll of *leather;* not on vellum, but on a soft, flexible leather, made of *goats' skins,* and *dyed red.* Of the six synagogue copies of the Pentateuch in rolls, which are all at present known in England, exclusive of those in the possession of the Jews, five are upon *skins* or *leather,* and the other upon vellum. One of these is in the Collegiate library at Manchester, and has never been collated. It is written upon *Basil,* or *brown African skins,* and measures in length one hundred and six feet, and is about twenty inches in breadth. The letters are black and well preserved, and the whole text is without points, accents, or marginal additions.§

* Percival's Account of Ceylon, ch. viii, pp. 205, 206.

† Yeates's Collation of an Indian Copy of the Heb. Pen., p. 2. 4to. 1812.

‡ The *Black Jews* are those who have been settled in India from time immemorial, and assimilated in colour to the Hindoos. The *White Jews* are of later settlement. (See Buchanan's "Christian Researches.")

§ See Yeates's Collation, p. 11.

The *skins of fishes* were also sometimes employed for writing upon; and Zonoras (Annal., lib. iii) relates, that the Iliad and Odyssey of Homer were written upon the *intestines of a serpent*, in characters of gold, forming a roll one hundred feet in length. This singular work is said to have been consumed in the dreadful fire which happened at Constantinople, in the fifth century, and destroyed nearly the whole city, together with the library, containing 20,000 volumes.*

From Job xix, 24, it appears to have been usual in his day to write or engrave upon plates of *lead*, which might easily be done with a *pen*, or *graver*, or *style of iron*, or other hard metal. Mountfaucon (Antiq. Expliquee, tom. ii, p. 378) assures us, that in 1699 he bought at Rome a book entirely of lead, about four inches long, by three inches wide. Not only the two pieces which formed the cover, but also all the leaves, in number six, the stick inserted into the rings which held the leaves together, the hinges, and the nails, were all of lead, without exception. It contained Egyptian Gnostic figures, and unintelligible writing.†

The "Works and Days" of Hesiod are also said to have been inscribed on *a leaden table*, carefully preserved in the Temple of the Muses, which, when shown to Pausanias, was almost entirely corroded, through age. According to Pliny the public documents were written in leaden volumes, after the use of the *pugillares*, or wooden tablets, had been laid aside. Thin plates of lead, reduced to a very great degree of tenuity by the mallet, were occasionally used, particularly for epistolary correspondence. Æneas Poliorceticus tells us, that they were beaten with a hammer, until they were rendered very thin and pliable; that they were sometimes sewed up between the soles of the shoes; that even the messenger who carried them was ignorant of the circumstance; and that while he slept, the correspondent to whom they were addressed unsewed the shoes, read the letters, replaced others, and thus carried on a secret intercourse without suspicion.‡

It was also an ancient practice to write upon thin smooth planks or *tables of wood*. Pliny says that table-books of wood were in use before the time of Homer. The Chinese, before the invention of paper, engraved with an iron tool upon thin boards, or upon bamboo; and in the Sloanian library at Oxford are six specimens of

* Mabillon De Re. Diplomat., l. 1, p. 31.

† Fragments, by the editor of Calmet's Dict., No. 74.

‡ Drummond's Herculanensia, Diss. 7, pp. 99, 100. Lond. 4to. 1810.

Kufic or ancient Arabic writing, on boards about two feet in length, and six inches in depth.*

The original manner of writing among the ancient Britons was by cutting the letters with a knife upon sticks, which were most commonly squared, and sometimes formed into three sides; consequently a single stick contained either four or three lines. (See Ezek. xxxvii, 16.) Several sticks, with writing upon them, were put together, forming a kind of frame, which was called *peithynen* or elucidator, and was so constructed, that each stick might be turned for the facility of reading, the end of each running out alternately on both sides of the frame.† A continuation of this mode of writing may be found in the *Runic*, or log almanacks of the northern states of Europe, in which the engraving on square pieces of wood has been continued to the present time. A late writer informs us, the Boors of Œsel, an island of the Baltic Sea, at the entrance of the Gulf of Livonia, continue the practice of making these rude calendars for themselves; and that they are in use likewise in the isles of Ruhn and Mohn.‡ Two curious specimens of the Runic almanacks are in the collegiate library at Manchester.

Bishop Nicolson, in his "English Historical Library," (2nd edit. fol. pt. i, p. 52,) remarks—"The Danes (as all other ancient people of the world) registered their more considerable transactions upon rocks, or on parts of them, hewn into various shapes and figures. On these they engraved such inscriptions as were proper for their heathen altars, triumphal arches, sepulchral monuments, and genealogical histories of their ancestors. Their writings of less concern (as letters, almanacks, &c.) were engraven upon wood: and because *beech* was most plentiful in Denmark, (though fir and oak be so in Norway and Sweden,) and most commonly employed in these services, from the word *bog*, which in their language is the name of that sort of wood, they and all other northern nations have the name of *book*. The poorer sort used *bark*; and the *horns* of reindeer and elks were often finely polished, and shaped into books of several leaves. Many of their old calendars are likewise upon *bones* of beasts and fishes: but the inscriptions on tapestry, bells, parchment, and paper, are of later use."

* Astle's Origin and Progress of Writing, ch. viii, p. 201.

† Davie's Celtic Researches, p. 271. Fry's Pantographia, pp. 304, 307. See Frontispiece, fig. 1.

‡ Gent. Mag., vol. lxxxii, pt. i, p. 625, where there is a fac simile of the Œsel almanack.

A singular custom still prevails at Pamber, near Basingstoke, in Hampshire. The court-leet, holden annually for that manor, is opened *sub dio*, in a small piece of ground called Lady Mead, which belongs to the tithing man for the year. Thence an adjournment is made to a neighbouring public house. The proceedings of the court are recorded on a *piece of wood*, called a *tally*, about three feet long, and an inch and a half square, furnished every year by the steward. One of these singular records was some time ago produced in evidence in a law-suit at Winchester.* The mode of keeping accounts by tallies, or cleft pieces of wood, in which the notches are cut on one piece conformably to the other, one part being kept by the creditor, the other by the debtor, is still practised in many parts of England, in particular cases. A tally continues to be given by the exchequer to those who pay money there upon loan; hence the origin of the *teller*, or tally writer of the exchequer; and also of the phrase *to tally*, to fit, to suit, or answer exactly.

The Scythians also conveyed their ideas by marking, or cutting, certain figures and a variety of lines upon splinters or billets of wood; and among the Lacedemonians, the *scytale laconica* was a little round staff, which they made use of to write their secret letters. In the Apocrypha (2 Esd. xiv, 24, 37, 44) we read of a considerable number, that is, two hundred and four books being made of *box-wood*, and written upon in the open field by certain swift writers. Aulus Gellius (lib. ii, ch. xii) says that the ancient laws of Solon, preserved at Athens, were cut in tablets of wood, and denominated *axones*. These were quadrangular, and so contrived as to turn on axes, and to present their contents on all sides to the eyes of the passengers. The laws on these wooden tables, as well as those on stone, were inscribed after the manner called *boustrophedon*, that is, the first line beginning from right to left, or from left to right, and the second in an opposite direction, as ploughmen trace their furrows; as in the following words, copied from an inscription on a marble, in the national museum at Paris:—

ΝΕΚΕΘΕΝΑΜ ΣΟΛΛΥ
ΑΡΙΣΤΟΚΙΔΕΣ ΝΟΕΣΕΝ

(em decalp sullyH"
(Aristocydes made me."

A somewhat similar mode of writing obtained among the ancient Irish, by whom it was denominated *cionn fa eite*.

* Gent. Mag., vol. lxxx, pt. i, p. 308.

The boustrophedon writing is said to have been disused by the Greeks, about four hundred and fifty-seven years before the Christian era, but was in use among the Irish at a much later period.*

It is highly probable also, that several of the prophets wrote upon tablets of *wood*, or some similar substance. (See Isaiah xxx, 8; Habakkuk ii, 2.) Zecharias, the father of John the Baptist, when required to name his son, "asked for a writing-table, and wrote, saying, His name is John," Luke i, 63. These table-books the Romans denominated *pugillares*. Smaller tablets were also frequently in use, made of wood cut into thin slices, and finely planed and polished.† In the year 485, during the reign of the emperor Zeno, the remains of St. Barnabas are said to have been found near Salamis, with a copy of the gospel of St. Matthew in Hebrew, laid upon his breast, written with his own hand, upon leaves of thyine-wood, a kind of wood particularly odoriferous and valuable. (Suid. Lex. v, Θυινα.) Tablets of this kind were generally covered with wax, sometimes also with chalk or plaster; and written upon with styles or bodkins. In epistolary correspondence, they were tied together with thread, and the seal put upon the knot. These tablets, when collected and fastened together, composed a book, called *codex* or *caudex*, that is, a trunk, from its resemblance to the trunk of a tree, sawed into planks; but when they consisted of only *two* leaves, they were termed *libri diptychi*.

Waxen tablets continued to be occasionally used till a very late period. Du Cange cites the following lines from a French metrical romance, written about A. D. 1376.‡

Les uns se prennent à ecrire,
Des greffes en tables de cire;
Les autres suivent la coustume
De former lettres à la plume.

Some with the antiquated style,
  On waxen tablets promptly write;
Others, with finer pen, the while
  Form letters lovelier to the sight.

There are many ample and authentic records of the royal household of France, of the thirteenth and fourteenth centuries, still pre-

* Astle's Origin and Progress of Writing, ch. v, p. 68. Vallancey's Antiquity of the Irish Language, p. 55, Dublin, 1772. 8vo.

† Horne's Introduction to Bibliography, vol. i, pp. 35–38. Astle's Origin and Progress of Writing, ch. viii, p. 200.

‡ Du Cange, v, *Graphium*.

served, written on *waxen tablets*. In the religious houses in France, they were constantly kept for temporary notation; and for registering the capitular acts of the monasteries. Specimens of wooden tables, filled up with wax, and constructed in the fourteenth century, were formerly preserved in several of the monastic libraries. Some of these contained the household expences of the sovereigns, &c., and consisted of as many as twenty pages, formed into a book by means of parchment bands glued to the backs of the leaves. One remaining in the abbey of St. Germaine des-prez at Paris, recorded the expences of Philip le Bel, during a journey that he made in the year 1307, on a visit to Pope Clement V.; a single leaf of this table-book is exhibited in the *Nouveau traité de diplomatique*, tom. i, p. 468. Among the monks of St. Victor of Paris, where the rule of silence was rigorously observed, certain signs were enjoined to prevent the necessity of speaking; Du Cange (v. *Signa*) notices many of them, and among others, those by which they asked for the style and tablet. In an account-roll of Winchester College for the year 1395, there is an article of disbursement, for a tablet covered with *green wax*, to be kept in the chapel, for noting down with a style the respective courses of duty alternately assigned to the officers of the choir. Shakspeare alludes to this mode of writing, in his "Timon of Athens:"

————"My free drift
Halts not particularly, but moves itself
In *a wide sea of wax*."

Even so late as A. D. 1718, several of the collegiate bodies in France, especially the chapter of the cathedral of Rouen, retained these tablets, for the purpose of marking the successive rotation of the ministers of the choir.

Tables, or table-books, were sometimes made of *slate*, in the form of a small portable book with leaves and clasps. Such a one is engraved in Gesner's treatise *De rerum fossilium figuris*, &c. Tigur. 1565, 12mo., and copied by Douce in his "Illustrations of Shakspeare," vol. ii, p. 227. The learned author thus describes it: *Pugillaris é laminis saxi nigri fissilis, cum stylo ex eodem.* "A table-book made of thin plates of black stone, with a style of the same material."*

By a law among the Romans, the edicts of the senate were directed to be written on tablets of *ivory*, thence denominated *libri elephantini*. And Pliny (lib. viii, ch. iii) says, that from want of

* Warton's Hist: of Eng. Poetry, vol. iii, p. 151, note (k.) Douce's Illustrations of Shakspeare, vol. ii, pp. 227–229.

the *teeth* of the elephant, which are alone of ivory, they had lately begun to saw the *bones* of that animal.*

Dr. Shaw (*Travels*, p. 194) informs us, that in Barbary the children who are sent to school write on a smooth thin board, slightly daubed over with whiting, which may be wiped off or renewed at pleasure, and thus learn to read, to write, and get their lessons by heart, all at the same time. The Copts, who are employed by the great men of Egypt in keeping their accounts, &c., make use of a sort of pasteboard for that purpose, from which the writing is occasionally wiped off with a wet sponge.† References to a similar mode of writing are frequent in Scripture: see particularly Numbers v, 23; Nehemiah xiii, 14, *et al.* In India it has been the practice from time immemorial to teach children to read by writing in sand; and from thence are derived some parts of the present Madras and Lancasterian systems of instruction, practised by the Rev. Dr. Bell and Mr. Lancaster.

The old Egyptians used to write on *linen* things which they designed should last. There is a piece of writing of this kind now in the British Museum, which was taken out of an Egyptian mummy; and a similar book was found in a mummy by Mr. Denon, an engraved fac simile of which may be found in his Travels.‡ Livy (lib. iv, ch. vii) makes mention of linen books, as containing information not to be found in public documents. We find also from Vopiscus, that the emperor Aurelian wrote his journal or diary in linen books.§ Suidas (Lex. v, Πεπλος) reports, that at Athens, they wrote upon the *peplus*, or robe of Minerva, the names of their chief warriors. Silk also was frequently made use of in works of value. In the Harleian library, in the British Museum, there is a very valuable Greek MS. of the *Geoponics*, written on *silken leaves*, toward the close of the twelfth century. Montfaucon mentions many works written on silk, which are preserved in different libraries in Italy, executed chiefly in the thirteenth and fourteenth centuries. In the Chigian library, at Rome, there is a MS. on silk, containing all the prophets, with some things struck out; and asterisks or stars, and some Hexapla readings, that is, of the six different translations, in the margin. In the library of St. Mary, at Florence, is the whole New Testament on silk, with the liturgy,

* Drummond's Herculanensia, p. 105. Astle's Origin and Progress of Writing, *ubi sup.*

† Harmer's Observations, by Dr. A. Clarke, vol. iii, p. 127.

‡ Clarke's Harmer's Observations, vol. iii, p. 132.

§ Herculanensia, p. 107.

and short martyrology: at the end of it there is written in Greek, "By the hand of the sinner and most unworthy Mark; in the year of the world 6840, (that is, of CHRIST 1332,) Monday, December the 22nd;" and on the next page are several Greek alphabets.* In the south of India they have a kind of book, called *cudduttum*, or *curruttum*. It is thus composed: A slip of cotton cloth, from eight inches to one foot in breadth, and from twelve to eighteen feet in length, is skilfully covered with a compost of paste and powdered charcoal, which, when completely dried, is divided into equal parts by folding. To the two end-folds are fixed ornamented plates of wood, painted and varnished, resembling the sides of a book. It opens at either side, and when unfolded, draws out to the full length; and is preserved by being kept in a case of silk, or cotton; or else by being tied with a tape, or riband. The writing on it may be compared to that done on a slate, as the marks made by the pencil may be rubbed out, and renewed at pleasure.†

The *bark of trees* is another material which has been employed in every age and quarter of the globe; and was called *xylochartion* by the Greeks. Before the use of the papyrus became general, the *bark of the philyra*, a species of the linden-tree, was frequently made use of for writing upon; and books written on it existed in the third century. The *bark of oak* was also used for the same purpose. Hence the Latins called a book, *liber*, which signifies the *inner bark* of a tree; and the Greeks used the word φλοιος, (phloios,) which also means *bark*.‡

The use of bark for this purpose still prevails in some parts of Asia; thus the sacred books of the Burmans are sometimes composed of thin stripes of bamboo, delicately plaited, and varnished over in such a manner as to form a smooth and hard surface upon a leaf of any dimensions; this surface is afterward gilt, and the sacred letters are traced upon it in black and shining japan; the margin is illuminated by wreaths and figures of gold on a red, green, or black ground.§ The Battas also, one of the nations who inhabit the island of Sumatra, form their books of the inner bark of a certain tree: one of which, in the Batta character, is in the Sloanian library, (No. 4726,) written in perpendicular columns, on a long piece of bark, folded up so as to represent a book.‖

* Montfaucon's Travels through Italy, ch. xvii, p. 272; ch. xxv, p. 412.

† Gentleman's Magazine, vol. lxxxi, pt. i, p. 147. ‡ Herculanensia, p. 106.

§ Horne's Introduction of Bibliography, vol. i, p. 42.

‖ Horne's Introduction, &c., *ubi sup.*

Of the several kinds of PAPER, used at different periods, and manufactured from various materials, the *Egyptian* is unquestiona bly the most ancient. The exact date of its discovery is unknown; and even the place where it was first made is matter of dispute According to Isidore, it was first made at Memphis; and accord ing to others in Seide, or Upper Egypt. It was manufactured from the inner films of the *papyrus* or *biblos*, a sort of flag, or bulrush, growing in the marshes of Egypt.* The outer skin being taken off, there are next, several films or inner skins, one within another. These, when separated from the stalk, were laid on a table, and moistened with the glutinous waters of the Nile. They were afterward pressed together, and dried in the sun. From this papyrus it is, that what we now make use of to write upon hath also the name of *papyr* or paper; though of quite another nature from the ancient *papyrus*. Bruce, the well-known Abyssinian traveller, had in his possession a large and very perfect manuscript on papyrus, which had been dug up at Thebes, and which he believed to be the only perfect one known. "The boards," or covers for binding the leaves, "are," says he, "of papyrus root, covered first with the coarse pieces of the paper; and then with leather, in the same manner as it would be done now. It is a book one would call a small folio, rather than by any other name. The letters are strong, deep, black, and apparently written with a reed, as is practised by the Egyptians and Abyssinians still. It is written on both sides. I gave Dr. Woide leave to translate it, at Lord North's request: it is a Gnostic book, full of their dreams."† The form of the book in Mr. Bruce's possession appears to be different from that in general use among the ancient Egyptians, for Pliny (lib. xiii, ch. xxiii) affirms, that the books made of papyrus were usually *rolled up*; and that every such roll consisted of an indefinite number of sheets, which were fastened together by glue, care being taken always to place the best sheet of papyrus first, that which was next in superiority second, and so in gradation to the last, which was the worst sheet in the roll. This practice is confirmed by an ancient Egyptian MS. taken from a mummy at Thebes, and preserved in the British Museum, which, before it was expanded in the manner in which it is now seen, was closely rolled up; and which, if held up to the light, will be perceived to have the first sheet composed of a much finer piece of papyrus, than any of the succeeding sheets. Manuscripts of this kind are by far the most ancient manuscripts which have reached our times.

* See Frontispiece. † Bruce's Travels, vol. vii, p. 117, *et seq.* 8vo. edit.

The few which have been found, have been observed to lie close to the embalmed figure, underneath the resin and bandages, which have been employed to envelop the body. The mummies of distinguished persons are said to be seldom without one of these rolls; and no mummy has been known to contain more than two.*

Many manuscripts written upon papyrus have been found in the ruins of Herculaneum, which was destroyed by an eruption of Vesuvius, A. D. 79. The manuscripts thus obtained are completely calcined, though by incredible labour and patience fragments of some of them have been unrolled and copied.

Paper made of *bark* is said to have been anciently used for the imperial protocols, in order to render the forging of false diplomas more difficult. Montfaucon notices a diploma, or charter, written on bark, in the Longobardic character, about the beginning of the eighth century, preserved in the library of Antony Capello, a senator of Florence. It is a judgment given at Reate, about guardianship. The parties contending are either Goths, or, as is more likely, Lombards; the judges are Romans. It is remarkable, that the date was orginally inserted in it; but has been defaced by a mouse gnawing it, as it lay rolled up: it is, however, one of the first charters in which the Christian computation has been used.† The Chinese generally make their paper from the bark of the bamboo, and other trees; but occasionally manufacture it from other substances, as hemp, wheat, or rice straw, the cocoons of silk-worms, and even old paper. The Rev. Robert Morrison, an English Protestant missionary in China, sent out by the London Missionary Society in 1810, has translated into the Chinese language several portions of the Old and New Testament, some of which, beautifully printed on paper of Chinese manufacture, have been transmitted to England.

The Japanese make an exceedingly strong paper from the *morus papyrifera sativa*, or true paper-tree, by the Japanese called *kaadsit*. Several other Eastern nations employ bark also in the manufacture of paper.

A kind of paper has also been lately made of the *shavings of leather*. A sheet of it now lies before me, of a reddish yellow, or orange colour: it is exceedingly tough, and will bear ink, but is rather greasy to the pen.

According to Montfaucon, *charta bombycina*, or *cotton paper*,

* Beloe's Anecdotes of Literature, vol. i, pp. 54–57, Lond. 1807, 8vo.

† Montfaucon's Travels through Italy, ch. iv, p. 84.

was discovered toward the end of the ninth, or early in the tenth century. Casiri states paper to have been first manufactured in Bucharia; and that the Arabs ascribe its invention to Joseph Amru, in the year of the Hegira 88, of Christ 706. Other learned men have thought, that we are indebted for it to the Chinese, from whom it passed successively to the Indians, Persians, and Arabs; and by the latter was communicated to the western nations. The manufacture of cotton paper is said to be still carried on to considerable extent in the Levant.*

Paper, fabricated from *linen rags*, is now used throughout Europe, and almost every part of the world whither Europeans have penetrated; and is a much more valuable material for writing upon than the cotton paper. We are ignorant both of the inventor and of the date of this important discovery. Dr. Prideaux delivers it as his opinion, that *linen paper* was brought from the East, because many of the Oriental manuscripts are written upon it. Mabillon believes its invention to have been in the twelfth century. One of the earliest specimens of paper from linen rags, which has yet been discovered, is that in the possession of Pestel, professor in the University of Rinteln, in Germany. It is a document, with the seal preserved, dated A. D. 1239; and signed by Adolphus, count of Schaumburg.† But Casiri positively affirms, that there are many MSS. in the Escurial, both upon cotton and linen paper, written prior to the thirteenth century. This invention appears to have been very early introduced into England; for Dr. Prideaux assures us, he had seen a register of some acts of John Cranden, prior of Ely, made on linen paper, which bears date in the fourteenth year of King Edward II., A. D. 1320; and in the Cottonian library are said to be several writings on this kind of paper, as early as the year 1335. The *first* paper-mill erected in this kingdom is said to have been at Dartford, in 1588, by M. Spilman, a German.‡ Shakspeare, however, refers it to the reign of Henry VI., and makes Jack Cade (Henry VI., pt. ii) say, in accusation of Lord Sands: "Whereas, before, our forefathers had no other books but the score and the tally, thou hast caused printing to be used, and contrary to the king, his crown, and dignity, thou hast built a *paper-mill.*" During the same reign, the head of the duke of York, with a paper crown upon it, was placed on the walls of the city of York.

* Horne's Introduction to Bibliography, *ubi sup.*

† Peignot, Essai sur Parchemin, p. 55, note. Casiri, *ubi sup.*

‡ Astle's Origin and Progress of Writing, ch. viii, p. **206.**

But, although paper made from linen rags is preferable to most other materials for writing upon, it is, nevertheless, inferior to parchment or vellum.

Parchment is usually made of the skins of sheep and goats: *vellum*, which is a finer kind of parchment, is made of the skins of abortive, or at least of sucking calves. The invention has been generally attributed to Eumenes, king of Pergamus;* there is, however, reason to believe that parchment was in use long before his reign. Josephus (Antiq., lib. xii, ch. ii) states, that the copy of the law, presented by the seventy elders to Ptolemy Philadelphus, about 277 years before Christ, was written upon parchment or vellum; and excited the astonishment of the king, by the extraordinary fineness of the parchment, as well as by the artful manner in which the different skins were sewed together, and the exquisite execution of the writing, in letters of gold. The most probable opinion, therefore, is, that Eumenes, son of Attalus I., king of Pergamus, though not the inventor, introduced parchment into more general use, at the time when Ptolemy Epiphanes, from a wish to prevent the rivalry of other princes in amassing books, and forming extensive libraries, prohibited the exportation of the papyrus, or Egyptian paper.†

From the city of Pergamus, parchment received the name of *Pergamenum*, and *charta Pergamena*, as it did that of *membrana*, from being made of the skins of animals. The term parchment is a corruption of the word *Pergamenum*. Vellum is derived from the Latin *vitulus*, a calf.

A coarse kind of parchment or vellum has been fabricated also from the *skins of asses*. A late traveller informs us, that in the Royal library in Sweden, "there are two enormous Latin MSS., the vellum leaves of which are made of asses' skins, and are of an amazing size."‡

The manuscripts written on parchment, or vellum, were sometimes so large as to be obliged to be carried on the shoulder. Melchior Adam relates, that Paul Pfedershcimer, a converted Jew, having lent a Hebrew MS. of the prophets, accompanied with the Massorah, to Conrad Pellican, then a youth, and indefatigably industrious to acquire a knowledge of the Hebrew tongue;

* Pergamus, now *Bergamo*, was the capital of the kingdom of that name in Asia Minor This city is mentioned in the Revelation of St. John ii, 11. It was the birthplace of Galen.

† Peignot. Essai sur Parchmin, pp. 27–33, 41, 42.

‡ Carr's (Sir John) Travels round the Baltic, p. 130, 4to.

Paul Scriptor, the tutor of Pellican, who was travelling with him, assisted him on his journey, by carrying the huge manuscript, which had the appearance of an entire calf-skin, upon his shoulder, like a porter, from Mentz to Pfortzheim, and from thence to Tubingen.*

Table-books, as they were called, made of asses' skins, or some similar substance, were common in the sixteenth and seventeenth centuries. Mr. Southey, in his "Omniana," has given a curious description of one of them. "It is a little book," says he, "nearly square, being three inches wide, and something less than four in length, bound stoutly in calf, and fastening with four strings of broad, strong, brown tape. The title as follows: 'Writing Tables, with a Kalendar for xxiiii. yeeres, with sundrie necessarie rules. The tables made by Robert Triplet. London. Imprinted for the Company of Stationers.' The tables are inserted immediately after the almanack. At first sight they appear like what we call asses' skin, the colour being precisely the same, but the leaves are thicker; whatever smell they may have had is lost, and there is no gloss upon them. It might be supposed that the gloss had been worn off, but this is not the case, for most of the tables have never been written on. Some of the edges being worn, show that the middle of the leaf consists of paper; the composition is laid on with great nicety. A silver style was used, which is sheathed in one of the covers, and which produces an impression as distinct, and as easily obliterated, as that of a black lead pencil. The tables are interleaved with common paper."†

The ancient offices of the church were sometimes written upon long *slips* of parchment, pasted together, and forming a very narrow roll of considerable length. This was fastened at one end to a very short staff, and rolled upon it. Such rolls were termed *kontakia*, or *contacia*.‡

The variety of substances thus made use of as materials for writing upon, rendered it necessary to employ different INSTRUMENTS to trace the writing. For inscriptions on stone or metal, the *chisel* and the *graver* were adopted: thus JOB, ch. xix.

V. 23.—O! that my words were even now written down;
O! that they were engraven on a table;
V. 24.—With a *pen of iron* upon lead!
That they were sculptured in a rock for ever!

GOOD'S TRANS.

But for writing upon boards, waxed tablets, bark, and such kinds

* M. Adami Vit. Germ. Theolog., p. 267, Francf. 1653.

† Southey's Omniana, vol. i, pp. 133, 134. ‡ Du Cange, *v.* Contacium.

ot softer substances, the *style* or *graphium* was used. This was an instrument, sharp at one end, to write with, and broad at the other, to erase any miswritten words; hence the phrase *vertere stylum*, to correct or blot out, was common among the Romans. The style was sometimes made of iron, sometimes of gold, or silver, or brass, or ivory, or even of wood. The iron styles were dangerous weapons, and were therefore prohibited by the Romans. Suetonius relates, that Cesar seized the arm of Cassius, one of his murderers, and pierced it with his style. He also tells us, Caligula excited the people to massacre a Roman senator with their styles; and the emperor Claudius was so fraid of being assassinated, that he would scarcely permit the *librarii*, or public writers, to enter his presence, without the cases which contained their styles being first taken from them. Prudentius (De Coran., Hymn ix) thus emphatically describes the tortures to which Cassianus* was put by his scholars, who killed him with their *pugillares* and styles:—

Innumeri circum pueri, miserabile visu,
  Confossa paruis membra figebant stylis.
Unde pugillares soliti præcurrere ceras,
  Scholare murmur adnotantes scripserant,
Conjiciunt alii lapides, inq: ora tabellas
  Frangunt, relisa fronte lignum dissilit.
Buxa crepant cerata, genis impacta cruentis.
  Rubetq: ab ictu curta tumens pagina.
Inde alii stimulos, et acumina ferrea vibrant.
  Qua parte aratis cera sulcis scribitur,
Et qua secti apices abolentur, et æquoris hirti.
  Rursus nitescens innouatur area.†

O wretched sight!—unnumber'd youths around
With small, sharp *styles*, his painful members wound.
The tablets,—spread with wax,—for writing used,
O'er which so scholar-like they oft had mused,
They dash upon his face—(some throw rude stones!)
And cruelly break them on his bleeding bones.
The boxwood shivers, with the rapid stroke,
As lightnings rend the ancient forest oak;
And as it beats that visage mark'd with age,
Blood bathes his cheeks, and dyes the batter'd page.

* This Cassianus was a Christian schoolmaster, at Imola, the ancient Forum Cornelii, twenty-seven miles from Ravenna, in Italy. In 365 he was by order of the emperor Julian exposed to the merciless rage of his scholars, who cruelly murdered him.

† Sixt. Senensi Bibliotheca Sancta, lib. ii, p. 124. 4to. Col. Agr. 1616. Astle's Origin and Progress of Writing, ch. viii, p. 207.

Meanwhile, another crew, with deadliest hate,
Resume the *iron* to complete his fate;—
One end, a point, traced all the indented words
In written furrows on the waxen boards;
The other, with a broad and level face,
Shall smooth the roughness, and the lines erase,
Till the whole area is again renew'd,
The seat of other thoughts, refined or rude.—
These horrid tools they whet and point afresh,
For keener tortures on his martyr'd flesh. D. M'NICHOLL.

Our Saxon ancestors appear to have sometimes used the style without ink, when writing upon parchment or vellum: H. Wanley instances in fol. 109, and 113 b. of the *Textus S. Ceddæ*, or St Chad's Gospel.* But for writing with ink, or coloured liquids, *reeds* or *canes*, and afterward *quills* were employed; and sometimes *pencils made of hair.*

The most beautiful *reeds* for this purpose grew formerly in Egypt, near Cnidus, a city and district in the province of Caria in Asia Minor, and likewise in Armenia, and Italy. Chardin (Travels, vol. v, p. 49) speaks of reeds which grow in the marshes of Persia, and are much sought after in the Levant. "Their writing pens," says he, "are made of reeds, or small hard canes, of the size of the largest swan quills, which they cut and slit in the same manner as we do ours, but they give them a much longer nib."† The Tartars and Indians still write with small reeds, bearing the hand exceeding lightly.

Pencils made of hair are used by the Chinese for their writing: they first liquefy their ink, and then dip their pencils into it. The curious large capital letters used in Italy, in the decline of the Roman empire, and until the sixteenth century, were made with hair pencils. After the invention of printing, they were drawn by the illuminators.‡ Specimens of these are in plate viii, of Astle's "Origin and Progress of Writing."

Quills of geese, swans, pelicans, peacocks, crows, and other birds, have been long used in these western parts, but the exact date of their introduction is uncertain. St. Isidore of Seville, who died in 636, describes a pen as in use in his time. "The instruments necessary for a scribe are the reed and the *pen*."§ In the same century Aldhelm wrote a short poem on a writing pen. In

* Nichols' Literary Anecdotes, vol. i, p. 541. Lond. 8vo. 1812.

† Beckmann's History of Inventions, by Johnston, vol. ii, pp. 207, 208. London, 8vo. 1797.

‡ Astle's Origin and Progress of Writing, ch. viii, p. 208.

§ Isid. Hisp. Orig., lib. vi, ch. xiv.

the eighth century writing pens are mentioned by Alcuin, after which period, proofs of their use occur so frequently as to place the matter beyond all doubt. Mabillon (*De Re. Diplomat*, in Supp., p. 51) saw a MS. of the Gospels, which had been written in letters of gold, in the ninth century; in which the four evangelists were represented with *quills* in their hands. In the twelfth century, Peter de Clugny, who by scholastic writers is called the Venerable, and who died in 1157, wrote to a friend, exhorting him to assume the *pen*, instead of the plough, and transcribe the Scriptures, instead of tilling the land.*

But notwithstanding the great advantage which quills have over reeds, in writing, the latter seem to have continued long in use, even with the former. Men of letters assure us, that writing reeds were used along with quills, in the eighth century, at least in France; and that the latter first began to be common in the ninth. The papal acts, and those of synods appear, however, to have been written with reeds much later. In monasteries they were retained for text and initials; while for small writing quills were every where employed. When the learned Reuchlin was obliged by the cruelties of his enemies, and by famine, and the plague, to fly from his country, and to leave behind him all his property, he was supplied with the most common necessaries by Perkheimer. Among other articles, the latter sent to him, in the year 1520, writing materials, good paper, penknives, and, instead of peacock's feathers which he had requested, the best swan quills; and that nothing might be wanting, added also proper reeds, of so excellent a sort, that Reuchlin considered them to be Egyptian or Cnidian. About the same period Reuchlin sent three of these reeds to Erasmus, who gratefully acknowledged the present, and expressed a wish that when he procured more, he would send some of them to a learned man in England, who was a common friend to both. About the year 1433 writing quills were so scarce at Venice, that men of letters could scarcely procure them. Ambrosius Traversarius, a monk of Camaldule, sent from Venice, to his brother, a bunch of quills together with a letter, in which he said: "They are not the best, but such as I received in a present. Show the whole bunch to our friend Nicholas, that he may select *a quill;* for these articles are indeed scarcer in this city than at Florence." Ambrosius also complains, that at the same period, he had scarcely any more ink, and requested that a small vessel filled with it might be sent to him!†

* Beckmann's Hist. of Inventions, vol. ii, pp. 216–219.

† Beckmann, vol. ii, pp. 222, 223.

The use of INKS, or coloured liquids, was early known among the ancients. Jeremiah, who flourished about six hundred years before the Christian era, speaks of writing with ink: (ch. xxxvi, 18:) "Then Baruch answered them; He pronounced all these words unto me with his mouth, and I wrote them with ink in the book." The term *deev*, used by the sacred writer, signifies *blackness*; as does also the word *ater*, from whence *atramentum*, the Latin term for ink. But although *black* ink was evidently the first in use, yet afterward inks of different colours were occasionally used. *Golden* ink was used by various nations, as may be seen in several libraries, and the archives of churches. *Silver* ink was also common in most countries. *Red*, *blue*, *green*, and *yellow* inks, were not uncommon. Metallic characters were also sometimes burnished, or varnished with wax.*

Lamp black, or the black obtained from burned ivory, formed the basis of the inks of the ancients, which was made in the sun, without the aid of fire. Red ink was obtained from vermilion, cinnabar, and carmine; purple, from the murex, or purple fish. (See Pliny, Nat. Hist., lib. ix, ch. lx.) Blue, yellow, and green colours, were made from pulverized gold and silver, sulphureted, and submitted to the action of fire; and were used for ornamenting and enriching manuscripts.†

Various methods were also adopted by the ancients, in order to *preserve* their writings, and to facilitate the reading of them. Those upon skins or papyrus, &c., were glued or sewed together, and rolled up, generally on cylinders of wood, and called rolls, or *volumes*, from the Latin *volvendo*, to roll up. To this form of the ancient writings there are many references in Scripture. Psa. xl, 7; Jeremiah xxxvi, 2; Ezekiel ii, 9. The literal rendering of Luke iv, 17, would be, "and *unrolling* the book, he found the passage," &c., evidently attributing to our Lord the action of unrolling a book, and afterward rolling it up again. Revelation vi, 14, also refers to this mode of rolling up the ancient writings.

The cylinder, on which the writing was rolled, was named *umbilicus*, and was generally formed of wood, particularly ebony, cedar, box, or cypress; sometimes also of ivory or bone. The ornaments of gold, or silver, or ivory, with which the ends were capped, were termed *cornua;* and the handle, or lower end, by which the roll was held in the hand, was probably what was in

* Hugo, De Prima Scrib. Orig., ch. viii, pp. 103–109. Astle's Origin and Progress of Writing, ch. viii, p. 210.

† Horne's Introduction to Bibliography, vol. i, p. 140.

Alfred's time denominated, by our ancestors, the *æstel*. The side of the parchment, or roll, which was written upon, was called *pagina*, or page, from *pango* to write, or compose; and as only one side of the roll was, in general, written upon, the written side was termed the *recto*, and the blank side *verso*, words still in use among bibliographers.* When the volume was rolled up, the outside was named *frons*, and frequently decorated with paintings: the bands with which the roll was fastened when rolled up were denominated *lora*, and were variously ornamented.†

Many of the manuscripts which have been discovered in the ruins of Herculaneum are in rolls; so are those also which have been taken out of Egyptian mummies. The Hebrew MSS. are written in columns, and are unrolled and read from the right hand to the left, and usually attached to an *umbilicus*, or cylinder, at each end;‡ many other Oriental manuscripts are unrolled perpendicularly. At present, books are seldom made to roll up in the East: many, indeed, of the very fine Persian and Arabic MSS. are written upon a kind of thin pasteboard, like paper; and being jointed at the back and front, fold up like pattern-cards.§

The Romans deposited their most valuable works in cases or chests called *scrinia*, made of cedar-wood; they also used an oil expressed from the cedar-tree, to preserve them from becoming mouldy or worm-eaten. Paintings obtained from Herculaneum prove, that the cases in which the rolls of writing were preserved, were frequently circular boxes, in which the different volumes were inserted with one of the ends downward, and a small label, containing the *titulus* or title, affixed to the upper one. The Greeks deposited their forensic, or legal instruments, in certain brazen or earthen vessels, called *Echini*. (Suidas, v. Εχινος.) The two Greek versions of the Old Testament, which Origen published in his Hexapla, and numbered five and six, he found preserved in an earthen vessel.‖ A similar mode of preserving writings was adopted by the prophet Jeremiah, ch. xxxii, 14. Leland, in his *Collectanea*, (tom. iii, p. 137,) has the following notice: "A writen booke of a twenty leves founde in a holow stone kyvered with a Stone in digging for a foundation at Yvy church by Sarisbyri." The Roman historians affirm, that the books of Numa, which had been buried more than five hundred years, looked, when

* Peignot, Essai sur Parchemin, pp. 93, 94.

† See Frontispiece. Hugo, De Prima Scrib. Orig., ch. xxxv, pp. 586–610.

‡ See Frontispiece.

§ Clarke's Harmer's Observations, vol. iii, p. 130, note by Edit.

‖ Calmet, Dissert. sur la forme des livres, &c.

taken up, as if perfectly new, from having been closely surrounded with wax candles; wax cloth being then probably unknown. The Arabs, and other Oriental nations, are wont to wrap up their sacred books in rich cases of brocaded silk; or some such rich materials. There is a fine specimen of this in the library of the East India Company in Leadenhall-street, a MS. containing the poetical works of the king of Persia, richly adorned, and wrapped up in costly velvet, &c., a present by himself to the governor general of India. A mode also of *binding books* similar to our present one seems to have been in use among the ancients, as may be seen in engravings copied from drawings found in the ruins of Herculaneum. See FRAGMENTS, *by the Editor of Calmet's Dictionary.*

To these ancient modes of writing, and the materials employed, the etymology of many words now in use may be traced. Not again to mention *paper* from *papyrus*, or *volume* from *volvendo;* the very word BIBLE, which means, by way of eminence, *the book*, is derived from the Greek word *biblos*, or *byblos*, a book, but which originally signified the inner bark of a tree. The word *book* is also derived from the Saxon *boc* or *bocce*, the beech-tree, probably from tablets or leaves of that tree having been used for writing upon. Hence also the term *leaf*, applied to a part of a book, and the use of the word *style*, for a person's manner of writing.

From the view that has been given of the various modes of writing at different periods, it is evident, that there is nothing inconsistent with ancient Oriental customs, either in the opinion of Dr. Kennicott, or of Dr. A. Clarke, as to the manner in which the transpositions in the Pentateuch have been occasioned. The same supposition also easily accounts for the narrative of the death of Moses forming the concluding chapter of Deuteronomy; which probably formed originally the commencement of the book of Joshua, from whence it was accidentally separated, and afterward appended to the books of Moses.*

* See Dr. A. Clarke's Commentary on Deuteronomy, ch. xxxiv.

CHAPTER II.

Inspired Penmen—Malachi—Ezra—Autograph of Ezra—Jewish Divisions of the books of Scripture—Targums—Masora—Hebrew MSS.—First Edition of the Hebrew Bible—Septuagint Version—Codex Vaticanus—Codex Alexandrinus—Cyril Lucar—Versions of Aquila—of Theodotian—of Symmachus—Hexapla—Persecution of Antiochus Epiphanes—Jewish Academies---Doctors---Scribes.

THE great Jewish legislator was followed by a succession of other writers, historical and prophetical, who with singular impartiality narrated the history of their nation; and with an originality, sublimity and purity of doctrine and morality, which could only have proceeded from divine inspiration, instructed and warned the chosen people of God, through a series of ages, extending from the decease of Moses to the time of Malachi, Ezra, and Nehemiah, who closed the sacred canon of the Old Testament, about four hundred years before the incarnation of the Redeemer.

MALACHI is called by the Jews, "The seal of the prophets;" and the rabbins say, that from the time the latter prophets, Haggai, Zechariah, and Malachi, died, the Holy Spirit was taken away from Israel. The outpouring of the Spirit on the day of Pentecost afterward, was therefore a full proof that the Mosaic dispensation was concluded, and that the new dispensation of the Messiah had restored the prophetical spirit, according to the promise by Joel, ii, 28.

EZRA, who was a ready scribe in the law of Moses, is allowed, by the universal consent of antiquity, to have been the restorer, collector, and publisher of the canon of the Old Testament Scriptures, which had existed before only in separate parcels; and had suffered much from the ignorance and carelessness of transcribers.*

A copy of the Pentateuch, purporting to be the *autograph* of Ezra, was some time ago preserved in the library of the Dominicans at Bologna, in Italy. The following account is given of it by the learned Montfaucon in his *Diarium Italicum*, or Journey through Italy: "I had long been desirous to turn over the manuscript, which I was told had been many years preserved among the relics of St. Dominic; which at my request was courteously granted by the Dominican fathers. But in regard that the said jewel is locked up under two keys, one of which is kept by the

* Dr. A. Clarke's Succession of Sacred Literature, vol. i, p. 36. Kennicott's Second Dissertation, ch. iii, pp. 232, 248.

magistrates, and the other by the friars, they took care to have them both brought; and produced a vast volume or roll. It is a calf-skin, dressed and pliable, containing, not the book of Ezra, as many give out, but the Pentateuch, in the nature of the books still preserved in the synagogues of the Jews: I took notice of some few marginal notes by a more modern hand. The letters have scarce lost any thing of their blackness, which is attributed to the skin, a mighty preserver of ink. The manuscript was presented to the monastery by the Jews, when Aymericus was general of the order, that is, about the beginning of the fourteenth century: an inscription sewed in about the middle of the roll, declares it to this effect:—

" 'This is the roll of the law written by Ezra, the scribe, with his own hand, when the children of the captivity under Cyrus returned to Jerusalem, and built the second temple, which was finished in forty-two years; and stood four hundred and twenty, that is, till forty-two years after the passion of Christ. That this is the very same, has been received by the constant report of ancient Jews, who were examined in several synagogues, where it was also preserved. From ancient times, it was looked upon as such among the Jews, from generation to generation; and as such it was received by the reverend general of the order, Aymericus, whose it is. Such some learned Jews proved it to be, having made certain *literal* experiments, in the presence of me brother Marsilius, and of the reader Perpynian, and of brother Peter Labius. Which tokens, either are not the same, or not so perfect in older rolls, as I have found by experience in many very ancient rolls. This roll therefore is to be looked upon as genuine, and to be handled with reverence, because written by so great an author; and ordered by the Holy Ghost, after the burning of the law; given as an original for other manuscripts; and preserved so many ages. And what is no less, that we and the Jews believe, it was shown in the temples on the greatest solemnities, in the presence of the Fulfiller of the Law, God himself, and our Lord JESUS CHRIST.'

"This appears by the character," says Montfaucon, "to have been written in the days of Aymericus, general of the order, who enjoyed that dignity in the year of our Lord 1308. This makes it plain, that they are much mistaken who think there are no Hebrew Bibles written above four hundred years ago. For it is four hundred years since this manuscript was presented to Aymericus, which was then looked upon as so very ancient; and though what they say of its being written by Ezra's own hand looks like a fable, yet it cannot be denied to have been of some antiquity when presented to Aymericus."

" Besides the Latin inscription above inserted, there is one in *Hebrew*, written by a skilful hand, now almost erased, (which in English is thus :)

"'This is the Book of the Law of Moses, which was writ by Ezra the scribe; and he read it in the sight of the multitude, men and women; and he stood in a wooden tower,' (that is, a pulpit.)"

This inscription is supposed to have been written at the same time with the Latin one above mentioned; for the Jews, when they made Aymericus that present, produced it with such a testimony of its pretended antiquity.* Dr. Kennicott doubts the fact of its being the autograph of Ezra; he nevertheless considers it as very ancient, and at least, not less than nine hundred years old.† Montfaucon describes another ancient MS. Hebrew copy of the book of Esther, in the library of the canons regular, at Bologna. It is a roll of dressed calf-skin, very ancient, worn with using, and appears to be older than the Pentateuch before mentioned.

Ezra having collected together all the books of which the Holy Scriptures then consisted, disposed them in their proper order, and divided them into three parts : the *Law* ; the *Prophets* ; and the *Cetubin*, or Hagiographa, that is, the Holy Writings. This division our Saviour himself notices in Luke xxiv, 44, when he says, " These are the words which I spake unto you, while I was yet with you, that all things might be fulfilled which are written in the Law, and in the Prophets, and in the Psalms concerning me." By the *Psalms*, he there means the whole third part called the Hagiographa; which beginning with the Psalms, was for that reason then commonly called by that name.‡

The five books of the Law are, by the Jews, divided into fifty-four sections. One of these sections was read in the ancient Jewish synagogues every sabbath-day. The number of these sections was fifty-four, because in their intercalated years (a month being then added) there were fifty-four sabbaths. Till the time of the persecution of Antiochus Epiphanes, they read only the Law. But then being forbid to read it any more, they substituted fifty-four sections out of the Prophets, the reading of which they ever after continued. When the reading of the Law was again restored by

* Montfaucon's Travels through Italy, pp. 436–438.

† Kennicott's Dissert. on Chronicles xi, &c., p. 309.

‡ Prideaux's Connections, vol. ii, p. 394.

the Maccabees, the section which was read every sabbath out of the Law served for their first lesson, and the section out of the Prophets for their second lesson. This was also the practice in the time of the apostles; and therefore when Paul entered into the synagogue at Antioch, in Pisidia, it is said that he stood up to preach, "after the reading of the *Law*, and the *Prophets*," Acts xiii, 15.

These sections were divided into verses, which the Jews called *pesukim*. This division was most likely invented by Ezra, for the sake of the Targumists, or Chaldee interpreters. For after the Hebrew language ceased to be the mother tongue of the Jews, and the Chaldee grew up into use among them instead of it, (as was the case after their return from the Babylonish captivity,) their usage was, that in the public reading of the Law to the people, it was read to them, first in the original Hebrew, and after that rendered by an interpreter into the Chaldee language; and this was done period by period. Nehemiah viii, 8. The Christian practice of reading two lessons in the churches, one out of the Old Testament, and another out of the New Testament, owes its rise to this custom of the Jews.

The TARGUMS of the Jews originated also in the necessity of translating the Scriptures into a language understood by the people. The word *Targum* signifies the translation of a book from one language into another, and is applied by the Jewish rabbins to the translation of the sacred writings from Hebrew into any other language, as Chaldee, Syriac, Persian, or Greek. There are several Targums, but the two principal ones are those of Onkelos and Jonathan. The first by Onkelos is a very literal translation of the five books of Moses into pure Chaldee, and was probably written prior to the Christian era; the latter is also a paraphrastical translation of all the Prophets into pure Chaldee, but not so elegant as the former, nor written at so early a date.*

Soon after the time of Ezra, the celebrated Jewish critics called MASORITES, or MAZORETES, began their criticisms and grammatical remarks upon the sacred text. They had their name from the Hebrew word *masar*, to deliver from one to another, because they professed to deliver the Scriptures to posterity in the state of purity in which they were found previous to the Babylonish captivity. To this end they not only numbered every verse, word, and letter, but even went so far as to ascertain *how often each letter*

* Lewis's Antiq. of Heb. Repub., vol. ii, b. 3, p. 441; vol. iv, b. 8, p. 336. Clarke's Succession of Sacred Literature, vol. i, p. 48.

of the alphabet occurred in the whole Bible! Thus sacredly did they watch over their records, in order to prevent every species of corruption.*

These Jewish critics were not a society, but rather a succession of men; and the *Masora*, or Masoretical criticisms, the work of many critics and grammarians who lived at different periods from the time of Ezra to about the year of Christ 1030, when the two famous rabbins, Ben Asher and Ben Naphtali, flourished; since whose time, almost all that has been done has been to copy after them, without making any more corrections or Masoretical criticisms. These two rabbins were chief teachers, or rectors of the great schools of the Jews, at Babylon, and in Palestine. Each of them, we are told, laboured to produce a correct copy of the sacred Scriptures; and their respective followers corrected theirs by that of their master; the Eastern, or Babylonian Jews, adhering to the copy of Ben Naphtali; the Western Jews, or those inhabiting Palestine, following that of Ben Asher. Maimonides, who wrote about the middle of the twelfth century, says, "The copy whereon we depend is the well-known copy in Egypt, which contains the twenty-four books, and which was many years at Jerusalem for the purpose of correcting copies from it; and upon it all of them depend; for Ben Asher revised it, and minutely corrected it; and revised it many times over: and upon the same I rely in the copy of the Law, which I have written according to his rule."† Another copy in high estimation among the modern Jews is said to have been corrected by R. Hillel, and for several centuries to have been kept at Toledo, in Spain. Elias Levita, a learned Jewish Masoretic critic of the sixteenth century, born in Germany, and the author of several grammatical and lexicographical works, mentions also two other celebrated copies; the *Hieriuchan*, or copy brought from Jericho; and the *Arabian*, or one preserved at Sinai.‡

The Masoretic notes, called by the Jews *the fence or hedge of the Law*, were at first written in separate rolls, but are now usually placed in the margin, or at the top and bottom of the page, in printed copies. Some transcribers, out of a design to decorate their MSS., have contrived to form the marginal lines of the

* Clarke's Succession of Sacred Literature, vol. i, p. 46. Waltoni Proleg. 8, *passim.*

† Yeates' Collation, p. 29. Kennicott, Dissert. 2, pp. 451, 457.

‡ Waltoni Proleg. 4, sec. 10, 11. Simon. Hist. Crit. du V. T., liv. i, ch. xxii. Kennicott, Dissert. 2, pp. 460–464.

Masora into all sorts of fanciful devices; such as triangles, circles, knots of various kinds, birds, beasts, &c. Such a one was presented by the emperor Maximilian I. to Reuchlin. It had originally been written for R. Aben Ezra in the twelfth century, in extremely small characters, not lineally, but in the form of certain animals. It is said to be still preserved in the library of the margrave of Baden.*

The first printed edition of the Masora was in Bomberg's Great Hebrew Bible, printed at Venice in 1526, in two volumes folio, and again in 1549, under the direction of R. Jacob Ben Chaim, a learned Jew of Tunis. A Latin translation of his celebrated preface, written originally in the rabbinical character, may be seen in Kennicott's Second Dissertation, pp. 229–244. The variations of the copies of Ben Naphtali and Ben Asher are also printed in the sixth volume of the London Polyglott.

Elias Levita, in the sixteenth century, wrote a standard work upon the Masora, which he intituled *Masoreth Hammasoreth*, having spent twenty years in the study of it. To this work the elder Buxtorf was under considerable obligations, in his celebrated *Tiberias*, or Masoretical Commentary, which he published in 1665, and to which he gave the title of *Tiberias*, from a celebrated Jewish school or academy, which flourished at Tiberias for several centuries. The notes affixed by the Masorites to the end of the different books of the Hebrew Bible, ascertaining the number of greater and smaller sections, chapters, verses, and letters, are translated and subjoined to the respective books by the Rev. Dr. Adam Clarke, in his valuable and learned Commentary.

The Jews still bestow extraordinary care on the copies of the sacred writings designed for their synagogues. "It is a constant rule with them, that whatever is considered as corrupt shall never be used, but shall be burned, or otherwise destroyed: a book of the Law, wanting but one letter, with one letter too much, or with an error in one single letter, written with any thing but ink, or written upon parchment made of the hide of an unclean animal, or on parchment not purposely prepared for that use, or prepared by any but an Israelite, or on skins of parchment tied together by unclean strings, shall be holden to be corrupt; that no word shall be written, without a line first drawn on the parchment; no word written by heart, or without having been first pronounced orally by the writer; that before he writes the name of God, he shall wash his

* Waltoni Proleg. 8, sec. 11.

pen; that no letter shall be joined to another; and that if the blank parchment cannot be seen all around each letter, the roll shall be corrupt. There are settled rules for the length and breadth of each sheet of parchment, and for the space to be left between each letter, each word, and each section."* Certain letters of the more splendid and highly finished copies are ornamented with *tagin*, or crowns. These are certain fine *radii*, ascending from the tops of the letters, in the manner of horns, and are said to be done in imitation of the glory Moses saw in the divine writing delivered to him on Mount Sinai. The *Codex Malabaricus*, presented to the University of Cambridge by the Rev. Dr. C. Buchanan, and collated by Mr. Yeates, exhibits a formation of particular letters peculiar to itself, especially the *Heth* and *Lamed*, the former being sometimes formed with an *arched*, and sometimes with an *angular* cap; and the latter having an indented or *hooked* top.†

The text of the synagogue-rolls of the Pentateuch is not divided into verses; and is also without the points of distinction, (:) called *soph-pesuk*. Buxtorf, in his *Tiberias*, ch. xi, p. 113, quotes the following note from Elias Levita: "It is a certain truth, and of which there is no doubt, that this Law, which Moses set before the Israelites, was plain; without points, and without accents, and without any distinction of verses, even as we see it at this day: and according to the opinion of the Cabalistic doctors, the whole Law was as one verse, yea, and there are that say, as one word."‡

Those who have not seen the rolls used in the synagogues can have no conception of the exquisite beauty, correctness, and equality of the writing. Some that I have seen have been equal to any Hebrew typography, for beauty and regularity.

The first *printed* edition of the *whole* of the Hebrew Scriptures was executed by Abraham Ben Chaim, at Soncino, in Italy, in 1488, in two vols. folio; ornamented with initial letters and words, from engravings in wood.

A very curious copy of the *Chetubin*, or *Hagiographa*, printed at Naples the preceding year, was presented by Dr. Pellet to the valuable library of Eton College. It is on vellum, in two volumes folio; and is considered as unique. Dr. Pellet supposes the whole edition to have been destroyed, except this copy, which by singular good fortune escaped the flames.§

* Butler's Horæ Biblicæ, vol. i, p. 47. Oxford, 1799, 12mo.

† Yeates' Collation, &c., pp. 6, 38. ‡ Yeates, *ubi sup.*, pp. 35, 36.

§ Kennicott, Dissert. 1, p. 520; and Dissert. 2, p. 472.

The celebrated SEPTUAGINT, or Greek version of the Old Testament, was made in the reign of Ptolemy Philadelphus, king of Egypt, who reigned about two hundred and eighty years before Christ. The most ancient account of this famous version is in a treatise written in the Greek language by Aristeas, who professes to have been an officer in the guards of the king of Egypt at the time it was made; and is delivered by way of letter to his brother Philocrates. The following is the substance of his narrative:—

"Ptolemy Philadelphus, king of Egypt, wishing to establish an extensive library at Alexandria, committed the charge of it to Demetrius Phalereus, a noble Athenian, who collected from various quarters twenty thousand volumes. In the course of his inquiries after curious and valuable books, he was informed of the LAW OF MOSES. This information he communicated to the king; and urged the importance of a translation of it into Greek. Ptolemy adopted measures for obtaining it; and accordingly directed that an embassy should be sent to Eleazar, the high priest, at Jerusalem, to request him to transmit a correct copy of the Law, and to send a certain number of grave and learned men, who should be capable of translating it out of Hebrew into Greek. Aristeas, Sosibius of Tarentum, and Andreas, three noblemen of Ptolemy's court, and persons friendly to the Jews, embraced the opportunity for soliciting the liberation of the Jewish captives taken prisoner by Ptolemy Soter, and still detained in slavery. Their suit was successful, and the king ordered twenty drachmas to be paid for each of them, whether man, woman, or child. The sum expended in their ransom was six hundred and sixty talents, liberating one hundred and ninety-eight thousand captives. Aristeas and Andreas were afterward commissioned to carry the official letter from Ptolemy to Eleazar, and their embassy was accompanied with gifts for the temple, and money for the sacrifices there offered, and the general service of the sanctuary; viz., one hundred talents; fifty talents in utensils of gold; and twenty talents in utensils of silver, besides the precious stones with which they were adorned, and which were of twice the value of the gold. Their embassy succeeded; and Eleazar sent to the Egyptian king a copy of the Law, written in letters of gold, upon skins of parchment of exquisite fineness and beauty. Six elders out of every tribe, men of acknowledged reputation and learning, were chosen to execute the translation, who returned to Alexandria, with the messengers of Ptolemy. On their arrival, the *seventy-two* elders were graciously received by the king, who not only expressed his satisfaction at receiving the Law, and his astonishment at its execution, but also feasted the elders for several days, and during the festival fully satisfied himself of their wisdom and ability, by proving each of them by seventy-two different questions. The seven days of feasting being ended, each of the elders received three talents, as a mark of the royal favour; and were then conducted by Demetrius to a sumptuous habitation, prepared for them in a retired situation in the Isle of Pharos, near Alexandria. Here they pursued their important undertaking with the utmost diligence, daily collating their separate versions with each other, and then dictating the approved version to Demetrius, who acted as their scribe. In seventy-two days they completed the whole translation, which was afterward read in the presence of the king, who expressed his approbation in the most decided manner, and rewarded each of the elders with three rich garments, two talents of gold, and a cup of gold of the weight of one talent. He afterward sent them honourably back to Jerusalem, loaded with the most valuable gifts to Eleazar the high priest; and commanded the version itself to be lodged with the utmost care in the Alexandrian library.* Such is the account given by Aristeas. It has, however, been called in question by many of the learned, especially by Dr. Hody, who, in a work expressly written on the subject, has so fully exposed the inconsistencies and anachronisms of the author, that the history of Aristeas is now generally considered as spurious.

But although the story, as narrated by Aristeas, is certainly in some measure fabulous, the general fact must be allowed; since writers prior to the Christian era, or nearly coeval with it, have attested its truth. Aristobulus, Josephus, Philo, Clemens Alexandrinus, Justin Martyr, and Eusebius, and even the Talmudical writers, all concur in the leading facts of the history of this version.† Dr. Masch supposes that this translation was promoted by Ptolemy, on political grounds, in order to secure the residence of the Jews in Egypt, by preventing the necessity of a constant intercourse with Judea, for want of the Law. The specious pretence of obtaining a copy of the Law for the library which had been erected at Alexandria, he conjectures to have originated with Demetrius. The transcription of the Law into the Greek charac-

* Hody, De Bibliorum Textibus Originalibus; Aristeæ Hist., pt. i, vol. xxxv, fol. Oxon. 1705.

† See Bibliotheca Sacra, edit. Masch., pt. ii, vol. ii, *in Præfat.* Waltoni Bib. Polyglott, Proleg. 9. Hamilton's Introduction to the Heb. Scriptures, ch. vi.

ters, and the version of it into the Greek language, he considers to have been the effect of coercion, not of choice; and the account of Aristeas to have been written for the purpose of giving a plausible colouring to the whole transaction.* This opinion, if adopted, affords a reason why the Hellenist Jews celebrated the translation of the Law by an annual feast, and the Jews of Palestine marked it by an annual fast.† It is probable that only the Law, or five books of Moses, were at first translated, and that the other books of the Old Testament were done at different times, by different hands, as the necessity of the case demanded, or the providence of God appointed; and being added to the books already translated, were comprehended with them in the general term *Septuagint*, or Septuagint version, so called from the number of translators employed.‡

By this translation of the Scriptures into Greek, divine Providence prepared the way for the preaching of the gospel which was then approaching, and facilitated the promulgation of it among many nations, by the instrumentality of the finest, most copious, and most correct language that was ever spoken, and which became common to all the countries conquered by Alexander: and to this version many of the most celebrated heathen philosophers were indebted for their most correct notions of the being and perfections of God, as well as for their best and purest sentiments of moral duties.§

The two most noted MSS. of the Septuagint version are the Codex Alexandrinus and the Codex Vaticanus. The Codex Vaticanus, or Vatican copy, is so called from belonging to the Vatican library, at Rome; and contains not only the Old Testament, but also the New. It is supposed to have been written in the fifth or sixth century; and is executed in the uncial, or square characters, (what we commonly term capitals,) without distinction of chapters, verses, or words. Cardinal Carafa edited the first printed edition of this MS. by order of Pope Sixtus V., in folio; but without the New Testament. The cardinal and his associates were employed nine years upon this edition, which was printed at Rome, by Franciscus Zunetti, in 1587.

The *Codex Alexandrinus*, or Alexandrian copy, was presented

* Bibliotheca Sacra, edit. Masch., *ubi sup.* in Præfat., p. 12.

† Hamilton's Introduction to Heb. Scriptures, ch. vi, pp. 114–117.

‡ Hody, De Bib. Text. Orig., lib. ii, ch. vii, ix. Owen's Inquiry into the Present State of the Septuagint Version, sec. i, pp. 2, 3.

§ Gale's Court of the Gentiles, *passim*.

to King Charles I. by Sir Thomas Roe, from Cyril Lucar, patriarch of Constantinople, who accompanied the MS. with the following note written by his own hand:—

"*Liber iste Scripturæ Sacræ Novi et Veteris Testamenti, prout ex traditione habemus, est scriptus manu Theclæ nobilis fœminæ Egyptiæ ante mile* (pro *mille*) *et trecentos annos circiter paulo post concilium Nicænum. Nomen Theclæ in fine libri erat exaratum; sed extincto Christianismo in Egypto a Mahometanis, et libri una Christianorum in similem sunt redacti conditionem; extinctum ergo et* (lege *est*) *Theclæ nomen et laceratum, sed memoria et traditio recens observat.*

"*Cyrillus* Patriarcha *Constantinopolitanus.*"

(TRANSLATION.)

"This book of the Holy Scriptures of the New and Old Testament was written, according to tradition, by the hand of Thecla, a noble Egyptian woman, about thirteen hundred years since,* a little after the council of Nice. The name of Thecla was formerly written at the end of the book, but Christianity being suppressed in Egypt by the Mohammedans, the books also of the Christians shared the same fate. But though the name of Thecla be blotted and torn out, yet memory and tradition continue to preserve it.

"*Cyril,* Patriarch of Constantinople."†

It is written on parchment, and, like all the most ancient manuscripts, in uncial characters, without distinction of chapters, verses, or words, and originally without accents. It consists of four folios, three of which contain the Old Testament, and the fourth the New Testament. It formerly belonged to the king's library, from whence it was transferred, in 1753, to the British Museum. A fac-simile edition of the New Testament of this MS. was published in 1786, by Dr. C. G. Woide, with types cast for that purpose, line for line, without intervals between the words, as in the manuscript itself. It is a splendid folio; and is accompanied with a learned preface, containing an accurate description of the manuscript, with an exact list of all its various readings. In 1814, the British House of Commons ordered that a fac-simile

* Cyril's note was written in the year 1628. The council of Nice was held at a city of that name in Nicomedia, in 324. The most strenuous advocates of this MS., however, consider this date as too early, and it is much more probable that it is about the same age as the Codex Vaticanus.

† Eclectic Review, vol. ii, pt. i, p. 216. Marsh's Michaelis, vol. ii, pt. ii, p. 651

edition also of the Old Testament should be executed at the public expense. The Rev. Henry Harvey Baber, one of the librarians of the British Museum, and editor of a beautiful edition of "Wicliff's New Testament," printed in quarto, 1810, was appointed the editor, and has since published the book of Psalms, for which he had issued proposals prior to his appointment; and several other parts of it.

The tragical fate of Cyril Lucar, who presented the Alexandrian manuscript to King Charles I., demands the tear of sympathy from every pious and candid lover of literature and religious liberty. A native of Crete, educated at Venice, and extensively learned, he was successively patriarch of Alexandria and Constantinople. In his younger days he had travelled over a considerable part of Europe, and understood not only the Greek, Arabic, and Turkish languages, but also the Latin and Italian. Possessing a mind superior to the slavish condition of his country, he formed various plans for the promotion of the common cause of Christianity, and the particular church under his care. He collected an excellent library, which he furnished with the choicest manuscripts; the Alexandrian MS. was one of them. He also patronized a Greek, named Nicodemus Metaxa, who had resided some years in England, and who having learned the art of printing, had procured a printing-press and types from London; and employed him to print catechisms and other books for the instruction of the Greeks in the principles of their religion. With the same benevolent design of aiding the interests of religion, he promoted an edition of the New Testament in the vernacular Greek, undertaken by Maximus Calliopolitus, at the instance of Cornelius Haga, the Dutch ambassador at Constantinople, and printed at Geneva in 1638, in quarto. To this edition he wrote a preface, in which he vindicated the propriety of translating the Scriptures into the vulgar tongues, and the right of all persons to read them. With the utmost liberality he also forwarded the designs of Dr. Pocock, and other learned men, who visited Constantinople, in order to acquire a more extensive and accurate knowledge of the languages, customs, and literature of the East.

During his travels, his inquiries had been directed to the disputes between the Romish and reformed churches; the result of which had been an attachment to the doctrines and discipline of the latter: he therefore now ventured upon the bold step of printing, at Constantinople, a "Confession of the faith and doctrines of the Greek Church," dedicated to the English monarch, Charles I

He also conceived the design of reforming the Greek Church, and rendering its doctrines and ritual more Scriptural. He occasionally attended public worship in the British ambassador's chapel, and even undertook to be godfather to the infant son of Sir Peter Wych, who was named Cyril, after the patriarch.

His attachment to the Reformed Church, and correspondence with its learned members, exposed him, however, but too fatally to the machinations of his determined enemies. For nearly twenty years, the Jesuits, aided by the credit and influence of the French ambassador, perplexed and misrepresented him. In this nefarious business his adversaries were assisted by the stratagems of some perfidious Greeks, particularly Cyril, bishop of Berea, a man of a dark, malignant, and violent spirit. Sometimes he was represented as the enemy of Islamism, and his arguments in defence of the divinity of Christ as blasphemy against Mohammed; at others, as employing the Greek press for the purpose of circulating inflammatory and seditious publications. At one time he was deposed; at another heavily fined; but the influence of the British government, and the exertions of its ambassadors, shielded him from the ultimate designs of his enemies, till the fatal deed was effected by Bairam, a bashaw, in 1638.

Bairam, being a favourite of the grand seignior, and bribed for the purpose, took advantage of the grand vizier's absence to persuade the sultan Morad, then on his way to the siege of Bagdat, that the death of Cyril was necessary for the safety of the state. An order was immediately signed for his execution, and sent to the governor of Constantinople, who apprehended and confined him in one of the castles on the Bosphorus; and afterward, on the 27th of June, delivered him to a band of Janizaries, to execute the sentence of the sultan. The venerable patriarch was then carried out to the sea, as though he was to be again banished; but scarcely had they quitted the shore before he perceived they intended to take away his life, and kneeling down, prayed with great fervency and recollection; while the Turkish officers inhumanly insulted him, and, fastening the bow-string round his neck, strangled him; then stripped him, and threw his body into the sea, which, being driven to the shore, was buried by his friends. The rage of his enemies pursued him to the grave, they dug up his corpse, and again cast it into the sea: it was, however, recovered a second time, and buried in a Greek chapel, on a small island over against the bay of Nicomedia, from whence it was afterward brought to Constantinople, and decently interred. Such was the end of the great and good Cyril Lucar, whose piety and sufferings will endear his memory to distant generations!*

The valuable manuscripts which enriched the library of Cyril were, after his death, obtained by the Dutch resident, who, fearing the attempts of the new patriarch to recover them, sent them away by a ship returning to Holland. The vessel arrived safely at the intended harbour the next day; but, by the violence of an extraordinary storm, sunk there with all its cargo, and was lost. The Alexandrian MS., so called from having been brought from Alex andria, will remain a lasting memorial of Cyril's generosity and piety.†

The *autograph*, or original copy of the Septuagint version, was, most probably, consumed in the fire which destroyed the Alexandrian library, in the time of Julius Cesar, about fifty years before the Christian era; but the translation was preserved by the numerous transcripts taken for the use of the different synagogues in Egypt, Greece, and Italy, and which were sure to be copied with the utmost accuracy and care. Other copies were also taken for the use of individuals. The evangelists, and apostles, and primitive fathers, made their quotations from this translation; all the Greek churches used it; and the Latins, till the time of Jerome, had no version of the Old Testament but what had been translated from it; and nearly all the older Oriental versions, as well as several of the Western, are derived from it.

The Hellenist Jews, that is, those who spoke the Greek language,‡ continued the use of this version from the time of its formation till about one hundred years after the incarnation of our Lord, when they began to disuse it, and formed another for themselves. For as this version grew into use among the Christians, it grew out of credit with the Jews; and they, being pressed in many particulars urged against them out of this version by the Christians, resolved to make a new one that might better serve their purpose. The person who undertook this charge was AQUILA, a native of Sinope, a city of Pontus. He had been brought up a heathen, but becoming a Christian, was excommunicated for

* Twell's Life of Dr. Edward Pocock, prefixed to his Works, pp. 11–13, fol. Lond. 1740. Bibliotheca Sacra, edit. Masch, pt. ii, vol. ii, sec. ii, p. 325. Account of the Sufferings of Cyrillus Lucaris, in Arminian Magazine, vol. xiii, pp. 537, 590. Mosheim's Ecclesiastical History, vol. v, pp. 248, 249, Lond. 1803, 8vo.

† Twell's Life of Dr. Pocock, p. 13.

‡ "Ελληνες sunt pagani, Ελληνισαι Judæi Græcis Bibliis in Synagogis utentes."—*Io. Scaliger* apud *Hody*, *De Bib. Text. Orig.*, p. 221.

addicting himself to magic and judicial astrology; he then turned Jew, got himself admitted into the school of Rabbi Akiba, the most celebrated Jewish teacher of his day, and having made considerable proficiency in Hebrew, was thought sufficient for the translation which he undertook, and published in the year of our Lord 128.* Of this version nothing now remains but some scattered fragments; yet it appears from these that the translation was strictly a literal one. Dr. Geddes says, "He is an uncouth, barbarous writer, the Arias Montanus, or Malvenda of his day; who seems to have purposely chosen a servile mode of translating, to hide the malevolence of his views, and to make his strict adherence to the letter of the Hebrew a plausible pretext for deviating so widely from the old version."† It is, however, to be regretted that his translation is lost, as it would have been singularly useful, both for discovering the state of the Hebrew text at that time, and affording the literal meaning and etymology of many words, the signification of which it is now difficult to ascertain. Encouraged by the Jews, Aquila undertook and published a second edition of his version, accompanied with a commentary, that rendered it still more acceptable to them.

The version of Aquila was followed by that of THEODOTION, which he published about A. D. 184. This writer is, by some, said to have been born at Sinope, and by others, at Ephesus, and flourished in the time of the Roman emperor Commodus. He had been first a disciple of Tatian, then a Marcionite, and lastly an Ebionite, or Jew. He altered, added to, or retrenched from the old Alexandrian version, wherever he found it to differ from the Hebrew manuscripts, which the Jews had put into his hands. This device succeeded according to his wish. The Jews were well pleased with his version, because it was conformable to their ideas; and the Christians were not offended, because it so much resembled the Septuagint. In many particular passages, and even in one whole book, that of Daniel, they preferred it to the Septuagint itself; especially after Origen had made use of it to correct the supposed faults of the latter, in order to make it agree with what he considered the Hebrew verity: hence it is, that much more of this version has been preserved than of that of Aquila.‡

At the close of the second, or the beginning of the third century,

* Prideaux's Connections, &c., vol. iii, pt. ii, b. i. Hody, De Bib. Text. Orig., lib. iv, p. 573.

† Geddes' Prospectus of a New Translation, p. 27, Glasg. 1786, 4to.

‡ Hody, De Bib. Text. Orig., lib. iv, pp. 579–585. Geddes' Prospectus, p. 28.

SYMMACHUS, a learned Samaritan, but who was become a convert to the Ebionites, whose system was compounded of Judaism and Christianity, published a *fourth* Greek translation, which was highly esteemed by some of the ancient fathers. This work was accomplished for the use of the Ebionite communion; the style of it was neat and clear, and the whole translation elegant and perspicuous. Not servilely literal, like the version of Aquila; nor altered from the Septuagint, like that of Theodotion; his version is a kind of comment, where we often meet with some striking examples of the theology of his sect.*

Besides the Greek versions of the Old Testament, there are three others mentioned by the ancient fathers, called the *fifth*, *sixth*, and *seventh;* because their respective authors or editors are unknown. They seem to have comprehended only, or chiefly, the poetical books of Scripture. All these versions were collated by the indefatigable ORIGEN, in the third century, and placed together with the Septuagint, and the original Hebrew text, in his famous Hexapla. In A. D. 1718, Abraham Tromm, an aged Protestant divine of Groningen, published a most valuable CONCORDANCE to the Septuagint, in two volumes folio; to which is annexed a Lexicon of all the words contained in the fragments of Origen's Hexapla, published by Father Montfaucon, in 1713, in two volumes folio.

About one hundred and twenty years after the completion of the translation of the Law by the LXX, Antiochus Epiphanes, king of Syria, raised a dreadful persecution against the Jews, suppressed the sacrifices, and all the observances of the Jewish religion; polluted the temple by the most detestable sacrifices and idolatries; carried away the vessels of the sanctuary; and commanded the books of the Law to be destroyed. Those who secreted any of the sacred books were ordered to be put to death. Many of the copies of the law were burned; others were torn to pieces, or defiled by having the likenesses of idols painted in them. 1 Maccabees i, 56, 57; iii, 48. Mattathias, and his son Judas Maccabæus, roused by the cruelties exercised upon their countrymen, the apostacy of many of the Jews, and the defilement of the temple, displayed extraordinary zeal and valour in defence of their religion and liberty; and were ultimately successful in reforming the worship of the Jews, and re-establishing the ritual of Moses. Several copies of the Law were recovered; and where any of them had been profaned by the idolatrous paintings of the heathens, the paintings were defaced, and

* Dr. Owen's Enquiry into the present state of Sept. Ver., pp. 109–112. Hody, De Bibl. Text. Orig., lib. iv, p. 586.

the copies permitted to be used. The temple-service was restored, and the Law, as formerly, read in the synagogues; to which were now added certain portions out of the Prophets, which first began to be read in the synagogues, during the persecution, while the Law was forbidden.*

The books called the APOCRYPHA, and appended to our Bibles, are so denominated from the Greek word αποκρυπτω, (apokrupto,) *to hide*, either because they are of doubtful or hidden authority; or because in the first ages of Christianity they were not read publicly in the churches, but only permitted to be read privately at home. Theodotion has been supposed to be the first person who collected them together; but except by the Romish Church they have never been admitted into the sacred canon, or collection of authentic and inspired writings. Some of them are highly absurd, and but little superior to the fables of the Talmudists: such are the stories of Bel and the Dragon; Susannah and the Elders; &c. Others of them wear more the appearance of authenticity, as the books of the Maccabees, especially the *first* of them. One of the earliest notices of the Apocryphal writings being read in the churches is about the end of the fourth century, in Jerome's preface to the books written by Solomon. He observes, "that as Judith, Tobit, and the books of Maccabees, were read in some churches, though not received as *canonical*, so the books of Wisdom and Ecclesiasticus might be read for the edification of the people; but not as authority in the doctrines of the church."† This judgment of Jerome has been adopted by the Church of England, in her sixth article of religion. The popish council of Trent, on the contrary, decreed in 1546, that several of the Apocryphal books should by the Romish Church be received as *canonical*. The Apocryphal books were rejected by the Jews, whose particular glory it was, "that unto them were committed the oracles of God," Rom. iii, 2. And although they frequently made the Word of God of no effect, by the traditions of their elders, they never placed the writings of their doctors in the canon of Scripture. A brief view of their academies, doctors of the law, and scribes, may not be unacceptable to the reader; nor improperly conclude this part of our "Illustrations."

The first notice we have of ACADEMIES, or *public schools* among the Jews, is in the time of the prophet Samuel, who has, with some

* 1 Maccabees ii, 48; iii, 48; iv, 52, 53, 59. Josephus, Antiq., b. xii, ch. v–vii Millar's (of Paisley) Hist. of the Church, *Works*, vol. iii, pp. 349, 354.

† Bingham's Antiq. of the Chris. Church, vol. vi, b. xiv, ch. iii, p. 433.

probability, been considered as the founder of the *schools of the prophets*. These appear to have been places of education, where the most hopeful young persons of the Levites, and the Nazarites out of other tribes, were instructed in religion and morals. Over these colleges, some venerable prophet, at first, presided, from whose mouth the students or scholars received the inspired dictates of prophecy, and delivered them to the people, when their president was otherwise employed. After the destruction of the first temple, we hear nothing of the schools of the prophets; but *academics*, or seminaries for instruction in the Law of Moses, were established in various places. Over these certain doctors of the Law presided. Gamaliel, the tutor of St. Paul, was one of them. The Jews say, that until the time of Gamaliel, the scholars stood while the Law was explained to them; but that afterward they sat at the feet of the rabbi who taught them. The author of the commentary which goes under the name of Ambrose, distinguishes the scholars into two classes: "The rabbins," says he, "are seated on elevated chairs, the older and more learned of the scholars are placed on benches below them; while the junior scholars sit upon mats, on the ground." (*Ambros.* in 1 Cor. xiv.) The scholars were expected also to hearken in silence, and pay the utmost deference to the instructions of the master. They were never, even in his absence, to call him by his name, but to address him, or speak of him, by some title of honour; they were not to sit in his presence till he bade them, nor afterward to rise without his permission; while sitting they were to behave as in the presence of a king; and when they withdrew, they were to retire without turning their faces from the master; when they walked with him, they were not to step before him, nor to walk at his side, but were to follow him at a respectful distance. Many other similar rules for the conduct of the scholars may be met with in Maimonides, *De studio legis*, where the subject is treated at large.*

In the times preceding the publication of the Talmud, the doctors of the Law were inducted into their office, first by imposition of hands; and then giving into the hands of the candidates the *five books of Moses*, and *a key*, to show them that they were at liberty to open the mysteries of the Law; and afterward authorizing them to declare what was lawful, and what unlawful, by saying to each of them, "Take thou liberty to teach what is *bound*, and what

* Lewis's Hebrew Antiquities, vol. i, b. ii, ch. xv. Calmet, Dissertation sur les Ecoles des Hebreux. Maimonides, De Studio Legis, a Rob. Clavering., cap. v and vi, Oxon. 1705, 4to.

is *loose.*' Simeon, the son of Hillel, (who is supposed to have taken our Saviour in his arms,) is said to have been the first doctor with a title, and he was called *Rabban.* From his time, titles came into request, and none was more common than *Rabbi.* These distinguishing titles implied mastership, doctorship, or principality, and were in respect and dignity one higher than the other. *Rabbi* was a more excellent name than *Rab; Rabban* was more excellent than Rabbi; and the simple name, as Haggai, Zechariah, or Malachi, was more excellent than Rabban. *Rab* was the more proper title of the Babylonian doctors, *Rabbi* of the Judean, and *Rabban* was ascribed to seven men only.* And as there were different titles, there were also different orders of doctors. The first and most honourable were the *men of the great synagogue,* who flourished in the time of the latter prophets. Among these they enumerate Haggai, Zechariah, and Malachi; Ezra, Nehemiah, Seraiah, Zerubbabel, and Mordecai. From the time of the men of the great synagogue to the publishing of the Mishna, they were called *Tannaim,* or traditionaries; and are the Mishnical doctors, who are said to have received the oral law, or Mishna, from the prophets, and out of whose traditions and doctrines the Mishna was composed. From that time to the publication of the Babylonish Talmud, they were called *Aemourain,* or dictators, because they dictated the explanations or commentaries upon the Mishna, contained in the Gemara. For about a hundred years after the publication of the Talmud, they obtained the name of *Seburaim,* or opinionists, because they only inferred opinions by disputation, and probable arguments, from what had been before dictated, and received in the Mishna and Gemara, and did not advance any peculiar doctrines themselves. After that, they had the appellation of *Gaonim,* or sublime and excellent doctors, being so called from the excellence and sublimity of their learning. Since then, the general name of *Rabbi* is that whereby their learned men are distinguished, except that those among them who minister in their synagogues are called *Chacamim,* or wise men.†

The Jewish SCRIBES were a body of the most learned men of the nation, and generally of the tribe of Levi, who were distinguished by the title of *scribes of the clergy;* those who were not of the Levitical stock being called *scribes of the people;* thus

* Basnage's History of the Jews, b. v, ch. v, p. 412. Lond. 1708, fol. Dr. A. Clarke's comment. on Matthew xviii, 18. Lewis's Heb. Antiq., vol. i, b. ii, ch. xxii. Lightfoot's Works, vol. i, Harmony, sec. 52, p. 307. Lond. 1684, fol.

† Levi's Ceremonies of the Jews, pp. 240, 246, 276, 302, 310. 8vo. Lewis, *ut sup.*

distinguishing them from such as were the private secretaries of particular men. The business of the lay scribes was to undertake to copy the Scriptures for any who desired it; for so great and various is the accuracy and exactness of the Scripture text, and of such importance that the copies should be correct, that it was deemed improper to permit the transcription of the sacred books by any but select transcribers. On this account, a particular order of learned men was established among the Jews, whose office it was to guard and preserve the purity of the text in all Bibles that should be copied out, that no corruption might creep into the original of the sacred writings; and these were denominated *scribes of the people.* Those who were men of learning and scholastic education were likewise employed as public notaries, in the sanhedrims and courts of justice; and as registrars in the synagogues. The scribes, therefore, not only transcribed the books of the Law, but wrote out the *phylacteries;* the *mezuzoth,* or sentences to be affixed to the door-posts, bills of contracts, or divorcements; and other matters of civil or religious concern. Out of these, it is probable that some of the most accomplished were made choice of to attend upon the king, as his secretaries, called the *king's scribes.* To qualify them for these offices, they were entered as students in some public academy, of which there were forty-eight belonging to the tribe of Levi; where they studied till they were accounted capable of these employments.*

The office of the *scribes of the clergy* was to preach in public, and to instruct the people, being the most certain and regular interpreters and expounders of the Law in sermons; and more constant teachers than any other of the clergy. Thus, Ezra was a *ready scribe* in the Law of Moses, both for copying, and preserving pure the text of the Scripture, and also for expounding it by his sermons. Ezra vii, 6.

* Lightfoot's Works, vol. i, p. 439. Lewis's Heb. Antiq., vol. ii, ch. xxi.

PART II.

FROM THE BIRTH OF CHRIST TO THE INVENTION OF PRINTING.

CHAPTER I.

First, second, and third Centuries—Books of New Testament—Autographs of sacred Writers—Jews in China—Syriac and Latin Versions—John Albert Widmanstadt—William Postel—Carolus Schaaf—Vetus Italica—Thomas Hearne—Peter Sabatier—Sahidic and Coptic Versions—Dr. C. G. Woide—Dr. David Wilkins—Origen—Pamphilus—Eusebius of Cesarea—Lucian—Hesychius—Bibliomancy—Gymnasia—Libraries—Public Readers—Persecutions—Traditores—Instances of extraordinary Memory.

IN the year of the world 4000, or 4004, JESUS, the CHRIST, that is, the MESSIAH, appeared among men, and became incarnate for us men, and for our salvation. To him be glory and dominion for ever and ever. Amen.

After the ascension of our Lord, his apostles, or disciples, or their contemporaries, committed to writing the various books which compose the canon of the New Testament; and which, being written under the inspiration of the Holy Spirit, are an inestimable compilation of divine truths, containing the records of human redemption.

It is not easy, perhaps it is impossible, to ascertain with exactness the different times at which the respective portions of the New Testament were written; but the following chronological arrangement, &c., extracted from Dr. A. Clarke's "Introduction to the Four Gospels, and to the Acts of the Apostles," will probably prove acceptable to the reader:—

Chronological Arrangement of the Books of the New Testament; the Places where written, according to Dr. Lardner; and the enumeration of all the Books, Chapters, and Verses.

THE GOSPELS.

BOOKS.	Places where written.	Time when written.	Books.	Chapters.	Verses.
Matthew	Judea	A. D. 64	1	28	1071
Mark	Rome	" 64	1	16	678
Luke	Greece	" 63 or 64	1	24	1151
John	Ephesus	" 68	1	21	880
Acts	Greece	" 63 or 64	1	28	1006

1

ST. PAUL'S EPISTLES.

Books.	Places where written.	Time when written.	Books.	Chapters.	Verses
I. Thessalonians	Corinth	A. D. 52	1	5	89
II. Thessalonians	Corinth	" 52	1	3	47
Galatians	Corinth or Ephesus	" 52 or 53	1	6	149
I. Corinthians	Ephesus	Beginning of 56	1	16	437
I. Timothy	Macedonia	A. D. 56	1	6	113
Titus	Macedonia or near it	Before the end of 56	1	3	46
II. Corinthians	Macedonia	October, 57	1	13	256
Romans	Corinth	February, 58	1	16	434
Ephesians	Rome	April, 61	1	6	155
II. Timothy	Rome	May, 61	1	4	83
Philippians	Rome	End of 62	1	4	104
Colossians	Rome	End of 62	1	4	95
Philemon	Rome	End of 62	1	1	25
Hebrews	Rome or Italy	Spring of 63	1	13	303

THE CATHOLIC EPISTLES.

James	Judea	A. D. 61 or 62	1	5	108
I. Peter	Rome	" 64	1	5	105
II. Peter	Rome	" 64	1	3	61
I. John	Ephesus	" 80	1	5	105
II. John	Ephesus	Between 80 and 90	1	1	13
III. John	Ephesus	Between 80 and 96	1	1	15
Jude	Unknown	A. D. 64 or 65	1	1	25
Apocalypse	Patmos or Ephesus	" 95 or 96	1	22	405
		Total	27	260	7959

St. Matthew's Gospel is generally allowed to have been written in the Hebrew or Syro-Chaldaic language, being designed for the immediate use of the inhabitants of Palestine. Irenæus, who lived in the second century, expressly says, (Adv. Steres, lib. iii, ch. i,) that "Matthew, among the Hebrews, wrote a Gospel in their own language, while Peter and Paul were preaching the gospel at Rome, and founding the church there." Papias, the companion of Polycarp, had still more early affirmed, that "Matthew wrote his Gospel in the Hebrew tongue." "We are fools," says Isaac Vossius, (Præf. App. in Lib. de 70 Interpr.,) "if we spend our time in confuting all the idle dreams which trample upon the unanimous testimony of all antiquity, and the authority of all churches, which conspire in assuring us that the Gospel of St. Matthew was originally written in the Syro-Chaldaic language."* This Gospel was afterward translated into Greek, as we

* Those who wish to be fully acquainted with the controversy respecting the language in which St. Matthew's Gospel was originally written, may consult Marsh's Michaelis, vol. iii, pt. i, ch. iv, sec. 3–9; Dr. Campbell's Preface to Matthew's Gospel,

have it at present, in the time of the apostles; possibly by the evangelist himself, though some say by St. James, others by St. John; and being approved by them, has always been considered as holding the place of the original; the copies of the Hebrew having been early so corrupted by the Nazarenes and Ebionites as to destroy all confidence in them.

The Epistle to the Hebrews also appears to have been written by St. Paul in Hebrew, and afterward to have been translated into Greek by St. Luke, according to Clement of Alexandria, (Eusebii H. E., lib. vi, ch. xiv,) but according to Eusebius, (H. E., lib. iii, ch. xxxviii,) by Clement of Rome.*

Cardinal Baronius, in his *Annales Ecclesiastici,* has attempted to prove that St. Mark wrote his Gospel in Latin. This hypothesis, so contrary to the testimony of antiquity, is, however, universally exploded. The arguments by which he endeavoured to support his opinion were the subscriptions of certain Syriac manuscripts, and the supposed autograph of St. Mark preserved at Venice; but it is well known that no dependance can be placed on such subscriptions in general, and in particular that the subscriptions of a version made in the East immediately from the Greek can be of no authority in regard to the language in which St. Mark wrote in Rome.†

The pretended autograph of St. Mark's Gospel, kept in St. Mark's treasury in Venice, is written upon paper made of cotton (charta bombycina) of a faded green colour, and forms a thin square volume, covered with plates of silver gilt. The dampness of the place long ago rendered the writing nearly illegible, and caused the leaves to cling together, so that they could scarcely be separated without tearing. The illegibility of the writing occasioned Misson, an eminent lawyer, to affirm that it was written in Greek, but more accurate observations have proved it to be Latin, and written in the sixth century. It was conveyed from Aquileia to Venice in the fifteenth century. The emperor Charles IV., in 1355, obtained from Aquileia, through his brother Nicholas, the patriarch of that city, the last eight leaves, which are kept at Prague;‡ and on receipt of which a testimonial was given in Latin, of which the following is a translation:—

in his excellent Translation of the Four Gospels; and Simon's Histoire Critique du Texte du N. T., ch. v, vi, vii, viii. See also Butler's Lives of the Saints, vol. ix, pp. 284, 285, note.

* Marsh's Michaelis, vol. iv, ch. xxiv, sec. 9–12.

† Simon, Hist. Critique du N. T., ch. xi. Marsh's Michaelis, vol. iii, ch. v, sec. 8. Kortholtus, De variis S. S. Editionibus, cap. vii, pp. 3, 4. Kilon. 1668, 4to.

‡ Michaelis (vol. iii, pt. i, ch. v, p. 226) says, the two quaternions, or quires,

"I CHARLES IV., by the grace of God king of the Romans, always august, and king of Bohemia, saw the book of St. Mark's Gospel, written with his own hand, entire from the beginning to the end, in seven quires, in the custody of the patriarch of the church of Aquileia; which book was preserved in the said church by the blessed Hermagoras, and by the said church of Aquileia to this day; which said blessed Hermagoras received that book from the hands of St. Peter; and also from St. Peter, at the request, and by the resignation of St. Mark, had the prelateship of the said church of Aquileia; of which book, upon my request to the patriarch and chapter of the said church of Aquileia, I obtained these two last quires of the aforesaid book; and the other five going before them, remained in the aforesaid church; and this I writ with my own hand, in the year of the incarnation 1355, on the eve of All Saints, the ninth of my reign."*

The fragment now kept at Prague was published by Joseph Dobrowsky, in 1778, in 8vo., under the title *Fragmentum Pragense Evangelii S. Marci vulgo autographi.* And from a letter by Laurentius a Turre, printed in Blanchini's *Evangeliorum Quadruplex*, pt. ii, p. 543, it appears that the manuscript of St. Mark's Gospel was brought to Venice from Friuli, the ancient Forum Julii, where a very ancient Latin MS., containing the Gospels of St. Matthew, St. Luke, and St. John, is still preserved; and consequently that the twenty leaves at Venice, with the last eight leaves at Prague, making the whole Gospel of St. Mark, complete the Foro-julian MS., which contains the oldest copy of Jerome's version of the Gospels; and has been published by Blanchini in his *Evangeliorum Quadruplex*, printed at Rome in 1748.†

The claims of the Venetian MS. being disproved, it will be granted that none of the autographa or original manuscripts of the New Testament are now in existence, though there is evidence, that, at least, some of them were for many years carefully preserved among the ancient Christian churches. Tertullian, who flourished at the close of the second, and the commencement of

contained sixteen leaves; but this is probably an error for *pages*, since the Baron De la Tour remarks, in his letters inserted in Montfaucon's Journey through Italy, (Diarium Italicum,) that a quaternion was the size of the fourth part of a sheet; two sheets or quaternions would therefore be eight leaves or sixteen pages.

* Montfaucon's Journey through Italy, pp. 75, 76. Lond. 1712, 8vo.

† Marsh's Michaelis, vol. iii, pt. i, ch. v, sec. 8. Butler's Lives of the Saints, vol. iv, p. 272, Edinburgh, 1798, 8vo. See also Calmet, Dissert. sur l'Evangile de S. Marc.

the third century, refers to many autographa as still extant. See his treatise *De Præscriptionibus*, sec. 36. "If you will indulge your curiosity," says he, "and give it both a useful and extensive range, in the affair of your salvation, be pleased to take a view of, and run over the apostolic churches, where the chairs of the apostles do now preside in their respective places, where their authentic and original epistles, (authenticæ literæ,) the very images of their voice and person, are now recited and exhibited. Do you live in Achaia? There is Corinth. Are you not far removed from Macedonia? You have Philippi and Thessalonica. Are you nigh unto Asia? There is Ephesus. Or if you border upon Italy, there is Rome."

Peter, an Alexandrian bishop of the fourth century, says, "The Gospel of the evangelist John, written with his own hand, is, by divine goodness, still preserved in the most holy church of the Ephesians, where it is held in veneration by the believers."*

Frickius supposes that the autographa were preserved by the primitive Christians in their archives, or *tabularia sacra*, and not suffered to be generally read, lest they should be injured by the frequent handling of the readers; and conceives that Ignatius refers to these archives in his Epistle to the Philadelphians, sec. 8, when he says, "I have heard some persons say, If I find it not (εν τοις αρχαιοις,) or rather (εν τοις αρχειοις,) in the archives, I believe it not." Usher, Dodwell, and others have adopted the same opinion.† The final loss of the autographs is probably to be attributed, principally, to the dreadful persecutions which raged against the Christians in the early ages, and to the exertions of their barbarous persecutors to destroy all their sacred books; a loss from which has arisen the necessity of collecting and collating manuscripts of the original Greek, and of the different early versions: a measure which has been pursued with much laudable industry and perseverance, especially in modern times, and which has completely proved the general accuracy of our present copies.

Transcriptions of the different parts of the New Testament were, however, very early made, and circulated among the Christian churches; and soon after the death of the apostles began to be collected into volumes. But so cautious were the first Christians not to receive any writings as *inspired* without the most

* Frickii Commentatio de cura Ecclesiæ Veteris circa canonem Sacræ Scripturæ, cap. iv, sec. 5, p. 130, 4to. Ulm. 1728.

† Frickius, *ubi sup*.

indubitable evidence, that it was not till after a considerable lapse of time that the Epistle to the Hebrews, the second Epistle of St. Peter, the second and third Epistles of St. John, the Epistles of St. James and St. Jude, and the Revelation of St. John, were admitted into the sacred canon.

During the FIRST CENTURY a colony of Jews settled in China, whom Bishop Walton has slightly noticed in the Prolegomena to his Polyglot Bible; (Proleg. iii, sec. 41 ;) but of whom the best account will be found in Brotier's Tacitus, vol. iii, p. 567, *et seq.*, from which the subsequent statement is chiefly extracted. Gabriel Brotier obtained his information from the manuscript letters of certain Jesuits, who were sent at the close of the seventeenth, or commencement of the eighteenth century, by the Roman Catholic Church, as missionaries to the Chinese nation; and who were requested to prosecute every possible inquiry into the state, customs, religious opinions, and sacred books of the Jews in China. From these sources the celebrated editor of Tacitus learned, that the ancestors of the present Chinese Jews settled in China during the dynasty of Han, in the reign of Ming-ti, and in the year of our Lord 73, two years before the death of Ming-ti, and three years before the destruction of Jerusalem. They appear to have emigrated from Persia, and to have consisted of at least seventy sings, or families, (viz., all those who are of the same origin, equivalent to the term "house," as made use of by the translators of the authorized English version.) In the last century only seven families remained, amounting to about six hundred persons. For a long time after their settlement in China their affairs were in a flourishing state, so that many became eminent for their attainments, especially in Chinese literature; others were dignified with the offices of state, others became rulers of provinces, and some were even advanced to the rank of mandarins. Their principal residences were Nimpo, Ning-hia, Ham-tcheon, Peking, and Cai-fong-fou. The affairs of the Jews gradually declining, many of them became the followers of Mohammed, so that the Jews of Cai-fong-fou, the capital of the province Honan, and about one hundred and fifty leagues from Peking, are now the only ones known and acknowledged. In the year of our Lord 1446 their synagogue was destroyed by an inundation of the river Ho-ang-ho; and again by fire at the commencement of the reign of the emperor Ouan-li, who governed from A. D. 1573 to A. D. 1620; and a third time by a flood in A. D. 1642. It was then rebuilt, and still exists.

These Jews are called by the Chinese Hoei-Hoei, a name given to them in common with the Mohammedans; but they call themselves Tiao-Kin-Kiao, that is, the law of those who cut out the sinews, because they cut away the sinews and veins, that they may abstain from blood. Their synagogue is large and magnificent. The most sacred part of the synagogue is the Bethel, or house of God. It is square on the outside, and circular within. In this Bethel, on the top of thirteen tables, thirteen *ta-kings*, that is, thirteen rolls of the Law, or Pentateuch, are placed; and each roll is covered with silk. At the very end of the temple or synagogue, behind Bethel, the tables of the Law are conspicuously written in Hebrew characters of gold; and on both sides of the tables are repositories, in which are kept the books which the Jews commonly use.

By the term *ta-king*, which signifies the great writing, the Chinese Jews solely designate the Pentateuch. Every ta-king is written upon long Chinese paper, many leaves of which are glued together, to make the paper thicker, and to cause it to turn more readily round the central stick of the roll. Every roll contains the whole law, without any distinction of books, chapters, or verses, but divided into fifty-three sections. In these rolls there are no vowel points, nor the distinctive letters of the sections, either single or triple; and only the space of one line intervenes between them. When the Jews of China were asked why there were no *points* in their *ta-kings*, they replied, that the Law was so rapidly dictated by God, that Moses had not time to affix the points. They affirm that the points were afterward added by the doctors of the West.

A roll of the *ta-king*, compactly wound round its stick, is about two feet high; its diameter rather exceeds the measure of a foot. One of these ta-kings, being very ancient, is held in the highest estimation. According to the representation of the Chinese Jews to father Ricci, the most ancient MS. of the Jews in China was about six hundred years old, at the commencement of the seventeenth century, and therefore about eight hundred years old at present. When the synagogue at Cai-fong-fou was burned, and the books destroyed, in the reign of the emperor Ouan-li, this copy of the Pentateuch was obtained from a Mohammedan, whom the Jews met with in the city Ninghia, in the province of Chen-si. This Mohammedan had received it from a Jew at the point of death, in the city of Canton, who committed it to him as a precious treasure of antiquity and religion. This roll is now held in very great veneration, because their other ta-kings have been copied from it; and because it was preserved in the second inundation, which happened in the year of our Lord 1642, of which calamity it now bears many marks.

Among the books in their repositories are many copies of the Law, that is, of the five books of Moses. The whole of the Law is not contained entire in any one book; for every section completes a book; it is therefore necessary to have fifty-three of these books to possess the whole Law. These books are four or five inches high, and about seven inches broad; they are written in larger letters than the ta-kings, and seldom have more than ten lines in a page. They consist only of a few leaves, rendered thicker by two or three being glued together; for the Jews never size with alum the thin paper of the Chinese, to enable them to write on both sides of it. Each of these books has a square mark about the middle of the first page, in which the first word of the book or section is written, without vowel points; and which is ornamented with silk, or with the colours green, blue, or white. The pages are marked at the top with the numerals, in words at full length, in the inward, and not according to our custom, in the outward margin. The sections of the Law are the same as in our Bibles, except that they connect our fifty-second and fifty-third sections together; hence we reckon fifty-four sections, and they only fifty-three.

The Jews of China are not acquainted with our distinction of Keri and Ketib; though in their books there are some letters larger and some smaller than the usual size. In the books kept in their repositories they use the vowel points and accents, as well as some other marks of distinction peculiar to themselves; and the number of verses of which every book or section consists is placed at the end of it.

Besides the Law of Moses, they have other books in their repositories, which they denominate San-tso, a word signifying supplementary and distinct books, and which contain certain imperfect parts of several of the historical and prophetical books; but among them are no portions whatsoever of the books of Proverbs, Job, the Song of Solomon, or Ecclesiastes; nor of the books of the prophets Ezekiel, Hosea, Joel, Amos, Obadiah, or Malachi; and of the book of the prophet Daniel they possess only a few verses of the first chapter. They have also one copy, which they greatly prize, of the two books of the Maccabees, which they name Manthiochium, or Mathathies. They have also in the same repositories a book of ceremonics or prayers, &c., arranged for all the sabbaths and festivals throughout the year, almost all of them taken from the Scriptures, and chiefly from the Psalms. In these repositories they have, lastly, some books, ill arranged, which they term in the Chinese language Tiang-tchang, or the Interpreters.

These Chinese Jews are, in general, very ignorant of the Hebrew language; for although by constant study, they, for the most part, understand the five books of Moses, they are not so skilful in reading their other books. They excuse their ignorance by saying, that they have a long time ago lost their *Tou-king-puen*, or grammatical books, and that for some centuries they have seen no Jew from Si-yu, that is to say, from the West. To their sacred books they pay so much reverence, that they seldom or never keep them at home, but lodge them in the repositories of the *li-pai-se*, or temple; yet this apparent veneration is nothing more than a mere superstitious practice, for when any one has copied, or caused to be copied, the books of the Law, and has placed them in the *li-pai-se*, he deems himself to have discharged all the duties of religion; and sometimes never afterward makes his appearance in the synagogue.

In copying the sacred books the Chinese Jews esteem it an act of impiety to make use of either Chinese pencils or Chinese ink; for this purpose therefore they cut a reed, called bamboo, into pens; and use very black ink, prepared after the European manner, in the beginning of the year, immediately after the feast of tabernacles; and which they keep with great care throughout the year. When the Law is read in the synagogue, the roll of the *ta-king* is placed in the chair of Moses, and as it is unrolled, a Jew, covered with a blue cap, and having a cotton or fustian cloth spread over his head, reads it aloud, or rather sings it, in a manner similar to that of the Jews of Italy: a monitor stands close to the reader, and corrects him when he errs. On the twenty-fourth day of their seventh month they celebrate the feast of the Law, when they carry about their thirteen manuscripts of the *ta-king* in solemn procession: and on which occasion the *tchang-kiao*, or ruler of the synagogue, wears a remarkable silk scarf, of a red colour, hanging from the right shoulder, and brought under the left, and there fixed by a knot.

Fathers Gozeni, Domege, and Gaubil, were desirous of collating the Hebrew Bible, with the books of the *li-pai-se*, and more especially the entire Pentateuch, with the ta-kings preserved in the Bethel of the synagogue; but the prejudiced opinions of the Chinese Jews always prevented their desire, since it appeared to them impious to trust their books to men who ate black flesh, for so they termed swine's flesh. An expectation was indulged some years afterward, (A. D. 1768,) by Dr. Kennicott, that books might be obtained from the repositories, either by exchange or money. A copy of the Hebrew Bible, printed at Amsterdam, by Vander Hooght was offered to them, which they praised exceedingly at first, on account of the beauty and thickness of the paper, and the compact binding of the book; but afterward despised it, and would not so much as supply from it the deficiencies of their own books. Money, however, had more weight with them; and one of them named Naai-ven had already promised that he would take his copy of the books of Joshua, Judges, Samuel, and Kings from the *li-pai-se*, and sell it at a stated price. But as soon as he had secretly conveyed it away, he was discovered, and severely reprimanded; for there is an ancient proverb well known among them, that "he who sells his sacred books, sells his God." Another Jew, named Cao-ting, who made the same promise, went to the ruler of the synagogue, and redemanded the books of the Law, sumptuously written, which he had received from his uncle when at the point of death, and which he had recently deposited in the li-pai-se; but instead of obtaining them he was severely rebuked, and sent away with ignominy. Thus every effort hitherto made to obtain possession of the books of the Chinese Jews has completely failed.*

Quitting for the present the colony of Jews in China, and again directing our views westward, we perceive the invaluable doctrines of Christianity rapidly extending their benign influences on every side; so that not only transcripts of the sacred Scriptures, especially of the New Testament, are multiplied, to aid the private devotions, or the public worship of those who understand the original tongues, but *translations* are made into various languages, for the accommodation of those who cannot read the Hebrew and Greek Scriptures, or who read them with difficulty. Within the first two centuries of the Christian era, the whole, or parts of the sacred writings, were translated into the *Syriac* and *Latin*, two of the most ancient versions of the New Testament, one of which was spread throughout Europe and the north of Africa; the other

* See the translation of the whole of G. Brotier's account of the Chinese Jews in *Jewish Expositor*, vol. i. No. 3, 4, for 1816. Kennicotti Dissertatio Generalis, p. 65, fol.

propagated from Edessa to China. This ancient Syriac translation is usually called the *Peshito*, or literal, or correct and faithful version; and is thus distinguished from the more modern versions, especially the one made under the patronage of Philoxenus, in A. D. 508, and from him denominated the *Philoxenian* version. The Rev. Dr. Claudius Buchanan, in his late tour through British India, to examine into the state of Christianity, was presented, by the Syrian bishop in Argamalee, with a most valuable Syriac manuscript, which had been deposited in one of the remote churches, near the mountains. It was supposed to have been preserved for near a thousand years. "It contains the Old and New Testaments, engrossed on strong vellum, in large folio, having three columns in a page; and is written with beautiful accuracy. The character is Estrangelo-Syriac; and the words of every book are numbered. But the volume has suffered injury from time or neglect. In certain places the ink has been totally obliterated from the page, and left the parchment in its state of natural whiteness: but the letters can, in general, be distinctly traced from the impress of the pen, or from the partial corrosion of the ink."* It is now deposited with other Syriac manuscripts, in the public library of the University of Cambridge.

The *Peshito* version was first made known to Europe by Moses of Marden, in Mesopotamia, a Maronite priest, who was sent by Ignatius, patriarch of the Maronite Christians at Antioch, to pope Julius III., to acknowledge the supremacy of the Roman pontiff; and to obtain the printing of the Syriac New Testament, that it might be more generally dispersed through the East. For the purpose of facilitating the latter design, he brought with him two Syriac MSS.; which appear not to have been duplicates of the whole Syriac Testament, but two different volumes, the one containing the Gospels, the other the Acts and the Epistles. One of them, containing the Gospels, said to have been written at Mosul, on the Tigris, is still preserved in the Imperial library at Vienna. For some time no one could be found to undertake a work, which would not only be very expensive, but also require much judgment and care to execute correctly; but at length Albert Widmanstadt who had formerly projected the same design, prevailed with the emperor Ferdinand I. to be at the expense of an undertaking so likely to prove advantageous to the church in general, and to the churches of Asia in particular. The care of the impression was committed to Widmanstadt, and Moses of Marden, who were as-

* Buchanan's Christian Researches, p. 129, Edin. 1812, 8vo.

sisted, particularly in the formation of the matrices for the types, by William Postel. This edition was completed, and neatly printed at Vienna, in 1555, in two volumes, 4to. It wants, however, the two last Epistles of St. John, the second Epistle of St. Peter, the Epistle of St. Jude, and the Revelation of St. John, which appear not to have been received into the sacred canon so early as the period when the translation was first made. A thousand copies were printed, of which the emperor reserved to himself five hundred for sale, sent three hundred to the two Syrian patriarchs, and made a present to Moses of two hundred copies, together with twenty dollars; these copies Moses disposed of by sale, prior to his return to Syria. This rare and valuable edition is considered as a perfect pattern of the genuine *Peshito*. The character of it by Michaelis is too interesting to be omitted. "The *Peshito*," says he, "is the very best translation of the Greek Testament that I have ever read; that of Luther, though in some respects inferior to his translation of the Old Testament, holding the second rank. Of all the Syriac authors with which I am acquainted, not excepting Ephrem and Bar Hebræus, its language is the most elegant and pure, not loaded with foreign words, like the Philoxenian version, and other later writings, and discovers the hand of a master in rendering those passages where the two idioms deviate from each other. It has no marks of the stiffness of a translation, but is written with the ease and fluency of an original; and this excellence of style must be ascribed to its antiquity, and to its being written in a city (Edessa) that was the residence of Syrian kings. It is true that the Syriac version, like all human productions, is not destitute of faults, and, what is not to be regarded as a blemish, differs frequently from the modern modes of explanation: but I know of none that is so free from error, and none that I consult with so much confidence, in cases of difficulty and doubt."*

This version is supposed to have been made at Edessa, where Abgarus, to whom certain spurious epistles have been ascribed, as passing between him and Jesus Christ, reigned from the eighth year after the birth of our Lord to the year 45. He is also said to have built there a Christian church, in the form of a temple, with a row of steps leading to the holy place; from whence the custom of erecting churches in the form of temples was communicated to the Christian countries in Europe. Of the translator of this version we have no certain knowledge. By the Syrians themselves, it has been asserted, that part of the *Old Testament* was

* Marsh's Michaelis, vol. ii, part i, sec. ii–vi, pp. 4–33, 40, 41.

translated in the time of Solomon, for the use of Hiram, king of Tyre, and the rest under Abgarus, king of Edessa, by Thaddeus, or one of the apostles. But whoever was the translator, there is internal evidence that the Old Testament was translated subsequent to the New, and therefore probably not translated by the same person.*

The first printed edition of the Syriac Old Testament was that by Le Jay, in the celebrated Polyglot of Paris, in 1645. The editors of the first printed edition of the Syriac New Testament were, as we have already noticed, Albert Widmanstadt, Moses of Marden, and William Postel.

JOHN ALBERT WIDMANSTADT, or WIDIMANSTADTER, chancellor of Germany under Ferdinand I., was a native of Nalinga, in the district of Ulm, in the circle of Suabia. He acquired the first rudiments of learning under George Bauler; and at thirteen years of age began to study the Greek tongue, under the famous Reuchlin, or Capnio, and afterward attended the lectures of James Jonas, at Tubingen. His knowledge of the Syriac language was obtained after his entrance upon public life, and was occasioned by a singular occurrence, thus related in his preface to the Syriac New Testament. Accompanying the court of Charles V. to Bologna, in 1529, he lodged in a house adjoining a monastery, where Theseus Ambrosius, a learned and aged civilian, then resided. One day visiting the monastery, he accidentally met a venerable old man, whom he courteously saluted. It was Theseus himself, who entering into conversation with him, and learning his desires to examine the literary treasures of the house, readily undertook to assist him. Having conducted Widmanstadt into the library, Theseus opened the doors of one of the book-cases, and taking out a Syriac MS. of the Gospels, said with a sigh, "My friend, I have for fifteen years devoted myself to these studies, and have loved them hitherto without a rival. But how earnestly do I wish that I could meet with some one of a prompt and ready genius, who would be willing to acquire from one whose days are nearly ended, and would transmit to others, the knowledge of a language consecrated by the holy lips of Jesus Christ." Widmanstadt professed himself to be ready to undertake the task, and as far as opportunity would permit him, to endeavour to fulfil the desire of the good old man, if he would afford him his assistance in acquiring the language. Theseus accordingly instructed him during his stay at Bologna, so that by indefatigable application, he soon became a

* Marsh's Michaelis, *ubi sup.* Calmet, Dictionnaire de la Bible;—*Bible en Syriaque Thadée.* Simon, Hist. Critique du V. T., liv. ii, ch. xv.

proficient in the Syriac tongue, in which he was afterward perfected by Simeon, bishop of the Syrians of Mount Libanus. In 1533 he met with a copy of the Syriac Gospels, in one of the continental libraries, which he transcribed; and being at Rome, was desirous of printing it under the auspices of Pope Clement VII., but was prevented by the decease of that pontiff. When in Italy, he assumed the name of *Johannes Lucretius.*

After the death of Clement, Widmanstadt returned into Germany. On his journey, meeting with Cardinal Pole, who himself had translated the Lamentations of Jeremiah out of Hebrew into Latin, and who was then going as the pope's legate to England, he was persuaded to interest himself in the printing of the Syriac Testament. His exertions were successful, and produced the rare and beautiful edition of 1555. He died about A. D. 1559. After his death, his library was purchased by the duke of Bavaria.*

WILLIAM POSTEL was born of obscure parents, in the province of Normandy. Possessing a genius naturally suited to study, and being ardently desirous of acquiring knowledge, he conquered the various difficulties which opposed themselves to his success, and finally became one of the most eminent linguists of the sixteenth century, and regius professor of the mathematics and languages, in the university of Paris.

Led by desire to see the world, he quitted France, and travelled into the East, visiting Rome, Constantinople, Alexandria, Jerusalem, and other famous cities. While in the East, he was employed by Francis I. to procure Oriental MSS. for the Royal library, and executed his commission in a manner highly satisfactory to his royal master.

Returning to Venice, after an absence of sixteen years, he unfortunately adopted several singular and mystical opinions, which being deemed heretical and dangerous by the magistrates, he was obliged to escape into Germany, where he resided for some time at the court of Ferdinand; but abjuring his errors, was permitted to return to France. He, however, returned to his former opinions, and by a decree of the parliament was banished to the monastery of St. Martin, where he died at a very advanced age A. D. 1581.†

"The very best edition of the Syriac New Testament is un-

* Le Long. Biblioth. Sacra, ed. Masch, pt. ii, vol. i, sec. 4, pp. 74, 75. Marsh's Michaelis, vol. ii, pt. i, ch. vii, sec. 2, pp. 8, 9. Freheri Theatrum Virorum Eruditione Clarorum, pt. i, sec. 2, p. 38. Noriberg. 1688, fol. Schelhornii Amœnitates Literariæ, tom. xiii, pp. 223–240. Francfort and Leips. 1730, 12mo.

† Freheri Theatrum Viror. Clar., pt. iv, pp. 1474, 1475. Leigh's (Edward) Trea-

doubtedly that of Leyden, published by Schaaf in 1709, and reprinted in 1717. The very excellent Lexicon which is annexed to it will ever retain its value, being, as far as regards the New Testament, extremely accurate and complete, and supplying in some measure the place of a concordance."*

CAROLUS SCHAAF, who was a native of Holland, and teacher of the Oriental languages, was assisted in the former part of this edition by the celebrated Leusden, professor of Hebrew at Utrecht, who died in 1699, when the work was printed as far as Luke xv, 20. Schaaf died in 1729.

The old Latin translations which were made prior to the time of Jerome have received the common denomination *Vetus Italica*, or ancient Italic version. The revised translation of Jerome is distinguished by the term *Vulgate*. Dr. Mills (Proleg., p. 41, &c.) conjectures, that a translation was made in the second century. Augustus, who lived in the fourth century, thus states the origin of the ancient Latin versions. In his treatise *De Doctrina Christiana*, lib. ii, cap. xi, he says, "The number of those who have translated the Scriptures from the Hebrew into the Greek may be computed; but the number of those who have translated the Greek into the Latin cannot. For immediately upon the first introduction of Christianity, if a person got possession of a Greek manuscript, and thought he had any knowledge of the two languages, he set about translating the Scriptures." In another part of his works, lib. ii, cap. xv, he observes further, "*in ipsis autem interpretationibus Itala ceteris præferatur, nam est verborum tenacior cum perspicuitate sententiæ*. Among the translations themselves, the Italic is to be preferred, because the most literal and perspicuous."†

These high terms of commendation have raised a general wish that the *Vetus Italica* should be discovered and published. The first publication of the kind was that of Flaminius Nobilius, printed at Rome in 1588, in one volume folio, under the auspices of Sixtus V. In 1695, Dom Martianay published at Paris, in octavo, what he supposed was the *Vetus Italica* of the Gospel of St. Matthew, and of the Epistle of St. James, besides the books of Job and Judith. To these was added, in 1715, the Acts of the Apostles, printed at Oxford, in a fac-simile edition of a Greek and Latin

tise of Religion and Learning, p. 298, fol. Postelli Absconditorum e Constit. Mundi Clavis. edit. Franc. de Monte S., pp. 110–118. Amster. 1646, 24mo.

* Marsh's Michaelis, vol. ii, pt. i, ch. vii, sec. 2, p. 17.

† Millii Proleg. fol. xli. Butler's Horæ Biblicæ, vol. i, pp. 181–185. Lond. 12mo. Mosheim's Commentaries on the Affairs of the Christians, translated by R. S. Vidal, Esq., vol. ii, p. 33. Note. Lond. 1813, 8vo.

MS. of the seventh century, preserved among the Laudian MSS. in the Bodleian library. The editor was the famous antiquary, Thomas Hearne, who printed only one hundred and twenty copies, by which means the edition is become extremely scarce. This was the first *fac-simile* edition ever printed. A copy of it is in the Collegiate library, in Manchester.

Thomas Hearne, M. A., the editor of this valuable edition of the Acts of the Apostles, and the indefatigable collector and editor of ancient books and manuscripts, particularly of our old chronicles, was the son of George Hearne, parish clerk of White Waltham, in Berkshire, in which parish he was born in 1678. Having but little opportunity for learning, and his father being poor, he was at an early age obliged to earn his subsistence as a day-labourer. Happily for him his abilities were discovered and fostered by Francis Cherry, Esq., in whose house he had lived as a menial servant, but who, on perceiving his talents, placed him at the free school of Bray, in his native county, and afterward educated him as his son. In 1695 he was entered of Edmund-hall, Oxford. Dr. Mill, the principal of the college, soon marked the bent of his studies, and employed him as his assistant in the laborious task of collating MSS. for his edition of the Greek Testament. Dr. Grabe also availed himself of his useful talents in transcribing and collating various old MSS. In 1699 he took his bachelor's degree, which was soon followed by a proposal from his tutor, Dr. White Kennet, to go to Maryland, as one of Dr. Bray's missionaries; but this proposal, not according with his views, was declined, and in a short time he obtained the situation of assistant to Dr. Hudson, the librarian of the Bodleian library. In 1703 he took his master's degree. In 1715 he was appointed archetypographus of the university and esquire-beadle of the civil law. These offices he soon after resigned, because of his objections to take the oaths to government, being in political principles a Jacobite. From the same conscientious motive he refused several other advantageous preferments. The latter part of his life was devoted to the study of antiquities, and the editing and republishing of numerous curious antiquarian works. He died at Oxford, June 10, 1735. His taste for those researches, which formed the business of his life, was seen at a very early period; for when he had only attained the knowledge of the alphabet, he was continually pouring over the old tomb-stones in the church-yard. But nothing can more correctly characterize this plain and laborious man than the following thanksgiving found among his papers after his decease

"O most gracious and merciful Lord God, wonderful in thy providence, I return all possible thanks to thee, for the care thou hast always taken of me. I continually meet with most signal instances of this thy providence, and one act yesterday, when I unexpectedly met with *three old MSS.*, for which, in a particular manner, I return my thanks, beseeching thee to continue the same protection to me, a poor, helpless sinner, and that for Jesus Christ his sake."*

Celebrated editions of the *Old Italic* were also edited by Blanchini and Sabatier. The most important and magnificent one is that of the four Gospels, by F. Joseph Blanchini, of Verona, a priest of the Oratory, taken from five genuine manuscripts of this version, or more properly from four copies of this version, one of them containing only the corrected version of Jerome. It was printed at the expense of John V. king of Portugal, at the instigation of Cardinal Carsini, and was published by order of Pope Benedict XIV., who was highly valued by the Protestant as well as by the Roman Church. The title of this work, which consists of two parts, forming four volumes, is, *Evangeliorum Quadruplex Latinæ versionis antiquæ, seu Italicæ, nunc primum in lucem editum ex codicibus manuscriptis aureis, argenteis, purpureis, aliisque, plusquam millennariæ ætatis sub auspiciis Joannis V. regis fidelissimi Lusitaniæ, a Josepho Blanchino. Anno Domini* CIↃ IↃ CCXLVIII. The four MSS. made use of for this edition were found at Corbie, Vercelli, Brescia, and Verona. That from Vercelli is said to be in the hand-writing of Eusebius, bishop of that city, and martyr. The fifth MS., which is taken from Jerome's corrected edition, is the *Codex Foro-juliensis*. Till Dr. Kennicott's "Collation" appeared, Blanchini's work was considered as the most splendid that had issued from the press during the eighteenth century. The beauty and largeness of the types, the great number of learned treatises, and the copper plates with which it is ornamented, make the work so very expensive, that it is seldom to be found in private libraries.†

While Blanchini was engaged in preparing the *Evangeliorum Quadruplex*, P. Sabatier published at Rheims, in three large volumes folio, his *Bibliorum sacrorum Latinæ versiones antiquæ, seu vetus Italica.* 1743. Of which a new edition was published in 1749–1751. To the third volume of the first edition, which

* Chalmers's Gen. Biog. Dictionary, vol. xvii, pp. 275–284.

† Marsh's Michaelis, vol. ii, pt. i, ch. vii, sec. 22, pp. 109, 110, &c., and ch. viii, p. 274. Butler's Horæ Biblicæ, vol. i, pp. 183, 184.

contains the New Testament, a memoir of Sabatier is prefixed, he having died before its completion. The following brief account of him is extracted from it :—

Peter Sabatier was born at Poictiers, in France, in 1682. At an early age he removed to Paris, where he studied in the Mazarine College under the most celebrated professors. As soon as he had attained the years prescribed by the ecclesiastical laws, he determined to assume the religious habit, and accordingly enrolled himself under the standard of St. Benedict, and took the vows upon him in the neighboring monastery of St. Faro, bishop of Meaux. That he might more successfully pursue his theological studies, he entered into the congregation of St. Maur, in the monastery of St. Germain, the scene of the labours of Mabillon, Ruinart, and other learned men, by whose example and friendship he was stimulated to those literary exertions which have given celebrity to his name. His friendship for Ruinart, in particular, led him to become first the associate with Ruinart, and after his decease the continuator of the *Annalium Benedictorum.*

In 1727 he quitted Paris, and went to Rheims, where he commenced, carried on, and nearly completed his celebrated edition of the *Vetus Italica*, or Italic version. This undertaking was for some time suspended, by his being delegated to form the catalogue of the library belonging to the abbey of St. Nicasius, which having executed in a masterly manner, and accompanied with an excellent index, he returned to his favourite design, and pursued the arrangement and collation of the manuscripts requisite for his work with the most indefatigable diligence ; and after having devoted many years to this object, he succeeded in printing the first volume, and preparing the other portions for the press, from which the second volume was about to issue when the fatal disease seized him which terminated his useful life, after an illness of fifteen days, borne with the most pious resignation, March 22, 1742. In stature, he was of the middle size ; in conversation, affable and cheerful, sometimes enlivened by wit ; his countenance mild and open, but inclined to melancholy. Study and prayer were his delight, prayer softening and solacing the severity of study.*

In 1793 a fac-simile edition of a very ancient Greek and Latin manuscript of the Gospels and Acts of the Apostles was published in a magnificent folio at Cambridge, by Dr. Thomas Kipling.

* Bib. Sac. Latinæ Versiones Antiquæ, *Lectori Benevolo*, pp. xxviii, xxix, tom. ii, Remis. 1743, fol.

This manuscript is usually denominated the *Codex Bezæ*, from the donor of it, or *Codex Cantabrigiensis*, from belonging to the University of Cambridge. It was obtained, by the reformer Beza, from the monastery of St. Irenæus in Lyons, where it had lain covered with dust for many years, till discovered during the civil wars in 1562; and in 1581 was presented by him to the University of Cambridge, which, in 1787, came to the resolution of printing the whole MS. in letters of the same form and magnitude as the original hand-writing, and accordingly committed the publication of it to Dr. Kipling.*

At a very early age of Christianity the Scriptures were translated also into the EGYPTIAN language, including the dialects both of Upper and Lower Egypt; the former called *Sahidic*, the latter *Coptic*. The *Sahidic* version is supposed to be as old as the second century. Several manuscripts, or rather fragments of manuscripts, of this version, are preserved in the libraries of Rome, Paris, Oxford, Berlin, and Venice. From the quotations in a Sahidic MS. in the British Museum, which contains a work entitled *Sophia*, and written by Valentinus in the beginning of the second century, Dr. Woide has endeavoured to prove, not only that a Sahidic version of the New Testament existed in the second century, but that there was also a translation of the Old Testament into Sahidic, from which the author frequently quoted.†

After the learned Woide had published his fac-simile edition of the Alexandrian MS. of the New Testament, in 1786, he engaged in preparing for the press an edition of several fragments of the Sahidic version, comprehending about a third part of the New Testament, for which he had issued proposals in 1778. This work, which he designed as an appendix to his Alexandrian New Testament, he intended to accompany with a Latin translation, and a dissertation upon the antiquity and various readings of the Sahidic version. That the publication might be as perfect as the small resources of Egyptian learning would admit, he did not confine himself to the Oxford MSS., and such other as might be found in this country, but enlisted in his service one or two scholars on the continent, who favoured him with collations; and G. Baldwin, Esq., an English gentleman, at that time resident in Egypt, in an official situation, sent over to him several Sahidic MSS., which he had collected together from different parts of that country. The work was put to press at Oxford, under the

* Marsh's Michaelis, vol. ii, pt. i, ch. viii, sec. 6, pp. 236–241, pt. ii, p. 688.

† Ibid., vol. ii, pt. ii, p. 595.

patronage of its delegates, in the year 1788. Death, however, prevented him from bringing it to a close. At the time of his decease the printing had advanced as far as Luke; and with a view to the further prosecution of the work, the delegates purchased his papers, and committed them into the hands of Dr. Ford, the late principal of Magdalen-hall, Oxford, and professor of Arabic in that university, who completed it in the year 1799. In addition to the fragments of the New Testament in the Sahidic version, and an able dissertation on the Egyptian versions, written by Woide himself, this work contains an accurate description of the various MSS. of that dialect, which are to be found either at Oxford or in other libraries, to which Woide and his friends had access. The collation of the Vatican MS. which is inserted at the close of the volume, was made by Dr. Bentley. To the work is prefixed an elegant and learned preface, by Dr. Ford, containing some particulars concerning Woide and his studies. The work itself forms a magnificent folio volume, bearing the following title: *Appendix ad editionem Novi Testamenti Græci e codice MS. Alexandrino a Carolo Godofredo Woide, descripti in qua continentur Fragmenta Novi Testamenti, juxta interpretationem dialecti Superioris Ægypti quæ Thebaidica vel Sahidica appellatur, e codicibus Oxoniensibus maxima ex parte desumpta, cum Dissertatione de Versione Bibliorum Ægyptiaca. Quibus subjicitur codicis Vaticani Collatio.**

The *Coptic* version, or that in the dialect of Lower Egypt, is probably of rather later date than the Sahidic, though not more modern than the *third*, if not the second century. Antonius, an illiterate Egyptian monk, who resided, in the third century, in a monastery of Alexandria where the Sahidic was not understood, had read the New Testament, and as he was ignorant of Greek, must have had a translation into his native dialect. Another proof of the early existence of a Coptic or vulgar Egyptian translation is, that in one of the rules of Pachomius, for the conduct of the Egyptian monks, it is ordered, that "all persons admitted to the order of monk, if unable to read, shall learn the letters of the A B C, that they may be able to read and write; after which they shall learn every day by heart some passages of Scripture." Men therefore of such profound ignorance would not have been able to read the Bible, unless they had possessed a translation in their native language.†

The Coptic dialect is now become obsolete, except as it is pre

* Appendix ad Edit. N. T. *ut. sup.* in Præfat.

† Marsh's Michaelis, vol. ii, pt. ii, p. 587.

served in the Scriptures and books of devotion. About the end of the fifth century of the Hegira, the calif Walid I. prohibited the Greek tongue throughout his whole empire, by which means the Coptic, the characters of which are derived from the Greek, as well as many of its words, ceased, like the other languages of the nations subdued by the Saracens, to be a spoken language. Niebuhr, in his Description of Arabia, p. 86, relates, that though the Gospels are still read in the Coptic version in the public service, it is not understood even by the priests; and that immediately after the lessons have been read in Coptic, the same are read in Arabic, which is the present language both of Upper and Lower Egypt.*

The only printed edition of the Coptic New Testament is the one edited at Oxford in 1716 by Dr. David Wilkins, accompanied with a Latin translation. The typographical execution of the work is beautiful. The title, which is an engraved one, is the following:—*Novum Testamentum Ægyptium, vulgo Copticum. Ex MSS. Bodlejanis descripsit, cum Vaticanis et Parisiensibus contulit et in Latinum sermonem convertit David Wilkins Ecclesiæ Anglicanæ Presbyter. Oxonii e Theatro Sheldoniano typis et sumptibus Academiæ.* 1716. It is in quarto. The editor, in his Prolegomena, supposes this version to have been made in the second century, but certainly not later than the commencement of the third century: *Versionem Novi Testamenti in linguam Ægyptiacam primis a Christo nato seculis, scilicet vel secundo, vel tertii initio factam esse nullus dubito asserere. Scriptores equidem illius ævi alto silentio annum et auctores pii hujus operis nobis haud detegunt, non obscuro tamen argumento ex Athanasio et Palladio elici potest Novum Testamentum Ægyptium jam circa medium seculi tertii exstitisse.*†

Dr. Wilkins also published an edition of the Coptic Pentateuch, printed at London, by Bowyer, in 1731. The impression consisted of only two hundred copies.

Egyptian literature is so much indebted to the learned editors of the Egyptian versions of the Scriptures, and particularly to Dr. Woide, that the subsequent biographical notices will probably gratify the reader. They are principally taken from Dr. Ford's Preface to the "Fragments of the Sahidic version;" and Nichols' "Literary Anecdotes of the Eighteenth Century," vols. i and ix.

CHARLES GODFREY WOIDE was a native of Poland. While at the University of Leyden in 1750, he was employed in transcribing

* Butler's Horæ Biblicæ, vol. i, p. 169. Marsh's Michaelis, vol. ii, pt. ii, p. 586.

† Le Long, Bibliotheca Sacra, a Masch, pt. ii, tom. i, sec. 10, p. 188.

the Coptic Lexicon of La Croze, formerly librarian to the king of Prussia, at Berlin. This work he undertook at the request of the Rev. Christian Scholtz, chaplain in ordinary to the king of Prussia, who was engaged in completing a grammar of both the Egyptian dialects, under the sanction of Dr. Jablonsky, his brother-in-law, an eminent professor at Frankfort Some time afterward he came over to England, where his first preferment was the preachership of the Dutch chapel in the Savoy, (succeeding the Rev. Bernard Drimel, a native of Frankfort on the Oder, who died in June, 1770,) to which he soon after added the readership of the same chapel. In 1773 and 1774 he was sent under the auspices of his present majesty* to Paris, for the purpose of transcribing several Sahidic and Memphitic MSS., where he resided about four months. In 1775 he revised through the Clarendon Press, Scholtz's *Lexicon Ægyptiaco-Latinum*, 4to. He was elected F.S.A. in 1778; and distinguished himself the same year by publishing a Coptic and Sahidic grammar, under the following title:—*Christ. Scholtz Grammatica Ægypti utriusque dialecti quam breviavit, illustravit, edidit C. G. Woide.* 4to. In 1782 Mr. Woide was appointed an assistant librarian at the British Museum; at first, in the department of natural history; but very soon after, in one more congenial to his studies, that of printed books. In 1786 came out his truly valuable edition of the Alexandrian MS. of the New Testament, dedicated to the then archbishop of Canterbury; on which occasion he was introduced to his majesty at the levee, and had the honour of presenting him with a copy of his work. He was this year admitted to the honorary degree of LL.D. in the University of Oxford. He had before obtained the degree of D.D. from the University of Copenhagen. In 1788 he was elected F.R.S. The latter part of his life was chiefly devoted to examining and collating the fragments of the Sahidic version of the New Testament, and in preparing them for the press. He also revised and corrected the Greek quotations in Bishop Hurd's edition of Warburton's Works. On May 6th, 1790, while at Sir Joseph Banks's with a select party of literary friends, he was seized with an apoplectic fit; every assistance was administered to him, and he was attended by Dr. Carmichael Smith, but died the next day, at his apartments in the British Museum. He left two orphan daughters, having been bereaved some years before of Mrs. Woide, who died August 12th, 1782.

* George the Third.

DAVID WILKINS, D.D., F.S.A., was a native of Memel, in Prussia, and eminent as an Oriental and Saxon scholar. About the year 1715 he was appointed by Archbishop Wake to succeed Dr. Benjamin Ibbot as keeper of the Archiepiscopal library at Lambeth; and in three years drew up a very curious catalogue of all the MSS. and printed books in that valuable library in his time, in which was incorporated the earlier catalogue of Mr. Henry Wharton, which is still preserved. As a reward for his industry and learning, Archbishop Wake constituted him his chaplain, collated him to several valuable livings, and, in 1720, to a prebend of Canterbury; to which was afterward added, his grace's option of the archdeaconry of Suffolk. Besides the Coptic New Testament and Pentateuch, he published a fine edition of *Leges Anglo-Saxonicæ ecclesiasticæ et civiles*, fol. 1721; *Seldeni Opera Omnia*, 3 vols. fol. 1726; and *Concilia Magnæ Britanniæ*, &c., 4 vols. fol. 1736. In 1725 he married the eldest daughter of Thomas Lord Fairfax, of Scotland; he died September 6th, 1745, and was buried at Hadleigh, in Essex.

Dr. Samuel Pegge, in his *Anonymiana*, (cent. i, p. 22,) thus speaks of Dr. Wilkins, with particular reference to a Polyglot Bible projected by him:—"The late Dr. David Wilkins, prebendary of Canterbury, a man of indefatigable industry, but grievously afflicted with the gout, had formed a design, as he told me, of publishing a European Polyglot, in order to illustrate the Scriptures of the Old and New Testament, by exhibiting, in one view, the authorized translations of the different nations of Europe, together with the best private ones of certain particular learned men, whereby the sense they severally put upon many of the more difficult texts might the more commodiously appear. But, alas! the doctor died before he had made any great advances in his project."

The THIRD CENTURY was eminently distinguished by the learned and critical labours of Origen, Pamphilus, Eusebius of Cesarea, and other individuals of sincere piety and multifarious learning.

ORIGEN was born at Alexandria, in Egypt, A.D. 185. Leonidas, his father, early taught him to exercise himself in searching the Scriptures, enjoining it upon him as a daily task to learn some portion of them by heart, and repeat it. This laid the foundation of an intimate acquaintance with the holy writings, and probably of that diligent study of them for which he was afterward so famed.

When he was seventeen years old, his father suffered martyrdom, leaving behind a wife and six children. In his son Origen, Leonidas found a steady encourager in the faith. Gladly would the son have suffered with his father; and when, to prevent him, his mother hid his clothes, he wrote a most persuasive letter, exhorting him, "Father, take heed; let not your care for us make you change your resolution." In his eighteenth year he was chosen master of the catechetical, or grammar school, at Alexandria. This situation he afterward relinquished, that he might apply himself entirely to theological studies. His library, containing the works of the heathen philosophers and poets, &c., he sold to a buyer, who engaged to give him *four oboli* (about sixpence) a day: and on this he subsisted for several years, sleeping on the floor, walking barefoot, and going almost naked; devoting not only the day, but also the greater part of the night, to the study of the Holy Scriptures.

He was a most voluminous writer; but the works which have immortalized his name are his HEXAPLA, or Collation of the Septuagint version, which Father Montfaucon supposes must originally have made fifty volumes; and his Vindication of Christianity against Celsus, the Epicurean philosopher.

In the collation of the Septuagint he laboured with indefatigable industry; and having acquired a perfect knowledge of the Hebrew tongue, and purchased from the Jews the *original*, (perhaps the autograph of Ezra,) or most authentic copies of the Hebrew Scriptures; and having also obtained a correct copy of the Septuagint, or Greek version, he transcribed them, and placed them in parallel columns. In the *first* column was the Hebrew text in Hebrew characters; in the *second*, the same text in Greek characters. In other columns he placed the Septuagint, and other Greek translations, particularly those of Aquila, (see p. 64,) and of Symmachus and Theodotion, two Ebionite Christians. The differences between the Hebrew copies and the Septuagint were noted by various marks. The name HEXAPLA, or *Sextuple*, was derived from the *six* principal Greek versions employed in the collation. Some fragments excepted, this work has been long irrecoverably lost. All that could be gathered from the works of the ancients was collected and published, A.D. 1713, by Montfaucon, in two volumes folio.*

An ancient MS. of the book of Genesis, written in Greek capitals, was brought from Philippi by two Greek bishops, who pre-

* Eusebius's History of the Church, b. vi, ch. ii, iii, xvi, xix, xxiii; b. vii, ch. i. Waltoni Proleg. 9. Clarke's Succession of Sacred Literature, vol. i, pp. 179–182.

sented it to King Henry VIII., telling him, at the same time, that tradition reported it to have been Origen's *own book.* Queen Elizabeth gave it to Sir John Fortescue, her preceptor in Greek, who placed it in the Cottonian library, now in the British Museum. Archbishop Usher considered it as the oldest manuscript in the world: and although it is impossible to ascertain whether this book belonged to Origen or not, it is probably the oldest manuscript in England, perhaps in Europe; unless it be supposed, with Matthai, that the copy of the Gospels preserved at Moscow is more ancient, which is at least very doubtful. It was almost destroyed by a fire which happened in the library in the year 1731; nor is it one of the least singular circumstances respecting this MS., that, in consequence of the fire, the capital letters in which it is written have been contracted from *large* into *small* capitals; and Mr. Dibdin supposes the *illuminations* to have undergone a similar metamorphosis.*

This manuscript contained one hundred and sixty-five folios or leaves, and two hundred and fifty most curious paintings, twenty-one fragments of which were engraved by the Society of Antiquaries of London.

Previous to the publication of the Hexapla, Origen composed what is called the TETRAPLA, or *Quadruple*, containing only the Septuagint, and the versions of Aquila, Symmachus, and Theodotion. The original work, which was deposited by him, with his other writings, in the library of Cesarea, is supposed to have perished when that city was taken and destroyed by the Saracens, in 653, after a siege of seven years.

He died a natural death, in the sixty-ninth year of his age, at Tyre, in 254, after having suffered much for the testimony of Christ: "A man," says Mosheim, "of vast and uncommon abilities, and the greatest luminary of the Christian world that this age exhibited to view. Had the justness of his judgment been equal to the immensity of his genius, the fervour of his piety, his indefatigable patience, his extensive erudition, and his other eminent and superior talents, all encomiums must have fallen short of his merit. Yet, such as he was, his virtues and labours deserve the admiration of all ages; and his name will be transmitted with honour through the annals of time, as long as learning and genius shall be esteemed among men."†

* Astle's Origin and Progress of Writing, ch. v. See a fac-simile of part of it in plate iii, fig. 3, of this work. Dibdin's Bibliog. Decameron, vol. i, p. xlviii, note.

† Mosheim's Eccles. Hist., vol. i, p. 270.

Pamphilus was a presbyter of Cesarea. He lived A. D. 294. In him were united the philosopher and the Christian. Of an eminent family, and large fortune, he might have aspired to the highest honours; but he withdrew himself from the glare of temporal grandeur, and spent his life in acts of the most disinterested benevolence. He was remarkable for his unfeigned regard to the sacred writings, and for his unwearied application in whatever he undertook. A great encourager of learning and piety, he not only lent books, especially copies of the Scriptures, to read, but, when he found persons well disposed, made them presents of his manuscripts, some of which were transcribed with the greatest accuracy by his own hand. "He erected (or rather enlarged) the library at Cesarea, which, according to Isidore of Seville, contained thirty thousand volumes. This collection seems to have been made merely for the good of the church, and to lend out to religiously disposed people. St. Jerome particularly mentions his collecting books for the purpose of *lending them to be read;*" and "this is, if I mistake not," says Dr. A. Clarke, "the first notice we have of a CIRCULATING LIBRARY."*

Of this library some traces remain even to the present day. Montfaucon assures us, that in the Jesuits' College, at Paris, there is a beautiful MS. of the Prophets, in which there occurs a note, signifying that it was transcribed from the very copy made by Pamphilus, in which were written these words: "Transcribed from the Hexapla, containing the translations; and corrected by Origen's own Tetrapla, which also had emendations and scholia in his own hand-writing. I Eusebius added the scholia; Pamphilus and Eusebius corrected."† The same learned writer mentions also a very ancient MS. of some of St. Paul's Epistles, preserved in the French king's library, which contains the following note: "This book was compared with the copy in the library at Cesarea, in the hand-writing of St. Pamphilus."‡

The death of this eminent, holy, and useful man did not discredit his life. For when a persecution was raised against the Christians, and Urbanus, the Roman president of Cesarea, an unfeeling and brutal man, required him to renounce his religion or his life, Pamphilus, the *gentle* Pamphilus, made the latter choice, and cheerfully submitted to imprisonment, to torture, and to death. The reflections of a late writer on the death of Pamphilus are so ap-

* Hieronymi Opera, tom. i, fol. 132, Basil. 1516, folio. Clarke's Succession of Sacred Literature, vol. i, p. 227.

† Montfaucon, Præf. in Hex. Orig., p. 4.

‡ Montfaucon, Bib. Coislin., p. 262.

propriate and impressive, that there can need no apology for inserting them :—

"When I peruse the account which Eusebius gives of the cruelties which this gentle and amiable spirit was forced to endure, and which he, and eleven others who were put to death with him, suffered with the most noble bravery and undaunted fortitude, I am struck with admiration at the greatness of that power which could raise men so much above themselves, and enable them so completely to overcome all the weakness of humanity. At all times there have been men ignorant, ferocious, and brutal, who have set death at defiance, and despised pain ; but it was reserved for Christianity to exhibit a new kind of sufferers—men who joined cool reason to heroic resolution, and tender sensibility to inflexible fortitude. The tiger and the bear will always retain their own manners ; but where is he, who shall give the feelings of the lion to the modest deer, or the gentle lamb ?—THEY ONLY CAN NOBLY SUFFER WHO CAN TENDERLY FEEL. Farewell, then, excellent Pamphilus ! reluctant we leave thee, bright STAR OF HUMAN EXCELLENCE ! obscure in the register of men ! illustrious in the CALENDAR OF HEAVEN !"*

EUSEBIUS, bishop of Cesarea, the friend of Pamphilus, was probably born in Cesarea about A. D. 270. Through affection to his friend he assumed his name, and was ever after termed EUSEBIUS PAMPHILUS. Origen excepted, he was the most learned of all the writers of antiquity. He is justly styled *the father of ecclesiastical history*. His most celebrated works are, his "Ecclesiastical History," "Evangelical Preparation," and "Evangelical Demonstration." His "History" begins at the birth of our Lord, and comes down to the defeat of Licinus. In his "Evangelical Preparation" he refutes the errors of paganism, demonstrates the excellence of the Hebrew Scriptures, and shows that the most eminent and learned nations, the Greeks especially, transcribed from them whatever dignity or truth is to be met with in their philosophy. His "Evangelical Demonstration," designed to prove that Jesus was the Messiah, is an invaluable work. Dr. Harwood observes, "It is a treasure of knowledge and good sense ; and contains all the arguments in favour of the credibility and divine authority of the Christian religion that have been advanced by Chandler, Leland, Benson, Butler, Brown, and other modern advocates of Christianity, against the Deists."†

* Christie's Miscellanies, p. 174, printed by J. Nichols, 1789, 8vo.

† Clarke's Bibliographical Dict., vol. iii, p. 209 ; and Succession of Sacred Litera-

He was made bishop of Antioch A. D. 313, was present at the council of Nice in 325, and at the council of Antioch in 331. He was high in the favour of the emperor Constantine, and is supposed to have died about A. D. 338 or 340.

Lucian, a presbyter of Antioch, and Hesychius, an Egyptian bishop, flourished about the same period, and are deservedly ranked among the Biblical scholars of that age. LUCIAN is generally supposed to have been born at Samosata, a celebrated city of Syria. He lived about the year 290. Eminent for piety and extraordinary knowledge of the divine Scriptures, as well as for polite learning, he laboured sedulously to produce a faithful and correct edition of the Septuagint version of the Old Testament, by collating the common Greek versions, and correcting the collation by the Hebrew. This edition was afterward read in all the churches from Constantinople to Antioch. The autograph of Lucian is said to have been found, in the reign of Constantine the Great, among the Jews, secreted in a wall. He suffered at Nicomedia, for confessing the name of Christ, in the reign of Maximin, and was buried at Helenopolis, in Bithynia.

HESYCHIUS was bishop of a city in Egypt, about the close of the same century. He also formed an edition of the Septuagint version, upon the same plan as that of Lucian, from copies collected in Egypt. To the Old Testament he added an edition of the New. His revision of the Septuagint was received and adopted by the churches of Egypt; so that the three editions by Origen, Lucian, and Hesychius shared the world among them; and from one or other of them are derived all the manuscript copies of the Septuagint that are now extant, or at least known. Hesychius obtained the crown of martyrdom in 311, during the persecution of Dioclesian.*

But while these pious and learned men were thus indefatigably labouring to promote the knowledge and circulation of the Holy Scriptures, various forms of superstition were insinuating themselves into the church of God. "Being mingled among the heathen," the Christians "learned their works," Psalm cvi, 35. One of the abuses thus introduced was *bibliomancy*, or divination by the Bible.

This kind of divination was named SORTES SANCTORUM, or

ture, vol. i, p. 265. Houtteville's Method of the principal Authors who wrote for and against Christianity, p. 92.

* Cavei Hist. Literar., p. 108. Lond. 1688, fol. Owen's Enquiry into the present State of the Sept. Version, p. 149.

SORTES SACRÆ, *lots of the saints, or sacred lots;* and consisted in suddenly opening, or dipping into the Bible, and regarding the passage that first presented itself to the eye as predicting the future *lot* of the inquirer. The *sortes sanctorum* succeeded the *sortes Homericæ*, and *sortes Virgilianæ* of the pagans, among whom it was customary to take the work of some famous poet, as Homer or Virgil, and write out different verses on separate scrolls, and afterward draw one of them; or else, opening the book suddenly, consider the first verse that presented itself as a prognostication of future events. Even the vagrant fortune-tellers among them, like some of the gipsies of our own times, adopted this method of imposing upon the credulity of the ignorant. The nations of the East still retain this practice. The late Persian usurper, Nadir Shah, twice decided upon besieging cities by opening upon verses of the celebrated poet Hafiz.*

Superstitious as this practice was, it nevertheless gained ground by the countenance of certain of the clergy, some of whom permitted prayers to be read in the churches for this very purpose.† Others, however, endeavoured to suppress it, for in the council of Vannes, held A. D. 465, it was ordained, "That whoever of the clergy or laity should be detected in the practice of this art, should be cast out of the communion of the church."‡ In 506, the council of Agde renewed the decree; and in 578, the council of Auxerre, among other kinds of divination, forbade the *lots of the saints*, as they were called, adding, "Let all things be done in the name of the Lord."§ But these ordinances gradually became slighted, for we find the practice again noticed and condemned in a capitulary, or edict of Charlemagne, in 793. In the twelfth century, this mode of divination was adopted as a means of discovering heretical opinions! One Peter of Thoulouse, being accused of heresy, and having denied it upon oath, a person who stood near took up the Gospels, on which he had sworn, and opening them suddenly, the first words he lighted upon were those of the devil to our Saviour, (Mark i, 24,) "What have we to do with thee, thou Jesus of Nazareth?" Which, says the relator, agreed well with such a heretic, "who indeed had nothing to do with Christ!!"‖

Francis of Assise, who founded the order of Franciscans, in

* Sir W. Jones's Works, Traité sur la Poesie Orientale, vol. v, p. 463, 4to.

† Heinault's Chronolog. Abridgment of the Hist. of France, A. D. 506.

‡ S. S. Concilia, Concil. Venet. Anno Christy 465, vol. iv, p. 1057. Bingham's Antiq. of the Chris. Church, vol. vii, b. xvi, ch. v, p. 278.

§ S. S. Concilia, vol. vii, p. 989.

‖ Gataker, Of the Nature and Use of Lots, p. 330.

1206, says of himself that he was tempted to have a *book:* but as this seemed contrary to his vow, which allowed him nothing but coats, a cord, and hose, and, in case of necessity only, shoes; he, after prayer, resorted to the Gospel, and meeting with that sentence, "It is given unto you to know the mysteries of the kingdom of heaven, but to them it is not given," Matthew xiii, 11; concluded that he should do well enough without books, and suffered none of his followers to have so much as a Bible, or Breviary, or Psalter!!*

Bibliomancy was also practised, not only in the common occurrences of life, and by private individuals, but by the highest dignitaries of the church, on the most public occasions, and particularly in the election of bishops. When a bishop was to be elected, it was customary to appoint a fast, usually for three days; afterward the Psalms, the Epistles of St. Paul, and the Gospels were placed on one side of the altar, and small billets, with the names of the candidates upon them, on the other; a child or some other person then drew one of the billets, and the candidate whose name was upon it was declared to be duly elected. On one of these occasions, St. Euvert caused a child to be brought which had not yet learned to speak; he then directed the infant to take up one of the billets; the little innocent obeyed, and took up one on which the name of St. Agnan was inscribed, who was proclaimed to be elected by the Lord. But for the more general satisfaction of the multitude, Euvert consulted the sacred volumes. On opening the Psalms, he read, "Blessed is the man whom thou choosest, and causest to approach unto thee, that he may dwell in thy courts." In the Epistles of St. Paul he found, "Other foundation can no man lay, than that is laid, which is Jesus Christ." And in the Gospels he opened upon the words, "Upon this rock I will build my church, and the gates of hell shall not prevail against it." These testimonies were accounted decisive in favour of Agnan, all the suffrages were united, and he was placed in the episcopal chair of Orleans, amid the acclamations of the people.† A similar mode was pursued at the installation of abbots, and the reception of canons.

This usage was not confined to the Latins, it was equally adopted by the Greeks. Two facts may prove its existence, and injurious tendency. The first is that of Caracalla, archbishop of Nicomedia,

* Gataker, Of the Nature and Use of Lots, p. 346.

† Memoires de l'Academie des Inscriptions: *Recherches Historiques sur les Sorts appelés. Sortes sanctorum*; par M. l'Abbé du Resnel, tom. xix, pp. 287, 296. Paris, 1753, 4to.

who consecrated Athanasius on his nomination to the patriarchate of Constantinople, by the emperor Constantine Porphyrogenitus. Having opened the books of the Gospels upon the words, "For the devil and his angels;" the bishop of Nice first saw them, and adroitly turned over the leaf to another verse, which was instantly read aloud, "The birds of the air may come and lodge in the branches thereof." But as this passage appeared to be irrelevant to so grave a ceremony, that which had first presented itself, became known to the public almost insensibly. To diminish the unpleasant impression it had produced, the people were reminded that on a similar occasion, another archbishop of Constantinople had accidently met with a circumstance equally inauspicious, by lighting upon the words, "There shall be weeping and gnashing of teeth," and yet his episcopate had neither been less happy nor less tranquil than formerly. The historian, nevertheless, remarks, that whatever had been the case under former archbishops, the church of Constantinople was violently agitated by the most fatal divisions during the patriarchate of Athanasius. The other instance is that of the metropolitan of Chersonesus, the first prelate consecrated by Theophanes, after his translation from the metropolitan see of Cyzicus to the patriarchate of Constantinople, and who having received the book of the Gospels at his hands, and opened it, according to custom, met with these words, "If the blind lead the blind, both shall fall into the ditch," which were regarded by the public as prognosticating evil to both the patriarch and the metropolitan.*

The Abbé du Resnel informs us, that this custom was continued in the cathedral of Boulogne, and at Ypres, and St. Omer, so late as the year 1744, only with this difference, that at Boulogne the newly chosen canon drew the lot from the Psalms, instead of the Gospels. The late M. de Langle, bishop of Boulogne, who regarded the custom as superstitious, and perceived, that when the new canons accidentally opened upon passages containing imprecations, or reproaches, or traits of depravity, an unmerited stigma attached to their character, issued an order for its abrogation, in 1722. But the chapter, who claimed exemption from episcopal jurisdiction, treated the order with contempt, and persevered in their superstition, except, that as it had been customary to insert in the letters of induction given to each canon the verse which had been drawn for him, it should in future be added, that this was done according to the ancient custom of the church of Terouanne;

* Memoires de l'Academie des Inscriptions, tom. xix, p. 303.

out of which the churches of Boulogne, Ypres, and St. Omer, had risen, after its destruction by Charles V. "I have in my possession," says the abbé, "one of these acts, dated in 1720, in which are the following words: *Et secundam antiquam ecclesiæ Morinensis, nunc Boloniensis consuetudinem, hunc ex psalmo sortitus est versiculum: Ipsi peribunt, tu autem permanes, et omnes sicut vestimentum veterascent:* "And according to the ancient custom of the church of Terouanne, (now Boulogne,) this verse was drawn from the Psalms: 'They shall perish, but thou shalt endure; yea, all of them shall wax old like a garment.'"*

Another species of bibliomancy, not very dissimilar from the *sortes sanctorum* of the Christians, was the bath-kol, or *daughter of the voice,* in use among the Jews. It consisted in appealing to the first words heard from any one, especially when reading the Scriptures, and looking upon them as a *voice from heaven,* directing them in the matter inquired about. The following is an instance: Rabbi Acher, having committed many crimes, was led into thirteen synagogues, and in each synagogue a disciple was interrogated, and the verse he read was examined. In the first school they read these words of Isaiah, (ch. xlviii, 22,) "There is no peace unto the wicked:" another school read Psalm l, 16, "Unto the wicked God saith, What hast thou to do to declare my statutes, or that thou shouldest take my covenant in thy mouth?" and in all the synagogues something of this nature was heard against Acher, from whence it was concluded he was hated of God!† This species of divination received its name from being supposed to succeed to the oracular voice, delivered from the mercy-seat, when GOD was there consulted by URIM and THUMMIM, or *light* and *perfection,* (Exodus xxviii, 30,) a term most probably used to express the clearness and perfection of the answers which God gave to the high priest. The Jews have a saying among them, that the Holy Spirit spake to the Israelites, during the tabernacle, by URIM and THUMMIM; under the first temple by the prophets; and under the second temple by BATH-KOL.‡

Nearly allied to the practice of bibliomancy, was the use of the *amulets* or *charms,* termed PERIAPTA, and PHYLACTERIA, and sometimes LIGATURÆ, and LIGATIONES. They were formed of ribands, with sentences of Scripture written upon them, and hung about the neck, as magical preventives of evil. They were worn by many

* Memoires de l'Academie des Inscriptions, *ubi sup.*

† Basnage's History of the Jews, b. iii, ch. v, p. 165, fol.

‡ Lewis's Antiquities of the Heb. Republic, vol. i. b. ii, ch. iii, pp. 112, 114, 198,

of the Christians in the earlier ages, but considered by the wisest and most holy of the bishops and clergy as disgraceful to religion, and deserving the severest reprehension. Chrysostom frequently mentions them, and always with the utmost detestation. The council of Laodicea, A. D. 364, can. 36, condemns those of the clergy who pretend to make them, declaring that such phylacteries or charms are bonds and fetters to the soul; and ordering those who wore them to be cast out of the church. And Augustine thus expostulates with those who used them: "When we are afflicted with pains in our head, let us not run to enchanters, and fortune-tellers, and remedies of vanity. I mourn for you, my brethren, for I daily find these things done. And what shall I do? I cannot yet persuade Christians to put their trust only in Christ. With what face can a soul go unto God, that has lost the sign of Christ; and taken upon him the sign of the devil?" Basil and Epiphanius also make similar complaints, and express equal abhorrence of the practice.* These phylacteries of the Christians were most probably derived from the *tephilim*, or phylacteries of the Jews.

The Jewish PHYLACTERIES were small slips of parchment or vellum, on which certain portions of the Law were written, enclosed in cases of black calf-skin, and tied about the forehead, and left arm. The Jews considered them as a divine ordinance and founded their opinion on Exodus xiii, 9, and similar passages. The design of them was believed to be, *first*, to put them in mind of those precepts which they should constantly observe; and *secondly*, to procure them reverence and respect, in the sight of the heathen. They were afterward degraded into instruments of superstition, and used as amulets or charms, to drive away evil spirits. Dr. Lightfoot thinks it not unlikely, that our Saviour wore the Jewish phylacteries himself, according to the custom of the country; and that he did not condemn the *wearing* of them, but the pride and hypocrisy of the Pharisees in making them "broad," and visible, to obtain fame and esteem for their devotion and piety.†

The council of Rome, under Gregory II., in A. D. 721, condemned the phylacteries of the Christians: and the council of

* Suiceri Thesaurus, vol. ii, pp. 668, 1465. Amstel. 1682, fol. Du Cange, Glossar. sub. v, *Ligaturæ*, and *Legationes*, &c. Bingham's Antiquities, &c., vol. vii, b. xvi, ch. v, sec. vi, p. 285.

† Wagenseilii Sota., ch. ii, pp. 397, 415. Altdorf. 1674. Buxtorfii Synagog. Jud., ch. ix, p. 170. Edit. Basil. 1661. Lightfoot's Works, vol. ii, p. 232, fol. Wotton's Miscellaneous Discourses, vol. i, p. 194. Fleury's Manners of the Israelites, by Dr. A. Clarke, pt. iii, ch. vi, p. 227, note. 8vo.

Trullo ordered the makers of them to be cast out of the church, and forbade all making and using of charms or amulets, as the relics of heathen superstition still remaining among the weaker and baser sort of Christians.*

Happily these baneful practices were partially restrained, by the pious and liberal endeavours of many of the early Christians to promote all useful knowledge. Accurate copies of the Holy Scriptures were everywhere multiplied, and that at such moderate prices, as rendered them of easy purchase; while translations into various languages were carefully published, in correct editions, many of the more opulent members of the Christian church generously contributing a great part of their substance to the carrying on these pious and excellent undertakings. All possible care was taken also to accustom their children to the study of the Scriptures, and to instruct them in the doctrines of their holy religion: and for this purpose SCHOOLS were erected, even from the very commencement of the Christian church. But besides the ordinary schools for children, there existed among the primitive Christians GYMNASIA, or *academies*, in which those who aspired to be public teachers were instructed in the different branches, both of human learning and of sacred erudition. None of these schools, or academies, were of more note than that which was established at Alexandria, commonly called the *Catechetical School*, and generally supposed to have been erected by St. Mark. This school was rendered famous by a succession of learned doctors; for after the death of St. Mark, Pantænus, Clemens Alexandrinus, Origen, and many others, taught in it the doctrines of the gospel. Similar schools were established also at Rome, Antioch, Cesarea, Edessa, and several other places, though not of equal reputation.†

Nor had they only schools, but at a very early period LIBRARIES, and these not the collections of private and curious persons, but public repositories belonging to various churches, containing copies of the sacred writings, the works of the Christian teachers, and also the profane authors. Alexander, who was elected bishop of Jerusalem about the beginning of the third century, "was rendered illustrious by a union of virtues seemingly opposite; remarkable for the mildness and gentleness of his general manners, he was at the same time resolute, magnanimous, and inflexible, wherever the great interests of truth were concerned. He was twice brought before heathen magistrates, in whose pre-

* Bingham's Antiquities, &c., vol. vii, p. 292.

† Mosheim's Eccles. Hist., vol. i, pp. 118, 277, Lond. 8vo.

sence he avowed his sentiments with undaunted freedom, for which he was at last thrown into prison, and died there."* To him the church at Jerusalem was indebted for a noble library, which he erected at that place. Eusebius found preserved in it the letters of several learned men who had lived in former times; and he tells us that it furnished him with many of the materials of his Ecclesiastical History.† Julius Africanus, a native of Palestine, and a man of the most profound erudition, founded in this century the library at Cesarea, which the excellent Pamphilus afterward enriched and greatly enlarged. Jerome compares it to the libraries of Demetrius Phalereus and Pisistratus, and informs us that Pamphilus sought all over the world for curious books and works of genius to deposit in it; and was so zealous for its improvement, that he wrote out for it the greatest part of Origen's works with his own hand. He adds also that this library contained the Hebrew copy of St. Matthew's Gospel.‡

The libraries formed by the early Christians were generally placed in the churches, in which were *cubicula*, or rooms appropriated to the use of those who were desirous of retirement and meditation. These *cubicula* or *secretaria*, as they were sometimes called, were erected with the church; one being generally placed on the right side of it, and another on the left. The sacred writings were preserved in one of them, and the sacramental utensils in the other. Paulinus, bishop of Nola, having erected a church there, placed appropriate inscriptions over each of the *cubicula*. Over that designed to be the repository of the sacred Scriptures was written,

Si quem sancta tenet meditandi in lege voluntas,
Hic poterit residens sanctis intendere libris.

"If any one be desirous of meditating in the Law of
God, he may here sit down and read the holy books."

Over the room designed for the sacred utensils was inscribed,

Hic locus est veneranda penus qua conditer, et qua
Promitur alma sacri pompa Ministerii.

"This is the place where the holy food is reposited, and whence we take provision and furniture for the altar."§

* Christie's Miscellanies, p. 127. † Hist. Eccles., lib. vi, ch. xx

‡ Hieronymi Catalog. Script. Eccles.. Opera, vol. i, fol. 132, Basil, 1516. Lomeier, De Bibliothecis, ch. vii. p. 127.

§ Bingham's Antiquities, &c., vol. iii, b. viii, ch. vi, pp. 210, 211, and ch. vii, p. 226, 8vo.

In the *third century* also a distinct order of PUBLIC READERS of the sacred Scriptures began to be generally established in the churches. Their office was to read the Scriptures to the congregation from the *pulpitum* or reading-desk, in the body of the church. The office was accounted an honourable one, and was sometimes held by confessors, as those were denominated who had avowed their attachment to the gospel in the face of the greatest dangers, and in the presence of the enemies of Christianity. Sometimes also young persons, who had been dedicated to the service of God from their infancy, were permitted to officiate as readers. The council of Carthage directs, that when a reader is ordained the bishop shall address the people, and declare to them the faith, and life, and talents of the candidate; and delivering to him a copy of the Scriptures, shall say to him, "Take this book, and be thou a READER of the WORD OF GOD, which office if thou fulfil faithfully and profitably, thou shalt have part with those that minister in the word of God."*

INTERPRETERS were established in the church at about the same period, whose business it was to render one language into another, as there was occasion, both in reading the Scriptures and in the homilies addressed to the people. Procopius, the martyr, is said to have borne the three distinct offices of reader, exorcist, and interpreter of the Syriac tongue, in the church of Scythopolis. This office, however, appears to have principally existed in those churches where the people spoke different languages, as in the churches of Palestine, where probably some used Syriac, and others the Greek tongue; and in the churches of Africa, where both the Latin and Punic were spoken.

Another custom observed in the ancient churches was that of having Bibles *in the vulgar tongue* placed in a convenient part of the church, for the people at their leisure to employ themselves in reading the Scriptures before or after divine service; a practice rendered peculiarly necessary by the enormous expense of transcribing so large a volume as the Bible prior to the invention of printing.

To these salutary measures, wisely adopted for the diffusion of sacred knowledge, a most formidable obstacle was presented by the cruel persecution of Dioclesian, the Roman emperor, which commenced in the year 303. When this emperor first assumed the purple in A. D. 284, he showed himself favourable to

* Bingham's Antiquities, &c., vol. ii, b. iii, ch. v, pp. 27–33.

Christianity; but instigated by the heathen priesthood, and counselled by his colleague Galerius, he at length threw off the mask, and in the nineteenth year of his reign commanded the churches to be razed, *the Bibles to be burned*, those who had borne offices of honour to be degraded, and those of inferior stations, if they persisted in their avowal of Christianity, to be made slaves. This edict was followed by others, ordaining that all who anywhere presided in the church should be imprisoned; and that they should by every means be compelled to sacrifice to the heathen deities. In one month no fewer than seventeen thousand martyrs suffered death! In the province of Egypt alone one hundred and forty-four thousand persons died by the violence of their persecutors; and seven hundred thousand died through the fatigues of banishment, or of the public works to which they were condemned! Gildas, the most ancient British historian we have, relates, that by this persecution of Dioclesian "the churches were thrown down, and *all the books of the Holy Scriptures that could be found were burned in the streets*, and the chosen priests of the flock of our Lord, with the innocent sheep, murdered, so that in some parts of the province no footsteps appeared of the Christian religion."* Our ancient chronicler, Robert of Gloucester, has left an account of this persecution in these old rhymes:—

"Twei emperoures of Rome, Dyoclician,
And an other, ys felaw, that het Maximian,
Were bothe at on tyme, the on in the Est ende,
And the other in the West, Cristendom to schende,†
For the luther‡ Maximian Westward hider sogte,
And Cristenemen, that he fonde, to strong deth he brogte.
Chirches he fel al a doun, ther ne moste non stonde,
And al the bokes, that he mygte fynde in eny londe,
He wolde lete hem berne echon amid the heye strete,
And tho Cristenemen alle sle, and none o live lete.
Seththe God was y bore, ther nas for Cristendom
In su lute stond y do so gret martirdom.
For ther were in a moneth seventene thousant and mo
Y martired for our Lorde's love."§

The most dreadful tortures were inflicted upon those who refused to deliver up the sacred volumes to the fury of the heathen; but every torture, and even death itself, were braved with the most

* Millar's Hist. of Propagation of Christianity, *Works*, vol. vii, p. 235.

† *Schende*, spoil, destroy.

‡ *Luther*, cruel, wicked, base.

§ Robert of Gloucester's Chronicle, by T. Hearne, p. 81. Oxford, 1724. 8vo.

heroic constancy by many Christian worthies, to whom the Book of God was more precious than life. Felix of Tibiura, in Africa, being apprehended as a Christian, was commanded by Magnilian, curator or civil magistrate of the city, to deliver up all books and writings belonging to his church, that they might be burned. The martyr replied, that it was better he himself should be burned. This magistrate sent him to the proconsul at Carthage, by whom he was delivered over to the prefect of the Prætorium, who was then in Africa. This supreme officer, offended at his bold and generous confession, commanded him to be loaded with heavier bolts and irons, and, after he had kept him nine days in a close dungeon, to be put on board a vessel, saying he should stand his trial before the emperor. For four days he lay under the hatches of the ship, between the horses' feet, without eating or drinking. He was landed at Agragentum, in Sicily; and when brought by the prefect as far as Venosa, in Apulia, his irons were knocked off, and he was again asked whether he had the Scriptures, and would deliver them up; "I have them," said he, "but will not part with them." The prefect instantly condemned him to be beheaded. "I thank thee, O Lord," said this honest martyr, "that I have lived fifty-six years, have preserved the Gospel, and have preached faith and truth. O my Lord Jesus Christ, the God of heaven and earth, I bow my head to be sacrificed to thee, who livest to all eternity."* Adopting the words of a valuable writer,† "I judge it not amiss to distinguish this man. The preservation of civil liberty is valuable, and the names of men who have suffered for it with integrity are recorded with honour. But how much below the name of Felix of Tibiura should these be accounted! He is one of those heroes who have preserved to us the precious word of God itself." Euplius of Catana, in Sicily, suffered in the same cause. Let his name be remembered with honour, together with that of Felix. Being seized with the Gospels in his hand, he was examined on the rack, "Why do you keep the Scriptures forbidden by the emperors?" He answered, "Because I am a Christian. Life eternal is in them; he that gives them up loses life eternal." When ordered away to execution, the executioners hung the book of the Gospels, which he had with him when he was seized, about his neck, and the public crier proclaimed before him, "This is Euplius, the Christian, an enemy

* Milner's History of the Church, vol. ii, p. 18, 8vo. Butler's Lives of the Saints Oct. 24, vol. x, p. 525.

† Rev. J. Milner, *ut sup.*

to the gods and the emperors." He was beheaded on the 12th of August, in the year 304.*

But all were not thus faithful; the clamours of the heathen, who were exclaiming on every side, "Burn your Testaments," and the dread of torture and death, intimidated many cowardly and perfidious spirits, who, deserting the sacred cause of Christianity, surrendered up the Holy Scriptures, and the different moveables of the church. At Cirta, in Numidia, Paul, the bishop, ordered a subdeacon to deliver up the treasures of the church to a Roman officer, thus betraying his sacred charge, and violating in the grossest manner every principle of Christian integrity.

This base and cowardly conduct met with merited indignation from the more faithful Christians, who denominated them *traditores*, or traitors, and anathematized them as guilty of profane and sacrilegious acts. The first council of Arles, held immediately after this persecution, decreed that every clergyman who had betrayed the Scriptures, or any of the holy vessels, or the names of his brethren, to the persecutors, should be deposed from his office: and St. Austin went so far as to affirm, "that if the charge of this crime could be made good against Cecilian, bishop of Carthage, and those who ordained him, by the Donatists, who threw out the reflection upon them, they should be anathematized even after death."† In this persecution, which continued for about ten years under Dioclesian and his successors, St. Alban, the first person who suffered martyrdom for Christianity in England, was beheaded at Verulam, in Hertfordshire, since called St. Albans, from the abbey founded in memory of the martyr, A.D. 795, by Offa, king of the Mercians.‡

Eusebius, in his account of the martyrs who suffered in Palestine under this persecution, presents us with some instances wherein those who suffered discovered the ardour of their love to the Bible, by having committed the whole or considerable portions of it to memory. He particularly mentions Valens, a deacon of Ælia, and John, an Egyptian. The former was an aged man, but "one above all others conversant in the divine writings; so that, when occasion offered, he could, from memory, repeat passages in any part of Scripture, as exactly as if he had unfolded the book and read them." The latter "had been formerly bereaved of

* Butler's Lives, Aug. 12, vol. viii, p. 158.

† Milner's History of the Church, vol. ii, p. 18. Kortholtus, De Persecutionibus Eccles. Prim., ch. x, pp. 444, 449. Kiloni, 1689, 4to.

‡ Bedæ Hist. Eccles., lib. i, ch. vii.

sight, and was, together with the rest of the confessors, not only maimed in one foot, but he had the heated iron thrust into his eyes, already blind. The transcendent perfection of his memory was such, that he had the whole books of the sacred Scriptures written, 'not on tables of stone,' as the divine apostle says, or on the skins of animals, or on paper, apt to be consumed by moths, and by time; but indeed 'on the fleshly tables of his heart,' so that, whensoever he willed, he brought forth, as from a repository of science, and repeated, either the Law of Moses, or the Prophets, or the historical, evangelical, and apostolical parts of Scripture."*

The tenaciousness of memory exhibited by these ancient worthies is almost without parallel in ancient or modern times, except in that prodigy of memory, the late Rev. THOMAS THRELKELD, of Rochdale, Lancashire. He was a perfect living concordance to the English Scriptures. If three words only were mentioned, except, perhaps, those words of mere connection which occur in hundreds of passages, he could immediately, without hesitation, assign the chapter and verse where they were to be found. And, inversely, upon mentioning the chapter and verse, he could repeat the words. This power of retention enabled him, with ease, "to make himself master of many languages. Nine, or ten, it is certainly known that he read; not merely without difficulty, but with profound and critical skill. It is affirmed, by a friend who lived near him, and was in the habits of intimacy with him, that he was familiarly acquainted with every language in which he had a Bible or New Testament." After his decease I had opportunity of examining his library, and noticed Bibles, or New Testaments, in English, Greek, Latin, Hebrew, French, Italian, Spanish, German, Welch, Dutch, Swedish, Gaelic, and Manks; besides grammars, &c., in other languages. In the Greek Testament, his powers of immediate reference and quotation were similar to those he possessed in the English translation; since he could in a moment produce every place in which the same word occurred, in any of its forms or affinities. In the Hebrew, with its several dialects, he was equally, that is, most profoundly skilled; and it is believed that his talent of immediate reference was as great here as in the Greek, or even in the English.†

* Eusebius, Of the Martyrs in Palestine, translated by Dalrymple, pp. 61, 87.

† See a sermon preached at Rochdale, April 13th, 1806, on occasion of the death of the Rev. T. Threlkeld, by Thomas Barnes, D.D.

CHAPTER II.

FOURTH CENTURY.

Opposition to Christianity—Constantine—Gregory the Illuminator—Councils—Chrysostom's Writings illustrative of Sacred Literature—Julian—Apollinarii—Valentinian—Valens—Gothic Version—Codex Argenteus—Francis Junius—Dr. Thomas Marshall—George Stiernhelm—Eric Benzel—Edward Lye—Ulphilas—Ethiopic Version—Frumentius—Juvencus—Proba Falconia—Epiphanius—Vulgate—Jerome.

In the year 304, or 305, Dioclesian resigned the empire, and Maximian, his colleague, reluctantly followed his example. They were succeeded by Galerius in the East, and by Constantius in the West. Galerius, the successor of Dioclesian, chose Maximin, his nephew, to be his *Cesar*, or subordinate governor. Maximin inherited the savageness and the prejudices of his uncle, and was even his superior in the arts of persecution:—"Paganism was expiring, and it behooved the prince of darkness to find or qualify an agent who should dispute every inch of ground with persevering assiduity."* Persons of quality filled the highest offices of idolatry, pains were taken to prevent Christians from erecting places of worship, or from following their religion in public or private; and, incited by the example of the tyrant, all the pagans in his dominions exerted themselves to effect the ruin of the Christians, and human ingenuity was put to the stretch to invent calumnies in support of the kingdom of darkness. "At length," says Eusebius, "having forged certain acts of Pilate concerning our Saviour, which were full of all sorts of blasphemy against Christ, they caused them, by the decree of Maximin, to be dispersed through all the parts of his empire; commanding, by their letters, that they should be published to all persons in every place, both in cities and country places; and that schoolmasters should put them into the hands of children, to be committed to memory."† This mode of promoting the cause of infidelity, by associating false and vicious ideas with the names of the eminent characters mentioned in the Scriptures, has been since followed by the Jews, in their *Toldoth Yesu*, and by Voltaire and his associates, in the *Taureau Blanc*, and other infamous publications.

* Milner's History of the Church. † Eusebius, Hist. Eccles., lib. ix, cap. v.

By a decree of the Roman senate, CONSTANTINE, usually styled the *Great*, the son of Constantius, and a native of Britain, being declared First *Augustus*, or chief emperor, and Licinius his associate; they, in the year 313, published an edict, in their joint names, in favour of the Christians. Licinius afterward persecuted the church of Christ; Constantine and he quarrelled, and a war soon commenced between the two princes. Constantine was victorious, and in A. D. 324 became sole master of the empire. From that time he professed himself a convert to the religion of Jesus, and more than ever laboured, not only to defend the Christians, but, after his manner, to spread Christianity itself.* We lament, however, that the methods he adopted savoured more of the savage barbarity of a pagan warrior, than of the mild and persuasive disposition of a true Christian. Elmacin, or El-Makin, relates, that as it was supposed many of the Jews had professed to be Christians, while they continued Jews in their hearts, swine's flesh was boiled, and cut into mouthfuls, and a portion placed at the doors of every church. All that entered were obliged to eat a piece of the flesh. Those that were Jews in their hearts refused; thus they were detected, and immediately put to death.† A much wiser method, and one more congenial with the religion he professed, was adopted by him, when he placed Bibles in the churches, for the use of the people. Eusebius informs us, that he himself was ordered by the emperor to provide fifty Greek Bibles, or more probably, only the principal books, at the public expense, for different churches. The following is a copy of Constantine's letter to Eusebius:—

"*Victor Constantinus Maximus Augustus, to Eusebius.*

"In that city which bears our name, [Constantinople,] by the assistance of God our Saviour's providence, a vast multitude of men have joined themselves to the most holy church. Whereas, therefore, all things do there receive a very great increase, it seems highly requisite that there should be more churches erected in that city. Wherefore do you most willingly receive that which I have determined to do. For it seemed fit to signify to your prudence, that you should order *fifty copies of the Divine Scriptures*, (the provision and use whereof you know to be chiefly necessary for the instruction of the church,) to be written on well-prepared parchment, by artificial transcribers of books, most skilful in the art of

* Eusebius's Life of Constantine. Camb. 1682. fol.

† Hottingeri Eccles. Hist., vol. i., pt. i, ch. iv, pp. 197, 198. 1651, 12mo.

accurate and fair writing; which (copies) must be very legible, and easily portable, in order to their being used. Moreover, letters are despatched away from our clemency, to the rationalist of the diœcesis,* that he should take care for the providing of all things necessary, in order to the finishing of the said copies. This therefore shall be the work of your diligence, to see that the written copies be forthwith provided. You are also empowered, by the authority of this our letter, to have the use of two public carriages, in order to their conveyance. For by this means, those which are transcribed fair, may most commodiously be conveyed even to our sight; to wit, one of the deacons of your church being employed in the performance hereof. Who, when he comes to us, shall be made sensible of our bounty. God preserve you, dear brother!"

This munificent order, for such it was considered, was immediately attended to, and completed; and, in the words of Eusebius, "sent him in volumes magnificently adorned."†

A similar display of liberality was made by this prince when he transferred the seat of his empire to Byzantium, or Constantinople, in the year 336; for being desirous of making reparation to the Christians for the injuries they had sustained during the reign of his tyrannical predecessor, he commanded the most diligent search to be made after those books which had been doomed to destruction; caused transcripts to be made of such books as had escaped the Dioclesian persecution; added others to them, and with the whole, formed a valuable library in the city of the imperial residence. On the death of Constantine, the number of books contained in the imperial library was six thousand nine hundred, but in the time of Theodosius the younger, it contained one hundred thousand. Of these, more than half were burned in the eighth century by command of the emperor Leo III., in order to destroy all the monuments that might be quoted in proof against his opposition to the worship of images. In this library was deposited the only authentic copy of the council of Nice, which was unfortunately consumed, together with a magnificent copy of the four Gospels, bound in plates of gold, to the weight of fifteen pounds,

* Diœcesis, or diocœsis, was originally a civil government, composed of divers provinces; and the *katholikon* or rationalist, one of the civil governors, or officers. Hence the ecclesiastical term *diocess*, for the jurisdiction of a bishop, and *diocesan*, applied to a bishop in relation to his clergy.

† Eusebius's Life of Constantine, lib. iv, cap. xxxvi.

and enriched with precious stones, which had been given by Pope Gregory III. to the church dedicated to our Saviour.*

Early in the FOURTH century, Gregory, the apostle and bishop of Armenia, surnamed the Illuminator, with laudable zeal obtained the approbation of the sovereign of the country to establish schools, or academies, in every city, and to appoint doctors and masters over them; and published through all the cities invitations to the inhabitants to send their children, that they might be taught the knowledge of the Holy Scriptures.†

During this century, also, various councils were held, which published canons considerably illustrative of the opinions and practices of the age. The council of Nice, convened by Constantine, A. D. 325, ordained, "That no Christian should be without the Scriptures." The council of Antioch, held A. D. 341, decreed, "That any person coming into the church, and only staying to hear the Scriptures, and neither uniting in the prayers, nor partaking of the eucharist, should be excommunicated." The council of Laodicea, in 367, enjoined in its sixteenth canon, "That the Gospels, with the other Scriptures, ought to be read on the sabbath-day;" by which was meant, that in the public assemblies, which were in that age held on the *sabbath-day*, as the Saturday was then usually called, the Scriptures should be read in the same order as on the *Lord's-day*, or Sunday, and not be omitted to be read. The seventeenth canon of the same council directs, "That the psalms shall not be sung one immediately after another, but, that a *lesson* shall be read after every psalm." And the fifty-ninth canon ordains, "That psalms composed by private men, or uncanonical books, should not be read in the church, but only the canonical books of the Old and New Testament."‡

The writings of Chrysostom, the eloquent patriarch of Constantinople, furnish us with much additional and interesting information respecting the sacred Scriptures, during this century and the commencement of the following; especially in those churches which were subject to the Greek patriarch. From him we learn, that the Scriptures, or parts of them, were very generally dispersed among the people, since he repeatedly exhorts even the poorest of them to make the Scriptures their daily study, to read

* Horne's Introduction to Bibliography, vol. i, p. xxiii. Lomeir, De Bibliothecis, cap. vii, sec. 2, pp. 131–134.

† Usserii Hist. Dogmat. de Scripturis, &c., p. 18. Butler's Lives of the Saints, vol. ix, Sep. 30.

‡ Usserii Hist. Dogmat. de Scripturis, &c., cap. vii, sec. i, pp. 193–195. Johnson's Clergyman's Vade Mecum, vol. ii, 4th edit., Lond. 1731.

them after their usual meals, and in the hearing of their wives and children; assuring them, that "the servant and the rustic, the widow and the infant, might understand them." The excuses made by some for their neglect of the sacred writings, present the monks of that day in a favourable light, as students in the word of God: "We have not renounced the world," said they; "we are not monks; we have wives and children." "Are the Scriptures then to be read only by monks?" replies the worthy patriarch, "or are they not still more necessary for you, as the man, who is daily exposed to danger and to wounds, stands most in need of the physician?" From the same source we acquire the knowledge, that it was usual for the deacons, during the reading of the lessons in the churches, frequently to command "silence," and direct the attention of the congregation to the reader, by loud calling, "Attend!" And for the reader, on rising to read the Scriptures, to commence by solemnly saying, "Thus saith the Lord." We are also informed, that it was common, especially for women and children, to have the Gospels hung round their necks, and constantly to carry them about with them; and that many of the rich, in their book-cases, or studies, preserved magnificent copies of the sacred writings, executed in the most beautiful characters, on the finest vellum.*

Complete copies of the Scriptures were, nevertheless, extremely rare, and could seldom be obtained by any but the most affluent; as the following circumstance, which shows the high value set upon a single copy of the Gospels, sufficiently proves. Hilarion, the first instituter of the monastic state in the East, having embarked at Paretonium, in Libya, with one companion, for Sicily, landed at Pachynus, a famous promontory on the eastern side of the island, now called Capo di Passaro. Upon landing, he offered to pay for his passage, and that of his companion, with *a copy of the Gospels*, which he had written in his youth with his own hand; but the master seeing their whole stock consisted in that manuscript, and the clothes on their backs, refused to accept of it, and generously forgave the debt.†

In the year 361, Julian, the Apostate, was advanced to the empire. During the reign of Constantius he had acted with the most profound dissimulation, and so far proceeded in his hypocritical profession of Christianity as to be ordained reader, in the church

* See the different quotations from Chrysostom's Works, in Usher's Hist. Dogmat. de Scripturis et Sacris Vernaculis, cap. ii, pp. 33–50. Lond. 1690, 4to.

† Butler's Lives, vol. x, Oct. 21. Gibbon's Decline and Fall, vol. vi, ch. xxxvii, p. 246, 8vo.

of Nicomedia; but, on his accession to the throne, he threw off the disguise, and became the avowed and active patron of paganism, and every art that the most refined policy could suggest, was practised for its advancement, and for the depression and overthrow of Christianity. To effect his purpose, he endeavoured to render the Christians ignorant and contemptible; and with this view, forbade the Christian professors to teach Gentile learning, "lest being furnished," says he, "with our armour, they make war upon us with our own weapons." He also commanded, that the writings of Christian authors should be destroyed, but that those of profane authors should be preserved. His epistle to Ecdicius, prefect of Egypt, respecting the library of George, of Cappadocia, the Arian archbishop of Alexandria, so fully delineates the character of Julian, that I will present it to the reader:—

"*To Ecdicius, Prefect of Egypt.*

"Some delight in horses, some in birds, and others in wild beasts. I, from my childhood, have always been inflamed with a passionate love for books. I think it absurd to suffer these to fall into the hands of wretches, whose avarice gold alone cannot satiate, as they are also clandestinely endeavouring to pilfer these. You will therefore oblige me extremely by collecting all the books of George.* He had many, I know, on philosophical and rhetorical subjects, and many on the doctrine of the impious Galileans. *All these I would have destroyed;* but lest others more valuable should be destroyed with them, let them all be carefully examined. The secretary of George may assist you in this disquisition, and if he acts with fidelity, he shall be rewarded with freedom; if not, *he may be put to the torture.* I am not unacquainted with this library, for when I was in Cappadocia, George lent me several books to be transcribed, which I afterward returned to him."†

The prohibition of human learning decreed by this emperor, induced the APOLLINARII, father and son, to invent something which might serve as a substitute for the loss. The father, a native of Alexandria, was a presbyter of the church of Laodicea, the son occupied

* George of Cappadocia was the rival of Athanasius. On the accession of Julian, he was dragged in chains to the public prison, and at the end of twenty-four days massacred by an infuriated and superstitious mob, who forced open the prison, and after murdering the archbishop, carried his lifeless body in triumph through the streets, on the back of a camel.

† Duncombe's Epistles of Julian, ep. ix, pp. 17–19.

the place of reader. Both were teachers of Grecian literature; the father taught grammar, the son rhetoric; both were persons of superior capacity; the son, particularly, was one of the greatest men of his time, in learning, genius, and powers of argument; and his answer to Porphyry is looked upon as the best defence of Christianity sgainst paganism. To compensate for the loss of the classical authors, from which the Christians were debarred, by the edict of the emperor, they composed a grammar on a Christian model, turned the books of Moses into *heroic* verse, paraphrased the historical books, in imitation of the Greek tragedians; and in the various works which they composed, adopted all the different kinds of verse, and modes of writing, employed by the most celebrated Greek authors. The translation of the Psalms into Greek verse, by the younger Apollinarius is still extant, and highly commended;* but how far their other writings merited the rank of classics cannot now be ascertained, for on the death of Julian, in 363, the prohibition ceasing, Christian scholars returned to their former studies, and the classical imitations of the Apollinarii sunk into disuse.

Jovian, an avowed Christian, succeeded Julian in the empire; and on the death of Jovian, which happened suddenly, not without suspicion of poison, in 364 Valentinian was advanced to the purple by the suffrages of the army. Thirty days after his own elevation, he associated his brother Valens in the empire. Both were Christians, but adopted different measures in the churches under their respective government. In the West, Valentinian adhered to the orthodox faith, while in the East, Valens countenanced the Arian principles, and persecuted those who dissented from the creed he maintained. At Edessa, the orthodox, driven from the churches, were wont to assemble in a field. At first, Valens ordered them to be dispersed; but the resolution of a woman, who hastened thither as on purpose to suffer martyrdom, staggered his mind, and caused him to cease from the attempt. Afterward, he sent the pastors of Edessa into banishment. Among those who were conducted to Antinous, a city in Thebais, in Egypt, was one named Protogenes. Desirous of communicating a knowledge of the truths of the Scriptures to the inhabitants, of whom the greater part were pagans, he commenced a school, in which he taught the children the art of writing sifwtly, (ad celeri manu scribendum,) and then dictated to them the Psalms of David, and suitable pas-

* Cavei, Historia Literaria, pp. 176, 202. Lond. 1688, fol. Milner's Hist. of the Church of Christ, vol. ii, pp. 126, 248.

sages of the New Testament, thus rendering the instruction in writing subservient to the multiplication of copies of the principal portions of the Holy Scriptures, and to the more extensive spread of the gospel.* On the other hand, Ambrose, the excellent bishop of Milan, who died about the year 397, "admired, regretted, and lamented, by the whole Christian world," affirms, that the Arians corrupted the word of God, and gives us, as an instance of the frauds practised by them, the erasure of John iv, 24, from the sacred volume, which he says took place at Milan, in the time of his Arian predecessor Auxertius.†

In the reign of Valens, Ulphilas, bishop of the Goths, immortalized his name by his Gothic translation, from the Greek, of the whole, or a considerable part of the Scriptures. A man of superior genius and endowments, he not only laboured with unwearied assiduity to transfuse the sublime doctrines of holy writ into a barbarous dialect, but invented, and taught his countrymen, the use of letters more suited to the Scriptures and a state of civilization than those of the barren Runic alphabet, to which they had hitherto been accustomed. Philostorgius asserts, that Ulphilas omitted the book of Kings, from an apprehension that the martial spirit of his nation might be roused by the relation of the Jewish wars; but this circumstance has been controverted by several learned men, who consider Philostorgius unworthy of credit; Gibbon, however, remarks, that the Arianism "of Philostorgius appears to have given him superior means of information."‡

Of this important version the principal remains are contained in the famous Codex Argenteus, or *Silver Book*, a MS. preserved in the library of the University of Upsal, in Sweden. It is impressed, or written, on very fine, thin, smooth vellum, of a quarto form, and purple colour, though some sheets have a pale violet hue; and has received the name of Argenteus, from its *silver letters;* but the three first lines of the Gospels of St. Luke and St. Mark are impressed with *golden* foil, as those of St. Matthew and St. John would most probably be found to be, were they still in existence. When the commencement of a section, or capitulary, takes place at the beginning of the line, the whole is distinguished by golden characters; but if in the middle, or any other

* Usserii Hist. Dogmat. de Scripturis, &c., p. 30. Milner's Hist. of the Church, vol. ii, p. 161.

† Ibid., vol. ii, p. 236.

‡ Gibbon's Decline and Fall, vol. vi, ch. xxxvii, p. 269, note. Lond. 8vo. 1807. Philostorgii Eccles. Hist., lib. ii, cap. v. Genev. 1642. 4to.

portion, such part of a line only is thus splendidly ornamented. The beginning of the Lord's Prayer, and the titles of the evangelists, are also illuminated in gold. Unfortunately it has suffered several mutilations. It is supposed to have been the property of Alaric, king of Thoulouse, whose kingdom and palace were plundered and destroyed by Chlodovic, (commonly named Clovis,) in the year 507; or of Amalaric, whom Childebert overcame in battle in the year 531. For many centuries this book was preserved in the monastery of Werden, in Westphalia, where it was discovered in 1597 by Anthony Marillon, who extracted a few passages, which were inserted in a "Commentary on the Gothic Alphabet," published by Bonaventura Vulcanius. Soon afterward, Arnold Mercator observed it in the same library, and transcribed a few verses, which Gruter gave to the world in his *Inscriptiones Antiquæ*. When that district was ravaged by the triennial war, in the seventeenth century, it was transmitted to Prague, for security. Subsequently Count Konigsmark took this city by storm, when it came into the possession of the Swedes, and afterward enriched the library of Holme. After lying some time in the library of Queen Christina, it suddenly disappeared, without any one being able to account for the loss, and was again brought to light in the Netherlands. Some have supposed that Isaac Vossius received it as a present from the queen, others that he brought it away by stealth. The latter is the more probable, since, during the confusion which preceded Christina's abdication, he is said to have pillaged the royal library, and carried away many rare books and MSS. The recollection of these literary depredations is perpetuated by a curious collection called *Furta Vossiana*, still preserved in the library at Leyden, and supposed to have been stolen by him while in Sweden. Puffendorf, journeying through Holland in 1662, found it in his possession, and purchased it for Count de la Gardie for four hundred rix-dollars, (Coxe says two hundred and fifty pounds,) who presented it to the royal library at Upsal, where it now remains.*

This part of the Gothic version has been several times printed; first at Dort, in 1665, 4to., in Gothic letters, or such as are found in the *Codex Argenteus*, by Francis Junius and Thomas Marshall, who borrowed the MS. from Vossius, and accompanied with a "Glossary" and "Observations." Again in Latin letters by the

* Henshall's Gothic Gospel of St. Matthew, pp. 35, 36, 44–47. Marsh's Michaelis, vol. ii, part i, sec. 32, pp. 133, 134. Coxe's Travels in Poland, &c., vol. iv, b. vii, ch. vi, pp. 173–180.

learned Stiernhelm, in 1671, at Stockholm, accompanied with the Icelandic, the Swedish, and the Latin Vulgate. But the best edition hitherto published is the one prepared for the press by the Swedish archbishop Benzel, who was head librarian at Upsal. This excellent man had devoted whole years to the study of the Codex Argenteus, but, after having taken a fresh copy, and written a Latin translation, he died in 1743, aged seventy, before the work was published. The task, however, was finished by the Rev. Edward Lye, to whom he had transmitted his collations and translation before his death, who prefixed a short, but valuable preface, and a Gothic grammar. It was printed at Oxford in 1750.

The following brief notices of the editors of the *Codex Argenteus* may be acceptable to the reader:—

Francis Junius, or Du Jon, son of Francis Junius, professor of divinity at Leyden, and coadjutor of Tremellius in the translation of the Old Testament from the Hebrew, was born at Heidelberg in 1589. He received the early part of his education at Leyden, but, on the death of his father in 1602, directed his studies to a preparation for a military life, which he had determined to embrace. The conclusion of the war, in 1609, altered his plans; he devoted himself to literature, published some of his father's works, and then travelled to France and England. For thirty years he resided in England, in the family of Thomas, earl of Arundel; and having frequent opportunities of visiting Oxford, he applied with unwearied assiduity to the study of the Gothic and Saxon tongues, and the various dialects derived from them. While on a visit to the continent, to obtain more accurate information relative to the ancient Saxon language, he met with the MS. of the Gothic version of the Scriptures, which he published, accompanied with the notes of Dr. Marshall. In 1674 he returned into England; and in 1677 died of a fever at Windsor, aged eighty-eight. He made a deed of gift of all his MSS. and collections to the public library of Oxford. The chief of these was his *Glossarium Gothicum*, in five languages, contained in nine volumes, which Bishop Fell caused to be transcribed for the press. The *Etymologicum Anglicanum* was published in 1743, in folio, by Edward Lye, M.A.*

Thomas Marshall, D.D., born at Barkby, in Leicestershire, about 1621, was entered of Lincoln College in 1640; but, on the breaking out of the civil wars, bore arms in defence of King

* Chalmers's Gen. Biog. Dict., vol. xix, pp. 198, 199. Lempriere's Univ. Biog.

Charles; and was therefore, in 1645, admitted B.A. without paying fees. He afterward went to Rotterdam, and became preacher to the English merchants there and at Dort. In 1661 he was made B.D., and in 1688 chosen fellow, without his solicitation or knowledge. In 1669 he commenced D.D., and in 1672 was elected rector of his college. He was afterward appointed chaplain in ordinary to his majesty, and rector of Bladen; and in 1681 was installed dean of Gloucester. He died at Lincoln College in 1685. He prefixed "An Epistle for the English reader" to Dr. Thomas Hyde's translation into the Malayan tongue of the Four Gospels and the Acts of the Apostles. Oxford, 1677.*

George Stiernhelm was a Swedish nobleman, a native of the province of Westmania, counsellor of war, and president of the Royal College of Antiquities of Stockholm. He flourished about A.D. 1671.†

Eric Benzel, or Benzelius, was born in 1673, at Upsal, in Sweden, where he began and completed his studies. Having travelled into Germany, England, and France, he returned to Upsal in 1702, and was appointed librarian to the university, an office which he held for twenty-two years. In 1724 he was nominated professor of divinity; and successively created bishop of Gottenburg and Lindkioping, and archbishop of Upsal, of which his father had previously enjoyed the dignity. The review of Swedish books, &c., commenced by Benzel and his associates in 1720, under the title of *Acta Literaria Sueciæ*, and continued for ten years, laid the foundation of the Royal Academy of Sciences at Upsal. He died in 1743.‡

Edward Lye was a learned linguist and antiquary, born at Totness, in Devonshire, in 1704, and educated under his father, and at Hart-Hall, (now Hertford College,) Oxford, where he took his degree of M.A. in 1722. Having been ordained priest, he was soon after presented to the living of Houghton-parva, in Northamptonshire. In this retreat he gained much of his knowledge of the Anglo-Saxon language; and published Junius's *Etymologicum Anglicanum*. In 1750 he became a member of the Society of Antiquaries, and about the same time was presented by the earl of Northampton to the vicarage of Yardley Hastings, where he died in 1767. His great work, the "Anglo-Saxon and Gothic Dictionary," left in manuscript at his death, was published,

* Chalmers's Gen. Biog. Dict., vol. xxi, pp. 350, 351.

† Le Long, vol. i, *Index Auctor.*

‡ Coxe's Travels, vol. iv, p. 185, note.

with two grammars, by the Rev. Owen Manning in 1772, in two volumes folio.*

In 1763 F. A. Knittel published another fragment of the version of Ulphilas, taken from the CODEX CAROLINUS, in the library of Wolfenbuttel. In this library an ancient MS. is preserved written in the eighth or ninth century, of the *Origines* of Isidore of Spain, a part of which is written on vellum, on which part the version of Ulphilas had been written in Gothic characters, accompanied with an old Latin version, in a parallel column. Through ignorance of its nature, the vellum leaves had been gradually torn out to serve for coverings to other books, but, being fortunately discovered by Knittel before the whole was destroyed, he with very great difficulty deciphered both the Gothic and the Latin, and published them with learned notes and essays, under the following title:—*Ulphilæ versionem Gothicum nonnullorum capitum epistolæ Pauli ad Romanos.* This part contains only the few following passages:—Rom. xi, 33–36; xii, 1–5, 17–21; xiii, 1–5; xiv, 9–20; xv, 3–13. These fragments are also inserted at the end of vol. 2 of Lye's "Saxon, Gothic, and Latin Dictionary."†

ULPHILAS, or WULPHILAS, the author of this version, was a descendant from some of the bishops who had been carried captive by the Goths, in their incursions into Asia during the reign of Gallienus. He flourished in the latter part of the *fourth century.* Several occurrences prove the high estimation in which he was universally held; in particular, the various and difficult embassies in which he was employed, and always with success. Coming ambassador to Constantine, he was ordained first bishop of the Christian Goths by Eusebius, of Nicomedia. Returning to his charge he discovered a holy zeal in his sacred office, and earnestly laboured for the conversion of the surrounding pagans. His missionary exertions were rewarded with numerous conversions, though accompanied with no small degree of danger to himself. He is also said to have contributed much toward the civilization of the barbarous people under his care.

His learning must have been extensive for the age in which he lived. Versed not only in the Gothic and Greek, but also in the Latin, it was still necessary for him to possess a critical knowledge of the formation of language in general, to enable him to invent letters, and construct new words and sentences expressive of the sense of the sacred Scripture, and suited to the genius of

* Chalmers, vol. xxi, pp. 9, 10.

† Marsh's Michaelis, vol. ii, part i, p. 136. Bibliog. Dict., vol. vi, p. 216.

the language in which he wrote. His manners, if we judge from circumstances, appear to have been mild and persuasive, dignified and gentle, uniting the courtier and the Christian bishop.

Sent by Fritigern to the court of Valens, to implore aid against Athanaric, the sovereign of the Ostrogoths, he succeeded in his embassy; but unfortunately, was induced by Eudoxius, bishop of Constantinople, to regard the dispute respecting Arius as a mere verbal difference, and to communicate with the Arians, in which he was followed by the rest of the Gothic Christians. At length, after a life of unwearied zeal in the cause of religion, and of patriotic labours for the welfare of his country, he sunk into the grave in a good old age; and "the memory of the just shall be blessed!"*

The Ethiopic version also is generally supposed to have been made during this century. Chrysostom, who lived toward the close of that age, in his first homily on the Gospel of John, says, "The Syrians, the Egyptians, the Indians, the Persians, the Ethiopians, and a multitude of other nations, having translated this Gospel into their own languages, the barbarians have learned to be philosophers."†

The ancient capital of Ethiopia, or Abyssinia, was *Saba;* and the queen whom the wisdom of Solomon attracted to Palestine was the sovereign of that country. The Ethiopic language, into which the translations of the holy writings were made, and which was denominated *Gheez*, is the ancient and learned language of Abyssinia, not the language now in use. The language which it nearest resembles is the Arabic, but it differs from that, and all the kindred languages of the East, by being written from the left to the right hand, and expressing the vowels by determinate characters, and not by points.‡ The following is the statement of Mr. Bruce, the celebrated traveller, on the Ethiopic Scriptures, as they exist in Abyssinia: "The Abyssinians have the Scriptures entire, as we have, and reckon the same number of books; but they divide in another manner, at least in private hands; few of them, from extreme poverty, being able to purchase the whole, either of the historical or prophetical books of the Old Testament. The same may be said of the

* Sacror. Evang. Versio Gothica, Præfat. Benzelii, cap. viii, pp. xxx-xxxv. Oxon. 1750, 4to. Cavei Hist. Lit. Sæc. iv, p. 182. Milner's History of the Church, vol. ii, pp. 168, 240.

† Marsh's Michaelis, vol. ii, pt. ii, p. 611. Waltoni Proleg. xv.

‡ Butler's Horæ Biblicæ, vol. i, p. 172.

New; for copies containing the whole of it are very scarce. Indeed nowhere, except in churches, do you see more than the Gospels, or the Acts of the Apostles, in one person's possession, and it must not be an ordinary man that possesses even these. Many books of the Old Testament are forgotten: so that it is the same trouble to procure them even in churches, for the purpose of copying, as to consult old records long covered with rubbish."*

Mr. Bruce, on his return from Abyssinia, in 1773, brought a number of Ethiopic MSS., among which were the following, said by his biographer to be in the library at Kinnaird, the family residence.

1. The Old Testament, in five large quarto volumes, each about a foot in length and breadth. These contain all the books in our canon, except the Psalms, and several of the Apocrypha. A book called the *Prophecies of Enoch* is inserted before that of Job. The Psalms are common in Abyssinia, but by some accident Mr. Bruce had no copy of them.

2. Two copies of the Gospels, in four volumes, two of which are in small quarto.

3. The Acts of the Apostles, and all the Epistles in our canon, with the Revelaton of St. John, in two small quarto volumes, uniform with the Gospels before mentioned.

4. A copy of the Song of Solomon, in the Amharic, the Falashan, the Gafat, the Agow, the Tcheretz Agow, and the Galla languages, along with a vocabulary of these languages.†

The Ethiopic version of the *Psalms*, with the *Song of Solomon*, were printed at Rome so early as 1513. The *Psalms* were reprinted in 1515 at Cologne; and again with the *Song of Solomon* in the London Polyglot. The celebrated Ethiopic scholar, Ludolf, published two editions at Francfort in 1701. The one was accompanied with a Latin translation, for the benefit of Europeans; the other was solely Ethiopic, being destined for the use of the natives, and was sent by the Dutch for that purpose to Abyssinia. The only portions of the historical books of the Old Testament which have been printed are the four first chapters of *Genesis* and the book of *Ruth*, the former repeatedly; the latter by J. G. Nisselius, in 1660. Of the Prophets only *Joel*, *Jonah*, *Zephaniah*, and *Malachi* exist in print, of various dates, and by different

* Owen's History of the British and Foreign Bible Society, vol. ii, p. 362. Murray's Account of the Life and Writings of James Bruce, Esq. Append., p. 297 Edinb., 1808, 4to.

† Murray's Life, &c., of James Bruce, Esq., *ubi sup.*

editors. The NEW TESTAMENT was printed in Ethiopic at Rome, in 1548, under the direction of three native Ethiopians, whose names were *Tesfa-Sion*, *Tensea-Wald*, and *Zaslask*, and who were all sons of Tecla Haimanot, of the Romish monastery of Mount Libanus. They assumed the Latin names of *Petrus*, *Paulus*, and *Bernardinus*. This edition was afterward reprinted in the London Polyglot, with a Latin translation by Dudley Loftus. It has been reprinted since, with a more accurate Latin translation by Professor Bode, at Brunswick, in 1752–1755, in two volumes quarto. The *Epistles of St. James*, *St. John*, and *St. Jude*, were printed at Leyden, in 1654, accompanied with an Arabic translation by Theod. Petræus.* The ancient Ethiopic version is generally supposed to have been made by Frumentius, who first preached Christianity in Ethiopia, in the fourth century.

FRUMENTIUS, the apostle of Ethiope, called FREMONAT by the Abyssinians, was the nephew of Meropius, a philosopher of Tyre. Meropius, undertaking a voyage to India, carried with him two of his nephews, Frumentius and Edesius, with whose education he was intrusted. In the course of the voyage homeward, the vessel touched at a certain port of the Red Sea, to take in provisions and fresh water. The barbarians of that country, who had a little before broken their league with the Romans, seized the ship, and murdered all the passengers and crew, except the two youths, who were studying their lessons under a tree at some distance. Their innocence and tender age moved the barbarians to compassion; their lives were spared: and being presented to the king, who resided at Axum, then the capital of Ethiopia, but now a mean village, called *Accum*, he was so charmed with their wit and sprightliness, that he not only took special care of their education, but in a short time took them into his service, making Edesius his cup-bearer, and Frumentius, who was the elder, his treasurer and secretary of state, intrusting him with all the public writings and accounts. These offices they fulfilled with integrity and honour, and so much to the satisfaction of their royal patron, that on his death-bed he thanked them for their services, and gave them their liberty. After his decease, the queen, who was left regent for her eldest son, entreated them to continue at court, to assist her in the education of her son, and the government of the state. The prin-

* Le Long. Bib. Sacra. ed. Masch, vol. i, pt. ii, sec. 6, pp. 145–157. Marsh's Hist. of Translations, pp. 95, 96. Marsh's Michaelis, vol. ii, pt. i, ch. vii, sec. 17, and pt. ii, p. 612.

cipal management of affairs was committed to Frumentius, who, by his fidelity and ability, proved the greatest support and comfort to the queen. But the pious mind of Frumentius was not so absorbed by attention to secular business as to neglect the promotion of Christianity; for which purpose he engaged several Christian merchants, who traded there, to settle in the country; and procured for them great privileges, and all the conveniences for their religious worship; and by his own fervour and example strongly recommended the true religion to the Ethiopians. When the young king, whose name was Aizan, came to age, and took the reins of government into his own hands, the brothers resigned their posts; but though entreated to stay, Edesius returned to Tyre, and Frumentius to Alexandria. On his arrival at Alexandria, Frumentius related to the patriarch Athanasius his whole history, and earnestly entreated him to send missionaries to Ethiopia, not doubting but their labours would prove successful to the conversion of that nation to Christianity. Athanasius summoned his clergy together, and, by their unanimous advice, ordained Frumentius himself bishop of the Ethiopians. Vested with the sacred character, Frumentius went back to Axum, where he had already been distinguished by his intregrity and capacity, and had gained the esteem and veneration of the people, by the administration of the secular concerns of government, and by the education of their sovereign. Eminently successful in his missionary labours, he was able to number the sovereign, and his brother Sazan, whom he had associated in the throne, among the converts to the Christian faith; churches were everywhere erected; and at length Christianity became the avowed religion of the nation. Constantius, the Roman emperor, laboured to bring them over to the adoption of the principles of Arius, and strove to obtain the deposition of Frumentius, but in vain; for the difficulty of access to this region, which has since proved prejudicial to the advancement of knowledge among its inhabitants, was at that time a happy preservative to the infant church, and placed the country out of the reach of his imperial bigotry. The time of the decease of Frumentius is not exactly ascertained: the Latins commemorate him on the 27th of October; the Greeks on the 30th of November; but of the year we are entirely ignorant. The Abyssinians still honour him as the apostle of the Axumites, and place the two kings, Aizan and Sazan, or Abreha and Atzbeha, among their saints.*

* Socrat. Scholast. Eccles. Hist., lib. i, cap. xix. Butler's Lives of the Saints, vol. x, Oct. 27. Milner's History of the Church, vol. ii, ch. vi, pp. 103, 104.

The old translation of the Ethiopic Scriptures having become nearly obsolete, by being written in the ancient and learned language of the country, attempts have been made, in more modern times, to translate the sacred volume into the *Amharic*, or vulgar dialect of Abyssinia; particularly under the direction of M. Asselin, the French charge d'affaires at Grand Cairo, who, in a communication to the British and Foreign Bible Society in 1814, states, that the Amharic, as spoken at Gondar, is the prevalent dialect in the eastern parts of Africa, which border on the equator; and that it is through this dialect all intercourse is maintained between the natives of Abyssinia and the Arabians and the negroes of the interior; and concludes by informing the society, that he has transmitted to England *Genesis* and *Exodus* in that dialect. Baron Silvester de Sacy, of Paris, also, in a report presented to the Royal Institute of France, on the labours of M. Asselin, affords the following interesting information respecting the Amharic dialect: "The language," says he, "which we commonly call *Ethiopic*, and which the Abyssinians call *Lisana Gheez*, that is to say, the language of the kingdom, is that of the province of Tigre, to which appertained the celebrated city of Axum. It was the common language of Abyssinia, down to the period at which Axum ceased to be the royal residence, and when the authority passed into the hands of the princes who spoke the Amharic dialect. The *Gheez*, however, continued to be the only dialect used in public worship, and in all acts of government; the only dialect, in short, used in writing. Thus the Egyptians call it the *language of books*, while the Amharic, as being that of the reigning family, is called the *royal language*. By the help of the Amharic, one may travel through all the provinces of Abyssinia, notwithstanding the different idioms which they respectively use. Before M. Asselin, the missionaries from the Jesuits, who resided long in Abyssinia, had there translated different portions of the sacred Scriptures into the Amharic language. None of these productions have reached Europe; nor is it known in what they consist, or what is become of them." In consequence of these, and other communications to the British and Foreign Bible Society, a sub-committee was appointed, of which the learned and celebrated travellers, Viscount Valentia, and Henry Salt, Esq., were constituted members, for the purpose of considering the best means of furnishing the Abyssinians with the Holy Scriptures.*

* Owen's Hist. of the Brit. and For. Bible Society, vol. ii, pp. 359–363. Twelfth Report of B. and F. Bible Society, Appendix, No. xlviii.

Reverting to the *fourth century*, we find a work of that age, entitled *Historia Evangelica*, in four books, written in good hexameter verse. It is properly the history of our Lord, as recorded in the Four Evangelists, and expressed, as nearly as possible, in the words of the sacred writers themselves; and is said to have been the first attempt to deliver the evangelical history in *verse*. The author, Caius Vettius Aquilinus Juvencus, was a Christian priest and poet, born of a noble Spanish family. He flourished about A. D. 330, and was author of several other poetical works. The *Historia Evangelica* has been several times printed, and may be found in the *Bibliotheca Patrum*, tom. iv, p. 55.*

The *Cento Virgilianus* of Proba Falconia may also be noticed, as an instance of the singular manner in which some of the Christians of this age pressed the heathen poets into the service of Christianity. It is a poem of some length, the subjects of which are the history of the creation, the deluge, and of Christ, and are narrated in centos from Virgil. Above seven hundred lines are so curiously selected from the works of the Mantuan bard, and so placed, that with the aid of titles to the different portions, the principal events of these Scripture histories are described in his words.

Proba Falconia was the wife of a noble Roman, and eminently distinguished by piety and benevolence. The most celebrated characters of her age valued her friendship, and honoured her in their works. After the capture of Rome by Alaric, in 410, she fled, having lost her husband, with her daughter Juliana, and her grand-daughter Demetria, into Africa, where she found an asylum, and lived upon the wreck of her fortune, honoured with the esteem of the great Augustine. The time of her death is uncertain.

Epiphanius, a father of the Christian church, as he has been called, is another author who claims our regard. He was born in Palestine, about A. D. 310. "To qualify himself for the study of the Holy Scriptures, he learned in his youth the Hebrew, the Egyptian, the Syriac, the Greek, and the Latin languages." About the year 367 he was chosen bishop of Salamis, then called Constantia, in Cyprus. His principal work appeared in 374, under the title of *Panarium*, or "Box of Antidotes against all Heresies;" in which he gives the history of twenty heresies before Christ, and of fourscore since the promulgation of the gospel. A commentary on the Canticles was discovered among the MSS. in the Vatican library, by Monsignor Foggini, prefect of the library, who pub-

* Cavei Hist. Lit. Sæc. iv, pp. 150, 207. Clarke's Succession of Sacred Literature, vol. i. Turner's History of the Anglo-Saxons, vol. ii, p. 334. Lond. 1807, 4to.

lished an accurate edition of it at Rome, in 1750, with a learned preface. The works of Epiphanius prove him to have been a man of extensive reading, yet credulous and superstitious; but his writings are rendered valuable by his numerous quotations from profane and ecclesiastical writers, known only by the fragments which he has preserved. In his book against heresies, he says, that the Gospel of St. John, and the Acts of the Apostles, translated into Hebrew, were kept in the treasury of the Jews at Tiberias. He died in 403, as he was returning from Constantinople to Salamis.*

But the most eminent Biblical scholar of the fourth century was Jerome, whose *revision* of the Latin version of the Bible constitutes the principal difference of the *Vulgate* from the old *Italic*. This renowned monk was born at Stridon, now Sdrigni, a small town upon the confines of Pannonia, Dalmatia, and Italy, near Aquileia, about the year 331. His father, Eusebius, who was a Christian, sent him to finish his education at Rome. In this city he perfected his knowledge of the Latin and Greek tongues, his native dialect being the Illyrican; read the best authors in both languages; and made such progress in oratory, that he for some time pleaded at the bar. While a student at Rome, he used on Sundays to visit, with his fellow-students, the catacombs or cemeteries of the martyrs: "When a boy," says he, "I studied the liberal arts at Rome, and was wont to make a round to visit the tombs of the apostles and martyrs, with others of the same age and inclinations, and often to descend into the caves which are dug deep into the earth, and have for walls on each side the bodies of those that are interred there."

During his residence at Rome, it was Jerome's greatest pleasure to collect a good library, and acquaint himself with all the best authors in different languages; and such was his thirst for knowledge, that in pursuing it, he not unfrequently forgot to take his usual repasts. Cicero and Plautus were his chief delight. He purchased a great many books, copied several, and procured many to be transcribed by his friends. Being arrived at man's estate, and desirous of improving his studies, he resolved upon travelling. Accompanied by his friend Bonosus, he made a tour through Gaul, where the Romans had erected several famous schools, especially at Marseilles, Toulouse, Bourdeaux, Autun, Lyons, and Triers, examining libraries, and collecting information from all quarters.

* Butler's Lives, vol. v. May. Le Long, Biblioth. Sacr., tom. i, p. 62.

At Triers he copied St. Hilary's book "On Synods," and his "Commentaries on the Psalms;" and while in this city experienced what he regarded as a "merciful conversion to God;" and resolved upon following the profession of a monk, which, in his day, meant chiefly the life of a private, recluse Christian, unfettered by any certain rules or vows.

Having collected whatever he could meet with in Gaul to augment his literary treasure, he repaired to Aquileia, where, at that time, flourished many eminent and learned men. With many of them Jerome contracted so great an intimacy that their names appear often in his writings; Cromatius, first priest, and afterward bishop of that city, and to whom he dedicated several of his works, was one of them; Toranius Ruffinus, famous primarily for his friendship, and subsequently for his controversies with Jerome, was also a monk of Aquileia. The monastery of this city was the first into which Jerome retired; but afterward he withdrew into the inhospitable desert of Chalcis, in Syria, where he devoted himself to reading and study, with immense industry. It was in this retirement that he commenced learning the Hebrew tongue: writing to the monk Rusticus, he says, "I became a scholar to a monk who had been a Jew, to learn of him the Hebrew alphabet; and after I had most diligently studied the judicious rules of Quintilian, the copious flowing elegance of Cicero, the grave style of Fronto, and the smoothness of Pliny, I inured myself to hissing and broken-winded words. What labour it cost me, what difficulties I went through, how often I despaired and left off, and how I began again to learn, both I myself who felt the burden can witness, and they also who lived with me. And I thank our Lord that I now gather sweet fruit from the bitter seed of those studies."

At length, however, wearied by the opposition of the monks of Meletius's party, who persecuted him, because in speaking of the divine nature, he used the word *hypostasis;* and afflicted with an infirm state of health, he left the wilderness, after having passed four years in it, and went to Antioch. Here he was ordained a presbyter of the church, but would never proceed any further in ecclesiastical dignity. Soon after his ordination he went into Palestine, and visited the principal holy places situated in different parts of that country, but made Bethlehem his most usual residence. He had recourse to the ablest Jewish doctors, to inform himself of all particulars relating to all the remarkable places mentioned in the sacred history; and neglected no means to perfect himself in the knowledge of the Hebrew tongue. For this purpose he addressed himself to the most skilful among the Jews; one of his masters in particular, by whose instructions he exceedingly improved himself, spoke Hebrew with such gracefulness, true accent, and propriety of expression, that he passed among the Jewish doctors for a true Chaldean.

About the year 380 Jerome went to Constantinople, to study the Scriptures under Gregory Nazianzen, who was then bishop of that city; but upon Gregory's leaving Constantinople in 381, he returned into Palestine, from whence he was soon afterward called to Rome, where he was detained by Pope Damasus as his secretary, and employed by him in writing his letters, in answering the consultations of bishops, and in other important affairs of the church.

Jerome soon gained at Rome universal esteem for his piety, learning, and eloquence; and many among the nobility, clergy, and monks, sought to be instructed by him in the Holy Scriptures. The illustrious Paula, Marcella, and other opulent and devout ladies, profited also by his instructions, and became proficients in Hebrew. Marcella, Paula, Blesilla, Eustochium, he tells us, could read and recite with equal ease, the Psalter in the Hebrew, Greek, and Latin tongues. One of his most useful letters is that addressed to Laeta, wife of Toxotius, Paula's son, containing rules for the education of her infant daughter. A few sentences from it may induce the reader to examine the epistle itself. "Let her be brought up," says he, "as Samuel was in the temple, and the Baptist in the desert; in utter ignorance of vanity and vice. Let her never hear, learn, or discourse of any thing but what may conduce to the fear of God. Let her never hear bad words; but as soon as she can speak, let her learn some parts of the Psalms. Let her have an alphabet of little letters, made of box or ivory, the names of all which she must know, that she may play with them, and that learning may be made a diversion. When a little older, let her form each letter in wax with her finger, guided by another's hand: then let her be invited, by prizes and presents suited to her age, to join syllables together, and to write the names of the patriarchs down from Adam. Let her have companions to learn with her, that she may be spurred on by emulation, and by hearing their praises. She is not to be scolded or brow-beaten, if slower; but to be encouraged, that she may rejoice to surpass, and be sorry to see herself outstripped, and behind others; not envying their progress, but rejoicing at it, and admiring it, while she reproaches her own backwardness. Great care is to be taken that she conceive no aversion to studies, lest their bitterness remain in riper years. A master must be found for her, who is a man both of virtue and learning; nor will a great scholar think it beneath him to teach her the first elements of letters, as Aristotle did Alexander the Great. That is not to be contemned, without which nothing great can be acquired. Care is necessary that she never learn what she will have afterward to unlearn. The eloquence of the Gracchi derived its perfection from the mother's elegance and purity of language; Alexander, the conqueror of the world, could never correct the faults in his gait and manners, which he had learned in his childhood from his master Leonidas."

After the death of Damasus, which happened in December, A. D. 384, Jerome returned to Palestine, and retired to Bethlehem, where Paula built a monastery for him, and where she also founded a nunnery, of which she was the governess. Being obliged to enlarge his monastery, he sold an estate for that purpose, which he still had in Dalmatia; and not only enlarged the monastery, but also erected a hospital, in which he entertained strangers; and when many fled to Bethlehem, on the plundering of Rome by Alaric the Goth, in 410, he joyfully received them, and afforded them every possible succour and comfort. In this retreat he continued to pursue his studies with unwearied diligence, and though considered as a master in the Hebrew, he applied again to a famous Jewish rabbi, called Bar-Ananias, who for a sum of money came to teach him in the night, that he might not offend his brethren the Jews; and with indefatigable labour he acquired also the Chaldee and the Syriac. Toward the end of life the studies of Jerome were interrupted by an incursion of barbarians, who penetrated through Egypt into Palestine; and some time afterward by the violence and ravages of the Pelagians, who, after the council of Diospolis, in 416, relying upon the protection of John of Jerusalem, sent the year following a troop of seditious banditti to Bethlehem, who set fire to all the monasteries, and reduced them to ashes, Jerome himself escaping with difficulty, and being obliged to retire to a strong castle. After the storm he resumed his labours, and continued them till near his death, which was occasioned by a fever, on the 30th of September, A. D. 420, in the ninetieth or ninety-first year of his age.*

* Butler's Lives, vol. ix, Sep. 30, pp. 369–412. Milner's Hist. of the Church of Christ, vol. ii, pp. 470–472. Hody, De Bibliorem Text. Orig., lib. iii, ch. ii, pp 350, 359, 360.

Jerome was a man of a most vigorous mind, but of a haughty spirit, and inclined to superstition; hence his numerous controversial writings are too frequently embittered by a sarcastic severity, unworthy a character so generally excellent; and many of his theological treatises are alloyed by the superstitious sentiments prevalent in that age. But as a Biblical critic and translator his fame is secured, and after the lapse of fourteen hundred years remains undiminished in its lustre. The revisions and translation of the Latin Scriptures constitute his most important labours. It is probable that he was first induced to examine the accuracy of the old Latin, or *Italic* version, and to collate it with the Septuagint, from which it was a translation, by a wish to silence the cavils of the Jews, who were constantly objecting to the Christians that their translations were inaccurate; to which he was further urged by the importunity of several of his friends, and particularly of Pope Damasus, by whom also he was commissioned to undertake a critical revision of the New Testament. At first he only marked the variations of some of the books of the Old Testament, especially the Psalms, from the Greek and Hebrew, by obeluses and asterisks, after the example of Origen; but at length, convinced of the insufficiency of the Old Latin version, even with all his own corrections and improvements; and having also lost the greater part of the manuscripts which contained the revision of the Old Testament, through the treachery of a person to whom they had been intrusted, and who either secreted or destroyed them, he seriously set about making a new one from the best Hebrew copies he could procure. This he accomplished at different intervals, and rather by starts than a continued labour, in the space of fifteen years, amidst many contradictions, reproaches, and bitter invectives. The four books of Kings were first published in the year 391; soon after followed the Prophets, then the books of Solomon, Job, the Psalms, Ezra, Nehemiah, Chronicles, and last of all the Octateuch, viz., the five books of Moses, and Joshua, Judges, and Ruth, about the year 405. His qualifications for the work, and the peculiar advantages he possessed as a translator of the Holy Scriptures, are thus described by a late critic*:—"His learning, whether sacred or profane, was not less extensive than Origen's; his judgment and taste were more correct and exquisite. He had a perfect knowledge of the Greek and Latin languages, and was

* Geddes's Prospectus of a New Translation of the Holy Bible, pp. 46, 47. Glasgow, 1786, 4to.

sufficiently versed in the Hebrew. He had correct copies of the Hexapla, if not the autograph itself before him. He was at no great distance from a famous school, (Tiberias,) of Jewish rabbins, whom he might consult as he saw occasion. He had traversed the land with his own feet, and seen with his own eyes the principal places mentioned in sacred history. He was acquainted with the manners and customs of the country. He knew its plants, its animals, and its other productions. With all these advantages, and his superior talents, it was impossible he should not succeed."

The critical revision of the NEW TESTAMENT he completed in the year 392, or a few years earlier; the four Gospels having been published before the death of Damasus. This revision of the New Testament, with Jerome's translation of the Old, form the ground work of the present VULGATE, so far as relates to the canonical books, except that the Psalms of the Italic version have been retained, and several corrections introduced in other parts from Aquila, Theodotion, and Symmachus, as well as from the Italic. Jerome also translated the books of Judith and Tobit from the Chaldee, which form a part of the Vulgate copy of the Apocrypha. His revision of the Psalms is sometimes used in the services of the Roman Catholic Church, and has received the name of the Gallican Psalter.

It has been justly observed, "that Jerome's version had the fate of many considerable works of genius. It had warm advocates, particularly among the truly learned; and violent enemies, particularly among the ignorant." Lucinius Bœticus, a noble Spaniard, and zealously attached to the Scriptures, sent six short-hand writers or copyists from Spain to Bethlehem, in 394, to take copies of his version, and of his other works. Sophronius, at whose request Jerome had translated some parts of the Hebrew Scriptures into Latin, retranslated a part of his version into Greek; and Augustine, who at first violently opposed the translation from the Hebrew, afterward so highly approved of it, that he extracted those passages from it which composed his *Speculum* or "Mirror," a work which contained a selection of the choicest parts of Scripture, designed for those who were too poor to purchase, or too engaged to read the whole of the sacred writings. Yet nearly two hundred years elapsed before this translation received the sanction of the church, many of the contemporaries of Jerome regarding a translation from the Hebrew as a dangerous innovation: for, strange as it may appear, the Septuagint version was more respected in the Latin Church than the Hebrew original. At that time the now exploded story of seventy-two interpreters, all translating by divine inspiration, all translating independently, yet each of them producing the same translation, was firmly believed in the Latin as well as the Greek Church; and this belief, united with a hatred of the Jews and an ignorance of the Hebrew, gave to the Septuagint version a higher rank than to the original itself. At the close of the sixth century Pope Gregory the Great gave to Jerome's translation the sanction of papal authority, by acknowledging that he considered it as superior to any other of the Latin versions, and therefore made use of it himself; and in a short time after, Isidore of Seville wrote, that all churches made use of it. In the sixteenth century the VULGATE was declared authentic by the popish council of Trent; and continues to be the only publicly authorized version of the Roman Catholic Church. Most of the first European translations were made from it.

Jerome was a rapid and voluminous writer. The translation of Tobit was finished in one day; and the three books of Solomon he calls "the work of three days." And besides his revisions and translations of the Scriptures, he was the author of Commentaries on the Prophets, Ecclesiastes, Matthew, and the Epistles of Paul to the Galatians and Ephesians, Titus and Philemon; of a History of Ecclesiastical Writers; of various treatises on different subjects, and of a number of elegant and useful epistles.* The *editio princeps*, or first printed edition of his works, was edited by Erasmus, and printed by Frobenius, at Basle, in five volumes folio, 1516. The edition of D. Vallarsius, printed at Verona in eleven volumes, 1734–42, is usually accounted the best. The genuine version of Jerome, from a beautiful manuscript at Paris, was published in 1693, by D. Martianay and D. Pouget, and forms the first volume of the Benedictine edition of his works, in five vols. folio.†

* On the revisions, and translations, &c., of Jerome the author has principally consulted Hody, De Bibl. Text. Orig., pt. ii, cap. ii, iii, iv.; Fabricy, Titres Primitifs, vol. i, pp. 233–237, and vol. ii, pp. 92–124; Calmet, Dissertation sur la Vulgate; Marsh's Lectures, lec. 4.

† Bibliog. Dict., vol. iv.

CHAPTER III.

FIFTH CENTURY.

Armenian Version—Mesrobe—Nonnus—Eudoxia—Theodosius—Lectionaria—Chrysography and illuminated MSS.—Ornamented Hebrew MSS.—Talmuds—Karaites—Irish Letters—St. Patrick—Irish Version.

THE translation of the Scriptures into the ARMENIAN tongue was executed nearly at the same period as the Latin version of Jerome, and illustriously distinguished the commencement of the *fifth century.* For this inestimable work, which La Croze calls "the queen of versions," the Armenian Church is indebted to Mesrobe, or Miesrob, minister of state, and secretary to Warasdates, and Arsaces IV., kings of Armenia. By some, indeed, it has been supposed that Chrysostom translated the whole, or part of the Scriptures into Armenian; but the evidence is doubtful, and no remains of such translation now exist. The version of Mesrobe has continued in use among the Armenians ever since it was first made, and many illustrious instances of enlightened piety occur in their history.

In the seventeenth century manuscript copies of the Bible were become so scarce in Armenia, that a single copy cost one thousand two hundred livres, or fifty pounds. Such being the rarity of copies of the Scriptures, a council of Armenian bishops, assembled in 1662, resolved to call in the art of printing, of which they had heard in Europe. For this purpose they applied first to France; but the Roman Catholic Church having refused their request, Uscan,* minister of Erivan, the seat of the Armenian patri-

* USCAN, or OSGAN, the celebrated editor of the Armenian Bible, was a minister of the gospel at Erivan, the capital of Persian Armenia. From the Armenian pronunciation of his name, he has sometimes been erroneously designated *bishop of Yuschuavanch*; from the place of his residence, *bishop of Erivan;* and from being confounded with Garabeid Wartabied, the editor of the Armenian psalms, in 1666, *Uscan Wartabied.* He was sent to Europe about the year 1662, by Agopus (Jacobus) Caractri, patriarch of the Armenians, for the purpose of having an edition of the Armenian Scriptures printed under his inspection. According to the commission of the patriarch, he went to Rome, where he remained fifteen months, and then removed to Amsterdam, where he established an Armenian press, and printed the *Bible*, and other works in that tongue. His chief assistant was Solomon de Leon, a deacon, his nephew, who afterward married a young lady at Marseilles; his printers' names were Etzmiatzneus and Sergius. In 1669 Uscan obtained permission from the king of France to establish an Armenian printing office at Marseilles, under the restriction of printing nothing contrary to the Catholic faith. The court of Rome immediately adopted every precaution to prevent

arch, printed the Bible at Amsterdam, in 1666, in 4to., and an edition of the New Testament in 1668, in 8vo., which was reprinted in 1698 in a still smaller form. A second edition of this Bible was published at Constantinople in 1705, 4to., and a third at Venice in 1733, corrected by Mehitar, a monk of the monastery of St. Lazarus, which is esteemed by the Armenians to be the most correct. Editions of the Psalms are said to have been published at Rome, 1565; Venice, 1642; Amsterdam, 1661, 1666, 1672, 1677; Marseilles, 1673; and Constantinople, *without date;* though Masch doubts whether the Amsterdam edition of 1677 ever appeared, as the Armenian press had been removed to Marseilles prior to that date. But notwithstanding these editions, the Armenian Scriptures had become so scarce by the close of the eighteenth century, that Dr. Buchanan informs us, (Christian Researches, p. 245,) that in Persia they bore no proportion to the Armenian population, and that in India a copy was scarcely to be purchased at any price; and in 1813 the committee of the Russian Bible Society report, that copies of both the editions of the Armenian Bible were become so scarce, that "they were hardly to be found anywhere," and that in consequence of this scarcity of the Scriptures, they had undertaken and completed an edition of five thousand copies of the New Testament, at the Armenian printing office of St. Petersburg, kept by the learned and reverend archdeacon of the Armenian Church, Joseph Joannis, every sheet of which had been examined by Joannis, the Armenian archbishop at Astrakan, to whom the sheets had been sent as they came out of the press.*

Dr. Buchanan, in 1811, remarks respecting the Armenians, that "they are to be found in every principal city of Asia, are the general merchants of the East, and are in a state of constant motion

any errors being inserted in the publications printed by the Armenians of Marseilles. A written confession of faith was demanded from Uscan, and an Armenian priest, named John Agolp, sent to watch the press. While Uscan, who was a man of great prudence, lived, the printing establishment was conducted peaceably; but after his death, which appears to have been before A. D. 1677, several lawsuits were commenced. These being terminated, Solomon de Leon continued the establishment, but not without considerable uneasiness, occasioned by Thomas Herabied, an Armenian priest, who had been appointed inspector of the press, in the place of John Agolp. The printing establishment was finally transferred to Constantinople. See Simon, Letters Choisies vol. ii, let. 22, 23, pp. 137–166. Le Long, edit. Masch, pt. ii, vol. i, sec. 9, pp. 175 176, 179. Clement, Bibliotheque Curieuse, vol. iii, p. 428.

* Marsh's Michaelis, vol. ii, pt. i, sec. 18, and pt. ii, pp. 615, 616. Butler's Horæ Biblicæ, vol. i, p. 173. Twelfth Report of the B. and F. Bible Society, p. 106. Le Long, edit. Masch, pt. ii, vol. i, sec. 9, pp. 173–181

from Canton to Constantinople. Their general character is that of wealthy, industrious, and enterprising people. They are settled in all the principal places of India, where they arrived many centuries before the English. Wherever they colonize, they build churches, and observe the solemnities of the Christian religion in a decorous manner. Their ecclesiastical establishment in Hindostan is more respectable than that of the English. They have three churches in the three capitals, one at Calcutta, one at Madras, and one at Bombay; but they have also churches in the interior of the country. The bishop sometimes visits Calcutta; but he is not resident there. The proper country of these Christians is Armenia, the greater part of which is subject to the Persian government; but they are scattered all over the empire, the commerce of Persia being chiefly conducted by Armenians. Their patriarch resides at Erivan, not far from Mount Ararat. They retain their ancient Scripture doctrines and worship, to this day."* When the British envoy, Sir Harford Jones, was sent to the court of Persia, in 1808 and 1809, he was met about four miles from Ispahan by an advanced part of the inhabitants. "First came the merchants of the city, in number about three hundred, all in their separate classes. Then followed a deputation from the *Armenian clergy*, composed of the bishop and chief dignitaries, in their sacerdotal robes. They carried silken banners, on which was painted the passion of our Saviour. The bishop, a reverend old man with a white beard, presented the EVANGELISTS, bound in crimson velvet, to the envoy, and proceeded on with his attendant priests, chanting their church service."†

MESROBE, or MIESROB, the author of the Armenian version, was a native of Hasecas, in the province of Taron. His father, whose name was Vardan, caused him to be educated in the sciences and literature of the Greeks. Early in life he was appointed secretary to the king, and notwithstanding the unsettled and ruinous situation of the national affairs, executed his official duties with extraordinary ability and prudence. But being fond of retirement, and desirous of devoting himself entirely to the practice of religious duties, he retired from office, and withdrew into another province. The vigorous mind of Mesrobe was not, however, to be satisfied with mere monastic exercises; instead therefore of confining himself to the cell, or the desert, he successfully attempted the conversion of various idolatrous sects then subsisting in Armenia, and

* Christian Researches, pp. 242, 243.

† Morier's Journey through Persia, &c., p. 161. Lond., 1812, 4to.

the adjacent countries. In this arduous and pious undertaking, a chief difficulty was the want of Armenian characters to express his ideas in writing, and afford the people the advantage of written instruction; the Armenians having at that time no letters peculiar to their own language, but making use either of the Persian, or Syrian, or Greek. To remove this obstacle to the progress of the gospel, as well as to render an essential service to the state, by enabling the secretaries to transact their business without having recourse, as formerly, to the Persian letters, he employed himself assiduously to the invention of characters suited to the pronunciation and genius of his native tongue. In this project he was sanctioned by the sovereign and the bishops; and in particular by Isaac, the great patriarch of Armenia. To accomplish his design he applied to most of the learned men of his day, and among others to a Syrian bishop, called Daniel, who professed to have already formed a set of characters suited to the Armenian tongue; but which, on examination, proved to be radically defective. Disappointed in his expectations of assistance, he is said to have betaken himself to prayer, and in a vision to have seen a hand describing on a stone certain figures, by the recollection of which, he with Ruphan, an anchoret, who was eminently skilled in the Greek, completed the formation of the Armenian alphabet.*

Suitable characters being invented, Mesrobe applied himself to the translation of the sacred Scriptures, commencing with the book of Proverbs. This translation Isaac, the patriarch of Armenia, and he, made from the Syriac; Meruzen, a Persian general, and an enemy to the Christians, having ordered all the books written in Greek to be destroyed, that no other letters might be used than the Persian; and the Persian governors not permitting even the Greeks who lived in their part of Armenia to use any other language than the Syriac. Having completed his version of the Scriptures, Mesrobe travelled into various provinces, and, penetrating into Iberia and Albania, was singularly successful in establishing schools for the instruction of youth, and, by the transcriptions furnished by his disciples and scholars, extensively diffusing the knowledge of the Holy Scriptures.

Isaac and Mesrobe engaged a second time in a translation of the Scriptures from the Syriac, in order to render the Armenian version still more perfect. But having afterward received from the council of Ephesus a correct copy of the Greek Bible, they cheer-

* For the Armenian alphabet, see plate 1.

fully submitted to the task of again translating what they had translated twice before. In this last version they were assisted by Moses of Chorene, the celebrated historian, whom they sent with others to the famous school of Alexandria to obtain more perfect knowledge of the Greek, that nothing might be wanting to the perfection of their translation. Such being the care bestowed by these Armenians, it is no wonder that they succeeded in their endeavours, and produced a version superior to most others.

After a life spent in unwearied exertions to promote the diffusion of the gospel and the circulation of the Scriptures, Mesrobe died a few months after his friend the great Isaac, in the city of Valarsapatam, in the first year of the reign of Isdegird, king of Persia, and was honourably buried at Asacan. Moses of Chorene, his disciple and coadjutor, describes him as being "handsome in person and elegant in manners; at once free from haughtiness and meanness; mild and benevolent in disposition; sound in judgment and eloquent in speech; cautious and prudent, yet firm and persevering in duty; indefatigable in teaching; skilled in reproving; patient, faithful, and sincere in all his conduct."*

Theodoret, a Syrian bishop, who lived at the beginning of the fifth century, speaks of the existence of other translations besides those we have noticed; but we have no fragments of them remaining, nor any account of the translators. His words are: "The Hebrew books are not only translated into the language of the Grecians, but also of the *Romans*, the *Indians*, *Persians*, *Armenians*, *Scythians*, *Sarmatians*, *Egyptians*, and, in a word, into all the languages that are used by any nation."†

But, notwithstanding our ignorance of some of those translations of which Theodoret speaks, several important facts induce us to believe that during this century considerable attention was paid to the sacred writings. Nonnus, a native of Panapolis, in Egypt, who lived about A.D. 410, was the author of a Paraphrase of St. John's Gospel, in Greek hexameter verse; a work from whence various readings have been carefully selected by Mill, Bengel, Wetstein, and Griesbach. It has been frequently printed. The best edition is by D. Heinsius, with a Latin translation, in octavo, printed at Leyden, 1627.

The empress Eudoxia, or Eudocia, may also be ranked among the Biblical scholars of this age. She was the daughter of Leon-

* Moses Chorenensis, Hist. Armen., lib. iii, cap. xlvii, lii, liii, liv, lx, lxvii, et Pref. Lond. 1736, 4to.

† Sixt. Senens, lib. iv. Usserii Hist. Dogmat. de Script. Vernacul., p. 53.

tius, a Gentile philosopher, and received a learned education. Being engaged in a lawsuit with her brothers respecting a share in the patrimonial estate, she carried her cause personally by appeal to Constantinople, where she obtained the friendship of Pulcheria, sister to Theodosius II. Embracing Christianity, she was baptized by the name of Eudoxia, or Eudocia, her former name being Athenais; and was soon afterward married to the emperor. Their union lasted a considerable time; but the machinations of Chrysapius creating jealousy in the emperor, Eudoxia retired to Jerusalem, where she spent many years in erecting and adorning churches, and relieving the poor. Cave assures us she was afterward reconciled to the emperor, returned to Constantinople, and continued with him till his death; after which she revisited Palestine, and spent the remainder of her days in works of piety. On her death-bed she took a solemn oath that the suspicions of Theodosius respecting her chastity were utterly groundless. She died A.D. 459.

She wrote a poetical Paraphrase of the Octateuch, or first eight books of the Bible; and another Paraphrase, in prose, of the Prophecies of Daniel and Zechariah. Photius says, she adhered so sacredly to the original text in these paraphrases, neither adding nor changing any thing, that they might justly be accounted legitimate versions of the sacred books. She also wrote the Histories of St. Cyprian and of Justina, in heroic verse, besides a Life of Christ, and other poetical works.

The emperor Theodosius himself, a prince of retired and literary habits, devoted much of his time to the transcription and adorning of the sacred books; and was so fair and elegant a writer, that he obtained the name of *Calligraphes*, or "the fair writer." In particular, he is said to have written a copy of the Gospels with his own hand, in *letters of gold*, and to have devoted his days and nights to the study of the Scriptures.* Where the sovereigns themselves set so pious an example, the people were sure to imitate them. The CODEX BEZÆ, or Codex Cantabrigiensis, which is supposed to have been written during this century,† may possibly, therefore, have been written in the reign of Theodosius. The selection and appointment of proper lessons to be read in the churches on all holydays, whether saints' days or others, is also referred to this century. The Scriptures had indeed been read

* Gibbon's Roman Empire, vol. v, p. 420, 8vo. Blanchini Evangel. Quadrup., vol. ii, part ii, fol. DXCII. Rom. fol. Cavei Hist. Lit. Sæc., vol. v, p. 312.

† Marsh's Michaelis, vol. ii, part ii, p. 720.

publicly from the earliest ages of Christianity, but selections for general devotion date their commencement only from about the year 450, for in that year Claudianus Mamercus composed a *Kalendar*, or *Lectionarium*, for the church of Vienna; and Musœus, a priest of Massilia, (now Marseilles,) applied himself to compose one for that church in 480, at the request of Bishop Venerius. Both these are now lost, and the oldest extant is the *Lectionarium Gallicanum*, published by Mabillon, from a manuscript which he supposed to be above a thousand years old.* About the same time Scripture histories began to be painted upon the walls of the churches, which Paulinus, bishop of Nola, who first commenced the practice in the church of St. Felix, called "the books of the ignorant."† At this period none were permitted to sit in the time of divine service, especially during the reading of the Scriptures, but those who were unable to stand on account of old age or infirmity: and so sacred were the Scriptures accounted, that even private Christians washed their hands before they read the Bible; and in the Eastern churches lights were carried before the Gospels when they were going to be read. Asterius, bishop of Amasia, in Natolia, about the commencement of this century, in his homily on Dives and Lazarus, describes the Grecians as wearing garments with various figures upon them, so that, walking in public, they seemed like painted walls: "You see there lions, panthers, bears, bulls, dogs, woods, rocks, and hunters." Others of the more devout had *Scripture histories woven in them:* "You may there also see the marriage of Galilee and the water-pots; the paralytic man carrying his bed upon his shoulders; the blind man cured by being anointed with clay; the woman with the bloody flux touching the hem of Christ's garment; the woman who was a sinner falling at the feet of Jesus; Lazarus returning from the sepulchre to life; Christ and all his disciples, and all the miracles he wrought."‡ Superstitious, however, as some of the preceding practices may appear, they sufficiently evince the profound reverence which the Christians entertained for the sacred writings, and the high estimation in which copies of them would be held by those who could procure them.

Similar esteem for the inspired volumes produced those magni-

* Bingham's Antiquities, &c., vol. vi, p. 416. Wheatley's Illustration of the Book of Common Prayer, ch. iii, p. 141, folio.

† Butler's Lives of the Saints, vol. vi, p. 310.

‡ Bingham's Antiquities, vol. vi, p. 427. Wheatley's Illustration, ch. iii, p. 144. F. Combefis, Græco-Lat. Patrum Novum Auctarium, vol. i, pp. 2, 3. Paris, 1648, fol.

ficent specimens of CHRYSOGRAPHY and of ILLUMINATION, or ornamental decorations of Biblical manuscripts, which, though found in writings of later ages, were most frequent in the fourth and fifth centuries. Jerome, who lived in the fourth century, mentions that there were in his time books written on parchment of a purple colour, in letters of gold and silver; and that whole books were written in large characters, such as are commonly used at the beginning of sentences, and called *uncial*, initial, or capital letters.* In the Imperial library at Vienna there is a famous MS. fragment of the book of Genesis and of the Gospel of St. Luke, generally allowed to be at least fourteen hundred years old. It is written upon *purple* vellum, in letters of gold and silver, and consists of twenty-six leaves, adorned with forty-eight pictures in water colours. Dr. Holmes published a copy of this MS. in 1795; and the pictures are engraven in volume third of the catalogue of Lambecius, printed at Vienna in 1670.† There is also a small fragment of a MS. of the New Testament in the Cottonian library in the British Museum, written on papyrus, (charta Ægyptiaca,) or on paper of a *purple* colour; and Wetstein assures us that he himself had seen two Psalters, the one Greek, preserved in the library of Zurich, the other Latin, kept in the monastery of St. Germain, at Paris, both written upon *purple* or red parchment, or paper.‡

In the history of the emperors of Constantinople, mention is made of *chrysographi*, or writers in letters of gold, an employment which appears to have been deemed honourable. Simeon Logotheta says of the emperor Artemius, that before he came to the empire he was a *chrysographus*, or writer in letters of gold; gold letters being very early used in titles and capitals of books, and sometimes whole books being written in letters of gold.§ D'Herbelot observes, that several of the works of the most excellent Arab poets who flourished before the times of Mohammedanism were called *Al Moallacat*, that is, suspended, because they were successively affixed, by way of honour, to the *Caaba*, or gate of the temple of Mecca; and also *Al Modhahebat*, which signifies *gilded*, because they were written in letters of gold upon Egyptian paper:‖ and Harmer conjectures that the 16th, 56th, 57th, 58th,

* Hieronymi Opera, in Lib. Job. Præfat., vol. iv, fol. 10. Basil. 1506.

† Astle's Origin and Progress of Writing, ch. v, p. 71.

‡ Wetsteinii Proleg., cap. i, p. 1, et cap. ii, p. 16. Amstel. 1730, 4to. Du Cange, Glossar. v. "Membraneum Purpureum."

§ Montfaucon's Antiquity explained, vol. iii, ch. iv, p. 220, fol.

‖ D'Herbelot, Bibliotheque Orientale, p. 591. Maestricht, fol.

59th, and 70th Psalms are distinguished by the epithet MICHTAM, or golden, on account of their having been, on some occasion or other, written in letters of gold, and hung up in the sanctuary, or elsewhere.* Among the Harleian MSS. in the British Museum is a noble exemplar of the four Gospels, in capital letters of gold, written in the eighth century: every page of the sacred text, consisting of two separate columns, is enclosed within a broad and beautifully illuminated border: the pictures of the evangelists, with their symbolic animals, are curiously painted in the front of their respective Gospels; the initial letter of each Gospel is richly illuminated, and so large as to fill an entire page: to the whole are prefixed the prologues, arguments, and breviaries; two letters of Jerome to Damasus; the canons of Eusebius; his letters to Carpian; and a capitular of the Gospels for the course of the year; all of them written in small golden characters.† In 670, the famous Wilfrid, among other donations for decorating the church of Rippon, ordered a copy of the four Gospels to be written for it, in letters of the purest gold, upon leaves of parchment, *purpled* in the ground, and coloured variously upon the surface: but that such copies were extremely rare, especially in England, is evident from Bede speaking of it as a kind of prodigy, unheard of before in those days.‡

The reason for thus preparing the skins of vellum or parchment, and staining them *purple*, was to render the appearance of the gold and silver letters more brilliant and splendid. Casiri (*Biblioth. Arabico-Hispana*, p. 9) says that he had seen many instances in which the lustre of the parchment, whether stained *red* or *black*, was such that it reflected objects like a mirror. But this expensive and magnificent mode of writing was appropriated chiefly to those copies designed for princes or nobles; hence Theonas (tom. xii, Spicil, p. 549) admonishes Lucian, the grand chamberlain, not to permit copies to be written upon *purple* vellum, in *gold* or *silver* letters, unless specially required by the prince. It was also principally confined to the transcription of the sacred books, which were thus executed to induce the greater reverence for them. Boniface, bishop of Mentz, the apostle of Germany, in the eighth century, gives this intimation in his epistle to the abbess Eadburga: "I entreat you," says he, "to send me the Epistles of the apostle St. Peter, written in *letters of gold*, that by exhibiting them,

* Clarke's Harmer's Observations, vol. iii, p. 150.

† Selection of curious Articles from Gent. Mag., vol. ii, p. 19.

‡ Whitaker's Cathedral of Cornwall, vol. i, p. 111. Lond. 1804, 4to.

in preaching, to the eyes of the carnal, I may procure the greater honour and reverence for the Holy Scriptures." Such was the book of the Gospels, written in letters of gold, which Lewis the Pious gave to the monastery of St. Medard, at Soissons, and now in the royal library of France. Of the same kind is the book of the Gospels belonging to the church of the Blessed Mary, at Rheims. To which may be added the legacies of Count Everard, who bequeathed to his son Berengarius a Psalter written with gold, and to Adelard a Lectionary of the Epistles and Gospels, written also with gold. Princes sometimes caused their usual books of prayer to be written in this manner; such, for instance, is the beautiful one written in letters of gold, upon purple vellum, bound in ivory, and studded with gems, preserved in the celebrated Colbertine library, formerly belonging to Charles the Bald; and another very similar work, belonging to the same prince, written on vellum, and executed in letters of gold, formerly preserved in the Parthenon of Zurich, but now in the Imperial library. This latter work was edited at Ingolstadt, in 1585, by Felix, bishop of Scala, who observes, that there is also a book of the Gospels, of the age of Charles the Bald, written in letters of gold, preserved in the church of St. Emmeran, at Ratisbon.*

That the practice of writing with solutions of gold and silver is a most ancient one is proved by various other instances besides those already adduced. The copy of the sacred books sent to Ptolemy by the high priest Eleazar, and presented to him by the seventy-two interpreters, was written upon the finest vellum in letters of gold; and Matthew Paris, in his "History of the Abbey of St. Albans," relates, that during the abbacy of Eadmer, the ninth abbot, a number of workmen being employed to erect a church on the site of the ancient city Verolamium, as they were digging the foundation, they discovered the remains of an ancient palace, and found, in a hollow part of one of the walls, several small books and rolls, one of which, written in a language not understood, was most beautifully ornamented with the title and inscriptions in *letters of gold.* It was covered with oaken boards, and tied with silken bands, and in a great measure retained its pristine strength and beauty, uninjured either in its form or writing by the length of time it had lain undiscovered. M. Paris adds, that after much inquiry they found a learned man, but decrepit with age, whose name was Unwoman, who understood and read

* Blanchini Evangel. Quadrup., vol. ii, part ii, fol. DXCII. See also Dibdin's Biographical Decameron, vol. i, p. xxxi. Lond. 1817, 8vo.

distinctly the writing both of that and of all the other books, and from whom they learned that they were written in the language of the ancient Britons, at the time they inhabited *Warlamcestre*. They also found the Life of St. Alban, written in Latin.*

Diplomatic instruments were likewise sometimes executed in letters of gold. "Among these," says Mabillon, "I find a charter of Aripert, king of the Lombards, confirming the gift of the patrimonial estate of Alpius Cottiarus, ordered to be written in letters of gold." This is related by Paul Warnefrid, in his History of the Lombards. Another charter, executed in a similar manner in the reign of Edgar, is mentioned by the author of the *Monasticon Anglicanum*, tom. i, p. 211. Puricellus, in his work on the antiquity of the church of St. Ambrose, at Milan, assures us that the originals of the charters of the kings Hugo and Lotharius were written in golden letters; and that these, as well as other charters of different kings and emperors, executed in *characters of gold upon the skins of fishes*, are still extant among the archives of the church.†

The art of writing in letters of gold was called *chrysographia*. In the royal library at Paris there is a Greek work, (formerly No. 618,) written in the low and vulgar style of the latter ages, bearing the title Περὶ χρυσογραμμίας, in which the art of preparing the golden liquid for writing is explained. Lambecius and Montfaucon notice other works upon the same subject; and Peignot, in his *Essai sur l'Histoire du Parchemin et du Velin*, gives several different processes for liquefying gold, &c.‡ It has even been conjectured that the celebrated Argonautic expedition was undertaken to obtain a work written on skins, containing a treatise on the art of writing in gold letters.§

The *purple* colour most esteemed by the ancients, and considered as of the highest value, was of a dark cast, as deep as bull's blood, and had a strong smell; it was restrained to the "person and palace of the emperor; and the penalties of treason were denounced against the ambitious subjects who dared to usurp the prerogative of the throne. But there were also other colours denominated *purple*, one of them approaching our scarlet, another nearly violet; there was even a white colour which bore

* Blanchini, Evangel. Quadrup., *ubi sup.*

† Mabillon, De re Diplomatica, lib. i; viii, p. 44. Peignot, Essai sur Parchemin, pp. 77–83.

‡ Blanchini, *ubi sup.*

§ Suidæ Lex. v. Δερας., edit. Kuster. Chandler's Defence of the Prime Ministry of Joseph, p. 448.

the name of purple."* Anastasius (in Versione Concilii vi, Actione x) calls the purple "saffron colour, or yellow." "The term *purple*," says Laurentius a Turra, "is not confined to those *Codices* or copies which are of a scarlet or red colour, but it is also used to denote a violet colour, of which I have seen a very large number; such, for instance, are two preserved in the library of St. Germain, one of them a Latin Psalter, the other the Gospel of St. Matthew. The latter is written from the beginning to the end in most beautiful characters of gold. I have also seen another of the same sort, in the royal library at Naples, (S. Joannis de Carbonaria,) and many others, the first pages of which were of a purple or violet colour."†

Since the invention of printing this mode of writing has been imitated, by printing upon paper of different colours. At the sale of M. Renouard, in 1804, a Hebrew Bible without points, printed by Plantin, at Antwerp, in 8vo., upon *yellow* paper, sold for nineteen livres; a Latin Bible also was printed at Nuremberg, in 1629, on *yellow* paper. Count M'Carthy lately possessed a Greek New Testament, in 16mo., printed in 1587 upon *lemon-coloured* paper; and an Armenian New Testament, in two vols., 12mo., printed upon *blue* paper.‡ Some works have also been printed in *golden* letters by M. Crapelet; and proposals have been issued for an edition of Magna Charta, (from the original MS. deposited in the British Museum,) to be executed in *burnished gold* letters, on royal purple satin, and on superfine vellum paper, by the inventor, Mr. John Whitaker.§

It was not only by the chrysographic mode of writing that the ancient Christians ornamented their manuscript copies of the Scriptures, they also frequently embellished them, at an immense expense, with *miniatures* and other paintings, collectively termed ILLUMINATIONS. In the Harleian library there is deposited a MS. of the four Gospels of St. Jerome's version, together with his prologues, &c., the canons of Eusebius, and the parallel passages, written in letters of gold, in the tenth century. This manuscript is superbly illuminated, and adorned with pictures of the following subjects, painted upon purple grounds, viz., before the Gospel of St. Matthew, in a circle, are first, the representation

* Gibbon's Roman Empire, vol. vii, ch. xl, p. 90, 8vo. Goguet, Origine des Loix, et des Arts, pt. ii, liv. ii, ch. ii, pp. 196–198.

† Blanchini, *ubi sup.*

‡ Peignot, Repertoire de Bibliographies speciales., 8vo., 1810, pp. 156, 175, 178.

§ Horne's Introduction to Bibliography, vol. i, p. 225.

of our Saviour, sitting as enthroned, holding in his right hand the book of the New Law, that of the Old Law lying in his lap, with the four evangelists in the angles, kneeling; secondly, our Saviour standing, with St. John resting his head on his bosom: thirdly, the portrait of St. Matthew; and fourthly, the salutation of the Virgin. Before St. Mark's Gospel are the portrait of that evangelist and the salutation of the Virgin Mary. At the beginning of St. Luke's Gospel are his portrait and the crucifixion of our Saviour; and before the Gospel of St. John are the picture of that evangelist and the ascension of our Lord.* In the same rich collection, as well as in the other principal libraries in Europe, are many other beautifully executed and superbly illuminated MSS. of the Gospels, Psalms, and other parts of the sacred writings, forming altogether an invaluable treasure. In Blanchini's *Evangeliarium Quadruplex*, p. 2, vol. ii, fol. DXCIII, is a list of the principal illuminated MSS. of the Scriptures, preserved in the different European libraries.

The practice of thus illuminating manuscripts with paintings is of the most remote date. In an ancient Egyptian MS. on papyrus, taken from a mummy at Thebes, and brought into England by William Hamilton, Esq., and presented by him to the British Museum, the writing, which is from right to left, is divided into five columns, the first of which is imperfect; each column is accompanied by a drawing, which represents one or more objects of Egyptian adoration.† The time and patience which were required to execute the illuminations of some manuscripts is truly astonishing. Fifty years were sometimes employed to complete a single volume; an evidence of which occurred at the sale of the late Sir W. Burrell's books, in 1796. Among these was a MS. Bible, beautifully written on vellum, and illuminated, which had taken the writer, Guido de Jars, half a century to execute. He began it in his fortieth year, and did not finish it until he had accomplished his ninetieth, in the year 1294, in the reign of Philip the Fair, as appeared by the writer's own autograph at the front of the book.‡ The art of illuminating manuscripts was much practised by the clergy, and even by some in the highest stations of the church, especially during the middle ages. Writers or transcribers of books first finished their part, and the illuminators then embellished them; and in the infancy of the

* Selection of curious articles from Gent. Mag., vol. ii, p. 20.

† Beloe's Anecdotes of Literature, vol. i, pp. 54, 55.

‡ Lemoine's Typographical Antiquities, p. 1.

art of printing the first letter of a book or chapter was frequently left blank, for the purpose of being illuminated at the option of the purchaser.

Gerhard Tychsen, professor of philosophy and Oriental literature, at Rostock, has attempted to furnish a rule by which to distinguish the Hebrew MSS. written and illuminated by Christians, from those executed by Jews. He observes, that all MSS. of the Masorah or Jewish criticisms, with figures of dragons, sphinxes, bears, hogs, or any other of the unclean animals; all MSS. of the Old Testament, with the Vulgate translation, or corrected to it, or to the Septuagint version; all MSS. not written with black ink, or in which there are words written in golden letters, or where the words, or the margin is illuminated; and all MSS. where the word ADONAI is written instead of the word JEHOVAH, were written by Christians, and not by Jews.* Professor Michaelis, however, warmly controverts the former part of these observations, and affirms, "The Jewish MSS. of the Bible are often ornamented with figures of animals, plants, trees, sphinxes, &c., from which none but a *Tychsen* will ever infer that these MSS. were made not by Jews, but by monks. (See *Joseph. Bell. Jud.*, v, 5, 4.—*Antiq.*, xv, 11, 3.) *He*, however, is the first man upon the face of the earth who has entertained such an opinion; for before he told them, mankind did not know that the monks of the middle ages were such eminent Hebræans; and the Jews recognise those copies of the Hebrew Scriptures that are thus bedaubed with figures as of Jewish workmanship."† In another part of the same work he says, "On the triumphal arch of Titus Vespasian, we have yet extant a representation of the sacred candlestick, as carried in his triumph, (see Reland, *De Spoliis templi Hierosolymitani in Arcu Titiano Romæ conspicuis*, p. 6, where is given a plate as well as a description,) the foot of which is formed of sphinxes. In still later times we find some MSS. of the Bible of which the large initial capital letters are ornamented with figures of sphinxes and lions. (See an instance on the plate at p. 604 of *Blanchini Evangeliarium Quadruplex*, p. ii, t. ii."‡§) Some beautiful specimens of ornamental Hebrew *printing* may

* Tentamen de variis Codicum Hebræorum Veteris Testamenti MSS. Rostock, 1772, cited in Butler's Horæ Biblicæ, vol. i, p. 44.

† Michaelis's Commentaries on the Laws of Moses, translated by Alexander Smith, D. D., vol. iv, p. 54.

‡ Michaelis, *ut sup.*, vol. iii, p. 225.

§ These specimens are engraved in plate 3 of the present work.

be seen in Dibdin's Bibliographical Decameron, vol. ii, pp. 317, 318.

The substitution of ADONAI for JEHOVAH in the Hebrew manuscripts has arisen out of the superstitious reverence of the Jews for the TETRAGRAMMATON, or *word of four letters*, as it is frequently termed, from being formed of the four consonants J. H. V. H. The name JEHOVAH imports necessary or self existence, and is expressive of the incommunicable nature of the divine Being: on this very account it is forbidden to be read by the Jews, who instead of it read ADONAI, or *Lord*, a term denoting authority or dominion. The Septuagint also has employed the word *Kyrios*, of similar import with *Adonai*, probably from the superstitious opinion of the Jews; and the writers of the New Testament, who wrote in Greek, have so far conformed to the usage of their countrymen, that they have never introduced this name into their writings. The generality of Christian translators have in this imitated their practice. Our own, in particular, have only in four places of the Old Testament used the name JEHOVAH; in all other places, which are almost innumerable, they render it THE LORD. But, for distinction's sake, when this word corresponds to JEHOVAH, it is printed in capitals.* Still we cannot but regret that any other word has been substituted, since many passages are thereby obscured to the common reader which would otherwise have clearly identified the person of the Redeemer with the INCOMMUNICABLE NAME, and shown more clearly the Godhead of the ever-adorable Saviour.

Origen, Jerome, and Eusebius, mention that in their day the Jews wrote the name JEHOVAH, in their copies of the Scriptures, in the ancient Samaritan characters, and not in the Chaldee or common Hebrew letters, in order to conceal it more fully from other nations.† It was also in the ancient Hebrew or Samaritan letters that the ineffable name was embossed on the gold plate of the high priest's mitre. The modern Jews either use the word *Adonai*, or express the name by circumlocution, as "The name of four letters," "The ineffable name," &c., or else make use of symbols, as two *Yods*, or (J's,) or three *Yods* in a circle, and sometimes three *radii* or *points*.‡ They assure us, that after the Babylonish captivity it was never pronounced but by the high priest, and by him only once a year, on the great day of expiation,

* Campbell's Translation of the Four Gospels, Prelim. Dissert. 7.

† Calmet, Dict. de la Bible, "Jehovah."

‡ Maurice's Indian Antiquities, vol. i, p. 127; and vol. iv, p. 581.

and then so as not to be heard by the people; and that after the destruction of Jerusalem it was never pronounced, so that the true pronunciation of it is now lost, and cannot be recovered till their restoration to the holy city, when it will be taught them by the Messiah. They do not even scruple to affirm, that he who should know how rightly to pronounce the word would be able to work the most stupendous miracles; that it was by pronouncing this name that Moses slew the Egyptian; and by its being written upon his rod that he was enabled to perform his wonders before Pharaoh. And some of them, in the heat of opposition to Christianity, have ventured to declare that Jesus stole this name out of the temple, secreted it, and by it wrought his miracles.* So great is the blindness which hath happened unto Israel!

The chief part of the doctrines and opinions of the Jews is to be found in those voluminous compilations, THE TALMUDS. There are two Talmuds, one called the Jerusalem Talmud, the other the Babylonish Talmud. The *Jerusalem Talmud*, compiled principally for the Jews of Palestine, was composed about A. D. 250. The principal, or *Babylonish Talmud*, was begun by Rabbi Asseh, and completed by his successors about A. D. 500. The Talmuds are divided into two parts, the Mishna and the Gemara. The MISHNA is the *oral Law*, which the Jews say GOD delivered to Moses on Sinai, as explanatory of the written Law. These unwritten traditionary explanations were delivered, say they, by Moses to Joshua, by Joshua to the elders, and so on to the year of Christ 150, or, according to others, 190; when Rabbi Judah Hakkadosh, or the Holy, collected all the traditions, and committed them to writing, that they might not be lost. These are the "traditions" which our Saviour condemned as destructive of the law of God. Mark vii, 7–13. The English reader who is desirous to see a specimen of the vain and frivolous distinctions attributed to the Father of lights by the Talmudical writers, may indulge his curiosity by perusing the translation of two of the Misnic titles, viz., "On the Sabbath," and "Sabbatical Mixtures," published by Dr. Wotton in his "Miscellaneous Discourses relating to the Traditions and Usages of the Scribes and Pharisees, &c.," vol. ii. The GEMARA, or *Completion*, as it is called, contains the commentaries and additions of succeeding rabbins. "The *Mishna*," says a Jewish writer, "is the text, and the *Gemara* the comment; and

* Maimonidis More Nevochim, pt. i, ch. lxi, lxii, p. 106. Basil, 1629, 4to. Wagenseilii Tela Ignea in Lib. TOLDOS IESCHU, p. 6. Altdorf, 1681, 4to. Kennicott's Dissertation on 1 Chronicles, ch. xi, &c., p. 321.

both together is what we call the Talmud;" a word signifying doctrine, or teaching.*

Surenhusius published the Mishna, with a Latin translation, in six volumes folio, at Amsterdam, in 1698.

So great is the estimation in which the TALMUD is held by the Jews, that the rabbinical writers frequently prefer it to the SCRIPTURES! They compare "the Scriptures to water, the Mishna to wine, and the Talmud, or Gemara, to aromatic spices." "The oral Law," say they, "is the foundation of the written Law;" and they exhort their disciples to "attend rather to the words of the scribes than to the words of the Law." "The words of the scribes," say they, "are lovely, above the words of the Law; for the words of the Law are weighty and light, but the words of the scribes are all weighty." And again, "The words of the elders are weightier than the words of the prophets."† But enough of such blasphemies!

Very differently were the Talmudical collections estimated by several popes, who, too suspicious of their baneful tendency, and too violent in their measures, instituted processes by which immense numbers of Jewish writings were destroyed. In 1230 Gregory IX. condemned the Talmudical volumes, and ordered them to be burned. In 1244 Innocent IV. adopted the same measures. At a later period, when, by the invention of printing, copies of the Talmud had been greatly multiplied, Julius III., by a new edict, ordered inquiry to be made after them, and all the copies that could be met with in all the cities of Italy to be seized and burned, while the Jews were celebrating the feast of the Tabernacles, in September, A.D. 1553; and, according to the calculation of the Romish Inquisition, twelve thousand volumes of the Talmud were committed to the flames by order of his successor, Paul IV.‡

The Jerusalem Talmud was printed at Venice, by Dan. Bomberg, about the year 1523, in one volume folio; and afterward, with marginal notes, at Cracow, in 1609.

The Babylonish Talmud has been printed several times. The principal editions are those of Bomberg, in twelve volumes folio, printed at Venice in 1520; and of Bebenisti, in quarto, printed at Amsterdam in 1644.

* Levi's Rites and Ceremonies of the Jews, p. 301. Leusdeni Philologus Hebræo-Mixtus, Diss. 12, 13, 14, 15.

† Lightfoot's Horæ Heb. and *Talmud.*, *Works*, vol. ii, p. 199.

‡ Leusdeni Philolog. Hebræo-Mixt., Diss. 15, p. 105.

Besides the Mishna, the Jews pretend to have received from the divine Author of the Law another and more mystical interpretation of it. This mystical exposition they term CABBALA, a word signifying *tradition*, or *reception*, and designed to intimate that this mystical comment was *received* from GOD by Moses, who *transmitted* it orally to posterity. The *Mishna*, say they, explains the manner in which the rites and ceremonies of the Law are to be performed; but the *Cabbala* teaches the mysteries couched under those rites and ceremonies, and hidden in the words and letters of the Scriptures. They give as an instance the precepts relating to phylacteries. The *Mishna* teaches the *materials* of which they are to be prepared, the *form* in which they are to be made, and the *manner* in which they are to be worn; but the *Cabbala* shows the mystical reasons of these directions, and informs them why the slips of parchment are to be enclosed in a *black* calf skin, in preference to any other colour; why the phylacteries for the head are to be separated into four divisions; why the letters written upon them are to be of such a particular form, &c., &c. They divide this mystical science into thirteen different species, and, by various transpositions, abbreviations, permutations, combinations, and separations of words, and from the figures and numerical powers of letters, imagine the Law sufficient to instruct the *Cabbalistic* adept in every art and science.* Happy would it have been for the Christian church had the Cabbalistic doctors of the Jews been the only interpreters of Scripture who had substituted their own fancies for the word of God!

It is the excellent remark of one of the best Jewish writers, and deserves the attention of every expositor of the sacred writings, "That in explaining the Scriptures, and especially the parables, the general scope and intention of the writer is to be regarded, and not every word and syllable of the parable; else the expositor will lose his time in endeavouring to explain what is inexplicable, or make the author say many things he never intended."†

The principal interpretations and commentaries of the Cabbalists are contained in the book ZOHAR, said to have been written by Rabbi Simeon Ben Jochai, who died about the year of Christ 120; but it is probably of a much later date. An edition of it was

* Menasseh Ben Israel, Conciliator, Quæst. in Exod. 50. Waltoni Proleg. 8. Basnage's History of the Jews, b. iii, ch. x–xxvi, fol.

† Maimonidis More Nevochim in Præfat.

printed at Mantua, A. D. 1558, in quarto, and another at Cremona in 1559, in folio.*

Dispersed by the destruction of Jerusalem and the heavy calamities that followed, the Jews, at an early period of the Christian era, had been scattered through various countries, and associated with nations of languages widely different from their own. Obliged in their civil and commercial intercourse to adopt the speech of the people among whom they dwelt, the Hebrew so far ceased to be their vernacular tongue, that the Hellenist, and other Jews, preferred the use of the Greek and other versions, even in their synagogue service. But in the reign of the emperor Justinian, A.D. 552, there arose disputes upon the subject. Some contended that the Law ought to be read in a language understood by the people, many of whom were but imperfectly acquainted with the Biblical Hebrew. Others insisted that the language in which the Law was originally written was *sacred*, and maintained that the Holy Scriptures ought not to be read in any other. The decision was referred to the emperor, who ordered that the Scriptures should be read in the language of the country, whether Hebrew, or Greek, or Latin, or any other. In the use of *Greek* versions he recommended the Septuagint, though he did not forbid the use of others. He also prohibited the use of the Mishna, or *Second Edition*, as it was called, because it did not belong to the body of the Scripture, nor had been delivered by the prophets, but was merely the invention of men, who had nothing divine in them, and who spake only of the earth. And lest the Archipheracites, or men of authority among the Jews, should frustrate the design of this edict, he denounced corporal penalties against those priests or rabbins who should, by anathemas or other censures, endeavour to prevent the people from reading the Scriptures.†

This dispute respecting the language in which the Law should be read in the synagogues originated in the debates between the Christians and Jews. The Christians pressed the Jews with arguments in favour of Christianity, drawn from the prophecies respecting the Messiah; and the rabbins, dreading the result of such arguments, forbade the Scriptures to be read in any other language than the Hebrew. So true it is that truth courts investigation and inquiry, and rejoices in the light; while error fears examination, and seeks for refuge in darkness! The edict of Justinian, however, was but transient in its influence; the Jews obsti-

* Buxtorf, De Abbreviaturis Hebraicis, p. 199; and Bibl. Rab., p. 55.

† Gothofredi Corpus Juris Civilis, Novel. 146, vol. ii, p. 580.

nately adhered to the practice of reading the Scriptures in *Hebrew* in their synagogues; a practice which still continues to be universally adopted.*

It will be easily discovered that the preceding account of the Jews refers to the great body of them, who are denominated *Rabbinists*, and are thus distinguished from the *Karaites*, a small sect among them who reject tradition and contend for the sufficiency of Scripture. One of their own writers observes, "Truth is known by reason, which draws it from the prophecies. An argument is known to be solid when it agrees with the words of a prophet; only, some articles are too profound for the understanding. However, they are received with respect, because they were dictated by a prophet. Could man apprehend every thing, neither the prophets nor prophecies had been necessary."†

The best account of the modern KARAITES is that which is given by Dr. E. D. Clarke, in his "Travels into Various Countries, &c.," in 1800, &c., from which the following extract is made:—

"The morning after our arrival" at Baktcheserai, the capital of the Crimea, "Colonel Richard Durant, a native of Smyrna, and an officer in the Russian service, residing in Baktcheserai, accompanied us on horseback, to climb the steep defile leading from the city to the Jewish colony of Dschoufoutkalé,‡ situate upon a mountain, and distant about five *versts*. These Jews are of the sect called *Karai:* they inhabit an ancient fortress, originally constructed by the Genoese, upon a very lofty precipice. Advancing along the defile, and always ascending, we passed above the re mains of that quarter of the city which belonged to the Greeks. We now came to the lower verge of some steep cliffs, and beheld upon the summit the walls of Dschoufoutkalé. In a recess upon our right hand appeared the cemetery, or "field of dead," belonging to the Karaite Jews. Nothing can be imagined more calculated to inspire holy meditation. It is a beautiful grove, filling a chasm of the mountains, which is rendered gloomy by the shade of lofty trees and overhanging rocks. A winding path conducts through this solemn scene. Several tombs of white marble present a fine contrast to the deep green of the foliage; and female figures, in white veils, are constantly seen offering their pious

* Basnage's History of the Jews, b. iii, ch. vi, p. 170. Lightfoot's Works, vol. ii, p. 798.

† Basnage's History of the Jews, b. ii, ch. viii, p. 106.

‡ *Dschoufout* is a name, originally, of reproach, bestowed upon the Jews: and *Kalé* signifies a fortress.

lamentations over the graves. An evening or a morning visit to the sepulchres of their departed friends constitutes, perhaps, all the exercises of the Jewish women, as they seldom leave their houses; in this respect their customs are similar to those of Tahtars and Turks.* The ascent from the cemetery to the fortress, although short, is so steep that we were forced to alight from our horses, and actually to climb to the gateway. Several slaves, however, busied in conveying water upon the backs of asses, passed us in their way up. The spring which supplies them is below, in the defile; and a very copious reservoir, cut in the rocks above, is prepared for the use of the colony. As we passed the gateway and entered the town, we were met by several of the inhabitants. Colonel Durant inquired for a Jew of his acquaintance, one of the principal people in the place. We were conducted to his house; and found him, at noon, sleeping on his divan. He rose to receive us, and presently regaled us with various sorts of confectionary; among these were conserved leaves of roses and preserved walnuts; we had also eggs, cheese, cold pies, and brandy. A messenger was despatched for the rabbi, whom he invited to meet us, and who soon after made his appearance This venerable man was held in very high consideration by them all, and with good reason; for he was exceedingly well informed, and had passed a public examination with distinguished honour in Petersburgh, after being sent for expressly by the empress Catherine. We were highly interested in their conversation, as well as in the singular circumstance of having found one *Jewish* settlement, perhaps the only one upon earth, where that people exist secluded from the rest of mankind, in the free exercise of their ancient customs and peculiarities.† The town contains about twelve hundred persons of both sexes, and not more than two hundred houses. The principal part of each dwelling belongs to the women; but every master of a family has his own private apartment, where he sleeps, smokes, and receives his friends. The room wherein we were entertained was of this description: it was filled with MSS., many in the hand-writing of our host;

* "This little Valley of Jehoshaphat is so highly valued by the Jews, that whenever the ancient Khans wished to extort from them a present, or to raise a *voluntary* contribution, it was sufficient to threaten them with the extirpation of those sacred trees, under the plausible pretence of wanting fuel or timber."—*Pallas's Travels*, vol. ii, p. 35.

† "It seems singular that such fortresses should have been possessed by such a people; yet, in Abyssinia, the *Falasha* appear similarly situated; and Jackson mentions a Jew's rock in Morocco."—*Heber's MS. Journal.*

others by those of his children; and all in very beautiful Hebrew characters. The Karaites deem it to be an act of piety to copy the Bible, or copious commentaries upon its text, once in their lives. All their MS. copies of the Old Testament begin with the book of Joshua: even the most ancient did not contain the Pentateuch. This is kept apart, not in manuscript, but in a printed version, for the use of the schools.* In their synagogues, with the exception of the books of Moses, every thing was in manuscript. The rabbi asked if we had any of their sect, KARAI, in England; a question we could not answer. He said there were a few in Holland. The etymology of their name is uncertain. The difference between their creed and that of Jews in general, according to the information we received from the rabbi, consists in a rejection of the Talmud; a disregard to every kind of tradition; to all rabbinical writings or opinions; to all marginal interpolations of the text of Scripture; and in a measure of their rule of faith by the pure letter of the Law They pretend to have the text of the Old Testament in its most genuine state."

"Being desirous to possess one of their Bibles, the rabbi, who seemed gratified by the circumstance, permitted us to purchase a beautiful manuscript copy, written upon vellum, about four hundred years old; but having left this volume in the Crimea, to be forwarded by way of Petersburgh, it was never afterward recovered. It began like all the others, with the book of Joshua.

"The character of the Karaite Jews is directly opposite to that generally attributed to their brethren in other countries, being altogether without reproach. Their honesty is proverbial in the Crimea; and the word of a Karaite is considered equal to a bond. Almost all of them are engaged in trade or manufacture. They observe their fasts with the most scrupulous rigour, abstaining even from snuff and from smoking for twenty-four hours together. In the very earliest periods of Jewish history this sect separated from the main stem: such at least is their own account: and nothing concerning them ought to be received from rabbinists, who hold them in detestation. For this reason the relations of Leo of Modena, a rabbi of Venice, are not to be admitted. Their schism is said to be as old as the return from the Babylonish captivity. They observe extraordinary care in the education of their children, who

* "The reason given by the rabbi for the omission of the books of Moses in their manuscript copies was, that the Pentateuch, being in constant use for the instruction of their children, was reserved apart, that the whole volume might not be liable to the injuries it would thereby sustain."

are publicly instructed in the synagogues; and in this respect the Tahtars are not deficient. We rarely entered any Tahtar village, in the day time, without seeing children assembled in some public place, receiving their instruction from persons appointed to superintend the care of their education; reciting with audible voices passages from the Koran, or busied in copying manuscript lessons placed before them. The dress of the Karaites differs little from that worn by the Tahtars. All of them, of whatsoever age, suffer their beards to grow. The Karaites wear also a lofty, thick, felt cap, faced with wool: this is heavy, and keeps the head very hot. The Turks and Armenians often do the same; and in warm climates this precaution seems a preservative against the dangerous consequences resulting from obstructed perspiration."*

Returning to the occurrences of the fifth century, we remark an event, which, from its influence upon Christian literature, deserves to be recorded: this was, *the instruction of the Irish in the use of the Roman letters*, by St. Patrick, the apostle of Ireland. PATRICK was born in Scotland, near Dunbarton. In his sixteenth year he was carried into captivity by certain barbarians, together with many of his father's vassals and slaves, taken upon his estate. They took him to Ireland, then called Scotia, where he was obliged to keep cattle on the mountains, and in the forests, in hunger and nakedness, amidst snows, rain, and ice. Here he learned the language and customs of the country, from whence he was afterward, by some pirates, conveyed into Gaul; and after various adventures returned a volunteer into Ireland, with a view to undertake the conversion of the barbarous natives, among whom the worship of idols still generally reigned. To effect his benevolent purposes, he travelled over the whole island, and not only preached frequently, but maintained and educated many children, and instructed the natives in the use of the Roman letters; for, before their conversion, the Irish were utterly unacquainted with the Latin language, without the knowledge of which, St. Patrick considered that his new converts would be incapable of reading the Scriptures, the ecclesiastical offices, and other good books; and consequently not be able to make such a progress in learning and religion, as was necessary to enable them to instruct the rest of their countrymen. On the other hand, these newly converted Christians, being well skilled in their native letters, readily became proficients in the elements of the Latin, so that Fiec, who, prior to his conversion,

* Clarke's Travels in various countries of Europe, Asia, and Africa, pt. i, Russia, Tahtary, and Turkey, vol. ii, ch. iv, pp. 185–194. Lond. 1816, 8vo. See also "Extracts of Letters from the Rev. Robert Pinkerton, &c.," pp. 17–20, Lond. 1817, 8vo.

had been a disciple of Dub' t' ac', arch-poet to Leogar, king of Ireland, became such a proficient that he could read the Latin Psalter in fifteen days. General Vallancey mentions, as being in his possession, an old vellum MS., treating of the state of the Christian church in Ireland, in the first century after St. Patrick's arrival, written in Latin, and in the Irish character.

The labours of St. Patrick proved eminently successful, and Christianity was very generally embraced throughout the island. Fiac, one of his converts, whom he appointed bishop of the church of Sletty, wrote a poem in his praise, containing thirty-four distiches, which is yet extant. In one of the verses of this poem, he says, "He daily sang the Apocalypse, and Hymns; and the whole Psalter he sang thrice; he preached, and baptized, and prayed; and he incessantly praised God." In another verse he notices that one of his usual acts of mortification was to stand "every night in the fountain of Slan, which was never dry, while he sang a hundred psalms."* He died about the year 460, at an advanced age.†

The schools of Ireland long maintained a high reputation. Camden observes, (Brit. de Hibern., p. 730,) that the English Saxons anciently flocked to Ireland, as to the mart of sacred learning; and this is frequently mentioned in the lives of eminent men among them. Thus, in the life of Sulgenus, in the eighth century, we read,

Exemplo patrum, commotus amore legendi,
Ivit ad Hibernos, sophia mirabile claros.
"With love of learning and examples fired,
To Ireland, famed for wisdom, he retired."

In 791, two Irishmen going into France, were there admired for their incomparable learning, and gave birth to the two first universities in the world, namely, those of Paris and Pavia: and our great king Alfred, in 891, listened to three learned Irishmen in his projects for the advancement of literature. In the beginning of the ninth century, no fewer than seven thousand students visited the schools of Armagh; while there were three more rival colleges in other cities, with many private seminaries in the remoter provinces.‡ And Camden conjectures, that the Anglo-Saxons bor-

* This superstitious practice was not confined to St. Patrick. St. Neot, the kinsman of Alfred, St. Chad, and even Aldhelm, used to chant the Psalter, standing in wells or springs of water. See *Whitaker's Hist. of the Cathedral of Cornwall*, vol. ii, pp. 312, 313.

† Milner's Hist. of the Church of Christ, vol. ii, p. 486. Butler's Lives of the Saints, vol. iii, March 17, pp. 176–185. Vallancey's Grammar of the Irish Language, ch. ix, pp. 146, 147; and ch. x, p. 168. Dublin, 1773, 4to.

‡ Butler's Lives of the Saints, vol. v, pp. 173, 174. Note [a.] Berington's Literary History of the Middle Ages, p. 182.

rowed their letters from the Irish, because they used the same, or nearly the same which the Irish at this day still make use of in writing their own language. The reader may compare the two alphabets, by referring to plate 2 of the present volume.*

It is not improbable that about this period a translation of some parts at least of the Scriptures was made into the *Bearla Feni*, or ancient Irish tongue. General Vallancey, in his "Essay on the Antiquity of the Irish Language," quotes a valuable old MS. in his possession, in what he calls the Phenician dialect of the ancient Irish, and which he supposes to be part of a copy of the Old Testament, brought to Ireland by St. Kieran, St. Aillu, St. Declan, or St. Ibar, the precursors of St. Patrick.† This MS. contains only the lives of the patriarchs and Moses : it is written after the manner termed *Cionne fa eite*, a mode of writing somewhat similar to the *Boustrophedon* of the Greeks, denoted frequently in ancient MSS. by this mark, ƆC, which implies that a sentence finishes, and that the reader is to go to the next line, from the end of which he is to turn to the *Cionne fa eite*.

From this old MS. the learned author of the "Essay, &c.," has

* Butler, *ut sup.*

† St. Kieran, or Kiaran, called by the Britons Piran, was a native of Ireland, born about A. D. 352. At thirty years of age he went to Rome, and after receiving fuller instruction in the principles of the Roman Catholic Church, returned to Ireland with several companions, and made many converts to Christianity, particularly among the inhabitants of Ossory. The Irish writers say he was ordained bishop, and established his see at Saigir. He founded a monastery for himself, and another for his mother. Toward the close of life he passed into Cornwall, where he lived as a hermit, and the place where he died has obtained the name of St. Pirans in the Sands.—*Butler's Lives*, vol. iii, p. 33.

St. Aillu, or Albeus, the chief patron of Munster, was converted by certain Britons, travelled to Rome, and on his return home became the friend and fellow-labourer of St. Patrick. He was the first archbishop of Munster, and fixed his seat at Emely, now removed to Cashel. King Engus bestowed on him the isle of Arran, where he founded a great monastery. His preaching and example appear to have rendered him eminently successful as a Christian minister, "possessing a wonderful art," says his biographer, "of making men not only Christians, but saints." He died in 525.—*Ibid.*, vol. ix, p. 130.

St. Declan, first bishop of Ardmore in Ireland, was baptized by St. Colman, and preached Christianity in his native country, a little before the arrival of St. Patrick.—*Ibid.*, vol. vii, p. 352.

St. Ibar, or Ivor, preached in Meath and Leinster, and built a monastery in Begerin, or Little Ireland, a small island on the coast of Kenselach, which was anciently a considerable province in Leinster. He was afterward abbot of the monastery of Magarnoide, in Kenselach. He is said to have been ordained bishop either at Rome, or by St. Patrick. His sister Mella was married to Cormac, king of Leinster. He died about the year 500.—*Ibid.*, vol. iv, p. 264.

given two extracts, which he supposes to have been designed as a version of Genesis, &c. His translations of them are here presented to the reader.

"Buid in righam," &c.—"The queen, viz., Rebecca, hearing this discourse, after the people were gone to hunt, she straightway rose and went to Jacob, where he was tending his sheep. She told him he should receive the blessing instead of the other son. How shall I do that, quoth Jacob? Do this, says she; viz., kill a kid, replied the mother, and dress it and give it to him, and then I will sew the skin of the kid upon thy hands to resemble Esau, for the hands of Esau are hairy. Jacob did so, and dressed the kid, and brought with him the pottage, and presented it to his father; and he said to him, Eat this mess. O son, says Isaac, you are returned this day from hunting earlier than any former day, if you tell the truth. At the first hunt I quickly found wherewith to make you a mess of pottage, and that is the reason, says Jacob, I returned so soon. Tell not a lie, says he, for thou art Jacob, and thou art not Esau. Truly, replied he, I would not tell a lie before thee. Stretch forth thy hands, says Isaac, that I may know thou art Esau. He stretched forth his hands to him, with the skin of the kid about them; Isaac took the hand. Thou art long suspicious of me, says Jacob; I am Esau. Isaac feeling the hand said, This is the hand of Esau, and it is the voice of Jacob," &c. Vide Genesis xxvii.

"Therefore after Jacob had been with his father, he presented divers gifts to Esau his brother, as the pledge of his brotherly peace and friendship thenceforward; these are the gifts, viz., two hundred ewes, and two hundred she-goats, and thirty camels, and forty cows; twenty rams, twenty young bulls," as the poet has said,

"Two hundred Ewes, XX He-Goats
Two hundred She-Goats, he generously bestowed.
XX Rams without fault he gave,
XL Kine, which proudly herd together.
Twenty Bulls with massy hides,
And XXX Camels giving milk.
XX very fair She-Asses,
And XX Colts along with them.
These were the Peace Offerings to Esau,
From Jacob most sincerely given;
For having wandered from the truth,
These are the numbers of the hundreds (given.")

Vide Genesis, ch. xxxii, 13.*

* Vallancey's Essay on An. of Irish Lan., pp. 55-60. Dub. 1772, 8vo.

CHAPTER IV.

SIXTH CENTURY.

Theodoric the Goth—Cassiodorus—Avitus—Philoxenian Syriac Version—Philoxenus—Mar Abba—Georgian Version—Councils of Agde, Toledo, and Vaison—Monastery of Iona—Columba—Culdees—Baithen—Arator—Gregory the Great—Augustine—Library of first Christian Church at Canterbury—Codex Ephremi—Codices Rescripti—Abbreviations.

THE close of the fifth, and the commencement of the SIXTH century, presented the singular fact of an illiterate *Goth* promoting the interests of literature. THEODORIC, the sovereign of the Ostrogoths, having invaded and conquered Italy, caused himself to be proclaimed king. By a wise and conciliatory policy he continued his new subjects in the possession of their former laws, which he commanded to be inviolably observed; retained the same form of government, the same distribution of provinces, the same magistrates and dignities; and exercised the most liberal toleration toward those whose religious tenets differed from his own. Educated among his own barbarous countrymen, and his education a military one, he was extremely illiterate, and incapable of writing his own name. For the purpose of signing the royal edicts, the four Greek letters ΘΕΟΔ., forming the abbreviations of his name, were cut for him in a plate of gold, and the plate being laid upon paper, he traced the letters with a pen. This, however, does not detract from the real merit of Theodoric, who, rising above the prejudices of his education, became the warm patron of learning in others. A proof of his discriminating mind was given in choosing for his principal adviser a man of great learning and integrity, the celebrated Cassiodorus. Theodoric died in 526.*

MARCUS AURELIUS CASSIODORUS was born in Calabria, of an illustrious family. To his counsels Italy was indebted for its repose, and Theodoric for his fame. He had experienced the patronage of Odoacer; but under Theodoric had been raised to the highest offices of the state, which he continued to administer under his successors till the commencement of the Gothic war.

* Berington's Literary Hist. of the Middle Ages, pp. 103, 104. Beckmann's Hist. of Inventions, vol. ii, p. 214.

He then retired from all public employments, and in A. D. 542 built a monastery, which he provided not only with the necessaries, but also with the conveniences, and even the elegancies of life, such as fish-ponds, baths, fountains, sun-dials, &c. In his retirement he applied himself to subjects adapted to his new calling. He employed his monks in the meritorious labours of transcription; he was instrumental in procuring translations of Greek authors, and he enriched his monastery with a copious collection of books. Such of the monks as were not good scribes he employed in agriculture and gardening, which he directed them to conduct on scientific principles. In his writings he highly commends those who laboured to procure and multiply accurate copies of the sacred writings. "The transcriber (antiquarius,") says he, "inflicts as many wounds on Satan as he produces copies." In his own monastery he neglected nothing that might tend to the accuracy of the transcriptions of the Bible. "For what benefit," he inquires, "can result from a multitude of copies that are incorrect?" And even in the copying of other MSS. he was so strenuous with his monks to preserve the phraseology and orthography of the most rude and obsolete writings which they copied, that he informs us, they clamoured against him for refusing to permit them to modernize some of the works they transcribed, and thereby preventing the entertainment and profit they should otherwise derive from them. In the library of his monastery he placed the Hebrew and Greek originals of the Old and New Testament, together with the Septuagint version, and that of Jerome as well as the old Italic; and took care to have correct copies taken of them for the use of the monks; to whom he recommended a careful comparison of the different versions, and especially of the original text, for the solution of the difficulties they might meet with in the perusal of the Scriptures, as well as to ascertain, in general, the true sense of the Holy Scriptures. He was also careful that the copies of the Scriptures, transcribed under his direction, should be written in a uniform and fair hand; and that the various sections and divisions into which the Bible had been first divided by Jerome, from the example of profane authors, should be cautiously preserved for the accommodation of the reader. He did more; for he not only promoted the interests of sacred literature, by the accuracy and number of his transcriptions of the Bible, but also illustrated the sacred writings by the delineations of his pencil. Bede, (De Tabernaculo., lib. ii,) who flourished about two hundred years after Cassiodorus, mentions having seen a sciographic delineation of the tabernacle, formed from the description given by Moses in the twenty-sixth chapter of Exodus. This great man closed a long life of piety and usefulness about the year 562.* A list of his works may be seen in Cave's *Historia Literaria*. They have been several times printed, but the best edition is by J. B. Garet, printed at Rouen, in 1672, in two vols. folio. They are also in the *Bibliotheca Patrum*, tom. xi, p. 1094.

About the commencement of this century ALCIMUS ECDICIUS AVITUS, a nobleman of Gaul, and archbishop of Vienna, became celebrated by his writings and pious and successful labours in his episcopal office, particularly in reclaiming Gundobald, king of Burgundy, and his son Sigismund, with others, from the errors of Arius. Besides other poems, he wrote one in hexameter verse, in five books, each book being appropriated to some Biblical subject: the first was, "Of the Origin of the World;" the second, "Of Original Sin;" the third, "Of the Judgment of God;" the fourth, "Of the Deluge;" and the fifth, "Of the Passing over the Red Sea." His poetry is said to have been uncommonly elegant for the rude age in which he lived. He died February the 5th, A. D. 523.†

PHILOXENUS, bishop of Hierapolis, now Pambouk, in Syria, was another eminent character of this age. To him we owe the Syriac version of the New Testament, called from him the *Philoxenian*. This translation was made at his request, and under his patronage, by Polycarp, his chorepiscopus, or rural bishop,‡ from the Greek, in A. D. 508. In 616 Thomas, a native of Harkel, in Palestine, and bishop of Germanicia, undertook a critical revision of this version, and for this purpose visited Egypt

* Sixt. Senensi, Biblioth. Sanct., lib. iv, p. 261, Colon. Agrip. 1626, 4to. Simon's Critical Hist. of the Versions of the N. T., pt. ii, ch. viii, x. Bibliog. Dictionary, vol. ii, p. 138.

† Berington, *ubi sup*. Simondi Opuscula, vol. ii, *S. Aviti Opera*. Paris, 1643.

‡ "Those to whom the instruction and management of the surrounding country churches were committed by the diocesan, were termed chorepiscopi, that is, τῆς χῶρας ἐπισκοποὶ, "rural bishops." Persons of this description are doubtless to be considered as having held a middle rank between the bishops and the presbyters; for to place them on a level with the former is impossible, since they were subject to their diocesan; but, at the same time, it is manifest that they were superior in rank to presbyters, inasmuch as they were not accustomed to look up to the bishop for orders or direction, but were invested with constant authority to teach, and in other respects to exercise the episcopal functions."—*Mosheim's Commentaries on the Affairs of the Christians before the time of Constantine, translated by R. S. Vidal*, vol. i, p. 234.

in order to collate it with some of the best MSS. in the Alexandrian library; the various readings of which he afterward placed in the margin of his own copy, from whence they appear to have been transcribed by other copyists. In the twelfth century Dionysius Barsalibæus, who was bishop of Amida, now called Diarbekir, from A. D. 1166 to A. D. 1171, again revised the Philoxenian version, and published a new edition of it. It was, however, but little known in Europe before the middle of the last century, when the attention of Biblical scholars was directed to it, by the excellent copies of it sent from Amida, by Mr. Palmer, to the Rev. Gloster Ridley, minister of Poplar, near London, and afterward prebendary of Salisbury. The learned Wetstein visited England to examine these MSS., and in his Prolegomena, prefixed to his valuable edition of the Greek New Testament, favoured the public with a particular description of them. A still more elaborate account of them was given in 1761, by Mr. Ridley, who, at the request of Professor Michaelis, published an excellent essay on this version, entitled *Dissertatio de Syriacarum Novi Fœderis versionum indole atque usu; Philoxenianam cum Simplici e duobus pervetustis Codd. MSS. ab Amida transmisis conferente Glocestrio Ridley.* The four Gospels copied from these MSS. were printed at Oxford in 1778, by Dr. White, professor of Arabic, who has since published the Acts of the Apostles and the Catholic Epistles.*

Philoxenus, or Xenayas, was a Persian, born in the city of Tahal. He was of the sect of the Monophysites, and by his zeal for the doctrines he had embraced, and his opposition to image worship, which already greatly prevailed in the Greek Church, so irritated his opponents that they seized every opportunity to calumniate him, and even to stigmatize him as a Manichæan. Being advanced to the bishopric of Hierapolis, or, as it was called by the Syrians, Mabug, he warmly espoused the cause of Severus, a celebrated Monophysite priest, and procured him the see of Antioch. Having incurred the displeasure of the emperor Justin, he was banished into Thrace, and from thence into Paphlagonia, where his enemies cruelly murdered him, by suffocating him in a room filled with smoke. The Monophysites place him among their martyrs. His death happened about A. D. 520, after having occupied the see of Hierapolis nearly forty years. A list of his works is given by Asseman, in his *Bibliotheca Orien-*

* Marsh's Michaelis, vol. ii, pt. i, ch. vii, sec. 11, and pt. ii, pp. 568–580.

talis, vol. ii, pp. 23–46. Except a commentary on the Scriptures, and a translation of Syriac prayers into Arabic, they consist chiefly of controversial treatises in defence of his peculiar tenets.*

The Old Testament was also translated from Greek into Syriac, by Mar Abba, about the same time as the Philoxenian version of the New. This MAR ABBA was mafregan, or primate of the East, between the years 535 and 552. He was by birth a Persian, educated in the religion of Zoroaster, without any instruction either in Greek or Syriac; but after he was converted to Christianity he learned Syriac at Nisibis, and Greek at Edessa, from a Jacobite Christian, of the name of Thomas, whom he afterward accompanied to Alexandria, and there applied himself to making translations.† There was also another version of the Old Testament from the Greek into Syriac, executed some years afterward by Paulus, bishop of Tela, of Mauzalat. Scarcely a fragment now remains of these two versions.‡

Professor Adler, in his "Biblical and Critical Journey to Rome," printed at Altona, in 1783, gives a description of a *Lectionarium*, which he met with in the Vatican library, containing portions of a Syriac version of the New Testament, in the dialect spoken in Jerusalem, and which he supposes, in point of antiquity, to hold a middle rank between the Peshito and the Philoxenian versions.§

Asseman, in his *Bibliotheca Medicea*, notices an illuminated MS. of the Syriac version of the Gospels, written A. D. 586; and gives twenty-six plates, illustrative of the illuminations. And in his *Bibliotheca Orientalis*, he mentions another MS. of the Syriac Gospels which bears the date A. D. 548.‖

At the end of the sixth, or beginning of the seventh century, the Scriptures were also translated into the GEORGIAN language. When Sir John Chardin visited the East, in the seventeenth century, he found this version still in use, though the language of it was become nearly obsolete. His words are, "There is not a man among 'em," (in Mingrelia,) "that understands the Bible, or that reads it; there being very few among 'em that can read or under-

* Assemanni Biblioth. Orient., vol. ii, pp. 10–23. La Croze, Histoire du Christianisme d'Ethiopie, pp. 36–39.

† Marsh's Michaelis, vol. ii, pt. i, p. 53. ‡ Classical Journal, vol. vii, p. 196.

§ Marsh's Michaelis, vol. ii, pt. i, p. 75; and pt. ii, pp. 582–585.

‖ Dibdin's Biographical Decameron, vol. i, p. xxxiii. Marsh's Michaelis, vol. ii, pt. i, p. 21.

stand the *Georgian*, which is the only language wherein they have the Holy Scriptures written. But as for the women, they are not altogether so ignorant as the men; so that you shall have some of them who will rehearse several stories of the Gospel, which they have read and got by heart." At the beginning of the eighteenth century the whole of the New Testament, with a part of the Old, consisting of the Psalms and the Prophets, were printed at Teflis, in Georgia, by order of the prince Vaktangh. In 1743 the whole Georgian Bible was printed at Moscow, under the inspection of the Georgian princes, Arcil and Bacchar; and in 1815 the Moscow Auxiliary Bible Society printed an edition of five thousand Georgian New Testaments.*

Those which have been already mentioned are the only translations of the Scriptures into the vernacular tongues which appear to have been made during the sixth century, unless we add to them some unimportant Latin ones, designed to accompany copies in other languages, and placed in parallel columns with them, as the Greek and Latin, and Gothic and Latin versions.†

The council of Agde, a city of France, held A. D. 506, in which Cæsarius, bishop of Arles, presided, made a number of canons relating to discipline, one or two of which may be mentioned as referring to the Scriptures. One of these forbade auguries and divinations, and *the opening of the Scriptures*, with a view to make an omen of the first words that offered, under penalty of excommunication. Another orders "laymen to remain in the church till the blessing is pronounced," since it had become a practice with some persons to leave the church as soon as the Scriptures had been read. Cæsarius one day observing some persons going out of the church, to avoid hearing the sermon, cried out with a loud voice, "What are you about, my children? Where are you going? Stay, stay for the good of your souls; at the day of judgment it will be too late to exhort you." He also frequently caused the church doors to be shut after the Gospel was read, in order to prevent the impious practice. His just and charitable zeal at length proved successful, and his people were reclaimed.‡ The council of Toledo, in Spain, held A. D. 581, enjoined that the clergy should read the Scriptures at the hours of refreshment

* Marsh's Hist. of the Translations of the Scriptures, p. 32. Chardin's Travels into Persia, &c., vol. i, p. 103. Lond. 1686, fol. Twelfth Report of the B. and F. Bible Society, p. 17.

† Marsh's Michaelis. vol. ii, pt. i, pp. 133, 136.

‡ Milner's History of the Church of Christ, vol. iii, pp. 10, 11.

to exclude trifling and unnecessary conversation, and to edify and instruct their minds.*

In 529 a council was held at Vaison, at which were present twelve bishops, of whom Cæsarius was one. They decreed, according to the custom observed in Italy, that all country priests should receive into their houses young men who might be readers in the church; that they should educate them with a paternal regard, causing them to learn the Psalms, to read the Scriptures, and to be acquainted with the word of God; and in this way provide themselves with worthy successors.†

Of the SCHOOLS or SEMINARIES of this age, none excelled, in the study of the Holy Scriptures, the monastery of Iona, or *Icolmkill*, an island of the Hebrides, "once the *luminary* of the Caledonian regions," (as Dr. Johnson calls it,) "whence savage clans, and roving barbarians, derived the benefits of knowledge, and the blessings of religion."

COLUMBA, the founder of this monastery, was of royal extraction, and born at Gartan, in the county of Tyrconnel, in Ireland, in the year 521. He received his education first under Cruinechan, a devout presbyter, and afterward under Finian, bishop of Cluain-iraird, or Clonard; he also spent some time with Ciaran, the founder of the monastery of Clon, upon the Shenan. In 546 he was advanced to the priesthood, and soon began to be celebrated for his admirable lessons of piety, and sacred learning. About the year 550 he founded the great monastery of Dair-Magh, now called Durrogh, in King's county, besides several other smaller ones. He at length turned his attention to the isles, and northern parts of Scotland, which were still covered with darkness, and held in the shackles of superstition, and resolved to become the apostle of the Highlands. Accordingly, in the year 563, or 565, "he set out," says his biographer, "in a wicker boat, covered with hides, accompanied by twelve of his friends and followers, and landed in the isle of Hi, or Iona, near the confines of the Scottish and Pictish territories."

By the preaching and virtues of Columba, many of the northern Picts were led to embrace Christianity, who gave him the small island on which he first landed. Here he built his monastery, which became the chief seminary of learning at that time, perhaps in Europe, and the nursery from which not only the monasteries of his own island, and above three hundred churches, which he

* Bingham's Antiquities of the Christian Church, vol. ii, p. 340.

† Milner's Hist. of the Church of Christ, vol iii, p. 21.

himself had established, but also many of those in neighbouring nations were supplied with learned divines, and able pastors. In this seminary, which might justly have been called a missionary college, the students spent much of their time in reading, and in transcribing the Scriptures and sacred hymns, which Columba was at pains should be done with the greatest care and accuracy, in which he was surprisingly successful. Baithen, one of his disciples, requested him on one occasion to permit one of the brethren to read over, and correct a copy of the Psalter, which he had written; Columba replied, that it had been already examined, and that there was only *one* error in it, which was the want of the vowel *i*, in a single instance.

The followers of Columba were called CULDEES, or *Keldees*, a term, the etymon of which has exercised the ingenuity of the learned, who have offered a variety of plausible derivations, of which the most satisfactory are those that refer it to the religious life they led, and consider it as equivalent to "servants or worshippers of God." They were taught to confirm their doctrines by testimonies brought from the unpolluted fountain of the word of God, and to teach that only to be the divine counsel which was found there. To those who were under his immediate instruction, Columba explained the difficult passages of Scripture with a happy perspicuity and ease. In his earlier studies he seems not to have confined himself to theology, but to have extended his inquiries much further into the general circle of science. For his knowledge of physic, or skill in healing diseases was so great, that his cures were often considered as miracles. And in the history, laws, and customs of different nations he was so well versed, that he made a principal figure in the great council held at Drimceat, about the right of succession to the Scottish throne. But whatever degree of knowledge and education Columba might have received in his earlier years, he never ceased by intense study and application to add to it. Every moment which so active and pious a life could spare from its main business was devoted to study. Sometimes he heard his disciples read, and sometimes he read himself; sometimes he transcribed, and sometimes read and corrected what had been transcribed by others. In his life we find mention made occasionally of various books of his writing and copying; Odonellus says, not less than three hundred! And Sir William Ware (Antiq. Hib.) mentions a MS. copy of the four Gospels of St. Jerome's translation, adorned with silver plates, formerly preserved in the abbey of Durrogh, and still extant, in the beginning of which is an inscription, which testifies that it was written by Columba, in the space of twelve days.

Having continued his labours in Scotland for more than thirty years, and conscious of his approaching end, he said to his attendant Dermit, "This day is called the sabbath, that is, the day of rest, and such will it truly be to me; for it will put an end to my labours." He afterward ascended a little eminence above his monastery, where he stood, and lifting both his hands to heaven, prayed God to bless it, and make it prosper. From thence he returned to his closet, and as he wished his usefulness to man to be commensurate with the moments of his life, and to make a part of his ultimate preparation for heaven, he spent some time in transcribing the Psalter. When he came to that passage in the thirty-fourth Psalm, where it is written, "They that seek the Lord shall not want any good thing," he said, "Here I have come to the end of a page, and to a very proper part to stop at; for the following words, 'Come, ye children, hearken unto me; I will teach you the fear of the Lord,' will better suit my successor than me. I will therefore leave it to Baithen to transcribe them." He then rose and went to evening service in the church; and after coming home, sat down on his bed, and gave a charge to Dermit, to deliver to his disciples, as his dying words. After this he remained silent, till the bell was rung for vigils at midnight; when hastily rising, and going to church, he arrived there before any other, and kneeled down at the altar to pray. Dermit, without waiting for the lamps, followed him, and found him in the dark, lying before the altar, in a praying posture. When the lights were brought, it was discovered that he was dying; and though his voice had failed, he looked round upon the monks, who had flocked to their beloved master, and with a smile of inexpressible cheerfulness, raised his right hand, and making a motion which he used in giving his benediction, breathed his last. Thus died this great and good man, on the 9th of June, A. D. 597, and in the seventy-seventh year of his age.*

Baithen, the cousin, favourite disciple, and immediate successor of Columba, as abbot of Iona, was much renowned for his wisdom, learning, and sanctity. In a very ancient account of his life, it is said that no man ever saw him idle, but always engaged in reading, praying, or working; that next to Columba, he was

* Smith's Life of St. Columba, Edin. 1798, 8vo. *passim*. Jamison's Historical Account of the ancient Culdees, pp. 3–5, 29, 309. Edin. 1811, 4to. Butler's Lives of the Saints, vol. vi, June 9th.

deemed to be the best acquainted with the Scriptures, and to have the greatest extent of learning on this side the Alps.*

IONA continued to be the seat of learning and piety for ages; and many who received their education there, became zealous and successful missionaries among the idolaters, especially in the north of Europe. In the ninth century, the Danes dislodged the monks, and the *Cluniacs* were the next order that settled there; but it would appear, that prior to that period learning had considerably decayed among them, for it is a singular fact, that, whether it was owing to the depredations of the Danes, or to the indifference of the Culdees of Iona to the works of the fathers, the only book of this description which they possessed in that century was one of the works of Chrysostom. Many of the kings of Scotland, and Ireland, and of the isles, were buried in the island; and in former times, it was the place where the archives of Scotland, and many valuable old MSS. were kept, most of which are supposed to have been destroyed at the Reformation; and others are said to have been carried to the Scotch college, at Douay, in France; and such is at present the neglected state of the island, that this once illustrious seat of learning and piety has now no school for education, no temple for worship, no instructer in religion, except when visited by the parish minister of Kilfinichin. "The name Iona is now also quite lost in the country, and it is always called I, (sounded like *ee*,) except when the speaker would wish to lay an emphasis upon the word, then it is called *I-colum-kill*." (Stat. Acc., vol. xiv, p. 198.) The ruins, however, are kept in better preservation than most ruins of this sort in Scotland, by the attention of the family of Argyle.†

In the sixth century, also, flourished the Latin poet ARATOR. He was by birth a Ligurian, and his profession that of an advocate or lawyer. Athalaric, the Gothic king, advanced him to an office of considerable rank and confidence; but, wearied with the pomp and anxiety attendant on the life of a courtier, he at length entered into the church, and was chosen sub-deacon. About the year 540 he composed a metrical version of the Acts of the Apostles, in two books; which was publicly recited in the church of St. Peter, at Rome, before Pope Vigilius, with unbounded applause. He likewise addressed a poetical epistle to Parthenon, to whom he transmitted his *Historia Apostolorum*, or "Acts of the Apostles," for

* Smith's Life of St. Columba, p. 43, *note*.

† Jamison's Historical Account of the ancient Culdees, p. 36. Encyc. Perth. *Icolumkill, Iona*.

circulation in Gaul. His poems have been several times printed. The most noted editions are, one printed at Salamanca, in 1516, in folio, with the notes of Arrius Mendosa, and another in the *Bibliotheca Patrum*, tom. x, p. 125.*

A few years afterward, the Christian church witnessed the rare instance of a Roman pontiff sedulously endeavouring to promote an acquaintance with the sacred Scriptures among all ranks of persons under his influence. GREGORY I., surnamed the Great, had been called to the papal chair A.D. 590, in defiance of his wishes and most determined opposition. A man of rank, of education, and of talents, he had in early life distinguished himself in the senate, and been raised by the emperor to be prefect or governor of Rome; but finding courts and the anxieties of magistracy unfavourable to religion, had abandoned his worldly honours for retirement and religious pursuits. The unanimous suffrages of the papal electors, the voice of the people, and the decision of the civil power, at length forced him from his solitude, and obliged him to assume the triple mitre. On his elevation he adopted the title of "Servant of the Servants of Jesus Christ;" and distinguished himself by the earnestness with which he urged the reading of the Scriptures. These he compared to a river; in some places so shallow that a lamb might easily pass through them; and in others so deep that an elephant might be drowned in them. "The SCRIPTURES," said he, "are infinitely elevated above all other instructions. They instruct us in the truth; they call us to heaven; they change the heart of him who reads them, by producing desires more noble and excellent in their nature than what were formerly experienced;—formerly they grovelled in the dust, they are now directed to eternity. The sweetness and condescension of the Holy Scriptures comfort the weak and imperfect; their obscurity exercises the strong. Not so superficial as to induce contempt, not so mysterious as to deserve neglect, the use of them redoubles our attachment to them; while, assisted by the simplicity of their expressions and the depth of their mysteries, the more we study them the more we love them. They seem to expand and rise in proportion as those who read them rise and increase in knowledge. Understood by the most illiterate, they are always new to the most learned." To eulogiums on the sacred writings Gregory united the most animated persuasions. Writing to a physician, he represents the word of God as an epistle addressed

* Cavei Hist. Literaria, p. 410. Sixt. Senens., lib. iv, p. 247.

by the Creator to his creatures; and as no one would disregard such an honour from his prince, wherever he might be, or whatever might be his engagements, but would be eager to examine its contents; so ought we never to neglect the epistles sent to us by the Lord of angels and men, but, on the contrary, read them with ardour and attention. "Study, meditate," said he, "the words of your Creator, that from them you may learn what is in the heart of God toward you, and that your soul may be inflamed with the most ardent desires after celestial and eternal good." This great man not only used persuasions, but adduced examples, and particularly referred to the conduct of a poor paralytic man, who lived at Rome, called Servulus; who, unable himself to read, purchased a Bible, and, by entertaining religious persons, whom he engaged to read to him, and at other times persuading his mother to perform the same office, had learned the Scriptures by heart; and who, even when he came to die, discovered his love to them, by obliging his attendants to sing psalms with him.

The last letter he ever wrote, addressed to Theodelinda, queen of the Lombards, discovers, by the present with which it was accompanied, his value for the Scriptures. "I send," says he, "to the prince Adoaldus, your son, a cross, and a book of the Gospels in a Persian box, and to your daughter three rings; desiring you to give them these things with your own hand, to enhance the value of the present."*

Gregory's decided opposition to persecution was scarcely less remarkable than his love to the Scriptures. It was a maxim with him that men should be won over to the Christian religion by gentleness, kindness, and diligent instruction, and not by menaces and terror. "Conversions owing to force," says he, in one of his letters, "are never sincere; and such as are thus converted scarcely ever fail to return to their vomit when the force is removed that wrought their conversion." Happy had it been for mankind if the successors of Gregory had possessed the same attachment to the Scriptures, and adopted the same views of persecution!†

It was this Gregory who, zealous for the conversion of the inhabitants of Britain, sent over the monk Augustine, or *Austin*, with forty companions, on a mission to the Anglo-Saxons.‡

* See Gregory's Works, as cited in Usserii Hist. Dogmat., pp. 92, 93. Chalmers's Gen. Biog. Dict., vol. xvi, p. 260.

† Bower's History of the Popes, vol. ii, p. 274.

‡ Bedæ Eccles. Hist., lib. i, ch. xxiii, and lib. ii, ch. i.

Christianity, indeed, had been planted in Britain at a very early period, either by the apostles themselves, as many have supposed, or, according to those ancient British records, "The Triads," by Bran or Brennus, the father of Caradoc, or Caractacus, the famous British general; who, being taken prisoner with his son, and carried to Rome, A.D. 51 or 52, embraced Christianity, and on his return became anxious to evangelize the country of the *Silures*, or Britons, who inhabited South Wales.* But such had been the cruelty and persecutions of the Saxons and others, united to the influence of pagan conquests, that, prior to the mission of Austin and his companions, heathenism had again overspread the land, except in Wales, Cornwall, and Cumberland, where the Britons still retained some footing.

Austin and the other missionaries were favourably received by Ethelbert, king of Kent, who had married Birtha, a Christian princess of great virtue and merit; an audience was granted them in the open air; and afterward, permission given them to use their best endeavours to convert the people from the worship of idols, and turn them to the true and living God. The attempt was, to a certain extent, successful, but was disgraced by the directions received from the Roman pontiff to accommodate the ceremonies of the Christian worship to the usages of the idolaters. Heathen temples, where they could be obtained, were to be preferred to churches specially erected for Christian worship, that the new converts might not be startled by too great a change: and because the heathens had been accustomed to sacrifice oxen to the devil, and feast upon the sacrifices, Christians were to be allowed, on certain festivals, to erect booths or tabernacles near the churches, when oxen were to be killed, and the people to feast together to the honour of God. Nay, so far was this principle of accommodation carried, that Venerable Bede, one of our oldest ecclesiastical historians, who was born A.D. 672, assures us that there was in the same temple one altar for the sacrifices of idolatry, and another for the services of Christianity;† and Procopius, who lived about the middle of the *sixth* century, affirms, that even human sacrifices continued to be offered by those Franks who had embraced the Christian religion!!‡

* Henry's Hist. of Great Britain, vol. i, b. i, ch. ii, sec. 2, p. 183, 8vo. Hughes's Horæ Britannicæ, vol. ii, ch. i, p. 19. Lond. 1819, 8vo.

† Bedæ, Hist. Eccles., lib. i, ch. xxx, and lib. ii, ch. xv.

‡ Procopius, De Bello Gothico, b. ii, cited in Borlase's Antiquities of Cornwall, b. ii, ch. xxiii, p. 154.

Gregory, who had been desirous to establish this mission long before his advancement to the pontificate, neglected nothing which he supposed would contribute to its success. That the missionaries, therefore, might perform the public duties of religion with decency and propriety, he sent over a number of vestments, sacred utensils, and relics, accompanied by a valuable present of *books;* a present peculiarly wanted, from the impossibility of procuring books in Britain; it being doubtful whether the pagan conquerors had not utterly destroyed every thing of the sort, and, by the time of the arrival of Austin, not left one book in the whole island.*

A curious account of the books belonging to the *first* Christian church erected at Canterbury by the monkish missionary and his companions, is furnished by H. Wanley, in his *Catalogus Librorum Veterum Septentrionalium,* from the *Liber Cantuarensis,* preserved in the library of Trinity College, Cambridge. The following is an abridged translation of the catalogue of them:—

"The GREGORIAN BIBLE, in two volumes. In the first volume the title of the book of Genesis is written in red letters; and in both volumes, several splendid purple and rose-coloured leaves are inserted at the beginning of each book."

"A PSALTER, called the 'Psalter of Augustine,' from having been presented to him by Gregory himself."

"The FOUR GOSPELS, denominated St. Mildred's; and of which it is related, that a rustic, in the isle of Thanet, having sworn falsely upon them, he was struck with blindness."

"A PSALTER, ornamented with a miniature painting of Samuel the priest; and adorned on the outside with the image of Christ and the four evangelists, on a plate of silver."

"The FOUR GOSPELS."

"A MARTYROLOGY, containing the Sufferings of the Apostles, the Life of St. John, and the Dispute of St. Peter and St. Paul with Simon Magus; ornamented with the image of Christ, embossed in silver."

"A MARTYROLOGY, beginning with Apollinaris, and terminating with Simplicius, Faustinus, and Beatrice, and adorned with an image of the divine Majesty, in silver gilt, and enriched with precious stones."

"An EXPOSITION OF THE GOSPELS AND EPISTLES, appointed to be read from the third Sunday after the octave of Easter, to the fourth Sunday after the octave of Whitsunday; richly ornamented

* Bedæ, Hist. Eccles., lib. i, cap. xxix. Henry's History of Great Britain, vol. iv, b. ii, ch. iv, p. 20.

with a large beryl, set round with diamonds and other precious stones."

"These," adds the ancient writer, "are the first-fruits of the books belonging to the whole Anglican Church.* But it may be remarked, that, besides these, Austin brought with him a copy of Gregory's work on the "Pastoral Care."

Leland (De Script. Brit., pp. 299, 300) intimates that this library was afterward considerably enlarged by the exertions of the monkish archbishop. "Augustine," says he, "collected by his friends in Italy many volumes both Latin and Greek, and took care to have them sent him, all of which he left at death to his monks, as pledges of his kindness toward them; the *Greek* are lost, partly by the violence of times, partly by fire, partly, too, by theft; but as to the *Latin*, written after the manner of the ancients, in the large kind of Roman characters, these even now remain, presenting an incredibly majestic air of antiquity in their aspect, namely, two volumes containing the four Gospels, but in a version different from that of the Vulgate; a Psalter, dedicated even by Jerome himself to Damasus, the Roman pontiff, which I would willingly believe to be the very original; besides two most elegant Commentaries on the Psalms, which, from their too great age, admit no reader, except one that is very keen-eyed."† Astle, in his "Origin and Progress of Writing," notices several of the volumes originally belonging to this library, which are yet extant, and of which he gives fac-similes. But that Christian library must certainly be deemed extremely defective which contained no more of the Old Testament than the *Psalter;* nor of the New Testament more than the *four Gospels*, and an *Exposition of some parts of the Epistles!*

The Acts of the Apostles, the Epistles, and the Apocalypse, or Revelation, were in this age but rarely copied, and consequently but seldom read. The four Gospels were what were chiefly transcribed, and many persons of the most illustrious rank seem to have possessed no other portions of the Holy Scriptures. Gregory of Tours relates a singular occurrence that took place toward the close of the sixth century, which illustrates this fact. Childebert, king of Austrasia, in one of his victories over the Goths, having obtained possession of the treasures of the church, as a part of the spoils, found among them sixty chalices, or cups; fifteen patens, or plates for the use of the communion; and twenty

* Hickesii Ling. Vet. Sept. Thesaurus, vol. ii, p. 172, fol.

† Whitaker's Ancient Cathedral of Cornwall, vol. ii, p. 324.

boxes, or *cases to hold the books of the Gospels*, all of pure gold, and richly ornamented with jewels. The celebrated copy of the Gothic translation, called the Codex Argenteus, is, with some probability, supposed to have been found in one of the cases.*

The Codex Ephremi, preserved in the royal library in Paris, and which Wetstein supposes to have been written before A. D. 542, forms an exception to the general practice, being originally a copy of the whole Greek Bible, both of the Old and New Testaments. It is written on vellum, and is what is termed by Biblical critics a *Codex Rescriptus*, that is, a manuscript which has been defaced, and another work written upon it on the same vellum or parchment; and is a demonstrative proof of that scarcity of materials for writing upon which prevailed during the middle ages, and of that barbarous ignorance which overspread Europe for several centuries. It is called the *Codex Ephremi* from the fact of several Greek works of Ephrem the Syrian having been written over the more ancient writing of the Bible. The traces, however, of the earlier writing are visible, and in many parts so far legible as to be read by a person of good eyesight.†

A very valuable *Codex Rescriptus* was discovered about thirty years since, by the Rev. Dr. Barrett, senior fellow of Trinity College, Dublin. While he was examining different books in the library of that college, he accidentally met with a very ancient Greek MS., on certain leaves of which he observed a two-fold writing, the one ancient, and the other comparatively recent, transcribed over the former. The original writing on these leaves had been greatly defaced, either by the injuries of time, or by art. On close examination he found, that this ancient MS. consisted of the three following fragments; the Prophet Isaiah, the Evangelist St. Matthew, and certain orations of Gregory Nazianzen. The fragment containing St. Mathew's Gospel he carefully transcribed, and the whole has been accurately engraved in fac-simile, by the order and at the expense of the university, presenting to the reader a perfect resemblance of every page, line, and letter of the original. Only sixty-four leaves remain of the original fragment of St. Matthew's Gospel, and even those are in a very mutilated state. Each page contains one column, and the columns consist of twenty-one lines, and sometimes, though rarely, of twenty-two or twenty-three; the lines are nearly of equal lengths, and consist ordinarily of eighteen or twenty letters. Dr. Barrett with great probability fixes

* Greg. Turon. Hist. Franc., lib. iii, cap. x. Marsh's Michaelis, vol. ii, pt. i, p. 146.

† Marsh's Michaelis, vol. ii, ch. viii, pt. i, sec. 6, p. 258

its age to the sixth century. The doctor gives the following rea sons for this opinion, which at once display his critical sagacity, and present the reader with interesting information :—

1. It is written in the square or uncial character, which is that of the most ancient MSS. and inscriptions: it began to be disused in the seventh century, and soon afterward gave place to the small, oblong, and inclined character, the uncial being only preserved in the *titles* of books, &c.

2. It not only possesses internal marks of very high antiquity; but is destitute of all those which characterize MSS. of a modern, or comparatively modern date. It has neither *spirits* nor *accents*, which, in the opinion of the learned Montfaucon, were first introduced in the seventh century: and though the writing is both accurate and extremely elegant, yet it has no *flourished* or *ornamented* letters, which prevailed in MSS. of the ninth and following centuries.

3. It agrees with the most ancient MSS. in its readings, &c., and particularly with the Codex Bezæ, and omits the doxology, Matthew vi, 13.

4. Though the Ammonian sections are exhibited in this MS., the Eusebian canons usually connected with them are wanting, as in the *Cod. Cant.*—yet these are found connected in MSS. which boast the remotest antiquity, such as the *Codex Ephrem:* and the *Codex Alexandrinus.*

5. The vellum on which this MS. is written was originally of a *purple* colour, which is allowed by the best judges to be a proof of the greatest antiquity.

6. There are evidences that the original writing on this vellum had not been removed by art, in order to write another work in its place, but had faded through the long lapse of time; as there are found in it unquestionable proofs of an attempt to retrace some of the evanescent letters with fresh ink, previously to the rescript.

The *later writing* contains several tracts of some of the Greek fathers, and is attributed by Dr. Barrett to a scribe of the thirteenth century.*

The writers of the *Codices Rescripti*, or, as they were sometimes called, *Codices Palimpsesti*, employed various methods to obliterate the ancient writings; sometimes they pared off the surface of the parchment or vellum MSS., sometimes they boiled them in water; at other times discharged the ink by some chemical

* See Review of Dr. Barrett's *Evangelium Secundum Matthæum*, &c., in Eclectic Review, vol. iii, pt. i, p. 193.

process, particularly by the use of quick-lime ; and sometimes only partially defaced the writing with a sponge; or where it was already faded through age, pursued their transcriptions without further erasure.* These processes, so destructive to literature, were commenced at an early period, for in the canons of the council of Trullo, held in the seventh century, we find one made expressly against this and similar practices:—Can. 68. "They that tear, or cut the books of the Old or New Testament, or of the holy doctors, or sell them to *depravers of books*, or apothecaries, or any one who will make away with them, unless they be worn out and useless, is excommunicated for a year: they that buy them, except to keep, or sell again for the benefit of themselves or others, or *go about to corrupt them*, let them be excommunicated."† Montfaucon, who was perhaps better qualified than any other man in Europe to give an opinion on this subject, informs us, that these destructive processes were in most frequent use in the twelfth, thirteenth, and fourteenth centuries, and that they were seldom applied to any other material than parchment or vellum, since he had only met with one instance in which the writing on cotton paper, (charta bombycina,) had been effaced, that another work might be written in its stead, although the major part of the works on parchment, which he had seen, of the twelfth and subsequent centuries, were written upon parchment, from which some former work had been erased.‡

By this barbarous operation religion and science were equally outraged, and the very words of God obliterated, to make way for such writings as have yielded but little to the instruction or amelioration of posterity. For as there are always persons to be found with whom gain is godliness, some of the wretched *librarii*, or transcribers of books, scrupled not to efface even the sacred Scriptures, in order to write more modern or more popular works upon the parchment which had contained them. Nor was the practice confined to the obliteration of the sacred records only ; many classical works of high reputation were also sacrificed to gain or superstition. Thus, in the place probably of some of the finest writers of antiquity, philosophers, poets, historians, and grammarians, we

* Peignot, Essai sur l'Histoire du Parchemin, pp. 83–88. Classical Journal, No. xxiii. Wetstenii Proleg., ch. i, p. 8. Amstel. 1730, 4to.

† Johnson's Clergyman's Vade Mecum, vol. i, p. 280. Wetstenii Proleg., ch. i, p. 8.

‡ Montfaucon, Palæogr. Gr., lib. iii, p. 231 ; and lib. iv, p. 319. Memoires de l'Academie Royale des Inscriptions, &c. *Dissertation sur la Papyrus*, vol. vi, p. 606 Paris, 1729, 4to.

have missals, confessionals, monkish rhymes, and execrable and puerile legends. In the fourteenth and fifteenth centuries the erasure of writing became so common in Germany, that, fearing the use of *erased* parchment in public instruments might prove injurious to the public, efficacious measures were adopted to prevent this disorder. Accordingly the patents by which the emperors elevated persons to the dignity of count, with power to promote imperial notaries, usually contained the following clause:—"On condition that they shall not employ *old* and *erased* parchment, but that it shall be *virgin*, (that is, made of abortive skins,) and quite new."*

These literary depredations were occasioned, as has been already intimated, by that extraordinary scarcity and dearness of materials for writing upon, which existed during several ages in most parts of Europe. Great estates were often transferred from one owner to another by a mere verbal agreement, and the delivery of earth and stone before witnesses, without any written deed. Parchment, on which nearly all their books were written, was so scarce, that about the year 1124, one master Hugh, being appointed by the convent of St. Edmundsbury, in Suffolk, to write and illuminate a grand copy of the Bible for their library, could procure no parchment for this purpose in England! And in the great revenue-roll of John Gurveys, bishop of Winchester, A. D. 1226, there is an item of five shillings, expended for parchment in one year; a considerable sum for such a commodity, at a period when wheat was only from two to three shillings a quarter, or eight bushels; and when within a few years afterward, in 1283, we find the following short entry in the annals of the priory of Dunstable:—"This year, in the month of July, we sold our slave William Pyke, and received one mark (thirteen shillings and four-pence) from the buyer."†

The scarcity and dearness of parchment were doubtless the causes of another abuse, that of *abbreviations*. Under the pretext of rendering manuscripts less voluminous, and consequently cheaper; of economizing the time of those who were employed in transcribing; and lastly, for the purpose of comprising several volumes in one, abbreviations became so multiplied, especially in the middle ages, that it requires more than common ability to understand and read them. These abbreviations continued in use subsequent to the invention of printing. In Okam's *Logic*, printed

* Peignot, Essai sur Parchemin, p. 86.

† Henry's History of Great Britain, vol. iv, p. 81; vol. vi, p. 306; and vol. viii, p. 340. 8vo. Warton's Hist. of Eng. Poetry, Dissert. ii, On Learning.

at Paris, in 1488, in folio, the words are so abbreviated as to be almost unintelligible. The following is a specimen:—*Sic hic e fal sm qd ad simplr a e pducibile a Deo g a e. et silr hic a n e g a n e pducible a Do.* These abbreviations are meant for the following sentence: but who could understand them? *Sicut hic est fallacia secundum quid ad simpliciter. A est producibile á Deo, ergo A est, et similiter hic: A non est, ergo A non est producibile á Deo.*

Toward the close of the fifteenth century, these abbreviations became so frequent and excessive, both in manuscripts and printed books, that it became necessary to procure works to explain them, and facilitate the reading of works thus abbreviated. Of this description was a treatise by John Petit, entitled, *Modus legendi abbreviaturas in utroque jure*, Paris, 1498, 8vo., and another printed at Cologne, in 1582, entitled, *Modus legendi abbreviaturas passim in jur. tam civil. quam pontifical. occurrent.** Buxtorf also published a useful work on *Hebrew* abbreviations, entitled, *De abbreviaturis Hebraicis. Franeq.* 1696, 12mo. Sertorius Ursatus's *Explanatio Notarum et Literarum, &c.*, Paris, 1723, 12mo., is a valuable little work on the *Latin* abbreviations. The *Palæographia Græca* is well known; and the various abbreviations and contractions of *Greek* words and letters which are found in inscriptions, MSS., and books, are beautifully engraved in Hodgkin's *Calligraphia Græca et Poecilographia Græca,* small folio, Lond. 1807. These plates are published in the Classical Journal, Nos xvii, xviii, xix, xxi.

CHAPTER V.

SEVENTH CENTURY.

Illiteracy of Ecclesiastics—Theodore, Archbishop of Canterbury—Paulicians—Caedmon—St. Cuthbert's Gospels—St. Chad's Gospels—Ina—Aidan—Aldhelm—Dagæus—Ultan—China.

THE proofs of illiterate barbarism which have been adduced in the former chapter were only the commencements of that universal and profound ignorance which exercised its gloomy sway during the SEVENTH, and several subsequent centuries. Princes and prelates, clergy and laity, all felt its baneful influence. The eighth council of Toledo, in Spain, held about the year 653, found it necessary to forbid the ordination of any who were not, at least,

* Peignot, Essai sur Parchemin, pp. 89, 90.

acquainted with the Psalms and hymns used in the services of the church, and with the ritual of baptism; and also to enjoin, that those who had been ordained already, but were, through ignorance, incapable of the duties of their office, should either voluntarily acquaint themselves with the services of the church, or be compelled to it by their superiors.* In a former synod, held at the same place, in 633, a canon had been made which declared, "Ignorance is the parent of error, and is therefore to be avoided, especially by the priests, whose duty it is to minister to the people; agreeably to the admonition of St. Paul, who enjoins the frequent reading of the Scriptures."† Withred, king of Kent, in a charter whereby he granted lands to the church or convent of St. Mary, at Liminge in that county, A. D. 693, acknowledges, that being illiterate, (pro ignorantia literarum,) he had marked it with the *sign* of the holy cross.‡ Crosses, instead of seals, were used by the ecclesiastics, who introduced the practice of conveying property by written instruments, and this custom prevailed invariably till the conquest, and for near a century afterward. Archbishops and bishops were frequently too illiterate to write their own names, and only made their *marks* to the acts of councils. Hence the phrase *signing*, for subscribing to a deed, is taken from persons making the *sign* of the cross, in place of their name, and proves how universal this practice must have been formerly. In the acts of the councils of Ephesus, and Chalcedon, many examples occur where subscriptions are to be found in this form: *I, such a one, have subscribed by the hand of such a one, because I cannot write.* And, *such a bishop having said that he could not write, I, whose name is underwritten, have subscribed for him.*§ A celebrated ecclesiastical historian‖ remarks, "Nothing can equal the ignorance and darkness that reigned in this century; the most impartial and accurate account of which will appear incredible to those who are unacquainted with the productions of this barbarous period."

Toward the close of this century the number of books was so inconsiderable, even in the Papal library at Rome, that Pope Martin requested Sanctamond, bishop of Maestricht, if possible to supply this defect from the remotest parts of Germany.¶ But nothing

* S. S. Concil., vol. vi, Conc. Tolet. 8, p. 406.

† Usserii Hist. Dogmat. de Scripturis, p. 196.

‡ Antiquarian Repertory, vol. ii, pp. 131–133. Lond. 1779, 4to.

§ Du Cange, Gloss. v, *Crux*, *Signum*.

‖ Mosheim, Eccles. Hist., vol. ii, p. 165.

¶ Warton's Hist. Eng. Poetry, vol. i, dissert. ii.

more completely proves the scarcity of books at this period, than the bargain which Benedict Biscop, a monk, and founder of the monastery of Weremouth, concluded a little before his death, A. D. 690, with Aldfred, king of Northumberland, by which the king agreed to give an estate of eight hides of land, or as much as eight ploughs could labour, which is said to have been eight hundred acres, for *one* volume on cosmography, or the history of the world!* This book was given, and the estate received, by Benedict's successor, the abbot Ceolfrid.

"Any remains of learning and philosophy that yet survived were, a few particular cases excepted, to be found principally among the Latins, in the obscure retreats of cloistered monks. The monastic institutions prohibited the election of any abbot to the head of a convent who was not a man of learning, or at least endowed with a tolerable measure of the erudition of the times. The monks were obliged to consecrate certain hours every day to reading and study: and, that they might improve this appointment to the most advantageous purposes, there were, in most of the monasteries, stated times marked out, at which they were to assemble, in order to communicate to each other the fruits of their study, and to discuss the matters upon which they had been reading. The youth also, who were destined for the service of the church, were obliged to prepare themselves for their ministry, by a diligent application to study; and in this they were directed by the monks, one of whose principal occupations it was to preside over the education of the rising priesthood. It must, however, be acknowledged, that all these institutions were of little use to the advancement of solid learning, or of rational theology, because very few in these days were acquainted with the true nature of the liberal arts and sciences, or with the important ends which they were adapted to serve."†

ENGLAND, it is true, was happier in this respect than the other nations of Europe. This was principally owing to THEODORE, archbishop of Canterbury. A native of Tarsus in Cilicia, a monk of Rome, and originally a Greek priest, he had been consecrated archbishop, and sent into England, by Pope Vitalian, in 668. He was skilled in the metrical art, astronomy, arithmetic, church music, and the Greek and Latin languages; and brought with him what was then called and esteemed a large library, consisting of

* Henry's Hist. of Great Britain, vol. iv, b. ii, ch. iv, p. 20. Russel's Hist. of Modern Europe, vol. i, let. 12, p. 102.

† Mosheim, *ubi sup.*

copies of the Scriptures, and many Greek and Latin books; among which were *Homer*, in a large volume, written on paper with most exquisite elegance; the *Homilies of Chrysostom*, on parchment; the *Psalter* and *Josephus's Hypomnesticon*, all in Greek. He was accompanied into England by ADRIAN, a Neapolitan monk, and a native of Africa, learned in the Holy Scriptures, versed in monastic and ecclesiastical discipline, and excellently skilled in the Greek and Latin tongues; who having declined the honour of the ecclesiastical primacy, in favour of his friend Theodore, had been appointed by the pope to the abbacy of St. Austin's, at Canterbury. They were both escorted from Rome, by BENEDICT BISCOP, a Saxon youth, a native of Northumberland. Theodore, in conjunction with Adrian, expounded the Scriptures publicly, endeavoured to excite a taste for letters, by delivering lectures to the most crowded audiences his exertions could procure; and established schools in most parts of England. These honourable labours produced the most pleasing effects, and it is recorded by Bede, that when he himself wrote, individuals were found among the scholars of those learned masters to whom the Latin and Greek languages were as familiar as their native tongue. To account for the possibility of an African delivering lectures to an English or Saxon audience, it should be remembered that Latin was the common language of all the ecclesiastics of the Romish Church;—that Benedict Biscop had not only acted as interpreter, but as teacher of the Saxon;—and that the principal hearers of Theodore were persons engaged in ecclesiastical offices, or educating for them.* "To his [Theodore's] memory," says a modern writer, "we owe respect and gratitude; he brought into our island a most invaluable library of Greek† and Latin books, *with several copies of the Scriptures*, which happily survived the wreck of ages; *he planted among us the language of the Gospels*, and sowed those seeds both of divine and human learning, which, under the blessing of Providence, have grown and flourished in our country, have exalted our religion, and consequently our morality, expanded our minds, embellished them with science, and added to our physical enjoyments the comforts of the arts. Those who unfortunately cannot relish the animated, pious effusions of Chrysostom, (which, however, would have equally served religion and virtue had they

* Bedæ, Hist. Eccles., lib. iv, ch. xxi. Warton's Hist. of English Poetry, vol. i, diss. 2. Cavei Hist. Litt., p. 464.

† "The copies of Homer, David's Psalms, and Chrysostom's Homilies, brought by Theodore, were still extant at the beginning of the last century."

been less severe upon women,) may at least respect the man who brought the *επεα πτεροεντα* of Homer to our shores."*

On the return of Benedict Biscop to Northumberland he founded the monastery of Weremouth. For the erection of the church he procured workmen from France, who constructed it of *stone*, after the Roman fashion; for before that time stone buildings were very rare in Britain; even the church of Lindisfarne was of *wood*, and covered with a thatch of straw and reeds, till Bishop Eadbert procured both the roof and the walls to be covered with sheet lead. Benedict also brought over *glaziers* from France, the art of glass-making being then unknown in Britain. The walls and roof of the church he adorned with pictures, which he purchased at Rome, representing the Virgin Mary, the twelve Apostles, the Gospel history, and the visions of the Apocalypse. He afterward added a noble library of rare Greek and Latin works.†

While Theodore held the archiepiscopal dignity, a council was summoned at Rome respecting the ecclesiastical affairs of Britain. In this council it was decreed, that "bishops, and all whosoever profess the religious life of the ecclesiastical order, shall not use weapons, nor keep musicians of the female sex, nor any musical concerts whatsoever, nor allow of any buffooneries or plays in their presence. For the discipline of the holy church permits not her faithful priests to use any of these things, but charges them to be employed in divine offices, in making provisions for the poor, and for the benefit of the church; *especially let lessons out of the divine oracles be always read*, for the edification of the churches, that the minds of the hearers may be fed with the divine word, even at the very time of their bodily repast."‡ From the same records we learn, that it was the practice, on holding a council, to place a *copy of the sacred Gospels* in open view, in the church where the council was held, during its deliberations; with the intention, most certainly, to intimate that all their decisions ought to be according to the word of God.

But though the Scriptures were thus enjoined to be read in the WEST, a singular circumstance which occurred during this century, and ultimately gave rise to the sect of the PAULICIANS, gives us reason to believe that they were already forbidden to the laity in the EAST; and proves the extreme rarity of copies of the sacred writings. A Syrian deacon, returning from captivity to his native

* Storer's Cathedrals of Great Britain, Canterbury, A. D. 690.

† Bedæ, Hist. Eccles., lib. iii, cap. xxv. Warton, *ut sup.*

‡ Johnson's Collection of Eccl. Laws, &c., A. D. DCLXXIX.

country, passed through Mananalis, an obscure town in the neighbourhood of Samosata. Here he was entertained for some days by an hospitable but indigent Armenian, whose name was Constantine. On leaving the place, the deacon, as a recompense for Constantine's generosity, presented him with *two* manuscripts, which he had brought with him from Syria, containing the Gospels, and the Epistles of St. Paul. Constantine was overjoyed with the present he had received, and resolved to study only the Gospels and the Epistles, to the exclusion of every other work; and, from this attachment to the writings of St. Paul, he and those who followed his example were denominated PAULICIANS. This was about the year 653. The narrator of these facts is Petrus Siculus, who was sent from Rome to the Paulicians in Armenia in 870, by the emperor Basil the Great, to negotiate for an exchange of prisoners. The intemperate language which he adopts on this occasion sufficiently discovers that, in his opinion, the Scriptures ought to be withheld from the laity, and not be left to their indiscriminate perusal and interpretation. He considers the resolution of Constantine as being formed by the instigation of the devil, (dæmone instigante,) and his conduct as pregnant with the direst ills. The relation which he has given of the way in which the Paulicians spread their opinions is too curious to be omitted. SERGIUS, the great and active promoter of their cause, became a convert to their doctrines, as Petrus Siculus informs us, through the reasoning and conversation of a female. "I hear, Sergius," said this advocate for the Paulician doctrines, "that you excel in literature and knowledge; and that you are a good man in every respect. Tell me, therefore, why you do not read the holy Gospels." The unsuspicious youth replied, "*It is not lawful for us profane persons to read them, but for the priests only.*" "You are mistaken," said she, "for there is no respect of persons with God, who will have all men to be saved and come to the knowledge of the truth. But your priests, because they adulterate the word of God, and hide the mysteries contained in the Gospels, do not read to you the whole of the Scriptures, but only some parts, and omit others, lest you should come to the knowledge of the truth. For in them (Matt. vii) it is written, 'Many shall say, Lord, Lord, have we not cast out devils in thy name, and in thy name done many wonderful works? But the King shall profess unto them, I never knew ye.' Search and see whether it be not thus written. And who are they, think you, to whom the Lord will say, 'I never knew ye?'" Sergius hesitating to reply, the woman proceeded: "To us there is no great difficulty in explaining the words of the Gospel. There are persons in the present day who honour the Christian life, and appear to live piously, and by certain incantations cast out devils, and cure diseases, and are called exorcists. Like some we read of in the Acts of the Apostles, they adjure those who are possessed with devils, by Christ whom Paul preached, 'Depart out of these men,' and at the hearing of the name of Christ the devils flee, filled with terror." In the same way the female Paulician continued to quote the Scriptures, and affix her own sense to them, till she had so far prevailed upon Sergius, that he determined to examine the Scriptures for himself. Having examined them, he became one of the most zealous promoters of the Paulician sentiments; and, like the other principal teachers who adopted names from the New Testament, he assumed that of *Tychicus*. The *text* of the Scriptures made use of by the Paulicians was, by the confession of their enemies, allowed to be genuine and uncorrupted, and their doctrines consequently deduced from the *pure* word of God.* With some show of probability, it has been supposed that the *Waldenses* derive their origin from these ancient defenders of the truth.

Returning to our Saxon ancestors, we find proofs still remaining of their attachment to those Scriptures, which were thus early, in the East, concealed from the eyes of the vulgar. Such are, for instance, the fragments of Caedmon's poetical paraphrases of the books of Genesis and Daniel; and the magnificent copies of St. Cuthbert's and St. Chad's Gospels.

Caedmon, a pious monk of Streaneshalch, or Whitby, in the *seventh century*, employed his poetical genius in the composition of a paraphrastical and metrical version of some of the most remarkable portions of sacred history. It is the earliest specimen of Saxon poetry, and was printed by Junius, at Amsterdam, 1665, 4to. It opens with the fall of angels and the creation of the world, and proceeds to the history of the first parents of mankind; of the deluge, of the departure of the children of Israel from Egypt, and their entrance into the land of promise. It recounts also some of the actions of Nebuchadnezzar and Daniel. It abounds with periphrasis and metaphor, the earliest figures and the universal characteristics of ancient poetry.†

The following fragment, on the first verse of the book of Genesis, is preserved in Alfred's Saxon translation of Bede's Ecclesi-

* Maxima Biblioth. Vet. Patrum, tom. xvi, pp. 759, 761, 762.

† Bedæ, Hist. Eccles., lib. iv, cap. xxiv. Baber's Saxon and English Versions, prefixed to his edition of Wicliff's New Testament. Lond. 1810, 4to.

astical History. It is made on waking in a stall of oxen, which he had been appointed to guard during the night.

Now we should praise
The Guardian of the heavenly kingdom;
The mighty Creator,
And the thoughts of his mind,
Glorious Father of his works!
As he, of every glory
Eternal Lord!
Established the beginning;
So he first shaped
The earth for the children of men,
And the heavens for its canopy.
Holy Creator!
The middle region,
The Guardian of mankind,
The Eternal Lord,
Afterward made
The ground for men,
Almighty Ruler!*

Nu we sceolan herigean
Heafon rices weard;
Metodes mihte
And his mod gethane
Weorc wuldor fæder
Swa he wuldres gehwaes
Ece drihten
Ord onstealde;
He ærest gescop
Eorthan bearnum,
Heofen to rofe
Halig scyppend!
Tha middan geard,
Mon cynnes weard,
Ece drihtne!
Æfter teode
Firum foldan
Frea almihtig!

Translations from other parts of Caedmon's Paraphrase, as published by Junius, are given in Sharon Turner's valuable "History of the Anglo-Saxons," vol. ii, b. xii, ch. i, pp. 309–316. Caedmon died in 680.

The *Textus Sancti Cuthberti*, or St. Cuthbert's Gospels, generally called the Durham Book, is a copy of the four Gospels in Latin, written about A. D. 680, in the time of St. Cuthbert, by Egbert or Eadfrid, a monk of Lindisfarne or Holy Island, with great care and labour. Eadfrid succeeded Cuthbert in the bishopric of Landisfarne, in 687, and was himself succeeded, in 721, by Ethelwold, who held the see till his death, in 737. The Latin text is of extraordinary fine penmanship, in round Roman characters. The letters are in a high state of preservation, the ink shining black as ebony. Ethelwold ornamented the MS. at his own cost, with golden bosses and precious stones; and with the assistance of Bilfrid, an anchoret, decorated it with illuminations of the most intricate and elaborate workmanship. "To give additional value to this venerated monument of British antiquity, to propagate the divine truth contained in its pages, written in an unknown language to the natives of the country, in the vulgar tongue, and to incorporate homely useful knowledge with splendid decorations and Latin literature,"* Aldred, a priest, added an

* Turner's Hist. of the Anglo-Saxons, vol. ii, p. 278, 4to. 1807.

interlinear Saxon version about the time of Alfred, which is the finest specimen of Saxon calligraphy and decoration extant. Mr. Henshall, who published Aldred's translation of the Gospel of St. Matthew, says, that the Gospels were originally in separate volumes, and that St. Matthew's Gospel was peculiarly appropriated by the writer to St. Cuthbert's minister; St. Mark's, to the bishop of the island; St. Luke's, to the holy fraternity resident in the island; and St. John's, to God, and St. Cuthbert, for his future salvation.

These Gospels were at first deposited in the Episcopal church of Lindisfarne; but when this religious edifice was ruined by the predatory Danes, in 793, the monks were obliged to leave their abode in the holy island, and to seek for another asylum. In their passage to the Northumberland coast, this book of the Gospels, which they had borne away as their most revered treasure, fell into the sea. Some historians relate, that it was three days in the water; others say, that the tide ebbing much further than usual, it was found upon the sands three miles from the shore. After its recovery it was deposited in a monastery at Chester, where it remained till the monks were again obliged by the Danes to emigrate. In the year 995 they settled at Durham. The recovery of this volume from the destruction with which it had been threatened by the devouring deep was an event from which the monks of Durham derived considerable emoluments. They pretended that this book was endowed with miraculous powers, and imposed upon the ignorant and credulous with great success. It is now preserved among the Cotton MSS. in the British Museum. The ornaments of this book which now remain (for of its gold and precious stones it has been long since plundered) are pictures of the evangelists prefixed to their respective Gospels, many capital letters beautifully illuminated, and four tessellated tablets, each most laboriously executed, and containing a fanciful design of the cross, painted with a rich variety of brilliant body colours. The pictures of the evangelists are to be seen engraved in Strutt's *Horda Angel Cynnan*, vol. iii, and there is a fac-simile of an illuminated capital letter in Astle's "Origin and Progress of Writing." The interlineatory version by Aldred is in red ink, but in some places a little faded.*

A Latin copy of St. John's Gospel, which St. Cuthbert was in

* Astle's Origin and Progress of Writing, pp. 100, 101, fol. Henshall's Gothic Gospel, pp. 53–63. Baber's Historical Account of Saxon and Eng. Versions, prefixed to Wicliff's N. T. 1810, 4to.

the habit of reading, was put into his coffin when he was buried, and was afterward found in his tomb. It was said to be not long ago in the possession of Mr. Thomas Philips, canon of Tongres, to whom it was presented by the earl of Litchfield; and to have been pronounced genuine by the ablest Protestant antiquarians.*

The *Textus Sancti Ceddæ*, or St. Chad's Gospel, is a fine MS. of the Latin Gospels, preserved in the church of Litchfield. It was many years ago presented to the church of Llandaff, by Gelhi, who gave for the purchase of it one of his best horses; and about the year 1020, being deposited in the cathedral church of Litchfield, was dedicated to St. Chad, the fifth bishop of that see; the book has thence been called by his name. This MS. was written in England about the time of St. Cuthbert's Gospels, in the seventh century, in (what Astell calls) the *Roman-Saxon* character. In the margin of it are several annotations in Latin and Saxon, and some in the ancient British and Welsh, which last Mr. Edwards Lhuyd supposes to be of about nine hundred years standing. A fac-simile of the writing of this MS. is given in Astle's "Origin and Progress of Writing."†

The immense donation of Ina, king of the West Saxons, to the church of Glastonbury, deserves also to be mentioned, as affording a proof of the veneration for the holy Gospels. He caused a chapel, or case modelled in the form of a chapel, to be formed of silver and gold, with ornaments and vases equally gold and silver; and placed it within the great church of Glastonbury, delivering two thousand six hundred and forty pounds of silver for forming the chapel; for the altar he gave two hundred and sixty-four pounds of gold; for the chalice and paten, ten pounds of gold; for the censer, eight and twenty mancuses of gold; for the candlesticks, twelve pounds and a half of silver; for the *coverings of the books of the Gospels*, twenty pounds and sixty mancuses of gold; for the water vessels and other vases of the altar, seventeen pounds of gold; for the basins for the offertory, eight pounds of gold; for the vessels for the holy water, twenty pounds of silver; for images of our Lord and the Virgin Mary, and the twelve apostles, a hundred and seventy-five pounds of silver and thirty-eight pounds of gold, the twelve apostles being in silver, but our Lord and the Virgin Mary in gold; the pall for the altar, and the vest

* Butler's Lives, vol. ii, Feb. 23, p. 221; and vol. iii, March 20, p. 228.

† Astle, *ut sup.*

ments for the priests were also artfully interwoven on both sides with gold and precious stones.*

AIDAN and ALDHELM flourished also during the seventh century, and enlightened the nation by their pious labours. Aidan was a native of Ireland, and a monk of Iona; and, on account of his extraordinary mildness, was appointed missionary to Northumberland, where Oswald then reigned, who had requested that the Irish sovereign and bishops would send him a bishop and assistants, by whose means his subjects might be confirmed in the Christian religion. Oswald bestowed on Aidan the isle of Lindisfarne for his episcopal seat; and was so edified by his learning and zeal, that before the bishop could successfully speak the English language, he acted as his interpreter, and explained his sermons and instructions to the people. In his ministerial labours Aidan was indefatigable, travelling on foot through the rudest and most uncultivated parts of his newly formed diocess; constantly aiming to communicate instruction, both to the rich and poor, to the Christian and infidel. He was particularly studious in the Scriptures, and not only read them himself, but obliged those who travelled or associated with him to spend their time either in *reading the Scriptures* or *learning the Psalter by heart*. He rarely would go to the king's table, and never without taking with him one or two of his clergy; and always after a short repast made haste away to read, or to pray in the church, or in his cell. He died on the 31st of August, A. D. 651.†

ADHELM, or ALDHELM, was born among the West Saxons, and was a near relation of King Ina, but educated under Adrian, at Canterbury. In 675, Maidulf resigned to him the abbey of Maidulfsbury, or, corruptly, Malmsbury, in Wiltshire. By his means this abbey was rendered one of the most famous in England, and numerous donations and privileges were granted to it by the pope, and various kings and princes. After having held the abbacy for about thirty years, he was chosen the first bishop of Sherborn, in Dorsetshire. But this dignity he did not long possess, for he died in the fifth year of his episcopacy, while in the visitation of his diocess at Dullinge, in Somersetshire, on the 25th of May, 709.‡

This excellent bishop was one of the most learned men and best poets of the age in which he lived. Under Maidulf, or Maildulf,

* Whitaker's Cathedral of Cornwall, vol. ii, pp. 291, 292.

† Bedæ Hist. Eccles., lib. iii, cap. iii, v. Butler's Lives of the Saints, vol. viii, Aug. 31, pp. 569, 570.

‡ Ibid., vol. v, pp 329, 330.

who founded the abbey of Malmsbury, and supported himself by teaching scholars, he became thoroughly versed in Greek and Latin; and was the first of the English nation who wrote in Latin. In a letter to his old preceptor, he expresses his love of study, and mentions the objects to which his attention was directed: among these we find the Roman jurisprudence, the metres of Latin poetry, arithmetic, and astronomy. His learning and poetic powers he devoted to the most benevolent and pious purposes. Before his advancement to the bishopric, and while abbot of Malmsbury, he employed his poetic genius in a singular manner, for the instruction of the people. Observing his barbarous countrymen to be inattentive to grave instructions, and to run home immediately after the singing of mass, he composed a number of little poems, ingeniously interspersed with passages of Scripture; and having an excellent voice, and great skill in music, frequently placed himself upon a bridge that joined the town and country, and professing himself skilled in singing, stopped the passengers, while he sang his poems in the sweetest manner. By this means he gained the favour of the populace, who flocked about him, and by so specious a mode of instruction were brought to a sense of duty, and a knowledge of religious subjects.

Toward the close of life he translated the Psalter into Saxon; and in his book *De Virginitate*, praises the nuns to whom he wrote for their industry and attention in daily reading and studying the Holy Scriptures; a practice highly deserving commendation at all times, but particularly so at this period. For "to a nation whose minds were so untutored in knowledge as the Anglo-Saxons, the Jewish and Christian Scriptures must have been invaluable accessions. From these they would learn the most rational chronology of the earth, the most correct history of the early states of the East, the most intelligent piety, the wisest morality, and every style of literary composition. Perhaps no other collection of human writings can be selected, which would so much interest and benefit a rude and ignorant people. We shall feel all their value and importance to our ancestors if we compare them with the Edda, in which the happiest efforts of the northern genius are deposited."* Aldhelm's translation of the Psalms was probably lost or destroyed through the incursions of the Danes.

This great and good man was not satisfied with only personally promoting the knowledge of the Scriptures; he endeavoured to engage others in the same blessed work. The copy of a letter is

* Turner's Hist. of the Anglo-Saxons, b. xii, p. 360.

still extant, which he wrote to Ehfrid or Eadfrid, bishop of Lindisfarne, with this design. It is a curious specimen of Aldhelm's epistolary style, and of the barbarous and monkish Latin then in use. As a *poet*, King Alfred the Great declared Aldhelm to be the best of all the Saxons, and notices one of his pieces as being universally sung in his time, near two hundred years after the decease of its author. His poetical works which remain are: *De Laude Virginum*, *De Octo principalibus Vitiis*, and *Ænigmata*.

The principal prose work of Aldhelm is his treatise in praise of virginity. A beautifully illuminated copy of this work is preserved in the archiepiscopal library, at Lambeth Palace. In the catalogue of this library, published in 1812, folio, by the Rev. H. J. Todd, a fac-simile is given of the first leaf of this MS., supposed to be, according to Mr. Todd, of the *eighth*, or, according to Mr. Dibdin, of the *tenth* or *eleventh* century, representing Aldhelm seated in a chair, with a group of virgins standing round him, as if approving of his work. Mr. Astle, in his "Origin and Progress of Writing," p. 71, has given also a specimen of the characters in which it is written. This singular treatise contains a profusion of epithets paraphrases, and repetitions, conveyed in long and intricate periods. But in an age of general ignorance, his diction pleased and informed by its magnificent exuberance. His imagery was valued for its minuteness, because, although usually unnecessary to its subject, yet, as these long details contained considerable information for an uncultivated mind, and sometimes presented pictures which, if considered by themselves, are not uninteresting, it was read with curiosity, and praised with enthusiasm. "It is, however, just to his memory to say, that he was a man of genius, though of wild and uncultivated taste. His mind was as exuberant of imagery as Jeremy Taylor's. Many of his allusions, though fanciful, are apposite, and some are elegant and vigorous, both in the conception and the expression."*

Dagæus and Ultan, two Irish monks, deserve also to be mentioned. Dagæus flourished in the early part of the *sixth* century, and died 587. He was abbot of Inniskilling, (Iniscеltraensis,) and an eminent calligraphist; and not only wrote many books with his own hand, but also manufactured and ornamented bindings in gold, silver, and precious stones. Ultan was the first bishop of Ardbraccan, in Meath, in Ireland. Among his virtues, his charity has been particularly mentioned. Ethelwolf, in a metrical epistle to

* Turner's Anglo-Saxons, vol. ii, b. xii, pp. 367, 368. Dibdin's Bibliographical Decameron, vol. i, p. lii, *note*.

Egbert, at that time resident in Ireland, with a view of collecting MSS., extols him for his talent in adorning books; Leland also (Collect., vol. ii, p. 364) designates him as a first-rate calligraphist and illuminator; and Harpsfield says, he used to transcribe the Holy Scriptures in the most beautiful manner.* He died in 656.

Such were the worthies, who rose liks stars in our hemisphere, and beamed their rays across the gloom, at a time when ignorance and barbarism so universally reigned, that in Britain the fair sex were treated with indignity, and our ancestors bought their wives as they purchased their cattle; parents exported their children to be sold for slaves; and men were yoked in teams like oxen !† But from such recollections we turn to the more pleasing subject of the introduction of the Scriptures into the immense empire of China.

From a curious monument discovered at Sighan-fu, in the province of Xen-si, in 1625, we learn, that under the reign of the emperor Thai-cum, about the year 637, a Christian missionary named Olopen visited the imperial residence at Cham-ghan, or Sighan-fu. The emperor, hearing of his arrival, sent his prime minister, and other noblemen of his court, to meet him, and after discoursing with him on the object of his mission, to conduct him to the palace. The result of his interview with the emperor was important; Fam-hiven-lim, the prime minister, one of the most learned men in the empire, was ordered to translate the Scriptures, brought by Olopen, into the Chinese language, and the doctrines of the Gospel were permitted to be divulged and preached.‡ Succeeding emperors, alas! pursued a different conduct; the *bonzes*, or pagan priests, raised violent persecutions; the Scriptures in the vernacular language were ultimately destroyed or lost, and for many ages that vast empire remained without a complete copy of the Bible, and almost without the smallest portion of the sacred writings in the Chinese tongue. Two separate translations have, however, lately been completed of the whole of the New Testament into this most difficult language; the one at Serampore, by Dr.

* Dibdin's Bibliographical Decameron, vol. i. p. cxxi. *note*. Butler's Lives, vol. ix, p. 39.

† Johnson's Ecclesiastical Laws, A. D. DCII. Turner's Anglo-Saxons, vol. ii, b. viii, ch. ix, pp. 99, 100.

‡ D'Herbelot, Bibliotheque Orientale, Supp., p. 165, fol. 1780. Marsh's Michaelis, vol. iv, p. 447. Gibbon's D. & F. of the Rom. Emp., vol. viii, ch. xlvii, p. 345, *note*. Mosheim's Eccles. Hist., vol. ii, pp. 151, 152.

Joshua Marshman, a Baptist missionary, the other at Canton, by Dr. Robert Morrison, a missionary sent out by the London Missionary Society. They are now proceeding with the translation of the Old Testament, notwithstanding the imperial edicts forbidding them to be read by the natives of China.

CHAPTER VI.

EIGHTH CENTURY.

Arabic Version—Venerable Bede—Willibrord—Boniface—Churches of Wood—Willehad—Alcuin—Illiteracy—Military Ecclesiastics—Canons of Councils—Scriptures in Saxon Characters—Egbert's Library—Instruction of Children.

EARLY in the EIGHTH century, the Scriptures were translated into ARABIC. The conquests of the Saracens, or Moors, had rendered the Arabic common in Spain; and John, archbishop of Seville, desirous that the people should read and understand the Holy Scriptures, undertook a translation of them into that tongue, which he completed about A. D. 717.* Between this and the version of Saadias Gaon, in the tenth century, other translations probably were made, but their exact date is not ascertainable. "If a conjecture is allowable," says Dr. Marsh, "on a subject where history leaves us in the dark, we may suppose that most of the Arabic versions were made during the period that elapsed between the conquests of the Saracens in the seventh century, and the Crusades in the eleventh; especially about the middle of this period, when the Syriac and the Coptic, though they had ceased to be living languages, were still understood by men of education; and Arabic literature, under the patronage of Al Mamon, and his successors, had arrived at its highest pitch."†

The Arabic version found in the Tritaglot Pentateuch, preserved in the Barberini collection at Rome, is probably one of the oldest now extant. J. J. Bjornstahl has described this very valuable MS. in a letter subjoined to Fabricy's *Titres Primitifs*, tom. i, and a specimen of the version has been presented to the public by And. Christ. Hwiid, in a small work entitled, *Specimen ineditæ versionis Arabico Samaritanæ Pentateuchi e codice manuscripto Bibliothecæ Barberinæ. Romæ.* MDCCLXXX.

* Basnage, Hist. de l'Eglise, tom. i, liv. ix, cap. iv, p. 471, fol. Brerewood's Enquiries touching the Diversity of Languages, p. 237.

† Marsh's Michaelis, vol. ii, pt. ii, p. 600.

From these it appears that this important MS. was purchased at Damascus, in 1631, for Nicholas Fabricius Peiresc, by whom it was bequeathed to Cardinal Barberini, nephew to Pope Urban VIII. It was transcribed at Damascus in 1227, for the use of the public synagogue of the Samaritans in that city. It is written on parchment, and forms one volume in large folio. Each page is divided into three collateral columns. The Hebræo-Samaritan occupies the column on the right, the Arabic version is in the middle, and the Samaritan version on the left. The Arabic version is made from the Hebræo-Samaritan text, to which it exactly corresponds, sentence for sentence, line for line, and, as nearly as possible, word for word. Both the versions, as well as the Hebræo-Samaritan text, are in the Samaritan character. The specimen adduced is the forty-ninth chapter of Genesis.

A translation of the Gospel of St. John into Anglo-Saxon was made also in the eighth century, by the Venerable Bede.

Beda, or Bede, the great ornament of his age and country, was born in 673. At the close of his "Ecclesiastical History," he gives the following simple, unaffected narrative of his life :—"Born in the territory of the same monastery," (of Weremouth, in the kingdom of Northumberland,) "I was, by the care of my relations, committed at seven years of age to the reverend abbot Benedict, (Biscop) in order to be educated; and afterward to Ceolfrid. From that period I have resided constantly in this monastery, and have applied myself wholly to the study of the Holy Scriptures; and in the intervals of the observance of regular discipline, and the daily care of singing in the church, have always found it sweet to be either learning, or teaching, or writing. In the nineteenth year of my life I received the order of deacon, and in my thirtieth that of priest, both by the ministry of the most reverend bishop John," (of Beverly, bishop of Hexham,) "and the command of abbot Ceolfrid. From the time of my receiving the office of priest to the fifty-ninth year of my age, I have been engaged in either briefly noting from the works of the venerable fathers, for the necessities of me and mine, these things* on the Scriptures, or in adding some new comment to their sense and interpretation."

It has been justly remarked, that "he never knew what it was to do nothing. He wrote on all the branches of knowledge then cultivated in Europe. In Greek and Hebrew he had a skill very uncommon in that barbarous age; and by his instructions and example he raised up many scholars." A year before his death

* Alluding to the catalogue of writings which he subjoined to this narrative.

he wrote a letter to Ecgbright, or Egbert, archbishop of York, which deserves to be noticed for the solid sense it exhibits, and the information it conveys. The following are extracts from it:—

"Above all things avoid useless discourse, and apply yourselves to the study of the HOLY SCRIPTURES, especially the Epistles to Timothy and Titus; to Gregory's Pastoral Care, and his Homilies on the Gospel. It is indecent for him who is dedicated to the service of the church to give way to actions or discourse unsuitable to his character. Have always those about you who may assist you in temptation; be not like some bishops, who love to have those about them that love good cheer, and divert them with trifling and facetious conversation."

"Your diocess is too large to allow you to go through the whole in a year; therefore appoint presbyters in each village, to instruct and administer the sacraments; and let them be studious, that every one of them may learn by heart *the Creed and the Lord's Prayer;* and that, if they do not understand Latin, they may repeat them in their own tongue. *I have translated them into English* for the benefit of ignorant presbyters. I am told there are many villages in our nation, in the mountainous parts, the inhabitants of which have never seen a bishop or a pastor, and yet they are obliged to pay their dues to the bishop."*

The high opinion which Bede entertained of a faithful minister of the gospel, is discoverable in his Life of St. Cuthbert, written in hexameter verse; it begins thus:—

"Multa suis Dominus fulgescere lumina seclis
Donavit, tetricas humanæ noctis ut umbras
Lustraret divina poli de culmine flamma,
Et licet ipse Deo natus de lumine Christus
Lux sit summa, Deus sanctos quoque jure lucernæ
Ecclesiæ rutilare dedit, quibus igne magistro
Sensibus instet amor, sermonibus æstuat ardor
Multifidos varium lychnos qui sparsit in orbem
Ut cunctum nova lux fidei face fusa sub axem
Omnia sidereis virtutibus arva repleret."

"That many lights should shine in every age,
T' illume the loathsome shades of human night
With his celestial flame, the Lord permits:
And though our light supreme is Christ divine,
Yet God has sent his saints with humbler rays
To burn within his church. With sacred fire,

* Milner's Hist. of the Church of Christ, vol. iii, pp. 134, 139.

1

Love fills their minds, and zeal inflames their speech.
He spreads his numerous torches through the world,
That the new rays of burning faith diffused
With starry virtues, every land may fill."*

Bede died in the year 735, and the circumstances of his death are thus described by his pupil Cuthbert, afterward abbot of Jarrow:—

"About two weeks before Easter he began to be much troubled with shortness of breath, yet without pain: and thus continued, cheerful and rejoicing, giving thanks to Almighty God day and night, nay, even every hour, till the day of our Lord's ascension. He daily read lessons to us his scholars; the rest of the day he spent in singing psalms. The nights he passed without sleep, yet rejoicing and giving thanks, unless when a little slumber intervened. When he awoke he resumed his accustomed devotions, and, with expanded hands, never ceased returning thanks to God. Indeed, I never saw with my eyes, nor heard with my ears, any one so diligent in his grateful devotions. O truly blessed man! He sang that sentence of St. Paul, 'It is a fearful thing to fall into the hands of the living God;' and many other things from the Scripture, in which he admonished us to arouse ourselves from the sleep of the mind. He also recited something in our English language, for he was very learned in our songs; and putting his thoughts into English verse, he repeated it with much feeling. For this necessary journey no one can be more prudent than he ought to be, to think before his going hence what of good or evil his spirit after death will be judged worthy of. He also sang anthems, according to his and our custom, one of which is, 'O glorious King, Lord of hosts, who triumphing this day, didst ascend above all the heavens, leave us not orphans, but send the promise of the Father, the Spirit of truth upon us. Alleluia.' When he came to the words *leave us not*, he burst into tears, and wept much. By turns we read, and by turns we wept; indeed, we always read in tears. In such solemn joy we passed the fifty days. But during these days, besides the daily lessons which he gave, and the singing of psalms, he endeavoured to compose two works. The one was a translation of St. John's Gospel into English, as far as where it is said, 'But what are these among so many;' the other some collection out of St. Isidore's book of Notes. On Tuesday before ascension day his breathing began to be very strongly affected,

* Turner's Hist. of the Anglo-Saxons, vol. ii, b. xii, c. iii, p. 347.

and a little swelling appeared in his feet. All that day he dictated cheerfully, and sometimes said, 'Make haste, I know not how long I shall hold out; my Maker may take me away very soon.' It seemed to us he knew well he was near his end. He passed the night awake in thanksgiving. On Wednesday morning he ordered us to write speedily what we had begun. This being done, we walked till the third hour, with the relics of the saints, as the custom of the day required. Then one of us said to him, 'Most dear master, there is yet one chapter wanting. Do you think it troublesome to be asked any more questions?' He answered, 'It is no trouble, take your pen and write fast:' he did so. But at the ninth hour he said to me, 'I have some valuables in my little chest. Run quickly, and bring all the priests of the monastery to me.' When they came, he distributed his small presents to them, and exhorted each of them to attend to their masses and prayers. They all wept when he told them they would see him no more; but rejoiced to hear him say, 'It is now time for me to return to Him who made me. The time of my dissolution draws near. I desire to be dissolved, and to be with Christ. Yes, my soul desires to see Christ, my King, in his beauty.' In this manner he continued to converse cheerfully till the evening, when the pupil mentioned before said to him, 'Dear master, one sentence is still wanting.' He replied, 'Write quickly.' The young man said, 'It is finished.' He answered, 'Thou hast well said, all is now finished. Hold my head with thy hands, for I shall delight to sit at the opposite side of the room, on the holy spot at which I have been accustomed to pray, and where, while sitting, I can invoke my Father.' When he was placed on the pavement of his little place, he sang, 'Glory be to the Father, and to the Son, and to the Holy Ghost,' and expired as he uttered the last words."* Such was the happy, the glorious conclusion of life to this first of scholars! "He was called the *wise Saxon* by his contemporaries," says Dr. Henry, "and *venerable Beda* by posterity; and as long as great modesty, piety, and learning, united in one character, are the objects of veneration among mankind, the memory of Beda must be revered."†

The study, or oratory, of this illustrious presbyter, which appears to have been in a building erected for the purpose, and detached

* Cuthberti Epist. in Bed. Hist. a Smith, pp. 793, 794. Butler's Lives of the Saints, vol. v, May 27.

† Henry's Hist. of Great Britain, vol. iv, p. 30.

from the monastery, was long preserved from destruction. Simeon, the historical monk of Durham, who flourished in 1164, and Leland, who lived in the sixteenth century, both speak of it as remaining in their time. "Even the place," says Simeon, "is shown at this day where he had his little mansion of stone, and, free from all disturbance, was accustomed to sit, to meditate, to read, to dictate, and to write." And Leland remarks, "The oratory of Bede is still remaining entire, a building low in its pitch, small in its size, and vaulted in its roof; having an altar within it, but neglected, yet bearing in the middle of its front a piece of serpentine marble, a marble of a dusky green in the ground, and of a lively green in the spots, inlaid into the substance of it." This, therefore, was the altar at which Bede, equally devout and learned, happily sensible, amid all his learning, that he derived his intellect, and the illumination of it, from the awful "Father of lights," kneeled down at his private devotions; and to which he was carried in his dying moments, and where, resting upon a rug, he prayed, and died in the act of prayer. The very chair, too, a rude oaken one, in which he used to sit, is still kept, carefully locked up in the vestry of the old monastic chapel, converted into a parish church, but recently rebuilt.* A copy of some of St. Paul's Epistles, in the hand-writing of Bede, is also said to be preserved in the library of Trinity College, Cambridge.†

Several other eminent men, chiefly Englishmen, distinguished for their zeal and love of the Scriptures, flourished about the same period as Bede.

Willibrord, the apostle of Friesland, was born in the kingdom of Northumberland about the year 658. When he was about thirty-three years of age, he, and eleven of his countrymen, crossed over the sea into Holland, and laboured among the Frieslanders with extraordinary success, till driven from the country by the violent persecutions raised against them by the idolatrous sovereign Radbod. They then passed into Denmark, and preached the gospel there during the life of Radbod; but at his decease returned into Friesland, where Willibrord was ordained bishop of Wiltenburgh, now Utrecht, by the Roman prelate. During the rest of his life he was indefatigable in his exertions for the conversion of the idolaters around him, and for the general spread of divine truth. With this design he erected schools at Utrecht, which afterward became famous; and an abbey at Epternach, near

* Whitaker's Cathedral of Cornwall, vol. ii, ch. vii, pp. 338–340.

† Hickesii Thesaurus, vol. ii, p. 241.

Treves, in the duchy of Luxemburgh, then a dreary waste, for the purpose of educating missionaries. He died, in the eighty-first year of his age, about A. D. 738. Alcuin says, "He was of a becoming stature, venerable in his aspect, comely in his person, graceful, and always cheerful in his speech and countenance, wise in his counsel, unwearied in preaching and all apostolic functions, amid which he was careful to nourish the interior life of his soul by assiduous prayer, singing of psalms, watching, and fasting."*

At Epternach were kept, a few years ago, two MSS. in Saxon letters, supposed to have been brought from England by Willibrord. The one a copy of the four Gospels, which in the colophon is said to be corrected from the original text of St. Jerome: "Prœmendavi ut potui secundum codicem de bibliotheca Eugipi præspiteri, quem ferunt fuisse S. Hieronymi, indictione vi, post consulatum Basilii v̄c̄. anno septimo decimo." The other, St. Jerome's Martyrology, which the Bollandists have caused to be engraved in their collection of the Lives of the Saints. In the margin of this calendar is written, in Willibrord's hand: "Clement Willibrord came from beyond the sea into France in 690; though unworthy, was ordained by the apostolic man, Pope Sergius, in 695; is now living in 728," &c. Another valuable MS., but probably of the *tenth* century, was also preserved in the same monastery. It is a copy of the four Gospels, written upon exquisitely beautiful vellum, in letters of gold. The life of Jesus is represented in miniature paintings. In the crucifixion he is clothed in raiment of a *violet* colour, and nailed to the cross with four nails: the thieves also appear clothed. The emperor Otho, and the queen Theophanu, are represented on the cover; from which it is conjectured to have been given to the monastery by that emperor.†

Winfrid, afterward called Boniface, was another of the distinguished characters of this age. He was an Englishman, born at Kirton, in Devonshire, about the year 680. From thirteen years of age he was educated in the monastery of Escancester, or Exeter, under the abbot Wolphard. After he had spent some years there, he removed to the monastery of Nutcell, in the diocess of Winchester, where he continued his studies under the learned abbot Winbert. Here he made unusual progress in poesy, rhetoric, history, and the knowledge of the Scriptures; and was afterward appointed by his abbot to teach the same sciences: of which duty

* Butler's Lives, vol. ii, pp. 152–161.

† Voyage Litteraire de deux Religieux Benedictins, tom. ii, pp. 197, 198. Paris, 1717, 4to.

he acquitted himself with great profit to others, at the same time improving himself with that redoubled advantage which maturity of years and judgment, and a diligent review of a well-digested course of former studies, give to masters of an elevated genius. At the age of thirty he was ordained priest, on the recommendation of his abbot, and laboured with much zeal in preaching the word of God. His spirit was ardent, and he longed to be employed as a missionary in the conversion of pagans. With this design, he, with two other monks, went over into Friesland about the year 716; but finding that circumstances rendered it impracticable, at that time, to preach the gospel in those parts, he returned into England, with his companions, to his monastery.

On the death of the abbot of Nutcell, the society would have elected Winfrid in his stead, but he firmly refused to accept the presidency; and having obtained recommendatory letters from the bishop of Winchester, proceeded to Rome, where he obtained from Pope Gregory II. a most ample and unlimited commission to endeavour the conversion of infidels.

With this commission Winfrid went into Bavaria and Thuringia. In the first country he reformed the churches; in the second he was successful in the conversion of infidels. He afterward co-operated for three years with Willibrord, in Friesland. Willibrord declining through age, chose Winfrid for his successor; an offer which he declined, because the pope had enjoined him to preach in the eastern parts of Germany, and he felt himself bound to fulfil the injunction. He accordingly laboured to spread the gospel through various parts of Germany, particularly Hesse, and succeeded in erecting the standard of truth even to the confines of Saxony; supporting himself at times by the labour of his hands, and repeatedly being exposed to imminent danger from the fury of the obstinate pagans.

In 732 he received the title of archbishop from Gregory III., who supported his mission with the same spirit as his predecessor Gregory II. The increase of his dignity did not, however, lessen his zeal; he still continued his pastoral care over the many churches he had founded, held various councils with his clergy, promoted several monastic institutions, and extended the gospel to different barbarous and uncivilized nations. In 746 he laid the foundation of the great abbey of Fuld, or Fulden, which continued long the most renowned seminary of piety and learning in all that part of the world. His principal residence he fixed at Mentz, from which he has usually been called the archbishop of that city.

His care for the churches, and his earnestness in the service of God, increased with his years, so that in 755, though oppressed with age and infirmities, and universally revered by the Christian world, he determined to return to Friesland. He therefore appointed Lullus, an Englishman, his successor as archbishop of Mentz; and wrote to the abbot of St. Denys, to request the king of France to be kind to him, and the other missionaries, who were struggling with indigence and difficulties. Having settled the affairs of his church, he went by the Rhine into Friesland, where, assisted by Eoban, whom he had ordained bishop of Utrecht after the death of Willibrord, he brought great numbers of the pagans into the pale of the church. Having appointed the eve of Whit-sunday to confirm those whom he had baptized, he pitched a tent on the banks of the Bordne, a river which then divided East and West Friesland, and was waiting, in prayer, the arrival of the new converts, when, instead of the friends he expected, a band of enraged pagans, armed with shields and lances, rushed furiously upon them, and slew Boniface and all his company, fifty-two in number. He died exhorting his followers not to fight, but to meet with constancy and cheerfulness a death which would be to them the gate of light. This was in the seventy-fifth year of his age. The barbarians, instead of the valuable booty of gold and silver which they had expected, found nothing of any value, but *books*, which they scattered about the fields and marshes. *Three* of these were afterward recovered, and kept in the monastery of Fuld, or Fulden; a Book of the Gospels, written in Boniface's own hand; a Harmony, or Canons of the New Testament; and a book, containing the letter of St. Leo to Theodorus, bishop of Frejus; and the discourse of St. Ambrose, "On the Holy Ghost," with his treatise, *De bono Mortis*, or, "On the Advantage of Death."*

A collection of Boniface's letters has been preserved and published. The following extracts from them will discover his love to the Scriptures, and his desire to promote an acquaintance with them in others. His epistle to the abbess Eadburga has been already mentioned. To Nithardus he writes, "Nothing can you search after more honourably in youth, or enjoy more comfortably in old age, than the knowledge of Holy Scripture." To Daniel, bishop of Winchester, he addresses a request, to send him the Book of the Prophets, "which," says he, "the abbot Winbert, formerly my master, left at his death, written in very distinct

* Milner's History of the Church of Christ, vol. iii, ch. iv, pp. 172–182. Butler's Lives, vol. vi, June 5.

characters. A greater consolation in my old age I cannot receive; for I can find no book like it in this country; and as my sight grows weak, I cannot easily distinguish the small letters, which are joined close together in the sacred volumes which are at present in my possession." In other letters also he begs for books, especially those of Bede, whom he styles the "Lamp of the Church."* Boniface's letters are all written in Latin; but, as Verstegan justly observes, the language of the English Saxons, and that of the inhabitants of most parts of Germany, were so nearly the same, that, in their preaching and general intercourse, he and his companions seem to have had no need of interpreters.†

Another celebrated missionary, in this "age of missions," was WILLEHAD, or VILLEHAD, usually called the apostle of Saxony. He was an Englishman, born in Northumberland, and educated in learning and piety. Crossing over the sea to the continent, he commenced his mission in Dockum, where Boniface was murdered, about the year 772. From Dockum, he made his way through the country now called Over-Yssel, and from thence to Trentonia, or Drentia, from whence he proceeded into Wigmore, where Bremen now stands, and was the first missionary who passed the Elbe. After labouring thirty-five years in his missions, he died at a village called Bleckensee, now Plexam, in Friesland, having been bishop of Bremen two years. Holy reading and meditation were his favourite exercises; and he usually recited the whole Psalter every day, and frequently two or three times a day. His attention and love to the Scriptures were discoverable in his copying, with his own hand, the Epistles of St. Paul, besides other books. His cathedral at Bremen he built of wood: his successor, Willoric, afterward rebuilt it of stone.‡ This mode of erecting churches was practised in other places where architecture was at a low ebb. Sulpicius Severus tells us, "that in the deserts of Libya, near Cyrene, he went with a priest with whom he lodged into a church which was made of small rods or twigs interwoven one with another, and not much more stately and ambitious than the priest's own house, in which a man could hardly stand upright. But the men who frequented these churches were men of the golden age and the purest morals." (S. Sulpic. Sev. *Dial.* 1, ch. ii.) Bede also informs us, that anciently there was not a stone

* Milner, *ut sup.*

† Verstegan's Restitution of Decayed Intelligence, p. 147, 4to.

‡ Milner's Hist. of the Church of Christ, vol. iii, pp. 187, 188. Butler's Lives, vol. ii, Nov. 8.

church in all this island, but that the custom was to build them all of wood; so that when Bishop Ninyas built one of stone, it was such an unusual thing, that the place was called from it *Candida Casa*, Whithern, or Whitchurch. (Hist. Eccles., lib. iii, cap. iv.) The church erected on the place where St. Edmund was martyred at Bedricksworth, or Kingston, since called St. Edmundsbury, was built after the same manner. Trunks of large trees were sawn lengthways in the middle, and reared up with one end fixed in the ground, with the bark or rough side outermost. These trunks being made of an equal height, and set up close to one another, and the interstices filled up with mud, formed the four walls, upon which was raised a thatched roof. Of the low rough manner of building in use among our ancestors, we have, or lately had, an example still standing, in part of Greensted church, near Ongar, in Essex. In this church, the most ancient part, the nave or body, was entirely composed of the trunks of large oaks split, and rough hewed on both sides. They were set upright and close to each other, being let into a sill at the bottom, and a plate at the top, where they were fastened with wooden pins. "This," says Ducarel, "was the whole of the original church, which yet remains entire, though much corroded and worn by length of time. It is twenty-nine feet nine inches long, and five feet six inches high, on the sides, which supported the primitive roof." But perhaps nothing more satisfactorily proves the general practice of building with wood than the Anglo-Saxon verb commonly used when buildings are spoken of being erected. It is *getymbrian*, "to make of wood." Where Bede says of any one that he built a monastery or a church, Alfred, in his translation of Bede's Ecclesiastical History, uses the word *getimbrade*.*

But to return from this digression.—ALCUIN, called also FLACCUS ALBINUS, another learned Englishman of this age, was so eminent for learning and science, that Charlemagne selected him for his literary friend and preceptor. The place of his birth has been disputed, but he says of himself, that he was nourished and educated at York, where he learned Latin and Greek, with the elements of the Hebrew language, and went through the sacred studies under Egbert, and Elbert, who taught a great school in that city, till they were successively placed in the archiepiscopal chair. When Elbert succeeded Egbert in that dignity, in 766, he committed to Alcuin the care of the school, and of the library be-

* Butler's Lives, vol. ii, pp. 336, 339. Turner's Hist. of the Anglo-Saxons, vol. ii, p. 412. Ducarel's Anglo-Norman Antiquities, p. 100.

longing to that church. Eadbald succeeding his uncle Elbert as archbishop, in 780, sent Alcuin to Rome to bring over his pall. On his return, Charlemagne met him at Pavia, and was so struck with the wisdom of his discourse, that he earnestly requested him to fix his residence at his court, as soon as he had accomplished his mission. To an invitation so flattering, Alcuin gave his consent, provided he could obtain the permission of his king and archbishop, and might be allowed to revisit his country. The requisite permission being granted, he returned to France, where he devoted himself to the instruction of his royal pupil, and the general interests of religion, literature, and science; and such were his indefatigable exertions for the encouragement and dissemination of learning, that they were not only successful in France, but greatly contributed to the general promotion of it throughout Europe.

From the numerous possessions and jurisdictions which Alcuin enjoyed, Elipand, a bishop of Spain, in a theological dispute with him, took the opportunity to reproach him severely for his riches, and the number of his vassals or slaves. "Elipand," says he, in a letter to the bishop of Lyons, "objects to me, my riches, servants and vassals, which amount to the number of twenty thousand, not reflecting that the possession of riches is vicious only from the attachment of the heart. It is one thing to possess the world, and another to be possessed by the world. Some possess riches, though perfectly disengaged from them in their hearts: others though they enjoy none, yet love and covet them." And it is but justice to the character of this great man, to remark, that these vassals belonged to the several abbeys of which the king had compelled him to undertake the administration, that he might establish regular discipline in them, and employ the surplus of the revenue in alms, agreeably to the intention of such foundations. Charlemagne had also made him his general almoner, and appointed him a house for the reception of strangers. It will nevertheless serve to mark the manners of the age, to remember, that the vassals or slaves belonging to the different abbeys "were obliged to go with their carts fifty miles or upward, whenever their abbot commanded, and were not permitted to marry, or change their abode, without first receiving his express consent; that they were compelled to cultivate the land three days in the week, while their master solely enjoyed the fruits of their industry; and that in several instances the abbots exercised the jurisdiction of life and death over them."

So far was the mind of the pious Alcuin from being corrupted by his prosperity, that he frequently entreated the king to permit him to resign those gifts, which he had only accepted upon the pressing solicitation of the sovereign.

After repeated and sincere solicitations on the part of Alcuin, and frequent refusals from Charlemagne, he was permitted to retire to the abbey of St. Martin at Tours, as a private monk. In this retirement, all his studies were bent toward theology; and it has even been affirmed, that notwithstanding his early attachment to the classic writers, in his advanced age he found fault with Ricabode, archbishop of Treves, for poring over the Æneid, instead of fixing his thoughts entirely upon the four Evangelists. Some of the last years of his life he employed in a work of great importance, the *revision of the Latin Bible.* From the carelessness of transcribers, the copies of the Scriptures, in general use, were become exceedingly incorrect; Alcuin, therefore, at the instance of Charlemagne, undertook to revise the Vulgate version of the Old and New Testament, and bring it as near as possible to its original purity. For this purpose he examined and collated a number of valuable MSS., and with indefatigable industry completed his laborious work so much to the satisfaction of his august patron, that it became the authorized edition read in the churches. Some copies of this revision are extant, particularly *two*, one preserved in the library of the fathers of the oratory, at Rome, and the other in that of the monastery of St. Paul without the walls. After enjoying imperial confidence and affection in a degree seldom experienced, he breathed his last in the abbey of St. Martin, at Tours, on the 19th of May, 804. His works were published by Frobenius, in 1777, in four volumes, 4to.*

Unfortunately, the invaluable labours of these and other pious and learned men proved insufficient to dispel the thick darkness which overspread the Western world at this period, extending its influence over both clergy and laity, and producing a correspondent laxity of morals and barbarism of manners. Alcuin, in a letter to Offa, king of Mercia, says, "I was ready to return into my native country of Northumberland, loaded with presents by Charlemagne; but, upon the intelligence I have received, I think it better to remain where I am than venture myself in a country where no man can enjoy security, or prosecute his studies. For, lo! their churches are demolished by the pagans, their altars polluted with

* Card's Reign of Charlemagne, ch. iv. Lond. 1807, 8vo. Turner's Hist. of the Anglo-Saxons, vol. ii, pp. 355, 374. Butler's Lives, vol. v, pp. 115–117. Fabricy, Titres Primitifs, tom. ii, pp. 99, 133.

impiety, their monasteries defiled with adulteries, and the land wet with the blood of its nobles and princes."* So great was the ignorance of the clergy in this and several of the succeeding centuries, that instructions were given by the pope to the bishops, to make inquiries through the parishes of their respective districts, whether the officiating clergy could read the Gospels and Epistles correctly, and give a literal interpretation of them. Gislemar, an archbishop of Rheims, being called upon before his consecration to read a portion of the Gospels, was found so shamefully ignorant as not to understand the literal meaning of the passage.† In Germany, a certain priest was so totally unacquainted with the Latin, the common language of the church offices, that he baptized in the name *Patri, Filia, et Spiritus Sancta;* and a question arising as to the legitimacy of the baptism, it was judged proper to refer it to Pope Zachary for his decision.‡ This was the same pope who imprisoned Virgilius for asserting the existence of the antipodes; though Butler, in his "Lives of the Saints," vol. iii, p. 173, endeavours to prove that the error of Virgilius was that of maintaining that there were other men under the earth, another sun and moon, and another world; or, in other words, another race of men, who did not descend from Adam, and were not redeemed by Christ; and that this being contrary to the Scriptures, he was justly censurable. But whether he taught the spherical form of the earth, or the plurality of worlds, his condemnation is sufficient to prove the low state of scientific acquirements, by even the highest dignitaries of the church.

In France, the martial spirit which prevailed during the government of Charles Martel, the grandfather of Charlemagne, extended its influence to the church. "In order to acquire consideration in the eyes of their martial prince, and to give a decisive check to future grants of their estates to laymen, the bishops and abbots embraced the singular resolution of following him to battle, in the character of soldiers: so that it became no uncommon spectacle to behold dignified ecclesiastics, at the head of their vassals, vie with laymen in feats of military skill and valour; while swords adorned with precious stones, fastened to costly belts, and golden spurs, alike characterized the dress of both." Charlemagne, in common with the whole nation, felt the indecency and disgrace of a warlike clergy; and an edict was issued, which ordained that

* Henry's Hist. of Great Britain, vol. iv, p. 45.

† Enfield's Hist. of Philosophy, vol. ii, b. ii, ch. ii, p. 344. London. 8vo.

‡ Lomeier, De Bibliothecis, p. 153.

priests should not attend the army, except for the purpose of saying mass, and administering spiritual consolation to the troops. He likewise forbade them the use of arms, to hunt, or to keep falcons; but declared that by these prohibitions he did not intend to diminish the dignity or property of the bishops; but, on the contrary, their wealth and honours should be increased in proportion to the amendment of their lives, and their devoted attachment to their holy calling.* These wise regulations checked, for a while, the military and secular appearance and conduct of the priesthood; but the clergy gradually reassumed the laical character, so that Du Cange informs us, the deans of many cathedrals in France entered on their dignities habited in a surplice, girt with a sword, in boots and gilt spurs, and a hawk on the fist. Carpentier adds, that the treasurers of some churches, particularly that of Nivernois, claimed the privilege of assisting at mass, or whatever festival they pleased, without the canonical vestments, and carrying a hawk. And the lord of Sassay held some of his lands by placing a hawk on the high altar of the church of Evreux, while his parish priest celebrated the service, booted and spurred, to the beat of the drum instead of the organ. We even find them sometimes conferring the titles of secular nobility on the apostles and saints; thus St. James was actually created a *baron* at Paris; and among the many contradictions of this kind which entered into the system of the middle ages, may be reckoned the institution, in 1181, of the *Knights Templars*. This was an establishment of armed monks, who made a vow of living, at the same time, both as anchorets and soldiers.† Their professed object was to defend the holy places and pilgrims from the insults of the Saracens; and to keep the passes free for such as undertook the voyage to the Holy Land. They were suppressed by the council of Vienne, in 1312.

The different canons promulgated by various councils and synods in this age prove but too fully the dissolute manners of both clergy and laity: several of these relate to crimes too abominable to be mentioned; the reader, therefore, who wishes to pursue the subject, may consult Wilkins' *Leges Anglo-Saxonica*, the canons of the different councils, and the capitulars of Charlemagne. Some that refer to less atrocious actions shall be noticed. In the canons or *Excerptions* of Ecgbright, or Egbert, framed in 740, the following is the 14th: "That none who is numbered among the priests

* Card's Reign of Charlemagne, pp. 92–97.

† Warton's Hist. of English Poetry, vol. ii, p. 345, *note*. Du Cange, Gloss. Lat. v. *Decanus*.

cherish the vice of drunkenness, nor force others to be drunk by his importunity."* The 19th enjoins, "That no priest swear an oath, but speak all things simply, purely, truly." The 70th decrees, "That an abbot or monk may not give freedom to a slave of the monastery: for it is impious that he should damage the church who hath given nothing to it." The 147th is, "That no Christian observe pagan superstitions, but express all manner of contempt toward all the defilements of the Gentiles." The 154th says, "A clerk ought not to bear arms, nor go into the wars, but rather trust in the divine defence than in arms." In Cuthbert's canons, made at Cloves-hoo, in 747, it is enacted by the 20th decree, "That bishops, by a vigilant inspection in their parishes, take care that monasteries, as their name imports, be honest retreats for the silent and quiet, and such as labour for God's sake; not receptacles of ludicrous arts, of versifiers, harpers, and buffoons; but houses for them who pray, and read, and praise God." And that "nunneries be not places of secret rendezvous for filthy talk, junketing, drunkenness, and luxury, but habitations for such as live in continence and sobriety, and who read and sing psalms; but let them spend their time in reading books and singing psalms, rather than in weaving and working party-coloured, vain-glorious apparel." By the Legantine canons of the council of Cealchythe, A. D. 785, can. 16th, the children of nuns are declared "spurious and illegitimate;" and in the 19th canon several superstitious and singular practices of our ancestors are noticed; I shall therefore transcribe the whole of it. It is there enjoined, "That every Christian take example by catholic men; and if any pagan rite remain, let it be plucked up, despised, and rejected; for God created man comely and sightly, but pagans, by the instinct of the devil, sacrifice themselves, as Prudentius says,

Tinxit et innocuum maculis sordentibus humor.

"He seems to do an injury to the Lord, who defiles and depraves his workmanship. If any one should undergo this blood-letting for the sake of God, he would on that account receive great reward; but whoever does it out of heathenish superstition, does no more advance his salvation thereby, than the Jews do by bodily circumcision, without sincere faith."

* Archbishop Boniface observes, in his Epistles, (Epist. Bonifacii, Wilkins, 1, 93,) "that drunkenness was so common in his time, that even the bishops, instead of preventing, were themselves partakers in it: and not content with this, compelled others to drink from large cups till they also became inebriated." (Sharpe's William of Malmsbury's History, &c., b. i, ch. viii, p. 171, *note*.)

"Ye wear garments like those of the Gentiles, whom your fathers, by the help of God, drove out of the world by arms. A wonderful stupid thing! to imitate the example of them whose manners ye hate."

"Ye also, by a filthy custom, maim your horses, ye slit their nostrils, fasten their ears together, make them deaf, cut off their tails, and render yourselves hateful in not keeping them sound when ye may."

"We have heard, also, that when you have any controversy between yourselves, ye use sorcery, after the manner of the Gentiles, which is accounted sacrilege in these times."

"Many of you eat horse-flesh, which is done by none of the Eastern Christians: take heed of this too. Endeavour that all your doings be honest, and done in the Lord."*

Other attempts were made to prevent these unchristian practices, by injunctions to the clergy, with respect to reading the Scriptures to the people, and instructing them in their duty. Thus in the "Excerptions" of Ecgbright, it is ordained, can. 3, "That on all festivals and Lord's days, every priest preach Christ's *gospel* to the people;" and, can. 6, "That every priest do with great exactness instil the *Lord's Prayer* and *Creed* into the people committed to him, and show them to endeavour after the knowledge of the whole religion, and the practice of Christianity." By Cuthbert's canons it was enacted, can. 3, "That every bishop do every year visit his parish; and call to him, at convenient places, the people of every condition and sex, and plainly teach them who rarely hear the word of God:" it was also decreed, can. 7, "That bishops, abbots, and abbesses, do by all means take care, and diligently provide that their families incessantly apply their minds to reading: for," adds the canon, "it is sad to say how few, nowadays, do heartily love and labour for sacred knowledge, and are willing to take any pains in learning; but they are, from their youth up, rather employed in divers vanities, and the affectation of vain glory; and they rather pursue the amusements of this present unstable life, than the assiduous study of the Holy Scriptures. Therefore let the boys be confined and trained up in the schools to the law of sacred knowledge, that being by this means well learned, they may become in all respects useful to the church of God: and let not the rectors† be so greedy of the worldly labour [of the boys] as to

* Johnson's Collection of Eccl. Laws, Canons, &c., vol. i, An. 740, &c.

† "*Rectors* were the heads of religious houses, and *incumbents,* as we now speak in lesser churches, who had their schools for training up young monks and clerks, and

render the house of God vile for want of spiritual adornment." In the tenth decree of the same council they further taught, "That priests should learn to know how to perform, according to the lawful rites, every office belonging to their orders; and then let them who know it not learn to construe, and explain in our own tongue, the *Creed* and *Lord's Prayer*, and the sacred words which are solemnly pronounced at the celebration of mass, and in the office of baptism." By can. 14 it was ordained, "That the Lord's day be celebrated by all, with due veneration, and wholly separated for divine service. And let all abbots and priests instruct the servants subject to them from the oracles of the Holy Scripture." It was also decreed, "That on that day, and on the great festivals, the priests of God do often invite the people to meet in the church, to hear the word of God, and to be often present at sacraments of the mass, and at preaching of sermons." One of the canons of the same council, relating to the practice of psalmody, so much in use in the early and middle ages, offers so curious an argument in favour of singing in an unknown tongue, that it deserves to be transcribed. "Psalmody," say they, "is a divine work, a great cure, in many cases, for the souls of those who do it *in spirit* and in mind. But they that sing with the voice, without the inward meaning, may make the sound resemble something; therefore, though a man *knows not the Latin words that are sung*, yet he may devoutly apply the intention of his own heart to the things which are at present to be asked of God, and fix them there to the best of his power."*

A passage in Bede's Ecclesiastical History has led some writers to suppose that during this century some portions, at least, of the Scriptures were translated into the vernacular tongues of the different nations who inhabited Britain at this period. The words of Bede (lib. i, cap. i) are: "Hæc in præsenti juxta numerum librorum, quibus lex divina scripta est, quinque gentium linguis unam eandemque summæ veritatis et veræ sublimitatis scientiam scrutatur et confitetur, Anglorum videlicet, Britonum, Scotorum, Pictorum, et Latinorum quæ meditatione scripturarum cæteris omnibus est facta communis." "This island searches and confesses one and the same knowledge of the highest truth, and of the true sublimity, according to the number of books in which the divine law is written, in the language of five nations, viz., of the English, the

who obliged their scholars to bodily labour: therefore they were not here forbidden absolutely to labour, but only so far as was inconsistent with their learning."

* Johnson's Ecclesiastical Laws, *ubi sup.*

Britons, the Scots, the Picts, and the Latins, which last has become common to all the rest, by the meditation of the Scriptures." It must be acknowledged, however, that if any parts of the sacred writings were then translated into these different tongues, they were soon lost or destroyed, or neglected for the more common Latin versions, since we hear nothing of several of these translations from any contemporary or succeeding writer. Be this as it may, it is certain that it was customary to copy Latin and Greek works, in Saxon characters, for the convenience of Saxon or English readers, or learners. A MS. of the four Gospels, with prefaces and the Canons of Eusebius, written in Saxon characters in this century, is among the Royal Collection of MSS. in the British Museum:* and Astle, in his "Origin and Progress of Writing," has given fac-similes of others. A Psalter which had belonged to Aldhelm, written after the same manner, was kept at Malmsbury till after the Reformation.† In the Cotton library there is a MS. [Galba, A. 18] with the Lord's prayer in the Greek language, written in Saxon characters. "It is probably," says Mr. Turner, (Hist. of Anglo-Saxons, vol. ii, p. 361,) "a correct example of the pronunciation of Greek, as introduced into England by Adrian and Theodore, in the seventh century; but it certainly shows, in the division of the words, how little the writer understood of the language. I will transcribe it, placing the original by its side.

Pater imon oynys	*Πατερ ἡμῶν ὁ εν τοις*
uranis agiastituto onomansu-	*οὐρανοῖς ἁγιασθήτω το ὄνομα σου.*
elthetu ebasilias genithito	*Ελθετω ἡ βασιλεια σου γενεθητω*
to theli mansu. os senu	*το θελημα σου, ὡς εν*
uranu Keptasgis	*οὐρανῳ, και επι της γης.*
tonartonimon. tonepiussion.	*Τον αρτον ἡμων, τον επιουσιον,*
dos simin simero Keaffi	*δος ἡμιν σημερον. Και αφες*
simin. to offilemata imon	*ἡμιν τα οφειλειματα ἡμων,*
oskeimis affiomen. tus	*ὡς και ἡμεις αφιεμεν τοις*
ophiletas imon Kemies	*οφειλεταις ἡμων. Και μη εις-*
ininkis imas. isperas	*ενεγκῃς ἡμας εις πειρασ-*
mon. ala ryse imas	*μον αλλα ρυσαι ἡμας*
aptou poniru.	*απο του πονηρου.*

The character which I express by the K, seems placed for Καὶ."‡

Such instances as these must be considered as rare proofs of attachment to literature, when transcriptions were expensive, and

* Classical Journal, No. xv, p. 150.

† Whitaker's Cathedral of Cornwall, vol. ii, p. 326, *note*.

‡ Turner's Hist. of the Anglo-Saxons, *ut sup.*

the most noted libraries composed of few books. Alcuin has left us the following poetical catalogue of the authors in the celebrated library of Egbert, archbishop of York; "the oldest catalogue perhaps existing in all the regions of literature, certainly the oldest existing in England:"—

"Illic invenies veterum vestigia Patrum,
Quidquid habet pro se Latio Romanus in orbe,
Græcia vel quidquid transmisit clara Latinis;
Hebraicus vel quod populus bibit imbre superno,
Africa lucifluo vel quidquid lumine sparsit;
Quod pater Hieronymus, quod sensit Hilarius, atque
Ambrosius præsul, simul Augustinus, et ipse
Sanctus Athanasius, quod Orosius edit avitus,
Quidquid Gregorius summus docet, et Leo papa,
Basilius quidquid, Fulgentius atque, coruscant,
Cassiodorus item, Chrysostom atque Johannes;
Quidquid et Athelmus docuit, quid Beda Magister,
Quæ Victorinus scripsêre, Boetius atque;
Historici veteres, Pompeius, Plinius ipse;
Acer Aristoteles, rhetor quoque Tullius ingens;
Quid quoque Sedulius, vel quid canit ipse Juvencus;
Alcuinus, et Clemens, Prosper, Paulinus, Arator,
Quid Fortunatus, vel quid Lactantius edunt;
Quæ Maro Virgilius, Statius, Lucanus, et auctor
Artis Grammaticæ, vel quid scripsêre Magistri;
Quid Probus atque Focas, Donatus, Priscianusve,
Servius, Euticius, Pompeius, Commenianus.
Invenies alios perplures, lector, ibidem
Egregios studiis, arte et sermone magistros,
Plurima qui claro scripsêre volumina sensu:
Nomina sed quorum præsenti in carmine scribi
Longius est visum, quam plectri postulet usus."*

The following *imitation* will convey to the English reader a general idea of the contents of this celebrated library:—

"Here, duly placed on consecrated ground,
The studied works of many an age are found.
The ancient *Fathers'* reverend remains;
The *Roman Laws*, which freed a world from chains;
Whate'er of lore pass'd from immortal *Greece*
To *Latian* lands, and gain'd a rich increase;
All that *blest Israel* drank in showers from heaven;
Or *Afric* sheds, soft as the dew of even:
Jerome, the father 'mong a thousand sons:
And *Hilary*, whose sense profusely runs.

* Alcuinus de Pontificibus, &c., quoted in Henry's Hist. of Great Britain, vol. iv, pp. 33, 34.

Ambrose, who nobly guides both church and state ;
Augustine, good and eminently great ;
And holy *Athanasius*,—sacred name !
All that proclaims *Orosius*' learned fame.
Whate'er the lofty *Gregory* hath taught ;
Or *Leo* Pontiff, good without a fault ;
With all that shines illustrious in the page
Of *Basil* eloquent, *Fulgentius* sage ;
And *Cassiodorus*, with a consul's power,
Yet eager to improve the studious hour.
And *Chrysostom*, whose fame immortal flies,
Whose style, whose sentiment, demand the prize.
All that *Adhelmus* wrote ; and all that flows
From *Beda's* fruitful mind, in verse or prose.
Lo! *Victorinus*, and *Boetius* hold
A place for sage philosophy, of old.
Here sober *History* tells her ancient tale ;
Pompey to charm, and *Pliny*, never fail.
The *Stagyrite* unfolds his searching page ;
And *Tully* flames, the glory of his age.
Here you may listen to *Sedulian* strains ;
And sweet *Juvencus*' lays delight the plains.
Alcuin, *Paulinus*, *Prosper*, sing, or show,
With *Clemens*, and *Arator*, all they know.
What *Fortunatus* and *Lactantius* wrote ;
What *Virgil* pours in many a pleasing note.
Statius, and *Lucan*, and the polish'd sage,
Whose *Art of Grammar* guides a barbarous age.
In fine, whate'er th' immortal masters taught,
In all their rich variety of thought.
And as the names sound from the roll of fame,
Donatus, *Focas*, *Priscian*, *Probus*, claim
An honour'd place ;—and *Servius* joins the band ;
While also move with mien form'd to command
Euticius, *Pompey*, and *Commenian*, wise
In all the lore antiquity supplies.
Here, the pleased reader cannot fail to find
Other famed masters of the arts refined,
Whose numerous works, penn'd in a beauteous style,
Delight the student, and all care beguile ;
Whose names, a lengthen'd and illustrious throng,
I waive at present, and conclude my song.

" D. M'Nicoll."

Celebrated as this library was, it appears to have contained only fourteen fathers and ecclesiastical works, ten ancient classics, including two or three modern Latin writers, six grammarians and scholiasts, and six modern Latin poets ; yet this was the library of which Alcuin speaks in a letter to Charlemagne: " O that I had the use of those admirable books, on all parts of learning, which I enjoyed in my native country; collected by the industry of my beloved master Egbert. May it please your imperial majesty, in your great wisdom, to permit me to send some of our youth to transcribe the most valuable books in that library, and thereby transplant the flowers of Britain into France."*

It was also in the earlier part of this century that King Pepin of France requested some books from the pontiff Paul I. "I have sent to you," replied his holiness, "what books I could find." To such a benefactor as Pepin had been to the apostolic see, the selection, doubtless, was as munificent as good-will and gratitude could make it: and yet the pope could procure for the sovereign of France, and the libraries of Rome could supply, nothing more valuable than an *Antiphonale*, and a *Responsale*, a *Grammatica Aristotelis*, (a work now not known,) *Dionysii Areopagitæ Libros*, *Geometrian*, *Orthographian*, *Grammaticam*, all of which were Greek writers.† Though it is a singular fact, that England was regarded as so excellent a mart for books, that, as early as the year 705, books were brought hither for sale.

But notwithstanding the scarcity of books, and the barbarous ignorance that so generally reigned, care was taken, in many instances, to instruct even children in the knowledge of the Scriptures. Bede (Eccles. Hist., lib. iii, cap. xix) says of Furseus, that from his very childhood he had been well acquainted with the sacred Scriptures; and Boniface (in Vita Livini) relates of Livinus, that he was trained up in his youth by Benignus in the singing of David's psalms and the reading of the holy Gospels, and other divine exercises. The same is likewise noticed of Kilianus and others; and of the virgin Bitihildis it is related, that when lying upon her death-bed, she requested for several nights successively, that a light might be burned, and the Holy Scriptures be read to her.‡

* Henry's Hist. of Great Britain, vol. iv, p. 32.

† Berington's Literary History of the Middle Ages, b. ii, p. 124.

‡ Usher's Discourse of the Religion anciently professed by the Irish and British, p. 4. Lond. 1687, 4to.

CHAPTER VII.

NINTH CENTURY.

Charlemagne—Rabanus Maurus—Otfrid's Harmony—Walafrid Strabo—Anselm—Text and Gloss—Catenæ—Commentaries—Methodius and Cyril—Slavonian Version—Alfred the Great—Anglo-Saxon Psalter—Rushworth Gloss.

The close of the eighth and the commencement of the NINTH century, were marked by the military prowess, magnificence, and liberality, and even the inconsistency of the renowned CHARLEMAGNE, emperor of the West, and king of France. A monarch of the most vigorous and comprehensive mind, and the great patron of learning and learned men ; yet so neglected in his education that he could not write, and was forty-five years of age when he began to study the sciences under Alcuin. Though grossly sensual in his pleasures, he was plain in his dress, and frugal at his table Equally fired by the love of conquest and of science, the Danube, the Teisse, and the Oder, on the east, and the Ebro and the ocean, on the west, became the boundaries of his vast dominions ; and France, Germany, Dalmatia, Istria, Italy, and part of Pannonia and Spain, obeyed his laws. Superior to the prejudices and contempt of learning discovered by the laity of all classes, he assembled scientific and literary men from all parts of Europe, and "established schools in the cathedrals and principal abbeys, for teaching writing, arithmetic, grammar, and church music ; certainly no very elevated sciences, yet considerable at a time when many dignified ecclesiastics could not subscribe the canons of those councils in which they sat as members ; and when it was deemed a sufficient qualification for a priest to be able to read the Gospels and understand the Lord's Prayer."*

Led on by a blind and ambitious zeal for the propagation of Christianity, Charlemagne affixed an indelible stain on his character, by frequently attempting to dragoon the pagan nations whom he conquered into a profession of the gospel. At other times he acted in a spirit more congenial with religion, and laboured to promote among the clergy an attention to learning and

* Russel's Modern Europe, vol. i, pt. ii, let. 9, p. 64, 8vo.

the duties of their office, and to diffuse a knowledge of the Scriptures and morality among the laity. In his admonition to the presbyters, in 804, he charges the priests to acquaint themselves with the Scriptures, to gain right views of the doctrine of the Trinity, to commit the whole of the Psalms and the Baptismal Office to memory, to be ready to teach others, and to fulfil the duties of their station to the utmost of their power.* In 805 he confirmed the practice of reading the Scriptures publicly. "Let the lessons," says he, "be distinctly read in the church."† He also employed Paul Warnefrid, usually called *Paulus Diaconus*, or Paul the deacon, a learned monk, who had held important offices under the Lombard kings, and who was the author of a history of the Lombard nation, to reform the church service, and in particular, ordered him to select from the works of the fathers, homilies, or discourses upon the Epistles and Gospels, worthy to be recited by the faithful in the churches of God. In this work Paul is said to have been assisted by Alcuin.‡ In the council of Tours, in which Charlemagne presided, A. D. 813, it was ordered that every bishop should procure a book of homilies, containing the instructions necessary for his flock, particularly those respecting the resurrection of the dead, a future judgment, the final dispensation of eternal rewards and punishments, and the works to which everlasting life is promised or refused; which he should take care to have translated into the rustic Roman or Teutonic, (German,) that the people might more easily understand the doctrines delivered to them. For the Franks, then either retained the original Teutonic, or else adopted the rustic Roman, from which the modern French is derived.§ It has also been affirmed by different authors, that Charlemagne caused the Scriptures themselves to be translated into the Teutonic, or vulgar dialect of the Franks; but of this there is some doubt, as there are no copies of it now to be found, and as it does not appear that contemporary writers have mentioned any such translation. In 813 the second council of Rheims, held under his auspices, enjoined, "That the bishops and abbots should have the poor and indigent with them at their table; there read aloud the sacred Scriptures, and take their food with thanksgiving and

* S. S. Concilia, tom. vii, p. 1182, edit. P. Labbei.

† Ibid., tom. vii, p. 1183.

‡ Card's Reign of Charlemagne, p. 107. Berington's Lit. Hist. of the Middle Ages, p. 162.

§ S. S. Concilia, *Concil. Turonense III.*, tom. vii, p. 1263.

praise."* He directed his vigilance and circumspection equally to the inferior as to the higher classes of the clergy, and considered in what manner their time and faculties might be most advantageously employed; as is evident from an edict, which ordains, that "if after the repeated admonitions of their bishop to improve the poverty of their understandings by study, they should still show no traces of amendment, their ignorance should not only be punished with the loss of their office, but of whatever ecclesiastical preferment they held." He also discovered a just discrimination of merit in the ecclesiastics of his kingdom, and a disposition to reward it, as is demonstrated by the following anecdote:—Having received intelligence of the death of a bishop, he inquired how much of his property he had bequeathed to the poor; the answer was, two pounds of silver; upon which a young clerk exclaimed, "That is but a very small provision for so great a voyage." Charlemagne, pleased with the observation, instantly said to him, "Be thou his successor, but never forget that expression."†

To promote the instruction of the people, and the more general diffusion of knowledge, injunctions were issued, requiring the bishops to make inquiry in their diocesan visitations, "Whether the respective priests could read the Epistles and Gospels with propriety, and particularly whether they could explain the literal sense of them?" They were also enjoined to instruct their parishioners in the public prayers of the church, as well as in the Lord's Prayer, that they might know what they asked from God."‡ Various directions were likewise given relating to the chanting of the Psalms, and the other parts of public worship;§ and two schools of chant established, one at Soissons, and the other at Metz, from whence the professors of that art were distributed throughout the provinces. A knowledge indeed of the Roman chant, as settled by Pope Gregory the

* Le Long, Biblioth. Sacra, tom. i, p. 373. Paris, 1723, fol. Usserii Hist. Dogmat. p. 111, and Whartoni Auctarium, p. 457.

† Card's Reign of Charlemagne, pp. 109, 116.

‡ An opinion having been very generally and extensively propagated, that it was not lawful to celebrate divine service, or to possess or read the Scriptures in any other tongues than the Hebrew, Greek, or Latin, which were denominated *sacred*, from being the three tongues in which the Saviour's title was inscribed on the cross; the council of Frankfort, in 794, decreed, "That none ought to believe that they were not to pray to God except in one of the *three* tongues; for God might be adored in any language, and those who asked what was right would be heard whatever tongue they used in their petitions."

§ Whartoni Auctarium Hist. Dogmat. Usserii., pp. 345, 459.

Great, often exalted its possessor to the highest preferments of the church.*

By a capitular of 789, and by several subsequent ordinances, the bishops were exhorted to establish two sorts of schools in their respective diocesses. Reading and writing were to be taught in those established for the cultivation of the infant mind; in the others, which were to be opened in the cathedrals and monasteries, the arts of music, grammar, logic, and rhetoric were acquired. The instruction afforded in these schools was ordered to be gratuitous, and the scholars were to be treated with tenderness and affection. The churches were to be furnished with small libraries for their use, consisting principally of the Scriptures or ecclesiastical offices, ("ut in ecclesiis libri canonici veraces habeantur.") The chief aim of Charlemagne in founding these schools was, undoubtedly, to give the clergy a greater proficiency in their theological studies, and thus to qualify them for a proper performance of their sacred functions; but laics also, of every age and of every rank, were admitted into these seminaries, that the treasures of learning might not be exclusively confined to the teachers of religion. In the council of Toul or Savonieres, in Lorrain, held in 859, the same decree was renewed, while it was acknowledged and lamented that scarcely any vestige remained of a just understanding of the divine Scriptures.† In these institutions every study pointed toward religion; even *grammar* was taught chiefly with a view of comprehending better the Holy Scriptures, and of transcribing them with more correctness; and *sacred* music was then alone studied and commended.

Over the progress of the young scholars, Charlemagne watched with a degree of attention not to be expected from the multiplicity of his public concerns; and he took great delight in examining, with the masters, their different compositions. Having discovered, upon some remarkable occasion, that the children of the poorer classes of the people, whom he had caused to be educated among those of the nobles, left the latter far behind in their studies, he applauded their proficiency, and declared that his favours should be exclusively bestowed on them. Then turning to their high-born fellow students, he addressed them in words which evinced his fixed determination to stimulate and reward talents, even if they should be deduced from the lowest origin. "It is evident," says he, "that you rest your claims to promotion solely upon the merits of your ances-

* Card's Reign of Charlemagne, p. 106.

† Whartoni Auctarium, pp. 346, 347. Card's Reign of Charlemagne, pp. 102, 103.

tors : know, therefore, that they have received their recompense, and that the state renounces all obligations, except to those who are capable of promoting her interests and honour by their abilities."*

He likewise established an academy in his own palace. Here the study of the Greek language was introduced, and various sciences were cultivated, especially astronomy, rhetoric, poetry, history, and antiquities. Each of the members in this distinguished society assumed a literary and academic name. Alcuin assumed the name of Horace ; Angilbert, a young man of noble birth, and eminently skilled in the composition of Greek verses, styled himself Homer ; the celebrated Eginhard, secretary or chancellor of Charlemagne, was called Kalliopus ; Adalhardus, abbot of Corbie, received the title of Augustine ; Riculphus, archbishop of Mentz, that of Dametas ; Theodolphus, from his attachment to the lyrical productions of the Greeks, obtained the name of Pindar ; and Charlemagne himself, in consequence of his decisive predilection for ecclesiastical writings, as well as from having committed the whole of the Psalms to memory, received the appropriate name of David from Alcuin, who is justly regarded as the founder and president of his literary undertakings.†

In the academy just mentioned the emperor wished only to maintain the character of a simple member ; assisting at their meetings, and discharging with zeal and promptitude all the duties of an academician. In his more private studies he was careful to buy up every moment, not otherwise employed, for the acquirement of knowledge. During his meals, he listened to the Holy Scriptures, or some devotional book, which he never failed to have read to him ; probably the lives of those saints which he had ordered to be written in a small volume, and of which copies were dispersed throughout his dominions, for the improvement and edification of his people ; and a reader was constantly summoned to his frugal supper, for the express purpose of acquainting him with the history of his royal predecessors, that he might know how to avoid their faults, and imitate their virtues. He had also St. Austin's book, "On the City of God," laid every night under his pillow, to read if he awaked. He is said to have been skilled in astronomy, arithmetic, music, and the different branches of the mathematics ; and to have understood, though certainly not perfectly, the Latin, Greek, Hebrew, and Syriac, besides the Slavonian, and several other living languages. He wrote Latin verses, and even ventured to publish a Teutonic Grammar, though defective in his know-

* Card, p. 156. † Ibid., pp. 157–164.

ledge of composition, and incapable of expressing himself with grammatical accuracy.*

About a year before his decease, Charlemagne resigned the empire to his son Louis, at Aix-la-Chapelle, in the presence of the bishops, abbots, and nobles. After this important transaction he retired from public life, and devoted himself to study, meditation, and prayer. In his retirement he is said to have engaged in a collation of the four Gospels with the original Greek, and the Syriac version, in order to obtain a correct copy of the Vulgate Latin. Le Long notices a copy or two of this collation, richly illuminated, and still preserved in different libraries.† The correction of the Vulgate by Alcuin, under the auspices of this prince, has been already mentioned. It has also been affirmed, (See Le Long, Biblioth. Sacra, tom. i, p. 373, fol.,) that he ordered a version to be made of the New Testament, into the Frankish, or Teutonic tongue; but there does not appear sufficient proof to establish the fact. Charlemagne died January 28th, A. D. 814, after a reign of forty-seven, or forty-eight years, in the seventy-third year of his age. He was interred at Aix-la-Chapelle, with all the pomp of imperial magnificence. His body was embalmed, and deposited in a vault, where it was seated on a throne of gold, and clothed in imperial habits, over the sackcloth which he usually wore. By his side hung a sword, of which the hilt and the ornaments of the scabbard were of gold, and a pilgrim's purse, that he used to carry in his journeys to Rome. In his hands he held the Book of the Gospels, written in letters of gold; his head was ornamented with a chain of gold in the form of a diadem, in which was enclosed a piece of the wood of the true cross; and his face was covered with a winding-sheet. His sceptre and buckler, formed entirely of gold, and which had been consecrated by Pope Leo III., were suspended before him; and his sepulchre was closed and sealed, after being filled with various treasures and perfumes. A gilded arcade was erected over the place with the following inscription:—

SUB HOC CONDITORIO SITUM EST CORPUS KAROLI MAGNI ATQUE ORTHODOXI IMPERATORIS, QUI REGNUM FRANCORUM NOBILITER AMPLIAVIT, ET PER ANNOS XLVII. FELICITER REXIT. DECESSIT SEPTUAGENARIUS, ANNO AB INCARNATIONE DOMINI. DCCCXIV. INDICTIONE VII. V. KAL. FEBRUARIAS.‡

* Card, pp. 164–168. Butler's Lives, vol. i, p. 406.

† Le Long, Biblioth. Sacra, tom. i, pp. 237, 247. Paris, 1723, fol.

‡ Memoires de Literature, tom. iv, pp. 388, 389. Amsterdam, 1719, 12mo

"Beneath this tomb is placed the body of the orthodox em peror CHARLES the GREAT, who valorously extended the kingdom of the Franks, and happily governed it XLVII years. He died a Septuagenarian, February 23d, A. D. DCCCXIV."

In the eleventh century the tomb of Charlemagne was opened by order of Otho III., when the body was stripped of its royal ornaments, which had not been in the least injured by the hand of time. The Book of the Gospels, written on purple vellum, in characters of gold, found in the sepulchre, continues to be kept at Aix-la-Chapelle. With this volume, the imperial sword and hunting horn were also found. The copy of the Gospels interred with the "illustrious" sovereign of the Franks, appears to have been one of those executed by his order, and corrected according to the Greek and Syriac. In the library of the church of St. Germain-des-Prez, at Paris, a Latin Bible, in two volumes, folio, is still kept, written on vellum, which bears the date of 814.

Lambecius has also noticed several other copies of the Scriptures, written in the time of Charlemagne, and preserved in the Imperial library at Vienna, among which are the three following:—A Latin Psalter, executed in letters of gold, by order of Charlemagne, while king of the Franks, and designed as a present to Pope Hadrian I., as appears by the dedicatory verses composed by the monarch himself. It is written on vellum, and forms a large octavo volume. Another Latin Psalter, used during her life by Hildegard, wife of Charlemagne, and after her death presented by the emperor to the cathedral of Bremen in 788, where it was kept for several centuries, and annually exhibited to the venerating crowds, with the other relics deposited in that church. A copy of the Old and New Testament, on vellum, in folio, executed in letters of gold, and every page divided into three columns, written under the inspection, and at the expense, of Rodon, the eleventh abbot of the monastery of St. Vedast, in the province of Artois, during the first year of his abbacy, A. D. 795.*

It is worthy also of remark, that Gisla, one of the daughters of Charlemagne, and the friend of Alcuin, evinced a strong attachment to the sacred writings. In an epistle addressed by her and Rectruda to Alcuin, and prefixed to his commentary on John, we meet with the following passage, expressive of her high regard for the divine word:—"After we had obtained somewhat of the de-

* Peignot, Repert. de Bibliograph. Speciales, p. 150. Paris, 1810, 8vo. Le Long. Biblioth. Sacra, tom. i, pp. 236, 247, fol., 1723. Lambecii Comment. Biblioth. Vindob., lib. ii, ch. v, pp. 261, 295, 402.

lightful knowledge of the Scriptures, in which we were aided, venerable master, by your excellent exposition, we acknowledge that our desire daily became more ardent for these most sacred lessons; in which are contained the truths relating to the purification of the soul, the consolation of our mortality, and the hope of perpetual blessedness; and in which, according to the psalmist, the good man meditates day and night, counting the knowledge of them better than all the riches of the world."*

The name of RABANUS MAURUS, one of the pupils of Alcuin. must likewise be enrolled among the friends to Biblical literature. He was a native of Germany, and a monk of the abbey of Fulda; of which he was afterward elected abbot. By his learning and piety he raised the celebrity of the seminary of Fulda; uniting in it, as the chief teacher, the lessons of general science to the study of the Scriptures. "As the age of his pupils permitted, or their abilities seemed to require, he instructed some in the rules of grammar, others in those of rhetoric; while he conducted the more advanced into the deeper researches of human and divine philosophy, freely communicating whatever they wished to learn. At the same time they were expected to commit to writing, in prose or verse, the occurrences of the day."†

The jealousy and ingratitude of the monks, who accused him of neglecting the temporal interests of the monastery for literary pursuits, drove him for a while to the court of Louis the Meek. After a residence there of some months, he was raised to the see of Mentz, which he advanced by his virtues, as he had Fulda by his learning.‡

At the request of the emperor Louis, and of his son Lothaire, and of Freculf, the learned bishop of Lysieux, he compiled commentaries on most of the books of the sacred Scriptures, collected principally from the Latin fathers, in a regular series from Jerome to Bede. The deficiencies in the expositions of the fathers he supplied by his own, placing in the margin the names of the respective authors, and marking the passages most deserving attention.§ He was also the author of a Latin and Franco-Theotise glossary of the Bible, *Glossarium Latino-Theotiscum in tota Biblia Sacra Veteris et Novi Testamenti;* a copy of which is extant in the Imperial library at Vienna. This work is the more important because

* Whartoni Auctarium, p. 367.

† Trithemius, quoted in Berington's Lit. Hist. of the Middle Ages, b. iii, p. 171.

‡ Sixt. Senensi Biblioth. Sanct., lib. iv, p. 370.

§ Sixt. Senens. *ut sup.*

it is probable that Otfrid derived assistance from it in his rhythmical "Harmony of the Gospels." Among his other works are, "Homilies on the Epistles and Gospels;" a treatise on the invention of languages, entitled, *De Inventione Linguarum ab Hebræa usque ad Theodiscam;* a Latin glossary of anatomy, *Glossæ Latino-barbaricæ de partibus humani corporis;* "Miscellaneous Poems;" a Martyrology; a treatise on arithmetic, *De Computo;* and many controversial tracts, particularly against Gotteschalcus on predestination. A list of his various works, both edited and inedited, is given in Cave's *Historia Literaria*, sæc. ix.

The poems of this great man afford us instances of the barbarous taste which prevailed in that age, in the composition of Latin poetry. Leonine verses were formed into various figures, and the ingenuity of the writer was exercised more in the variety of the forms than in the harmony of the verses he composed. These laborious trifles assumed the different figures of men, angels, birds, quadrupeds, trees, crosses, rings, or any similar ones, according to the pleasure or skill of the composer: an instance of which may be found in the *Bibliotheca Sancta* of Sixtus Senensis, lib. iii, p. 225.

Homely as verses of this kind must appear to the classical reader, and whimsical as they confessedly were in their figure they nevertheless attracted attention, and served to disseminate the rudiments of knowledge, in an age when it required the mandate of imperial or episcopal authority to oblige the professed teachers of religion to acquire sufficient learning to teach their flocks the creed and the Lord's prayer, or even to read intelligibly the usual religious offices. At such a period not to have descended to the capacities and barbarous prejudices of the multitude where it could be innocently done, might, indeed, have secured the praise of elegance and taste in composition, from contemporary or succeeding scholars; but would not have gained the plaudit of "Well done," from Him who "went about doing good," and whom, when on earth the "common people heard with gladness."

Rabanus died about the year 856, with the general opinion, "that Italy had not seen his like, nor Germany produced his equal."* Mosheim says, "He may be called the great light of Germany and France, since it was from the prodigious fund of knowledge he possessed that these nations derived principally their religious instruction."† Rabanus, in conjunction with Haimo and Strabus,

* Trithemius, quoted in Berington's Lit. Hist. of Mid. Ages, p. 171.

† Mosheim's Eccles. Hist., vol. ii, p. 313.

is said to have engaged also in a translation of the Scriptures into the Teutonic, or ancient German; but if such a version were actually completed, it is irrecoverably lost, not a single fragment of it being extant. See Le Long, tom. i, p. 347.

Louis the Meek, the son and successor of Charlemagne, was, like his father, studious in the Scriptures, and the patron of Biblical scholars. It has been said that he gave it in charge to a learned Saxon to translate both the Old and New Testament into the vernacular tongue of that part of his empire; this, however, does not appear to be correct, for although there is a rhythmical dedication to Louis, prefixed with others to the *Harmony* of Otfrid, there is no evidence that the learned monk engaged in the work at his request. Louis died in 842, and, when dying, bequeathed to his son Lothaire his crown, his sword, and a book of the Gospels, richly ornamented with gold and precious stones.*

A Græco-Latin Psalter, of the ninth century, written in a very fair and legible hand, with the Greek in Roman characters, was sold to the marquis of Douglas for £110. 5s., at the late Mr. Edwards' sale, in 1815.

The Libri Evangeliorum, or *Harmony* of Otfrid, alluded to above, was the arduous attempt of a pious and learned monk to communicate to his rude countrymen the knowledge of the principal facts and doctrines recorded in the four Gospels. It is written in the Teutonic, or ancient German tongue, accompanied with a Latin translation; both the versions are metrical. It has obtained the name of a Harmony from being selected from the different Gospels; and is divided into five parts, the *first* of which includes the nativity and baptism of Christ, and the doctrines taught by John the Baptist; the *second* relates to the calling and instruction of his disciples, and the signs by which the Saviour established his doctrine in the world; the *third* treats of the miracles, and proofs of the Messiahship of Christ; the *fourth* treats of the perspicuity of the doctrines and miracles of Jesus, and their reference to the Jews; the *fifth* records his resurrection and ascension, and points out the solemnities of a future judgment. Two acrostical dedications are prefixed to the work, one of them addressed to the emperor Louis, whom he styles sovereign of Germany, *Rex Orientalium Regnorum;* the other to Solomon, bishop of Costnitz, or Constance; these are followed by a prefatory epistle to Luidbert, archbishop of Mentz. The work itself is divided into two columns; the one containing the *Teutonic*, the

* Usserii Hist. Dogmat., p. 113.

other the *Latin* translation. In most places the passages from which the poetic paraphrase is taken are quoted from the Vulgate, and inserted between the columns. The following are Otfrid's Teutonic and Latin versions of the Lord's Prayer:—

TEUTONIC.	LATIN.
"Fater unser guato	"Pater noster bone
bist Druhtin thu gimuato	es Dominus tu gratiosus
In himilon io hoher	In cœlis altissimis
Uuih si namo thiner	Sanctum sit nomen tuum
Biqueme vns thinaz richi	Adveniat nobis regnum tuum
thaz hoha himilrichi	altum illud regnum cœlorum,
Thara uuir zua io gingen	Ad id ut penetremus
ioh emmizigen thingen.	idque assiduo frequentemus.
Si uuillo thin hiar nidare,	Sit voluntas tua hic inferius
So s'er ist ufan himile.	sicut est in cœlis.
In erdu hilff vns hiare	In terra juva nos hic
So thu engilon duist nu thare.	sicut angelis facis jam illic.
Thia dagalichun zuhti,	Quotidianum panem
gib hiut vns mit ginuhti.	da hodie nobis cum satietate.
Joh follon ouh, theist mera	Atque imple etiam, quod plus est
thines selbes lera.	tuo ipsius verbo.
Seuld bilaz uns allen	Debitum dimitte nobis omnibus
so uuir ouh duan uuollen	quod nosquoque facere volumus
Sunta thia uuir thenken,	Peccata quæ nos cogitamus
ioh emmizigen uuirken.	et continuo operamur.
Ni firlaze unsih thin uuara	Ne derelinquat nos tuum tutamen
in thes uuidaruuerten fara	in adversarii tentamine
Thaz uuir ni missi gangen	Ut nos ne aberremus
thara ana ni gifallen,	eoque ne cadamus
Losi unsih io thanana	Libera nos quoque abhinc
thaz uuir sin thine thegana,	ut nos simus tui famuli
Joh mit ginadon thinen	Et cum gratia tua
then uueuuon io bemiden, Amen."	Gehennam effugiamus. Amen."*

The prefatory epistle to Luidbert assigns the reasons for the work, and states the difficulties Otfrid had to conquer in the prosecution of his undertaking. The following translation† will be interesting to the Biblical and philological reader:—

Epistle of Otfrid the monk, to Luidbert.‡

"To LUIDBERT, by divine grace, the most dignified archbishop of the city of Mentz, OTFRID, an unworthy man, yet by devotion a

* Schilteri Thesaurus Antiquitatum Teutonicarum, tom. i, lib. ii, cap. xxi, p. 148. Ulmæ, 1728, fol.

† For this translation I am indebted to the ingenious Mr. Jonathan Crowther, jun., of Frodsham, Cheshire.

‡ Luidbert was advanced to the archiepiscopal see, November 21st, 863; and died

monk, and a presbyter of mean consideration, wishes always the joy of eternal life in Christ."

"In transmitting to your most excellent prudence the style of this book for your approbation, I think it proper, first of all, to explain to you the reasons for my presuming to write it, lest, if you should not approve of it, the minds of any of the faithful should be disposed to lay the blame of it on my presumption."

"For some time the ears of certain most excellent men had been troubled with the sound of vain things, and their sanctity annoyed by the obscene songs of worldly people; I was, therefore, requested by some worthy brethren, and, especially, I was urged by the repeated solicitations of a venerable matron named Judith, to compose for them a part of the Gospels in *Teutonic*, in order that the singing of these words might destroy the trifling of worldly voices; and that they, being occupied with the sweetness of the Gospels in their own language, might be able to divert their attention from the noise of vain things. To this request they added a complaint, that whereas several of the heathen poets, as Virgil, Lucan, Ovid, &c., had celebrated the exploits of their countrymen in their native language, and the world abounded with their volumes; and whereas several most excellent men of our own sect, as Juvencus, Arator, Prudentius, and many others, had in the same way celebrated the miracles of Christ, yet I, though possessing the same faith, and the same grace, was too indolent to exhibit in my own language the brilliant splendour of the divine words."

"Being, therefore, unable any longer to refuse this favour to their importunate charity, I have at last done it for them, not from any opinion I had of my own abilities, but because I was compelled by the requests of the brethren. Supported by the assistance of their prayers, I have composed a part of the Gospels in *Francic*,* and have intermingled here and there spiritual and moral words, in order that whoever is afraid of the difficulty of a foreign language may understand the sacred word in his own language; and understanding the law of God in his own language, may be afraid to deviate from it ever so little in his own mind. In the *first* and *last* parts of this book, I have taken a middle way between the

September 7th, 889. Serarius observes, he was "a truly venerable and learned man, wise, liberal, patient, humble, kind, and universally esteemed."—*Schilteri Thesaurus*, tom. i, p. 12.

* A dialect of the Teutonic.—C.

four Evangelists, and have inserted in its proper order what one and another has related. But in the *middle*, lest the reader should be wearied with the superfluity of words, I have omitted many things concerning the parables and miracles of Christ, and also concerning his doctrine; this, however, I have done reluctantly, not so much from weariness, (though I have very lately published it,) as from the necessity before mentioned: and so I have endeavoured to write, not in regular order as I did in the beginning, but as things occurred to my short memory. I have divided the volume into five books, of which the *first* speaks of the nativity of Christ, and ends with the baptism and doctrine of John: the *second* informs us how, after the call of the disciples, both by certain signs and by his famous doctrine, he was made known to the world: the *third* speaks a little of the clearness of his miracles, and of his doctrine, as addressed to the Jews: the *fourth* tells in what manner he drew near his passion, and of his own accord suffered death for us: the *fifth* gives an account of his resurrection, his conversation afterward with his disciples, his ascension, and the day of judgment. These, as I said before, I have divided into *five* books, (though there are only *four* of the Evangelists,) for this reason, because their *quadrate* equality sets off* the inequality of our *five* senses, and turns all the superfluities not only of our actions, but also of our thoughts, to the elevation of celestial things; and whatever we do amiss, either as it respects our *sight*, *smell*, *feeling*, *taste*, or *hearing*, we purge away the depravity in the remembrance of the reading of these things. Let the useless sense of *sight*, then, be obscured, being illuminated by the words of the gospel;—let not the depraved *hearing* be injurious to our heart; let the *smell* and the *taste* restrain themselves from wickedness, and join themselves to the sweetness of Christ; and let the heart be always *touching*, by means of the memory, these lessons in Teutonic. But now the barbarism of this language, as it is uncultivated and incapable of discipline, and has never been accustomed to be taken by the regular bridle of the grammatical art, so also in many words it is difficult to be written, either because of the combination or unknown sound of the letters. Sometimes, for instance, it requires in sound three *u*'s, (as I think,) the two first consonants, and the third a vowel: sometimes I have not been able to pronounce the sound of either *a*, or *e*, or *i*, or *u*, and then I have thought it best to write the Greek γ; and yet even this letter cannot always be used in this language, which sometimes, in certain

* Or, perhaps, "fills up."

sounds, cannot easily be referred to any character at all. This language also, frequently, contrary to the usage of Latinity, makes use of the letters *k* and *z*, which grammarians will have to be superfluous letters: the *z*, I judge they use in this language to represent a hissing through the teeth; and the *k*, for a guttural sound, (or rather a sound in the *fauces*.) Moreover, it allows too much the figure antithesis, though not always that species of it which teachers of grammar call synalæpha, or elision; and unless those who read are aware of this, they pronounce some words rather awkwardly, sometimes retaining the letters as they are written, and at other times omitting them, after the manner of the language of the Hebrews, who are accustomed in poetry, as some say, entirely to omit and pass over some letters by way of synalæpha; not that this writing of mine is regulated by metrical exactness, but it uniformly follows the homoioteleuton, or rhyming scheme. For both in this and in the former reading, the words require a congruous and similar final sound; and for the sake of this congruity, it is proper to use the figure elision, not only between two vowels, but very often between other letters also; indeed, unless this be done, the extension of the letters sounds very awkwardly. Now we shall find, on close examination, that we do the very same thing in our common conversation; for the beauty of this language requires, that those who read should use a soft and easy collision of synalæpha, and that those who write should pay regard to the homoioteleuton, that is, to the similar termination of words; and sometimes the sense ought to be suspended for two, three, or four lines, in order that the reader may better understand what the words mean. Very often, too, the vowels *i* and *o*, and in the same manner other vowels, are found written together; sometimes continuing distinct vowels in sound, sometimes making only one sound, the first being taken as a consonant. Also, whereas in Latin two negatives make an affirmative, in the usage of this language they almost always make a stronger negative. Of this I have generally been aware, though I have still taken care to write according to the established mode of common conversation. Again, the idiom of this language allowed me to regard neither number nor genders, for sometimes I have rendered by the feminine in this language what in the Latin was masculine; and so in the same manner I have been obliged to confound the other genders. I have changed the plural number for the singular, and the singular for the plural, and have thus sometimes been found to fall into a barbarism, or solecism. I would lay down examples of these faults in Teutonic from this book, but I wish to avoid incurring the derision of the reader. For, to see the uncultivated words of a rustic language mingled with the smoothness of Latinity would certainly excite his laughter; for this language is reckoned, as it were, a rustic one, not having been *polished* by writing, nor any useful art, by our own countrymen,* inasmuch as they do not, like many other nations, record the history of their predecessors, nor do they set off their exploits with a love of glory. If such a thing has ever happened, they have preferred writing in the language of other nations, that is, in Latin or Greek: they are careful of other languages, and are not ashamed of the deformity of their own. They are afraid in other languages to transgress rule, even in a single letter, and yet in their own make mistakes at almost every word. A most astonishing thing truly! that such great men, devoted to prudence, excelling in carefulness, supported by activity, extensive in wisdom, famous for sanctity, should transfer all these excellences to the glory of a foreign language, and have no use of writing in their own! It is fit, however, that by some means or other, whether in incorrect, or in strictly grammatical language, mankind should praise the Author of all things, who has given them the instrument of the tongue, to sound the word of his praise; who seeks not the flattery of polished words, but the pious affection of our thought; not an empty servitude, but a series of works performed with pious diligence."

"I have taken care, therefore, to send to your sagacious prudence this book for your approbation; and because my littleness was educated in time past by Rabanus, of venerable memory, formerly the worthy president of your place, I have commended it to the dignity of your presidentship, and to your equal wisdom. If it is acceptable to the regard of your sanctity, and you judge it not altogether to be rejected, let your authority grant, to the faithful, permission to use it lawfully. But if it appear improper, and like my negligence, let the same venerable and sound authority despise it. My small humility commands the matter to be determined in either case by your judgment. May the Supreme Trinity and

* Otfrid denies the Teutonic language to have been polished by writing, or the grammatical art, prior to his time; but not that it had been reduced to writing, though in a rude and unpolished manner: for, in fact, Charlemagne had ordered the ancient songs to be collected and committed to writing; there also existed a translation into Teutonic of the conversation of Christ with the woman of Samaria; and a fragment of a letter to his sister Florentina by Isidore of Spain, who flourished near two hundred years before Otfrid.—*Schilter.*

Perfect Unity deign long to preserve you safe, and in the right way to be a universal blessing! AMEN."*

OTFRID was a native of Germany, and a monk of the monastery of Weissenburg in Alsace, of the order of St. Benedict. He had been the hearer, and became the disciple, of Rabanus Maurus, the celebrated abbot of Fulda. Trithemius says, "He was profoundly versed in the knowledge of the Holy Scriptures, and extensively acquainted with literature in general; a philosopher, a rhetorician, and a famous poet; eloquent in speech, and excellent in disposition His prose and poetical works were numerous, and have transmitted his name with honour to posterity. After the example of Charlemagne, he attempted to reduce the barbarous language of the ancient Germans to grammatical rule, and partially succeeded."

Besides the *Liber Evangeliorum*, or Harmony, he wrote a metrical paraphrase on the Psalms. A MS. containing this paraphrase, with the addition of a translation of the poetical parts of Scripture, the Apostles' and Athanasian Creeds, and the Lord's Prayer, is preserved in the Imperial library at Vienna. Lambecius, in his *Commentarius de augustissima Bibliotheca Cæsarea Vindobonensi*, lib. ii, p. 461, has transcribed the first Psalm, and the Lord's Prayer, from this MS., which he considers as coeval with the author. Otfrid wrote also two tracts, on the "Last Judgment," and the "Joys of the Kingdom of Heaven," besides a book of poems, and another of epistles. "He composed many others," says Trithemius, "which are now lost through the negligence of those who lived in former times, or have been erased and torn by ignorant monks."

He flourished under the emperors Louis, Lothaire, and Charles, and died about the year 870.†

The best edition of Otfrid's LIBER EVANGELIORUM, or Harmony, is that published by Schilter in his *Thesaurus Antiquitatum Teutonicarum, Ecclesiasticarum, Civilium, Litterarium.* Ulmæ, 1728, fol., tom. i.

A Teutonic metrical version of the Gospels has been attributed, by Beatus Rhenanus and others, to Waldo, or Valdo, bishop of Freising; but this appears to be a mistake, and to have arisen from the transcription of Otfrid's work, by the presbyter Sigebert, undertaken at the request of Waldo.‡

* Schilteri Thes., tom. i, pp. 10–12. Maxima Biblioth. Pat., tom. xvi, pp. 764, 765.

† Vit. Otfridi, ex Catalog. J. Trithemii,—apud Schilteri Thesaurus, tom. i, Whartoni Auctarium, pp. 369, 370.

‡ Usserii Hist. Dogmat., p. 125; et Whartoni Auctarium, p. 370.

Another German monk, named WALAFRID STRABUS, or STRABO, became celebrated during this century for his *Glossa Ordinaria.* This was a Latin comment on the Bible, selected, like that of Rabanus, from the expositions and sayings of the fathers, and accompanied with the names of the respective authors; and which for several centuries was held in universal esteem. The author, who was a monk of Fulda, had studied under Rabanus, and been employed by him as a scribe. He afterward was chosen abbot of Reichenau, in the diocess of Constanz, and died in 849.*

At a later period, ANSELM, a scholar and deacon of the church of Laon in France, who flourished at the close of the eleventh, and commencement of the twelfth century, invented the *Glossa Interlinearis,* or Interlineary Exposition, so called from being inserted in smaller characters between the lines of the sacred text. It consists of brief explanations of difficult words, or sentences; an example is given from it in the *Bibliotheca Sancta* of Sixtus Senensis, lib. iii, p. 200.

The etymology and application of the terms TEXT and GLOSS are well explained in the following remarks of a late learned antiquary.† "There are few who are ignorant of the sense and meaning of the word TEXT, but how it grew to signify the WORD OF GOD, many, perhaps, would be glad to know. We have it from the Romans, who, from the similitude subsisting between spinning and weaving, and the art of composing, both in verse and prose, applied to the latter several expressions proper to the former; hence Horace,

> —*tenui deducta poemata filo:*
> "That fine-spun thread, with which our poem 's wrought;"
> EP. 2, l. 225:

and Cicero *texere orationem* and *contexere carmen.* Among the latter Roman writers, TEXTUS occurs often in the sense of a *piece,* or *composition,* and by excellence came to denote the WORD OF GOD, just as the general word SCRIPTURA also did. But this is not all; the method of writing the Scriptures, (and some few other books,) before the art of printing was invented, was thus, as I here represent it, from an old manuscript of the New Testament, of the Vulgate version, now before me.

* Le Long, Biblioth. Sacr., pt. ii, sec. 3, tom. iii, p. 353, edit. a Masch.

† Rev. S. Pegge, under signature of "Paul Gemsege,"—in Selection of Curious Articles from Gent. Mag., vol. ii, p. 46.

MATTHEW VII, 23.

Nonnovit lux tenebras I. non aspicit, quas si aspiceret, tenebræ non essent.

Et tunc confitebor illis quia

in nullo approbavi, sed reprobavi.

nunquam novi vos. discedite a me omnes qui opera-

quia
non hos novit, ergo eos, qui mandata ejus custodiunt.

mini iniquitatem.

qui operamini. non dicit qui operati estis ne tollat pœnitentiam, sed qui injudicio licet non habeatis facultatem peccandi tamen habetis affectum.

"The sentences at the sides are the *gloss;* the middle, which is in larger hand, is the *text;* and between the lines of that is put the *interlineary gloss*, in which place a translation or version, in some ancient manuscripts in the Cottonian and other libraries, is sometimes inserted. The TEXT here means the WORD OF GOD, as opposed to the *gloss*, both the *lateral* and the *interlineary gloss;* and because the text was usually written, as in this manuscript, in a very large and masterly hand, from thence a large and strong hand of that sort came to be called *text-hand.* By GLOSS is meant a commentary or exposition, generally taken out of the Latin fathers, St. Hieronyme, St. Augustine, &c. It is originally a Greek word, and at first meant a single word put to explain another, as appears from the ancient Greek and Latin glossaries, but afterward it came to signify any exposition or larger commentary. From hence are derived our English expressions *to put a gloss upon a thing*, that is, a favourable interpretation or construction; *gloss*, a fair shining outside; and to *glose*, to flatter."

The Greek commentators of this age chiefly employed themselves in forming CATENÆ, or *chains of commentaries*, consisting entirely in collections of the explications of Scripture that were scattered up and down in the ancient writers. The more modern work of the learned Poole, entitled *Synopsis Criticorum*, in five large folio volumes, is a somewhat similar compilation, selected with judgment, and displaying the most profound erudition.

PHOTIUS, patriarch of Constantinople, who flourished about A. D. 870, was the most celebrated of his contemporaries; he wrote a *Catena* on the book of Psalms, compiled from the writings of Athanasius, Basil, Chrysostom, &c., and a Commentary upon the Prophets, both of which are yet extant in MS.* He also composed a book of Questions relating to various passages of Scripture, entitled *Amphilochia*, from its having been addressed to

* Mosheim's Eccl. Hist., vol. ii, p. 325.

1

Amphilochius, bishop of Cyzicum. These questions on the Bible are, however, interspersed with others of a philosophical and literary kind; they are also extant in MS. in different public libraries. But his most celebrated works are his *Nomocanon* and *Myrobiblion*, or *Bibliotheca*. The *Nomocanon* is a collection which includes, under fourteen titles, all the canons acknowledged in the church, from the times of the apostles to the seventh œcumenic council. The *Myrobiblion*, or Library, is a review of the works of two hundred and eighty authors, theologians, commentators, philosophers, historians, orators, physicians, and grammarians. It was undertaken at the request of his brother Tarasias, and composed while he was a layman, and, as it seems, during an embassy at the court of Bagdat. It is one of the most precious remains of antiquity; and is the model on which the critical journals have been formed, which, in modern times, have so much engaged the learned of different nations, and contributed to the advancement of literature. An interesting account of this most learned and accomplished scholar is given in Berington's "Literary History of the Middle Ages," App. i, pp. 554–562. His *Myrobiblion*, or Library, has been several times printed. The best edition is that of And. Schottus, Rothom., folio, 1653.*

The propriety of explaining and illustrating the sacred Scriptures by COMMENTS has been very generally allowed, though the mode and extent of them have been various, at different periods. "At first the insertion of a *word* or *sentence* in the margin, explaining some particular word in the text, appears to have constituted the whole of the comment. Afterward these were mingled with the text, but with such marks as served to distinguish them from the words they were intended to illustrate; sometimes the comment was *interlined* with the text; and at other times it occupied a space at the bottom of the page."

"Ancient comments, written in all these various ways, I have often seen," says Dr. A. Clarke, "and a Bible now lies before me, written probably before the time of Wicliff, where the glosses are all *incorporated* with the text, and only distinguished from it by a *line underneath*; the line evidently added by a later hand." The following are specimens:—

Blynde men seen, crokid men wandren, mesels ben maad clene, deef men heeren, deed men rysen agein, pore men ben taken to prechynge of the gospel, or ben maad kepers of the gospel. *Matt.* xi, 5.

Heroude tetraarcha, that is, prince of the fourth parte. *Luke* iii, 1.

* See also Cave's Hist. Lit. Sæc., vol. ix, p. 552; and Bibliog. Dict., vol. v.

"Comments written in this way have given birth to multitudes of the *various readings* afforded by ancient MSS., for, the notes of distinction being omitted or neglected, the *gloss* was often considered as an integral part of the text, and entered accordingly by succeeding copyists."

"This is particularly remarkable in the *Vulgate*, which abounds with explanatory words and phrases, similar to those in the preceding quotations. In the *Septuagint*, also, traces of this custom are easily discernible, and to this circumstance many of its *various readings* may be attributed."* A sketch of the principal Jewish and Christian commentators, and their works, may be found in the *General Preface* to the learned commentary of Dr. A. Clarke, vol. i, pp. 1–23.

Directing now our inquiries to the more northern states of Europe, we learn, that in the course of the NINTH century many of them received the Gospel, through the pious and indefatigable labours of two Greek monks, Methodius and Cyril, brothers, and natives of Thessalonica, descended from an illustrious senatorian Roman family. CYRIL, who in early life had borne the name of Constantine, received his education at Constantinople, and, by his great progress in learning, obtained the surname of *The Philosopher*. Remarkable also for his piety and zeal, he was promoted to the priesthood, and sent on a mission to the Chazari, a tribe of the Turci, the most numerous and powerful nation of the Huns in European Scythia. Already acquainted with the Slavonian, Greek, and Latin languages, he seems to have learned also the Turcic, which was at that time spoken by the Huns, Chazari, and Tartars. After having accomplished the object of his mission, he returned to Constantinople, absolutely refusing to accept any part of the great presents with which the prince of the Chazari would have honoured him.

Cyril's second mission was to the Bulgarians, a nation of the Slavi, who had possessed themselves of the ancient Mysia and Dacia, now Walachia, Moldavia, and part of Hungary; in this mission his brother METHODIUS, a monk, was his chief assistant. From Bulgaria our two missionaries passed into Moravia, being invited thither by Rastices, who had received the crown of Moravia from Louis, king of Germany, in 846. Stridowski, in his *Sacra Moraviæ Historia*, styles Cyril and Methodius the apostles of Moravia, Upper Bohemia, Silesia, Cazaria, Croatia, Circassia,

* Dr. A. Clarke's Commentary, *Gen. Pref.*, pp. i, ii.

Bulgaria, Bosnia, Russia, Dalmatia, Pannonia, Dacia, Carinthia, Carniola, and almost all the Slavonian nations.*

For the more effectual promotion of the sacred work in which they were engaged, these two indefatigable and judicious missionaries translated the Scriptures, and the Liturgy of the church, into the Slavonian tongue. For this purpose they invented an alphabet, principally formed from the Greek capitals, and gave to each letter of the alphabet the name of a word beginning with the letter. These characters are usually termed, from one of the inventors, *Cyrillian;* and the alphabet, the *Servian* or ancient *Russian.* (See plate 1.) About the year 880, Pope John VIII. addressed an epistle to a Slavonian prince, in which he observes, "We approve of the Slavonian letters invented by the philosopher Constantine; and we order that the praises of Christ may be published in that language. It is not contrary to the faith, to employ it in the public prayers of the church, and in reading the Holy Scriptures. He who made the three principal tongues, Latin, Greek and Hebrew, made the rest also for his own glory. Nevertheless, to show the more respect to the Gospel, let it first be read in the Latin, and then in the Slavonian, for the sake of the people who understand not Latin; and according to the practice of some other churches, &c."

Of the importance of the Slavonian translation, some idea may be formed from the various dialects of the Slavonian tongue enumerated by Reland, in his *Dissertationes Miscell.*, pars iii. He has, at the end of that work, given the Lord's Prayer in the following dialects of the Slavonian, viz., *Cyrillic, Bulgaric, Dalmatic, Croatic, Slavonic, Bohemic, Polonic, Vandalic, Lusatic, Muscovitic or Russic, Carniolic, Nova-Zemblic, Walachic.*† Cyril died about A. D. 870. Methodius lived to an advanced age, but the year of his death is uncertain.

The MS. of the Slavonian or Russian version, supposed to be the oldest now extant, is one of the New Testament, written in the time of the grand duke Wladimir, in the *tenth* century, and which was used in the Ostrog edition of the Bible, printed in 1581, in folio, at the expense of Constantine, prince of Volhinia, a copy of which is in the valuable library of Earl Spencer. But the most ancient MS. of the *whole* Slavonian Bible, is probably one preserved in the

* Butler's Lives, Dec. 22, vol. xii, pp. 287–300.

† Bacmeister, Essai sur la Bibliotheque, &c., de St. Petersbourg, p. 5, 1776, 8vo. Relandi Dissert. Miscell., pt. iii, Traject. ad Rhenum, 1708, 12mo. Jortin's Remarks on Eccl. Hist., vol. iii, p. 104. Lond. 1805, 8vo.

library of the Holy Synod, written in the year 1499, in the time of the grand duke Ivan Wasiljewitsh. The oldest printed edition of the Slavonian Scriptures, and the first book printed in the language, is the Pentateuch, in 4to. It was translated by Francis Scorino, a physician, and printed at Prague in 1519, on good paper, in beautiful Cyrillian characters, and with few or no abbreviations. The second page of the title is ornamented, or rather *disgraced*, with a representation of angels combating with infernal spirits; above them the Holy Trinity, under the form of an old man with three faces, lifting up his hand as if to bless them, while the angels offer him crowns. There is a preface to each book; and a summary of contents to each chapter. The chapters are not divided into verses. The whole is adorned with wood cuts, capitals, and vignettes. Scorino was also the author of a paraphrase on Chronicles; and of a translation of the Acts of the Apostles, which was printed at Wilna, in 1517, in 8vo. The famous Socinian, Budny, made use of Scorino's version when translating the Bible into the Polish tongue. Methodius and Cyril translated from the Greek of the Septuagint; Scorino from the Vulgate Latin.*

The *first* book printed at Moscow was the Acts and Epistles of the Apostles, in 1654, in the time of the czar Ivan Wasilovitsch. The characters and paper are excellent: the latter was probably obtained from England; since in this undertaking, the czar applied to those nations who were most capable of affording him aid and instruction in the establishment of printing in his dominions. In the library of the Academy of Sciences at Petersburg, a copy of this rare edition is preserved, which a soldier found by chance, and presented to the academy in 1730. At the end of the volume is the following mandate of the czar, relating the principal circumstances that led to the printing of this edition.

"By the will of the Father, the assistance of the Son, and the operation of the Holy Spirit.—By order of the orthodox czar and grand duke of all the Russias, Ivan Wasilovitsch; and by the benediction of Macar, the most venerable metropolitan of all the Russias, many churches have been erected in Moscow, and its environs; and in all the cities of Russia, but chiefly in the city of Casan, and in the country round about, which have been lately enlightened. These churches the orthodox czar has ornamented with venerable images, sacred books, moveables, and vestments, and other things belonging to public worship, according to the traditions and rules of the

* Bacmeister, Essai sur la Bibliotheque, &c., de l'Academie des Sciences de Saint Petersbourg, pp. 91–94. Marsh's Michaelis, vol ii, pt. i, ch. vii, p. 154.

apostles and blessed fathers, and the ordinances of the Greek emperors of blessed memory, who have reigned at Constantinople, Constantine the Great, Justinian, Michael, Theodore, and other pious princes. The orthodox czar and grand duke of all the Russias commanded also the sacred books, such as the Psalms, the Gospels, the Acts, and Epistles of the Apostles, and many others, to be purchased at the public marts, and distributed to the churches; but very few could be found that were correct, and fit for use; the others being falsified and disfigured, by the ignorance and inaccuracy of the copyists. Of this, the czar had scarcely been informed, before he thought of the means of causing books to be printed, in his states, similar to those in Greece, at Venice, in Phrygia, or among other nations, in order to possess more correct copies of the sacred books; and having declared his intention to the most venerable metropolitan of all the Russias, the holy man rejoiced exceedingly, gave thanks to God, and assured the czar that he regarded the thought as a gift from Heaven. Inquiry was accordingly made respecting the manner of printing, by order of the czar, and under the benediction of the metropolitan, in the year of the world 7061, (A. D. 1553,) and the thirty-first of his reign. The orthodox czar afterward caused a house to be builded at his own proper charge, designed for the printing; and advanced a sum out of the public treasury to the workmen Ivan Fedor, deacon of the church of the miraculous, Nicholas de Gostun, and Peter Timofeew Motislavzov, sufficient for the expenses of the printing, and for their own support until the work should be finished. The impression of the present book, which contains the Acts of the Apostles, the Catholic Epistles, and those of St. Paul, was begun on the 19th of April, the anniversary of the blessed father Ivan Palevret, in the year of the world 7071, (A. D. 1563,) and was completed on the 1st of March in the year of the world 7072, (A. D. 1564,) being the first of the ministry of the archbishop and metropolitan Athanasius; in honour of the all-powerful and quickening Trinity of the Father, of the Son, and of the Holy Ghost. Amen."*

The whole Bible, from the version of Methodius and Cyril, was printed at Ostrog, 1581, fol., and again at Moscow, 1663, fol. The Slavonian, or ancient Russian, is still the authorized version of the Russian Church, though scarcely intelligible to the common people.

Reverting to the occurrences of the ninth century, England claims

* Bacmeister, *ut sup.*, pp. 98–101.

our attention. ALFRED, justly surnamed the Great, a prince not inferior in talent to Charlemagne, and infinitely his superior in piety and suavity of manners, ascended the throne in 871. Born when his country was involved in the most profound darkness, and deplorable confusion; and when learning was considered rather as a reproach than an honour to a prince, he was not taught to know one letter from another till he was above twelve years of age, when a book was put into his hand by a kind of accident, more than by previous design. Judith, his step-mother, was sitting one day surrounded by her family, with a book of Saxon poetry in her hands. As Aldhelm and Caedmon had written poems of great popularity, it might contain some of theirs. With a happy judgment, she proposed it as a gift to him who would soonest learn to read it. The elder princes thought the reward inadequate to the task, and retired from the field of emulation. But the mind of Alfred, captivated by the prospect of information, and pleased with the beauty of the writing, and the splendour of the illuminations, inquired if she actually intended to give it to the person who would soonest learn it. His mother repeating the promise, with a smile of joy at the question, he took the book, found out an instructer, and learned to read it; recited it to her, and received it for his reward. Religion continued the stimulus which the pleasures of poetry had first created. He made a collection of the devout offices for the day, with prayers, and psalms adapted to pious meditation; and always carried this treasure in his bosom for perpetual use.*

Difficulties were, however, thrown in the way of Alfred's acquisition of learning, which, to a mind less vigorous than his, would have been deemed insurmountable. For not only was his kingdom for many years the seat of war, during which he is said to have fought in person fifty-six battles, by sea and land; but at that time few or none among the West Saxons had any learning, or could so much as read with propriety and ease; and when he had attained the age of maturity, he became subject to a disease which incessantly tormented him, and which his physicians could neither remedy nor explore. But his ardent thirst for knowledge surmounted every obstacle, and in 887 he obtained the happiness he had long coveted, of reading the Latin authors in their original language; and even became a profound scholar for those times, a grammarian, a rhetorician, a philosopher, an historian, a musician, the prince of Saxon poesy, and an excellent architect and geometrician.†

* Turner's Hist. of the Anglo-Saxons, vol. i, b. ii, ch. viii, p. 193.

† Spelman's Life of Ælfred the Great, p. 210. Oxford, 1709, 8vo.

One of the principal features of Alfred's useful life was his ardent piety; and it forms a shining trait in his character, that an author, who lived at the period of the Norman conquest, in mentioning some of the preceding kings with short, appropriate epithets, names him with the simple, but expressive addition of "THE TRUTH TELLER." He was accustomed daily to attend divine service, especially the eucharist; making use also of prayers and psalms in private. He kept the established hours of prayer, being every third hour, both night and day; and frequently entered the churches secretly in the night for prayer, after lamenting with sighs his want of more acquaintance with divine wisdom. He used also, with careful solicitude, to hear the Scriptures of God from the recitations of natives, or even (if by chance any arrived from abroad) to hear prayers equally from foreigners. Asser, the bishop of St. David's, the friend and biographer of Alfred, speaking of his own reception and attendance at the court of Alfred, says: "I was honourably received in the royal city of Leonaford, and that time staid eight months in his court. I translated and read to him whatever books he wished which were within our reach; for it was his peculiar and perpetual custom, day and night, amid all his afflictions of mind and body, either to read books himself, or to have them read to him by others."* Some of the last instructions of Alfred to his son Edward have been preserved, and deserve to be quoted for their pathetic simplicity and genuine piety, their political wisdom, and the proof which they afford of his anxiety for the welfare of his subjects.

"Thus, quoth Alfred, worldly wealth at last cometh to the worms, and all the glory of it to the dust, and our life is soon gone. And though one had the rule of all this middle world, and of the wealth in it, yet should he keep his life but a short while. All thy happiness would but work thy misery, unless thou couldst purchase thee CHRIST. Therefore, when we lead our lives as God hath taught us, we then best serve ourselves. For then be assured that he will support us; for so said Solomon, that wise man; well is he that doth good in this world, for at last he cometh where he findeth it."

"Thus, quoth Alfred: My dear son, set thee now beside me, and I will deliver thee true instructions. My son, I feel that my hour is coming; my countenance is wan. My days are almost done. We must now part. I shall go to another world, and thou

* See Asser, as cited by Turner, in Hist. of Anglo-Saxons, vol. i, p. 293; Whitaker in Life of St. Neot, p. 161; and also Turner's Anglo-Saxons vol. i, ch. ii, p. 309.

shalt be left alone in all my wealth. I pray thee, (for thou art my dear child,) strive to be a father and a lord to thy people; be thou the children's father and the widow's friend; comfort thou the poor, and shelter the weak; and with all thy might, right that which is wrong. And, son, govern thyself by law, then shall the Lord love thee, and God above all things shall be thy reward. Call thou upon him to advise thee in all thy need, and so he shall help thee the better to compass that which thou wouldst."*

No sovereign ever studied the public interest more than Alfred. He seems to have considered his life but as a trust, to be used for the benefit of his people; and his plans for their welfare were intelligent and great. He fought their battles, regulated the administration of justice, compiled a body of laws, corrected the abuses of the realm, extended their commercial relations and knowledge by an embassy to India, cultivated the arts and sciences, established public seminaries for the education of youth, and was the munificent patron of religion and learning. To him Englishmen are indebted for the TRIAL BY JURY, for the foundation of their COMMON LAW, and for the division of the kingdom into HUNDREDS and TYTHINGS; and the sentiment expressed by him in his will will never be forgotten: "IT IS JUST THAT THE ENGLISH SHOULD FOR EVER REMAIN FREE AS THEIR OWN THOUGHTS."†

Stimulated by a laudable anxiety for the mental and moral improvement of his subjects, Alfred searched his dominions for men of literary attainments, invited learned foreigners to his court, and munificently rewarded the exertions of their talents. He also added the powerful influence of his own example, by composing a variety of poems, fables, and apt stories; and by translating into the Anglo-Saxon, then the vernacular language of the kingdom, the "Consolation of Philosophy," by Boëtius, the "Histories" of Arosius and Bede, and the "Pastorals" of Gregory. To this last mentioned work he prefixed a prefatory epistle to Wulfsig, bishop of London, which deserves to be transcribed; the following is Spelman's literal translation:—

"ÆLFRED, king, wisheth greeting to Wulfsig, bishop, his beloved and friendlike, and thee to know, I wish, that to me it cometh very often in mind, what manner of wise men long ago were throughout the English nation, both of the spiritual degree and of the temporal, and how happy the times then were among all the English, and how the kings, which then the government had of the people,

* Spelman's Life of Ælfred the Great, pp. 130, 131.

† Russell's Hist. of Modern Europe, vol. i, pp. 102, 104.

God, and his written will obeyed, how well they behaved themselves both in war and peace; and in their home government, how their nobleness was spread abroad, and how they prospered in knowledge and in wisdom. Also the divine orders, how earnest they were, as well about preaching as about learning, and about all the services that they should do to God; and how men from abroad, wisdom and doctrine here in this land sought, and how we the same now must get abroad if we would have them. So dear has learning fallen among the English nation, as that there has been very few on this side the Humber that were able to understand the English of their service, or turn an epistle from Latin into English: and I wot there were not many beyond the Humber that could do it. There were so few as that I cannot bethink me of one on the south side of the Thames, when I first came to reign. God Almighty be thanked that we have ever a teacher in pulpit now. Therefore I pray thee that thou do, (as also I believe thou wilt,) that thou that wisdom, that God has given thee, bestow all about on them thou canst bestow it; think what punishment shall for this world befall us, when as neither we ourselves have loved wisdom, nor left it to others; we have only loved the names that we were Christians, and very few of us the duties. When I minded all this, methought also that I saw (before all was spoiled and burned) how all the churches throughout the English nation stood filled with books and ornaments, and a great multitude of God's servants; and at that time they wist very little fruit of their books, because they could understand nothing of them, for that they were not written in their own language. So they told us, that our ancestors, that before us held those places loved wisdom, and through the same got wealth, and left it to us. A man may here yet see their swath, but we cannot inquire after it, because we have let go both wealth and wisdom; for that we would not stoop with our minds to the seeking of it. When I thought of all this, then wondered I greatly that their godly wise men, that were everywhere throughout the English nation, and had fully learned all those books, would turn no part of them into their own language; but I then again quickly answered myself, and said, they weened not that ever men should become so reckless, nor that this learning would so decay, therefore they willingly let it alone, and wot that here would be the more wisdom in the land, the more languages that we understood. Then I called to mind how that the LAW was first found written in the *Hebrew* speech; and after that the *Greeks* had learned it, then turned they it into their own speech wholly, and also all other books. And then the *Latin* people, a little after they had learned it, they translated all through wise interpreters into their own language; and all other Christian people also have turned some part thereof into their own tongue. Therefore methinketh it better, if you so think, that we also some books, that be deemed most needful for all men to understand, into that language turn, that we all know; and that we bring to pass (as we easily may, with God's help, if we have quietness) that all the youth of free-born Englishmen (such as have wealth that they may maintain them) be committed to learning, that, while they no other note can, they first learn well to read English writing, afterward let men further teach in the *Latin* tongue those that they will further teach and have to a higher degree. When I minded how this learning of the Latin tongue heretofore was fallen throughout the English nation, though many skill to read English writing, then began I, among divers and manifold businesses of this kingdom, to turn into English that book which in Latin is named *Pastoralis*, and in English, the *Herd-man's Book*, sometimes word for word, sometimes understanding for understanding, even as I learned them of Plegmond my archbishop, of Asser my bishop, and Grimbald my mass-priest, and John my mass-priest. After that I had learned of them how I might best understand them, I turned them into English, and will send one to each bishop's see in my kingdom: and upon each there is a *style*,* that is of fifty marks; and

* Various meanings have been affixed to the Saxon word ÆSTEL, which is here translated *style*. Mr. Wise and Dr. Pegge support the adoption of the term *style*, an instrument which they conceive was chiefly designed, in the present case, for the use of the master or teacher, to whom it might be subservient in a double capacity; that is, both for writing, and by way of *indicatorium* or *festuca*; and, supposing the books to have been written with a pen, they apprehend the latter use accounts very well for their being accompanied by a *stylus*, or *style*; though they affirm that waxen table-books were not yet grown into disuse: and in reply to the objection that these *styli* could not be worth fifty *mancussæ* apiece, or £18 15*s*. of our present money, Dr. Pegge remarks that the handles of them might be enriched, in the materials and workmanship, to almost any sum; and that the king might be desirous of exciting his subjects, by this extraordinary act of liberality, to the love of learning; and conjectures that a curious jewel of gold, enamelled like a bulla or amulet to hang round the neck, circumscribed in Saxon characters, ÆLFRED MEC HEHT GEWYRCAN, *Alfred caused me to be made*, which was found in the Isle of Althelney, formed the handle of one of these styli. This jewel is engraved in Hickes's Thesaurus, vol. i, p. 142. See *Pegge on the Æstel in the Archæologia*, vol. ii, pp. 68–74, 4to.

Mr. Hearne and Dr. Milles controvert this translation, and observe, that the *styli* were usually implements of small value, made either of iron or bone, or some such cheap materials; that in Alfred's time vellum had taken place of waxen tablets, and consequently pens succeeded to styles; to which Dr. Milles adds, that, supposing

I command in God's name, that no man the style from the books, nor the books from the minster take, seeing we know not how long there shall be so learned bishops as now, God be thanked, everywhere there are. Therefore I would they should always remain in their places, except the bishop will have them with him, or that they be lent somewhither until that some other be written out."

The last literary work in which this excellent monarch engaged was a translation of the Psalms of David into Anglo-Saxon, which, however, he did not live to finish, but which was afterward completed by another hand. This translation appears to have been part of a princely design to translate the whole of the Old and New Testaments into the vernacular tongue, for the general benefit of

waxen tablets not to have been entirely laid aside, it was, nevertheless, very improbable that they would have been used for so many copies of a book, when they might have been written in a more convenient and durable manner by ink, on vellum; and the more so as it was not usual to commit things of great importance to these tablets, but only such as were in common and daily use; and that a stylus was superfluous, when no addition nor alteration was to be made in the work. Mr. Hearne's idea of the *æstel*, in which he is supported by Dr. Milles, is, that it was the *umbilicus* of the volume on which this book was written, or rather, the two handles or knobs at the extremities, like those affixed to our modern maps, (see frontispiece,) by the means of which the volume was to be rolled up or opened; and on which each copy of the book was sent to the respective cathedrals. In this sense of the word the æstel was a very proper, and indeed a necessary appendage of the book, and it adds great propriety to the king's request, "that no one would take the æstel from the book;" which, if they had been tempted to do, by the value of this ornament, they would have deprived the volume, not only of its beauty, but in some measure, also, of its use. Mr. Hearne also justifies the use of this word from Chaucer, who, in the letter of Cupide, calls a handle a *stele* or *stail*, as it is still used in the northern parts of England—

"And when that man the pan hath by the stele."

He further supposes that this handle might be magnificently chased and carved, like the jewel of Alfred, mentioned by Hickes. Dr. Milles, however, thinks there is no necessity for such a supposition, since the value of six pounds three ounces in silver, or the weight of seven ounces and a half in gold, might be easily worked up in forming the *umbilicus*, or rather the two handles at the extremities of it, without the additional expense of sculpture and ornament. For by these mancussæ all the ornaments and furniture of gold among the Saxons were weighed, a mancussa weighing about sixty-eight troy grains, and equiponderant with three Saxon pennies. Dr. M. thinks that there is no other ground for the supposition that the jewel of Alfred might have been the top or extremity of the æstel, than that they were both the property of the same king; and that there is no analogy between the shape of that jewel and that of a stylus or manubrium to the book, and that the weight of it, which was about one ounce and five-eighths, does not at all coincide with the weight of the æstel.—*Leland's Itinerary*, vol. vii, pp. xix–xxii. *Archæologia*, vol. ii, pp. 75–79.

his subjects. The old Chronicle of Ely affirms this to have been done; and Boston of Bury says, *Totum fere Testamentum in linguam Anglicanum transtulit*—"He translated the whole of the Testament into the English tongue." Spelman endeavours to reconcile these varying accounts by supposing that "the king began with the most principal, and translated the New Testament first, and that done, he set upon the Old Testament, and so as his time served him he went on, till (as he was going through the Psalms) his work was interrupted by his death."* But the testimonies of Asser and William of Malmsbury are too express to be superseded by more modern ones, unless supported by corroborating circumstances, which, however, is not the case; on the contrary, it is a probable conjecture, that if Alfred had completed a translation of even any detached book of the sacred volume, he would have taken the same method to preserve and publish it for the religious benefit of his subjects, as he did with his translation of Gregory's Pastoral, by sending copies to every bishop's see in the kingdom, to be kept in the cathedrals. It may be further added, that if Alfred had translated all, or most of the books of the Bible, there would have been little or no need for Ælfric, abbot of Winchester, and others, to have undertaken the translations which he completed in the following century. A Latin Psalter, with an interlineary Saxon version, formerly belonging to Alfred, and probably written by an Italian scribe, was in the possession of the late learned antiquary, Mr. Astle, who has an engraved fac-simile of it, in Plate XIX, No. 6, of his "Origin and Progress of Writing;" and from which Plate IV. of this work is copied.

This extraordinary prince; "this victorious warrior; this sagacious statesman; this friend of distress; this protector against oppression; who, in an age of ignorance, loved literature, and diffused it; who, in an age of superstition, could be rationally pious; and in the station of royalty could discern his faults, and convert them into virtues; was called away from the world on the 26th day of October, in the year 900, or 901."† He died at the age of fifty-two, after a life, literally a life of disease. The ficus molested him severely in his childhood. This, after many years, disappeared; but, at the age of twenty, was replaced by another of the most tormenting nature, probably an internal cancer. Its seat was internal and invisible, but its agony was incessant. Such was the dreadful anguish it perpetually produced, that if for one

* Spelman's Life of Ælfred the Great, pp. 212, 213.

† Turner's History of the Anglo-Saxons, vol. i, b. iv, ch. v, p. 284.

short hour it happened to intermit, the dread and horror of its inevitable return poisoned the little interval of ease. The skill of his Saxon physicians was unable to detect its nature, or alleviate its pain. Alfred had to endure it unrelieved. It is not among the least admirable circumstances, therefore, of this great prince, that he withstood the fiercest hostilities that ever distressed a nation, cultivated literature, discharged his public duties, and executed all his schemes for the improvement of his people, amid a perpetual agony, so horrible, that it would have disabled a common man from the least exertion.*

To the endeavours of Alfred to promote literature among his subjects we probably owe the celebrated RUSHWORTH GLOSS, so called because it formerly belonged to John Rushworth, Esq., of Lincoln's Inn, though it is now deposited in the Bodleian library at Oxford. It contains the four Gospels in Latin, written in a large hand, similar to that of the Durham-book, and probably about the same time; and over each line of the Latin is a corresponding one of Saxon, written in the ninth or tenth century. At the conclusion of St. Matthew's Gospel these words are added: *Farmen, presbyter, thas boc thus gleosode*—"Farman, presbyter, this book thus glossed." And at the end of the volume: *The min bruche, gibidde fore Owun the thas boc gloesede, Farmen thæm preoste æt Harawuda*—"He that of mine profiteth, bead (pray) he for Owen, that this book glossed, and Farman, the priest at Harewood." After this follow, in Saxon characters, these words: *Macregol dipinxit hoc euangelium quicumque legerit et intellegerit istam narrationem orat pro Macreguil scriptori*—"Macregol delineated this Gospel: whoever hath read and understood its recital, pray he for Macregol, the writer." From the volume itself, therefore, we are informed that the Saxon version was the joint production of Farman and Owen, and that Macregol was the scribe, and its decorator. Its ornaments consist of delineations of the four evangelists, and divers coloured initial letters. The volume is in a small degree imperfect, wanting a few leaves at the beginning.†

In 1807, the Rev. Samuel Henshall, A.M., rector of St. Mary, Stratford Bow, Middlesex, published the Gospel of St. Matthew from the Durham-book, in a work entitled "The Etymological Organic Reasoner," and afterward published it with the Gothic Gospel of St. Matthew, under the title of "The Gothic Gospel of

* Turner, *ut sup.*, b. v, ch. iii, p. 331.

† Baber's Saxon and English Versions, prefixed to Wiclif's New Testament, p. lx. Henshall's Gothic Gospel, p. 64.

St. Matthew, from the Codex Argenteus of the Fourth Century; with the corresponding English or Saxon, from the Durham-book." 1807, 8vo. In this work he has given the various readings of the Rushworth Gloss.

CHAPTER VIII.

TENTH CENTURY.

Scarcity of Books—Feast of the Ass—Ordeal—Scriptoria—Antiquarii—Calligraphy—Bruno—Gerard de Groot—Thomas à Kempis—Value of Books—Superb Bindings—Athelstan—Edgar's Canons—Ælfric—Saxon Gospels—German Versions—Arabic Version—Celebrated Jews.

THE TENTH century, which presents one of the darkest periods of the Christian era, was an age of the profoundest ignorance, and of the most degraded superstition. Some, who filled the highest situations in the church, could not so much as read; while others, who pretended to be better scholars, and attempted to perform the public offices, committed the most egregious blunders. In Spain, books were become so scarce, that one and the same copy of the Bible, St. Jerome's epistles, and some volumes of ecclesiastical offices and martyrologies, served several different monasteries: and in the famous monastery of Iona there seems to have been, in the ninth century, no other work, even of the fathers, than one of the writings of Chrysostom. Gennadius, a Spanish bishop, by his will, bearing date A.D. 953, bequeathed about sixteen volumes of books to certain religious houses, with the express condition that no abbot should be permitted to transfer them to any other place, but that they should be kept for the monks of the monasteries specified in the will, who should accommodate each other as much as possible in the use of them. The will is subscribed by the king and queen, as well as by bishops, and other persons of rank.*

Of the deplorable state of religion, and of the wretched superstition that reigned in this and several succeeding centuries, no other proof need be adduced than that of the *Feast of the Ass*, celebrated in several churches in France, in commemoration of the Virgin Mary's flight into Egypt. This festival was celebrated at Beauvais, on the 14th of January. They chose a beautiful young woman, whom they richly attired, and placed a lovely infant

* Warton's History of English Poetry, vol. i, dissert. 2. Jamieson's Historical Account of the Ancient Culdees, p. 316. Mabillon, Annales, tom. iii, lib. xli, p. 351.

in her arms. She then mounted an ass richly comparisoned, and rode in procession, followed by the bishop and clergy, from the cathedral to the church of St. Stephen, where she was placed near the altar, and high mass commenced. Instead, however, of the usual responses by the people, they were taught to imitate the braying of the ass; and at the conclusion of the service the priest, instead of the usual words with which he dismissed the people, *brayed* three times, and the people *brayed* or uttered the imitative sounds *hinham, hinham, hinham!* During the ceremony the following ludicrous composition, half Latin, half French, was sung with great vociferation, in praise of the ass :—

	TRANSLATION.
" Orientis partibus	" From the country of the East
Adventavit asinus ;	Came this strong and handsome beast,
Pulcher et fortissimus,	This able ass beyond compare,
Sarcinis aptissimus.	Heavy loads and packs to bear.
Hez, Sire Asnes, car chantez ;	Now, Seignior Ass, a noble bray ;
Belle bouche rechignez ;	That beauteous mouth at large display ;
Vous aurez du foin assez	Abundant food our hay-lofts yield,
Et de l' avoine à plantez.	And oats abundant load the field
Lentus erat pedibus,	True it is, his pace is slow,
Nisi foret baculus ;	Till he feel the quick'ning blow ;
Et eum in clunibus	Till he feel the urging goad,
Pungeret aculeus.	On his buttock well bestow'd,
Hez, Sire Asnes, &c.	Now, Signior Ass, &c.
Hic in collibus Sichem.	He was born on Shechem's hill ;
Jam nutritus sub Ruben ;	In Reuben's vales he fed his fill ;
Transiit per Jordanem,	He drank of Jordan's sacred stream,
Saliit in Bethlehem.	And gamboled in Bethlehem.
Hez, Sire Asnes, &c.	Now, Signior Ass, &c.
Ecce magnis auribus !	See that broad majestic ear !
Subjugalis filius ;	Born he is the yoke to wear ;
Asinus egregius,	All his fellows he surpasses !
Asinorum dominus !	He 's the very lord of asses !
Hez, Sire Asnes, &c.	Now, Signior Ass, &c.
Saltu vincit hinnulos,	In leaping he excels the fawn,
Damas et capreolos,	The deer, the colts upon the lawn ;
Super dromedarios	Less swift the dromedaries ran,
Velox Madianeos.	Boasted of in Midian.
Hez, Sire Asnes, &c.	Now, Signior Ass, &c.
Aurum de Arabia,	Gold, from Araby the blest,
Thus et myrrham de Saba,	Seba myrrh, of myrrh the best,
Tulit in ecclesia	To the church this ass did bring ;
Virtus asinaria.	We his sturdy labours sing.
Hez, Sire Asnes, &c.	Now, Signior Ass, &c.

Dum trahit vehicula Multa cum sarcinula, Illius mandibula Dura terit pabula. Hez, Sire Asnes, &c.	While he draws the loaded wain, Or many a pack, he don't complain; With his jaws, a noble pair, He doth craunch his homely fare. Now, Signior Ass, &c.
Cum aristis hordeum Comedit et carduum; Triticum à palea Segregat in area. Hez, Sire Asnes, &c.	The bearded barley and its stem, And thistles, yield his fill of them; He assists to separate, When its thresh'd, the chaff from wheat. Now, Signior Ass, &c.
Amen, dicas, asine,* Jam satur de gramine: Amen, amen, itera; Aspernare vetera. Hez va! hez va! hez va hez! Bialx Sire Asnes car allez; Belle bouche car chantez."†	Amen! bray most honour'd ass, Sated now with grain and grass; Amen repeat, Amen reply, And disregard antiquity."‡

The final chorus, as given by Du Cange, is certainly an imitation of asinine *braying;* and when performed by the whole congregation must have produced a most inharmonious symphony.

M. Millin has published an account of this festival as practised in the cathedral of Sens, in the thirteenth century. The details are taken from a MS. missal of that church, now kept in the town library, originally composed by Pierre Corbeil, archbishop of Sens, who died June, 1222. The MS. is said to be beautifully written, and the cover of it to be ornamented with representations of all the operations of vintage, and other analogous mythological subjects. At the time the missal was written the ceremonies were become entirely bacchanalian and impious. The priests were besmeared with lees of wine, and entered the choir dancing and singing obscene songs; the deacons and subdeacons profaned the altar by eating in the filthiest manner, and playing cards upon it while the priest was celebrating mass; pieces of old shoes were put into the censer, and burnt instead of incense; and the deacons and their companions were afterward carried through the streets in carts, practising various indecencies. For several days the most disgusting and extravagant actions were continued, and riot, drunkenness, and wanton singing universally prevailed both among clergy and laity.

Attempts were made at different periods to suppress these sottish superstitions, but unfortunately without success. Mauri-

* Here he is made to bend his knees. † Du Cange, Glossarium, v. *Festum.*

‡ Literary Panorama, vol. ii, pp. 585–588; and vol. vii, pp. 716–718.

tius, bishop of Paris, who died in 1196, laboured to abolish them, but the missal already noticed, which appears to have been drawn up *ex officio*, shows how completely he failed. In 1245, Odo, bishop of Sens, prohibited the offensive disguises, and repressed some of the mummeries and licentiousnesses which had become part of this festival; but did not remove the whole, for in 1444 the Faculty of Theology, at the request of several bishops, wrote to all the prelates and chapters to abolish this custom. It is, nevertheless, evident by the acts of the council held in 1460, that the grossnesses merely of this ceremony were retrenched; the council forbids caricature habits, false and uncouth singing, and orders, that on the *precentor of the fools*, as he was called on this occasion, *not more than three pails of water, at most, should be thrown*, and on the other naked men *only one pail each*, and that not *within the church;* the other ceremonies, if practised out of the church, were permitted. From so gentle a remonstrance it could not be expected that the festival would be materially checked; and we are not surprised to learn that it was officially permitted by acts of the chapter of Sens, in 1514 and 1517. Still later permissions are found, but with gradual prohibition of indecencies, till at length it ceased toward the end of the sixteenth century.*

This ridiculous festival was not limited to France; Michaelis, who supposes that annual fairs originated in the conventions of the people for religious purposes, conjectures, that one of the German annual fairs, denominated *Missen*, from the *masses* formerly said at those times, owed its rise to some ceremony of this kind. The fair is held on the Wednesday after Easter, near Querfurt, in the place called the Asses Meadow.† In England Robert Grosseteste or Greathead, bishop of Lincoln, in the eleventh century, ordered his dean and chapter to abolish the Feast of Asses, which had been annually celebrated in Lincoln cathedral on the feast of the circumcision, on account of its licentiousness.‡

The festival itself probably derives its origin from that principle of accommodation to the manners and prejudices of the people, which led to the adoption of rites and ceremonies in imitation of the pagans; the coronation of the ass was a part of the ceremony

* Literary Panorama, vol. ii, pp. 585–588; and vol. vii, pp. 714–719. See also Tilliot, Memoires pour servir a l'histoire de la Fete des Foux, *passim*.

† Michaelis's Commentaries on the Laws of Moses, vol. iii, p. 198.

‡ Warton's Hist. of Eng. Poetry, vol. ii, p. 367.

of the Feast of Vesta, an honour conferred upon this quadruped because, according to the pagan mythology, it had by its braying saved Vesta from being ravished by the Lampsacon god.

Among other superstitious practices of this century, the *trial by ordeal* is one of the most prominent. The following law of King Athelstan is sufficiently explanatory of its nature: "As to *ordeals*, we charge in the name of God, and by the precept of the archbishop, and all my bishops, that no one go into the church after the carrying in of the fire, with which the ordeal is to be heated, but the priest, and the person to be tried. And let nine feet be measured out from the stake to the mark, according to the length of the person's foot who is to be tried. And if it be the *water-ordeal*, let it be heated till it boils: and if it be a single accusation, let the hand be dipped to the fist only, to take out the stone; but if the accusation be three-fold, then let it be dipped to the elbow. And when the ordeal is ready, let two of each party come in, to see that it be sufficiently heated, and let an equal number of both sides enter, and stand on each side of the ordeal, along the church, and let them all be fasting, without having been with their wives the foregoing night; let them humble themselves at the priest's sprinkling the holy water upon them; and let the priest give them the Holy Gospel Book, and the sign of the holy cross to be kissed. And let no man increase the fire after the consecration is begun; but let the iron lie in the fire till the last collect, then let it be laid on the pillar.* And let nothing be said but prayers to God that he may reveal the truth; and let the person accused drink holy water, and let the hand in which he is to carry the ordeal be sprinkled with it. Let the nine measured feet be divided into three parts, containing each three feet. Let him place his right foot at the first mark at the stake; at the second mark let him put his right foot foremost; when he is come to the third, let him throw down the iron. Let him speed to the holy altar, and let his hand be sealed up. On the third day let inspection be made whether there be any filth† or not, in the place that was sealed up. If any one break these laws, let the ordeal be null, and a mulct of one hundred and twenty shillings be paid to the king."‡ The irrational and daringly impious practice of the modern *duellist* is almost the only remaining trace of this ancient appeal to the justice of God.

* *Super staples.* Some supporter made of stone or iron, from whence the person to be tried was to take the hot iron into his hands.—*Johnson.*

† If there was any matter or corruption, the person was condemned as guilty: if there was none, or the priest could see none, he was acquitted.—*Johnson.*

‡ Johnson's Collection of Ecclesiastical Laws, &c., vol. ii, A. D. DCCCCXXV.

But in the midst of the ignorance and superstition which so generally overspread the Western world, our acknowledgments of gratitude are due to those institutions, which, during the middle ages, preserved literature from utter extinction in Europe. Let our views be what they may of the general utility of monastic foundations, it is a well-known fact, that when literature was neglected everywhere else, it found a refuge in monasteries. In every great abbey there was an apartment called the SCRIPTORIUM, or *domus antiquarii*, where writers were constantly employed in copying psalters, missals, church music, and such other works as they could obtain. The monks, in these conventual writing-rooms, were enjoined to pursue their occupations in silence; and cautiously to avoid mistakes in grammar, or spelling, or pointing;* and in certain instances, authors prefixed to their works a solemn adjuration to the transcribers to copy them correctly. The following ancient one by Irenæus has been preserved: "I adjure thee who shalt transcribe this book, by our Lord Jesus Christ, and by his glorious coming to judge the quick and the dead, that thou compare what thou transcribest, and correct it carefully according to the copy from which thou transcribest; and that thou also annex a copy of this adjuration to what thou hast written."† When a number of copies were to be made of the same work, it was usual to employ several persons at the same time in writing it; each person, except the writer of the first skin, began where his fellow was to leave off.‡ Sometimes the writers wrote after another person called the *dictator*, who held the original, and dictated; hence the errors in the orthography of many ancient MSS., particularly Greek ones; thus in the very old fragments of the Greek Gospels, in the Cotton library, written in large ancient letters of silver and gold, CHIPAN is written for *σπεῖραν*, KYPHNEON for Κυρηναῖον; and many others.§

Musical notes intended for the choirs were also very frequently written from dictation. Till the eleventh century, musical notes were expressed only by letters of the alphabet, and till the fourteenth century they were expressed by large lozenge-shaped black dots, or points placed on different lines, one above another, and then first named *ut*, *re*, *mi*, *fa*, *sol*, *la*, to which *si* was afterward added; and they were all expressed without any distinction

* Du Cange, Glossarium, vol. i, Præfat., p. iv, and vol. vi, v. "*Scriptores*," and "*Scriptorium*." Venet. 1740, fol.

† Eusebius's Eccles. Hist., lib. v, cap. xx.

‡ Astle's Origin and Progress of Writing, ch. viii, p. 192.

§ Classical Journal, No. 24, December, 1815, p. 453.

as to length of time, and without any such thing as breves, semi breves, minims, crotchets, or quavers. The old Psalters, in many cathedral churches, are found thus written; and in consequence of this it was, that the *scriptoria* at Gloucester, and some other places, are found so contrived as to have long ranges of seats or benches, one beyond another, for the copyists; so that a master or person standing at one end, and naming each note, it might quickly be copied out by all, naming it in succession from one end to the other. Hence the Psalters were more easily copied than any other books; and it is not a little remarkable, that in the library at Worcester there is a copy of St. Matthew's Gospel set to music throughout, with these sort of notes.* In representations of these *scriptores*, or writers, in the act of writing, they are drawn with a pen in one hand, and an instrument to mark the lines with in the other; the inkhorn, an inverted cone, hanging on one side of the desk. Reeds were commonly used for writing the text and initials, and quills for the smaller writing.†

These writing monks were sometimes distinguished by the name of LIBRARII, the term applied to the common *scriptores*, who gained a livelihood by writing; but their more usual denomination was that of ANTIQUARII. Isidore, of Seville, says, "The *librarii* transcribed both old and new works; the *antiquarii* only those that were ancient; from whence also they derived their name."‡ Swift or short-hand writers obtained the name of *tachygraphi;* and elegant writers that of *calligraphi*. The works executed in large uncial or square characters were written by the latter; such for instance as the fifty copies of the Scriptures presented by Constantine the Great to the different churches, and the fifty copies sent by Athanasius to Constantius:§ and in the thirteenth century the scribes in Italy

* Savage's Librarian, vol. iii, p. 36. Lond. 1809, 8vo.

† Ducarel, in his Anglo-Norman Antiquities, p. 28, informs us, that in the cloisters of St. Owen, at Rouen, which appeared to be a more ancient building than the church, he "observed some old *stone desks* stuck to the pillars, and designed to place *books* upon;" and adds, "In the Benedictine convents it was anciently a custom, for all the monks to assemble together in the cloisters, at stated times in the day, and there cultivate their studies in common; some being employed in reading, while others were engaged in transcribing books; and for this purpose it was, that these desks were placed in the abbey cloisters." It may also be remarked, that the ancients, prior to the discovery of desks, wrote upon *scrolls*, placed upon their knees, and it is very questionable whether desks were at all in use before the seventh century. See also Fosbrooke's British Monachism, vol. ii, p. 179. Lond. 1802, 8vo.

‡ Isid. Hispal. Orig., lib. vi, cap. xiii, p. 48. Colon. Agrip. 1617, fol.

§ Nov. Test. Gr. a Woide, in Præfat., p. xiii.

called themselves *scriptores librorum*, or *exemplatores*.* It was the duty of the librarian, who was the *præcentor* of the monastery, to provide the writing monks with the books they were to copy, and whatever was necessary for their occupation; they were also forbidden to write any thing without his permission;† and in some of the great houses it was usual for the librarians to make some benefit, by letting others have copies made of the MSS. in their custody. The librarians were themselves generally fine writers and illuminators.‡

Besides being employed in the transcription of the Scriptures, and ecclesiastical works, and sometimes of the classics, the monks were the registrars of public events, of the age and succession of the king, and of the births of the royal family: and the constitutions of the clergy in their national and provincial synods, and (after the conquest) even acts of parliament were sent to the abbeys to be recorded by them. Instances also appear of the pope's sending orders for certain books to be made for him; and the monks used to transcribe the bulls of privileges, in books of a various nature, as missals, and others, as well as make marginal notes of the affairs of their abbeys in books of history; even the *Martyrologium* sometimes contained acts of general chapters.§

Those who were engaged in the transcription of books, were principally the novices and junior monks, but by a capitular of Aix-la-Chapelle, in 789, it was ordained, that "the Gospels, Psalters, and missals should be carefully written by monks of mature age."‖ Nuns were sometimes occupied in a similar way; but none of the Gilbertine nuns were to write books without leave of the grand prior, or hire or retain writers in their churches.¶

Calligraphy, or the art of beautiful writing, has been considered as having arrived at its summit of excellence in the monasteries of Spain; though it was not confined to them, for in England the Anglo-Saxon artists possessed eminent skill in the execution of their books, and the character they used had the honour of giving rise to the modern small beautiful Roman letter. But after the Norman invasion, degeneracy of skill occasioned the MSS. subse-

* Histoire des Arts, &c., cited in Literary Panorama, vol. iii, No. 4. January, 1816.

† Du Cange, Glossar., v. "*Scriptores.*"

‡ Nichols's Literary Anecdotes, vol. vi, pt. i, p. 77.

§ Tanner's Notitia Monastica, by Nasmith, Pref., p. xix. Camb. 1787, fol. Fosbrooke's British Monachism, vol. ii, pp. 177, 178.

‖ Du Cange, Glossar., vol. i, Præfat., p. iv.

¶ Fosbrooke, *ut sup.*

quent to that period, to be of difficult reading. The missals, and other books of divine offices, were indeed curiously done, through the extraordinary expense laid out upon works of this nature, and in compliance with an injunction, that no books should be brought into places of devotion which could not easily be read. Some copies were written in a larger hand, for more aged persons; and others illuminated with extraordinary beauty, for nuns of a superior quality, and other persons of distinction. At Godstowe there was a common library for the use of the nuns there, well furnished with books, many of which were in English, and divers of them historical; such of them as contained the lives of the holy men and women, especially of the latter, were curiously written *on vellum*, and many illuminations appeared throughout, so as to draw the nuns the more easily to follow their examples: and many of them "were finely covered, not unlike the Kiver of the Gospell book given to the chapel of Glastenbury, by King Ine."*

At the sale of the books belonging to the late James Edwards, Esq., of Pall-Mall, April, 1815, among many other very valuable MSS. were the following, thus described in the catalogue:—

"Psalterium Græco-Latinum, fol., a MS. of the *ninth* century, upon vellum, written in a very fair and legible hand, with this peculiarity, the Greek is written in Roman characters." Sold to the marquis of Douglas for £110 5s.

"Evangelia Quatuor, *Græce*, fol., a magnificent MS. upon vellum, of the *tenth* century, most elaborately executed. The subject of each page is designated at the top in letters of gold. This grand MS. is in the highest preservation, and is one of the finest Greek MS. of the Gospels extant. It is supposed to have been one of the Imperial collection saved at the capture of Constantinople. Bound in blue velvet, with bronze-gilt medallions of the birth of our Saviour, and the adoration of the magi, on the sides." Sold to Mr. Payne for £210.

"Evangelia Quatuor, *Latinè*, a most beautiful MS. of the *tenth* century, on vellum." Sold for £57 15s.

Michaelis, in his "Introduction to the New Testament," vol. ii, pt. i, p. 218, notices a Greek MS., (Basileensis, b. vi, p. 27,) which Wetstein supposes to have been written in the *tenth* century, and which is held in high estimation for its critical authority. It was given by Johannes de Ragusio to the monastery in Basil, and was borrowed from the monks by Reuchlin or Capnio, who kept it

* Hearne's edit. Guil. Neubrig., quoted in Dibdin's Bibliomania, p. 236, note. Fosbrooke's British Monachism, vol. ii, pp. 178, 179.

during thirty years, till the time of his death. It contains the whole of the New Testament, except the Revelation. It is written on vellum, with small characters and accents; and is ornamented with pictures, one of which appears to be a portrait of Leo Sapiens, and of his son Constantine Porphyrogenitus. Montfaucon also, in his "Journey through Italy," *passim*, notices many valuable MSS. of the middle ages, preserved in the different libraries of Italy; several of which are written upon *silk*, others upon vellum and purple paper, executed in the most superb manner.

Professor Tychsen, when noticing the beauty of certain MSS., '*where the letters throughout were so equal that the whole had the appearance of print*," adds, "Frequently, after reflecting on this singular circumstance, I have been inclined to think, that the monks, who cultivated the study of calligraphy with great eagerness, had the forms of all the letters of the alphabet impressed into or engraved out of thin plates: that whole pages or columns of these plates were placed under the parchment or vellum on which it was intended to write, so that, by drawing a pencil over them, the monks were able to produce this surprising equality of letters; or it may have been that the shapes or forms of the letters were first imprinted upon the parchment or vellum, and afterward filled up."* The celebrated Codex Argenteus, or Fragments of the Gothic Gospels, (see p. 118,) has been supposed to have been executed by heated metallic characters, or letters, impressed on gold or silver foil, attached to vellum by some glutinous or resinous cement, similar to the mode adopted by bookbinders in lettering and ornamenting their volumes. Ihre, the learned professor of the university of Upsal, in his *Ulphilas Illustratus*, 1752, 1755, 4to., and in his Preface to "Fragments of Ulphilas's Version of some Portions of the Epistle to the Romans," 1763, 4to., has endeavoured to establish the fact, by showing that the furrows of the letters in the *Codex Argenteus* are so palpably and deeply impressed, that when the vellum in every other part is highly polished and exceeding smooth, the lines present a rough surface, to be distinguished by the touch of the finger; and by observing that the delineation of the letters so perfectly corresponds throughout the whole volume, that they never vary in the least from each other, either in size or shape.† Meerman, in his *Origines Typo-*

* Butler's Horæ Biblicæ, tom. i, p. 46.

† The intelligent Mr. Coxe (Travels into Poland, &c., vol. iv, p. 173, 8vo.) has offered a different opinion as to the mode of forming the letters of the *Codex Argenteus*. "I was convinced," says he, "from a close inspection, that each letter was

graphicæ, has supported the same opinion; and in reply to an objection, that vellum would not admit of the application of heated iron types so frequently repeated, has stated that he ordered his bookbinder to stamp an entire folio of vellum, in the way that he lettered the backs of volumes; which he effected without difficulty, and with little injury to the smoothness of its surface.* This mode of imprinting letters with gold and silver foil has been thought to be what the Romans denominated the *encaustic* art.†

Particular lands were given, or a tax levied upon the community, to furnish the writing materials for these conventual *scriptoria*. A noble Norman, who was a great hearer and lover of books, (*diligens auditor et amator scripturarum*,) conferred upon the abbey of St. Albans, about A.D. 1086, two parts of the tithes of Hatfield, and certain tithes in Redburn, for the formation of

painted, and not formed, as some authors have asserted, by a hot iron upon leaves of gold and silver." In a note he adds, "They [the letters] appeared to me to be drawn or painted, in the same manner as the initial letters in several of the finest missals; and not stamped, as the learned Mr. Ihre conjectures, or imprinted on the vellum with hot metal types, in the like manner as the bookbinders at present letter the backs of books."

* To the works already mentioned, relating to the Gothic version of Ulphilas, may be added, the edition of that version by M. Zahn, preacher at Delitz-sur-la-Saale, near Weissenfels, in Saxony, printed at Weissenfels, 1805, large 4to. The text of the Gospels is chiefly from a corrected MS. of Chancellor Ihre's, who had meditated a new edition of the version; but being prevented from publishing by the appearance of Lye's edition, had presented his MS. to the celebrated Busching, at whose death it passed into the hands of M. Heynatz, professor at Frankfort on the Oder, who communicated it to M. Zahn. The Fragments of the Epistle to the Romans are taken from Knittel. The whole is accompanied with a completely literal interlineary Latin translation, by Charles Frederick Fulda, formerly pastor in the dutchy of Wirtemberg, well known for his various works on antiquities, and the genius of the German language. At the side of the text is Benzel's translation corrected by Ihre; and below are placed critical and explanatory notes, and the various readings by M. Zahn. A Mœso-Gothic Grammar is added by C. F. Fulda, revised, and a supplement subjoined, by M. Zahn. Annexed to the grammar is a glossary by C. F. Fulda, corrected by M. Reinwald, first librarian of the Ducal library of Meinungen. To the work is prefixed a preface by M. Zahn, in which he first gives a general idea of the work, and a biographical notice of Fulda; after which follows an ample introduction, divided into two parts; the first containing a history of the Goths and their language, drawn from a work of Adelung's of Dresden; the second presenting a review of the life of Ulphilas and his version, partly from a MS. of Adelung's. M. Zahn has also prefixed to his grammar a specimen of the Codex Argenteus, from Matt., ch. v, printed with fac-simile types, formed under the direction of M. Steenwinkel of Harderwick, who had projected, but not executed, a fac-simile edition.—*Millin, Magasin Encyclopedique*, tom. iii, Mai. 1806, pp. 61–68. Paris, 8vo.

† Henshall's Gothic Gospel, pp. 37–44.

volumes necessary to the church; and appointed a daily provision of meat to be allowed the writers, lest they should be hindered in their work. Paul, who was abbot at the time, and by whose persuasion the bequest was made, built the *scriptorium*, and caused some noble volumes necessary for the church to be placed there, written by writers selected and fetched from a distance, the copies being furnished by Archbishop Lanfranc. By the rules of Evesham, the præcentor was obliged to find, from the tithes and lands allotted him, *enamel* for all the writers of the monastery, and *parchment* for briefs,* and *colours* for illuminating books, and necessaries for *binding* them.† The *scriptorium* at St. Edmundsbury was endowed with two mills; and in the year 1171 the tithes of a rectory were appropriated to the cathedral convent of St. Swithin, at Winchester, *ad libros transcribendos*. For a similar purpose, *ad libros faciendos*, Nigel gave the monks of Ely two churches in 1160; and Hearne (*Ad Domerham*, Num. iii.) has published a grant from R. de Paston to Bronholm abbey, in Norfolk, of 12d. per annum, a rent charge on his lands, to keep their books in repair, *ad emendacionem librorum*.‡

The prices of the materials for writing upon, during the middle ages, have been already noticed when treating of the *Codices Rescripti*, to which the following entry in the *Compotus* of Bolton may be added:—

> XC
> "MCCVIII
> *Pro auro et coloribus ad picturam, et pro uno missali luminand' et ligand', XVIs.*"
>
> For gold and colours, and for illuminating and binding a missal, 16s.§

This was probably an elaborate and curious work; for *sixteen shillings* was one-third more than the yearly clothing of a canon cost, and equivalent to £12 at present.

The transcription of books, as a monastic employment, may be traced to an early era. In the *fourth* century, Martin, bishop of Tours, built the famous abbey of Marmoutier, the most ancient that now subsists in France, and which belongs to the congregation of St. Maur. The place was then a desert, enclosed by a high

* A term originally signifying heads, or contents of chapters.

† Whitaker's Cathedral of Cornwall, vol. ii, ch. vii, sec. 3, pp. 352, 353.

‡ Warton's History of English Poetry, vol. i, dissert. 2.

§ Whitaker's History of Craven, p. 384. Lond. 1812, 4to.

steep rock on one side, and by the river Loire on the other, and the entrance into it was only by one very narrow passage. The bishop had a cell built of wood; several of his monks had cells made in the same manner: but the greater part took up their dwellings in narrow holes, which they dug in the side of the rock. He had here, in a short time, about fourscore monks: among them, no one had any distinct property, no one was allowed to buy or sell, as was the practice of the greater part of the monks with regard to their sustenance and work. *No art or business was permitted among them except that of writing*, to which the younger were deputed, while the more ancient attended to prayer and spiritual functions.*

In the *sixth* century, Cassiodorus retired from the toil of political engagements, erected a monastery, and employed his monks in the meritorious labours of transcription: about the same period St. Columba, or Columb-Kill, who founded the monastery of Iona, directed his attention to sacred literature, and deserves to be praised for the correctness of the copies produced by him and his followers. In the library of Trinity College, Dublin, a copy of the Old Testament is preserved, written by Columba, on vellum, in the Roman character; at the beginning of which is a conveyance of land from the king of Meath to Columba and his successors in the abbey of Kells, written in the Irish character. The monks of Croyland also appear to have been diligent copyists; for Ingulph relates, that when the library of that abbey was burned in the year 1091, seven hundred volumes were consumed. Fifty-eight volumes were transcribed at Glastonbury, during the government of one abbot, about the year 1300; and in the library of this monastery, the richest in England, there were upward of four hundred volumes in the year 1248.†

In the eleventh century, Bruno, the celebrated founder of the Carthusian monks, was one of the active promoters of knowledge, by the attention which he paid to the multiplication of books by transcription. He was a descendant of an ancient and honourable family at Cologne, where he was born, about A. D. 1030. Removing to Rheims he became chancellor of that diocess, and doctor of divinity. Such was his reputation, that he was considered the ornament of the age in which he lived, and the model of good men. He was learned in Greek and Hebrew, and in the writings

* Butler's Lives, vol. xi, Nov. 11, p. 209.

† Vallancey's Grammar of the Iberno-Celtic, or Irish Language, ch. ix, p. 147. Warton's Hist. of Eng. Poetry, diss. 2.

of the fathers, particularly Ambrose and Augustine. His principal works are, comments on the Psalter, and on St. Paul's Epistles. After the legal deposition of Manasses, archbishop of Cologne, for simony, Bruno was offered the vacant archbishopric, but preferred a state of solitude. He, with six companions, withdrew into the desert of Chartreuse, in the diocess of Greenoble, selecting a barren plain, in a narrow valley, between two cliffs, near a rapid torrent, surrounded with high craggy rocks, almost all the year covered with snow; there he and his companions built an oratory, and very small cells, at a little distance from each other, similar to the ancient Lauras of Palestine. Such was the original of the order of Carthusians, which took its name from this desert. The name of *Chartreuse* is given to all other convents of this order, which by some has been corruptly called in English *Charter-house*, the term now constantly applied to their ancient residence in London. The Carthusians practised uncommon austerities; but their chief employment was that of *copying books*, by which they endeavoured to earn their subsistence, that they might not be burdensome to others; they were enjoined to keep almost continual silence, and to speak to each other by signs. Bruno was careful to provide for them a good library of useful and pious books. He died in 1101. This order, notwithstanding its excessive austerities, was at one period so extensive, that it possessed one hundred and seventy-two convents, and five nunneries; the nunneries were all situated in the Catholic Netherlands. By the rules of the Carthusians, the sacrist was ordered at a certain hour of the day, "to deliver out to the monks, ink, parchment, pens, chalk, and books to read or transcribe;" and the following remarks evince extraordinary literary ardour: "Books ought to be carefully preserved as the everlasting food of our souls; and since we cannot preach the word of God with our mouths, we do it by our hands, for the books which we transcribe, are so many sermons of truth which we deliver."*

In the fourteenth century, Gerard de Groot, or Gerard the Great, instituted a society called *Fratres Vitæ Communis*, or Brethren of the common life. Gerard was born at Deventer, in the year 1340. His parents, who were wealthy, bestowed great care upon his education, and at fifteen years of age sent him to Paris to perfect himself in theological and philosophical studies.

* Butler's Lives, vol. x, pp. 132–150. Milner's History of the Church of Christ, vol. iii, pp. 326, 327. D'Emillianne's Hist. of Monastical Orders, pp. 102–105. Mabillon, Annales, tom. iii, pp. 548, 549.

His acquirements in general knowledge afterward procured for him the distinctive appellation of *The Great;* but in the midst of his intellectual celebrity, he debased himself by levity, luxury, and dissipation. A private, but faithful reproof, from one of his former fellow-students, was the occasion of an entire change in his conduct. He now became grave, devout, and exemplary; he clothed himself in a doublet of gray, lined with hair, and retired to a monastery at Munikhuysen, where he devoted himself to prayer and the reformation of immoral characters. Meeting with unexpected success in this pious avocation, he instituted the fraternity before mentioned. "One heart, one soul, one common property, influenced and supported this illustrious society; whose glory it was that *they earned their livelihood by their pen.*" They were distinguished by wearing a gray coat, lined with hair next their skin. A black cowl hung down behind as low as the waist; and whenever they went abroad, they wrapped themselves in a large mantle, which descended to their heels. Their hair was closely cropped in a circular manner. Dibdin, in his "Typographical Antiquities," vol. i, p. 9, has given a representation of their dress, copied from "*Lambinet's Recherches,* &c." Successive popes confirmed and extended their privileges; and in 1402 seven monasteries had admitted their rules, and imitated their example.* Gerard died in 1384, in the forty-fourth year of his age, and was buried in the church of the Virgin Mary, at Deventer.†

Of all the disciples of Gerard, no one seems to have excelled the celebrated THOMAS A KEMPIS, either in piety, or manual skill. This excellent man was born in a village called Chempis, or Kempis, in the diocess of Cologne, about A. D. 1380. In his youth he studied at Deventer in the school of the "Brethren of the common life;" and in 1400 became a canon regular in the convent of Mount St. Agnes, near Zwoll, in the province of Over-Yssel. The sincerity of his piety, and the amiableness of his manners, caused him to be chosen sub-prior, and afterward procurator of the monastery. He died in 1471, in the ninty-first year of his age. In a painting near his tomb, he is represented as sitting in a chair; a monk on his knees before him inquires, "Thomas, where shall I, with certainty, find true rest?" To which he replies, "Never canst thou find certain rest but in the cell, in the Bible, and in Christ," (*in cellâ, Codice, Christo.*) He was the author of several works,

* Dibdin's Typographical Antiquities, vol. i, *Ames's Preface,* pp. 8–10, note. Lond. 1810, 4to.

† Freheri Theatrum, tom. i, pt. i, sec. 3, p. 80. Norib. 1688, fol.

the most noted of which are his Lives of Gerard de Groot, and his successors, Dr. Florentius, and John Cacabus, or Chetel; and his Imitation of Christ, or Christian Pattern. It has indeed been disputed whether he was the author of the last-named work, but the evidence preponderates in his favour. Trithemius, a German monk, in *Catalog. Virorum Illustrium*, says, there were two persons of this name, both of them regular monks, the elder of whom, who flourished about A. D. 1410, was the author of The Imitation of Christ; the younger lived in his own time, about A. D. 1495.* The incomparable work of The Imitation of Christ has been translated into most European languages, and even into Chinese. As a Biblical scribe, his immediate master, Radewyns, assures us, that "he excelled in this department, and devoted his earnings to the support of the common body." He is said to have been the copier of the Bible, in four large volumes; of a very large missal; of some Opuscula of St. Bernard; and of several minor works. The seventh plate in Meerman's *Origines Typographicæ* exhibits a specimen of works printed from his hand-writing.† A beautiful copy of the Bible is preserved in the library of the regular canons at Cologne, transcribed by him, as appears from the following colophon, at the end of the fifth volume:—

Completum est hoc volumen Novi Testamenti anno Domini MCCCCXXVII., in vigilia Pentacostes, per manus fratris Thomæ de Kempis ad laudem Dei.‡

"This volume of the New Testament was finished A. D. MCCCCXXVII., on the eve of Pentecost, by the hand of the brother Thomas de Kempis, to the glory of God."

If this be the same Bible as that referred to before, there must be an error in one case as to the number of volumes; but as transcription was his usual employment, it is probable that, in the course of a long life, he transcribed more than one copy of the Scriptures.

In the middle of the fifteenth century, the "Brothers of the common life" instituted public schools for the instruction of the poor and ignorant. Tho Brabant Chronicle informs us, that in the year 1460 the public magistrate at Brussels invited over a body of these "Brothers" to establish schools of instruction there, and appointed colleges for their reception. Lambinet (*Recherches*, &c.) says he saw at Louvain a most beautiful manuscript missal, *Se*

* Freheri Theatrum, tom. i, pt. i, sec. 3, pp. 92, 93.

† Dibdin's Typographical Antiquities, vol. i, p. 10.

‡ Voyage Litteraires de deux Religieux Benedictins, tom. ii, p. 266.

cundum consuetudinem Gallicorum, which was printed in 1481, and had been executed by one of these "Brothers." As they had taken St. Gregory and St. Jerome for their patrons, these scribes were sometimes called the "Brothers of St. Gregory," or "of St. Jerome."*

From the length of time requisite for the transcription of books, and the immense labour bestowed upon them, the expense of copying manuscripts was necessarily very great. This, joined to the cost of the materials for writing upon, rendered the purchase of books almost impossible to the poor, and persons of moderate fortune. In the year 1174, Walter, prior of St. Swithin's at Winchester, afterward elected abbot of Westminster, purchased of the canons of Dorchester, in Oxfordshire, St. Austin's Psalter and Bede's Homilies, for twelve measures of barley, and a pall, on which was embroidered in silver the history of St. Birinus converting a Saxon king.†

In the tenth century, *a single copy of the Bible*, and a few other books, not exceeding *sixteen* in the whole, were considered as a legacy of sufficient importance to be witnessed by the king and queen, and several bishops; and of so great value as to be bequeathed as the common property of several monasteries:‡ and in the thirteenth century, Elizabeth, the wife of Charles Robert, king of Hungary, mentioned two breviaries in her will, one of which she bequeathed to her daughter-in-law, and the other to Clara von Puker, but with this stipulation, that after her death it should belong to a monastery at Buda.§

In the *Compotus* of Bolton we have the following entries, which I transcribe, with the remarks of the historian of Craven upon them.

"MCCCV.

Pro quodam Libro Sententiarum empt. XXXs."

"The Book of Sentences, by Peter Lombard, one of the most fashionable books of school divinity in the middle age. The price of this volume was nearly that of two good oxen. How expensive must it have been to furnish a library with MSS.! But the canons of Bolton did not exhaust themselves in this way. I can only discover that they purchased three books in forty years!"

* Dibdin's Typographical Antiquities, vol. i, p. 10.

† Warton's Hist. of Eng. Poetry, vol. i, diss. 2.

‡ Mabillon, Annales Benedict., tom. iii, lib. xli, p. 351. Lutecia-Parisiorum, 1707, folio.

§ Beckman's Hist. of Inventions, vol. ii, p. 240.

"MCCCX.

Pro uno libro qui vocatur V' itates Theologie, VIs."

"*V' itates Theologie*—In the beginning of the fourteenth century, I can scarcely suppose there was a book with so profane or so bold a title as Vanitates Theologiæ; and therefore I understand this contraction to mean either Veritates or Utilitates."

"MCCCXIII.

Pro Chroniclis apud Ebor. scribendis, XIs."

"To the care and curiosity of the religious houses it is principally owing that the Old Chronicles of our country were preserved till the invention of printing."*

Besides the monks who were employed in the monasteries, in copying manuscripts, there were others who were engaged in illuminating and binding them when written. Gold and azure were, as has been already noticed, (p. 143,) the favourite colours of the illuminators. In binding their books, some were adorned with gold, silver, ivory, precious stones, or coloured velvet; but for common binding they frequently used rough white sheep-skin, with or without immense bosses of brass, pasted upon a wooden board; and sometimes the covers were of plain wood, carved in scroll and similar work.† About the year 790, Charlemagne granted an unlimited right of hunting to the abbot and monks of Sithiu, for making their gloves and girdles of the skins of the deer they killed, and for covers for their books.‡ In a copy of the will of Lady Ravensworth, the wife of Lord Fitzhugh, dated September 24th, 1427, we find the following bequests: "Also I wyl yat my son Robert [bishop of London] have a SAUTER, covered with rede velvet, and my doghter Margory a PRIMER, covered in rede, and my doghter Darcy a SAUTER, covered in blew, and my doghter Maulde Eure a PRIMER, covered in blew, and yong Elizabeth Fitzhugh, my god-doghter, a boke covered in grene, with praiers thereinne."§ About the year 1430, Whethamstede, the learned and liberal abbot of St. Albans, being desirous of familiarizing the history of his patron saint to the monks of his convent, employed Lydgate, as it should seem, then a monk of Bury, to translate the Latin legend of his life in English rhymes. It was placed before the altar of the saint, which Whethamstede afterward adorned with much magnificence, in the abbey church. He paid for the transla

* Whitaker's Hist. of Craven, pp. 388, 391, 393.

† Fosbrooke's British Monachism, vol. ii, p. 180.

‡ Warton, *ubi sup.*

§ Antiquarian Repertory, vol. iii, pp. 79, 80.

tion, writing, and illumination of the legend, *one hundred shillings*, and expended on the binding and other exterior ornaments upward of *three pounds!*"* These were immense sums to be laid out on such a work, since, in 1426, an *ox* was appraised at *three shillings and four pence;* a *cow* at *two shillings and eight pence*, and a *horse* at *three shillings*.†

A tolerably correct idea may be formed of the superb manner in which these works were bound, which were designed for the use of the principal churches, from the following extract from an inventory of copies of the Gospels belonging to the cathedral church of Lincoln, taken in 1536:—

"*Imprimis.* A Text after Matthew, covered with a plate, silver and gilt, having an image of the Majesty, [that is, of the Saviour,] with the four evangelists and four angels about the said image; having at every corner an image of a man, with divers stones, great and small; beginning in the second less: and a transmigration, wanting divers stones and little pieces of the plate."

"*Item.* One other Text after John, covered with a plate, silver and gilt, with an image of the crucifix, Mary, and John, having twenty-two stones of divers colours, wanting four, written in the second less: *Est qui prior me erat.*"‡

For less valuable works a plainer style of binding was adopted. When they were bound in thick boards, without any leather covering, it was usual to cut letters in the covers, which, in order to be better preserved, were placed in a hollow part, as might easily be done, when the boards were pretty thick. Scaliger also tells us "that his grandmother had a Psalter, the cover of which was two inches thick, in the inside of which was a kind of cupboard, wherein was a silver crucifix, and behind it the name of Berenica Codronia de la Scala." In such cases the crucifix was safely guarded by a metal door with clasps.

Many books were ornamented with metal or ivory figures, and silver or brass bosses on the outside of the cover. A Latin Psalter, with an interlineary Saxon version, probably of the ninth century, and preserved in the library at Stowe, is decorated, on the exterior of the oaken boards with which it is bound, with a large brass crucifix, about seven or eight inches in height, formerly, perhaps, covered or washed with silver. A MS. copy of the Latin Gospels, mentioned by Mr. Dibdin, (Decameron, vol. ii, p. 434,) is also said

* Warton's Hist. of Eng. Poetry, vol. ii, p. 53.

† Chronicon Preciosum, p. 103. London, 1707, 8vo.

‡ Dugdale's Monast. Anglic., vol. iii, p. 277, 2d edit., 1673, folio.

to have oaken covers, the outside of one of which was inlaid with pieces of carved *ivory:* the first consists of our Saviour, with an angel above him; the second of the Virgin with Christ in her lap, the Virgin being represented in half length: the third is a small whole length of Joseph with an angel above. A gilt *nimbus* or glory is round the head of each, but that which encircles the Virgin is perfect; and the compartment in which she appears (about five inches high) is twice the size of each of the others. The draperies throughout are good.*

Sometimes inferior writings were merely stitched in parchment covers. Bagford (Harl MSS., No. 5910) says, that "when old books and MSS. were done with, they were thrown under the desks by the scribes and monks, and there lay till the binders used them as waste parchment or vellum, to bind up with the new books transcribed."†

But neither the *writing* nor the *illuminating*, nor even the *binding* of books, was the work of the subordinate monks only. Ervene, one of the teachers of Wolstan, bishop of Worcester, was famous for caligraphy and skill in colours. To invite his pupils to read, he made use of a Psalter and Sacramentary, whose capital letters he had richly illuminated with gold. This was about the year 980. Herman, one of the Norman bishops of Salisbury, about the year 1080, condescended to write, bind, and illuminate books.‡ The Gospel written by Eadfrid, and illuminated by Ethelwold, has been already noticed. In the thirteenth century, when Michael Palæologus had usurped the Greek empire, and had had recourse to the barbarous policy of putting out the eyes of the rightful heir, then an infant, he basely accused Arsenius, the guardian of the emperor, and bishop of Nice in Bithynia, of certain crimes before an assembly of priests. The venal convocation condemned and banished Arsenius to a small island of the Propontis But, conscious of his integrity, the pious bishop bore his sufferings with serenity and composure; and requesting that an account might be taken of the treasure of the church, he showed that *three pieces of gold, which he had earned by transcribing psalms,* were the whole of his property.§

The reader who wishes to see the subjects of ancient illumina-

* Concise Hist. of Printing, p. 44. London, 1770, 8vo. Dibdin's Bibliomania, p. 158, 2d edit. Dibdin's Bibliographical Decameron, vol. ii, p. 434, *note.*

† Dibdin's Typographical Antiquities, vol. i. *Life of Caxton,* p. cxxx.

‡ Warton's Hist. of Eng. Poetry, diss. 2.

§ Milner's Hist. of the Church of Christ, vol. iv, ch. vi, pp. 15, 16.

tion and bookbinding discussed at large, may consult the Rev. T F. Dibdin's superb and entertaining work entitled "The Bibliographical Decameron," 3 vols. 8vo., Lond. 1817, *passim;* and Herman Hugo's erudite work, edited by C. H. Totz, *De Prima Scribendi Origine, et Universæ rei literariæ Antiquitate,* Traj. ad Rhen. 1738, 8vo.

Resuming the occurrences of the tenth century, we remark with pleasure, that amid the general ignorance which prevailed in Europe, some faint efforts were made to dispel the shades of illiterate barbarism, and to promote the interests of religion and learning. Edward, the son, and Athelstan, the grandson of Alfred, were not only the bravest, but the most intelligent princes of their age, and the greatest patrons of learning. EDWARD, if we may believe some of our ancient historians, was the founder or restorer of the university of Cambridge, as his father had been of Oxford; but the Danes, in 1010, again ruined the schools and town of Cambridge. Another proof which he gave of his regard to learning, was that of bestowing a very liberal education on his five sons and nine daughters, who excelled all the princes and princesses of their age in literary accomplishments.*

ATHELSTAN, the eldest son and successor of Edward, was a prince of uncommon learning for the age in which he lived. There is a catalogue of his books extant, which may not be unworthy of notice. It is in Saxon characters, in the Cotton library, (Domitian, A. 1,) in these words:—

"This syndon tha bec the Æthelstanes waeran; De natura rerum; Persius, de arte metrica; Donatum minorem; Excerptiones de metrica arte; APOCALYPSIN; Donatum majorem; Alchuinum; Glossa super Catonem; Libellum de grammatica arte qui sic incipit, &c. Sedulium . . . . .] 1 gerim waes Alfwoldes preostes, Glossa super Donatum. Dialogorum."†

During his reign a law was passed, which enacted, "that if any man made such proficiency in learning as to obtain priest's orders, he should enjoy all the honours of a thane," or nobleman.‡ It has also been asserted that this prince employed certain Jews, who then resided in England, to translate the *Old Testament* out of *Hebrew* into *Anglo-Saxon:* Leland, in his "Newe yeares Gyfte, enlarged by Johan Bale," says, "As concernynge the Hebrue, it

* Henry's Hist. of Great Britain, vol. iv, b. ii, ch. iv, pp. 69, 70.

† Turner's Hist. of the Anglo-Saxons, vol. i, b. vi, ch. ii, p. 363, *note*.

‡ Henry's Hist. of Great Britain, vol. iv, p. 71.

is to be thought, that many were therein well learned in the dayes of Kynge Athelstane. For at the instaunt request of his prelates, he caused the Scriptures out of that tungue to be by certen doctours translated into the Saxonysh or Englyshe speche, as in the Chronycles is mencyoned."* Archbishop Usher, in his *Historia Dogmatica*, &c., places this in the year 930. But the learned Hody, *De Bib. Text.*, lib. iii, p. 415, considers the fact as doubtful.

Athelstan is represented to have been a great benefactor to the monastic institutions. He rebuilt many; and was liberal to most, of books, ornaments, or endowments. In the Cotton library there are two curious MSS., which were presented by him to different religious institutions. One is a MS. of the Latin Gospels. Before these is a page of Latin in Saxon characters, of which the first part is—*Volumen hoc Evangelii Æthelstan Anglorum basyleos, et curagulos totius Britanniæ devota mente Dorobernensis cathedræ primatui tribuit*—"Athelstan, king of England, and governor of all Britain, with a pious intention, gave this volume of the Gospels to the cathedral church of Canterbury." One page is occupied by the letters LIB. in large gilt capitals, and by the rest of the first verse in small gilt capitals, on a lilac ground. The following verses, containing the genealogy, are in gilt capitals, on a dark blue ground. The first verses of the three other Gospels are in gilt capitals, on the uncoloured parchment. To each a painting of the evangelist is prefixed. The rest is written in ink, without abbreviations. In the beginning of the Gospels is a page with, *Incipit evangelium secundum Matthæum*, in large gilt capitals. Below these words are two crosses; opposite to one is ODDA REX, and to the other MIHTILD MATER REGIS; from which it appears probable that it was a present from Otho of Germany, whose name a contemporary writer spells Oddo, who married Athelstan's sister; and from Mathilda, the empress of Henry, and mother of Otho. It is said to have been used for the coronation oath of our Anglo-Saxon kings, but this is doubtful. The other MS. was presented by Athelstan to the monastery of Bath. It contains the proceedings of the sixth synod of Constantinople, in the seventh century. At the end of the MS. is a paragraph, stating that it was written in the time of Pope Sergius. Sergius was pope in 690. Besides these MSS., there is in the same valuable library a small sized volume, which has come down to us as the Psalter used by Athelstan. In the beginning of it is

* Lives of Leland, Hearne, and Wood, vol. i. Oxford, 1772, 8vo.

a very ancient calendar, in Saxon letters, written in 703. The rest is composed of prayers, the Latin Psalter, and several other hymns, very handsomely written. Every psalm is begun with gilt capitals, with a title preceding in red letters. It has several ornamental paintings.*

There were also during this century several ecclesiastical laws or canons published, which deserve attention, as illustrative of the state of Biblical knowledge. Among those ascribed to King Edgar are the following, designed, as we learn from the title, for "the regulation of the lives of ecclesiastical persons:"—

Can. 3. "That at every synod, every year, they have their books and vestments for divine ministration, as also ink, and parchment for [writing down] their instructions, and three days' provision."

12. "That no learned priest do reproach him that is half-learned, but mend him, if he know how."

17. "That every Christian man diligently win his child to Christianity, and teach him the Lord's Prayer, and the Creed."

34. "That every priest take great care to have a *good* book, at least a *true* one."

52. "That priests preach to the people every Sunday, and always give them a good example."

64. "That no priest be a hunter, or hawker, or player at dice; but entertain himself with his book, as becometh his order."†

In the canons drawn up by Elfric for Bishop Wulfsin, in which the seven orders appointed in the church are defined, it is observed, that

"The *lector* is to read in God's church, and is ordained to publish God's word."

"He is called the *acolyth* who holds the candle, or taper, at the divine ministration, when the Gospel is read, or the housel hallowed at the altar, not as if he were to drive away the obscure darkness, but to signify bliss by that light, to the honour of Christ, who is our light."

"The *deacon* is he that ministers to the mass-priest, and places the oblation on the altar, and reads the Gospel at the divine ministration."

By the can. 21 it is ordained that "the priest shall have the furniture for his ghostly work before he be ordained, that is, the Holy Books, the Psalter, and the Pistol-Book, Gospel-Book, and Mass-

* Turner's History of the Anglo-Saxons, vol. i, p. 363.

† Johnson's Collection of Ecclesiastical Laws, &c., A. D. DCCCCLX.

Book, the Song-Book and the Hand-Book, the Kalendar, the Passional, the Penitential, and the Lesson-Book."

Of these books it may be necessary to remark, that "the *Pistol-Book* did not contain the entire Epistles, or entire four Gospels, but such portions of them as were assigned to be read at the altar, at mass."

The *Song-Book*, sometimes called the *Antiphonar*, was a book of anthems to be sung with responses.

The *Manual*, or *Hand-Book*, contained directions for the administration of baptism, and extreme unction; the catechism; and the service for the dead.

The *Passional* was the same with the Martyrology.

The *Penitential* was the book which directed the priest what penance to enjoin for every sin confessed to him.

By can. 23 it is further enjoined that "the mass-priest, on Sundays and mass-days, shall speak the sense of the Gospel to the people, in *English*, and of the Pater Noster and the Creed, as oft as he can, for the inciting of the people to know their belief, and retaining their Christianity. Let the teacher take heed of what the prophet says: 'They are dumb dogs, and cannot bark.' We ought to bark and preach to laymen, lest they should be lost through ignorance. Christ, in his Gospel, saith of unlearned teachers, 'If the blind lead the blind, they both fall into the ditch.' The teacher is blind that hath no book-learning; and he misleads the laity through his ignorance. Thus are you to be aware of this, as your own duty requires."*

Among the Saxon Capitulars, translated from those of Theodulf, bishop of Orleans, by a bishop of uncertain date, probably by Elfric, the following is the 20th: "Mass-priests ought always to have a school of learners in their houses, and if any good man will commit his little ones to them to be taught, they ought gladly to accept them, and to teach them at free cost. Ye should consider that it is written, 'They that are learned shine as the brightness of heaven; and they who persuade and instruct men to right, as the stars for ever and ever;' yet they ought not to demand any thing of their relations for their learning, but what they of their own accord are willing to give."†

England had its scholars also, who befriended learning by their countenance and example. The haughty DUNSTAN, archbishop of Canterbury, was one of the most celebrated. Occasionally he

* Johnson's Eccles. Laws, &c., A. D. DCCCCLVII.

† Johnson, *ut sup.*, A. D. DCCCCXCIV.

employed himself in the transcription of books; though his more favourite pursuits were painting and music, chemistry and mechanics, and the sublime sciences of astronomy and geometry.

But of all the Saxon scholars, a monk named Elfric seems to have been the only one who attempted, by vernacular translations, to enable his countrymen to read the Scriptures in their native tongue. Very little is known of him accurately, except from the prefaces and dedications of his writings. From these we learn that he was a mass-priest and an abbot; that he had been the alumnus, or pupil, of Athelwold, bishop of Winchester, and that on the death of Athelwold he was sent by Bishop Elfeage to a monastery called Cernal, at the request of a nobleman named Æthelmer, during the reign of King Æthelred.* From the name of Elfric being subscribed to an authentic instrument, of the year 1001 or 1002, Cave† supposes him to have been afterward advanced to the archiepiscopal see of Canterbury. This opinion has been generally followed.

This pious and learned Saxon partly composed and partly translated a number of homilies, which were everywhere distributed among the priests, and ordered to be publicly read to the people on Sundays and holydays. In them he speaks in the highest terms of the Holy Scriptures, and strenuously enforces the constant reading of them. In his homily "On the Assumption of the Virgin Mary," he observes, "If we were to say many things respecting this festival, which are not read in the sacred Scriptures, which were appointed by the inspiration of God, we should be like those heretics who write falsehoods from their own inventions or dreams. It is sufficient for the faithful to read and learn what is true; and yet how very few are there who diligently search the whole Bible, dictated by God, or published by the inspiration of his Spirit. Let every one, therefore, whether of the clergy or laity, throw aside those heretical falsehoods which lead the incautious to destruction; and let him read or hear that sacred doctrine, which, if attended to, will guide us to the kingdom of heaven." In another homily, "On Reading the Scriptures," he thus expresses his sentiments: "Whoever would be one with God, must often pray, and often read the Holy Scriptures. For when we pray, we speak to God; and when we read the Bible, God speaks to us. The reading of the Scriptures produces a twofold advantage to the reader. It renders him wiser, by informing his mind; and also leads him from the vanities

* Turner's Anglo-Saxons, vol. ii, b. xii, ch. iv, p. 404.

† Historia Litteraria, sæc. x, p. 589.

of the world to the love of God. The reading of the Scriptures is truly an honourable employment, and greatly conduces to the purity of the soul. For as the body is nourished by natural food, so the sublimer man, that is, the soul, is nourished by the divine sayings, according to the words of the Psalmist: 'How sweet are thy words unto my taste! yea, sweeter than honey to my mouth.' Happy is he, then, who reads the Scriptures, if he convert the words into actions. The whole of the Scriptures are written for our salvation, and by them we obtain the knowledge of the truth. The blind man stumbles oftener than he who sees; so he who is ignorant of the precepts of Scripture offends more frequently than he who knows them," each of them being without guide.* His "Homily on Easter" was printed with an English translation by Fox, in his "Acts and Monuments," vol. ii, pp. 450–456, ed. 1641, folio. An edition of it, in Saxon and English, accompanied with a part of a letter of Elfric's to Wulfsin, bishop of Sherborn, was also published by Archbishop Parker, under the title of "A Testimonie of Antiquitie, showing the auncient Fayth in the Church of England, touching the Sacrament of the Body and Bloude of the Lord here publickely preached, and also receaved in the Saxons Tyme above 600 Yeares agoe." Imprinted at London by John Daye. It has no date.

Elfric was likewise the author of a Saxon Grammar, and Saxon and Latin Glossary, published by Somner, at the end of his *Dictionarium Saxonico-Latino Anglicanum; Oxon*, 1659, folio. In his preface, our author observes, that he undertook this work "for the promotion of sacred studies, especially among the young;" and adds, "It is the duty of the servants of God, and ecclesiastical men, to guard against such a want of zeal and learning in our day as occurred in England but very few years ago, when not a priest could either write or translate a Latin epistle, till Archbishop Dunstan and Bishop Athelwold encouraged learning in the monasteries." He also wrote the lives of certain saints, and various epistles and religious treatises; in particular, a "Compendium of the Old and New Testament," for Siward, or Sigward, a Saxon nobleman, published with an English version in 1638, 4to., by William L'Isle, Esq., of Wilburgham; to which was appended Archbishop Parker's "Testimonie of Antiquitie."†

In this "Compendium," we are informed of those parts of the sacred volume which Elfric translated into the vernacular language. The list is as follows:—

* Usserii, Hist. Dogmat., pp. 378, 379. † Idem, *ut sup.*

The PENTATEUCH.—The translation of Genesis is preceded by a prefatory address to the "Ealdorman Æthelwærd," who, he tells us, had requested him to translate it into English, as far as the history of Isaac, from which period some other person had made a version of it before his time. The preface concludes with the following adjuration:—"If any one transcribe this book, I adjure him, by the name of God, carefully to correct his copy by the autograph; lest by any mistake of the copier, persons should be led into errors; the guilt of which will, nevertheless, devolve upon the transcriber, and not upon me."*

JOSHUA.—"This book," he remarks, "I turned into English for Prince Ethelwerd."

JUDGES.

Some parts of the BOOKS OF KINGS. Under the Books of Kings were comprehended the Books of Samuel, of Kings, and of Chronicles.

ESTHER.

JOB.—All that we have of Job is probably collected from Elfric's Homily upon the History of Job.

JUDITH.—"Englished," says he in the Compendium, "according to my skill, for your example, that ye may also defend your country by force of arms against the invasion of a foreign host." This was written when the Danes used to invade the land.

MACCABEES,—two books.†

These translations were made by Elfric, from the Latin, for in his Preface to Genesis he remarks, "Nothing should be written in the English but what is found in the Latin; nor should the order of the words be changed, except when the Latin and English modes of expression differ. For he who interprets, or translates from the Latin into English, should carefully preserve the English idiom, or else those who are unacquainted with the idiom of the Latin may be led into many errors."

It must, however, be observed, that these are not complete versions of the above-mentioned books, since the object of the translator was to furnish his countrymen with a translation of those parts of the Scriptures only which he conceived to be most important for them to know; as for instance, in *Genesis*, several parts of the tenth, twenty-second, twenty-third, twenty-sixth, and thirty-sixth chapters are omitted; *Exodus* terminates with the fourth verse of the thirty-fifth chapter; *Leviticus* contains only

* Usserii, Hist. Dogmat., *ut sup.*

† Baber's Wicliff's New Testament, p. lxiii.

what relates to the moral law, nearly the whole of what refers to the ceremonial being omitted. *Numbers*, *Deuteronomy*, and *Joshua*, are also incomplete; and the Book of *Judges* concludes with the last verse of the sixteenth chapter. In many instances he has epitomized the history and precepts, and in others given a verbal translation.*

The Heptateuch, the Book of Job, and the imperfect History of Judith, were published in 1698, in 8vo., by Edward Thwaites, of Queen's College, Oxford. The Apocryphal Gospel of Nicodemus was added to this edition.

In the library of Benet College, Cambridge, is a MS. containing a Saxon version of the Gospels, by an unknown author. It was writtena little before the Conquest; and appears to be a transcript of an older MS. The Bodleian library contains a MS. of the same version, which bears evidence of having been written at various times, by different persons; and Dr. Marshall supposes, that the Gospel of St. Matthew alone had two different translators, or interpreters. He also tells us, that in the front of a Saxon MS. of the Gospels belonging to the public library at Cambridge, there is written, in an old hand, in Latin and Anglo-Saxon, "This book gave Leofric, bishop of the church of St. Peter, in Exeter, for the use of his successors;" and that this Leofric died A. D. 1071, or 1073.†

The Bodleian MS. belonged formerly to Matthew Parker, archbishop of Canterbury, under whose direction it was published by John Fox, the martyrologist, in 1571, 4to., and dedicated by him to Queen Elizabeth. The presentation copy, which was given by Fox into the queen's own hands, is in the British Museum. The Gospels were printed in large Saxon types, and accompanied with an English version, taken out of the Bishop's Bible. Being found to be inaccurately transcribed, and incorrectly printed, they were afterward revised by Junius, in conjunction with Dr. Marshall, and were published with the Mœso-Gothic Fragments ascribed to Ulphilas, at Dordrecht, or Dort, in 1665, in 4to., and afterward reprinted at Amsterdam, in 1684. Dr. Marshall enriched the volume with many observations upon this version, and has particularly noticed those passages which differ from the text of the present Latin Vulgate, but agree with the Codex Bezæ; from which it is concluded, that the Anglo-Saxon was translated from the Vetus Italica, or old Latin version, as it stood previous to the correction

* Usserii, Hist. Dogmat., pp. 385, 387.

† Baber's Wicliff's New Testament, p. lxi. Lewis's Hist. of Translations, pp. 6, 7.

of it by Jerome.* Besides these editions, William L'Isle published certain fragments of the Old and New Testament, at London, in 1638, in 4to. The Psalter was also published by the younger Spelman, at London, in 1640, 4to., from a MS. of his father's, and collated with three other copies. The various readings are placed in the margin. These translations are of uncertain dates, but are by the learned generally referred to some part of the eighth century.

In the Cotton library is a Latin MS. of the Proverbs of Solomon, partially glossed or translated; the Latin text of which was written in the ninth century; and the Anglo-Saxon interlineary gloss probably in the tenth.†

It appears also that about this period the whole of the divine offices either were performed in the vernacular tongue, or at least were translated into it, for the benefit of the unlearned; for in the library of Benet College, Cambridge, there is a Latin and Saxon Missal, probably of this age, to which the following note is prefixed:—"This book was usually called the *Derby-Red-Book*, in the mountainous parts of Derbyshire, where it was held in such veneration and honour, that it was commonly believed, that whoever should forswear himself on that book would lose his senses."‡

The old German, or Teutonic translation of the Psalms, and of the Book of Job, by Notker, is of rather uncertain date, though the evidence seems to place it at the conclusion of the tenth, or commencement of the eleventh century. This uncertainty has arisen, chiefly, from the work having been attributed to different persons of the same name, all belonging to the monastery of St. Gall, in Switzerland, and all of them men of learning and talents. The first of these, surnamed *Balbulus*, or the stammerer, was of a noble family, and the author of a number of hymns, some of which are still sung in the church. His death is placed in the year 912. The second was skilled in medicine, excelled in the art of painting, was grave and severe in his habits, illustrious in his virtues, and noble in his descent. His surnames were various: in particular, from his medical knowledge, he was denominated *Physicus*, or *Medicus*, the physician; from the severity of his monastic discipline, *Piperis Granum*, the grain of pepper; and from his skill in painting, *Pictor*, or the painter. He died about A. D. 975. The third, who was called *Labeo*, from his having thick lips, was a man of deep piety and extensive learning, and passed into a bet-

* Baber's Wicliff's New Testament, *ut sup.* Marsh's Michaelis, vol. ii, ch. vii, sec. 38, pt. i, p. 158, pt. ii, p. 637.

† Baber's Wicliff's New Testament, p. lxii. ‡ Usserii, Hist. Dogmat., p. 129.

ter world A. D. 1022. The translation of the Psalms is most generally attributed to Notker, surnamed *Labeo*, who is said to have undertaken it for the benefit of the monks under his care, that they might understand what they sung.* The following is a specimen of this version:—

PSALM I.

1. Der man ist salig, der in dero argon rat ne gegieng.
Noh an dero sundigon uuege ne stuont.
Noh an demo suhstuole ne saz.
2. Nube der ist salig, tes uuillo an Gotes eo ist, unde der dara ana denchet tag unde naht.†

The learned Schilter has published a correct edition of this translation of the Psalms, the Book of Job being lost, in his *Thesaurus Antiquitatum Teutonicarum*, with the title, *Notkeri Tertii Labeonis Psalterium: e Latino in Theotiscam Veterem Linguam versum, et Paraphrasi illustratum. E Manuscripto Codice pervetusto Dn. de la Loubere. Primus eruit, et describi, dum viveret, curavit. Tum interpretatione et notis ornavit Io. Schilterus. Ulmæ*, 1726. It is preceded by a Critical and Historical Dissertation, by Franck.

A copy of this version was written by the younger Ekkerard, a monk of Mentz, by order, and for the use, of the empress Cunegundis, wife of the emperor Henry II., about the year 1004. After the decease of the emperor, the pious empress embraced the monastic life, and spent her time chiefly in reading the Holy Scriptures, either privately, or to her attendants.‡

In the East an Arabic translation of the Scriptures was made by R. Saadias Gaon. Pocock, Walton, and several other Biblical critics affirm, that he translated the whole of the Old Testament; and Pocock assures us, that he had in his possession other portions of his translation besides the Pentateuch.§ Others, and in particular Wolfius, have asserted, that Saadias only translated the Pentateuch, and appeal to the Jewish writers, who notice his version of the Law; but are silent as to any translations of the other parts of the Scriptures by him.‖ The version of Saadias is irregular, and frequently more paraphrastical than literal. The Penta-

* Schilteri Thesaurus, tom. i, Franckii Dissert., pp. i–xv.

† Schilteri Thesaurus, pp. 1, 3.

‡ Le Long, Biblioth. Sacr., p. 375. Paris, 1723, fol. Usserii, Hist. Dogmat., p. 130.

§ Pocockii Specimen Hist. Arab., p. 361. Oxon. 1650, 4to. Ibid. Præfatis variis lect. Arab. in Waltoni Polyglott, tom. vi.—Waltoni Proleg. 14, sec. 15.

‖ Wolfii Biblioth. Heb., tom. i, p. 934. Hamb. and Lips. 1715, 4to.

teuch of this version was first printed by the Jews, at Constantinople, in the Hebrew letters, A. D. 1546, fol. It was accompanied with the Chaldee Targum of Onkelos; the Persic version by *R. Jacob*, surnamed *Tawosus*, or *Tusius*, from the city of Tus, where there was a celebrated academy; and the Commentary of R. Salomon Jarchi, or *Rashi*.* It was afterward published in the Polyglotts of London and Paris.

R. Saadias, surnamed *Gaon*, or the Excellent, a title of honour bestowed upon the more celebrated Jewish doctors during the middle ages, was a native of Al Fiumi, in Egypt, where he was born about A. D. 892. In 927 he was called out of Egypt by the æchmalotarch, or prince of the Captivity, David ben Zachai, and appointed rector, or head of the academy of Sora, with the general superintendency of the Babylonian schools. This important office he discharged with considerable success. His first care was to cure of their error those of his nation who held the doctrine of the transmigration of souls; an opinion prevalent among the Persians and Arabians, and which many of the Jews had entertained prior to the time of our Saviour. In this laudable undertaking he had made some progress, notwithstanding the inveterate prejudices of his countrymen; when an unfortunate dispute took place between him and David, the prince of the Captivity, who had requested him to sign a regulation he had made against the laws, which Saadias deeming unjust, had refused. The refusal incensed David; he upbraided Saadias with ingratitude, and sent his son to threaten him with the loss of his head, if he did not obey his orders. The rabbi informed his scholars of the threat he had received, who at once mutinied against the prince, and attacking him in a body, beat him severely. The nation followed the example of its heads, and divided into parties. The faction of Saadias for a while prevailed; David was deposed, and his brother Joseph proclaimed prince of the Captivity. But the authority of the newly elected prince did not last long; for David, supported by his friends, was soon enabled to resume the government; and Saadias was obliged to save himself by flight. He continued in retirement about seven years, during which time he wrote the greater part of his works. He at length returned, that he might be reconciled to the prince, and surviving him, enjoyed the peaceable possession of the academy. He died A. D. 942, aged fifty. He was the author of several grammatical, and other works, besides the Arabic

* Le Long, Biblioth. Sacr., vol. i, pt. ii, sec. 5, p. 118; and sec. 7, p. 159. edit. Masch. Bibliographical Dic., vol. i, pp. 243, 264.

translation of the Scriptures, and Commentaries on Job, Daniel, and the Song of Solomon.* He seems also to have contributed his part toward the Masora; for Leusden (Philolog. Heb. Diss. 22) tells us, that this laborious rabbi enumerated all the Hebrew letters in the Old Testament, and expressed their several numbers in a Hebrew poem.†

R. Moses was another celebrated Jew of this age. He was born in the East, and was taken, when on a voyage, by privateers, and carried with his son to the coast of Spain, where he was ransomed by the Jews of Cordovia. This they did out of charity, without any knowledge of his learning and worth. But some time afterward, placing himself in the corner of a school or academy, as a layman and beggar, clothed only with a sack, from which he was called *Moses clad with a sack*, he argued so profoundly upon all the questions that were proposed, that the president of the school was filled with admiration, and yielded up his place to him. This occasioned his appointment to the office of judge of the nation, with a liberal salary. His honours did not, however, prevent him from wishing to return to his native land, and to die there; and he had already formed the resolution to quit Spain, when the calif forbade his departure.

At the time of this event the Talmud was but very little known in Spain, so that when any controversy arose, the synagogues sent deputies to Bagdat, to obtain a decision. Even the prayers recited in the Spanish synagogues on the days of affliction, and particularly on that of the expiations, were composed by Armissim, head of one of the academies of Babylon. The calif Hakim was, therefore, exceedingly glad to find that *Moses clad with a sack* was capable of instructing the Jews under his government in the knowledge of the Talmud. This led to the detention of the rabbi, for the calif hoped by this means to prevent the deputations of his subjects to the East, where the Abassides, the enemies of his house, then reigned. Moses continued in possession of his judicial authority till his decease in 997, when he was succeeded in it by his son Enoch.

Haschem II. having ascended the throne of Cordova, not only continued the measures adopted by his father in behalf of his Jewish subjects, but also ordered that the Talmud should be translated into Arabic. R. Joseph, the disciple of Moses, undertook this

* Wolfii, Biblioth. Heb., vol. i, pp. 932–936. Fabricy, Titres Primitifs, tom. ii, pp. 242, 246, 257. Basnage's Hist. of the Jews, b. vii, ch. iv, p. 601.

† Kennicott's Dissertations on the Heb. Text, diss. 2, p. 453.

great work, and very successfully accomplished it; but grew so haughty upon it, that he could no longer bear that Enoch should be judge of the nation in preference to himself. This occasioned a violent quarrel between them, in which the different synagogues engaged; but Enoch's party being the most powerful, Joseph was excommunicated. He appealed to the calif, but in vain. Thus deprived of the protection he expected from the court, he left Spain for Bagdat, where he hoped to find a retreat near the famous Hay, head of the academies of *Pheruts Shibbur*, and *Pundebitha*, and also prince of the Captivity;* but in this too he was disappointed, for R. Hay gave him to understand, that he could not receive him, because he was excommunicated by the Spanish synagogues. He remained therefore at Damascus, where he died, without being able to obtain a revocation of the sentence which had been pronounced against him.†

CHAPTER IX.

ELEVENTH CENTURY

Dark State of England—Marianus Scotus—Saxon MSS.—Lanfranc—Anselm—Ingulph—Promotion of Literature—France—Theodoric—Ivo—Correction of Vulgate—Vernacular Translations—Latin Versions of Psalms, called the Gallican, Roman, and Hebraic—Germany---Willeram---Reimbold---MSS.---Gregory VII.---Crusades.

THE ELEVENTH century, to which we are now advanced, presents a scene still dark and gloomy. The following anecdote will serve to mark its character:—A considerable part of the gold and jewels belonging to the church of Laon, in France, had been stolen. The thief could not be discovered; a general meeting of the canons and principal citizens was therefore called. Uncertain what to do, they unanimously agreed to take the opinion of Anselm, the bishop of the city, who was universally regarded as an oracle. Anselm revolved the business in his mind, and, recollecting the passage in the Book of Joshua, where it is related in what manner

* The princes of the Captivity, or heads of the Captivity, called also *æchmalotarchs*, were the chiefs or leaders of the Jewish captives in Babylon and the East; as the Jewish patriarchs were in Judea and the West, and were installed with great pomp and ceremony. They conferred ordination on the heads of the synagogues, and exercised authority over all the Oriental Jews. See Lewis's Antiquities of the Hebrew Republic, vol. iii, b. vi, ch. vi; and Basnage's Hist. of the Jews, b. vi, ch. xiii.

† Basnage's Hist. of the Jews, b. vii, ch. v, p. 606.

a secret theft had been detected by the casting of lots; "It is my advice," said he, "having weighed the matter most deliberately, that you try to discover the author of this horrid crime by the ordeal of water. Let an infant be taken from each parish, and cast into a vessel of holy water: from the child which sinks will the guilty parish be known. Then, from each house of this parish take another infant: which will show you the guilty house. You can be no longer at a loss: throw every man and woman belonging to the house into tubs of holy water, and guilt will be concealed no longer." The experiment is supposed to have succeeded, and the thief is said to have been a person to whose care the rich ornaments of the church had been intrusted.*—A learned writer, therefore, justly remarks: in this "century the state of ENGLAND was superlatively wretched. In consequence of the successful invasion of the ferocious Danes, murder and rapine marched hand in hand through the kingdom, with wasteful triumph. This scene of horror and desolation was quickly abandoned by the muses, and, in the absence of learning, religion, corrupted by repeated abuses, soon degenerated into superstition. In these calamitous times, and for some ages after, those who presided over that hallowed fountain of living waters, the Scriptures, suffered them to flow with only a niggardly stream, and that polluted."†

In 1017 Canute the Dane obtained the English throne. Among the ecclesiastical laws issued by him, is one enjoining an acquaintance with the Lord's Prayer and Creed: "We charge that every Christian learn to know, at the least, the right faith, and be expert at *Pater Noster*, and *Credo*. For with one of them the Christian should pray to God, and with the other declare his right faith. Christ himself first sang *Pater Noster*, and taught that prayer to his disciples; and in this divine prayer are seven petitions. He that inwardly sings this, does his own message to God for every necessary want, either in relation to this, or the future life. But how can a man ever pray inwardly to God, unless he have an inward faith in him? Therefore, he hath no Christian communion in the consecrated places of rest, after death; nor is he capable of the housel (or eucharist) in this life, nor is he a good Christian who will not learn it: nor can he be surety for another at baptism, much more at the bishop's hands, (that is, confirmation,) till he have first learned well to rehearse it."‡

* Berrington's Lives of Abelard and Heloisa, b. ii, p. 59. Birmingham, 1788, 4to.

† Baber's Wicliff's New Testament, p. lxiii.

‡ Johnson's Ecclesiastical Laws, A. D. MXVII.

This law is, of itself, sufficient to prove the very low state of religious knowledge at this period; and the information to be gleaned from different writers, respecting the attention paid to the Holy Scriptures, during the reign of Canute, is exceedingly scanty. Warton mentions a Dano-Saxon Harmony of the Four Gospels, which formerly belonged to that king, and which is still in the Cotton library. It is adorned with paintings, and bears the title of *Evangelia IV. sermone Danico*, written by a later hand than the Harmony itself. The name *Jesus*, or *Christ*, is scarcely ever used in it, but instead of it the term, *Godes barn*, the Son of God.* In the British Museum a copy of the Latin Gospels is preserved, "remarkable for having in it the signature of King Canute: with a charter, in Saxon, confirming the privileges of the church. The last leaf of St. John's Gospel is wanting."† And in the Cotton library there is also a Latin Psalter, accompanied with the songs of the Old and New Testament, the Lord's Prayer, and the Athanasian and Apostles' Creeds; to which an interlineary Saxon version is added by an anonymous hand. By a computation at the end of the book it appears to have been written in the year 1049.‡

About the middle of this century, Marianus Scotus, having left the monastery of Dunkeld in North Britain, went to Germany, and settled at Ratisbon, where he, with several of his countrymen, taught both sacred and profane learning, and where he founded a monastery for the Scots, in 1074; he and his companions having acquired great reputation by their piety, zeal, and knowledge.§ From the journal of the indefatigable and learned Humphrey Wanley, it appears that the library of these missionaries was extant in the last century. The following are his words: "10 August, 1720, Mr. O'Sullivan likewise acquainted me, that the library of those learned men, who went from Ireland with Marianus Scotus, A. D. 1058, is yet remaining in some church at Ratisbon, and has lately been seen there."‖

The disturbed state of England, by the sanguinary contests of the Saxons, Danes, and Normans, and the frequent change of government, were, for many years, highly detrimental to the in-

* Wartoni Auctarium, pp. 388, 389.

† Classical Journal, No. 15, September, 1813, p. 150.

‡ Usserii, Hist. Dogmat., p. 132

§ Butler's Lives, vol. ix, Sep. 5, p. 61, *note*.

‖ Nichols's Literary Anecdotes of the Eighteenth Century, vol. i, p. 87. Lond. 1812, 8vo.

terests of religion and literature; but after the conquest by William of Normandy, letters were more cultivated, and learning began to reillume our island, though a long time elapsed before its benignant light beamed upon the science of theology. In the catalogue of Saxon MSS. compiled by H. Wanley, and forming the second volume of Hickes's *Thesaurus Linguarum Septentrionalium*, we meet with a few MSS. of the Psalter, sometimes accompanied by the sacred songs of the Scriptures, and the hymns of the church, apparently written about the time of the Conquest. Of the Gospels in the Normano-Saxon dialect there are only three MSS. yet discovered to exist; the one supposed to have been written in the reign of William the Conqueror, and the other two about the time of Henry II. The former of these is deposited in the public library at Cambridge; of the latter, one is among the Hatton MSS. in the Bodleian library, the other in the British Museum; and from the general agreement that subsists between the texts of these MSS., it is very manifest that they are all transcripts of the same version.* Saxon literature had, in fact, long been in its decline, and we may date its fall to about one hundred years after the Conquest, when the language had been so far changed as to have assumed that form which entitles it to the appellation of English. "Those of the clergy who were occupied in the pursuits of literature sought it rather in the paths to which they were directed by interest and ambition than by piety. Even among the few who, duly impressed with the importance and sanctity of their vocation, were diligent to inform themselves, that they might be better qualified to instruct others, little could be expected from their studies which would illuminate their own minds, or those committed to their solemn charge; for as their reading was seldom extended beyond scraps of Scriptural history, hideously disfigured, and incredible legends, which were equally at variance with reason and truth, they only produced feeble and erroneous expositions of the oracles of God, and delivered unedifying homilies."†

The attempt of the Conqueror to introduce the use of the French language into his newly acquired dominions, and the appointment of Norman ecclesiastics, who were ignorant of the vernacular tongue, to the best bishoprics and abbacies in the kingdom, checked the diffusion of knowledge among the English laity, and sunk the lower orders into superstitious darkness, while they served to restrict scientific information to the clergy, and to hasten the

* Baber's Wicliff's New Testament, p. lxiv. † Ibid.

decay of the Saxon dialect. The laws were ordered to be administered in French; and even children at school were forbidden to read in their native language, and ordered to be instructed in a knowledge of the Norman only. In the year 1095, Wolstan, bishop of Worcester, was deposed by the arbitrary Normans, who objected against him, that he was "a superannuated English idiot, who could not speak French," though he appears to have been a pious and diligent scholar; for it was his practice to have the Latin Scriptures regularly read at his table, when he explained them in English to the illiterate, and held conferences upon them with the more learned. It is true that in some of the monasteries, particularly at Croyland and Tavistock, founded by Saxon princes, there were regular preceptors in the Saxon language; but this institution was suffered to remain, after the Conquest, only as a matter of interest and necessity, since the religious could not otherwise have understood their original charters. In the reign of Henry II. the nobles constantly sent their children into France, lest they should contract habits of barbarism in their speech, which could not have been avoided in an English education. Even the transcribers of Saxon books changed the Saxon orthography for the Norman, and in the place of the original Saxon substituted Norman words and phrases, a remarkable instance of which appears in a voluminous collection of Saxon Homilies, preserved in the Bodleian library, and written about the time of Henry II. It was afterward, by various statutes, ordered that the students of our universities should converse either in French or Latin. But from the declension of the power of the barons, and the prevalence of the commons, most of whom were of English ancestry, the native language of England again gradually gained ground; till, in the reign of Edward III., an act of parliament was passed, appointing all pleas and proceedings of law to be carried on in English.*

Among the learned ecclesiastics invited into England by the Norman William, LANFRANC stands foremost. He was a native of Pavia, in Lombardy, born about the year 1005, of a noble family; studied eloquence and the laws at Bologna, and was professor of laws in his native city. This charge he resigned in order to travel into Normandy, where he made his monastic profession at Bec, or Bea, about the year 1042. Three years after he was made prior, and commenced a great school in that monastery,

* Warton's History of English Poetry, vol. i, pp. 3–7. Whartoni Auctarium Hist. Dogmat. Uss., pp. 393, 394.

which, by his extraordinary reputation, soon became the most famous at that time in Europe. It is related of him, that on one occasion, when a pedantic clerk, surrounded by a gorgeous train of attendants, waited upon him, Lanfranc, by conversing with him, discovered the extreme scantiness of his knowledge, and, to ridicule the ignorance of the pedant, laid a cross-row or alphabet before him; which, however, was so resented as to expose the teacher to serious dangers. In 1063 he was appointed first abbot of the monastery of St. Stephen, at Caen, by William, the founder, then duke of Normandy. Four years after his patron had obtained the crown of England he was called to the see of Canterbury, and was appointed by the pope to be his legate in England. In this high situation he exerted himself to reform the clergy and monasteries, and to promote the study of the sacred sciences, eloquence, and grammar.* By his constitutions, in 1072, the librarian is ordered to deliver a book to each of the religious at the beginning of Lent: a whole year is allowed for the perusal of the book; and at the returning Lent, those monks who had neglected to read the books they had respectively received are commanded to prostrate themselves before the abbot, and to supplicate his indulgence.† He was the author of a Commentary on St. Paul's Epistles, which has never been printed. Besides this, and some other smaller works, he is generally considered as having been the principal author of a *Correctorium Ecclesiasticum*, or critical correction of the Old and New Testaments, and ecclesiastical writers. For, having observed that various errors had crept into the sacred text and the works of the fathers, chiefly through the negligence of transcribers, he, with the assistance of his monks, carefully examined and noted the corruptions which had taken place in the sacred Scriptures and fathers, and even in the service books of the church. This work is said to have been held in high estimation both in England and France. His death happened on the 28th of May, 1089. He was buried in Christ Church, Canterbury.‡

ANSELM, who succeeded Lanfranc in the archbishopric of Canterbury, was born at Aoust, in Piedmont. In 1060 he commenced monk, at the age of twenty-seven, at Bec, or Bea, in Normandy, under Lanfranc. He afterward became prior of the monastery. His progress in religious knowledge was great; but mildness and

* Butler's Lives, vol. iv, p. 211, *note*. Berington's Literary History of the Middle Ages, p. 241.

† Warton's History of English Poetry, vol i, dissert. 2.

‡ Butler, *ubi sup*. Millii Proleg., p. civ.

charity seem to have predominated in all his views of piety. The book commonly called Augustine's Meditations was chiefly abstracted from the writings of Anselm. At the age of forty-five he became abbot of Bec. His old friend Lanfranc dying in 1089, William Rufus usurped the revenues of the see of Canterbury, and treated the monks of the place in a most barbarous manner. For several years, the profane tyrant declared that none should have the see while he lived; but his conscience being alarmed during a fit of sickness, he nominated Anselm to be the successor of Lanfranc, who with great difficulty was prevailed upon to accept the arduous office. The king, on his recovery, resuming his tyrannical measures, the archbishop retired into Calabria with two monks; one of whom, named Eadmer, wrote his life. On the death of his royal persecutor he returned to England, by the invitation of Henry I.; and although he became the strenuous defender of the papal authority, he seems to have been influenced more by the popular prejudices of his day than by a spirit of ambition, which certainly formed no part of his character. In a national synod, held at St. Peter's, Westminster, he forbade men to be sold as cattle, which had till then been practised. Another instance of his humane and pious disposition given by his biographers is, that one day, as he was riding to the manor of Herse, a hare, pursued by the hounds, ran under his horse for refuge; he stopped, and turning to the hunters, said, "This hare reminds me of a sinner upon the point of departing this life, surrounded with devils, waiting for their prey." The hare starting off, he forbade her to be pursued, and was obeyed. He died in the sixteenth year of his archbishopric, and in the seventy-sixth of his age, on the 21st of April, A.D. 1109.

The works of Anselm are partly scholastical, partly devotional, and demonstrate him to have been a man of genius, as well as piety. In the list of them we find one entitled "The Fool refuted," *Liber adversus insipientem*, written against those who ridiculed, and pretended to argue against the divine inspiration of the Scriptures. In this treatise, the ingenuity and acuteness of this great prelate are displayed with good effect. The archbishop was also the real inventor of the argument, erroneously attributed to Descartes, which undertakes to prove the existence of God from the idea of infinite perfection, which is to be found, without exception, in every man's mind.*

* Milner's History of the Church of Christ, vol. iii, pp. 307–317. Butler's Lives, vol. iv, April 21, pp. 210–224.

Ingulph, the abbot of Croyland, an Englishman, was another of the learned men of this age. He died in 1109. He is chiefly celebrated for his "History of the Abbey of Croyland," in which the reader is interested by the simple and ingenuous air of his narrative. It furnishes all the information which the most inquisitive would wish to possess concerning the abbey, its buildings, its various fortunes, its extensive possessions and immunities, its treasures, its monks, its occupations, and its statutes. From this history, however, it does not appear that any distinct period was allotted to study by the monks of the abbey; but an account is given of a present of forty large original volumes, of divers doctors, to the common library, and of more than a hundred smaller copies of books on various subjects. Sometimes, also, the names are mentioned of men said to have been "deeply versed in every branch of literature."* As the transcripts of books multiplied, the permission to inspect them was more liberally conceded than formerly. The historian gives us a specimen of their rules on this point: "We forbade," says he, "under the penalty of excommunication, the lending of our books, as well the smaller without pictures as the larger with pictures, to distant schools, without the abbot's leave, and his certain knowledge within what time they would be restored. As to the smaller books, as Psalteries, Donatus, Cato, 'et similibus poeticis ac quaternis de cantu,' adapted to the boys, and the relations of the monks, &c., we forbade to be lent more than one day without leave of the prior."† When the fire happened in 1091 which consumed this celebrated abbey, the library contained seven hundred volumes.

The seeds of knowledge having been sown, many persons began to contribute to the general progress of learning, by assiduously forming libraries; and more attention was paid in the monasteries to the art of neat and correct writing, that the copies of authors' works might not only be multiplied, but might also be accurate. Without this happy practice, the progress of literature must have been confined to a few individuals, because the cost of books was enormous; and their use, in the great libraries, was much restricted on account of their value. Osmund, who came over with William the Conqueror, and had been created earl of Dorset, and borne the highest offices of the state, having embraced a religious life, and been chosen bishop of Sherborn, or Salisbury, collected a noble library; and not only received with great liberality

* Berington's Literary History of the Middle Ages, b. iv, p 255.

† Turner's History of the Anglo-Saxons, vol. i, p. 410, *note*.

every ecclesiastic that was distinguished for learning, and persuaded them to reside with him, but copied and bound books with his own hand.* We have another "instance of an individual's patriotic exertion in Simon of St. Albans, who, from his own taste, maintained liberally two or three select writers in his chamber, where he prepared, says the authority, an invaluable plenty of the best books. He made it a rule in his monastery, that every future abbot should always keep a good writer."† Among the other works provided by Simon were two noble volumes, containing the Old and New Testaments with a gloss. They were kept in a painted press or book-case, with the other transcripts of different authors. This was in the twelfth century. A somewhat similar account is given of a former abbot, of whom it is recorded that he gave to this church twenty-eight notable volumes and eight Psalters, a Collectary, an Epistolary, a book containing the Gospel Lessons for the whole year, and two TEXTS, or complete volumes of the Scriptures, ornamented with gold, and silver, and gems; besides Ordinals, Consuetudinaries, Missals, Troparies, Collectaria, and other books.‡ The attempts of these learned ecclesiastics, aided by the endeavours of others equally ardent in the cause of literature and science, partially succeeded, and a foundation was laid for that diffusion of knowledge, which, after the lapse of some centuries, produced the Reformation.

In FRANCE, Theodoric, the learned abbot of St. Evroul, endea voured to unite an assiduous attention to the offices of religion with the study of the graphic art, and the diligence of the scribe. His monks were urged to the labours of transcription by the influence of example, and the promise of future recompense. Mabillon, the industrious annalist of the Benedictines, relates, that in order to add weight to his exhortations, Theodoric used to tell a legendary tale of a deceased monk, who, being brought to the tribunal of God, was accused, by the devils, of numerous crimes which he had committed, but from which he was successfully vindicated by the holy angels, who produced an enormous volume which had been transcribed by him, and in which there was a single letter more than the number of his crimes!

During the eight years that Theodoric presided over this monastery, he procured a transcription of all the books of the Old and

* Turner's Hist. of England, vol. i, pt. ii, ch. ii, p. 410. London, 1814, 4to. Butler's Lives, vol. xii, Dec. 4, pp. 73–75.

† Turner's Hist. of England, *ut sup.*

‡ Whitaker's Cathedral of Cornwall, vol. ii, p. 317.

New Testaments, and of the works of Gregory the Great. The *antiquarii*, or scribes of St. Evroul, became celebrated for their skill and diligence; and the names of Berengarius, afterward bishop of Venosa, Goscelinus, Rodulfus, Bernardus, Turchetillus, and Richard, are mentioned with honour, as transcribers of the works of the fathers for the library of the monastery of St. Evroul. Theodoric himself bequeathed a *Collectaneum*, or book of Collects, a *Graduale*, and an *Antiphonar*, written with his own hand; Rodolfus, his nephew, transcribed a Missal, and the Heptateuch, or five books of Moses, with Joshua and Judges; Hugo copied an Exposition of Ezekiel, the Decalogue, and the first part of Gregory's Morals; and Roger, a presbyter, transcribed the third part of the Morals, the books of Chronicles, and the books of Solomon.

The value of these labours will be best appreciated by recollecting the scarcity of books at this period, and the excessive prices paid for them by the few who were able to purchase them. Mabillon saw a necrology belonging to the monastery of Jumiege, in which prayers were appointed to be offered up on the 6th of March for those "who had made and given books on the first day of Lent;" the day on which books were distributed to the monks according to rule. Robert, abbot of Jumiege, and successively bishop of London and archbishop of Canterbury, presented to his monastery, during the time he held the bishopric of London, a book called a Sacramentary, containing all the prayers and ceremonies practised at the celebration of the sacraments. This present was accompanied also with various rich ornaments for the sacred services. At the close of the book an anathema was denounced against any one who should steal the book, or any of the ornaments of the monastery; which concluded in terms that strongly mark the value of books, and, in the donor's views, the preference of the book which he had given to the other articles of his donation:—"If any one take away this book from this place by force, or fraud, or any other way, let him suffer the loss of his soul for what he has done; let him be blotted out of the book of life, and not be written among the just; and let him be condemned to the severest excommunication who shall take away any of the vestments which I have given to this place, or the other ornaments, the silver candlesticks, or the gold from the table. Amen."*

Ivo, bishop of Chartres, who flourished about A. D. 1092, seems to have been desirous to promote the knowledge of the Scriptures,

* Mabillon, Annales Ord. Benedict., tom. iv, pp. 461, 462, 518, 519. Lut. Paris, 1707, folio.

both among the clergy and laity. In a discourse on the excellence of the sacred order, delivered before the synod, we meet with some judicious advice, addressed to those who, from their office, were denominated Readers: "Let those," says he, "who aspire to this degree, be well instructed in literature, that they may understand the meaning of words, and be acquainted with the use of accents, and read distinctly, lest their auditors should be prevented, by a confused pronunciation, from understanding what is read. Let them distinguish between what is to be read affirmatively, and what is to be read interrogatively; and carefully note the various stops and pauses of the discourse; for where they are neglected, they disturb the mind, and provoke the contempt of grammarians. A reader should consult both the heart and the ear."*

Among the more learned of the monastic orders, there were some who saw and deplored the corruptions which had taken place in the copies of the Holy Scriptures, by the carelessness and incompetency of the transcribers, and attempted to render them more correct. William, abbot of Hirsauge, in the diocess of Spire, was one of these enlightened and valuable men. In his monastery there was a monk of a noble family, who had made unusual progress in sacred literature, of the name of Theotger: this able scholar, with another of the same fraternity equally learned, named Haymon, he employed in correcting the Vulgate version, endeavouring to restore it to its original purity, amending the punctuation, and forming proper divisions. The revised copy, Trithemius says, was in his time still preserved in the library of the monastery. Theotger was the author of a work on music, of brief notes on the Psalms, and of sermons and epistles.†

The greater part of those studious monks who endeavoured to increase the general stock of knowledge by their literary productions, either spent their time in compiling the lives of saints, or devoted their talents to writing commentaries or glosses on select portions of the Bible, while but few were found who were willing to employ themselves in transcribing and multiplying correct copies of the Scriptures themselves: and even with respect to literary pursuits in general, there was an astonishing diversity of practice in the different orders, according to the views of their respective founders, and the consequent tenor of the rules by which they were governed; as well as in the different religious houses of the

* Usserii, Hist. Dogmat., p. 136.

† Trithemii Chronicon Hirsaugiense, tom. i, pp. 282, 283. Monast. S. Gall., 1690, folio. Mabillon, Annales, tom. v, p. 277.

same order, according to the abilities and dispositions of the favourable or unfavourable abbots, or the leading characters of the several fraternities. The bequests or donations of certain of the abbots of the famous monastery of Clugni will sufficiently evince the great dissimilarity of literary encouragement in the governors of conventual establishments: Hugo, who became abbot A. D. 1199, and died A. D. 1207, presented several valuable gifts to the monastery, "especially all his best books, among which was nearly the whole of a Gloss upon the Old and New Testament." Ivo I., the twenty-fifth abbot, who began to govern A. D. 1257, and died A. D. 1275, bestowed many costly gifts upon the monastery, among others, "a Missal; the Text of the Gospels; an Epistolarium, covered with silver; a Collectary, and a large book of Capitulars; also, an Exposition of the Gospels, to be read in the refectory; and twenty-two books placed in the cloister, fastened with chains." Andruinus I., the thirty-fourth abbot, who commenced his government of the abbey A. D. 1351, was afterward created cardinal, and died A. D. 1360: besides other donations, he gave as "many *books* as were estimated at upward of two thousand francs." Lastly, John III., the forty-second abbot, who was raised to that dignity A. D. 1456, and died A. D. 1485, was not only princely in other gifts which he presented to his monastery, but singularly generous in his literary donations, which prove him to have been an extensive book collector, and a great patron of the then newly invented art of printing, as well as what the moderns have designated a *bibliomaniac.* In the list of the books given by him to this convent are fifteen volumes on parchment, illuminated and bound, consisting of Augustine's City of God; Vincent's *Historiale Speculum*, &c.; twelve other volumes on parchment, including an Exposition of part of the New Testament, from II. Corinthians to Hebrews, inclusive; Comestor's *Historia Scho lastica; Legenda aurea*, &c.; all of which were in MS.; eighty-three other volumes, on paper, mostly printed, among which were, De Lyra's Commentary on the Old and New Testament; Turrecremata on the Psalms; S. Thomas Aquinas on Matthew, Mark, Luke, and John; Mamotrectus, &c.*

Some attempts were however made to render the Scriptures more generally useful, by translating select parts of them into some of the vernacular dialects of the continent. Le Long mentions a Psalter or two, still extant, written in the old French or

* Bibliotheca Cluniacensis, pp. 1663, 1664, 1667, 1672, 1681–1684. Lutet. Paris, 1614, fol

Norman dialect of the eleventh century; a translation of the books of Kings, probabiy made about the year 1080, and one of rather a later date, of the two books of the Maccabees. The principal translation of the Psalms into Norman-French, and one of those referred to by Le Long, is found in a magnificent Polyglott Psalter preserved in the library of Trinity College, Cambridge. It contains three of the most celebrated versions of the Latin Psalms, usually called the Gallican, the Roman, and the Hebraic, with a preface, prayer, and commentary, subjoined to each psalm. The Gallican Latin version is accompanied with a gloss, or brief commentary; the Roman with an interlineary Normano-Saxon version; and the Hebraic with the Norman-French version. The whole forms a large folio volume, written on vellum, and richly illuminated and ornamented with miniatures and historical paintings, by Eadwin, a monk, who is supposed to have flourished in the reign of Stephen, king of England, about A. D. 1136.*

The following remarks by Dr. Waterland, will elucidate the nature of these different Latin versions: "There are four kinds of Latin Psalters, which have passed under the names of Italic, Roman, Gallican, and Hebraic. The *Italic* Latin Psalter is of the old translation, such as it was before St. Jerome's time. The *Roman* Psalter is not very different from the old *Italic*. It is nothing else but the old version, cursorily, and in part, corrected by Jerome, in the time of Pope Damasus, A. D. 383. It has had the name of Roman, because the use of it began the soonest, and continued the longest, in the Roman offices. It obtained in Gaul nearly as soon as at Rome, but was laid aside in the sixth century, when Gregory of Tours introduced the other Psalter, since called Gallican. The *Gallican* Psalter is Jerome's more correct Latin translation, made from Origen's Hexaplar, or most correct edition of the Greek Septuagint, filled up where the Greek was supposed faulty, from the Hebrew; distinguished with obelisks and asterisks, denoting the common Greek version, in those places, to be either redundant or deficient. This more correct Psalter was drawn up by Jerome in the year 389, and obtained first in Gaul, about the year 580, or however not later than 595; from which circumstance it came to have the name of Gallican, in contradistinction to the Roman. From Gaul it passed over into England, before the year 597, and into Germany and Spain, and other countries. The popes of Rome, though they themselves used the other Psalter, yet patiently connived at the use of this in the Western churches, and

* Le Long, Biblioth. Sacra., vol. i, p. 323, 7. Paris, 1723, fol.

even in Italy; and sometimes privately authorized the use of it in churches and monasteries; till, at length, it was publicly authorized in the council of Trent, and introduced awhile after into Rome itself, by Pius V. It was admitted into Britain and Ireland before the coming of Augustine, the monk, and prevailed after, except in the church of Canterbury, which was more immediately under the archbishop's eye, and more conformable to the Roman offices, than other parts of the kingdom. It has been said, (Hodius de Text. Bibl. Orig., p. 384,) that this very Gallican Psalter is what is still retained in the Liturgy, called the *reading psalms*, in contradistinction to the other psalms in our Bibles of the new translation. But this is not strictly true; for the old translation, though it be taken in a great measure from the Gallican, has yet many corrections from the Hebrew, (where they were thought wanting,) first by Coverdale in 1535, and by Coverdale again in 1539, and last of all by Tonstall and Heath in 1541; according to which edition is the Psalter now used in the Liturgy. (Durell Eccles. Anglican. vindic., p. 306.) The *Hebraic* Latin Psalter means Jerome's own translation, immediately from the Hebrew, made in the year 391. This, though otherwise of great esteem, was never used in the public church offices."*

In GERMANY, the abbot Willeram was the author of a twofold paraphrase of the Canticles. The first of which is a rhythmical Latin one; the other a prose one, in the old Francic or German dialect. The best edition of this work is by Schilter, published in his *Thesaurus Antiquitatem Teutonicarum*, tom. i.

WILLERAM was a native of Franconia. His acquaintance with letters and philosophy was principally obtained in the schools of Paris, from whence returning into his native country, he was elected *scholasticus* of the church of Bamberg. But, notwithstanding his elevation to the ecclesiastical dignity, he continued his former friendships and habits; till, "at length," says Trithemius, "being convinced of the transitory nature of the vain glory of this world, and contemning worldly things for the love of God, he put on the habit of a monk in the monastery of Fulda; and by increasing in merit, was at last chosen abbot of Mersburg." Besides the paraphrase on Solomon's Song, he wrote a number of sermons and epistles. He flourished in the reign of Henry IV., about A. D. 1080.†

* Waterland on the Athanasian Creed, pp. 112–117. Cam. 1728, 8vo.

† Trithemius in Catal. Viror. Illustr. Germ. See Schilteri Thesaurus, tom. i, in Præfat Willerami in Cantic., &c.

Reimbold, first abbot of Muri, in Helvetia, about A. D. 1027, not only furnished the abbey with two bells, which he purchased at Strasburgh; but procured also transcripts of the Bible, hymns, homilies, and legends; the books of Homer, Æsop's Moral Apologues, some of Ovid's poems, the Histories of Sallust, and other valuable works. His monks, treading in his steps, established a school, where they taught the rudiments of science.*

Montfaucon, in his *Diarium Italicum*, or Travels through Italy, notices several works written or transcribed in the *eleventh* century, and deposited in the different libraries of Italy. They chiefly consist of copies of various parts of the Scriptures, of the works of the fathers, and books of ecclesiastical offices, and lives of the saints. Some of them have curious inscriptions. In the duke of Modena's library is a Psalter most elegantly written, on the front of which is inscribed in Greek: "This book is deposited in the holy monastery, for the remission of the sins of the monk Theodosius Xylata; let him who reads it through the Lord, praise him, and pray for his soul." In the library of the monastery of Mount Cassino is a MS. containing the lessons for the vigils, to which the following note is prefixed:—"In the year of the incarnation of our Lord, 1072, and tenth indiction, at the time when the venerable Desiderius, the thirty-seventh abbot after the decease of our most holy and illustrious father Benedict, presided in this venerable monastery of Mount Cassino, where the bodies of our said holy father and lawgiver, and of his renowned sister Scholastica, lie honourably buried; among the other monuments of his great works, wherein he wonderfully outdid all his predecessors, he also caused this most beautiful book to be writ, containing the lessons that are to be read on the vigils or eves of the principal festivals, that is, or the nativity of our Lord, St. Stephen, St. John the Evangelist, the Epiphany, the Resurrection, the Ascension, and Pentecost, which book, I, brother John of Marsicana, long since archpriest of the church, but now the meanest servant of that holy place, did cause to be composed at my own proper charge, for the salvation of me and mine; and devoutly offered it to the said most holy father Benedict, on his holy altar, on the day when I took his habit upon me. Further praying, that if any man shall, on any pretence whatsoever, presume to take it from this holy place, he may have his eternal mansion with those to whom CHRIST at the last judgment shall say: Depart from me into everlasting fire, prepared for the devil and his angels."

* Planta's Hist. of the Helvetic Confederacy, vol. i, ch. iii, p. 142. Lond. 1807, 8vo.

"But whosoever you are that read these lines, fail not also to read the distich underneath:"—

Hujus scriptorem libri, pie Christe, Leonem
In Libro Vitæ dignanter supplico scribe.

"Blest Saviour! in thy Book of Life divine,
May Leo's* favour'd name illustrious shine."

This MS. is accompanied with an historical painting, which Montfaucon has caused to be engraved, representing John of Marsicana receiving the monk's cowl from St. Benedict; and Desiderius presenting the volume to the saint.

Another MS., mentioned by the learned author of the *Diarium*, deserves to be noticed as a rare instance of the study of the sacred writings, in an age of darkness and illiteracy. It is a handsome volume on vellum; and contains, first, all the quotations and testimonies from the Old Testament that are to be found in the fourteen Epistles of St. Paul; and secondly, all the quotations from profane and apocryphal writers in those epistles. It is preserved in the library of the monastery of St. Basil, at Rome. In the same library there is also a Latin Bible, curiously written in this century, on vellum, containing Genesis, to the book of Judges, with Origen's notes in the margin; but imperfect at the beginning and end.†

From the tranquil pursuits of the man of letters, and the solemn stillness of the monastic library, we turn reluctantly to mark the conduct of an imperious pontiff. On the elevation of Hildebrand to the pontificate, in 1073, he assumed the name of GREGORY VII. The famous *Sentences*, relating to the supreme authority of the Roman pontiffs over the universal church and the kingdoms of the world, said to have been composed by him, and from him termed the *Dictates of Hildebrand*, sufficiently demonstrate the fierce impetuosity and boundless ambition of his character. The *twelfth* of these dictates affirms, "That it is lawful [for the pope] to dethrone sovereigns;" the *seventeenth* impiously declares, "That no book is to be deemed canonical without his authority;" and the *twenty-seventh* haughtily asserts, "That he may absolve the subjects of heretical princes (*iniquorum*) from their oath of fidelity." And although it may be disputed whether Gregory published the Dictates in their present form, it must be granted that the greatest part of them are repeated word for word in several places in his

* The transcriber of the book.—ED.

† Montfaucon's Travels through Italy, ch. iii, p. 44; ch. xv, p. 250; ch. xxii, p. 381.

Epistles, and that the whole of them are characteristic of that imperious pontiff.*

In 1080, Uratislaus, the king of Bohemia, expressed a wish to Gregory to have the offices, or prayers of the church, performed in the SLAVONIAN tongue, at that time the common language of the north of Europe; but the pontiff forbade it, and haughtily replied, "I will never consent for service to be performed in the Slavonian tongue. It is the will of God that his word should be hidden, lest it should be despised if read by every one; and if, in condescension to the weakness of the people, the contrary has been permitted, it is a fault which ought to be corrected. The demand of your subjects is imprudent. I shall oppose it with the authority of St. Peter; and you ought, for the glory of God, to resist it with all your power."† A decision very different from that of his predecessor John VIII. about A.D. 880. A request of a similar nature having been made to him, he replied by blessing God that the Slavonian characters had been invented, thereby enabling every man to praise the Lord in his own language; and, defending his conduct by the example of the apostles, remarked, that he apprehended no danger from the use of the public services in the vernacular dialect, provided that they read the Gospel in Latin first, and then interpreted it to the people, according to the practice of some other churches. A different policy from that of Gregory was also pursued by Innocent III. in 1215; for, in the council of Lateran, held in that year, it was ordained, that if persons of different nations, speaking different languages, dwelt in the same city, the bishop of the diocess should provide ministers for them, capable of performing service in their respective tongues.‡

But "what judgment," inquires a Catholic historian, "shall we form of the crusades, which were more extravagant in their origin, more contagious in their progress, more destructive in their consequences, than all the follies which had hitherto infuriated or depressed the human race, and which, toward the close of this century, took forcible possession of the minds of the Western world."§ Their object was the recovery of Jerusalem out of the hands of the infidels. "The scheme originated," observes the same intelligent writer, "in the cultivated mind of Gerbert, in the

* Usserii, Gravissimæ Questionis, &c., ch. v, p. 124. Lond. 1613, 4to. Mosheim's Eccles. Hist., vol. ii, p. 492, *note*.

† Basnage, Hist. de l'Eglise, tom. ii, p. 1575. Rotterdam, 1699, fol.

‡ Basnage, *ut sup.*

§ Berrington's Literary History of the Middle Ages, b. iv, p. 266.

1

first year of his pontificate; was nourished by Hildebrand; and carried into execution by the activity of Urban II., and the eloquence of Peter the Hermit. The first army marched in 1096, and in 1099 Jerusalem was taken."

The state of letters was necessarily affected by these wars. They occasioned dissipation in the minds of all men, whether civil or ecclesiastical, and a "new temper was generated, by which all sedentary occupations were suspended, and a mark of reproach fixed upon every undertaking which did not tend to, or was not connected with, the peculiar military mania of the times. Schools and convents felt the general contagion; if a few employed the remonstrances of wisdom, they were unheeded or despised. At the call of their prince, Duke Robert, the pupils of Bea deserted their masters; and no eloquence gained hearers but that of the hermit, or of popular declaimers on the same subject." Ignorance and barbarism marked the progress of the crusaders, and literature in every form was the object of indifference or contempt. In the summer of 1203 they appeared before Constantinople; and spent the following winter in the suburb of Galata. The city was taken by storm, and suffered all the horrors of pillage and devastation. "In order to insult the fallen city, the manners, the dress, the customs of the Greeks were exposed to ridicule or scorn in ludicrous exhibitions; and *pens, ink-stands, and paper were displayed in the streets, as the ignoble arms or contemptible instruments of a race of students and of scribes*."* What was the fate of some, or many, of the Byzantine libraries, is not related. "Paper or parchment held out no temptation to avarice; and the pilgrims, feeling no predilection for science, particularly when locked up in an unknown tongue, would not be solicitous to seize or purloin the works of the learned; but we cannot doubt that many perished in the three fires which raged in the city; and some writings of antiquity, which are known to have existed in the twelfth century, are now lost."†

The effects of these *Holy Wars*, as they were called, became visible in a variety of forms, and the crusades may be regarded as the date when *chivalry* assumed a systematic appearance; knighthood was invested with extraordinary splendours; and the science of heraldry may be traced to Palestine. New institutions arose to promote chivalry, at the expense of reason and propriety, and the lay orders were expected to produce prodigies, in uniting with the

* Berrington, App. I., pp. 601, 602. † Ibid., p. 606.

exercise of war the practice of religious duties. In every country in Europe the Christian knight drew his sword during the celebration of mass, and held it out naked, in testimony of his readiness to defend the faith of Christ.*

CHAPTER X.

TWELFTH CENTURY.

Waldenses—Gallican Clergy—Singular Customs—Cistercian Monks—Lambert of Liege—Petrus de Patis—Petrus de Riga—Matthæus—Joannes Burgundio—Peter Comestor—Nuns of the Paraclete—Sanson de Nanteuil—Romance—Legenda Aurea—England—English MS. Versions—Adrian IV.—Profligacy of Monks and Clergy—Religious Dramas—Biblical MSS.—Arabic Scholars—Learned Jews.

THE circumstances under which the TWELFTH century commenced were most inauspicious. Chivalrous superstitions and dissolute manners prevented the extensive circulation of the sacred writings, and checked the progress of Scriptural translations. The facts presented to the Biblical scholar are frequently unimportant and uninteresting, except in the instance of the Waldenses, who stood forward as the friends of Scriptural investigation and vernacular translations, amid sanguinary persecutions and unmerited calumnies.

The WALDENSES, called also Vaudois, or Vallenses, obtained their name from inhabiting the valleys of Piedmont, particularly those of Lucerne and Angrogne. Sometimes they were denominated *Leonists*, or *the poor men of Lyons*, from the city of that name; and at other times the *Sabatati*, or *Insabatati*, from the wooden shoes which they wore, and which, in the French language, are termed *sabots*. From the occupation followed by great numbers of them, the whole sect, in certain places, was called the *Sect of Weavers.*

They were properly the descendants of the *Cathari*, or Puritans, who arose in the church some centuries earlier than the time of PETER VALDO, or WALDO, to whom, by a mistake originating in the similarity of names, the rise of this sect has usually been attributed. But, though he was not the founder of the Waldensian churches, he became one of their most considerable friends and

* Introd. to the Literary History of the 14th and 15th Centuries, p. 169. Knox's Liberal Education, vol. ii, p. 280, *note*.

benefactors; and, by his writings, his preachings, and his sufferings, defended their cause and extended their influence. He was an opulent merchant, and citizen of Lyons. About the year 1160 a providential event gave the first occasion to his concern for religion. Being assembled with some of his friends, and after supper conversing and refreshing himself among them, one of the company fell down dead on the ground, to the amazement of all that were present. From that moment Waldo became a serious inquirer after divine truth, and soon after abandoned his mercantile occupation, distributed his wealth to the poor, and became the teacher of the multitudes who flocked to receive his bounty or hear his instructions. By the study of the Scriptures his mind was enlightened, he saw and strenuously opposed many of the errors of the Church of Rome.* With the design, therefore, of more effectually promoting religious knowledge, he made or procured a translation of the four Gospels, and probably of other parts of the sacred writings, into French. Stephen de Borbone, who died in 1261, says that Waldo, not being sufficiently learned for the work, employed and paid Stephen de Ansa, or Emsa, an ecclesiastic, and a noted grammarian, with another priest named Bernard Ydros, both of Lyons, to execute the translation, in which De Ansa dictated while Ydros wrote; and that they were engaged also in the translation of other religious works. Stephen de Ansa was afterward beneficed in the cathedral of Lyons, and died by a fall from a solarium or chamber which he had erected. Reinerius, however, an opponent of the Waldenses, who lived in 1250, says, that "being somewhat learned, he taught the people the *text* of the New Testament, for which he was reproved by the bishop:" and Matthias Illyricus, one of the Magdeburgh centuriators, or writers of the famous Ecclesiastical History, printed at Basil in the sixteenth century, observes, "He was himself a man of learning, as I understand from old parchments, nor was he obliged to employ others to translate for him, as some enemies of the truth have falsely affirmed."†

It is probably impossible to ascertain with correctness what portions of the sacred Scriptures were at this time translated into

* Milner's History of the Church of Christ, vol. iii, pp. 437–439. Usserii, Hist. Dogmat., pp. 145, 146. Du Cange, Glossarium, Lat. v. *Sabatati*. Mosheim's Eccl. Hist., vol. iii, pp. 120–127.

† Usserii, Hist. Dogmat., pp. 146, 147. Le Long, Biblioth. Sacra, tom. i, pp. 313, 314. Paris, 1723, folio. Usser., De Christ. Ecc. Success. et Statu, cap. viii, p. 217.

French. Thuanus and Massonus say, "He caused the writings of the prophets and apostles to be translated into the popular language, or French." Walter Mapes, who was chaplain to our Henry II., informs us, that during the council of Lateran, held in 1179, the Waldenses presented to Pope Alexander III. "a book containing the text of the Psalms, with a gloss; and the greater part of the books of *both Laws*," that is, of the Mosaic Law and the Gospel. It was alleged against them as a crime that they affirmed, "that when a preacher advanced any doctrine which he did not prove from the Old and New Testaments, such preaching ought to be regarded as false;" and according to Gretser, Reinerius assigns "the translation of the Old and New Testaments into the vulgar tongue," as one cause of the rapid increase of these early reformers.* But whether Waldo himself entirely performed the work, or encouraged others to do it, or, what is most probable, executed it himself with the assistance of others, it is certain that the Christian world in the West were indebted to him for the first translation of a great part, if not of the whole, of the sacred volume into French.

Besides the French translation of the Scriptures, executed more immediately for the disciples of Waldo, who had retired into Dauphiny, there appears to have been a translation into Waldensian, for the use of those who inhabited the valleys of Piedmont. Leger, who was one of their pastors for several years in the seventeenth century, says, that although, prior to his time, they had possessed a translation of the New Testament for several centuries, they had not a translation of the whole of the Old Testament, but only of certain parts of it, as Genesis, the Psalms, Proverbs, and Job.† In 1658, a number of MSS. and other pieces, collected by Sir Samuel Morland, during the time that he resided in Geneva, for the purpose of dispensing the bounty of the British nation to the poor persecuted Waldenses, were presented by him to the public library of the University of Cambridge. These papers consist altogether of twenty-one volumes, numbered A, B, C, &c. "In the volume F, are collected, and written on parchment, in that which is called the Waldensian language, of a very ancient, but fair and distinct character, the Gospel of Matthew, the first chapter of Luke, the Gospel of John, the Acts, 1 Corinthians, Galatians, Ephesians, Philippians, 1 Thessalonians, 2 Timothy, Titus, the eleventh

* Usser., De Christ. Ecc. Success. et Statu, cap. viii, pp. 220, 234, 235. Usserii, Hist. Dogmat., *ut sup.*

† Le Long, Biblioth. Sacra, tom. i, p. 368. Paris, 1723, fol.

chapter of the Hebrews, with 1 and 2 Peter, the two last imper fect."*

Le Long mentions a copy of the New Testament, in the Waldensian dialect, written by one of the Waldensian barbs or pastors, preserved in the library of the city of Zurich. It is on parchment, in 12mo., and is supposed to have been written after A. D. 1100.†

The poverty of the Waldenses, and the great expense of transcription, prevented the copies of the Scriptures being numerous among them; but this deficiency was amply compensated by the diligent perusal of those they possessed, and the extraordinary attention paid to them when publicly read. Reinerius, who was a Roman Catholic writer, and an inquisitor, acknowledges that he saw and heard a peasant recite the book of Job by heart; and that there were others among them who could perfectly repeat the whole New Testament.‡ In a book concerning their Barbs or pastors, we have this account of their vocation: "All who are to be ordained as pastors among us, while they are yet at home, entreat us to receive them into the ministry, and desire that we would pray to God, that they may be rendered capable of so great a charge. They are to learn by heart all the chapters of St. Matthew and St. John, all the canonical Epistles, and a good part of the writings of Solomon, David, and the Prophets. Afterward, having exhibited proper testimonials of their learning and conversation, they are admitted as pastors by the imposition of hands."§

The way in which these excellent men disseminated their sentiments, during the dreadful persecutions which raged against them, will be interestingly explained by the following extracts. The first is from Reinerius, who wrote against the Waldenses, in the thirteenth century. In his book *Contra-Waldenses*, cap. viii, *Quomodo se ingerant familiaritati magnorum*, he says, that it was the practice of some of the Waldensian teachers, the more readily to gain access to persons of rank, to carry with them a small box of trinkets, or articles of dress; and to introduce themselves by offering their articles to sale: "Sir, will you please to buy any rings, or seals, or trinkets? Madam, will you look at any handkerchiefs, or pieces of needlework for veils? I can afford them cheap." If, after

* Morland's Hist. of the Churches of Piedmont, p. 98, cited in Anderson's Memorial on behalf of the native Irish, App., p. 79.

† Le Long, Bibliotheca Sacra, tom. i, p. 369.

‡ Reineri Liber contra Waldenses, cap. iii, vide Biblioth. Vet. Pat., tom. xiii, p. 299. Colon. Agrip. 1618, fol.

§ Milner, vol. iii, p. 461.

a purchase, the company ask, "Have you any thing more?" the salesman would reply, "O yes, I have commodities far more valuable than these, and I will make you a present of them, if you will protect me from the clergy." Security being promised, on he would go. "The inestimable jewel I spoke of is the Word of God, by which he communicates his mind to men, and which inflames their hearts with love to him. 'In the sixth month the angel Gabriel was sent from God unto a city of Galilee named Nazareth:'" and so he would proceed to repeat the remaining part of the first chapter of Luke.* Or he would begin with the thirteenth of John, and repeat the last discourse of Jesus to his disciples. If the company should seem pleased, he would proceed to repeat the twenty-third of Matthew: "The scribes and Pharisees sit in Moses' seat—Wo unto you, ye shut up the kingdom of heaven against men; for ye neither go in yourselves, neither suffer ye them that are entering to go in. Wo unto you, ye devour widows' houses." "And pray," should one of the company say, "against whom are these woes denounced, think you?" he would reply, "Against the clergy and the monks. The doctors of the Roman Church are pompous, both in their habits and their manners, they 'love the uppermost rooms, and the chief seats in the synagogues, and to be called Rabbi, Rabbi.' For our parts we desire no such rabbies. They are incontinent; we live each in chastity with his own wife. They are the rich and avaricious, of whom the Lord says, 'Wo unto you, ye rich, for ye have received your consolation;' but we, 'having food and raiment, are therewith content.' They are voluptuous, and 'devour widows' houses;' we only eat to be refreshed and supported. They fight and encourage wars, and command the poor to be killed and burnt, in defiance of the saying, 'He that taketh the sword, shall perish by the sword.' For our parts, they persecute us for righteousness' sake. *They* do nothing but eat the bread of idleness: *we* work with our hands. They monopolize the giving of instruction, and wo be to them that take away the key of knowledge. But among us, women teach as well as men, and one disciple, as soon as he is informed himself, teaches another. Among them you can hardly find a doctor who can repeat three chapters of the New Testament by heart; but of us, there is scarcely a man or woman who doth not retain the whole. And because we are sincere believers in Christ, and all teach and

* The reader should keep in mind, that at this time the use of the Bible was not allowed to the laity; and that vernacular translations especially were discountenanced, and copies of the Scriptures, which were all MSS., rare and expensive.

enforce a holy life and conversation, these scribes and Pharisees persecute us to death, as their predecessors did Jesus Christ."*

The second extract is from the examination of Peironetta, a widow, before Anthony Fabri, the inquisitor general of Dauphiny, in 1494. To the first interrogatory she answered nothing: to the second, she said and confessed, "That about twenty-five years ago, or thereabouts; there came to the house of Peter Fornerius, her husband, two strangers in gray clothes, who, as it seemed to her, spake Italian, or the dialect of Lombardy, whom her husband received into his house, for the love of God. That while they were there, at night after supper, one of them began to read a godly book, which he carried about with him, saying, that therein were contained the Gospels, and other precepts of the Law;—and that he would explain and preach the same in the presence of all who were present; God having sent him to go up and down the world like the apostles, to reform the Catholic faith, and to preach to the good and simple, showing them how to worship God, and keep his commandments."†

The following curious passage from a MS. chronicle of the abbey of Corvey, supposed to have been written about the beginning of the twelfth century, is singularly descriptive of the character of these reformers, and of the mode of disseminating the knowledge of the Scriptures by the Waldensian laity, and of the extensive spread of their doctrines:—

"*Religionem nostram*, &c."‡ "Laymen from Suabia, Switzerland, and Bavaria, have been wishful to render our religion and the faith of all the Christians of the Latin Church contemptible;—men seduced from the ancient race of simple men who inhabit the Alps and their vicinity, and are always attached to what is ancient. Merchants of this description from Switzerland frequently enter Suabia, Bavaria, and the north of Italy, who *commit the Bible to memory*, and despise the rites of the church, which they hold to be novel. They forbid the worship of images, and condemn the relics of the saints; they live upon herbs, and seldom or never eat flesh. We therefore call them Manichees. There are also others who meet them from Hungary," &c.

The general habits of this interesting people are also well de-

* Biblioth. Vet. Pat., tom. xiii, p. 307. Colon. Agrip. 1618. Jones' Hist. of the Walaenses, pp. 390, 391.

† Allix's Remarks upon the Ancient Church of Piedmont, pp. 319, 322.

‡ Planta's Hist. of the Helvetic Confederacy, vol. i, b. i, ch. iv, pp. 179, 180. London, 1807, 8vo.

scribed by that great historian Thuanus, or De Thou, an enemy indeed to the Waldenses, though a fair and candid one. He is describing one of the valleys inhabited by them in Dauphiny, which is called the stony valley. "Their clothing," he says, "is of the skins of sheep; they have no linen. They inhabit seven villages; their houses are constructed of flint-stone, with a flat roof, covered with mud, which being spoiled or loosened by rain, they smooth again with a roller. In these they live with their cattle, separated from them, however, by a fence; they have besides two caves set apart for particular purposes, in one of which they conceal their cattle, in the other themselves, when hunted by their enemies. They live on milk and venison, being by constant practice excellent marksmen. Poor as they are, they are content, and live separate from the rest of mankind. One thing is astonishing, that persons externally so savage and rude should have so much moral cultivation. They can all read and write. They understand French, so far as is needful for the understanding of the Bible, and the singing of psalms. You can scarce find a boy among them who cannot give you an intelligible account of the faith which they profess; in this, indeed, they resemble their brethren of the other valleys: they pay tribute with a good conscience, and the obligation of this duty is peculiarly noted in the confession of their faith. If by reason of the civil wars they are prevented from doing this, they carefully set apart the sum, and at the first opportunity pay it to the king's tax-gatherers."

From the account of Thuanus, it appears that WALDO fled into Germany, and at last settled in Bohemia, where he ended his days in the year 1179, or before that time.*

The practices of the Gallican clergy of the middle ages present the most perfect contrast to the plain and modest manners of the Waldenses. On many occasions they assumed the military habit, and even officiated in it during the solemn services of the church; and at other times exhibited the most disgraceful attachment to the rude sports of the field. A custom equally indecorous prevailed in England from the early part of the reign of Edward I. till the time of Elizabeth. This was a most singular offering of a fat doe in winter and a buck in summer, made at the high altar of St. Paul's church in London, by Sir William de Baude and his family, and then to be distributed among the canons resident, in lieu of twenty-two acres of land in Essex, formerly belonging to the canons of this church. Weever, in his "Funerall Monu-

* Milner's Hist. of the Church of Christ, vol. iii, p. 455.

ments," has thus described it: "On the feast day of the commemoration of St. Paul, the bucke being brought up to the steps of the high altar in Paul's church at the hour of procession, the deane and chapter being apparelled in coapes and vestments, with garlands of roses on their heads, they sent the body of the bucke to baking, and had the head fixed on a pole, borne before the crosse in their procession, untill they issued out of the west dore; where the keeper that brought it blowed the death of the bucke, and then the horners that were about the citie presently answered him in like manner. For the which paines they had, each man, of the deane and chapter, foure pence in money, and their dinner; and the keeper that brought it was allowed during his abode there, for that service, meate, drinke, and lodging, at the deane and chapter's charges, and five shillings in money, at his going, together with a loafe of bread, having the picture of St. Paul upon it. There was belonging to the church of St. Paul, for both the daies, two especiall sutes of vestments, the one embroidered with buckes, the other with does, both given by the said Bauds."*

In this age of persecution and profligacy, the monasteries were the principal asylums of sacred literature. The writings of former ages were kept with religious care in several of the monastic libraries; and even where the general interests of science were neglected, the monks continued the employment of transcription: and it deserves to be recorded to the honour of Manegold, the seventeenth abbot of Hirsauge, about A. D. 1157, that, while he was in an inferior station as conductor of the singers, and keeper of the library, he caused sixty valuable volumes to be written upon parchment, for the use of the fraternity to which he belonged.†

The Cistercian monks allotted several hours in the day to manual labour, *copying books*, or sacred studies. Stephen Harding, an Englishman of an honourable and wealthy family, received his education in the monastery of Sherborn, in Dorsetshire, and there laid a very solid foundation of literature and sincere piety. He travelled into Scotland, and from thence to Paris and Rome. In 1098, he, with twenty companions, retired to Citeaux, a marshy wilderness, five leagues from Dijon, where they founded the Cistercian order. In 1109 he was chosen the third abbot of Citeaux, and, with the assistance of his monks, wrote during the same year a very correct copy of the Latin Bible for the use of the monastery. For this great work, which was equally creditable to his piety and

* Weever's Ancient Funerall Monuments, p. 603. London, 1631, folio.

† Trithemii Chronicon Hirsaugense, tom. i, p. 437.

his learning, he collated a number of MSS., and consulted many learned Jews on the Hebrew text of difficult passages, and in particular on the books of Kings, in which he found the errors were most numerous. This most valuable MS. copy of the Bible is preserved at Citeaux, in four volumes in folio, written on vellum.* He died March 28th, 1134.

Clairvaux was one of the dependencies of Citeaux. It was founded in 1115. Bernard, the son of a military nobleman, was its first abbot. He was born at Fontaines, a castle in Burgundy, and a lordship belonging to his father. From his infancy he was devoted to religion and study, and made a rapid proficiency in the learning of the times. He early formed a resolution to retire from the world, and engaged all his brothers, and several of his friends, in the same monastic views with himself. He became a Cistercian, the strictest of the orders in France, and entered the monastery of Citeaux. In this humble retirement, "I meditated," said he, "on the word of God, and the fields and forests taught me its secret meaning: the oaks and the beeches were my masters." He read the Scriptures without a comment, "for their own words," he observes, "explain their meaning best; and in those words may be found the real force of the truths which they convey." After two years this extraordinary youth was translated, with the jurisdiction of an abbot, to the new establishment at Clairvaux, a barren and neglected spot, the retreat of thieves, and, from its state of desolation, called the Vale of Wormwood. To encourage learning, Bernard was careful to furnish all the monasteries subject to him with good libraries; and several beautifully illuminated MSS., written in his time, are still shown at Clairvaux. In defending what he considered to be the truth, he had to contend with the noted Peter Abelard, whose base seduction and subsequent treatment of Eloisa have justly branded his name with infamy. By an abuse of the scholastic divinity, and the elation of applause and self-confidence, Abelard was led to adopt sentiments approaching to the Socinianism of more modern times. These opinions were successfully combated by Bernard; and Gaufredus, one of the writers of Bernard's life, thus expresses his gratitude: "Blessed be God, who gave to us a better master, by whom he confuted the ignorance of the former, and quashed his arrogance; by whom Christ exhibited to us three special objects in his sufferings,—an example of virtue, an incentive of love, and a sacrifice of redemp-

* Butler's Lives, vol. iv, Ap. 17, p. 167. Le Long, Biblioth. Sacra, tom. i, p. 239. Paris, 1723.

tion." His works which he has left behind him are various as they are numerous, and comprised under the principal heads of sermons, epistles, and moral treatises. He has acquired the appellation of the mellifluous doctor. His writings are pervaded by devotional fervour; and the facility with which, in almost every period, he introduces the words of Scripture, is really admirable, and their application is seldom forced or unappropriate. In the beginning of the year 1153 he fell into a decay, which on the 20th of August terminated his life. He was buried at Clairvaux.*

LAMBERT of Liege, a canon regular of St. Christopher, who died about the year 1177, is said to have translated the Acts of the Apostles into the Romance, or vulgar French dialect.†

PETRUS, or PIERRE DE PATIS, a Frenchman, who flourished A. D. 1200, was the author of a French paraphrastical version of the Psalms. The following specimen of it, from a copy in the royal library at Paris, written by a scribe called Linardin, is curious, and suggests the idea that the mode of glossing or commenting, in his day, was by appending the gloss or comment to the preceding sentence.

"*Beneure est cel home qui ne nala pas en le conseil des felons, et ne se aresta pas en la voie des pecheors, come fist Adam quand il mangea la poume.*"

"Blessed is the man who walketh not in the counsel of felons,‡ nor standeth in the way of sinners, as Adam did when he ate the apple."§

PETRUS DE RIGA, canon of Rheims, who flourished under the emperor Frederick I., was the author of a work entitled AURORA, or the *History of the Bible allegorized*, in Latin verses, some of which are in rhyme. The books of the sacred volume which he turned into verse were, Genesis, Exodus, Leviticus, Numbers, Deuteronomy, Joshua, Judges, Ruth, Kings, the Song of Solomon, Daniel, Job, Esther, the four Gospels, and the Acts of the Apostles; besides the apocryphal books of Tobit, Judith, and Maccabees. His version of Esther, in hexameter and pentameter verses, was published at Frankfort, in 1624, by Gasper Barthius,

* Butler's Lives, vol. viii, Aug. 20. Milner, vol. iii, cent. 12. Berrington's Literary Hist. of the Middle Ages, pp. 278–284.

† Le Long, Biblioth. Sacra, tom. i, p. 324, et Index Auctor. Paris, 1723.

‡ The propriety of using this term in reference to Adam is evident from its etymology; for, according to Spelman, it is derived from the Teutonic FEE, which signifies *fief*, and LON, which signifies *price* or *value*, so that *felony* was the act by which a vassal forfeited his estate to his lord. *Spelmanni Glossar.*

§ Le Long, Biblioth. Sacra, tom. i, p. 323. Paris, 1723.

in his *Adversaria.*, lib. 31, cap. 15, in folio. He also wrote *Speculum Ecclesiæ*, and other pieces in Latin poetry.* He died A. D. 1209.

About the same time MATTHÆUS, a presbyter of Vendasme, paraphrased the book of Tobit into Latin elegiacs from the Latin Bible of Jerome, under the title of the Tobiad, sometimes called the Thebaid, first printed among the *Octo Moralès*. Warton† says he flourished in 1170; but Sixtus Senensis‡ places him in the year 1400.

JOANNES BURGUNDIO was another of the learned men of this period, whose Biblical labours entitle him to notice. He was a citizen of Pisa, where he sustained a high judicial office, under the emperor Frederick I., surnamed Barbarossa. As a scholar, he was eminently skilled in the literature of Greece and Rome; and attended a council at Rome in 1163, carrying with him a translation from the Greek into Latin of the Gospel of St. John made by himself; he also acknowledged that he had translated the greater part of the book of Genesis. He died A. D. 1194.§

But besides these translations, which seem to have originated in a desire for the dissemination of truth, there were others produced by the chivalrous spirit which had been excited by the crusades. The books of Kings, the Maccabees, and other historical books, were translated into the vulgar French, under the title of *Plusieurs Battailes des Roys d'Israel en contre les Philistiens et Assyriens, &c.*, and other similar ones. Unfortunately, however, they were deeply tinctured with the deplorable superstition and barbarity of the age; and the translators made no scruple of embellishing their writings by the insertion of legendary tales and fabulous exploits Some of these interpolated versions were composed in rhyme, to render them popular, and easy to be sung.|| Leontius, or Leonine, a French monk of St. Victor, at Marseilles, about the year 1135, wrote a Latin heroic poem in twelve books, containing the "History of the Bible, from the creation of the world, to the story of Ruth." He was the most popular, and almost only Latin poet of his time in France. Leonine verses, which are probably the Roman hexameters, or pentameters rhymed, but which are sometimes

* Sixt. Senensis, Biblioth. Sanct., lib. iv. Warton's Hist. of Eng. Poetry, vol. ii, p. 167, *note*. Le Long, vol. ii, p. 929.

† Warton's Hist. of Eng. Poetry, vol. ii, p. 168.

‡ Sixt. Senens. Biblioth. Sanct., lib. iv, p. 345.

§ Le Long, Bibliotheca Sacra, tom. i, p. 309, et Index Auctor.

|| Warton's Hist. of Eng. Poetry, vol. ii, p. 107.

used as a term for Latin rhymes in general, are said to have obtained their name from having been invented, and first used by him; though some contend that Pope Leo II., a great reformer of the chants and hymns of the church, invented this sort of verse, about the year 680.*

One of the most celebrated works of this period was the *Scholastica Historia* of Peter Comestor, compiled about the year 1175, at Paris. It was a sort of Latin breviary of the historical parts of the Old and New Testaments, and Apocrypha, accompanied with elaborate expositions from Josephus, and many pagan writers; and so popular as not only to be taught in schools, but even to be publicly read in the churches.

Of this very singular and once popular work, the reader may form some idea, by the following translation, from an early printed copy of the work in my possession, of the prefatory epistle, and version or gloss of Gen. iii, 1-6.

Prefatory Epistle.

"To the reverend father and his lord William, by the grace of God, archbishop of Siena, Peter, a servant of Christ, and presbyter of Troyes, prayeth a good life and happy death.

"I have been induced to undertake this work by the earnest entreaties of my brethren, who, being engaged in reading the history of sacred Scripture in regular order, found it was made diffuse by numerous glosses, and that it needed considerable enlargement and explanation; and therefore urged me to compose a work to which they might have recourse for coming at the truth of the history. In doing this, my intention has been so to direct my pen, as not to leave the writings of the fathers, although novelty is pleasing and delights the ear. So beginning with the cosmography of Moses, I have continued a small rivulet of history to the ascension of the Saviour, leaving the ocean of my stories to more skilful hands, who may follow the useful and ancient, and invent new ones. Also, from the histories of heathen writers, I have inserted some things which fell in with the order of the times, thus making my work like a stream, which, while it fills the creeks that it finds in its course, at the same time continues to flow on. But as rough style needs a polish, I have reserved that business for you, that, if God will, this work may derive splendour from your correction, and perpetuity from your approbation. In all things blessed be God!"

* Warton's Hist. of Eng. Poetry, vol. i, diss. 2.

VERSION OR GLOSS OF GEN. III, 1, &c.

"The serpent was more subtle than all terrestrial animals, both naturally and incidentally. Incidentally, because it was full of the devil. For Lucifer, being banished the paradise of spirits, envied man who was in the paradise bodies, of knowing that, if he should make him commit transgression, he also would be banished. But fearing to be detected by the man, he tried the woman, who was both less prudent, and more easy to be moved to sin. And this he did by means of the serpent; for then it was erect like man, being afterward made prostrate by the curse; and it is said the *Phareas* walks erect even to this day. He chose also, says Bede, a certain kind of serpent, having a face resembling a virgin's, because like things delight in their like, and moved its tongue to speak, the serpent at that time knowing nothing of it, in the same way as he speaks by the mouth of fanatics and those who are possessed without their knowledge. And he said, 'Why hath God commanded you not to eat of every tree of paradise, to eat of the trees, but not of every tree?' He put this question that from the reply to it he might find occasion to say what he had come for: and so it happened. For, when the woman, as if in doubt, made answer: 'Lest peradventure we die;' because a person in doubt is easily moved any way, he, without taking any notice of the command, says, 'You will certainly not die; nay, but because he is unwilling that you should resemble him in knowledge, and knows that when you shall have eaten of this tree, you will be as gods, knowing good and evil, he hath, as it were through envy, forbidden you.' And the woman being lifted up and wishful to become like God, consented."*

GUIARS DES MOULINS, a canon of Aire, translated it into French, in 1291; and about the year 1271 it was translated into German rhymes. Vossius says that the original was abridged by Gualter Hunte, an English Carmelite friar, about the year 1460. There are numerous and very sumptuous manuscripts of this work in the British Museum. One of them, with exquisite paintings, was ordered to be written by Edward IV. at Bruges, A.D. 1470. Another was written in 1382. R. Simon says, that the French version of the Scriptures, ascribed to Guiars des Moulins, is no other than the translation of Comestor's *Historia Scholastica*, though it ap-

* Comestoris Scholastica Historia, *Proleg. Epist.* et Gen., cap. xxi. Basil, 1486, fol For the translation I am indebted to the kindness of Mr. Jonathan Crowther junr., master of the Classical Academy, Frodsham, Cheshire.

pears without the glosses or interpolations. In proof of this fact, he quotes the following passages from the preface of a MS. copy in the royal library at Paris:—"Because the devil every day molests, disturbs, and pollutes the heart of men, by idleness and a thousand snares, which he lays to entrap our hearts; never ceasing his endeavours to entice us to sin, that he may thereby draw us into hell with him, it is the business of our clergy, and priests of holy church, after their orisons, to employ themselves in doing some good work. And because the devil has many times drawn me into sin by idleness, that he may no more find me unemployed in good works, I that am priest and canon of St. Peter's of Aire, in the bishopric of Therovenne, by name Guiars des Moulins, called, first of all to the praise of God, the Virgin Mary, and all the saints; and next, to the profit of all those whom this book shall reach; wherein (at the request of a special friend, who much desired the profit of my soul) I have translated the historical books of the Bible. I desire all that shall read these translations, if they find any fault therein, to take for excuse what I here protest, viz., that I have not taken away, nor added any thing besides the pure verity as I have found it in the Latin Bible, and the scholastical histories; and those that will search may see that I have followed the pure verity in these translations, word for word, as I found it in the Latin. I began these translations in the year of grace 1291, and finished them in the year 1294, in the month of February." After the preface Des Moulins places a catalogue of the books of the Bible, professing to follow the order of the *Historia Scholastica*, by Peter Comestor, whom he calls master in history. As the Old Testament was not entire in Comestor's epitome, so he had only a Harmony or Agreement of the Gospels, which Des Moulins translated, commencing with the words *Chi commenchent les Evangilles en le maniere que li maistres en traite en Hystoires*: "Here begin the Gospels after the manner adopted by masters in history." The Acts of the Apostles are placed next after this Harmony; and St. Paul's Epistles supply the third place; the other Epistles follow, Jude being placed the last.* The *Historia Scholastica* was first printed at Augsburg, in 1473, fol., by Gunth. Zainer. The French translation was first published without date or place, in two tomes, with old wood cuts, about A. D. 1487.

The glosses and legendary tales rendered Comestor's work so pleasing to the major part of the readers, that father Simon says,

* Warton's Hist. of Eng. Poetry, vol. ii, pp. 107, 108. Simon's Critical Hist. of the Versions of N. Test., pt. ii, ch. xxviii.

"The study of the Holy Scriptures was neglected, because the Scholastical History was preferred to versions of the Bible;" and even so late as the sixteenth century it continued to be prejudicial in its influence, for in 1545 a French version of the whole Bible was printed, which the same writer assures us was only a revision of Des Moulins' translation of the *Historia Scholastica.**

PETER, surnamed COMESTOR, or the *Devourer*, from the avidity with which he read or *devoured* the Scriptures, was a Frenchman, born at Troyes. He became a priest in his native city, from whence he removed to Paris, where his extraordinary talents and learning were so fully appreciated, that he was elected chancellor of the university. Wearied with the anxieties of his official situation, he at length withdrew from public life, to spend his days in retirement as a canon regular of St. Victor, in the suburbs of Paris. He died in 1198. The following curious epitaph was made on him:—

> " *Petrus eram*, quem *petra* tegit dictusque *Comestor*
> Nunc *Comedor*. Vivus docui, nec cesso docere
> Mortuus; ut dicat, qui me videt incineratum:
> Quod sumus iste fuit, erimus quandoque quod hic est."†

" I who was once called *Peter*, (that is, a stone,) am now covered by a *stone*, (petra): and I who was once surnamed *Comestor*, (that is, Devourer,) am now *devoured*. I taught when alive, nor do I cease to teach, though dead. For he who beholds me reduced to ashes may say, 'This man was once what we are now, and what he is now we soon shall be.' "

Among the Biblical students of this age, it is a curious fact that the nuns of the Paraclete appear pre-eminent. This convent was erected in the forest of Nogent by Abelard, and placed under the care of the unfortunate and deserted Eloisa, whose history demonstrably proves, that the villain who can basely betray the confidence of unsuspicious innocence will not be reluctant to desert and treat with unfeeling indifference the wretched victim of his brutal passions; and that the unfortunate female who deviates from the path of virtue exposes herself to the pang of keen remorse, and the cold neglect of him whose faithless vows induced the irretrievable violation of her honour, and plunged her into crime and disgrace. The nuns of the Paraclete, with Eloisa at their head, studied the Latin, and Greek, and Hebrew tongues, applied them to the acquirement of a more accurate knowledge of the

* Simon, Hist. Crit. du V. T., liv. iii, cap. xi, et Hist. des Vers., pt. ii, cap. xxviii
† Cavei, Hist. Litteraria, sæc. 12, p. 682. Bibliog. Dict., vol. iii.

Holy Scriptures, and endeavoured, by a sedulous examination of the original texts, to derive sacred wisdom from its purest source. Eloisa died in 1163, when she had entered her sixty-third year; and, for many years after her death, the nuns of the Paraclete commemorated her learning and abilities at the feast of Whitsuntide, by performing the service of the day in Greek: a practice which only ceased when the knowledge of the language was lost among them.*

I know not whether it be worth observing, that about this time a practice prevailed of forming and reducing into parchment-rolls historical trees of the Old Testament. The invention of them has been attributed to Peter of Poictou, a disciple of Lombard, about the year 1170, who was desirous of aiding the poorer clergy by this employment. The rage of genealogizing lasted for ages, and extended to profane as well as sacred history. Roger Alban, a Carmelite friar of London, formed the descent of Jesus Christ from Adam, through the Levitical and regal tribes, the Jewish patriarchs, judges, kings, prophets, and priests. A vellum roll, supposed to be the original one, beautifully illuminated, is among the MSS. More in the public library at Cambridge. A pedigree of the British kings, from Adam to Henry the Sixth, written by the same compiler, and presented by him to the king about the year 1450, is now in Queen's College library, at Oxford. Juliana Barnes, a native of Roding, in Essex, prioress of Sopewell nunnery, was eminent for learning and personal accomplishments, but employed her talents in writing treatises on hunting, hawking, heraldry, &c. One of her tracts on "Armory," or heraldry, written about the year 1441, begins in the following curious manner: "Of the offspring of the *Gentilman* Jafeth come Habraham, Moyses, Aron, and the profettys, and also the kyng of the right lyne of Mary, of whom that *Gentilman* Jhesus was born, very god and man: after his manhode kynge of the land of Jude and of Jues, *gentilman* by his moder Mary, *prince of cote armure*."† This, however, was the less remarkable in an age when the rank and titles of secular nobility were sometimes conferred even on the saints. St. James was actually created a *baron* at Paris. Thus Froissart, tom. iii, cap. xxx: "Or eurent ils affection et devotion d'aller en pelerinage au *Baron* Saint Jaques." And in Fabl., tom. ii, p. 182, cited by Carpentier, sup. Lat. gloss, p. 469:—

* Berrington's Lives of Abelard and Heloisa, b. v, p. 258, and b. vii, pp. 395, 396.

† Warton's History of English Poetry, vol. ii, pp. 172, 177. Lempriere's Universal Biography.

"Dame, dist il, et je me veu,
Adieu, et au Baron Saint Leu,
Et s'irai au Baron Saint Jaques."*

Even the popular translations of the Scriptures were influenced by the spirit of the times. Sanson de Nanteul, a clerical rhymer, who lived in the reign of our Stephen, and to whom the versification of our ancient poetry is said to have been much indebted, was the author of a translation of the Proverbs of Solomon into the eight-syllable verse of Norman-French, with a copious "Glosse." His plan is, to give the Latin Vulgate of a verse or more, then his versified translation, and afterward his gloss, which is sometimes moral, and sometimes allegorical; in this way he has rhymed above twelve thousand lines into couplets. A copy of it, forming a beautiful specimen of the ancient calligraphy, is among the Harleian MSS., No. 4388, in the British Museum. "To us," says a competent judge, "the rhyme is the only mark of poetry in its composition; but as a collection of didactic aphorisms in familiar verse, it must have been an important present to the awakening thought of the unlearned population." It was written at the request of an Anglo-Norman lady; and notwithstanding the author classes the hearing of songs and tales among the acts of criminal voluptuousness, he styles his work a "Romanz:"—

"Ki ben volt estre engranz
Entendet dunc a cest *romanz*
Qi al loenge damne de
Et a senor al translate."†

This appellation, and that of the modern term romance, are derived from the name given to the corrupted Latin spoken chiefly by the Franks, after their settlement in Gaul or France. This new language varied in different provinces, for want of a regular standard of pronunciation and grammar. Among its dialects in Burgundy, it was intermixed with a great alloy of the old Burgundian language; in the southern provinces of France, the Provencal, Languedocian, and Gascon dialects with that of the Visigoths; and afterward that in Neustria with the Norman; so that these dialects are at this day often not intelligible to those who speak pure French. The Romance, or Romanciere language, began to be formed in the eighth century; but, except in some few unimportant instances, was not made use of in writing before the eleventh age: but all who preached or read any thing before an

* Warton's History of English Poetry, vol. ii, p. 345, *note.*

† Turner's History of England, vol. i, pp. 444, 445.

audience, in which there were many who did not understand Latin, used afterward to add, in the Romance tongue, some explication of what had been said or read in Latin. In the eleventh century some began to commit considerable translations to writing, and in the succeeding century some wrote books in the Romance language. The works thus written in the vulgar tongue were denominated *romanzes* or romances; and as fictitious narratives of imaginary adventures were the first compositions committed to writing in the vernacular dialects of France, while other writings continued still to be published in Latin, this species of historic fiction became distinguished by the term romance.* The general subject of many of the early romances were the triumphs of Christianity over paganism. Many of them were written by monks or clergymen; thus the Chronicle attributed to Turpin, or Tilpin, archbishop of Rheims, the contemporary of Charlemagne, and which professes to give the history of that monarch's expedition to the Peninsula, and his destruction of idolatry, is supposed to have been written by a canon of Barcelona about the end of the eleventh or the commencement of the twelfth century. Another work, similar to the Chronicle, and called *Philumena*, was written by a monk of the abbey de Grasse. These works of fiction were diligently sought after by the inmates of the monasteries, were eagerly read by them, and were placed in their libraries among their most valuable treatises. In that of Croyland abbey we find Turpin's Chronicle placed on the same shelf with Robert Tumbelay on the Canticles, and Thomas Waleys on the Psalter.†

One of the earliest of these religious fictions was the story of Barlaam and Josaphat, by Johannes Damascenus, or St. John of Damascus, a monk of Syria, who lived in the eighth century, during the reign of Leo Isauricus. This work seems to have been written with a view of promoting a taste for monastic seclusion. It details the successful endeavours of the hermit Barlaam to convert o the Christian faith the Indian prince Josaphat, who had from his infancy been placed in a state of seclusion from the world, by his idolatrous father Abenner, in order to avert the completion of a prophecy, which fortold his desertion of idolatry, and zealous adoption of Christianity. The style is formed on the sacred writings; and the artifice by which Barlaam is represented as gaining

* Du Cange, Glossarium, Lat. Præfat., p. vii. Butler's Lives, vol. viii, pp. 246, 247, *note;* and vol. x, p. 326, *note.*

† Dunlop's History of Fiction, vol. i, ch. iv, pp. 312, 313, 333. Warton's History of English Poetry, vol. iii, Diss. on the Gesta Romanorum, p. lxv.

admittance to the prince, will remind the reader of the modes of disseminating their principles, practised by the Paulicians and Waldenses. The hermit who had insinuated himself into the acquaintance of an attendant, informed him, that he wished to present to the prince a gem, which was of great price, and was endowed with many virtues. Under this similitude of a worldly jewel, he typified the beauties of the Gospel; and the prince having heard the story of the merchant, ordered him to be instantly introduced. Barlaam having obtained admittance, premised his instructions with a summary of sacred history, from the fall of Adam to the resurrection of our Saviour; and having in this way excited the attention and curiosity of Josaphat, who conjectures that this is the jewel of the merchant, he gradually proceeds to unfold all the mysteries, and inculcates all the doctrines of Christianity. This Greek romance was a great favourite during the middle ages, "and, as Prince Josaphat is represented in it as gradually acquiring, by unaided meditation, moral notions and ideas of disease and death, it has been considered as the origin of a fictitious work of Avicenna, in the beginning of the eleventh century, as well as of the celebrated Arabian story of *Hai Ebn Yokdhan*, written by Ebn Tophail, a Mohammedan philosopher who lived, toward the close of the twelfth century, in some part of the Saracenic dominions in Spain. In a more recent period it gave rise to more than one of the tales of Boccaccio; and became the model of that species of spiritual fiction which was so prevalent in France during the sixteenth and seventeenth centuries.*

A work of still greater celebrity was the *Legenda Aurea* of Jacobus de Voragine, a dominican friar, and archbishop of Genoa, in 1292. It consists of the biography of saints, "interspersed" it is said in the colophon of the book, "with many other beautiful and strange relations." The Lives of the Saints were denominated *legends*, from being statedly *read* in the churches; and this compilation received the epithet of *golden*, from its extraordinary popularity; or the supposed value of its contents. It was the delight of our ancestors, during the ages which preceded the revival of letters. The library of no monastery was without it. Every private person who was able, purchased it; and for a long time after the invention of printing no work more frequently issued from the press.† In the year 1555 the learned Claude D'Espence was

* Dunlop's Hist. of Fiction, vol. i, pp. 70–83; and vol. iii, pp. 328, 329.

† Dunlop's Hist. of Fiction, vol. iii, p. 7. C. Butler's Life of Alban Butler, prefixed to Lives of the Saints, p. 21.

obliged to make a public recantation, for calling it *Legenda Ferrea*, or the Iron Legend. A French translation of it was made in the fourteenth century, by Jean de Vignay, a monk hospitaler, the French translator of Vincent de Beauvais's famous *Speculum Historiale*. From De Vignay's version, the Legenda Aurea was converted into our language by the indefatigable Caxton, who printed an edition of his translation, which he completed in 1483, and dedicated to William, earl of Arundel, who, while it was printing, gave him annually a buck in summer, and a doe in winter. A magnificent, and perhaps the original French manuscript of this work was sold among the duplicates of Mr. R. Heathcote's books in 1803; said to be "near five hundred years old," and executed for the queen of Philip de Valois. It is described as being "an immense folio volume, perhaps the most curious work of the kind in the world; every leaf of the finest vellum; all the capital letters illuminated with gold, and rich colours; with upward of two hundred miniatures of the different saints, &c." It was purchased by the duke of Norfolk for £64. A copy of the English version of the same work, printed by Caxton in 1483, in folio, was, December 24th, 1814, sold by auction at the late residence of Mr. Brassey deceased, for ninety-three guineas!*

This excessive attachment to romantic, or legendary fiction, proved injurious to Biblical knowledge; it increased the number of apocryphal writings, and prevented the multiplication of copies of the Holy Scriptures. So rare and expensive were transcripts of the sacred writings, that when any person made a present of a copy to a church or monastery, it was deemed a donative of such value, that he offered it on the altar *pro remedio animæ suæ*, in order to obtain the forgiveness of his sins. In the collegiate church of Dreux, in France, a Latin Bible, fairly written in two volumes large folio, is preserved, at the close of which is a Latin deed of gift. The following is a translation of it:—

"Let all the sons of the church, whether present or future, know that Thomas, Seneschall of St Gervase hath, of his own free will, given this Library† to God and the holy protomartyr Stephen, for the remission of his own sins, and those of his wife Ermelina, of his son Herbert, and of his daughters Margaret and Fredeburga; the canons of the aforesaid church of the protomartyr have, therefore, conceded to them the benefits and prayers of the said church,

* Dibdin's Typographical Antiquities, vol. i, p. 190. Warton's Hist. of Eng. Poetry, vol. ii, p. 111. Gent. Mag., April, 1815, p. 349.

† The term *Bibliotheca*, or Library, was frequently applied to the Bible.

and after their removal from this world, the regular celebration of their anniversaries in the church, for ever. Offered by the hand of Thomas himself, and by the hand of his wife, on the altar of the protomartyr Stephen, on the day of the Nativity of our Lord, in the year of the Incarnation, one thousand one hundred and sixteen, in the reign of the most pious and sincere worshipper of God, King Louis the Sixth, son of King Philip the First."*

If we turn our attention to ENGLAND, we find that the ravages of the Danes, and the conquest of the Normans, had repressed the ardour of Biblical pursuits, and rendered copies of the sacred Scriptures, even in Latin, exceedingly scarce and difficult to be obtained. The Anglo-Saxon versions were become nearly obsolete; and the attempt of the conqueror to introduce the French had so altered the language of the nation, that the inhabitants of our island could understand but little of what had been the vernacular tongue of their ancestors. The Bible was consequently out of the reach of the illiterate and the poor; and the baneful opinion began to prevail, that the knowledge of the Scriptures was *unnecessary*, and that it was *unlawful* for private Christians to read them in their mother-tongue. William Butler, a Franciscan friar, went so far as to maintain, that "the prelates ought not to admit of this, that every one should at his pleasure read the Scriptures translated into *Latin*"——"A paradox," says Lewis, in his History of English Translations of the Bible, "which served indeed to justify or excuse many even of the priests of those times, who, as they knew nothing of the Scriptures but what they found of them in their *Portuises* and *Missals*, so they were not able to read those portions of them there with understanding; so utterly ignorant were they even of *Latin*."†

If any portion of the Bible was attempted to be transferred into the English language at this period, it appeared in a prolix paraphrase, shackled with metre, and with frequent violations of Scripture facts. The earliest production of this kind is a paraphrase of the Gospels, and the Acts of the Apostles, preserved in the Bodleian library. It is entitled *Ormulum*, from being written by one Orme, or Ormin. The style is that of Saxon poetry, without rhyme, in imitation of the most common species of the Latin tetrameter iambic. It is in the Saxon character, but in the English language, properly so called, in its dawn and infancy.‡

* Le Long, Biblioth. Sacra, tom. i, p. 238. Paris, 1723, fol. Robertson's Hist. of Charles V., vol. i, Proofs, &c., note x. † Lewis, *ut sup.*, p. 11.

‡ Baber's Wicliff's New Testament, *Saxon and English Versions*, p. lxiv.

There is also in the Bodleian library a prodigious folio volume, beautifully written on vellum, and elegantly illuminated, with this title: "Here begynnen the tytles of the book that is cald in Latyn tonge SALUS ANIME, and in Englysh tonge SOWLE-HELE." It was given to the library by Edward Vernon, Esq., soon after the civil war. Although pieces not absolutely religious are sometimes introduced, the scheme of the compiler or transcriber seems to have been, to form a complete body of legendary and Scriptural history in verse, or rather to collect into one view all the religious poetry he could find. In this ponderous volume is a metrical paraphrastic translation of the Old and New Testaments, supposed to have been executed before the thirteenth century. The following paraphrase of John xix, 25, 26, 27, will exhibit the nature of this curious work:—

"Oure ladi and hire suster stoden under the roode,
And seint John and Marie Magdaleyn with wel sori moode:
Vr ladi bi heold hire swete son i brouht in gret pyne,
Ffor monnes gultes nouthen her and nothing for myne.
Marie weop wel sore and bitter teres leet,
The teres fullen uppon the ston doun at hire feet.
Alas, my son, for serwe wel off seide heo
Nabbe iche bote the one that hongust on the treo,
So ful icham of serwe, as any wommon may beo,
That ischal my deore child in all this pyne iseo:
How schal I sone deore, how hast i yougt liven withouten the,
Nusti nevere of serwe nought sone, what seyst you me?
Then spake Jhesus wordus gode to his modur dere;
Ther he heng uppon the roode here I the take a fere,
That trewliche schal serve ye thin own cosin Jon,
The while that you alyve beo among all thi fon:
Ich the hote Jon, he seide, you wite hire both day and niht
That the Gywes hire fon ne don hire non un riht.
Seint John in the stude vr ladi in to the temple nom
God to serven he hire dude sone so he thider come,
Hole and seeke heo duden good that hes founden thore
Heo hire serveden to hond and foot, the lass and eke the more.
The pore folke feire heo fedde there, heo sege that hit was neode
And the seke heo brougte to bedde and met and drinke gon heom beode.
Wy at heore mihte yong and olde hire loveden bothe syke and fer
As hit was riht for alle and summe to hire servise hedden mester.
Jon hire was a trew feer, nolde nought from hire go,
He lokid hire as his ladi deore and what heo wolde hit was i do."

This sumptuous volume of religious poems was probably chained in the cloister, or in the church, of some capital monastery, where the novices were exercised in reciting portions from these pieces, many of them being metrical legends or lives of saints. Legendary poetry was sometimes sung to the harp, by the minstrels, on Sundays, instead of the romantic subjects usual at public entertainments. In the British Museum there is a set of legendary tales in rhyme, which appear to have been solemnly pronounced by the priest to the people on Sundays and holydays.*

In the valuable library of Corpus Christi College, Cambridge, is a poetical Biblical History, embracing the principal facts recorded in the books of Genesis and Exodus, apparently with the one before mentioned, but written in a different, the *northern* dialect. There is also in the same library a version of the Psalms in English metre, and in the northern dialect, which must be referred to about the same period. It is a translation, as close as verse will allow, of that edition of Jerome's Latin version which has been denominated the French, or Gallican. In the Bodleian library, and in the Cotton MSS. at the British Museum, are copies of this translation revised and improved, if not by the hand of the first translator, yet by some person who lived in or near his time.†

Clement, canon of the order of St. Augustine, and prior of the monastery of Lanthony or Llandennen, in Wales, who flourished about the year 1154, compiled, in Latin, a Harmony of the Gospels. He likewise wrote a Commentary on the four Gospels, in Latin. His Harmony was so esteemed by Wicliff, that he translated it into English. A very beautiful MS. of this version is in the British Museum, Harl. MSS., 1862. The Rev. H. H. Baber, assistant librarian, possesses another MS. copy of the fourteenth century, in 12mo.‡

About the year 1155, Nicholas Breakspear, an Englishman, who, by a train of singular adventures, had risen from the lowest condition to the papal dignity, under the name of Adrian IV., sent over for the use of the English people, who were directed to commit them to memory, metrical versions of the Creed and Lord's Prayer. These curious proofs of the high regard of the Roman pontiff for his countrymen are here copied from Stow's Chronicle:

THE CREED.

"I beleue in God Fadir almichty shipper of heuen and earth,
And in Jhesus Crist his onlethi son vre Louerd,
That is iuange thurch the holy ghost: bore of Mary maiden,

* Warton's Hist. of Eng. Poetry, vol. i, pp. 14, 19, 20.

† Warton, vol. i, p. 23. Baber's Wicliff's New Testament, *ubi sup.*

‡ Lewis's Life of Wicliff, p. 149. London, 1720, 8vo. Baber's Life of Dr. Wicliff. p. xlix, prefixed to New Testament.

Tholede pine vnder Pounce Pilat, picht on rode tree, dead and yburiid,
Licht into helle, the thridde day from death arose,
Steich into heauen, sit on his fadir richt honde God almichty,
Then is cominde to deme the quikke and the dede,
I beleue in the holy ghost,
All holy chirche.
Mone of alle hallwen : forgiuenis of sine,
Fleiss vprising,
Lif withuten end, Amen."

THE LORD'S PRAYER.

"Vre fadir in heuene riche,
Thi name be haliid eueriliche,
Thou bring vs to thi michil blisce,
Thi will to wirche thu vs wisse,
Als hit is in heuene ido,
Euer in earth ben hit also,
That holi bred that lasteth ay,
Thou sendhit ous this ilke day,
Forgiue ous all that we hauith don,
Als we forgiuet vch other mon,
He let us falle in no founding,
Ak scilde us fro the foule thing, Amen."*

This singular instance of a pope of Rome deeming it necessary to transmit to England a vernacular version of the Creed and Pater Noster, sufficiently indicates the low state of religious information among the inferior classes of the people, and certainly is not very creditable to the literary abilities of the Catholic clergy of that period.

The historian of Craven has noticed a dispute which occurred during this century between Ralph Hageth, abbot of Kirkstall, and his monks, that will serve still further to elucidate the state of Biblical literature. In the time of his abbacy, "a great calamity befell the brethren from without; for Henry II., by the evil counsel of Roger de Mowbray, deseised them of their best estate, the grange of Micklethwaite. This occasioned great murmurs; and the monks imputed to their abbot, not only the loss of the estate, but of some sacred utensils and ornaments which he had disposed of; for in order to conciliate the king's favour, he had presented him with a gold chalice and a MS. of the Gospels." "This," subjoins the indefatigable antiquarian, "may be added to the instances adduced of the extreme scarcity of MSS. in the middle ages. A copy of the Gospels here accompanied a gold chalice,

* Stow's Annales, or Generall Chronicle of England, pp. 150, 151. London, 1615, folio.

as a propitiatory offering to a king. I am pleased with the dissatisfaction of the monks on this account, and willing to hope they really prized the Gospels as gold. If it was their *only* copy, which is far from being improbable, their loss was indeed to be deplored." Compare this with the following account of a contemporary fact:

"HUGO Decanus Ebor. cum omnibus fortunis suis Fontes se contulct. Dives erat in libris scripturarum sanctarum, quos multis sibi sumptibus comparaverat. Hic primus armariolum de Fontibus suscitavit." "A library in the twelfth century, collected at a great expense, sufficed only to furnish a little closet, or perhaps even a small chest. It is to be supposed that as books multiplied, and wealth increased, the library at Fountains," of which these holy writings thus purchased and deposited there by Hugo were the commencement, "expanded in proportion."* It may also be deemed worthy of notice, as illustrating the practice of the age, that in the records of the exchequer we find an entry purporting that in the seventeenth year of the reign of Henry II. the sheriffs of London paid, by the king's order, "xxijs. *for gold to gild the Gospel* used in the king's chapel."†

The general manners of the age, and the too frequently depraved habits of the monks and priests, proved greatly injurious to the cause of religion and sacred learning. The crusades were everywhere preached, pilgrimages were undertaken, ceremonies were multiplied, and appeals were made to the traditions of the fathers, the opinions of doctors, and the decisions of councils, in preference to the Scriptures. The canons of synods and provincials exhibit the lamentable state of monkish and clerical morality. Of these canons, some of which refer to crimes "obstinately and profligately" practised, of a nature unfit to meet the public eye, and with which we cannot consent to pollute our pages, the following, selected from the acts of different English synods, may suffice.

From Anselm's canons passed at Westminster, A. D. 1102:—

Can. 9. "That priests go not to drinking bouts, nor drink to pegs."‡

* Whitaker's History of Craven, p. 63. Lond. 1812, 4to.

† Madox's Hist. and Antiq. of the Exchequer, ch. ix, p. 190. Lond. 1711, fol.

‡ "Such great drinkers were the Danes, who were in England in the time of Edgar, and so much did their bad examples prevail with the English, that he, by the advice of Dunstan, archbishop of Canterbury, put down many ale-houses, suffering only one to be in a village, or small town; and he also further ordained, that *pins* or *nails* should be fastened into the drinking-cups, or horns, at stated distances, and whosoever

Can 27. "That none exercise that wicked trade which has hitherto been practised in England, of selling men like beasts."

From Archbishop Richard's canons, made at London A. D. 1175 :—

Can. 5. "Because clerks for their ignorance, incontinence, defect of birth, title, or age, despairing of [higher] orders from their own bishops, procure or pretend themselves to be ordained by foreign bishops, and so bring seals unknown to their own diocesans; we therefore annul their orders, forbidding with the terror of *anathema* any to admit them to the exercise of their function."

Can 11. "Let none that would appear to be clerks wear or bear arms, but make their manners and clothes suitable to their profession; or else be degraded as despisers of the canons, and of ecclesiastical authority."

should drink beyond those marks at one draught, should be obnoxious to a severe punishment."—*Strutt, in Brand's Observations on Popular Antiquities*, App., p. 377.

"Our ancestors were formerly famous for compotation; their liquor was ale, and one method of amusing themselves in this way was with the *peg-tankard*. I had lately one of them in my hand. It had on the inside a row of eight pins, one above another, from top to bottom. It held two quarts, and was a noble piece of plate, so that there was a gill of ale, half a pint Winchester measure, between each peg. The law was, that every person that drank was to empty the space between pin and pin, so that the pins were so many measures to make the company all drink alike, and to swallow the same quantity of liquor. This was a pretty sure method of making all the company drunk, especially if it be considered that the rule was, that whoever drank short of his pin, or beyond it, was obliged to drink again, and even as deep as to the next pin. And it was for this reason that, in Archbishop Anselm's canons, made in the council of London A. D. 1102, priests are enjoined not to go to drinking bouts, nor drink to pegs. The words are, '*Ut presbyteri non eant ad potationes, nec ad pinnas bibant.*'—*Wilkin's Concil. I.*, p. 382. M. Du Fresne, in his Gloss., v. *Pinna*, cites Archbishop Anselm's canons of A. D. 1102, *Nec ad pinnas bibant*, and conjectures, '*forte legendum pilas*,' because *pila*, he finds, signifies sometimes *taberna*, a tavern, or drinking house. But this is a most unhappy conjecture, as the sense is so plain and intelligible without it; and all the MSS. agree in writing *pinnas*; and so Mr. Johnson, in his Collection of Ecclesiastical Laws, &c., translates the canon without scruple, '*nor drink to pegs.*'"—*Dr. Pegge, under the signature of T. Row, in Selection of Curious Articles from Gent. Mag.*, vol. i, pp. 262, 263.

William of Malmesbury, speaking of Dunstan, archbishop of Canterbury, says, "So extremely anxious was he to preserve peace even in trivial matters, that, as his countrymen used to assemble in taverns, and, when a little elevated, quarrel as to the proportions of their liquor, he ordered gold or silver pegs to be fastened in the pots, that while every man knew his just measure, shame would compel each, neither to take more himself, nor oblige others to drink beyond their proportional share."—*History of Kings of England, translated by Rev. John Sharpe, M. A.*, b. i, ch. viii, p. 171. Lond. 1815, 4to.

From Herbert Walter's canons, made at Westminster, A. D. 1200:—

Can. 5. "We, following the decrees of the Lateran councils, which are the most famous of any that have been ordained by the modern fathers, do forbid archbishops to exceed the number of forty or fifty men, and horses; bishops the number of twenty or thirty, in visiting parishes: let the archdeacon be content with five or seven; the deans under the bishops with two. And let them not make their progress with hunting dogs, or hawks; but like such as seek not their own, but the things of Christ."

The two following canons, both made under Archbishop Walter Herbert, the former at York, in 1192, the latter as above, in 1200, are highly creditable to that prelate:—

Can. 3. "Because the [canon or] secret part of the mass is frequently corrupted through the mistake of the writers, or the oldness of the books, so that it cannot distinctly be read, let the archdeacons take greater care that the canon of the mass be corrected according to some true and approved copy."

Can. 1. "Whereas an error in divine offices endangers both the souls and bodies of men, it is wholesomely provided by this council, that the words of the *canon** be roundly and distinctly pronounced by every priest, in celebrating [mass;] and not curtailed by a hasty, or drawn out into an immoderate length, by an affectedly slow pronunciation. In like manner that the *hours*,* and all the offices, be rehearsed plainly and distinctly, without clipping or mangling the words: the offenders, after these admonitions, are to be suspended, till they make just satisfaction. Saving in all things the honour and privilege of the holy church of Rome."†

One of the popular employments and entertainments of the ecclesiastics in the middle ages, and one of the modes adopted by them for the instruction of the people, in the place of the Bible, was writing and *exhibiting* RELIGIOUS DRAMAS: these being founded on Scripture narratives, or designed as emblematical representations of moral qualities, were variously designated as *Scripture Plays, Miracles, and Moralities;* and, from the festivals on which they were very generally performed, *Corpus Christi*, and *Whitsun Plays*. As the history of these religious and emblematical dramas is connected with Biblical literature, and is but little known, the

* The *canon*, or secret part of the mass, is from the end of the *trisagium* to the end of the consecration: the *hours* are certain prayers performed at stated hours of the day.

† Johnson's Ecclesiastical Laws, vol. ii, *sub ann.*

reader will excuse the digression of an attempt to present him with an outline of their rise, and progress, and influence; for which I am considerably indebted to Warton's "History of English Poetry," a work of astonishing research and information; to Riccoboni's curious "Historical and Critical Account of the Theatres in Europe;" and to Du Tilliot's *Memoires pour servir a l'histoire de la Fete des Foux.*

The theories which have been advanced to elucidate the origin of these theatrical exhibitions of Scripture histories are various: one supposes them to have been first exhibited at the public marts or fairs, held at certain periods in different parts of Europe; another conjectures that they had their rise at Constantinople; and a third believes them to have been introduced into the West by the pilgrims of the middle ages.

In support of the first of these theories it is remarked, that about the eighth century trade was principally carried on by means of fairs, which lasted several days. Charlemagne established many great marts of this sort in France; as did William the Conqueror, and his Norman successors, in England. The merchants, who frequented these fairs in numerous caravans or companies, employed every art to draw the people together. They were therefore accompanied by jugglers, minstrels, and buffoons; who were no less interested in giving their attendance, and exerting all their skill, on these occasions. In proportion as these popular amusements were attended and encouraged, they were rendered more seductive by numerous decorations and improvements; and the arts of buffoonery acquired additional importance in the eyes of the multitude. By degrees the clergy, observing that the entertainments of dancing, music, and mimicry, exhibited at these protracted annual celebrities, rendered the people less attentive to the duties of religion, by promoting idleness and a love of festivity, proscribed these sports, and excommunicated the performers. But finding that no regard was paid to their censures, they changed their plan, and determined to take these representations into their own hands. They turned actors; and, instead of profane mummeries, presented stories taken from legends, or the Bible. This was the origin of sacred comedy. The death of St. Catherine, acted by the monks of St. Denis, rivalled the popularity of the professed players. Music was admitted into the churches, which served as theatres for the representation of these religious farces. The festivals among the French, called the Feast of Fools, of the Ass, and of Innocents, at length became greater favourites, as they certainly were more capricious and absurd, than the interludes of the buffoons at the fairs.*

Another ingenious and novel theory on this subject supposes religious plays to have originated at Constantinople, where the old Grecian stage continued to flourish in some degree, and the tragedies of Sophocles and Euripides were represented, till the fourth century. About that period, Gregory Nazianzen, a bishop, a poet, and one of the fathers of the church, banished pagan plays from the stage at Constantinople, and introduced select stories from the Old and New Testaments. As the ancient Greek tragedy was regarded by the heathens as a religious spectacle, it is supposed that a translation was made on the same plan, and that the chorusses were turned into Christian hymns. Gregory wrote many sacred dramas for this purpose, of which the only one now extant is the tragedy called Χριστος πασχων, or Christ's Passion. In the prologue it is said to be in imitation of Euripides, and that this is the first time the Virgin Mary has been produced on the stage. The fashion of acting spiritual dramas, in which, at first, a due degree of method and decorum was preserved, was at length adopted from Constantinople by the Italians; who framed, in the depth of the dark ages, on this foundation, that barbarous species of theatrical representation called MYSTERIES, or *Sacred Comedies*, and which were soon afterward received in France. This opinion is rendered more probable by considering the early commercial intercourse between Italy and Constantinople; for although the Italians, at the time when they are supposed to have imported plays of this nature, did not understand the Greek language, yet they could understand, and consequently could imitate, what they saw. It may also be further observed, in defence of this hypothesis, that the Feast of Fools, and of the Ass, with other farces of that sort, so common in Europe, originated at Constantinople. They were instituted, although perhaps under other names, in the Greek Church, about the year 990, by Theophylact, patriarch of Constantinople, probably with a better design than is imagined by the ecclesiastical annalists,—that of weaning the minds of the people from the pagan ceremonies, particularly the Bacchanalian and Kalendary solemnities, by the substitution of Christian spectacles, partaking of the same spirit of licentiousness; a principle of accommodation, however, which cannot be too severely reprehended. The fact is recorded by Cedrenus, (Compend. Hist., p. 639,) one

* Warton's History of English Poetry, vol. ii, pp. 366, 367.

of the Byzantine historians, who flourished about the year 1050, in the following words, "Εργον εκεινον, κ. τ. λ." "Theophylact introduced the practice, which prevails even to this day, of scandalizing God, and the memory of his saints, on the most splendid and popular festivals, by indecent and ridiculous songs, and enormous shoutings, even in the midst of those sacred hymns which we ought to offer to the divine grace with compunction of heart, for the salvation of our souls. But he, having collected a company of base fellows, and placing over them one Euthymius, surnamed Casnes, whom he also appointed the superintendent of his church, admitted into the sacred service diabolical dances, exclamations of ribaldry, and ballads borrowed from the streets and brothels."* But at a much earlier period than that of Theophylact, attempts had been made to imitate the style and manner of the most elegant Greek classics in the composition of *Scriptural dramas*. The imitations of the *Apollinarii* in the fourth century have been already noticed; and the fragments of a much more early and more singular specimen of a dramatical representation of sacred history are yet preserved in the extracts from an ancient *Jewish* play on the *exodus*, or the departure of the Israelites from Egypt, under their leader and prophet, Moses. The author was Ezekiel, a Jew. Huetius, (Demonstrat. Evangelic., p. 99,) and Whitaker, (Origin of Arianism, pp. 213, 214, 219,) endeavour to prove that he wrote before the Christian era; but Warton (vol. ii, p. 372) deems it most probable that he flourished at the close of the second century, and composed his drama in Greek iambics, in imitation of the Grecian stage, after the Jews had been dispersed and intermixed with other nations. The principal characters in this piece are Moses, Sapphora, and God speaking from the burning bush. Moses delivers the prologue, or introduction, in a speech of sixty lines, and his rod is turned into a serpent on the stage. Clemens Alexandrinus, in his *Stromata*, and Eusebius, in his *Præparatio Evangelica*, have each preserved fragments of this writer. Portions of these extracts are copied, and translations given, in Whitaker's "Origin of Arianism." See also *Corpus poetar. Gr. Tragicor. et Comicor.*, Genev. 1614, fol., and *Poetæ Christian. Græci*, Paris, 1609, 8vo.

A third hypothesis respecting the origin of the Mysteries and Miracle-Plays is that of Menestrier and Boileau, who seem to think that the ancient *Pilgrimages* introduced them into France. The

* Warton, vol. ii, pp. 368–370.

pilgrims who returned from Jerusalem and other places esteemed holy, composed songs on their adventures; intermixing recitals of passages in the life of Christ, descriptions of his crucifixion, of the day of judgment, of miracles, and martyrdoms. To these tales, which were recommended by a pathetic chant, and a variety of gesticulations, the credulity of the multitude gave the name of *visions*. These pious itinerants travelled in companies; and, taking their stations in the most public streets, and singing with their staves in their hands, and their hats and mantles fantastically adorned with shells, and emblems painted in various colours, formed a sort of theatrical spectacle. At length their performances excited the charity and compassion of some citizens of Paris, who erected a theatre in which they might exhibit their religious stories in a more commodious and advantageous manner, with the addition of scenery and other decorations. At length professed practitioners in the histrionic art were hired to perform these solemn mockeries of religion, which soon became the principal public amusement of the people.*

A similar idea of the origin of these theatrical exhibitions is entertained by a sensible writer in a popular periodical work, who remarks, "that representations approaching as near as possible to the facts were annually exhibited in the church of the Holy Sepulchre at Jerusalem. These were the actions of our Saviour's sufferings:" and adds an observation by M. Millin, that in France, "the pilgrims, after vespers, exhibited dramatic representations upon the pavement in the open space before the doors of churches." He then proceeds to state his own opinion of the origin of the Moralities, &c., by saying, "it appears likely, that, in the East, certain celebrations were instituted, in which the original action was imitated by way of making the greater impression on the minds of spectators: those among these spectators who had no better employment, when they got home endeavoured to effect imitations of what they had seen abroad. It may not be easy to convince such as have never seen the continent, of the interest taken by spectators at the sight of those shows carried about in boxes, representing the '*Ecce Homo*,' the crucifixion, &c., or of the attention (formerly) paid to a *Chanteur de Cantiques*, who sung his carols with such images before him. Those who can recollect such sights, will think it very credible that these are traditionary memorials of the once popular festivities; as the custom of sing-

* Warton, vol. ii, pp. 372, 373. Burney's History of Music, vol. ii, p. 325. Lond. 1776, 4to.

ing Christmas carols is almost the only remaining vestige of these *Cantiques;* to which our ancestors, in the days of darkness, were indebted for a feeble ray of knowledge."*

"On the whole," says Warton, "the Mysteries appear to have originated among the ecclesiastics; and were most probably first acted, at least with any degree of form, by the monks. This was certainly the case in the English monasteries. The only persons who could read were in the religious societies; and various other circumstances, peculiarly arising from their situation, profession, and institution, enabled the monks to be the sole performers of these representations."†

The first spectacle of the kind that was ever attempted in England, at least with which we are acquainted, was exhibited under the direction of Geoffrey, a learned Norman, who had been invited from the university of Paris to superintend the direction of the school of the priory of Dunstable; where he composed a play, called the Play of Saint Catharine, which was acted by his scholars, about A. D. 1110. Matthew Paris, who first records this anecdote, says, that Geoffrey borrowed copes from the sacrist of the neighbouring abbey of St. Albans, to dress his characters. He was afterward elected abbot of that opulent monastery.‡ In the same century, Peter of Blois, who had been invited into England by Henry II., employed by him as his private secretary, and made archdeacon of Bath, congratulates his brother William, who was an abbot, on the fame he had acquired by his *tragedy of Flaura and Marcus*, and by his other *theological* works: and W. Fitz Stephen, a monk of Canterbury, who wrote a "Description of London" in 1190, *Descript. Lond.*, p. 7, says, "London, for theatrical spectacles, hath religious plays, which are representations of the miracles which holy confessors had wrought, and of the sufferings by which martyrs had displayed their constancy."§

In the north of Europe these dramatic exhibitions were encouraged by Albrecht, bishop of Livonia, who, after having dragooned the Livonians into a profession of Christianity, built the town of Riga, in 1201; and afterward instituted the performance of Scripture plays, as the means of instructing the people of his charge in the knowledge of Biblical history. "Of the methods employed in teaching" (by Albrecht) "history mentions only one.

* Literary Panorama, vol. vii, pp. 714, 715.

† Warton, *ubi sup.*

‡ Warton, vol. i, dissert. 2, and sec. 6, p. 236.

§ Henry's Hist. of Great Britain, vol. vi, b. iii, ch. vii, p. 375.

At Riga, in 1205, was acted a *prophetic play*, that is, a dramatized extract from the history of the Old and New Testaments. The design was by this means to allure the heathen to the adoption of Christianity, partly by attaching the converts to their new religion by sensible gratification; and partly to instruct them in the history of it. The Livonians, baptized and unbaptized, resorted to it in multitudes, and they were informed of the contents by an interpreter. The piece was probably in Latin. The number of performers must have been very great, (perhaps it consisted of the whole order, together with the chapter,) as battles and wars were represented; for instance, from the history of Gideon, David, and Herod. The first exhibition, however, was like to have been attended by very serious consequences. When the Israelites, under Gideon's command, were fighting at close quarters with the Midianites, the heathens took it into their heads that the armed troops were brought in under this pretence, in order to fall upon them. They, therefore, sought their safety in flight. Their mistake, however, being explained to them, they were persuaded to return, and the play was brought to a happy conclusion."*

The institution of the Fraternity *del Gonfalone*, in ITALY, in the year 1264, proves the frequency of these Scripture plays among the Italians at that period. In the statutes of that company, printed at Rome, in 1584, p. 74, we find the following notice of their constitution:—"The principal design of our fraternity being to represent the Passion of Jesus Christ, we ordain, that in case the mysteries of the said passion are represented, our ancient orders shall be observed, together with what shall be prescribed by the general congregation." It is probable, that it was about the same time also, that the Passion of our Lord began to be represented at the Coliseum at Rome, where it continued to be exhibited till the sixteenth century, when it was abolished by the pope. In the year 1298, on the feast of Pentecost, and the two following holydays, the representation of the Play of Christ, that is, of his passion, resurrection, ascension, judgment, and the mission of the Holy Ghost, was performed by the clergy of *Civita Vecchia;* and again in 1304, the chapter of Civita Vecchia exhibited a play of the creation of our first parents, the annunciation of the Virgin Mary, the birth of Christ, and other passages of sacred Scripture. In a feast made upon the Arno in 1304, a machine, representing hell, was fixed upon the boats, and a piece acted, toward the end of

* Tooke's View of the Russian Empire, vol. i, b. ii, sec. 2, pp. 390, 391

which the rich man in hell was seen begging relief, in vain, of the poor Lazarus in Abraham's bosom.*

In FRANCE, the first notice I have met with of these theatrical exhibitions is in 1313, when Philip the Fair gave a magnificent feast at Paris. He invited the king of England to it; and among other diversions, the people are said to have "represented divers shows, sometimes the joys of the blessed in heaven, and sometimes the punishments of the damned." In 1398 the mysteries of the passion were first represented, on a theatre at St. Maur, but were prohibited by the provost of Paris, by an order, whereby he forbade "all the inhabitants, &c., to act or represent any play by persons, either the lives of the saints or otherwise, without leave of the king." The actors in these representations formed a part of the royal household; and in order to make themselves more agreeable to the public, erected their society into a fraternity, by the name of "The Actors of our Saviour's Passion." Charles VI. went to see these shows, and was so well pleased with them that he granted the actors letters patent, dated the fourth of December, 1402. They also built the Theatre of the Hospital of the Holy Trinity, on which, during the space of almost one hundred and fifty years, they acted the Mysteries, or other pieces of a similar nature, under the common title of Moralities. Francis I., by his letters patent, dated in the month of January, 1518, confirmed all the privileges of this fraternity.†

These religious farces were also held in high estimation in the Greek Church, as well as in the Latin. Bertrandon de la Brocquiere, counsellor and first esquire-carver to Philip the Good, duke of Burgundy, who visited Palestine in 1432, tells us, that when he was at Constantinople, being desirous of witnessing the manner of the Greeks performing divine service, he went to the church of St. Sophia, on a day when the patriarch officiated. "The emperor was present, accompanied by his wife, his mother, and brother, the despot of Morea.‡ A *mystery* was represented, the subject of which was, the three youths whom Nebuchadnezzar had ordered to be thrown into the fiery furnace."§

* Riccoboni's Historical and Critical Account of the Theatres in Europe, pp. 40, 42, 43, 45, 50. Warton, vol. i, pp. 249, 250.

† Riccoboni, pp. 114, 122, 123. Warton, vol. i, p. 246.

‡ "This emperor was John Palæologus II.,—his brother Demetrius, despot or prince of the Peloponnesus,—his mother Irene, daughter to Constantine Dragases, sovereign of a small country in Macedonia,—his wife Maria Comnenis, daughter to Alexis, emperor of Trebisonde."

§ Travels of Bertrandon de la Brocquiere, translated by Thomas Johnes, Esq., p. 223, 8vo., 1807.

The composers of the Mysteries did not think the plain and probable events of the Holy Scriptures sufficiently marvellous for an audience who wanted only to be surprised. They frequently selected their materials from books which had more the air of romance, particularly the legends and pseudo Gospels. They also introduced into them the most ludicrous and licentious conversations and actions. In a mystery of the Massacre of the Holy Innocents, part of the subject of a sacred drama given by the English fathers at the famous council of Constance, in the year 1417, a low buffoon of Herod's court is introduced, desiring of his lord to be dubbed a knight, that he might be properly qualified to go on the adventure of killing the mothers of the children of Bethlehem. This tragical business is treated with the most ridiculous levity. The good women of Bethlehem attack our knight-errant with their spinning-wheels, break his head with their distaffs, abuse him as a coward and a disgrace to chivalry, and send him home to Herod, as a recreant champion, with much ignominy.* In the year 1327, a play of the Old and New Testaments was exhibited at Chester, at the expense of the different trading companies of that city. The following is the substance and order of the former part of the play:—God enters, creating the world; he breathes life into Adam, leads him into Paradise, and opens his side while sleeping. Adam and Eve appear naked, and *not ashamed;* and the old serpent enters, lamenting his fall. He converses with Eve. She eats of the forbidden fruit, and gives part to Adam. They propose, according to the stage direction, to make themselves *subligacula a foliis,* &c.; cover themselves with leaves, and converse with God. God's curse. The serpent *exit* hissing. They are driven from Paradise by four angels, and the cherubim with a flaming sword. Adam appears digging the ground, and Eve spinning.† In the part of the same play which refers to the entrance of Noah and his family into the ark, an altercation takes place between him and his wife, which occupies almost the whole of what is called the third *pageaunt.* The following extract is from Lyson's *Magna Britannia,* in which it is copied from the Harleian MSS. in the British Museum:—

"NOE AND HIS SHIPPE."

"Then Noe shall goe into the arke with all his familye his wife except, the arke must be borded rounde aboute and upon the bordes all the beastes and fowles hereafter rehearsed must be painted that there wordes may agree with the pictures."

---

* Warton, vol. i, p. 242. † Idem, vol. i, pp. 243, 244.

NOE.

"Wiffe come in, why standes thou there?
Thou arte ever frowarde I dare well sweare."

NOE'S WIFFE.

"Yea sir, set up your sayle
And row forth with evill haile,
For withouten faile I wille not out
Out of this towne;
But I have my gossippes every eich one,
One foote further I will not gone;
The shall not drowne by St. John,
And I may save there life;
But thou wylt let them into that cheist,
Else row forth Noe where thou list,
And get thee a new wife."

THE GOOD GOSSIPPES.

"The flood comes flitting in full fast,
One every syde that spreadeth full farr;
For feare of drowning I ame agaste,
Good gossippes let us draw neer;
And let us drinke or we departe,
For oft-tymes we have done soe,
For at a draught thou drinkes a quarte,
And soe will I doe or I goe;
Here is a pottell full of Malmeseye gode and stronge
Yt will rejoice both hart and tonge;
Though Noe thinke us never so longe,
Yet we will drinke alike."

JAPHAT.

"Mother, we pray you all together,
For we are here your owne children;
Come into the shippe for feare of the weather."

NOE'S WIFFE.

"That will I not for all your call,
But I have my gossippes all."

SEM.

"In fayth mother yet thou shalt
Whether thou wylt or not."

NOE.

"Welcome wife into this boat."

WIFE.

"Have thou that for thy note."
(et dat alapam.)*

NOE.

"Ha! ha! marye; that is hott,
It is good for to be still;

* "She gives him a box on the ear."

A ! children methinkes my boat remeves,
Our tarrying here highly me greeves ;
Over the lande the water spreades,
God doe as he will."*

The *Guare-mir*, or Miracle-Plays of Cornwall, were interludes, the subjects of which were taken from Scripture, and performed in the Cornish tongue, in places called *Rounds*, which were a kind of amphitheatre, with benches, either of stone or turf. Dr. Borlase, in his "Natural History of Cornwall," has given the plan of a very large and regular "Round," formed with the exactness of a fortification, in the parish of Piran-sand, called Piran Round. In the Bodleian library there are two MSS. which contain some of these interludes, or, as the author calls them, *Ordinalia*. The first, on parchment, written in the fifteenth century, exhibits three *Ordinalia;* the first treats of the creation of the world, the second of the passion of our Lord Jesus Christ, the third of the resurrection. The other MS. is on paper, written by William Jordan, in the year 1611. This has only one Ordinale, of the creation of the world and the deluge. The first Ordinale of the creation begins thus, (God the Father speaking :)

(CORNISH.)

"En Tas a Nef ym Gylmyr
Formyer pub tra a vydh gwrys
Onan ha tryon yn gwyr
En Tas, han Mab, han Spyrys.
Ha hethyn me a thesyr
Dre ou grath dalleth an Bys
Y lavaraf, nef, ha Tyr
Formyys orthe ou brys."

ENGLISHED.

"The Father of Heaven, I the Maker,
Former of every thing that shall be made,
One, and Three, truly,
The Father, the Son, and the Spirit.
Yes—this day it is my will
Of my especial favour to begin the world ;
I have said it—Heaven and Earth
Be ye formed by my counsel."

But the poetry is the least exceptionable part of these interludes. A person called the Ordinary was the chief manager ; every thing was done as he prescribed, and spoken as he prompted. The persons of these dramas are numerous ; in the first Ordinale of the creation, no fewer than fifty-six ; in the second, sixty-two ; and

* Lyson's Magna Britannia, vol. ii, pt. ii, p. 595. London, 1810, 4to.

in the third, sixty. Princes, patriarchs, saints, angels, (good and bad,) and even the persons of the ever blessed Trinity, are introduced. Unity of time, action, and place is not at all attended to; the first-mentioned play runs through a space of time from the creation to King Solomon's building the temple, and incongruously ordaining a bishop to keep it. It takes in also the fabulous legend of Maximilla, in which part the actors are, a bishop, a crosier-bearer, a messenger, four tormentors, the martyr, Gebal, and Amalek. The bishop gives to the tormentors, for putting the martyr to death, Behethlan, Bosaneth, and all Chenary, three places in Cornwall. King Solomon speaks the epilogue. The audience, with a strict charge to appear early on the morrow, in order to see the "Passion" acted, is dismissed in these words:—

(CORNISH.)

"Abarath an Tas
Menstroles a' ras
Pebourgh whare
Hag ens pub dre."

ENGLISHED.

"In the name of the Father,
Ye Minstrels holy,
Tune your pipes,
And let every one go to his home."*

This may serve to give a general notion of these interludes, which were all translated into English by Mr. John Keigwyn, of Mousehoule, at the desire of Sir Jonathan Trelawny, Bart., bishop of Winchester, in a literal manner, for the better understanding the language.

Carew, in his "Survey of Cornwall," says, "for representing it," (that is, the Guary Miracle,) "they raise an earthen amphitheatre in some open field, having the diameter of an enclosed plane, some forty to fifty feet. The country people flock from all sides, many miles off, to see and hear it. For they have therein devils and devices to delight, as well the eye as the ear."†

But whatever was the source of these exhibitions, or whatever were the inconsistencies in the delineations of characters, it is certain that our ancestors thought they contributed to the information and instruction of the people on the most important subjects of religion; so that while we lament the blindness of their guides, we must acknowledge, that where no just idea of decorum pre-

* Borlase's Natural Hist. of Cornwall, pp. 295–298. Oxford, 1758, folio.

† Johnson and Steevens' Shakspeare, vol. vii, p. 174. Dissert. Warburton. Lond., 1785, 8vo.

vailed, there would be but little sense of the ridiculous, and that what appears to us to be the highest burlesque, would on them make no sort of impression. That this opinion was formerly entertained of these plays, perhaps no stronger proof can be adduced than what is afforded by a proclamation issued at Chester, in 1533, for the Whitsun Plays, by William Newall, clerk of the Pentice, during the mayoralty of William Snead:—

"FORASMUCH as of ould tyme not only for the augmentation and increase of the holy catholic faith of our Saviour Jesus Christ, and to exhort the minds of common people to good devotion, and holsome doctrine thereof, but also for the comonwelth and prosperity of this city, a play and declaration of divers storyes of the Bible, beginning with the creation and fall of Lucifer, and endinge with the general judgment of the world, to be declared and played in the Whitson weeke, was devised and made by one Sir Henry Francis,* sometyme monke of this monasterye disolved, who obtayned and gat of Clement, the bushop of Rome, a thousand dayes of pardon, and of the bushop of Chester, at that tyme, forty dayes of pardon, graunted from thenceforth to every person resorting in peaceable manner, with good devotion, to hear and see the sayd playes, from tyme to tyme, as oft as they shall be played within the sayd cittie, (and that every person or persons disturbing the said playes in any manerwise, to be accursed by the authority of the sayd Pope Clement's bulls, untill such tyme as he or they bee absolved thereof;) which playes were devised to the honour of God, by John Arnway, then maior of this citty of Chester, (about A. D. 1328,) his brethren and whole cominalty thereof, to be brought forth, declared and played at the coste and charges of the craftsmen, and occupations of the said cittie; - - - - wherefore Mr. Maior, in the kings name streatly chargeth," &c.†

The clergy themselves were generally the performers in the Mysteries and Moralities. In the reign of Richard II. the clergy, and the scholars of St. Paul's school, presented a petition to him, praying his majesty "to prohibit a company of unexpert people from presenting the History of the Old Testament, to the great

* "A marginal note" to this proclamation, "in another hand, asserts that they were written by Randal Higden, to whom they are generally ascribed. It is probable that Sir Henry Francis only procured the pardons mentioned in the proclamation. It is said in a note prefixed to a copy of these (Whitsun) plays in the British Museum, Harl. MSS., No. 2124, that Higden was thrice at Rome, before he could obtain leave of the pope to have them represented in the English tongue."

† Lyson's Magna Britannia, vol. ii, pt. ii, p. 590.

prejudice of the said clergy, who have been at great charge and expense, in order to represent it publicly, at Christmas." Dr. Burney, referring to the Northumberland Household Book, pp. 343, 345, as his authority, states that about the year 1512, the nobility, in imitation of royalty, had, among other officers of their household, a *master of the revels*, "for the overseyinge and orderinge of *Playes*, and *Interludes*, and dressing, that is plaid in the twelve days of Crestenmas." Of these, the gentlemen and children of the chapel seem to have been the principal performers; for which, and for acting upon other great festivals, they were assigned particular rewards: "Item, my Lorde vseth to gyf yerely, when his lordeshipe is at home, in reward to them of his lordschip chappel that doith play upon shroftewsday, at night, Xs." And when they performed in the dramatic mysteries, such as "the play of the Nativity at Crestenmas, or of the Resurrection upon Esturday," they were allowed XXs.*

Other instances have already occurred, of the active part taken by the ecclesiastics in the representation of these religious dramas; to which may be added the relation of a performance of this nature recorded in the old *Chronique de Metz*, written by the rector of St. Euchaire. "The play of the Passion of our Lord," says the honest chronicler, "was performed the 3d of July, 1437, in the plain of Veximiel. The rector of St. Victoire, of Metz, personated our Lord, and would have died on the cross, had he not been relieved by another priest, who was affixed to the cross to complete the ceremony of the crucifixion for that time. The next day the same rector of St. Victoire personified the Resurrection, and accomplished his part excellently." Another priest, who was chaplain of Metrange, personated Judas, and through failure of the apparatus, was hung till he was nearly dead.† The great expense of exhibiting these plays occasioned the before-mentioned petition to Richard II. Warton informs us, that the chaplains of Abbeville, in the year 1455, gave four pounds ten shillings to the players of the *Passion;* and that in the year 1486, at Anjou, ten pounds were paid toward supporting the charges of acting the *Passion of Christ*, which was represented by masks, probably by persons hired for the purpose: he also adds from an ancient computus, that three shillings were paid by the ministers of a church, in the year 1537, for parchment, for writing *Ludus Resurrectionis Domini*.‡

These dramatic spectacles were at first exhibited in the open

* Riccoboni, p. 161. Burney's Hist. of Music, vol. ii, pp. 570, 571.

† Johnson's and Steevens' Shakspeare, *ubi sup.* ‡ Warton, vol. i, pp. 246, 247.

air; but it afterward became customary to perform them, on different festivals, in or about the churches. In several of our old Scriptural plays, we see some of the scenes directed to be represented *cum cantu et organis*, (a common rubric in the missal,) because they were performed in a church where the choir assisted. Fontenelle (*Hist. Theatr.*) says, that anciently among the French, comedies were acted after divine service, in the church-yard, *thus changing the mode of instruction. Au sortir du Sermon, ces bonnes gens alloient à la* Comedie, *c'est à dire, qu'ils changeoint le Sermon.* These, however, were Scriptural comedies, and they were constantly preceded by a *Benedicite*, by way of prologue. In Lambarde's Topographical Dictionary, written about the year 1570, there is a curious passage, which so completely exposes the burlesque and profane nature of these representations, especially in the times immediately preceding the reformation from popery, that I shall transcribe it for the information of the reader:—"In the dayes of ceremonial religion, they used at Wytney (in Oxfordshire) to set fourthe yearly in maner of a show, or interlude, the Resurrection of our Lord, &c. For the which purposes, and the more lyvely heareby to exhibite to the eye the hole action of the resurrection, the priestes garnished out certain smalle puppettes, representing the persons of Christe, the watchmen, Marie, and others; amongest the which, one bare the parte of a wakinge watchman, who espiinge Christe to arise, made a contiual noyce, like to the sound that is caused by the metynge of two styckes, and was thereof commonly called *Jack Snacker of Wytney.* The like toye I myself, beinge then a childe, once saw in Poule's church at London, at a feast of Whitsuntyde; wheare the comynge downe of the Holy Gost was set forthe by a white pigion, that was let to fly out of a hole that is yet to be sene in the mydst of the roofe of the great ile, and by a longe censer, which desendinge out of the same place almost to the verie grounde, was swinged up and downe at suche a lengthe, that it reached with thone swepe almost to the west gate of the churche, and with the other to the quyre staires of the same; breathinge out over the whole churche and companie a most pleasant perfume of such swete thinges as burned therein. With the like doome shewes also, they used everie where to furnish sondrye parts of their church service, as by their spectacles of the Nativitie, Passion, and Ascension."*

These plays were not only performed in the churches, they were sometimes acted also on the Sunday. In the year 1487,

* Warton, vol. ii, pp. 240, 241.

while Henry VII. kept his residence at the castle at Winchester, on occasion of the birth of Prince Arthur, he was entertained, on a Sunday, during the time of dinner, with a religious drama called *Christus Descensus ad Infernos*, or Christ's Descent into Hell. It was represented by the *Pueri Eleemosynarii*, or choir-boys, of Hyde abbey, and Saint Swithin's priory, two large monasteries at Winchester. An entertainment of a similar nature was furnished, in 1503, at the marriage of King James of Scotland, with the Princess Margaret of England, daughter of Henry VII. On the first Sunday of the magnificent festival, celebrated with high splendour at Edinburgh, "after dynnar, a MORALITE was played by master Inglyshe, and hys companyons, in the presence of the kyng and qwene." (Leland, Coll. iii, pp. 299, 300, appendix.) So late as the reign of Elizabeth, and even till that of Charles I., plays continued to be acted on Sundays by the choristers, or singing-boys of Saint Paul's cathedral, in London, and of the royal chapel.*

The enormity of these practices was long seen and lamented by different prelates, who attempted to prevent them. Innocent III., who sat in the papal chair at the commencement of the thirteenth century, prohibited all spectacles and plays being exhibited in the churches. In the chapter *Cum Decorem*, (lib. iii, *Decretal Tit.* 1, *de vita et honestate Clericorum*,) he says: "Shows and theatrical entertainments are sometimes exhibited in the churches, in which not only the most monstrous masks are introduced, but even the deacons, priests, and sub-deacons have the effrontery, on certain festivals, to practise those follies and buffooneries. We therefore enjoin you to exterminate from your churches the custom, or rather the disgrace and irregularity, of such spectacles and shameful entertainments, that their impurity may no longer pollute the honour of the church." The council of Basil, in 1435, acknowledges that in some churches, and on certain festivals, some persons clothed themselves in the pontifical robes, put on the mitre, held the crosier, and gave the benediction as bishops; others habited themselves like kings and dukes; stage-plays were exhibited; and men and women danced together, attracting a crowd of spectators, and producing the most dissolute mirth. The council, however, expressed its abhorrence of such disorders, and forbade the clergy, under pain of suspension from all their ecclesiastical revenues for three months, to permit such exhibitions in the churches or cemeteries.

* Warton, vol. ii, p. 206; vol. i, p. 241. Tilliot, Memoires pour servir a l'Histoire de la Fête des Foux, pp. 55, 56, 58, 59. Lausanne et Geneve, 1751, 12mo.

In the register of William of Wykeham, bishop of Winchester, under the year 1384, an episcopal injunction is recited against the exhibition of *Spectula*, or similar diversions, in the cemetery of his cathedral: *Canere Cantilenas, ludibriorum Spectacula facere, saltationes et alios ludos inhonestos frequentare, choreas*, &c. (Registr., lib. iii, fol. 88.) An interdiction of a similar nature is found among the statutes of the synod of the church of Liege, A. D. 1287; by which joculators or minstrels, actors and dancers, are forbidden performing in the church, cemetery, or portico:* "Joculatores, histriones, saltatrices, in ecclesia, cemetorio, vel porticu, nec aliquæ choreæ." (*Statut. Synod. Eccles. Leod.* apud Marten. *Thesaur. Anecd.*, tom. iv, p. 846.) So by the statutes of the church of Nantz, in 1405, joculators or minstrels are prohibited exhibiting in the church and cemetery: "Mimi vel joculatores, ad monstra larvarum in ecclesia et cemeterio." (*Statut. Eccles. Nannett. apud Marten. ut sup.*, p. 993.) In 1445, Charles VII. of France ordered the masters in theology at Paris to forbid the ministers of the collegiate churches to celebrate, at Christmas, the Feast of Fools in their churches, where the clergy danced in masks and antic dresses, and exhibited *plusieurs mocqueries spectacles publics, de leurs corps deguisements, farces, rigmeries*, with various enormities shocking to decency. In England, in the reign of Henry VIII., Bonner, bishop of London, issued a proclamation to the clergy of his diocess, dated A. D. 1542, prohibiting "all manner of common plays, games, or interludes, to be played, set forth, or declared within their churches, chapels, &c." For many other similar prohibitions, see Tilliot, *Memoires*, &c., *passim*. But so attached were the people to these representations, that they continued to be performed in *churches* even after the Reformation; for in a pamphlet published in 1580, entitled "The third Blast of Retrait from Plaies," &c., p. 77, the author says, the players are "permitted to publish their mamettrie in everie temple of God, and that throughout England." And in the year 1603 this abuse of acting plays in churches is mentioned in the canon of James I., which forbids also the profanation of churches by court-leets, &c.†

* The *porticus*, or *portico*, was not the same with what is usually called the *church-porch*, but either what is now commonly called the *side-aisle*, or a particular division of it, consisting of one arch with its recess, and was frequently distinguished by the name of some saint, as *Porticus Sti. Martini* in St. Augustine's church at Canterbury. See "Essays on Gothic Architecture," *Bentham's Essay*, pp. 28, 29. London, 1800, 8vo.

† Warton, vol. i, pp. 240, 241, 247.

1

They were, however, not only forbidden the churches, but royal and episcopal, and even papal authority were entirely, as we have seen, employed to suppress them. In France, the procureur general, in 1541, presented a request, in the name of the king, to the parliament, against the company established in the Hotel de Bourgogne, for the representation of the Mysteries. The three principal branches of his charge against them were, that the representation of the Old Testament stories inclined the people to Judaism; that the New Testament stories encouraged libertinism and infidelity; and that both of them lessened the charities to the poor. It seems that this prosecution succeeded; for in 1588 the parliament of Paris confirmed the company in the possession of the Hotel, but interdicted the representation of the Mysteries.* In Italy the representation of the Passion of our Saviour was abolished toward the end of the pontificate of Paul the Third, about A. D. 1546 or 1549.† In England, as the Reformation gained ground, and the Bible was permitted to be publicly read, Mysteries and Moralities gradually yielded to the purer and more rational instruction of the Scriptures themselves, as rendered accessible to the people by vernacular translations. The inconsistent Henry VIII., in the same law by which he forbade Tyndale's English Bible, decreed that the kingdom should be purged and cleansed of all religious plays, interludes, rhymes, ballads, and songs, which are equally pestiferous and noysome to the peace of the church.‡

The accession of Mary to the English throne revived the expectations of the Roman Catholics, and the performance of Mysteries and Miracles became again the medium of papistical instruction, in preference to the Bible. In the year 1556, a *goodly stage-play* of the Passion of Christ was presented at the Gray Friars, in London, on Corpus Christi day,§ before the lord mayor, the privy council, and many great estates of the realm! Strype also mentions, under the year 1557, a stage-play at the Gray Friars, of the Passion of Christ, on the day that war was proclaimed in London against France, and in honour of that occasion. (*Eccl. Mem.*, vol. iii, ch. xlix.) On Saint Olave's day, in the same year, the holyday

* Johnson and Steevens' Shakspeare, vol. vii, p. 176.

† Riccoboni, p. 41.

‡ Stat., Ann. 34, 35. Henr. VIII., cap. i, cited in Warton, vol. iii, pp. 202, 203.

§ The annual festival of *Corpus Christi* was instituted about the year 1246. The design of it was to impress upon the minds of the people a belief of the reality of transubstantiation. Besides a superb procession through the streets on the day of the celebration, there was commonly a Mystery, or interlude, which sometimes lasted eight days.

of the church in Silver-street, which is dedicated to that saint, was kept with much solemnity. At eight of the clock at night began a stage-play of *goodly matter*, being the miraculous history of the life of that saint, which continued four hours, and was concluded with many religious songs.* John Bale, a tolerable Latin classic, and an eminent biographer, embraced the Reformation, and was advanced to the bishopric of Ossory, by King Edward VI. Prior to his conversion from popery he composed many Scriptural interludes, chiefly from incidents of the New Testament; among them are, the Life of Saint John the Baptist, written in 1538; Christ in his Twelfth Year; Baptism and Temptation; the Resurrection of Lazarus; the Council of the High Priests; Simon the Leper; Our Lord's Supper, and the Washing of the Feet of his Disciples; Christ's Burial and Resurrection; the Passion of Christ; the Comedy of the three Laws of Nature, Moses, and Christ, corrupted by the Sodomites, Pharisees, and Papists, printed by Nicholas Bamburgh, in 1538, and so popular that it was reprinted by Colwell, in 1562; God's Promises to Man, which he calls "a Tragedie, or interlude, manyfestynge the chyefe Promises of God unto man, in all ages, from the begynnynge of the worlde to the deathe of Jesus Christe, a Mysterie, 1538." Our author, in his "Vocacyon to the Bishoprick of Ossory," informs us, that his comedy of John the Baptist, and his tragedy of God's Promises, were acted by the youths upon a Sunday, at the market-cross of Kilkenny.†

In Scotland these dramatic performances continued to be occasionally exhibited, even after the Reformation; for in the records of the Weekly Assembly of Perth there is the following entry:—"July 1st, 1577. The Weekly Assembly regret that certain inhabitants of this town, against the express command of the civil magistrate, and the prohibition delivered by the minister from the pulpit, have played Corpus Christi play upon the sixth day of June last, which day was wont to be called Corpus Christi day; whereby they have offended the church of God, and dishonoured this haill (whole) town; the said play being idolatrous and superstitious." The Assembly ordained that the guilty persons should receive no benefit from the church till they had showed evidence of their repentance. A similar offence occurred soon afterward. On the tenth of December, in the same year, usually called "Sanctoberti's eve," a very great number of persons passed through the

* Warton, vol. iii, p. 326.

† Ibid., vol. iii, p. 78. Baker's Companion to the Play-House, vol. ii.

town in disguised dresses, with piping and dancing, and striking a drum. They carried in their hands burning torches. One of the actors was clad in the devil's coat; another rode upon a horse, which went in men's shoes. It is probable the horse and its rider represented a part of the legendary history of the saint, who seems to have been the patron saint made choice of by the bakers' incorporation, as the offenders were of that trade.* In Germany, the mystery of the Passion of our Lord was represented on the stage at Vienna in the early part of the last century, but prohibited afterward by the archbishop, on account of the indecencies and profaneness introduced by the actors in the representation.† Riccoboni also mentions one of the Electoral cities, though without giving the name of it, in which, speaking of his own time, he says, "They commonly erect a theatre in the cathedral church on one of the days of the holy week, representing the garden of olives, where Christ, after returning from prayer, found his disciples asleep. All this is done by living persons: and he that represents Christ goes three times, and awakes the apostles, and as often returns to prayer. In a word," he adds, "we may there see a complete image of what happened in the garden of olives."‡ The same author assures us, that on certain festivals, in Flanders, they had chariots carrying stages through the streets, on which subjects were represented in dumb show, taken from the Old or New Testament, or allegorical objects of piety. At Genoa, in 1690, he saw several mysteries exhibited on the theatres erected at the corners of the streets on Corpus Christi day; and at Naples, at the Feast of the Holy Sacrament, they exhibited similar subjects. The Spanish *Autos Sacramentales* were sacred dramas, acted at certain seasons of the year, but especially at Christmas; consisting chiefly of allegorical personages, and are still continued, or were, till lately, in different parts of Spain. Even so late as the year 1738, we find the canons of the cathedral of Besancon, in France, celebrating a mummery in the cloisters and church on Easter-day, called *Bergeretta*, or the Song of the Shepherds:§ and in South America the Romish Church continues its theatrical exhibitions to the present time. Mr. Henry Koster, who visited Brazil in 1809, thus describes the service of Good Friday at Recife: "The church was much crowded, and the difficulty of getting in was considerable. An enormous curtain hung from the ceiling, excluding from

* Scott's History of the Reformers in Scotland, pp. 186, 187.

† Riccoboni, p. 211. ‡ Ibid., p. 117.

§ Ibid., pp. 115, 116, 95. Warton, vol. ii, p. 368.

the sight the whole of the principal chapel. An Italian missionary friar of the Penha convent, with a long beard, and dressed in a thick, dark brown cloth habit, was in the pulpit, and about to commence an extempore sermon. After an exordium of some length, adapted to the day, he cried out, 'Behold him!' the curtain immediately dropped, and discovered an enormous cross with a full-sized wooden image of our Saviour, exceedingly well carved and painted, and around it a number of angels represented by several young persons, all finely decked out, and each bearing a large pair of out-stretched wings, made of gauze; a man, dressed in a bob wig and a pea-green robe, as St. John; and a female kneeling at the foot of the cross, as the Magdalen, whose character, as I was informed, seemingly that nothing might be wanting, was not the most pure. The friar continued, with much vehemence and much action, his narrative of the crucifixion, and after some minutes again cried out, 'Behold, they take him down;' when four men, habited in imitation of Roman soldiers, stepped forward. The countenances of these persons were in part concealed by black crape. Two of them ascended ladders placed on each side against the cross, and one took down the board, bearing the letters I. N. R. I. Then was removed the crown of thorns, and a white cloth was put over, and pressed down upon the head; which was soon taken off, and shown to the people, stained with the circular mark of the crown in blood: this done, the nails which transfix the hands were by degrees knocked out, and this produced a violent beating of breasts among the female part of the congregation. A long white linen bandage was next passed under each arm-pit of the image; the nail which secured the feet was removed; the figure was let down very gently, and was carefully wrapped up in a white sheet. All this was done by word of command from the preacher. The sermon was then quickly brought to a conclusion, and we left the church."* (Travels in Brazil, pp. 18, 19.) In fine, wherever the Bible is withheld from the people, the most degrading superstitions extend their baneful influence over the minds, not only of the uncultivated, but too generally over those also who have enjoyed superior opportunities of mental cultivation. The circulation of the Bible produces the triumph of reason and of truth; and where the divine word is known, and studied, and followed, its

* After this detail, we do not wonder to hear that, although almanacks, and the Lives of the Saints, and certain books of devotion, are sold at the Benedictine convent, the Bible and Testament are not among them; and that at Pernambuco there is neither printing-press nor bookseller.

benign influence will accelerate the mental and moral improvement of all ranks of society.

From the details of ignorance, superstition, and profanity, into which we have been led by a desire to expose the insufficiency of those modes of instruction which have been substituted for the Scriptures, and for which we can only be excused by their intimate connection with the history of Biblical literature, we resume with pleasure our former subject, and proceed to present the reader with some proofs that, amid all the disadvantages of the twelfth century, there were various learned men who pursued their Biblical studies with good success.

In the British Museum, among the Harleian MSS., No. 5786, is a Polyglott Psalter, written in Greek, Latin, and Arabic. The date of it is 1153, but, from being faded, is read with difficulty.* The learned Joseph Scaliger possessed a copy of the four Gospels, in Arabic, written in the year of the world 6687, that is, A.D. 1179.† An Arabic Psalter is also preserved in the library of St. Lawrence, executed about the close of the twelfth century by Theodulus Aben Alfathl, a Melchite deacon of Antioch. It is a translation from the Greek version of the LXX. There is another Arabic Psalter in the Vatican library, translated from the Greek by a deacon named Abdallah *fil.* Alphadli, whom Le Long supposes to be the same with the preceding Theodulus. This latter copy is upon paper, in quarto.‡ At this period general science was diligently pursued among the Arabians. Among the African or Moorish Moslems we find Essachalli, a native of Sicily, celebrated for his geographical writings; and Ebn Albaithar, renowned for medical and botanical knowledge. In Spain were Avenzoar and Thophail; the first deemed the rational improver of Arabian medicine, the second the author of some admired works, and the faithful follower of Aristotle; both of them famed as the masters of the great Averroes, born at Corduba, and viewed by his contemporaries as a prodigy of science. In Asia flourished Gazzali, a man of uncommon acquirements as a philosopher, a Mohammedan theologian, a jurist, and a poet.§ Many of the learned productions of the Mohammedan Arabians were translated into Latin by the Christians; the high esteem in which the erudition of that people was held, together with a desire of converting the Spanish Sara-

* Classical Journal, No. xvi, December, 1813, p. 453.

† Le Long, Biblioth. Sacra, tom. i, ch. ii, p. 120. Paris, 1723.

‡ Ibid., p. 118, et Index Auctor., p. 584.

§ Berrington's Literary History of the Middle Ages, App. ii, pp. 671-680.

cens to Christianity, having excited many to study their language, and to acquire a considerable knowledge of their doctrine. Gerhard of Cremona, who was famous among the Italians for his eminent skill in astronomy and physic, undertook a voyage to Toledo, and translated several Arabian treatises. Mirimet, a French monk, travelled into Spain and Africa to learn geography among the Saracens. Daniel Morlach, an Englishman, who was extremely fond of mathematical learning, went to Toledo, and brought from thence a considerable number of Arabian books. Peter, abbot of Clugni, surnamed the Venerable, after having resided some time among the Spaniards, in order to make himself master of the Arabic language, translated into Latin the Alcoran and the Life of Mohammed. On his arrival in Spain, he found persons of learning from England, and other places, who were applying themselves with extraordinary assiduity and ardour to the study of astrology; a science which, however futile in its nature, has, at different periods, been enthusiastically pursued by men of considerable learning and talent in almost every nation.* Unhappily, the subtleties of the Stagyrite, and the conjectures of astrology, were preferred to the plain and impressive truths of the Scriptures, and, except in the instances we have adduced, and the Biblical labours of the Spanish Jews, but little evidence is afforded of the study of the Bible in this age by the scholars of Arabia, or the lovers of Arabian erudition.

The most eminent of those Jews who flourished in this century, in Spain, were Aben Ezra, Maimonides, David Kimchi, and Solomon Jarchi.

R. Aben Ezra was born about A. D. 1099. He was very greatly esteemed for his various learning and acquirements. His skill in different languages, and especially in the Arabic, appears in his commentaries, particularly in his criticisms on several parts of the book of Job. As an astronomer, his discoveries were sanctioned by the ablest mathematicians; and as a physician, his medical knowledge was extensive. But his greatest celebrity has arisen from his commentaries on all the books of the Old Testament. Instead of following the usual method of his predecessors, he endeavoured to exhibit the grammatical and literal sense of the sacred Scriptures; a plan by which he has secured the esteem of both Jews and Gentiles. These commentaries have been printed in the great Hebrew Bibles of Bomberg, and Buxtorf.

* Mosheim's Ecclesiastical History, vol. iii, pp. 40, 41.

Impelled by a thirst of learning, he spent a considerable part of his life in visiting those countries that were renowned for science and art. After passing through England, France, Italy, Greece, and other countries, he expired in the Isle of Rhodes, in his seventy-fifth year, about A. D. 1174.*

R. MOSES BEN MAIMON, better known by his abbreviated name MAIMONIDES, was born at Cordovea in Spain, A. D. 1131. His father, who sustained the office of judge, was highly respected both by Jews and Christians, for his knowledge of jurisprudence, and the ability and integrity with which he executed the difficult duties of the magistracy. The education of Moses was at first superintended by his father; and afterward intrusted to the most learned rabbins of his country. Possessing a mind vigorous, penetrating, and acute, he not only made rapid progress in rabbinical literature, but excelled also in mathematical, metaphysical, and medical sciences. To a knowledge of the Hebrew and Arabic, he added an acquaintance with the Chaldee, and Turkish, and Greek languages, besides other more modern dialects spoken in the countries in which he resided.

At the age of twenty-three he commenced his commentaries on the Mishna, which he completed seven years afterward in Egypt. Dr. Pocock, in his *Porta Mosis*, or Mishnical Dissertations of Maimonides, has given the history of this work, which was written in Arabic, and then translated into Hebrew, and from that version was published in Latin, by Surenhusius.

The violent persecutions to which the Jews were exposed in Spain, drove him from his native country into Egypt, where he resided during the remainder of his life. For want of other employment, he was reduced to the necessity of trading as a jeweller; but, embracing the opportunity of commencing a school, he soon became famous for his learning and talents; and his instructions were attended by numerous and respectable pupils. At length his merit introduced him to the notice of the sultan, who appointed him his physician, and allowed him a pension. In an epistle to his friend R. Samuel Aben Tybbon, he thus describes the daily occupations of his important situation:—"I generally visit the sultan every morning; and when either he, or his children, or wives are attacked with any disorder, I am detained in attendance the whole of the day; or when any of the nobility are sick, I am ordered to visit them. But, if nothing prevent, I repair to my own habitation

* Relandi Analecta Rabbinica, in Vit. Celeb. Rabbin., pp. 69–80. Basnage's Hist. of the Jews, b. vii, ch. viii, pp. 625, 626, fol.

at noon, where I no sooner arrive, exhausted and faint with hunger, than I find myself surrounded with a crowd of Jews and Gentiles, nobles and peasants, judges and tax-gatherers, friends and enemies, eagerly expecting the time of my return. Alighting from my horse, I wash my hands according to custom, and then courteously and respectfully saluting my guests, entreat them to wait with patience while I take some refreshment. Dinner concluded, I hasten to inquire into their various complaints, and to prescribe for them the necessary medicines. Such is the business of every day. Frequently, indeed, it happens, that some are obliged to wait till evening, and I continue for many hours, and even to a late hour of the night, incessantly engaged in listening, talking, ordering, and prescribing, till I am so overpowered with fatigue and sleep, that I can scarcely utter a word."*

During his residence in Egypt he wrote his *Yad Chazachah* or the Strong Hand, and *Moreh Nebochim* or Instructer of the Perplexed. The — יד חוזה, or Strong Hand, is an excellent digest or abridgment of all the laws and ordinances of the Talmud. It was printed at Soncini, in Italy, in 1490, folio, and has been several times republished, particularly at Venice, in 1550, and at Amsterdam in 1702, four volumes, folio. It is divided into fourteen titles or sections: a list of these, with the names of those learned men who have translated any of them into Latin, is given by Dr. Wotton in his "Miscellaneous Discourses relating to the Traditions and Usages of the Scribes and Pharisees, in our blessed Saviour Jesus Christ's time," volume ii, pp. 273-278.

The מורה נבוכים, or Instructer of the Perplexed, is a critical, philosophical, and theological work, in which the author endeavours to explain the difficult passages, phrases, parables, allegories, and ceremonies of the Old Testament. It is rendered particularly valuable by an excellent exposition of the grounds and reasons of the Mosaic Laws. An eminent Biblical critic has characterized it as "a very curious and important work, and one of the most rational that ever proceeded from the pen of a rabbin."† It was written in Arabic, and translated into Hebrew with his approbation, by his friend and disciple R. Samuel Aben Tybbon. In 1520 Justinian, bishop of Nebio, published a Latin version of this work in folio, printed at Paris by Badius Ascensius. The younger Buxtorf undertook a new translation of the Hebrew into Latin,

* Buxtorf, Moreh Nevochim, in *Præfat.* Basil, 1621, fol.

† Dr. Adam Clarke. See Bibliog. Dict., vol. ii, p. 87.

which was printed at Basil by J. J. Genath, 1629, 4to., and to which the translator prefixed a preface, including a biographical account of the author. The Hebrew, with a triple rabbinical commentary, was printed in 1553 at Venice, and at Jaznitz 1742. Other editions have also been printed of this celebrated work besides those now mentioned, but which it is needless to enumerate. About the close of the seventeenth century Dr. Thomas Hyde issued proposals for an Arabic edition, to be accompanied with notes and a new Latin version, a specimen of which, being all that was ever printed, was published by Dr. Gregory Sharpe, in the *Syntagma Dissertationum quas olim auctor doctissimus Thomas Hyde, S. T. P. separatim edidit*, vol. alter. pp. 433-448. Oxon., 1767, 4to.

Our great author, Maimonides, died in Egypt at the age of seventy, and was buried in the land of Israel. Such was the esteem in which he was universally held, that there was a general mourning for three whole days by the Egyptians as well as Jews, and the year in which he died was called *Lamentum Lamentabile*. "The memory of Maimonides," says Dr. Clavering, "still flourishes, and will for ever flourish."*

R. David Kimchi was a native of Narbonne, annexed at that period to the crown of Castile. Disputes having arisen among the Jews respecting the *Moreh Nebochim* of Maimonides, our rabbi became the zealous defender of that celebrated writer, and one of the chief instruments in terminating them in his favour, in 1232, after having been continued for forty years. These disputes being happily brought to a conclusion, he devoted his time and talents to the composition of various theological and grammatical works, which have obtained considerable celebrity. His commentary on the principal books of the Old Testament, and in particular on the prophet Isaiah, is still held in high estimation, and said to be excellent and useful. His grammatical works have afforded very great assistance to later Hebrew grammarians; and the learned *Sanctus Pagninus*, who wrote at the commencement of the fifteenth century, borrowed the most part of his Hebrew Lexicon and Grammar from the writings of Kimchi. Our rabbi had also a brother eminent for his literary accomplishments, whose name was Moses; he was the author of a work entitled "The Garden of Pleasure," in which he treated of the nature of

* Clavering, Mosis Maimonidis Tract. Duo. in *Dissert. de Maimonide*. Oxon. 1705, 4to. See also Basnage's Hist. of the Jews, b. vii, ch. viii. Lond. 1708, fol.

souls. It was never printed, but is preserved in MS. in the Vatican library, at Rome.*

Another eminent Jew, who flourished in the twelfth century, was R. Solomon Jarchi, or Isaaki, whose name is frequently abbreviated into *Rashi*, as that of R. David Kimchi is into *Radak*. He was by birth a Frenchman, being born at Troyes, in the province of Champagne, in 1105. At the age of thirty he travelled abroad, and not only visited Italy and Greece, but penetrated to Egypt, Palestine, Persia, Tartary, Moscovy, and other countries; and returned through Germany to his native city after an absence of more than five years. He wrote a commentary on the whole of the Old Testament, but it is said to be "so completely obscure in many places as to require a very large comment to make it intelligible."† During his travels he made collections of the decisions of the wise men in different Jewish academies, respecting the difficulties to be met with in the *Talmud*, to the study of which he had particularly dedicated himself. After his return he was accustomed to visit different Jewish universities and academies, and after disputing with the professors upon various questions, to throw down secretly the decisions upon them extracted from his collections, but without the name of the author. From these papers a gloss upon the Talmud was formed, which bears his name. He also composed a commentary on the Gemara, which has been considered so valuable as to render him deserving of the title of the prince of commentators. He died A. D. 1180, in the seventy-fifth year of his age, at Troyes, from whence his body was conveyed to Bohemia, and buried in the city of Prague.‡

* Relandi Analecta Rabbinica, *Vit. Celeb. Rab.*, pp. 81–102. Basnage's Hist. of the Jews, b. vii, ch. viii, pp. 620, 630.

† Dr. A. Clarke's Commentary, *Gen. Pref.*, p. 2.

‡ Relandi Analect. Rab., *Vit. Cel. Rab.*, pp. 59–69. Basnage, *ut sup.*

CHAPTER XI.

THIRTEENTH CENTURY.

Council of Toulouse—De Voragine—Italian and French Versions—German and Icelandic Versions—Grosseteste—Roger Bacon—Libraries—Scarcity of Bibles—Stationarii—MSS. of Scriptures—Expulsion of Jews—Biblical Pursuits—Division of the Sacred Text into Chapters—Stephen Langton—Hugo de S. Caro—Academical and Monastic Literature—Jews—Louis IX.

THE century on which we are now entering is chiefly famed for the growing celebrity of the Aristotelian philosophy; a philosophy which furnished the polemical disputant with weapons to wage an endless warfare with his opponents, and served to confound rather than to enlighten and convince the controversial combatants. We must not, therefore, expect to meet with many Biblical students, or to find the Scriptures in general circulation. On the contrary, the prevalent disposition of the Roman hierarchy being ambition, measures were taken to prevent the laity from the indiscriminate perusal of the word of God, and traditions, legends, and decrees were substituted in its stead.

The infamous council of Toulouse, held in the year 1229, by Romanus, cardinal of St. Angelo, and the pope's legate, formed the *first courts of Inquisition*, and published the *first canon which forbade the Scriptures to the laity*. Innocent III. about the commencement of this century had commissioned certain Cistercian monks to denounce heretics to the civil magistrate to be corporally punished; and Dominic, the celebrated Spaniard, founder of the order of Dominicans, or Preaching Friars, had afterward received a similar commission; but it was in the council of Toulouse that the Inquisition received its designation by the decree, for the erection in every city of a *council of inquisitors*, consisting of one priest and three laymen.* In 1233 Gregory IX. nominated two Dominican friars in Languedoc the first inquisitors, an office gone rally intrusted to that order by succeeding pontiffs.

The canon prohibiting the Scriptures is couched in the following terms:—

Prohibemus etiam, ne libros Veteris Testamenti aut Laici permittantur habere: nisi forte Psalterium, vel breviarium pro

* Mosheim's Eccles. Hist., vol. iii, p. 269. Butler's Lives, vol. viii, Aug. 1 Basnage, Hist. de l'Eglise, tom. ii, liv. 24, ch. ix, p. 1429. Amsterdam, 1629, fol.

*divinis officis, aut Horas Beatæ Mariæ, aliquis ex devotione habere velit. Sed ne præmissos libros habeant in vulgari translatos, arctissime inhibemus.**

"We also forbid the laity to possess any of the books of the Old or New Testaments, except perhaps some one out of devotion wishes to have the Psalter or Breviary for the divine offices, or the Hours of the Blessed Virgin. But we strictly forbid them having any of these books translated into the vulgar tongue."

A policy similar to this of the Church of Rome is still pursued by the idolatrous worshippers of Brahma, in Hindostan, as it was in past ages by the priests of Egypt, the idolaters of Rome, and many of the ancient heretical sects among the Christians; for none but the Brahmins or sacred tribe may read the *Vedas* or holy books; and none but the Khatries or military men may hear them read, while to the other two more populous castes or tribes, the Bhyse and the Sudra, or merchants and husbandmen, the *Sastras* only, or commentaries upon the Vedas, are accessible. This interdiction is also extended to the *Ramayana*, a sacred poem, which is so highly venerated that the Sudras are not permitted to read it. At the end of the first section of it is a promise of benefits to those who duly read or hear it; "a Brahmin reading it acquires learning and eloquence, a Kshettria will become a monarch, a Vaysia will obtain vast commercial profits, and a Sudra *hearing* it will become great."†

The nefarious attempt of the council of Toulouse was happily, however, only partial in its influence; vernacular translations were in some instances made into different languages, and individuals among the laity continued to read such portions of the Scriptures as the rarity of copies, or the poverty of their circumstances, permitted them to possess. Sixtus Senensis, in his *Bibliotheca Sancta*, says that James de Voragine, archbishop of Genoa, and author of a history of that republic, translated the Old and New Testaments into the Italian, with diligence and fidelity. And Father Simon speaks of this translation of Voragine, as the oldest in the Italian tongue, and remarks that the Jesuit Possevin objects to it as being inaccurate, but that by others it has been highly esteemed; the editor of his "Sermons" also states him to have been the *first* who translated the whole Bible into the Italian language. Le Long is,

* Labbei Sacro-Sancta Concilia, tom. ii, pt. i, p. 430.

† Moor's Hindu Pantheon, p. 189. Lond. 1810, 4to. Wrangham's Sermon on the Translation of the Scriptures into the Oriental Languages, p. 37, *note*. Camb. 1807. Usserii, Hist. Dogmat., cap. ix.

however, inclined to question the existence of such a version, and offers as his reasons, the silence of Antoninus, Trithemius, Castillus, and Voragine himself in his History of Genoa; and the information of Muratori, who had consulted the celebrated Magliabechi, that no copy of the Scriptures with the name of Voragine in the title was to be met with in the libraries of Rome or Florence, Modena or Milan: but as we do not think that the silence of the authors mentioned by Le Long is sufficient to oppose to the positive evidence of such Biblical critics as Sixtus Senensis and Simon; and as we can easily suppose that the author of a history of the Genoese republic might have been the translator of the Bible, without introducing the notice of it in his historical work; and since it is well known that many of the ancient translators of the Scriptures never affixed their names to their translations, we hesitate to blot De Voragine out of the list of translators of the Bible. It must nevertheless be acknowledged that F. Simon, in another of his works, conjectures that the archbishop only published an Italian translation of Comestor's *Historia Scholastica*, which was then very much esteemed, and read more frequently than the text of the Bible.*

James de Voragine, or Voraigne, was a native of Voragine, a town on the sea coast, not far from Genoa. He was celebrated for various and extensive reading, for eloquence in declamation, and elegance in writing, especially in his native tongue. Studious in the works of the fathers, he is said to have committed to memory nearly the whole of the writings of Augustine. As a writer of history, he attained at least to mediocrity; and as a Biblical scholar, secured the praise of succeeding critics. Agreeably to the practice of the age in which he lived, he employed a portion of his leisure hours in the compilation of his famous Golden Legend, or Lives of the Saints, in which he unfortunately studied entertainment at the expense of credibility, and, "in imitation of Livy, often made the martyrs speak his own language." He was a friar of the order of St. Dominic, and archbishop of Genoa. He died in 1298.

Besides the works already mentioned, he was the author of Latin Sermons for all the Sundays and Festivals in the year, and of one hundred and sixty sermons in Latin, entitled *Mariale*, on the titles

* Sixt. Senens. Biblioth. Sanct., lib. iv. Simon, Histoire Critique du V. T. *Bibles en Langue Vulgaire*, p. 595, 4to. Le Long, Biblioth. Sacra, tom. i, cap. iv, art. 2, p. 353. Paris, 1723. Simon's Critical Hist. of Versions of N. T., pt. ii, ch. xl, p. 335.

and virtues of the Blessed Virgin, alphabetically arranged; all edited by Rudolph Clutius, B. D., a Dominican; and printed by Pet. Cholin, at Mentz, 1616, 4to. He wrote also in defence of the Dominican order; and published a book *De Opusculis D. Augustini.**

A French version of the Bible is ascribed to Guiars des Moulins, canon of St. Peter's of Aire, who flourished in this century, but, as we have already seen, (p. 310,) it is probable that is was merely a translation of Comestor's *Historia Scholastica.*

The *Albigenses*, who inhabited some parts of Spain, were probably the authors of certain Spanish versions, interdicted by James I. king of Arragon, who died in 1276; and who, by a law which he passed, ordered, that "no one should possess the books of the Old or New Testaments in the Romance, or vulgar tongue; and that whoever possessed any of them, and did not bring them to the bishop of the place, in order to be *burned*, should be considered as suspected of heresy, whether they were of the clergy or laity."† Toward the close of this century, however, Alphonsus the Wise, king of Castile, acted with more pious liberality, by procuring a translation of the Bible into the Castilian dialect, and rendering it accessible to the most illiterate. This was about A. D. 1280.‡

In the Imperial library, at Vienna, there is a quarto MS. on parchment, containing fragments of the Old and New Testaments, in the old German tongue, chiefly in verse, and written as early as A. D. 1210. Goldastus, in his *Rerum Alimannicarum Scriptorum*, notices a most elegant Paraphrase of the Old Testament, in German verse, written at the request of the emperor Conrad IV. by Rodolph ab Ems, about A. D. 1260.§

The following extract from Petrus Undalensis, preserved by Arngrim, in his *Specimen Islandiæ Historicum*, affords reason to believe that an Icelandic version of the Scriptures existed in the thirteenth century, among a people who cultivated literature and science, at a period when many other parts of Europe were sunk in lethargy, and buried in monkish ignorance:—

"En Welburdig Norsk Mand, Erick Brockenhuss, som heden vved Anno 1567. haffde Mandals leen i Befalinngh sagde vvdi Sandhed, att haffne seet, den gandske Bibel vvdsett paa Islendske

* Sixt. Senens. Biblioth. Sanct., lib. iv. Le Long, *ut sup.* Jacobi de Voragine Sermones Aurei. Mogunt. 1616, 4to.

† Du Cange, Glossar., v. *Romancium.* Calmet, Dict. de la Bible, *Bibles Espagnoles.*

‡ Le Long, Biblioth. Sacra, p. 361.

§ Le Long, Biblioth. Sacra, p. 377. Usserii Hist. Dogmat., p. 152.

maal, skreffnen for 300. Aar seden, och, den forste Bogstaff i hver Capittel vvaar forgylltt, &c."

By which we learn, that Eric Brockenhusius, governor of Mandale, in Norway, asserted, that in the year 1567 he saw a copy of the Bible in the Icelandic tongue, which had been translated three hundred years previous to that date ; and that the initial letters of the chapters were embellished with gold. The probability of an attempt having been made about that time to communicate some knowledge of the Scriptures, in the vernacular idiom, is corroborated by the Rev. Dr. Ebenezer Henderson, in the Report of his visit to that island in 1814, for the purpose of carrying into effect the plans of the British and Foreign Bible Society. "Wherever I came," says he, "the people received me with open arms, and complained sadly of the dearth of the Scriptures. In the parish of Kalfafell, which contains seventy souls, I found only one Bible, besides that belonging to the church: and, what is remarkable, in the parish of Thyckvabæ Abbey, where, *about the middle of the thirteenth century, the first attempt was made to translate the Scriptures into the vernacular language*, not a single copy was found to exist at the present day !" In his subsequent, and very interesting publication, entitled "Iceland, or a Journal of a Residence in that Island," he has favoured the public with an historical view of Icelandic translations, in which he remarks, that the book which Brockenhusius saw, was, most probably, "a copy of the famous work entitled 'STIORN,' which was composed about the middle of the thirteenth century, by Brandr Jonson, at that time abbot of Thyckvabæ monastery, in the eastern quarter of Iceland, and afterward bishop of Holum." This work, which was written in 1255, by order of King Magnus Haconson, who rendered himself famous by reducing the different books of Norwegian law to one grand code, contains a view of the sacred history from the creation to the captivity of the Jewish kings. In many places, a literal version is given of the Vulgate text; in others, the sacred history is paraphrased, and interspersed with legendary tales and fanciful interpretations; and in some, nothing more is exhibited than a brief compendium of the contents of the Scripture accounts. The interpretations of the text are mostly taken from the *Historia Scholastica* of Peter Comestor; though considerable use is made of the *Speculum Historiale*, and the writings of the fathers. Dr. Henderson adds, "From the few documents that have been handed down to us, relative to the state of sacred literature in Iceland, during the reign of superstition, it would appear that copies even of the Vulgate were by no means common; and the learned bishop Jonson supposes, (*Hist. Eccles. Island.*, tom. ii, p. 183,) even that in many instances in which mention is made of the Holy Book (*helga boc*) being used in the administration of oaths, nothing more is meant than an image or representation of the Gospels cut in wood, and painted or cast in a mould; relics of which were still found in his time in the cathedral of Skalhollt. The Psalms of David in Latin, however, were more frequently to be met with; and such as were distinguishingly strict in their devotions, made conscience of repeating a third part of the Psalter daily. The only attempt that was made to communicate the knowledge of the divine oracles to others, seems to have been owing to the zeal of Thorlak Runolfson, who lived in the twelfth century, and of whom it is said in the Hungurvaka, that 'he read lectures on the sacred Scriptures;' but whether these lectures were public, and in the vernacular language, or merely delivered to such as were designed for the priesthood, cannot now be ascertained."*

In the Netherlands, the Waldenses turned the Scriptures into Low Dutch rhymes, according to the custom of those ages, and in imitation of those of the old Teutons, or Germans, who used to record their most memorable affairs in verse. Their reasons for this we shall give in their own words: "Dat daer in was groote nutschap; no boerte, no fabulen, no truffe, no falserde; mer were woerden. Dat hier endaer wel was een herde coerste, mer dat het pit ende die soethit van goet en selicheit der in wel was te bekinnen." "That there was great advantage in it, [the Bible,] no jests, no fables, no trifles, no deceits, but the words of truth. That indeed there was here and there a hard crust. But the marrow and sweetness of what was good and holy might be easily discovered in it."†

It has been questioned, and apparently with justice, whether any translation of the *whole* Bible into English took place during this century; for although Dr. Thomas James, in his treatise "Of the Corruption of the Scripture," supposes that three of the MS. Bibles preserved in the different libraries of Oxford are of this age; they are, with more probability, referred by other critics to a later date. Partial translations of the Bible, indeed, were made about this time, "but they were translations of only *some parts* of

* Henderson's Iceland, vol. ii, Append. I, pp. 252–261. Edin. 1818, 8vo. Arngrim, Specimen Islandiæ Historicum, pt. ii, Memb. 2, p. 128. Amstel. 1643, 4to. Twelfth Report of Brit. and For. Bible Society, p. 204.

† Brandt's Hist. of the Reformation, vol. i, b. i, p. 14. Lond. 1720, fol.

the old Testament, as the Psalter, the Church Lessons and Hymns, and of the New Testament, or rather of *some of the books* of it, and seem not to have been published, but made only for the translator's own use."* It deserves, however, to be noticed, that the learned Dr. A. Clarke, in the General Preface to his Commentary, gives several extracts from a *glossed* translation in his possession, which he says was "written, probably, before the time of Wicliff:" and that Sir William Thoresby, who was archbishop of York in the fourteenth century, caused a treatise to be drawn up in English, by a clergyman, of the name of Garryk, "in the whiche were conteyned the artycles of belefe, the vii. dedly sines, the vii. workes of marcy, the x. commaundements, and sent them in small pagyantes to the common people, to lerne it;" and in this treatise remarks, that, "a man of London, whose name was Myringe, had a Byble in Englyshe of Northern speche whiche was sene of many men, and it seemed to be C. yeres old."†

But although it is not ascertained whether any complete translation of the whole Bible was made or not, it is certain that there were some few eminent men who flourished at this period in England, and were strenuous advocates for the spread of Scriptural knowledge. Bishop Grosseteste, and Roger Bacon, in particular, merited the gratitude of the age in which they lived, by their opposition to papal corruptions, and their promotion of Biblical and scientific acquirements.

Robert Grosseteste, or Grosthead, seems to have been a person of obscure parentage, and born about the year 1175, at Stradbrook, in Suffolk. After having studied at Oxford, where he laid the foundation of his knowledge of the Greek and Hebrew tongues, and of the Aristotelian philosophy, he went to Paris, and there perfected his acquaintance with the sacred tongues, and became a perfect master of the French. Here also he acquired those stores of various learning, which not only rendered him one of the first theologians and philosophers of the age, but subjected him to the calumny of some of his ignorant contemporaries, who accused him of necromancy or magic.

In 1221, the Dominicans, who, from the colour of their upper garment, were called *Black Friars*, landed in this country; and within three years were followed by the Franciscans, or *Gray*

* Lewis's Hist. of English Translations, p. 17. Lond. 1739, 8vo. James's Treatise of the Corruption of Scripture, &c., pt. ii, p. 74. Lond. 1611, 4to. Baber's Historical Account of Saxon and English Versions, p. lxviii.

† Dibdin's Typographical Antiquities, vol. iii, pp. 257, 258.

Friars. The university of Oxford was their favourite station, where they soon opened their schools, and Grosseteste, from his partiality to the Franciscans, was induced to become their first lecturer. A curious anecdote is related of him and the superior of the order: "The superior, who was himself void of learning, but who gloried in the talents of his professor, was anxious to ascertain, if possible, what progress the scholars had made, and he accordingly entered the school one day as they were rehearsing their questions; when he found to his astonishment, that the subject before them was, Whether there be a God? 'Alas! Alas!' exclaimed the good man, 'ignorant simplicity is daily gaining heaven; while these learned disputants are arguing about the existence of heaven's Master.' After this he is said to have become solicitous to turn their minds to more substantial studies."*

The exalted virtues and reputation of our divine procured him the see of Lincoln, to which he was called in 1235. After his election, he religiously devoted himself to the duties of his office, and adopted vigorous measures for the reformation of abuses, and for the instruction of the priests and people of his diocess, who were lamentably deficient in the first rudiments of Christian knowledge. He went through the several archdeaconries and deaneries, called the clergy and people together, preached to the clergy, and caused some friar of the Dominican, or Franciscan order, to deliver lectures to the people, heard their confessions, and confirmed the children. He enforced the duties of the clerical vocation by authoritative injunctions, by personal advice, and by a treatise written expressly "On the Pastoral Care." One of his constitutions enjoins, "That the priests shall teach their parishioners the Decalogue," another commands "the rectors of churches, and parish priests, diligently to instruct the youth of their respective parishes, so that they may be able to say the Lord's Prayer, the Creed, and the Salutation of the Blessed Virgin;" and adds, "Because it is reported that many adults are ignorant of these things, we enjoin, that when the laity come to confession, they be examined, whether they know them or not; and if needful, that they be taught them by the priests." In his "Treatise on the Pastoral Care," he exhorts the priest diligently to preach the word of God, which is "the food of the soul;" and then proceeds, "If any one say, he knows not how, the proper remedy is for him to resign his benefice; nevertheless, I can tell him of a better remedy: let every such person or priest thoroughly learn, every week, the text alone (that is, without

* Berington's Literary Hist. of the Middle Ages, b. v, p. 364.

gloss or comment) of the Gospel lesson appointed for the following Sunday, that he may be, at least, able to repeat the history itself to the people. And this, I say, that if he understand Latin, and will pursue this practice regularly every week, he will, most assuredly, profit by it greatly. But, if he be ignorant of Latin, let him go to some one near him, who will cheerfully explain it to him, and by this means enable him also to teach his flock. Thus in one year he may repeat the Epistles for the Festivals; and in another the 'Lives of the Saints.'"* To the regents in theology, in the university of Oxford, he wrote a pathetic letter, earnestly entreating them to lay the foundation of theological learning in the study of the Scriptures; and to devote the morning hours to lectures on the Old and New Testaments. It appears also by the following passage, quoted from his writings by the author of an early English translation of the Bible, that he was a decided friend to vernacular translations of the Scriptures: "Deus voluit, ut plures interpretes S. Scripturam transferrent, et diversæ Translationes in ecclesiâ essent; idcirco ut quod unus obscuriùs dixerat, alter manifestiùs redderet."† "It is the will of God that the Holy Scriptures should be translated by many translators, and that there should be different translations in the church, so that what is obscurely expressed by one, may be more perspicuously translated by another."

He abolished the Feast of Asses, which used to be annually celebrated in Lincoln cathedral, on the Feast of the Circumcision: miracle plays; and the *Maii Inductio*, or ceremonies practised on the first of May.‡ He also forbade the archdeacons of his diocess to permit *Scot-Ales*§ in their chapters and synods, and other *Ludi*, or games and pastimes on holydays. (*Gratii Fascicul*, tom. ii, Ep. 22, 107, pp. 314, 382, 411, 412.)

* "The Legends, or Lives of the Saints were, formerly, constantly read in churches."

† Whartoni Auctarium Hist. Dogmat., cap. ii, pp. 416–418. Henry's Hist. of Great Britain, vol. viii, b. iv, ch. iv, p. 181. Gratii Fascic., tom. ii, Ep. 123, pp. 392, 410

‡ It was an ancient custom for the priest and people of country villages, to go in procession to some adjoining wood, on a May-day morning, and return in a kind of triumph, with a May-pole, boughs, flowers, garlands, and other tokens of the spring. This May-game, or rejoicing at the coming of spring, and termed *Maii Inductio*, was long observed, and traces of it still continue in some parts of England. It was derived from the heathen Feast of Flora, the goddess of fruits and flowers, celebrated with all manner of obscenity and lewdness, on the four last days of April, and the first of May. —*Brand's Observations on Popular Antiquities*, ch. xxv, p. 283, &c. Lond. 1810, 8vo. *Tiliot, Memoires pour servir a l'histoire de la Fete des Foux*, pp. 26–32. Lausanne et Geneve, 1751, 12mo.

§ *Scot-Ales*. The nature of these compotations will be best understood by the two

He was a universal scholar, and no less conversant in polite letters than in the most abstruse sciences. The Greek language he cultivated and patronized beyond most of his contemporaries. He translated Dionysius the Areopagite, and Damascenus, into Latin. He was also the author of the first Latin translation of the Greek Lexicon of Suidas, at that time almost a recent compi lation. He promoted John of Basingstoke to the archdeaconry of Leicester, chiefly because he was a Greek scholar, and possessed many Greek MSS., which he is said to have brought from Athens to England; and he entertained as a domestic in his palace Nicholas, chaplain of the abbot of St. Alban's, surnamed Græcus, from his uncommon proficiency in Greek. With the assistance of Nicholas he translated from the Greek into Latin "The Testaments of the Twelve Patriarchs," which had been discovered at Athens by Archdeacon Basingstoke, and was said to have been translated out of Hebrew into Greek by Chrysostom. This work, from the low state of criticism at that period, was regarded as an invaluable treasure, and the translator was supposed to have enriched Europe with the knowledge of a valuable monument of sacred antiquity. Modern critics have exposed its defects, and placed it in the list of spurious writings, except the eccentric Whiston, who attempted to defend it,* and published an

following constitutions; the first by Edmund Rich, archbishop of Canterbury, A. D. 1236; the latter by Simon Langham, archbishop of Canterbury, A. D. 1367. See Johnson's *Collection of Ecclesiastical Laws*, vol. ii, *sub. ann.*

"6. We wholly forbid clergymen the ill practice, by which all that drink together are obliged to equal draughts, and he carries away the credit who hath made most drunk, and taken off the largest cups: therefore we forbid all forcing to drink: let him that is culpable be suspended from office and benefice, according to the statutes of the council," (of Lateran, 1216, ch. xv,) "unless, upon admonition from his superior, he make competent satisfaction. We forbid the publication of *Scot-Ales* to be made by priests. If any priest or clerk do this, or be present at *Scot-Ales*, let him be canonically punished."

"2.—When a multitude of men, exceeding ten in number, stay long together in the same house for drinking sake, we declare these to be common *drinking bouts*. But we mean not to comprehend travellers and strangers, and such as meet (though in taverns) at fairs and markets, under this prohibition. Detesting those common drinking bouts, which, by a change of name, they call *Charity Scot-Ales*, we charge that the authors of such drinking bouts, and they who publicly meet at them, be publicly solemnly denounced excommunicate, till they have made competent satisfaction for it, and have merited the benefit of absolution." See also Du Cange, *Glossar. v.* "Scotallum."

* Warton's Hist. of English Poetry, vol. i, dis. 2. Whiston's Collection of Authentic Records, vol. i, pt. i, pp. 294–443. Lond. 1727, 8vo.

English translation of it in his Collection of Authentic Records belonging to the Old and New Testament.

Several of the bishop's popular works are in French, particularly his metrical compositions, which display a fondness for the metre and music of the French minstrels. His *Manuel de Peche*, or "Manual of Sin," is a long work, and treats of the Decalogue and the seven deadly sins, which are illustrated with many legendary stories. It was translated into English in 1303 by Robert Manning, or De Brunne, with a design to be sung to the harp at public entertainments. His *Chateau d'Amour*, or "Castle of Love," is a religious allegory, in which the fundamental articles of Christian belief are represented under the ideas of chivalry. "It has the air of a system of divinity written by a Troubadour."* The poem commences with the following lines, the sentiments of which are excellent, though the language is antiquated :—

"Ki pense ben, ben peut dire ;
Sanz penser ne poet suffise :
De nul bon oure commencer
Deu nos dont de li penser
De ki, par ki, en ki, sont
Tos les biens ki font en el mond."

They are thus paraphrased in a translation made, probably, in the reign of Edward I. :—

"That good thinketh, good may do,
And God wol help him thar to :
Ffor nas never good work wrougt
With oute biginninge of good thougt.
Ne never was wrougt non vuel† thyng
That vuel thougt nas the biginnyng.
God ffader, and sone and holigoste
That alle thing on eorthe sixt‡ and wost,
That one God art and thrillihod,§
And threo persones in one hod,||
Withouton end and biginninge,
To whom we ougten over alle thinge

* The *Troubadours* were French minstrels or poets, who chiefly flourished in Provence, during the twelfth and thirteenth centuries.

† Well, good. ‡ Highest. This is the explanation of the term as given by Warton ; but there is probably an error in the first letter, and that the word ought to be *fixt*, settled, placed, as the following word *wost* is evidently from the old verb *weet*, to know.

§ Trinity. || Unity.

Worschepe him with trewe love,
That kineworthe king art us above,
In whom, of whom, thorw whom beoth,
Alle the good schipes that we hire i seoth
He leve us thenche and worchen so,
That he us schylde from vre fo."*

He also began a comment on the Psalter, though he did not live to finish it. A list of his principal works is given in Cave's *Historia Litteraria*, sæc. xiii, pp. 716, 717. Lond. 1688.

Grosseteste was the resolute opposer of the extortionary system of the Roman court, which was at no time more severely felt; and the disgust he entertained at the conduct of the pope, who attempted to introduce his Italian minions into the most opulent benefices, was discovered in the contempt with which he treated the orders of the pontiff. Often he would indignantly cast the papal bulls out of his hands, and absolutely refuse to comply with them, saying, that he should be the friend of Satan if he should commit the care of souls to foreigners. He even refused to appoint the nephew of Innocent himself to a canonry in the cathedral of Lincoln, which so exasperated the pontiff, that he violently exclaimed, "Who is this old dotard who dares to judge my actions? By Peter and Paul, if I were not restrained by my generosity, I would make him an example and a spectacle to all mankind. Is not the king of England my vassal and my slave? And if I gave the word would he not throw him into prison, and load him with infamy and disgrace?" The cardinals, however, endeavoured to appease his resentment by representations of his own danger, and the great reputation of the bishop. But the fury of Innocent was not to be allayed, and he pronounced the sentence of excommunication against Grosseteste, and appointed Albert, one of his nuncios, to the bishopric of Lincoln. The high character of the bishop rendered the thunder of the Vatican harmless, the pope's commands were universally neglected, and the bishop continued in the quiet possession of his dignity.†

This excellent dignitary of the church died at Buckden, in Huntingdonshire, October 9, 1253.

Roger Bacon, the friend and contemporary of Grosseteste, was born at Ilchester, in Somersetshire, in the year 1214. After finishing the elementary studies of grammar and logic at Oxford,

* Warton's Hist. of English Poetry, vol. i, pp. 79, 80.

† Milner's Hist. of the Church of Christ, vol. iv, pp. 48, 51, 52. Fox's Actes and Monuments, vol. i, pp. 405–410. Lond. 1570, fol.

he visited Paris, to attend upon the lectures of the celebrated professors of that university. Here he sedulously applied himself to the knowledge of languages, history, jurisprudence, the mathematics, and medicine, completing the whole by the study of theology. The information which he could not obtain from living preceptors, he dug with indefatigable industry out of the mines of Grecian and Arabian learning. About the year 1240, having been admitted to the degree of Doctor, he returned to England, and assumed the Franciscan habit, and, in the retirement of his cell, prosecuted his studies with increasing ardour. Being chosen to deliver lectures to the university of Oxford, he expended immense sums in books, and other means of perfecting his knowledge and discoveries. "In twenty years," says he, "during which I have been particularly engaged in the study of wisdom, neglecting all vulgar attentions to money, I have expended more than *two thousand pounds* in books of secrets, in a variety of experiments, and in languages, and instruments, and tables, and other means of obtaining the friendship of the wise, and of instructing the minds of my hearers."* An almost incredible sum, when the income of a curate was but five marks, or £3 6*s*. 8*d*.; and the salary of a judge but £40!† and consequently equal in efficacy to £30,000 of our money at present. We are, indeed, at a loss which to applaud most, his generous friends and patrons, who enabled him to spend so large a sum; or the disinterestedness of the lecturer himself, who lost sight of his own emolument in the desire for the improvement of others. Seldom, however, has money been better employed; for in the course of his experiments, he is said to have made a greater number of useful and surprising discoveries in geometry, astronomy, physics, optics, mechanics, and chemistry, than ever were made by one man, in an equal space of time. Among the discoveries of this luminary of his age, are enumerated,—the discovery of the exact length of the solar year, and a method of correcting all the errors in the calendar; of the art of making reading-glasses, the camera obscura, microscopes, telescopes, and various other mathematical and astronomical instruments; of the composition of gunpowder, and the nature of phosphorus; the method of making elixirs, tinctures, solutions, and of performing many other chemical operations; of the art of combining and employing the mechanical powers in the construction of machines capable of producing the

* Leland. Coll. iii, 333, cited in Whitaker's Cathedral of Cornwall, vol. ii, ch. vii, sec. iii, p. 335.

† Chronicon Preciosum, pp. 131, 155, 156. Lond. 1707, 8vo.

most extraordinary effects; and of various remedies in the science of medicine.*

But however astonishing his attainments were as a natural philosopher, it is chiefly as a divine and a promoter of Biblical knowledge that he at present claims our regard; and it will with pleasure be discovered, that ardent as were his scientific pursuits, they not only did not prevent his study of the Scriptures, but were hallowed by their application to the sacred purposes of religion. In a treatise addressed to Pope Clement, he shows the necessity of understanding the Greek, and the Oriental languages, in order to ascertain the true sense and reading of the Scriptures, which he says were become miserably corrupted, chiefly through the profound ignorance of transcribers and pseudo-critics, who frequently corrupted them by attempting injudiciously to correct them. He also enters into a learned discussion of the translations made use of in the Greek and Roman churches, and particularly examines the translations of Jerome; and remarks, that the one generally adopted by the Latins was one of those which were executed by Jerome, and that it had obtained universal sanction and use on account of its accuracy and perspicuity: "Cujus editione generaliter omnes ecclesiæ utuntur, pro eo quod veracior sit in sententiis, et clarior in verbis." He further inveighs against the practice of theological lecturers, who preferred the philosophy of the schoolmen, or followers of Aristotle, to the plain truths of Scripture; and read lectures on the Sentences† in preference to the Bible, as one of the causes of general indifference to Biblical literature.‡

In another work, addressed to the same pontiff, and designed to obtain the papal sanction to his endeavours for a more general acquaintance with the original languages of the sacred volume, he undertakes to prove that the rudiments of all kinds of knowledge are to be found in the Scriptures; and that all the sciences may be rendered subservient to their illustration and explanation; that all the evils then existing under Christian governments arose from ignorance of the Scriptures; and in particular from the example and conduct of princes and prelates. "Causa namque quare

* Henry's History of Great Britain, vol. viii, b. iv, ch. iv, sec. 2, pp. 217–220. Enfield's Hist. of Philosophy, vol. ii, b. vii, ch. iii, pp. 376–378.

† Peter Lombard, a French divine of the twelfth century, wrote a theological system, which he entitled *Magister Sententiarum*, "The Master of Sentences," in which he illustrated the doctrines of the church by sentences collected from the fathers, with select questions for disputation; a work which obtained universal authority in the theological schools, and upon which innumerable commentaries were written.

‡ Hody, De Bibliorum Text. Orig., lib. iii, pt. ii, ch. xi, pp. 419–428.

fideles non convértuntur ad fidem, est quia principes et prelati eorum tenent eos in errore, et sic est in omni statu. Scilicet, infinitus est defectus in eis qui præsunt nunc temporis studio et vitâ : et ideo est quod subjecta multitudo errat in infinitis," (c. xxviii, *De Laude Sacræ Scripturæ.*) He maintains the necessity of an acquaintance with the Hebrew and Greek, in order accurately to understand the sacred writings, observing that the best translators, and even Jerome himself, have sometimes erred ; and that, during the preceding twenty years, the major part of Biblical MSS. had been depraved by scribes and sciolists, every one correcting according to his pleasure, and altering what he did not understand, a practice not allowed even in common writings : "quod quilibet corrigat pro suâ voluntate, et quilibet mutat quod non intelligit; quod non licet facere in libris poetarum." On this subject of acquiring a knowledge of Hebrew and Greek he carries his ideas so far as to suppose that Christians in general ought to learn them ; and especially as they are so easy of attainment. For he affirms that, by the universal grammar which he has invented, a person may learn the Hebrew, Greek, Latin, and Arabic in a few days. "I am certain," says he, "that in less than three days* I could teach any person of a diligent habit and retentive memory, who would be conformable to certain rules, to read Hebrew, and understand whatever wise and holy men have formerly said in explanation of the sacred text, or whatever relates to its correction and explanation ; and in three days more to understand the Greek, so as not only to be able to read and understand what relates to theology, but whatever has been written concerning philosophy, and the Latin tongue." To the objection, that even if these languages were generally attained, common Christians would nevertheless mistake the sense of Scripture, he replies, that the fear is groundless ; but, to prevent all danger, he intends to accompany his work with a manual, or introduction. He proceeds earnestly to entreat Clement not to withhold his sanction from a measure so pregnant with numerous and great benefits as the general knowledge of the original languages of holy writ, but to promote it by every mild and persuasive method ; and concludes by predicting the advantages that will result from the adoption of his plans. The principal of these are, that the "Divine Office," or prayers of the church, will be then understood by all Christians ; that the "Divine

* It is probable that our learned author has adopted a definite term for an indefinite one, expressive of a very short time ; still we cannot but regret that we are not in possession of his mode of instruction.

Law" being more generally known, it will not be so easily corrupted; that Christians, being instructed in the sacred oracles, will be better prepared to resist with firmness the future dangers of antichrist; and that the law of faith and the rule of life will be drawn from a pure and unpolluted source; to which may be added the conversion of infidels and schismatics, and the condemnation of those who cannot be converted. Every way, therefore, the languages are useful; every way, the knowledge of the Scriptures is necessary.*

The extraordinary abilities of our learned friar gained him the appellation of the *Wonderful Doctor*, while in their stupid admiration they ascribed his inventions to the black art. His knowledge of the Greek and Hebrew languages was regarded as the medium of intercourse with infernal spirits; and the suspicion was confirmed by the circles and triangles of his mathematical productions. The brethren of his order refused to admit his works into their libraries, and the general of the order confined him to his cell, and prohibited him from sending any of his writings out of his monastery, except to the pope. He languished in confinement for several years, till Clement IV., to whom he had sent a copy of his *Opus Majus*, in 1266, obtained some mitigation of his sufferings, if not his entire liberty. But, on pretence of some suspicious novelties in his works, he was again imprisoned by Jerome d'Ascoli, in 1278. This second imprisonment continued for about eleven or twelve years, when Jerome, who had occasioned his condemnation, being raised to the pontifical chair, by the name of Nicholas IV., was prevailed upon, by several noblemen, to release him from his confinement. Though now old and infirm, his love of science was unabated, and he continued to prosecute his studies, by polishing his former works and composing new ones, till death terminated his sufferings and labours about A. D. 1292.†

In an age when incarceration and contempt were the recompense of laborious research and extensive learning, it would be absurd to expect any thing but ignorance and the most puerile pursuits. The following method of attempting to cure the epilepsy, recommended by the most famous physicians of those times, correctly delineates the manners of the age, and fully proves the deplorable state of science in general. "Because there are many children and others afflicted with the epilepsy, who cannot take medicines," says John

* Whartoni Auctarium Hist. Dogmat. J. Usserii, pp. 420–424. See also Baconi Opus Majus, a Jebb. London, 1733, fol. et *in Præfat.*

† Henry's Hist. of Great Britain, vol. viii, b. iv, ch. iv, p. 218.

de Gaddesden, in his "Medical Rose," "let the following experiment be tried, which is recommended by Constantine, Walter, Bernard, Gilbert, and others, which I have found to be effectual, whether the patient was a demoniac, a lunatic, or an epileptic. When the patient and his parents have fasted three days, let them conduct him to a church. If he be of a proper age, and in his right senses, let him confess. Then let him hear mass on Friday, during the fast of *quatuor temporum*," (viz., March, June, September, or December,) "and also on Saturday. On Sunday let a good and religious priest read over the head of the patient, in the church, the Gospel which is read in September, in the time of vintage, after the feast of the holy cross. After this let the priest write the same Gospel devoutly; and let the patient wear it about his neck, and he shall be cured. The Gospel is,—This kind goeth not out but by prayer and fasting."*

The private libraries of many abbots afford another proof of the depressed and neglected state of sacred literature. Symon Gunton, in his "History of the Church of Peterburgh,"† has, with considerable labour, collected biographical notices of many of the abbots, and presented the reader with lists of the books belonging to them. The following are selected from them:—

ROBERTUS DE LINDESEY was monk and sacristan of Burgh, and paved his way to the abbacy by his liberality toward the church; "for whereas the windows were before only stuffed with *straw* to keep out the weather, he beautified above thirty of them with glasses; and his example brought the rest by degrees to the like perfection." Having been abbot seven years, he died October 25th, 1222. "He was not very rich in books; his library consisted only of these few:—

"Numerale Magistri, W. de Montibus, cum aliis rebus. Tropi Magistri Petri cum diversis summis. Sententiæ Petri Pretanensis. *Psalterium Glossatum.* Aurora.‡ *Psalterium non Glossatum.* Historiale."§

ALEXANDER DE HOLDERNESS. He was first a monk, then prior, and lastly abbot. Having been abbot four years he died, November 20th, 1226. "These were his books:—

"*Psalterium. Concordantiæ utriusq*; TEST. Claustrum Animæ. Opus alterum quod perfecit Rogerus de Helpston. Aurora. Pœnitentiale. Tria Breviaria. Concilium Lateranensi cum aliis rebus. Corrogationes Promet hei. Missale.‖"

---

* Henry's Hist. of Great Britain, b. iv, ch. iv, pp. 208, 209.

† Commonly written "Peterborough."

‡ The History of the Bible allegorized in Latin verse by Peter de Riga.

§ Gunton's Hist. of the Church of Peterburgh, pp. 27, 29. London, 1686, folio.

‖ Gunton, p. 29.

MARTINUS DE RAMSEY was a monk of Peterborough, and elected abbot after the death of Alexander. He died after being abbot six years. "His library was but thin:—

"Missale. Item Missale ad Altare S. Katharinæ. Capitula collecta Evangelica in 2 voluminibus ad magnum Altare."*†

WALTERUS DE S. EDMUNDO was first monk, then sacristan, and at length abbot, in 1233. "His library was copious in comparison of his predecessors, consisting of these books:—

"Decretale. Aurora. Claustrum Animæ. BIBLIA. Hexæmeron S. Cantuariæ versificé. Rabanus de Naturis Rerum, et Interpretationes Hebraicorum nominum in uno volumine. Versus M. W. de Montibus. *Psalterium gloss.* Summa Magistri J. de Cantia de Pœnitentia. Templum Domini cum arte confessionum. Regula S. Benedicti. *Psalterium cum hympnario.* Item *duo Psalteria.* Duo Missalia. Duo Gradualia. *Liber Evangeliorum.* Liber Orationum ad magnum altare."‡§

WILLIELMUS DE HOTOT, or HOTOFT, being a monk of Peterborough, was chosen abbot the 6th of February, 1246. "Having been abbot only three years, he surceased. Perhaps he had not time enough to gather more books than these into his library:—

"Antissiodorensis abbreviatus. Tractatus super Canonem Missæ. Templum Domini cum aliis rebus. Libellus de diversis rebus. Missale ad altare Michaelis."||

JOHANNIS DE CALETO. He was elected abbot in 1249. He is said to have been made lord treasurer by the barons. "His secular employments might take off his mind from books and plead for the poorness of his library." "This was his stock of books, as I find from an ancient MS.:—

"Flores Evangeliorum. Tractatus de Theologia, Concilium Lateranense. Templum Domini. Testamentum 12 Patriarcharum."¶

But we should be unjust to the abbots of Peterborough, if we were to suppose them to be more indifferent to literature than their contemporaries. The neglect of learning was nearly universal, and the following instances will evidence how extensively the scarcity of books was experienced. In an inventory of the goods of John de Pontissara, bishop of Winchester, contained in his palace of Wulvesey, all the books which appear are nothing more than *Septemdecem pecie librorum de diversis Scienciis*, "Fragments of seventeen books on different sciences." This was in the

* The Missal and Capitula seem to have been lent on account of the scarcity of books.

† Gunton, p. 30.

‡ Walter's library was creditable to him, and exhibits, most pleasingly, his love of Biblical literature;—a Bible, four Psalters, the Four Gospels, and a work on Hebrew names, were a rich treasure possessed by few or none beside!

§ Gunton, p. 33. || Gunton, pp. 33, 34. ¶ Gunton, pp. 34, 35.

year 1294. The same prelate, in the year 1299, borrowed of his cathedral convent of St. Swithin, at Winchester, *Bibliam bene Glossatam*, that is, The Bible with marginal annotations, in two large folio volumes, but gave a bond for due return of the loan, drawn up with great solemnity. A copy of the bond may be seen in the "Dissertation on Learning," prefixed to the first volume of Warton's History of English Poetry. This Bible had been bequeathed by Pontissara's predecessor, Bishop Nicholas de Ely: and in consideration of so important a bequest, and of one hundred marks in money, the monks founded a daily mass for the soul of the donor. About the year 1225, Roger de Insula, dean of York, gave several Latin Bibles to the university of Oxford, with a condition, that the students who perused them should deposite a cautionary pledge. Even the library of that university, before the year 1300, consisted only of a few tracts, chained or kept in chests, in the choir of St. Mary's church.* The prices of books were, consequently, excessively high, and almost beyond the reach of the inferior orders of the clergy, at a time when the annual allowance of a scholar of the university was but *fifty shillings*.† W. de Howton, abbot of Croxton, bequeathed to that abbey, at his death, in 1274, "a BIBLE, in nine tomes, faire written, and excellently well glosed by Solomon, archdeacon of Leicester, and paid for it *fiftie markes* sterling," or £33 6*s*. 8*d*.‡ And in a valuation of books bequeathed to Merton College, at Oxford, before the year 1300, a *Psalter*, with glosses, or *marginal annotations*, is valued at *ten shillings* ; and St. Austin on Genesis, and a *Concordantia*, or Harmony, are each valued at the same price.§ Let it also be remembered, that every charge should be multiplied by fifteen, to bring it to the average, or value of money at present;‖ and in some instances, the comparative value would be still too low, as, in the instance of the labouring men, whose pay, in 1272, was only three halfpence per day, and who must therefore have devoted the earnings of many years to purchase a Bible.¶ Whitaker, in his History of Craven, affords the additional information, that toward the close of the thirteenth, and at the commencement of the fourteenth cen-

* Warton's Hist. of English Poetry, vol. i, diss. 2.

† Chalmer's Hist. of the University of Oxford, vol. i, p. 6. Oxf. 1810, 8vo.

‡ Stow's Annales, p. 169. Lond. 1615, fol.

§ Warton, *ubi sup.*

‖ See Henry's Hist. of Great Britain, vol. vi, ch. vi, pp. 302–307; and vol. viii, ch. vi, p. 352. Whitaker's Hist. of Craven, p. 404.

¶ Dugdale's Warwickshire, quoted in Evang. Mag. 1807, p. 121.

tury, the average wages of a man-servant, with meat and clothing, were from three to five shillings only *per annum;* but that reapers were paid two-pence a day; that a sheep sold for a shilling, and thirty quarters of fossil-coal for seventeen shillings and six-pence.* Madox, in his History of the Exchequer, says, that in 1240, the building of two arches of London Bridge cost only twenty-five pounds; eight pounds less than the Bible bequeathed to the abbey of Croxton, by Abbot W. de Howton!†

The booksellers of this period were called *stationarii*, from their *stations*, or shops, a term still in use in the English word *stationer*. They not only sold books, but many of them acquired considerable property by *lending* out books to be read, at exorbitant prices, not in volumes, but in detached parts, according to the estimation in which the author was held. In Paris, the limited trade of these booksellers consisted principally in selling books for those who wished to dispose of them, and furnishing a depository for them while on sale. To prevent frauds being practised by these *stationaires*, as they were called, the university framed a law, or regulation, dated Dec. 8th, 1275, by which the booksellers were obliged to take an oath every year, or, at the furthest, every two years, or oftener if required, that they would act loyally, and with fidelity in their employment. By the same statute, which was the first ever passed in the university respecting booksellers, they were forbidden to purchase, on their own account, the books placed in their hands, until they had been offered to sale for a month; and were enjoined to expose them publicly, immediately on being lodged in their hands, with a label affixed, containing the title and price of the book; it was also further ordered, that this price should be received on behalf of the owner of the books, who should allow a certain commission to the vender, which was fixed by the university at four deniers per livre, according to the price of the book; and if any bookseller committed fraud, he was dismissed from his office, and the masters and scholars were prohibited trading with such persons, under pain of being deprived of all the rights and privileges of the university. Their stalls, or portable shops, were sometimes erected in the market-place;‡ and at other times in the *parvis*, or church-porch, where schools were also occasion-

* Whitaker's Hist. of Craven, p. 404.

† Madox's Hist. of the Exchequer, ch. x, pp. 249, 250. Lond. 1711, fol.

‡ The Latin term *statio*, sometimes means a place of public resort: see Pitisci Lex Antiq. Roman. *in voce:* sometimes also a *depository*, [Fr. *Entrepos.*] See Crevier Hist. de l'Univ. de Paris, tom. ii, p. 66, *note*.

ally kept. Matt. Paris says, that in 1250 a poor clerk of France was forced to drag on "a starving life in the *parvis*, keeping a school, and selling petty books;" and the portal at the north end of the cross aisle, in Rouen cathedral, is to this day called *Le Portail des Libraires*, or the porch of the booksellers.* These moveable booksellers' shops may appear to us at present as insignificant and unworthy the importance of literary traffic; but at the time of which we are writing, they served the interests of literature, and in an age of barbarous ignorance, promoted knowledge; nor ought we to forget, that in the preceding century, the monks of Cottenham, near Cambridge, were obliged *to hire a barn*, in order to give lectures to the students of that university. To this day markets for MSS. are continued in the East. Dr. E. D. Clarke, in his "Travels in various Countries," &c., remarks, "The bazar of the booksellers," of Constantinople, "does not contain all the works enumerated by D' Herbelot; but there is hardly any Oriental author, whose writings, if demanded, may not be procured; although every volume offered for sale be MS. The number of shops employed in this way, in that market and elsewhere, amounts to a hundred: each of these contain, upon an average, five hundred volumes; so that no less a number than fifty thousand MSS., Arabic, Persian, and Turkish, are daily exposed for sale. There are similar MS. markets in all the Turkish cities, particularly those of Aleppo and of Cairo."†

Tedious as was the process of transcription, several of the public libraries of Europe contain copies of the whole or parts of the Scriptures, especially the Psalter, written in this century. In a copy of the whole Latin Bible, in the British Museum, the name of the transcriber, and the date of the transcript, are thus preserved: "Hunc librum scripsit Willielmus de Hales, Magistro Thome de la Wile, quem vocavit Magister Radulphus de Hehham tunc Cancellarius Sarum: quibus Deus in hoc Sæculo et in futuro propicietur. Amen. Factus fuit liber anno 1254, ab incarnatione Domini."

Another MS., containing the Proverbs of Solomon, Ecclesiastes, Canticles, and Wisdom, with Prologues, has the following anathema, not uncommon in ancient MSS., inscribed in the beginning:

* Du Cange, Glossar., v. Stationarii. Whitaker's Cathedral of Cornwall, vol. i, p. 149. Berrington's Literary Hist. of the Middle Ages, b. v, p. 356. Crevier, Hist. de l'Université de Paris, tom. ii, liv. 3, pp. 66–68. Paris, 1761, 12mo.

† Berrington, *ut sup.*, p. 307. Dr. E. D. Clarke's Travels, vol. iii, pp. 65, 67. Lond. 1817, 8vo.

"Liber De Claustro Roffensi per Johannem Priorem: quem qui inde alienaverit, alienatum celaverit, vel hunc titulum fraudulenter deleverit, Anathema sit. Amen."—"This book belongs to the monastery of Rochester (given) by the prior John; if any one remove it, or conceal it when taken away, or fraudulently deface this inscription, let him be anathema. Amen."

Le Long, in his *Bibliotheca Sacra*, notices several MSS. containing the Latin Bible, written during this century, particularly one transcribed by the Premonstrants in 1263. It was made use of by Joannes Hentenius, in an edition of the Bible printed in 1547, and also by the deputies to the council of Trent.

Godefridus de Croyland, who was elected abbot of Peterborough in 1290 or 1299, during his abbacy entertained King Edward I., and also two cardinals, to one of whom, named Gaucilinus, he presented a Psalter, curiously written with golden letters, but the time when it was transcribed is uncertain.

Among the royal MSS. in the British Museum is a MS. Psalter, of this century, which belonged formerly to the church of St. Botolph, and having been taken from thence, was presented to Queen Mary by Ralph Pryne, a grocer of London, as appears by the following lines written in the first leaf:—

"God saue the most vertuus and nobull Quene Marys gras:
And send her to in Joye the crowne of Eyngland long tyme and spas.
Her ennimys to confunde, and hutterly to deface,
And to folo her godly proceydynges God giue us gras:
As euery subyegte ys bounde for her gras to praye
That God may preserve her body from all dangers both nyght and daye.
God save the Quene.

Be me humbull and poor Orytur Rafe Pryne, grocer of Londoun, wyshynge your gras prosperus helthe."*

During this century an important event took place, which, from its intimate connection with Biblical literature, demands particular notice. This was the expulsion of the Jews from England, and the confiscation of their property. From the time of William the Conqueror the Jews had been permitted to settle in the kingdom; and, notwithstanding the cruelties practised upon them at different times, under various pretences, and the tyrannical exactions they had suffered whenever the government was in want of money, they had spread themselves in vast bodies throughout most of the cities and capital towns in the land. In the reign of William Rufus, some

* Classical Journal, vol. viii, No. 15, pp. 150, 151. Le Long, Biblioth. Sacra, tom. i, cap. iv, p. 240. Paris, 1723, fol.

of the rabbins had been permitted to open a school in the university of Oxford, to instruct not only their own people, but Christian students, in the Hebrew language and literature. About two hundred years after their admission by the Conqueror, they were expelled again by Edward I., their synagogues profaned, their libraries dispersed, their goods seized, and many of them barbarously murdered. At Huntingdon and Stamford "all their furniture came under the hammer for sale, together with their *treasures of books*." These Hebrew MSS. were immediately purchased by Gregory of Huntingdon, prior of the abbey of Ramsey, who had been studying the Hebrew language for some time, and had been checked in his studies by the want of Hebrew books; and who no sooner heard of this auction, than "he hastily repaired to it from his neighbouring monastery, well furnished with money, and readily, at the fixed price, purchased their gold for his brass, and returned home exceedingly well pleased. Night and day he turned over his Hebrew volumes, until he had obtained a more intimate knowledge of the language from its fountain-head. He left also to his fellow-priests many excellent annotations from his own pen, which a learned posterity might read with pleasure. The catalogue of Ramsey library makes a distinct and honourable mention of the Hebrew books, most industriously collected by him."* Gregory bequeathed these valuable acquisitions to his monastery about the year 1250. At Oxford, great multitudes of the books which had belonged to the Jews fell into the hands of Roger Bacon, or were bought by his brethren, the Franciscan friars of that university.†

But the number of those who applied to the study of the Hebrew tongue were so few, that the famous Roger Bacon affirmed that there were not more than three or four persons among the Latins, in his time, who had any knowledge of the Oriental languages; though it must be acknowledged that, in this instance, the views of our learned friar were too gloomy, and that, whether known to him or not, there were others who were engaged in the study of Arabic and Hebrew principally, to enable them more effectually to refute the antichristian writings of the Jews. On the other hand, that species of theology known by the name of *school divinity* was cultivated with uncommon ardour; and the most celebrated of the scholastic divines were honoured with the pompous titles of *profound*, *sublime*, *wonderful*, *seraphic*, *angelic doctors*. In the preceding century the scholastic doctors had made the Scriptures the chief subject

* Leland, De Script. Brit., tom. ii, cap. cccxxiii, pp. 321, 322. Oxon, 1709, 8vo.

† Warton's History of English Poetry, vol i. dissert. 2.

of their studies, and the text of their lectures, as some few of them still continued to do, who for that reason were denominated *Bible divines.* But in the course of this century the Holy Scriptures, with those who studied or endeavoured to explain them, were neglected and contemned. The Bible doctors were slighted as men of inferior learning and acuteness. "He who lectures on the *Sentences* of Lombard," says the illustrious Roger Bacon, "is everywhere honoured, and preferred to him who adopts the sacred text as the subject of his lectures; for he who reads the *Sentences* chooses the most convenient hour, according to his pleasure, and obtains a companion and an apartment among the religious; while he who reads the *Bible* is deprived of these advantages, and only obtains an hour for lecturing, by begging it of the lecturer on the *Sentences*."*

The same spirit of scholastic divinity ascended the pulpit, and introduced a new and more artificial method of preaching. Before this period the clergy chiefly used the modes of preaching termed *postillating* and *declaring*. *Postillating* consisted in expounding a large portion of Scripture, sentence after sentence; a method of instruction still practised in some foreign churches, and in the church of Scotland, where it is called *lecturing*. *Declaring* was so termed, because the preacher, without naming any particular text, declared the subject of his sermon, in words to this purpose: "In my present sermon I design, by the grace of God, to discourse on such or such a subject, (on the fear of God, for example,) and on this subject I design to lay down some true and certain conclusions," &c. This last way of preaching was the most popular, and continued in use long after this period. The new method of preaching differed from both these ancient ones in several respects. At the beginning of his discourse the preacher read a text out of some book and chapter of the Old or New Testament, which had lately been divided into chapters and verses by Archbishop Langton, or Cardinal Hugo, as the theme or subject of his sermon. This text he divided into several parts, and the more numerous his divisions and subdivisions the greater divine and the better preacher was he esteemed. The younger clergy, especially, adopted this artificial method of preaching; but others condemned it, and Roger Bacon in particular speaks of it with contempt, and assigns a singular reason for the prevalence of it in his time: "The greatest part of our prelates," says he, "having but little knowledge in

* Hody, De Bibliorum Text. Orig., lib. iii, cap. xi, p. 420. Henry's Hist. of Great Britain, vol. viii, b. iv, ch. iv, pp. 180, 181.

divinity, and having been little used to preaching in their youth, when they become bishops, and are sometimes obliged to preach, are under a necessity of begging and borrowing the sermons of certain novices, who have invented a new way of preaching, by endless divisions and quibblings; in which there is neither sublimity of style nor depth of wisdom, but much childish trifling and folly, unsuitable to the dignity of the pulpit." The opposition to the textual mode of preaching continued for more than a century; it at length, however, prevailed universally, and still continues to be generally adopted.*

To this century also is to be referred the division of the sacred text into our present *chapters*. The most ancient Hebrew and Greek copies of the Old and New Testaments were written without any distinction, not only of chapters and verses, but even of words, so that the Jews were accustomed to say, that anciently the books of the Old Testament formed but a single *pesuk*, or verse. One of the oldest of the Greek MSS. of the New Testament, in which the words are distinctly divided, is the Codex Augiensis, so called from Augia major, the name of a monastery at Rhenau, to which it belonged at the time of holding the council of Basil. It is accompanied with a Latin version, and is supposed to have been written in the ninth century. The Greek text is written in capitals, and the Latin in Anglo-Saxon letters. The division of the Hebrew text into *chapters* was made by the Jews, in imitation of the division of the New Testament; but the division of the Old Testament into *sections* and *verses* was much earlier in its origin, and has been considered as coeval with Ezra. The first division of the text of the New Testament was into τίτλοί, *titles*, or larger portions, which received their denomination from the *titles* or subjects of those portions being written either in the upper or lower margin of the Greek MSS., and generally in red ink. They were called by the Latins *breves*, and the table of the contents of each *brevis*, which was prefixed to the copies of the New Testament, was called *breviarium*. Dr. Mills supposes that Tatian, who flourished A. D. 160, invented them for the purpose of constructing his work, called *Diatesseron*, or Harmony of the four Evangelists. From Tertullian we learn that in his time, about A. D. 200, the New Testament was divided into *capitula*, or small chapters, called by the Greeks κεφαλαία. These chapters, or smaller portions, were numbered on the side of the margin.

* Henry's History of Great Britain, vol. viii, pp. 182–186.

Both these divisions are very clearly represented in the editions of the Greek Testament by Erasmus, or in R. Stephens' edition of 1550. The chapters differ in different copies. The most celebrated and one of the most ancient divisions was that of Ammonius, a Christian philosopher, who lived at Alexandria in the third century. From him it had the appellation of the *Ammonian Sections*. Of these there are three hundred and fifty-five, and sixty-eight *tituli*, in the Gospel of St. Matthew. In the fourth century Eusebius adapted to these sections his ten tables or canons, which represent a harmony of the Gospels, and which were commonly prefixed to the Greek MSS. These tables may be seen in the editions of the Greek Testament by Erasmus, in Kuster's edition of Mills' Greek Testament, and in that of R. Stephens of 1550. From these tables of Eusebius the marginal references were taken that are found in many printed editions of the Greek.

Euthalius relates, that about the year 396 the Epistles of St. Paul were divided into chapters; as were also the Acts of the Apostles, and the Catholic or General Epistles, about the year 451. Andreas Cæsariensis, in the sixth century, or, according to others, Andreas Cretensis, in the seventh century, divided the Apocalypse into seventy-two chapters; and about the eleventh century Œcumenius is said to have divided the Acts into forty *capita* and two hundred and forty-seven *capitula;* a division something analogous to our chapters and verses. The division which obtained in the ancient Latin MSS. was different from that used by the Greeks.* In the thirteenth century the present chapters were invented or adopted by Archbishop Langton, or Cardinal Hugo de S. Caro. Our early biographers, Bale, Pitts, &c., ascribe the invention to the archbishop, but Biblical critics in general have allowed that the cardinal was the inventor, and that it was by his example and influence that the old division was entirely laid aside in the Latin Church, and in Latin MSS.; although the division in present use was not adopted in writing Greek MSS. till about the end of the fifteenth century.† The following biographical sketches of these two celebrated but very different characters may not be unacceptable to the reader.

STEPHEN LANGTON was by birth an Englishman. He received

* Marsh's Michaelis, vol. ii, pt. i, ch. viii, p. 210; and ch. xiii, p. 524; pt. ii, pp. 664, 905–908. Barrett, Evangelium secundum Matthæum, quoted in Eclectic Review, vol. iii, pp. 198, 199.

† Hody, De Bibliorum Text. Orig., lib. iii, pt. ii, p. 430. Butler's Horæ Biblicæ vol. i, p. 201, edit. 12mo.

his education at Paris, and became so eminent for scholastic learning, and for his application of it, in his explications of Scripture, that he was created chancellor of the university of Paris, canon of Paris, and dean of Rheims. Being called to Rome, he was placed among the cardinals by Innocent III. In 1207 he was nominated by the same pontiff to the archbishopric of Canterbury, vacant by the death of Hubert Walter, and was consecrated by the pope himself at Viterbo. This nomination being regarded as a usurpation of the rights of the king of England, as well as of those of the monks of Canterbury and the bishops of the province, met with violent resistance, especially from the king. The pope, enraged at the disappointment, laid both the king and kingdom under an interdict. For several years King John acted with more than usual firmness, and refused to acknowledge the appointment of Langton to the see of Canterbury. At length, dispirited by opposition from the pope and foreign princes from abroad, and from the barons and many of the clergy and people at home, he submitted to the election of Stephen, and purchased his peace with the Roman pontiff by a charter granted to certain prelates, and the payment of forty thousand marks.

In 1222 the archbishop called a council at Oxford, at which a number of constitutions were framed, from which the following are extracted, as illustrating the practice and manners of that age:

Constit. 10. "We strictly command parish priests to feed the people with the word of God, as God inspires them with it, lest they be justly thought dumb dogs: and let them remember that they who visit the sick shall be rewarded with the eternal kingdom; therefore let them cheerfully go, when sent for, to the sick."

21. "We forbid, with the terror of anathema, any one to retain *robbers* in his service, for committing robberies, or knowingly to let them dwell on his lands."

25. "Let archdeacons take care, in their visitations, that the canon of the mass be correct, and that the priest can rightly *pronounce* (at least) the words of the canon and of baptism, and that he knows the true meaning of them; and let them teach laymen in what form they ought to baptize in case of necessity, in some language or other."

31. "Let not clergymen that are beneficed, or in holy orders, publicly keep concubines in their manses, (or parsonage houses,) or have public access to them with scandal anywhere else."

36. "We decree that nuns and other religious women wear no silk veils, nor needles of silver or gold in their veils; that neither

monks nor canons regular have girdles of silk, or garnished with gold or silver; nor use burnet, (artificial brown,) or any irregular cloth. Let the dimensions of their clothes be commensurate to their bodies, not longer than to cover their feet, like Joseph's coat, which came down to the ankles. Only the nuns may wear a ring, and but one."*

On various occasions the archbishop discovered a haughty independence, particularly in his conduct toward his sovereign and the pope. He not only opposed the pope's legate in his exorbitant grants of benefices, but was the principal of those peers who declared against the validity of King John's resignation of his crown and kingdom to the see of Rome. The irritated pope excommunicated and suspended him, and reversed the election of his brother Simon Langton, who had been chosen archbishop of York. Prior, however, to the calling of the council at Oxford, these violent measures appear to have been relinquished.

He was the author of commentaries on many of the books of the Old and New Testaments, and of various other works. He died at Slindon, in Sussex, July, 1228, and was buried in the cathedral at Canterbury.†

Hugo de S. Caro, or, according to his French name, Hugues de St. Cher, was born at Vienne, in Dauphiné, and studied at Paris, where he became a Dominican friar in 1225. He was sent by Gregory IX. to Constantinople, to procure, if possible, a union of the Greek and Roman Churches. On his return he was chosen provincial of France, and, in 1245, received the dignity of cardinal from Innocent IV., being the first of the Dominicans who obtained that honour. In a synod held by him as the pope's legate, at Liege, in 1246, the feast of Corpus Christi was first ordered to be celebrated. Pope Urban IV. afterward, in 1264, fixed it on the Thursday after the Octave of Whitsunday, commanding it to be observed in the whole church with a solemnity equal to the four great festivals of the year.‡ But his truest honours were derived

* Johnson's Ecclesiastical Laws, &c., A. D. MCCXXII.

† Cavei Hist. Lit., sæc. xiii, pp. 702, 703. Fox's Actes and Monuments, vol. i, pp. 327–334. London, 1570.

‡ This festival, instituted in support of the doctrine of transubstantiation, was confirmed by different popes, and various privileges and indulgences were granted to those who honoured it by their devotions. Thus Pope Urban, in his bull of 1264, "To encourage the faithful to honour and celebrate this great feast, we grant to all that do confess their sins, and are truly penitent, who shall be found in the church at the *mattins* (midnight) of the said feast, one hundred days' pardon, and as many to

from his Biblical labours, which placed him in the first rank of sacred critics and patrons of sacred literature. To him we are indebted for the celebrated *Correctorium Bibliorum* of the Dominicans; the first Concordance of the Scriptures; a Comment on the Old and New Testament; and most probably for the division of the Bible into our present chapters.

The Correctorium Bibliorum, or Bible with *various readings*, was, in 1772, in the library of the Dominicans in the college of St. James, at Paris. It is fairly written upon parchment, with demi-Gothic letters, forming four large volumes in folio. The design of it was to introduce correct copies of the Scriptures into the public services of the church, and into general use, instead of the shamefully corrupt and incorrect ones commonly read. For this purpose Cardinal Hugo, aided by the authority of F. Jordan, general of the order, caused a collation to be made of the common copies with the oldest and most accurate that could be obtained, particularly of those transcribed by order of Charlemagne, under the inspection of Alcuin; and also ordered them to be compared with the original texts. The *Correctorium* is the result of this laborious and valuable collation. The various readings of the Latin, Hebrew, and Greek MSS. are placed in the margin, and the superfluous words which have been inserted in the text by careless transcribers or ignorant critics are marked by a line drawn underneath them. This important revision of the Latin Scriptures was made about A. D. 1236; and was succeeded by an injunction that all the copies made use of by the order should be corrected and punctuated according to this standard. So well was this revision received by the Dominican friars, that Humbert, another general of the order, at a chapter general held at Paris, in 1256, forbade all the religious of his order to make use of the corrections of the Latin Bible which had been made at Sens, with the same design as this by the cardinal.* Hugo's *Correctorium* consequently soon became general, and, till the declaration of the council of Trent, was

those who shall devoutly assist at mass," &c.—*Butler's Moveable Feasts*, &c., pp. 655–657. London, 1774, 8vo.

* The same Humbert, in his *Expositio in Regulam S. Augustini*, cap. cl, after earnestly pressing the importance of reading the Scriptures, and replying to those who refused to read or hear them, because they despaired of understanding them, (probably from not being in the vernacular tongue,) concludes by the following extraordinary and superstitious sentiment: "We ought to believe that the words of Scripture, (verba sacra) although not understood by those who read them, nevertheless possess a power against 'spiritual wickedness;' as the words of a charm against a serpent, though not understood by the charmer himself!" See *Whartoni Auctarium*, p. 420.

considered as the standard of the Latin Scriptures, and the editions of Sixtus V. and Clement VIII., and may be regarded as the source of all those MSS. which, under the titles of *Correctio, Correctiones*, or *Correctorium Bibliæ*, are still to be met with in many of the monasteries of the Dominican friars.*

The CONCORDANCE of the Latin Bible, compiled under the direction of the cardinal, was the first work of the kind, and must have demanded unwearied patience and indefatigable diligence; he is accordingly said to have employed five hundred monks,† in selecting, and arranging in alphabetical order, all the *declinable* words of the Old and New Testaments. It first appeared under the name *De Sancto Jacobo*, or the Concordance of St. James; the author himself being sometimes called *Hugo De Sancto Jacobo*, probably from residing a considerable time at Paris in the convent of St. James, where he gave lectures on the Holy Scriptures, and assisted, as doctor in theology, in the condemnation of a plurality of benefices by the faculty of theology, A. D. 1238. The idea of such a compilation was probably suggested by those very useful *Indexes* which, from a remote period, had been formed for assisting the student in his consultations of the works of different authors; though there was this difference between an index and a concordance, that the former referred only to particular subjects or passages, but the latter to words and sentences. John of Darlington, and Richard of Stavensby, assisted by other Englishmen, made considerable additions to the original work, which was afterward considerably improved by Conrad of Halberstadt, who flourished A. D. 1290. It was still further enlarged and improved in the fifteenth century, about the time of the council of Basil, by John of Ragusia, procurator general, and a monk of the order of preachers, or Dominicans, who added all the *indeclinable* words; and at length received its present form from Walter Scot, and John of Segovia. Sixtus Senensis, in his *Bibliotheca Sancta*, lib. iii, first published in 1566, has presented the reader with a specimen of an extensive and improved Concordance, invented by himself, and intended to serve not only as an index of words and sentences, but as a theological dictionary, and concordance of parallel passages: unfortunately there is no intimation that the work was ever completed. From the Latin Concordance of Cardinal Hugo are de-

* Fabricy, Titres Primitifs, tom. ii, p. 132–141.

† Chevillier (L'Origine de l'Imprimerie de Paris, p. 134) doubts the fact of so many monks being employed, but supposes the work to have been at first much less voluminous than at present, and to have increased by frequent revisions and improvements.

rived those Concordances in various languages which have so greatly aided the studies of Biblical scholars.*

The COMMENTARY, or *Postilla*,† of Hugo, on all the books of Scripture, is a series of notes on the sacred text, in which he endeavours to show the literal, allegorical, moral, and anagogical sense of the inspired writers, though all these different modes of exposition are not employed to explain every part of the sacred text, most generally only the literal and moral, or literal alone, and occasionally the allegorical, and anagogical or mystical; a brief extract will exhibit the nature of his work:—

JOHN, chap. v. "Search the Scriptures.] q. d. in them the Father testifies of me, if ye read them inwardly. Therefore search, that is, diligently investigate the spiritual sense, not satisfying yourselves with the literal merely."

"For in them ye think ye have eternal life: ye *think*.] because, as he shows, they only read the Scriptures literally, and therefore had not the knowledge of eternal life, but a mere opinion or conjecture."

"And they are they which testify of me,] q. d. the very grounds on which you found your hope of eternal life, testify of me. It is therefore evident that the hinderance to your believing in me is in your own depraved will, since the design of the Scriptures is to persuade you to believe in me."

2 TIM. iv. "The cloak that I left at Troas with Carpus, when thou comest, bring with thee.] According to Haymo, the penula, or cloak, was the consular vest of Paul's father, conferred upon him by the Romans, when he obtained the privilege of a Roman citizen:—according to Jerome, the book of the law is to be understood; but Chrysostom says, *phelonem* is a garment; and afterward adds, that he inquires for the cloak, to prevent the necessity of receiving from others. Acts xx. It is more blessed to give than to receive."

"And the books.] Chrysostom asks, What need was there of books for him who was about to go to God? And replies, there

* Le Long, Biblioth. Sacra, tom. i, cap. x, pp. 456, 457. Paris, 1723, fol. Chevillier, L'Origine de l'Imprimerie de Paris, pt. ii, ch. ii, pp. 133, 134. Paris, 1694, 4to. Sixt. Senens. Biblioth. Sanct., lib. iii, p. 185, et lib. iv, pp. 311, 273.

† The term "Postilla," frequently adopted by the commentators of that period, was generally applied to those explanatory notes which were placed *after* the text, and was probably derived from the Latin *postea*, or *postilla*, (sc. *verba*;) unless we suppose the word *postilla* to be a corruption from *posta*, a page.—*Du Cange, Glossar.*, v. *Posta, Postillæ.*

was then the greatest need, that he might deposite them with the believers. Another reason was, that they might afford him solace in tribulation; and give to others an example of study. 1 Maccab. xii. We have the holy books of Scripture in our hands, to comfort us. And it is an argument for study, since, on the eve of martyrdom, he either wishes to study them himself, or to recommend the study of them to others."

"But especially the parchments;] That I may write my epistles upon them. And let it be noted, that he who gloried that the Holy Spirit and Christ spake in him, 2 Cor. xiii, made use of parchments in this case, for [the assistance of] the memory."*

This work has been several times printed in six volumes, folio, and at Cologne, in 1621, in eight volumes, folio. This is usually supposed to be the first Bible divided into the present CHAPTERS, which, for the convenience of quotations and references, were subdivided again by the cardinal, by adding in the margin the letters A. B. C. D. E. F., a practice continued till the invention of the present verses by Robert Stephens in 1550, and adopted in our early English Bibles. Yet Cardinal Humbert, about A. D. 1059, cites the twelfth and thirteenth chapters of Exodus, and the twenty-third of Leviticus, according to our present division of chapters. Hugo died on the 14th of March, A. D. 1262, and was buried in the church of the Dominicans at Lyons.†

The school or academy of Paris has been repeatedly mentioned, as the resort of all who were desirous of completing a literary education; we may now further observe, that hitherto the public studies had been limited to certain branches of learning, denominated the *trivium* and the *quadrivium*; the *trivium* included grammar, rhetoric, and dialectics; the *quadrivium* comprehended music, arithmetic, geometry, and astronomy. He who was master of these had been thought to have no need of a preceptor, to explain any books, or to solve any questions which lay within the compass of human reason; the knowledge of the *trivium* having furnished him with the key to all language, and that of the *quadrivium* having opened to him the secret laws of nature. But as the views or desires of men became enlarged, the whole circle of the sciences, as far as the allotted period of time would allow, did not appear to be an object beyond the comprehension of youthful minds. Schools then, which professed to embrace *all* the sciences

* Ugonis de S. Charo, Opera, tom. vii, p. 230. Colon. Agrip. 1621, fol.

† Cavei Hist. Lit., sæc. xiii, p. 721. Jortin's Remarks, vol. iii, p. 126.

within their walls, and to appoint masters to each, were properly denominated *universities*, of which Paris, about the year 1215, is said to have set the example. This was soon followed in other countries, and particularly in Italy; where almost every city, owing to the beneficence of princes or of pontiffs, was honoured with the distinctive title. The civil and canon law, theology, and the more abstruse philosophical researches, were the studies most ardently followed: the two first as the path to preferment; the latter, as the way to secure celebrity and applause in the field of disputation.* But books were still scarce, as has been already noted, for the work of transcription was necessarily slow, laborious, and expensive; and where the monks laboured as scribes, their copies were generally enclosed in the cloister; and what was executed by hired artists in the universities could satisfy the demands only of a few. Wood's notice of the library of Merton College, Oxford, in its infant state, (Colleges and Halls, edit. Gutch, vol. i, p. 61,) is illustrative of the manners and learning of the times: "At first the society kept those books they had (which were but few) in chests, and once, sometimes twice, in a year, made choice for the borrowing of such as they liked, by giving a certificate under their hands for the restoring of them again to their proper place."† How arduous the pursuit of literature, and how slow its progress during the ages of transcription, and before the invention of printing! Nor did the allowance to students in the public academies, or universities, enable them to purchase many volumes for themselves. According to the statutes of Merton College, Oxford, founded in 1264, the allowance to scholars was only fifty shillings per annum for all necessaries; and the revenues of Baliol College, founded in 1263 or 1268, were at first so small, as to yield only eight-pence per week to each scholar, but afterward were so increased by the benefaction of Sir P. Somervyle, as to raise the weekly allowance of the fellows and scholars to eleven-pence, and in case of dearness of victuals to fifteen-pence.‡

Hearne, in the "Preliminary Observations" prefixed to the sixth volume of his edition of Leland's "Collectanea," has attempted to defend the monks of the middle ages against the general charge of ignorance and illiteracy; and if he have not been completely successful in rescuing them from the imputations of their contempo-

* Enfield's History of Philosophy, vol. ii, p. 337. Berrington's Literary History of the Middle Ages, b. v, p. 354.

† Chalmers's Hist. of the University of Oxford, vol. i, p 36. Oxford, 1810, 8vo.

‡ Ibid., pp. 6, 47–49.

rary opponents, his reasoning is nevertheless deserving of attention: "Nobody doubts," says he, "but the monasteries had divers members that could not be styled *learned*. But when we discourse of learned bodies, these ought not to be considered, at least their ignorance ought not to be looked upon as sufficient to denominate them unlearned. Add to this, that sometimes these illiterate persons were eminent upon some other account, and consequently might prove very serviceable to the monasteries. After all, 'tis very certain that a great number of the monks were men of very profound learning and of extraordinary abilities. Had they been otherwise, 'tis impossible to account for that incredible number of books written by them. No one that reads either Boston of Bury, or Leland, or other authors that say any thing of their writings, can justly suppose them to have been illiterate men. On the contrary, many of their writings are very judicious and full of learning, and what many of the best of our modern writers (notwithstanding the many advantages we have for acquiring learning that they wanted) need not be ashamed of: nay, in some parts of learning they exceeded any of our moderns, which is an argument, not only of excellent parts, but of their constant and unwearied diligence and application. Had it not been for this diligence and care, we had not had so many of the best authors of the first ages preserved. John Bale* himself, who was otherwise their mortal enemy, will allow them this praise, and 'tis for that reason he laments the havoc of so many of the books that they had preserved, at the dissolution. I know very well that the abbots had oftentimes a small quantity of books, sometimes not above five or six, in their own private studies; and perhaps many of the monks might not have had more. But we are not to measure the extent of any one's learning by the number of books; although, indeed, if this were any proof, we might allege in behalf of the religious, that however meanly furnished their own private studies might be, they might have continual access, if they pleased, to such libraries as were well stored; I mean the libraries that belonged in common to each abbey. We have accounts of the furniture of some of these libra ries; and if we may judge of the rest by these, 'tis certain they had a large as well as a noble stock of books, and that many of their libraries might vie for number with many of our best libraries since. And even such libraries as had not so great a store ex-

* John Bale, bishop of Ossory, in Ireland, was educated in the Roman Catholic religion, but afterward embraced the doctrines of the Reformation, and became a noted author. He died in 1563.

ceeded divers of our present libraries, by reason they were all MSS., and upon that score are to be looked upon as a valuable and precious treasure. In short, as the abbeys were very curious, fine, and magnificent piles of building, richly endowed, and continually found liberal benefactors, so I believe their libraries in every respect answered the other parts of the structures, and were all (notwithstanding the reflection made upon the Franciscan library at Oxford, just upon the dissolution) adorned with an extraordinary fine collection of books."*

Among the mendicant orders, particularly the Dominicans, there were some who, during this century, applied themselves to the study of the Oriental tongues, with the laudable design of attempting the conversion of the Jews and Mohammedans. In one of their general chapters, held at Valencia in 1259, it was ordained that the prior of Spain should institute a school in the convent of Barcelona, for the study of the Arabic tongue: "Injungimus Priori Hispaniæ quod ipse ordinet aliquod studium ad addicendam linguam Arabicam in conventu Barcinonensi vel alibi, et ibidem collocet fratres aliquos de quibus speretur, quod de hujusmodi studio possunt proficere."†

Raymond of Pennafort, or Pegnafort, so called from the place of his birth in Catalonia, general of the Dominicans, a man of piety, zeal, and learning, condemned the violence which had too frequently been employed to destroy rather than to convert the Jews, and endeavoured to promote their conversion by instruction, and the adoption of mild and persuasive measures. At his request, James I., king of Arragon, published several edicts to repress the insolence of the people, and to encourage those studies that might qualify them for disputing against the Jewish errors with success. Pope Gregory IX., to whom Raymond of Pennafort was chaplain and confessor, promoted the same plans; and countenanced the public disputations with the Jews. The most noted of these public conferences was one held in the palace, before the king of Arragon, about A.D. 1260. The disputants were Moses Bar Nachman, or Nachmanides, a learned Cabbalistic Jew, and Raymond Martin and Paul Christian, two Dominican friars. Both sides claimed the victory. In the acts of this conference, published by Wagenseil, in his *Tela Ignea Satanæ*, Altdorf. Noric. 1681, 4to., and written by Nachmanides, the author maintains, that the king was so well pleased with his conduct as to present him with three

* Leland's Collectanea, by Hearne, vol. vi, pp. 86, 87.

† Simon, Lettres Choisies, tom. iii, let. 16, p. 112.

hundred golden crowns for his intended journey. On the other side it is asserted, that the Jews were so confounded by their adversaries, that their advocate chose to quit Spain, and retire to Jerusalem, to avoid the reproach and shame of his defeat. Basnage, however, considers the "Acts" published by Wagenseil as spurious, though he allows the fact of a public disputation.*

R. MOSES BEN NACHMAN, frequently called RAMBAN, from the abbreviation of his name, was born at Gironne, in the year 1194. He applied himself first to physic; and at the same time made such progress in the study of the Law, as to obtain the names of the Father of Wisdom; the Luminary; the Flower of the Crown and of Holiness. A discourse delivered before the king, acquired him the title of the Father of Eloquence. At one period he despised the CABBALA, but afterward became one of the most strenuous of its defenders. He published various works, principally Cabbalistic expositions of the Law. After enjoying high reputation in Spain, his native country, for many years, he quitted it for Judea, and resided at Jerusalem, where he built a synagogue, and afterward ended his days. The exact time of his death is uncertain, different authors placing it in different years.†

Of PAUL, surnamed *Christian*, nothing more is known than what has been related, except that he obtained a decree from the king of Arragon, of which Wagenseil has given a copy, from which the following translation is made. It is addressed to the Jews:—

"We command and strictly charge you, that whenever our beloved son, Fr. Paul Christian, of the order of Friars Preachers, (or Dominicans,) whom we have sent to show you the way of salvation, shall come to you, to your synagogues, or houses, or any other place, for the sake of preaching the word of God, or of disputing, or conferring with you, together or separately, respecting the Holy Scriptures, in public or in private, or by way of familiar conversation; that ye come to him, and mildly and favourably listen to him; and, as far as ye know, answer his questions respecting faith and the Holy Scriptures, with humility and reverence, and without calumny or subterfuge. And that you also permit him to have the use of such of your books as he may want, in order to show you the truth; and the expenses which the said brother may have in curred in conveying from place to place such books as he deemed necessary for teaching you the truth, (the brethren of his order, by

* Basnage's History of the Jews, b. vii, ch. xv, pp. 660, 661. Wagenseilii Tela Ignea Satanæ, Disputatio, &c., pp. 2, 60.

† Basnage, *ut sup.*, pp. 655, 656.

their constitution, being freed from expenses,) be careful to discharge, placing them to our account, and deducting them from the tribute which ye should pay to us. Moreover we strictly charge and command all bailiffs, vicars, and other officers, in every part of our dominions, that if the Jews aforesaid do not freely comply with what is before mentioned, that they oblige them by our authority, as they desire our favour and affection. Given at Barcelona, IV. Calend. Sept. Anno Domini MCCLXIII."*

RAYMOND MARTIN was a monk of the order of St. Dominic, and had been chosen to study the languages, that he might be employed in the conversion of the Jews. With this design he not only applied himself diligently to the Hebrew, Chaldee, and Arabic tongues, but gained an extensive acquaintance with the rabbinical writings, and the general habits and character of the people for whose instruction his studies were immediately directed. After the public disputation with R. Moses Ben Nachman, he was appointed, with the bishop of Barcelona, and Raymond Pennafort, the general of his order, to examine and judge of the blasphemies inserted in the Jewish books, in consequence of complaints having been made to the king against them. He was also the author of a celebrated work against the Jews, entitled *Pugio Fidei*, or the Poniard of Faith, which, by the numerous quotations from the rabbins, proves that the author had diligently studied their works, and was well qualified for the controversy in which he had engaged. In 1651 an edition was published at Paris, in folio, at the expense of the order to which its author had belonged, edited by the learned Joseph de Voisin, and accompanied with remarks by the editor: another edition was published by Carpzovius, at Leipsic, in 1687, fol., with an introduction to Jewish theology, and a short account of the conversion of Herman, a Jew, to Christianity, written by himself. The celebrated German, Esdras Edzard, who died in 1708, took the trouble to verify all the references made by Raymond Martin to Jewish writings, by collating them with the printed editions of the several works. These researches have since been inserted by Wolfius, in the fourth volume of his Bibliotheca Hebræa, pp. 572–628. Unfortunately, Edzard did not specify the editions which he consulted, but Fabricy, in his *Titres Primitifs*, informs us, that the Abbé Poch has remedied this defect; he has revised the remarks of Edzard, indicated the different editions in which the quotations may be found, and pointed out several other passages which had escaped the researches of Edzard. His remarks

* Wagenseilii Tela Ignea Satanæ: *Disputatio*, &c., *in Præfat.*

and corrections, however, have never been published. Raymond Martin died in the convent of the Dominicans at Barcelona, in 1284.*

The character of James I., king of Arragon, in whose presence Nachmanides and the two Dominican friars held their public disputations, appears to have been singularly inconsistent. Basnage relates,† that such was his attachment to the Jews, that he received moral lectures from them; and procured books of devotion and piety to be composed by them. R. Jona, who lived in 1264, wrote to another Jew at Gironne, requesting his advice, how to fulfil the intention of the king of Arragon, who had commanded him to write a book to instruct man in the duties of religion and piety: the same Jona was probably the author of a celebrated work on the "Fear of God," translated into German and Spanish, under the title of *Tratado del Timor Divino*. Yet such was the capriciousness of this prince, that he prohibited his Christian subjects from reading the writings of the rabbins, and so far were these violent measures carried, that to have a rabbinical work in possession was deemed a sufficient proof of Judaism!‡

In France, Louis IX., who died in 1270, and was canonized by Pope Boniface VIII. in 1297, displayed "the magnanimity of the hero, the integrity of the patriot, and the humanity of the philosopher," and what was of still higher value, discovered the virtues of the Christian. He ranked the study of the Holy Scriptures among the essential duties of a prince, and literally "meditated therein day and night." His biographer, who had been eighteen years confessor to Queen Margaret, wife of Louis, tells us that his library consisted of the Bible accompanied with a Gloss, or Commentary; the originals of the works of St. Augustine; the writings of other saints; and certain works concerning the Scriptures. These he either himself read, or caused others to read to him every day after dinner; and when not otherwise engaged, sent for one of the monks, with whom he conversed concerning God, or the saints, or Scripture history. In the evening, when the last of the daily religious services, or *Compline*, had been read in the chapel by his chaplains, he usually retired to his chamber, and then, to use the expressions of the writer, "estoit alumée une Chandele de certaine longueur, c'est à savoir de trois piez ou environ; et endementieres

* Basnage's Hist. of the Jews, b. vii, pp. 660–662. Fabricy, Titres Primitifts, tom. ii, pp. 143–145. Simon, Lettres Choisies, tom. iii, let. 16, p. 113.

† Basnage's Hist. of the Jews, b. vii, ch. xv, p. 663.

‡ Du Cange, v. *Charta de Rabi*, vol. ii, col. 517.

que ele duroit, il lisoit en LA BIBLE, ou en un autre saint livre: et quant la chandele estoit vers la fin, un de ses chapelains estoit apelés, et lors il disoit complie avecques lui:" "a candle, (or wax taper,) of about three feet long was lighted, and while it lasted he read in the Bible, or some other pious book; and when it was nearly consumed, one of his chaplains was called, with whom he then said the Compline."*

Another of the biographers of this excellent sovereign communicates the information, that by his order a translation was made of the whole Bible into *French*, and adds, that he had seen a copy of the version.† Lelong notices an old French version of the Bible, now in the royal library at Paris, from which he has extracted the first chapter of Genesis, and part of the first Psalm, as specimens of the translation, and which he conjectures may be the one executed by the order of St. Louis. It is on parchment, illuminated and ornamented with figures; but is defective, wanting from the twelfth chapter of the Epistle to the Hebrews, to the end of the Revelation.‡

During the reign of Louis, ROBERT SORBON, a canon, and learned doctor at Paris, whom he had honoured with his particular friendship, founded the *Sorbonne*, a college in the university of Paris, appropriated to the study of divinity. It was endowed by Louis, and the confirmation of it obtained from Clement IV. about A. D. 1250. Cardinal Richelieu afterward magnificently rebuilt the college, and thus erected an honourable monument to his memory.§

It is however to be lamented, that about the same time it was ordered by the statutes of the university of Paris, that "none should read lectures on the Bible, unless he had studied seven years in that university;" (see Lewis's Hist. of the Eng. Translations of the Bible, p. 35;) and that several works were written and circulated in France and Italy, which could only serve to depreciate the sacred Scriptures, and promote superstition and the worst species of fanaticism. The principal of these were the Psalter of the Blessed Virgin; the Everlasting Gospel; and the Introduction to the Everlasting Gospel.

The PSALTER OF THE BLESSED VIRGIN was an impious parody

* Histoire de Saint Louis par Jehan Sire de Joinville, &c., &c. Vie de S. Louis, p. 322. Paris, 1761, fol.

† Joannes de Serres. See Le Long, Biblioth. Sacra, tom. i, cap. iv, pp. 314, 315, fol. 1723.

‡ Le Long, *ubi sup.*

§ Butler's Lives, vol. viii, Aug. 25, p. 385.

upon the Psalms, in which the author introduces the name and appellations of Mary, instead of those of the divine Being.

The following extracts will exemplify his manner :—

"Blessed is the man that loveth thy name, O Virgin Mary; thy grace shall comfort his soul."

"The heavens declare thy glory; and the fragrance of thine ointments is spread among the nations."

"O come let us sing unto our lady; let us make a joyful noise to Mary our queen, that brings salvation."

"O give thanks unto the Lord, for he is good; give thanks unto his mother, for her mercy endureth for ever."

"Lady, despise not my praise; and vouchsafe to accept this Psalter, which is dedicated unto thee."

"The Lord said unto our lady, Sit thou, my mother, at my right hand."*

This Psalter is generally ascribed to Cardinal Bonaventure, who was the author of several other works in praise of the Virgin Mary; but Alban Butler denies that he wrote the Psalter, and says "it is unworthy to bear his name."† John Peckham, archbishop of Canterbury, also composed a work of a similar nature, entitled *Psalterium Meditationum B. Mariæ*, but it has never been printed.‡

The Everlasting Gospel, as it was called, was a fanatical work, attributed, perhaps falsely, to Joachim, abbot of Sora, in Calabria, whom the multitude revered as a person divinely inspired, and equal to the most illustrious prophets of ancient times. It contained various predictions relating to the Church of Rome, and the future state of religion. The author divided the world into *three ages*, agreeing with the three dispensations of religion that were to succeed each other. The *two imperfect ages*,—by which he understood the age of the Old Testament, which was that of the Father, and the age of the New, which was under the administration of the Son,—were, according to his predictions, now past; and the *third* age, or that of the Holy Ghost, was at hand, in which *a new and more perfect Gospel* should be promulgated by a set of poor and austere ministers, whom God would raise up and employ for that purpose. The title of this production was taken from Re-

* Usher's Answer to a Challenge made by a Jesuit in Ireland, p. 367. Lond. 1686, 4to., where he refers to *Bonavent. Opera.*, tom. vi. Rom. 1588.

† Cavei Hist. Lit., sæc. xiii, pp. 728–730. Butler's Lives, vol. vii, p. 166, *note*.

‡ Usher's Answer to a Challenge, &c., p. 367.

velation xiv, 6, and was divided into three books; the first of which was entitled *Liber Concordiæ Veritatis*, that is, the "Book of the Harmony of Truth;" the second, *Apocalypsis Nova*, or the "New Revelation;" and the third, *Psalterium decem Chordarum*, or the "Ten-stringed Harp." The Franciscans applied the predictions to themselves, and to the austere rule of discipline established by their founder St. Francis, who, they maintained, was the angel whom St. John saw flying in the midst of heaven; and that it was he who delivered to mankind the true gospel.*

The Introduction to the Everlasting Gospel was the production of a Franciscan friar, and was evidently written by its fanatical author to delude the multitude into a high notion of the sanctity of the Mendicant orders, and to extend and establish their authority among the people. In this impious work it was maintained,

1. "That the *Everlasting Gospel* [viz. of Joachim] excelled the doctrine of Christ, and the Old and New Testaments."

2. "That the gospel of Christ was not the gospel of the kingdom, and that the church could not be built up by it."

3. "That the New Testament was to be done away with, like that of the Old."

4. "That the New Testament would cease to be of force after the year 1260."

5. "That another gospel would succeed the gospel of Christ; and another priesthood the priesthood of Christ."

6. "That none were suited to the instruction of men in spiritual and eternal things, but those who walked barefoot, that is, the Mendicant orders."†

A number of other detestable opinions, extracted from these works, are given by the learned Usher, in his work entitled *Gravissimæ Quæstionis, de Christianarum Ecclesiarum, in Occidentibus præsertim partibus, ab successione et statu, historica explicatio.* Lond, 1613, 4to.

When the Introduction to the Everlasting Gospel was published at Paris, in 1254, it excited the most lively feelings of horror and indignation, and the Roman pontiff, Alexander IV., was obliged to suppress it in the year 1255. But willing to spare the reputation of the Mendicants, he ordered it to be burnt in *secret*. The university of Paris, dissatisfied with such gentle and timorous proceedings, insisted upon the *public* condemnation of the book, and

* Mosheim's Eccl. Hist., vol. iii, p. 209–211.

† Usserius, De Christianarum Ecclesiarum, &c., pp. 277–280.

1

Alexander, at length, was reluctantly constrained to commit the Franciscan's performance publicly to the flames.*

Such were the occurrences of the Western churches in relation to the sacred Scriptures, and the circulation of them among the people; nor do we find a more general and effective promotion of Biblical knowledge in the churches of the East. Scanty and unsatisfactory is all the information that can be gleaned on this important and interesting subject. It is, however, certain that a number of transcriptions were made of the Greek Testament, and of the Psalms. Proofs of this exist in the various MSS. of this century, brought from mount Athos, and other places in the East, and still preserved in the different libraries of Europe.†

Toward the close of the thirteenth century, a translation was made of the New Testament, and of the Psalms of David, into the TARTAR language, by Johannes a Monte Corvino, in order to accelerate the propagation of the gospel among the dark and idolatrous nations to whom he had been sent as a missionary in 1288 by Pope Nicholas IV. He was originally an Italian friar, and derived his name from Mons Corvinus, where he was born in 1237. After having been employed in the mission for many years, he was appointed archbishop of Cambalu, the same with Pekin, at that time the celebrated metropolis of Cathay, now one of the capital cities of the Chinese empire; erected into an archbishopric, and conferred upon our laborious missionary, by Clement VII. in 1307; an honour which he enjoyed till his decease in A.D 1330.‡

The following letter, addressed by this zealous missionary to certain dignitaries of his church, is curious and interesting:—

"I, brother JOHN DE MONTE CORVINO, of the order of Friars Minors, left Tauris, a city of Persia, in the year 1291, and came into India, and remained in this country, at the church of St. Thomas the Apostle, thirteen months, and baptized about one hundred persons in divers places; here also Nicholas de Pistoris, of the order of Friars Preachers, and the companion of my life, died, and was buried in the church. From thence I came into Cathay, the kingdom of the emperor of the Tartars, who is called the great khan, and whom I invited to the faith of our Lord Jesus Christ, by the letters from the lord pope; but he was too obstinately at-

* Mosheim's Eccles. Hist., *ut sup.*

† Marsh's Michaelis, vol. ii, part i, and ii, ch. viii, sec. 6, *passim.*

‡ Mosheim's Ecclesiastical History, vol. iii, pp. 133, 299. Mosheimii Hist. Tartar Eccles., pp. 76–78, 97, 98, 111.

tached to idolatry, yet he conferred many benefits on the Christians, and I remained with him two years."

"In those parts, certain Nestorians, assuming the title of Christians, but differing in many things from the religion of Christ, had established themselves so firmly, that they permitted no Christian to practise ceremonies differing from theirs; nor to have ever so small an oratory; nor to promulgate any other doctrine than Nestorianism. And, forasmuch as no apostle, nor disciple of the apostles, ever visited these lands, the before-mentioned Nestorians, and others whom they had corrupted by money, raised violent persecutions against me, asserting, that I was not sent by the lord pope, but was a great spy, and one who made men mad; and after some time produced false witnesses in another way, saying, that an ambassador had been sent with great treasures to the emperor, whom I had robbed and murdered in India; and this machination continued for about five years, so that I was frequently dragged to judgment, with the imputation of murder. At length, by the will of God, through the confession of a certain person, the emperor was convinced of my innocence, and of the malice of my enemies, whom, with their wives and children, he sent into exile. In this foreign land I remained eleven years, without a companion, until brother Arnold, a German, from the province of Cologne, came to me, now more than a year ago. I have built a church in Cambalu, the chief residence of the sovereign, which I finished six years ago; and have made a belfry, in which I have placed three bells. I have also baptized, as I suppose, up to this time, about six thousand persons; and but for the before-mentioned accusations, I should have baptized thirty thousand; and I am still often baptizing. I have, besides, successively purchased one hundred and fifty boys, the children of pagans, from seven to eleven years old, who were at the time completely ignorant, having never been taught; these I have baptized, and taught them our ritual in Greek and Latin letters; and have transcribed Psalters for them, with thirty hymn-books, and two breviaries; with which, eleven boys now know our office, and hold *chorus* and *hebdomary*, as is done in the convents, whether I am present or not; many of them also copy Psalters, and other useful works: the emperor delights much in their singing. I ring the bells at all the [stated] hours, and perform divine service with the congregation of babes and sucklings; and we sing *secundum usum*, not having an office with the notes."

"A certain king, in this quarter, named George, of the sect of the Nestorians, a kinsman of the great king called *Prester John* of India, attached himself to me the first year I came, and being converted by me to the Catholic faith, entered the orders of the Friars Minors, and when I celebrated [divine service] ministered to me, clothed in the vestments. Some of the other Nestorians accused him of apostacy; but, notwithstanding, he brought over a great part of his people to the true Catholic faith, and erected a beautiful church, with royal magnificence, to the honour of our God, of the Holy Trinity, and of the lord pope, calling it the *Roman Church.* Six years ago this king George went to the Lord, leaving behind him an infant son and heir, who is now nine years old. The brethren of king George, however, adhering steadily to the errors of the Nestorians, after the death of the king subverted all those whom he had converted, by inducing them to return to their former schism. As I was alone, and could not quit the emperor the khan, I was unable to go to that church, which was distant twenty days' journey; yet, if some good coadjutors and coworkers should come, I hope in God that all might be reclaimed; for I still have the privilege granted by the deceased king George."

"I again say, that had it not been for the before-mentioned infamous calumnies, great fruit might have followed. If there had been two or three companions with me, to assist me, perhaps the emperor the khan might have been baptized. I request, therefore, that such brethren may come, if any be willing, who will studiously endeavour to set examples, and not to 'enlarge the borders of their garments.' Of the route, I may notice, that the shorter and safer way is through the country of the Goths, the governors of the Tartars of the north, by which they might come, with guides, in five or six months; the other way is longer, and more dangerous, including two voyages, the first as far as between Acho and the province of Provence, the second as far as between Acho and Angelia; and it may happen that the journey this way will scarcely be completed in two years, the former way having been for a long time rendered impassable by the wars. On this account I have not for twelve years received any news respecting the court of Rome, or our order, or the state of the West. Two years since a certain Lombard physician came, who spread incredible and blasphemous reports in these parts relative to the court of Rome and our order, which makes me anxious to know the truth."

"I request you, brethren, to whom this epistle may come, to take care that its contents be known to the lord pope, the cardinals, and the procurator of our order, at the court of Rome. I entreat the general of our order for an antiphonar, a legendary, a graduale, and a Psalter, with notes for a copy, since I have only a portable breviary with brief lessons, and a small missal. If I obtain a copy, the before-mentioned boys will transcribe others. I am now engaged in building another church, to separate the youths into several places. I am now old, and gray-headed, more by labour and trouble than by age, being only fifty-eight. I have completely learned the Tartar language and letters, as commonly used by the Tartars, and have translated into their tongue and letters *the whole* NEW TESTAMENT and PSALTER, which I have caused to be written in their most beautiful characters; and I write, and read, and preach, in that language, openly and clearly, the testimony of the law of Christ. I had also agreed with the aforesaid king George, if he had lived, to translate the whole Latin office, that it might be sung through the whole of his dominions; and as long as he lived, I celebrated mass in his church according to the Latin ritual, reading in that language, as well the words of the canon as of the preface. The son of the said king is called JOHN, after my name, and I hope in God he will imitate the steps of his father. Moreover, from what I hear and see, I believe there is no king nor prince in the world that can be equalled to the lord khan for extent of territory, multitude of people, and abundance of riches."

"Given in the city of Cambalu, in the kingdom of Cathay, January the 8th, in the year of our Lord 1305."*

An interesting relation of the discovery of the existence of a TARTAR version of the OLD TESTAMENT, among the Karaite Jews, by the Rev. R. Pinkerton, at Baktcheserai or Bahchisaray, in 1816, will be found in Pinkerton's Letters, &c. It is there said to have been made several centuries ago by the forefathers of the present Karaite Jews. Of this copy Dr. Pinkerton writes: "We returned to Bahchisaray by the same way we went; and it was not long before Aaron followed, and presented me with a most beautiful copy of *all the canonical books of the Old Testament* in the *Tartar* language, written on fine vellum paper, in the Hebrew character, comprised in four volumes quarto, for which I paid him two hundred rubles. I have seldom met with a more beautiful manuscript. It is elegantly bound in red goat's leather, and ornamented with gold. I shall endeavour to get it sent off in safety to St. Petersburgh,† where, with the assistance of one or two learned Tartars,

* Mosheimii Hist. Tartar. Eccles., p. 114, No. 33. Helmstad. 1731, 4to.

† This precious MS. arrived safely at St. Petersburgh, and a volume of it was sent

under my own direction, should it please God to spare me to return, it may be fairly written out in the character, and carefully revised and put to the press, with the translation of the New Testament made by the missionaries in Karass. The peculiar principles of the Karaites, in rejecting the Talmud, and all the traditionary fables of the Jews, and their strict adherence to the sacred text of Scripture alone, give me great reason to hope that we shall find this, their Tartar translation from the Hebrew, to be correct."*

Of the old Tartar translation, by Johannes a Monte Corvino, but little is known, as no copies of it are in any of the public libraries of Europe; nor, so far as can be ascertained, do any traces of it remain in Tartary or China.

In Armenia several important events took place intimately connected with Biblical literature. The churches of the lesser Armenia, or Cilicia, submitted to the authority of the pope; and Haitho, or, as he is more properly called, Hethom, who reigned from A. D. 1224 to 1270, became a Franciscan friar, a short time before his death. This prince was not only attached to the Church of Rome, but likewise acquainted with the Latin language; and published a new edition, or revision of the *Armenian* Bible, to which he added all the prefaces of Jerome. He has been charged with altering or corrupting his edition from the Vulgate, and inserting 1 John v, 7, from the Latin, because thirty-seven years after his death this passage was quoted at a council held at Sis, in Armenia, and is to be found in other Armenian records, though it is asserted the passage was not in the old Armenian MSS. But whether we allow the authenticity of the verse or not, Haitho is cleared from the charge of wilful corruption of the sacred text, by the acknowledged fact, that this verse is not to be found in any modern Armenian MS. of the New Testament.†

Gregorius Bar Hebraeus, or Abul-Farai, more generally called Abulpharagius, was also a native of Armenia. He was born in 1226, at Malatia, a city near the source of the river Eu

to the Scotch missionaries in Astrachan, who, after having examined it, pronounced it to be in a very different dialect from that spoken by the Nogay, Kasan, and Crimea Tartars, but regarded it as what would be of great use to them in a translation of the Old Testament into the same Tartar dialect in which the New Testament already exists. See *Prince Galitzin's Letter to Lord Teignmouth.*

* Extracts of Letters from the Rev. R. Pinkerton, on his Tour in Russia, &c., to promote the object of the British and Foreign Bible Society, pp. 18–20. Lond. 1817, 8vo. See also Thirteenth Report of British and Foreign Bible Society, pp. 74–76.

† Marsh's Michaelis, vol. ii, pt. i, p. 102; pt. ii, p. 616.

phrates. His father, whose name was Aaron, was a physician, of eminence in his profession. In his youth he devoted himself with ardour to the study of philosophy and theology; and acquired an intimate knowledge of the Greek, and Syriac, and Arabic languages. Under the instructions of his father, and other celebrated physicians, he pursued the study of medicine, and was famed for his excellence in that art. In the year 1243 Armenia was invaded by the Tartars, when he and his father were obliged to flee from Malatia, to avoid the fury of the invaders. The following year he went to Antioch, and retiring to a cave near the city, adopted the life of an anchoret. From Antioch he removed to Tripoli, or Tripolis, in Syria. In his twentieth year, Ignatius, the patriarch of the Jacobites, ordained him bishop of Guba; and the following year translated him to Lacabena. The patriarch Dionysius, whose cause he had espoused and defended against his opponent Johannes Bar Maadan, afterward raised him to the see of Aleppo; and the universal suffrage of the bishops called him in 1264 to be mafrejan or primate of the East, a dignity which he retained till his decease in 1286.*

The memory of this great man was honoured with the highest encomiums both by Christians and Mohammedans, who called him the Prince of Doctors, the most Excellent of the Excellent, the Model of his times, and the Glory and Phœnix of the age.† A list of his numerous works is given by Asseman, in the *Bibliotheca Orientalis*, tom. ii, the most important of which are his History of Dynasties, or Abridgment of Universal History, and *Horreum Mysteriorum*, or Commentaries on the Scriptures.

The History of the Dynasties, or Abridgment of Universal History, is a compendium of the general history of the world, from the creation to his own time. It is divided into ten dynasties or governments. The first comprehends the history of the ancient patriarchs, from Adam to Moses; the second, that of Joshua and the judges of Israel; the third includes the reigns of the kings of Israel; the fourth, the history of the Chaldeans; the fifth, of the Magi, or Persians; the sixth, of the idolatrous Greeks; the seventh, of the Franks, or Romans; the eighth, of the Greeks under Christian emperors; the ninth, of the Saracens; and the tenth, of the Mogul Tartars. The two last dynasties are esteemed the most correct, and by far the most interesting in point of information. In 1650, the very learned Dr. Edward Pocock published the intro-

* Assemani Biblioth. Orientalis, tom. ii, pp. 244–321. Romæ, 1728, fol.

† Pocockii Specimen Hist. Arab. in Præfat. Oxon, 1650, 4to.

duction to the ninth dynasty, with a Latin translation, under the title of *Specimen Historiæ Arabum, sive Gregorii Abul Farajii Malatiensis de Origine et Moribus Arabum succincta Narratio.* The Arabic text and translation extend only to thirty pages, but are rendered invaluable by the editor's notes, from more than one hundred MSS., forming by far the largest portion of the volume, which consists of three hundred and ninety pages, besides the preface. The extract from Abulpharagius contains a compendious account of the Saracens, or Arabians, prior to the time of Mohammed; of the impostor himself; of the religion which he introduced; and of the several sects into which his followers were divided. The notes are a collection of curious and important extracts from Arabian authors, and original discussions relative to Mohammed, and to the origin, manners, literature, and religion of the Arabians; in which the learned editor has introduced a description of Mecca; accounts of the ancient Zabii, worshippers of the heavenly bodies; and of the eastern Magi; a brief discourse from the works of an Arabian physician, respecting the influence of different kinds of food upon the temper and disposition; and critical remarks on several other interesting topics. The celebrated Orientalist, Simon Ockley, calls it "a golden work," and pronounces it to be a "key to all other Arabian authors."* Dr. Pocock also published the entire History of the Dynasties, with a Latin translation, in 1663, 4to., which he dedicated to King Charles II.

The *Horreum Mysteriorum*, or Storehouse of Mysteries, is a critical and expository edition of the Syriac Scriptures, in which the editor corrects the punctuation of the text; gives the various readings of an extensive collation of MSS. and versions; adduces the critical remarks of other writers; and accompanies the whole with brief explanatory scholia, or notes; thus emulating the labours of Jacob of Edessa, and Dionysius Barsalibæus, the former of whom was bishop of Edessa from 677 to 708, and wrote Remarks on the Book of Genesis; and the latter, bishop of Amida, from 1166 to 1171, and revised and published a new edition of the Philoxenian Syriac version of the New Testament.

The order in which Abulpharagius places and comments on the sacred books, is, first the Pentateuch, then the Books of Joshua and Judges, the First and Second of Samuel, the Psalms, the First and Second of Kings, Proverbs, Ecclesiasticus, Ecclesiastes, Song of Solomon, Wisdom, Ruth, the story of Susannah, Job, Isaiah, the Twelve Minor Prophets, Jeremiah with the Lamentations,

* Ockleii Introductio ad Linguas Orientales, p. 147. Lond., 8vo.

Ezekiel, Daniel, with the story of Bel and the Dragon. The four Gospels, the Acts of the Apostles, the Epistles of James, and Peter, and John; and lastly, the fourteen Epistles of St. Paul. To the Notes, or Commentary, are added several chronological and other tables; the Canons of Eusebius; the Genealogy of Christ; the Names and Sufferings of the Apostles; and the Names of the Seventy Disciples of our Lord.

The extensive erudition, and critical research of the author, are discoverable in the numerous versions and writers to which he has had recourse in the prosecution of his work. Among the copies of the Scriptures, are the Hebrew and Greek Texts of the Old and New Testaments; the Septuagint version; the Samaritan, Armenian, and Egyptian, or Coptic versions; the *Pentapla*, and *Hexapla* of Origen; the versions of Symmachus, Aquila, and Theodotion; and besides the Philoxenian version of the Syriac, which he closely follows, the Heraclean and Karkufite Syriac versions, the former of which received its denomination from Thomas of Harkel, (see p. 164,) and the latter from its being adopted by the Nestorian Christians who inhabited the mountains of Assyria, the Syriac term Karkufe meaning the head or the top of a mountain. Among the authors are Basil, Athanasius, Chrysostom, Nazianzen, Cyril of Alexandria, Epiphanius, Ephrem, Jacob of Edessa, Pope Julius, Severus of Antioch, Philoxenus, bishop of Hierapolis, Moses Bar-Cepha, Hippolytus, Theodore of Mopsuestia, or Mamestra, and several others.

The whole of this erudite work has never been printed; Asseman, in his *Bibliotheca Orientalis*, tom. ii, and Dudley Loftus, in the London Polyglott, tom. vi,* have made extracts from it; those in the Polyglott are from the notes on the Psalms, and were taken from a thick quarto MS. copy in the possession of Archbishop Usher.†

* The learned translator of Michaelis's Introduction to the New Testament, to whom Biblical scholars are so greatly indebted, and to whose valuable publications I have had frequent occasion to refer, is therefore mistaken, when he asserts, "the only few extracts which we have of this celebrated, and as is said, valuable work, are those which have been given by Asseman, in his Bibliotheca Orientalis." As he is also, when he supposes there was no edition of the Syriac version of the Revelation of St. John, published by De Dieu, 1627. That edition now lies before me. It is a beautiful thin quarto, printed by Elzevir, with an ornamented title-page, cut in wood. The Syriac text is placed in parallel columns, in Syriac and Hebrew characters; and underneath, in a similar manner, the Greek text and Latin translation: these are followed by forty-six pages of notes, forming, in the whole, a volume of two hundred and eleven pages, exclusive of the dedication and preface. See *Marsh's Michaelis*, vol. ii, pt. ii, pp. 581, 543.

† Assemani Biblioth. Orient., tom. ii, pp. 282, 283.

CHAPTER XII.

FOURTEENTH CENTURY.

State of Society—Council of Vienne—Libraries—French Version—Raoul de Presles—Jean de Vignay—Mendicant Friars—Nicholas de Lyra—Petrus Berchorius—Petrarch—Germany—Swedish Version—St. Bridget—Polish Version—Hedwige—Danish Version—Learned Greeks—Persian Gospels—Irish New Testament—Richard Fitzralph—Richard de Bury—Scripture Paintings—Old English Versions—John de Trevisa—Wicliff.

THE state of society at the commencement of the FOURTEENTH century was peculiarly unfavourable to the cultivation of sacred literature and the study of the Scriptures. Pride and luxury reigned among all orders of the clergy, and induced universal ignorance and profligacy. Their vices were the subject of satire in every country in Europe. In Italy, Petrarch exposed the depravity of the papal court; and in England, Chaucer satirised, with equal severity, the corruptions of both laity and clergy. Of Avignon, the residence of the Roman pontiff, Petrarch writes in an epistle to a friend, "In this city there is no piety, no reverence or fear of God, no faith or charity, nothing that is holy, just, equitable, or humane. Why should I speak of truth, where not only the houses, palaces, courts, churches, and the thrones of popes and cardinals, but the very earth and air, seem to teem with lies? A future state, heaven, hell, and judgment, are openly turned into ridicule, as childish fables. Good men have of late been treated with so much contempt and scorn, that there is not one left among them to be an object of their laughter."*

The poems of Chaucer abound with invectives against the vices of the clergy, particularly the Plowman's Tale, in which he charges them with ignorance, cruelty, covetousness, simony, vanity, pride, ambition, drunkenness, gluttony, and lewdness: an example or two will sufficiently discover the tenor of the poem.

"Such as can nat ysay ther crede,
With prayer shul be made prelates;
Nother canne thei the gospell rede,
Such shul now weldin hie estates."
* * * * * * *
"They use horedome and harlottrie,
And covetise, and pompe, and pride,

* Henry's Hist. of Great Britain, vol. viii, p. 361.

And slothe, and wrathe, and eke envie,
And sewine sinne by every side.
* * * * * *
"As Goddes godenes no man tell might,
Ne write, ne speke, ne think in thought,
So ther falshed, and ther unright,
Maie no man tell that ere God wrought."*

Wicliff, who wrote about the same time, says there were "many unable curates that kunnen not the Ten Commandments, ne read their Sauter, ne understond a verse of it."† Edward III., king of England, addressed a strong remonstrance to the pope against his encroachments, in which he represented that "the encouragements of religion were bestowed upon unqualified, mercenary foreigners, who neither resided in the country nor understood its language; by which means the ends of the priesthood were not answered, his own subjects were discouraged from prosecuting their studies, the treasures of the kingdom were carried off by strangers, and the jurisdiction of its courts baffled by constant appeals to a foreign authority," &c.‡ Lewis Beaumont, bishop of Durham, was one instance, among many, of the necessity of Edward's remonstrance. He was a very lame and illiterate French nobleman, so incapable of reading and spelling that he could not, although he had studied them, read over the bulls announced to the people at his consecration. At the word "*metropoliticæ*," he paused, tried in vain to repeat it, and at last said, "*Soit pour dit!*—Suppose that said!" Then he came to "*In Ænigmate;*" this puzzled him again: "*Par St. Louis*," said he, "*il n'est pas courtois qui a escrit cette parole ici*—By St. Louis! it could be no gentleman who wrote this stuff."§

At this period robbery was the reigning vice in all the nations of Europe; and the robbers, protected by the barons, who shared their booty, plundered all who came in their way, without distinction. A troop of these plunderers, commanded by Gilbert Middleton and Walter Selby, assaulted two cardinals, who were escorted by our illiterate prelate and his brother Lord Beaumont, attended by a numerous retinue of gentlemen and servants, near Darlington. The cardinals they robbed of their money and effects, and then permitted them to proceed on their journey; but carried the bishop and his brother, the one to the castle of Morpeth, and the other to the castle of Mitford, and detained them till they had paid certain

* Chaucer's Works, by Urry, pp. 179–189, folio.
† Lewis's Hist. of the Life, &c., of John Wicliff, D. D., p. 38.
‡ Henry's Hist. of Great Britain, vol. viii, p. 55.
§ Andrews' Hist. of Great Britain, vol. i, p. 425. London, 1794, 4to.

sums as ransoms. The same unfortunate prelate had his palace afterward plundered even to the bare walls, by Sir Joselin Deinville.*

Injurious as such a state of society must necessarily have been to the promotion of religion and learning, various instances occurred which proved that, in an age of strife, and ignorance, and depravity, there were, nevertheless, some who duly appreciated the sacred writings, and were convinced of the advantages resulting from the study of the Oriental languages. In 1311 the council of Vienne passed a decree, directing that the Hebrew, Chaldee, and Arabic languages, together with the Greek tongue, should be taught in the college of Rome, and in the universities of Paris, Oxford, Bologna, and Salamanca. Schools or academies were also erected at Cologne, Orleans, Cahors, Perusia, Florence, and Pisa; and opulent persons founded and amply endowed particular colleges in the public universities, in which, besides the monks, young men of narrow circumstances were educated in all the branches of literature. Libraries were also collected, some of which were successively augmented by the generous patrons of literature, and became eminent for the number and value of the books which they contained.† Sir Richard Whittington built the library of the Gray Friars, now called Christ's Hospital, in London, which was one hundred and twenty-nine feet long and twelve broad, (Pennant says thirty-one,) with twenty-eight desks and eight double settles of wainscot, and was also ceiled with wainscot. In three years it was filled with books to the value of £556, of which Sir Richard contributed £400, and Dr. Thomas Winchelsey, a friar, supplied the rest. About the year 1430, one hundred marks were paid for transcribing Nicholas de Lyra's Commentary on the Bible, in two volumes, to be chained in this library. Leland (*Script. Brit.*, p. 441, et *Collectan.*, iii, p. 52) relates that Thomas Walden, a learned Carmelite friar, who went by order of Henry V. to the council of Constance, and died approved in 1430, bequeathed to the same library as many MSS. of authors, written in capital Roman characters, as were then estimated at more than two thousand pieces of gold; and adds, that this library, even in his time, exceeded all others in London, for multitude of books and antiquity of copies.‡

* Henry's Hist. of Great Britain, vol. viii, p. 386. Andrews' Hist. of Great Britain, *ut sup.*

† Fabricy, Titres Primitifs, tom. ii, p. 150. Mosheim's Eccles. Hist., vol. iii, p. 305.

‡ Warton's Hist. of English Poetry, vol. i, pp. 291, 292. Pennant's Account of London, p. 198. London, 1791, 4to.

About the year 1320, Thomas Cobham, bishop of Worcester, began to make preparations for a library at Oxford, but dying soon after, little progress was made in the work until 1367, when his books were deposited in it, and the scholars permitted to consult them on certain conditions. A dispute arising between the university and Oriel College, it was not finally completed till about the year 1411. It appears to have been the first public library in that university. It was at first called Cobham's library, but in 1480 the books were added to Duke Humphrey's collection,* of which some account will be found in the succeeding chapter.

Another public library was established at Oxford, in Durham (now Trinity) College, by Richard of Bury, or Richard Aungerville, bishop of Durham, in the time of Edward III., who bequeathed his books to the students of this college. According to the practice of those times, these books were preserved in chests, till the year 1370, when Thomas Hatfield, who succeeded Richard of Bury in the see of Durham, built the library.†

In France, Charles V. might justly be considered as the founder of the KING'S LIBRARY, now deemed one of the finest in Europe. This prince, who was fond of reading, and to whom a book was an acceptable present, commenced his library with *twenty volumes*, left him as a royal legacy by his father!‡ These he afterward augmented to *nine hundred*, "a very large number for a time when the typographical art was not invented." They consisted of books of devotion, astrology, physic, law, history, and romance; a very few ancient authors of the classic ages, among which there was not a single copy of Cicero's works; of the Latin poets only Ovid, Lucan, and Boetius. To these were added some French translations of the BIBLE, of Augustine's City of God, of Livy, of Valerius Maximus, &c. Many of the volumes were most superbly illuminated by John of Bruges, the best artist in miniatures of that time. The whole were deposited in three chambers, in one of the towers of the Louvre, from thence called *La Toure de la Libraire*, the Tower of the Library. The rooms designed for their reception were, on this occasion, wainscoted with Irish oak, and ceiled with cypress curiously carved. The windows were of painted

* Chalmer's Hist. of the Colleges, &c., attached to the University of Oxford, vol. ii, p. 458. Oxford, 1810, 8vo.

† Ibid., *ut sup.*

‡ In the British Museum there is a beautiful MS. on vellum of a *French* translation of the *Bible*, which was found in the tent of King John, father of Charles V., after the battle of Poictiers, in which he had been taken prisoner by Edward the Black Prince.—*Warton's History of English Poetry*, vol. iii, p. 204.

glass, fenced with iron bars and copper wire. The English became masters of Paris in 1425, and the duke of Bedford, regent of France, sent into England the principal part of the books, valued at two thousand two hundred and twenty-three livres.* A saying related of Charles deserves to be remembered: some persons having complained of the respect he showed to men of letters, who were then called clerks, he replied, "Clerks cannot be too much cherished; for, so long as we honour learning, this kingdom will continue to prosper; but, when we begin to despise it, the French monarchy will decline."†

A new and more accurate translation of the Bible into French was also undertaken by order of the same prince. The versions prior to that period had generally been made from Comestor's *Historia Scholastica*, the chief of which was by *Guiars des Moulins*, canon, and afterward dean of St. Peter of Air, begun in June, 1291, and completed in February, 1294. King John had also enjoined John de Sy to translate the Scriptures into French, and to add an exposition of them, but he seems to have completed only Isaiah, Jeremiah, and five books of Solomon. Charles, therefore, with that wisdom which characterized his reign, formed the design of a new translation of the sacred Scriptures. Christina de Pisan,‡ a female poet and historian, patronised and pensioned by that prince, informs us that he "was fond of books, and by his liberality procured translations of the best authors into French; especially the Bible, which he caused to be translated in a threefold manner: first the text itself; then the text accompanied with a gloss; and lastly an allegorical exposition."§

This version has frequently been attributed to Nicolas Oresme, bishop of Lisieux, in Normandy, who died in 1382. Francis Grudé, Sieur de la Croix du Maine, is the earliest writer who

* Henault's Chronological Abridgment of the History of France, translated by Nugent, vol. i, *sub ann.* 1380, p. 268. Warton's Hist. of English Poetry, vol. i, diss. 2.

† Henault, *ut sup.*

‡ In the British Museum, among the *Harleian MSS.*, No. 4431, there is a large volume, containing part of the works of this celebrated female. It is a vellum MS., written in a small Gothic letter, in double columns. On the recto of the first leaf, in a large hand, is the following autograph: "Henry, Duke of Newcastle, his booke, 1676." The illuminations are by various hands: a beautiful sketch of a portion of the principal one is copied in Dibdin's Bibliographical Decameron, p. cxxxv, which represents the authoress presenting her book to the queen of France. About the period of the composition of her poems, or *balades*, the duke de Berry gave her not less than two hundred crowns for a set of them. See *Dibdin's Bibliographical Decameron*, vol. i, p. cxxxiv.

§ Le Long, Biblioth. Sacra, tom. i, cap. iv, pp. 321, 324. Paris, folio.

speaks of Oresme as the person deputed by the king of France to translate the Scriptures into the vernacular tongue. In his "Bibliotheque des Auteurs, &c.," printed at Paris in 1584, folio, he affirms, "Il a traduit la Bible de Latin en Francois"—"He translated the Bible out of Latin into French." Le Long has, however, proved that Raoul de Presles, and not N. Oresme, was the author of this translation; and accounts for the error which has been so generally adopted, by supposing that La Croix du Maine misunderstood a passage in the *Recueil General des Rois, et des affaires de France jusqu' à Louis XIII.*, by Jean du Tillet, bishop of Meaux, in which he says, "Nicolas Oresme, a learned man, whose counsel and advice was particularly followed by King Charles V., translated the works of Aristotle and Cicero, and many others, out of Latin into French. For the king greatly loved and admired letters and literary men. He also commanded the holy books of the Bible to be diligently and truly translated," &c. But though Bishop Oresme and the Bible are both mentioned by Du Tillet, he does not speak of Oresme as the translator.*

On the other hand, there is indubitable evidence that Raoul de Presles engaged in a translation of the Scriptures, at the request of the king; since, in a beautiful illuminated copy upon vellum, in folio, of an old French translation, we meet with the following Prologue, or Preface :—

"To the most excellent and mighty prince, Charles V., king of France; I, Raoul de Praelle, your unworthy servant and subject:

"When my most dread and sovereign lord directed me to translate the Bible into French, all that I could do was to deliberate whether I ought to undertake it, or decline it. On the one hand, I considered the greatness of the work, and my own slender ability; and on the other, that there was nothing I either could or ought to refuse you. I, moreover, regarded my age, and my unfortunate disorder, and the different works I had already composed, namely, the Translation and Exposition of St. Augustine's City of God, the book entitled *Compendium Historiale*, another called Musa, and various epistles. But while I debated with myself, I recollected having read, that human nature (like iron, which is valuable when in use, but, if disused, rusts and spoils) sustains less injury in every way by labour than by indolence, I judged it

* Le Long, Biblioth. Sacra, tom. i, cap. iv, p. 320.

better to be exhausted by exercise than consumed by idleness; for, according to the wise man's saying, leisure without letters is death. Let me therefore entreat your majesty graciously to accept my labours. As to the method to be pursued in my translation; where I conceive abridgment is necessary, I shall give the substance of the whole; and where I perceive a repetition of the same thing, as in Chronicles and the Second Book of Esdras, and elsewhere, I shall retrench; I shall also leave out many names of persons and places where they would be unedifying and wearisome to the reader; and where they would scarcely know whether they were proper names of persons, or of their fathers, or ancestors, or of towns or cities; acting in these things according to your command. I intend also to prefix prefaces, explaining what is necessary respecting the design of the books; and summaries at the beginning of the chapters, that the sense of them may be more easily comprehended; and to distinguish what is not in the text by a line drawn underneath; for without explanations the text is in many places exceedingly obscure, particularly to the laity, who are not versed in Holy Scripture. And let nothing that I have undertaken be imputed to pride, but let your command be my apology in all and every thing."

"Finally, I entreat all those who may see this work, when they discover inaccuracies, to bear with my defects; and whatever they find in it that is excellent, to ascribe it to our Lord, from whom cometh every thing that is good; and further, in every thing relative to faith, I submit to what is dictated by the (true) faith and to what is held by our holy-mother church."*

From this very rare translation, Le Long, in his *Bibliotheca Sacra*, has given considerable extracts.† Neither of the two manuscripts from which the extracts are made is perfect; both of them terminating with the Proverbs of Solomon; and the first leaf of the former, which originally belonged to John, duke of Berry, brother to King Charles V., having been torn away, probably for the sake of its ornamental decorations, and the latter being without the Prologue.

Raoul de Presles, the translator, was the illegitimate son of Raoul de Presles, secretary to Philip the Fair, to Louis X. and Philip V., and who founded the college at Paris which bears his name. He embraced the profession of the law, and became celebrated for his various and learned writings. One of his earliest

* Le Long, *ubi sup.* † Ibid., p. 319.

works was that which was denominated *Musa*, written in Latin, and dedicated to Charles V. It is an ingenious fiction, on the means of remedying the disorders of the age. About the year 1369 he composed a "Dissertation on the Oriflame," or Royal Banner of the Kings of France, in their wars against the infidels.* In this discourse the author dwells less upon the ancient banner than upon the necessity of imploring aid from Heaven, when engaged in warfare. About the year 1379 he was employed by the king to translate Augustine's "City of God" into French, and had a considerable pension allowed him for that purpose. This translation he commenced in 1371, and completed, with the addition of a Commentary upon it, in 1375. He also translated into French a book entitled the "Pacific King," supposed to be an historical and political work, probably the same as the *Compendium Historiale*. Another of his works was an abridgment of the *Somnium Viridarii*, or Dream of the Orchard, containing a dispute between the ecclesiastics, the temporalists, and seculars. But his greatest and most important undertaking was the TRANSLATION OF THE HOLY SCRIPTURES out of the Latin into the French, which appeared about A. D. 1377. La Croix du Maine saw a MS. containing De Presles' translations of the City of God, and of the *Compendium Historiale*, in two large volumes, on parchment. The former of these, accompanied with the Commentary upon it, was printed at Abbeville in 1486, in two volumes folio, and again at Paris, in two volumes folio. The Abbeville edition is extremely scarce, and is said to have been the first book printed in that city, though Marchand cites the *Somme Rurale* of Bouthellier, which was printed in the same year, as the first work which proceeded from the press

* The *oriflame* was anciently the chief standard borne by the kings of France in war. Our author thus defines it: "L'oriflambe, c'est à savoir, un glaive (une lance) tout doré, ou est attachée banniere vermeille"—"The oriflame is a gilded lance, to which a vermilion or flame coloured banner is affixed;" hence the appellation *auriflamma*, from whence the corrupted terms *oriflambe, oliflamma*, &c. It was originally the ensign of the abbey of St. Denis, and borne by the counts of Vexin, who held that earldom as a fief of this abbey, with the obligation of leading its vassals to war, and defending its lands and privileges, under the title of advocate. In peaceable times it was placed on the tomb of St. Denis, but when called for, to be borne to battle, it was delivered into the hands of the advocate by the abbot himself, who accompanied the delivery of the standard with certain prayers.

Vexin being in process of time united to the crown, the sovereign became the advocate of St. Denis, the standard was accounted sacred, and borne as the royal banner. The ancient cry of war by the French in battle, *Mont joie St. Denys*, took its rise from this circumstance. See Du Cange, Gloss. Lat., v. *Auriflamma. Advocati Ecclesiarum.*

at Abbeville. La Croix du Maine likewise notices a *MS.* copy of the abridgment of the *Somnium Viridarii*, written on vellum, and preserved in the library of the president Fauchet, at Paris. Of the Translation of the Bible, the indefatigable bibliographer Le Long never had seen more than the two copies from which his extracts are taken.

Raoul de Presles was made attorney-general in 1371, and master of requests, 1373. He died in 1382, aged about sixty-eight years.*

The dissemination of the Scriptures appears to have been a favourite object with Charles V. of France. For before Raoul de Presles was engaged in the new translation of the Bible, many transcripts had been made, by his order, of the version of Guiars des Moulins. Several of these, some of which are richly illuminated and adorned with exquisite miniature paintings, and formerly belonging to the king, and his brother John, duke of Berry, are still preserved in the king's and other libraries of France; among which particular mention is made of a large Bible in two volumes, which Charles used constantly to carry with him.† Molinæus, or, according to his French name, Charles du Moulin, in his work on the Origin and Progress of the French Monarchy, says, "He caused the Bible to be translated into French, and not only into the dialect of Paris, but also into the dialects of Picardy, Normandy, and the other provinces of the kingdom, that every one might have the Scriptures in his maternal language; many of which old translations are still extant, with the inscription, '*By the command of Charles the Fifth.*'" Anthony Du Verdiers says the same, and adds, "I possess one of these copies, written on parchment, in the dialect of Picardy."‡ It is probable that most of these translations, made by the king's order, were corrected copies of the version by Guiars des Moulins, since none appear in the provincial dialects, in the list of MSS. given by Le Long, ex cept those of that version. In the Cottonian library, in the British Museum, among other old French MS. copies of the whole or parts of the Scriptures, is one of an uncertain date, with the title, "L'Evangel translaté de Latine en franceys, in usum Laïcorum"—"The Gospel translated from the Latin into French, for the use of the laity."§

* R. de Juvigny, Les Bibliotheques Francoises de la Croix du Maine, et de Du Verdier, &c., tom. ii, pp. 347–350. Paris, 1772, 4to.

† Le Long, *ut sup.* ‡ Usserii Hist. Dogmat., p. 158. Le Long, *ut sup.*

§ Le Long, vol. i, p. 318.

An earlier translation than that of Raoul de Presles had been made of the Gospels and Epistles, contained in the Missal, by Jean de Vignay, or Du Vignes, at the request of Jane of Burgundy, queen of King Philip of France.*

Jean de Vignay, or Du Vignes, who flourished about A. D. 1306, was a hospitaller of St. James of Haut Pas, and the translator, as has been already noticed, of De Voragine's Golden Legend, and De Riga's *Speculum Ecclesiæ*. There is also a translation by him of The Game of Chess moralized.

Queen Jane also ordered several of the early Latin Christian writers to be turned into French, and for this purpose commissioned the archbishop of Rouen to undertake the task. But finding that this dignitary did not understand Latin, she employed a Mendicant friar to accomplish her design; for at this period the Mendicant orders had risen to considerable celebrity, by their learning and diligence.†

The Mendicants owed their rise, about the beginning of the thirteenth century, to the luxury and indolence of the monastic orders, which rendered it necessary to adopt measures for remedying the disorders created by their dissipation and licentiousness. For this purpose a new order of religious fraternity was introduced into the church, the members of which, being destitute of fixed possessions, might restore respect to the monastic institution, and recover the honour of the church, by the severity of their manners, a professed contempt of riches, and an unwearied perseverance in the duties of preaching and prayer.

The four orders of Mendicant or Begging Friars, established by a decree of the second council of Lyons, in 1274, were the Dominicans, Franciscans, Carmelites, and Augustines, or Austins. The Franciscans were often styled Friars Minors, or Minorites, and Gray Friars; the Dominicans were generally termed Friars Preachers, and sometimes Black Friars; the Carmelites bore the name of White Friars; and the Austins, of Gray Friars. The Dominicans and Franciscans were the most eminent. The popes, among other immunities, allowed them the liberty of travelling wherever they pleased, of conversing with persons of all ranks, of instructing youth and the people in general, and of hearing confessions without reserve or restriction: and as on these occasions, which gave them opportunities of appearing in public and conspicuous situations, they exhibited more striking marks of gravity and sanctity

* Rigoly de Juvigny, Les Bibliotheques Francoises, tom. i, pp. 605, 606.

† Warton's Hist. of English Poetry, vol. ii, p. 111.

than were observable in the deportment and conduct of the members of other monasteries, they were regarded with the highest esteem and veneration through all the countries of Europe.

In the mean time they acquired the most extensive influence, by the extraordinary assiduity and success with which they cultivated the various branches of literature then pursued. Most of the theological professors in the university of Naples, founded in 1222, were chosen from among them. They were the principal teachers of theology at Paris; and at Oxford and Cambridge, respectively, all the four orders had flourishing monasteries. The most learned scholars in the university of Oxford, at the close of the thirteenth century, were Franciscan friars; and, long after that period, the Franciscans appear to have been the sole support and ornament of that university. Their diligence in collecting books was proverbial; and every Mendicant convent was furnished with what was considered as a great and noble library, ("grandis et nobilis libraria.") They were the revivers of the Aristotelian philosophy, and obtained the merit of having opened a new system of science, which too soon degenerated into mere scholastic disputes and unintelligible jargon. The Dominicans of Spain applied themselves to the study of the Oriental languages and rabbinical literature, and were employed by the kings of Spain in the instruction and conversion of the numerous Jews and Saracens who resided in their dominions. To literary pursuits they joined the arts of popular entertainment, and were probably the only religious orders in England who acted plays. The Creation of the World, annually performed by the Gray Friars at Coventry, is still extant. Gualvanei de la Flamma, who flourished about the year 1340, has the following curious passage in his Chronicle of the Vicecomites of Milan. "In the year 1336," says he, "on the Feast of Epiphany, the first feast of the three kings was celebrated at Milan, by the convent of the Friars Preachers. The three kings appeared crowned, on three great horses, richly habited, surrounded by pages, body guards, and an innumerable retinue. A golden star was exhibited in the sky, going before them. They proceeded to the pillars of St. Lawrence, where King Herod was represented with his scribes and wise men. The three kings ask Herod where Christ should be born; and his wise men, having consulted their books, answer him, at Bethlehem. On which the three kings with their golden crowns, having in their hands golden cups filled with frankincense, myrrh, and gold, the star still going before, marched to the church of St. Eustorgius, with all their attendants, preceded by trumpets and horns, apes, baboons, and a great variety of animals. In the church, on one side of the high altar, there was a manger, with an ox and an ass, and in it the infant Christ in the arms of his mother. Here the three kings offer their gifts, &c. The concourse of the people, of knights, ladies, and ecclesiastics, was such as never before was beheld." During the same century a religious drama was performed at Eisenach, in Germany, so singular in its design, and so fatal in its effects, that it well deserves to be noticed. The Mystery of the Five Wise and Five Foolish Virgins was exhibited before the margrave Frederick. The "wise" virgins were represented as St. Mary, St. Catharine, St. Barbara, St. Dorothy, and St. Margaret. The "foolish" virgins applied to them for oil, which the actor interpreted to mean, prayers offered to them, to intercede with God in behalf of the suppliants, that they might be admitted to the marriage supper, that is, into the kingdom of heaven: but the wise refused to give them of their oil. The foolish virgins were now thrown into an agony of distress; they knocked, they wept, they entreated, but all in vain; oil was denied them, and they were commanded to go and buy for themselves. The scene, and the doctrine it insinuated of the inutility of praying to the saints, alarmed the prince, and threw him into the greatest consternation: "Of what use," exclaimed he, "is our faith, if neither Mary nor the other saints can be obtained to pray for us? To what end so many meritorious actions and good works, that by their intercession we might obtain the grace and favour of God?" His alarm produced apoplexy, which in four days terminated his life. He was buried at Eisenach. (*Adami Vit. Gobelin. Person.*, p. 3.)

The buildings of the Mendicant monasteries, especially in England, were remarkably magnificent. These fraternities being professedly poor, and by their original institution prevented from receiving estates, the munificence of their benefactors was employed in adorning their houses with stately refectories and churches. Persons of the highest rank bequeathed their bodies to be buried in the friary churches, which were esteemed more sacred than others, and were consequently filled with sumptuous shrines and superb monuments. In the noble church of the Gray Friars in London, finished in the year 1325, but long since destroyed, four queens, besides upward of six hundred persons of quality, were buried, whose beautiful tombs remained till the dissolution. These interments imported considerable sums of money into the Mendicant societies, so that it is not improbable but that they derived more benefit from casual charity than they would have gained from a regular endowment. The Franciscans indeed enjoyed from the popes the privilege of distributing indulgences, which produced a valuable indemnification for their voluntary poverty.

For the space of nearly three centuries, two of these Mendicant institutions, the Dominicans and Franciscans, appear to have governed the European church and state with an absolute and universal sway;—during that period, filling the most eminent ecclesiastical and civil stations, teaching in the universities with an authority which silenced all opposition, and maintaining the disputed prerogative of the Roman pontiff against the united influence of prelates and kings, with a vigour only to be paralleled by its success, and being, before the Reformation, exactly what the Jesuits have been since.*

At the time, therefore, when Queen Jane of France employed a Mendicant friar to execute the translations of certain Christian writers, that order ranked high in literary attainments, and produced, in different countries of Europe, learned men whose writings acquired them a just celebrity. This was Petrus de Bruniquello, bishop of Civita Nuova, an Austin friar, and a native of France, who wrote a work in which all the histories of the Old and New Testaments were reduced to alphabetical order; and compiled a commentary on the Old Testament.† NICHOLAS DE LYRA also, who illustrated this period by his learning and writings, particularly claims our regard. He was born of Jewish parents, at Lyre, a town in Normandy, in the diocess of Evreux. After having been instructed in the Hebrew tongue, and in rabbinical learning, he embraced Christianity, entered among the Franciscans at Verneuil, and afterward studied at Paris, where he obtained the degree of doctor, and taught in the university with great credit. By his merit he rose to the highest offices in his order, and gained the esteem of the great. Queen Jane, wife of Philip of France, appointed him one of her executors, in 1325. He died at a very advanced age, October 23d, 1340.‡

He is particularly celebrated for his Latin *Postillæ*, or brief comments on the whole Bible, which are allowed to be very judi-

* See Warton's Hist. of English Poetry, vol. i, pp. 288–294, from which the above account of the Mendicants is principally extracted.

† Le Long, Biblioth. Sacra, tom. ii, p. 900.

‡ Jewish Repository, vol. iii, p. 41. London, 1815, 8vo. Simon, Lettres Choisies, tom. iv, p. 213. De Juvigny, tom. v, p. 128.

cious. The following is the judgment of a learned foreign critic: "The commentaries of De Lyra not only manifest industry, but display considerable erudition, and deservedly place their author in the first rank of the Biblical expositors of his day. They discover the writer to be skilled in the Hebrew tongue, and to be well acquainted with rabbinical writings; but his knowledge of the Greek not being so extensive as that of the Hebrew, his commentary on the New Testament does not equal that on the Old, in felicity and accuracy. Among the Jewish writers, he generally follows R. Solomon Jarchi, and frequently applauds him in his notes. In explaining the literal sense of the Holy Scriptures, he excelled most of his contemporaries. On those passages of the New Testament which derive illustration from Jewish antiquities, he has thrown considerable light. Unshackled by the authority of the fathers, he thought for himself, as his works sufficiently discover; though he was not without defects, for he is sometimes inaccurate in what he attributes to the Jews, and sometimes rashly and incorrectly adopts the Aristotelian philosophy."*

The Notes of De Lyra were appended to an edition of the Latin Vulgate, printed at Rome, in 1472, in seven volumes folio, and were the first comment ever *printed*. They were also often joined to the *Glossæ Ordinariæ*, or a Comment of Walfridus Strabus, or Strabo; the Additions of Paul, bishop of Burgos; and the Replies of Matthias Doringk, or Thoringk, and printed with the Vulgate or Latin Bible. The best edition is that of Antwerp, 1634, six vols. folio. They are incorporated in the *Biblia Maxima*, edited by Jean de la Haye, Paris, 1660, nineteen vols. folio. A French translation was published at Paris, 1511 and 1512, in five vols. folio.

De Lyra was also the author of a Disputation against the Jews, published by Bratheringius, at Frankfort, in 1602; and translated into English from a copy prefixed to the Basil edition (1506, tom. 7) of Lyra's Commentary, by a Fellow of Queen's College, Cambridge, and printed in the Jewish Repository for 1815, Lond. 8vo. Another work written by him, and subjoined to his *Biblia*, is a treatise against a particular rabbi who made use of the New Testament to combat Christianity. Besides which Le Long (tom. 2) mentions a treatise entitled *Liber differentiarum Veteris et Novi Testamenti cum explicatione nominum Hebræorum*, an edition of which was very early printed at Rouen, in 8vo. It appears to have treated of the difference of the various translations from

* Walchius in Le Long, Bib. Sacra, edit. Masch., pt. ii, sec. 3, p. 357.

1

the Hebrew, &c. Other writings still remain unpublished; and Cave (*Hist. Lit.*) notices a small tract or two printed with the works of others.

Both Wicliff and Luther were considerably indebted to the *Postillæ* of Lyra. The author of the Prologue usually attributed to Wicliff, says, that our English reformer consulted Lyra's Commentary, in his translation of the Bible; and of Luther it has been affirmed,

Si Lyra non lyrasset,
Lutherus non saltasset.
"If Lyra had not *harped* on profanation,
Luther had never *planned* the Reformation."*

The writings of our author exhibit him as a defender of the novelty of the Hebrew vowel points, in opposition to the rabbinical opinion of their antiquity. "The points," says he, "are not an essential part of the letters, nor were they in being when the Scriptures were written, but were invented a long time afterward, to assist in reading; hence the rolls which are read in the synagogues are without points." They also inform us of the impious conduct of the Jews toward the Christians and the gospel. Speaking of the reasons why the Jews do not embrace Christianity, he observes, "Many turn away from the faith of Jesus for a threefold cause. One is, on account of the fear of temporal penury, for they are always avaricious; and in their Law an abundance of temporal things is always promised; therefore above measure they abhor poverty. Another cause is, because from their cradle they are nursed in hatred to Jesus; and they curse the Christian law, and the worshippers of Jesus, in their synagogues every day. But those things to which men are accustomed from their youth, become as it were a second nature; and consequently, they turn the judgment of the understanding from the truth which is contrary to them. The third cause is, on account of the difficulty and depth of those things which are proposed to be believed in the Christian faith; as by experience they know who frequently confer with them on these subjects.†

Another Franciscan friar of note was Petrus Aureolus, or Oriel, a native of France, and archbishop of Aix, in Provence. He was called the Eloquent Doctor. He taught publicly in the university of Paris, from A. D. 1318 to A. D. 1321, when he was removed to the archiepiscopal see. In 1345 he wrote *Breviarium Bibliorum*,

* Lewis's Life of Wicliff, p. 73. Dr. A. Clarke's Commentary, Gen. Pref., p. 5.

† Hody, De Bibl. Text. Orig., lib. iii, pars ii, p. 433. Jewish Repos., vol. iii, p. 324.

or Compendium of the Bible, printed at Paris, 1508, 8vo. He also wrote Commentaries on the Four Books of Sentences, and other works. He died on the 27th of April, but in what year is uncertain.*

Montfaucon, in his Journey through Italy, gives us another instance of the attention paid to learning by the Mendicant friars. At Bologna he was shown a very ancient HEBREW BIBLE, with this inscription prefixed :—

"This Hebrew Bible was given by brother William of Paris, of the order of Brother Preachers, confessor to the most illustrious king of France, to the monastery of Bologna, for the common library of the brethren, in honour of St. Dominic, *Ann.* 1310, the day before the ides of February. Whosoever reads in it is desired to pray for him. Amen."†

But learning, though principally cultivated by the Mendicants, was not entirely restricted to them ; there were some belonging to the other monastic orders who devoted themselves to study. Of this PETRUS BERCHORIUS, or PIERRE BERCHEUR, was an instance. He was a native of Poitou, and a monk of the order of St. Benedict. His learning was various and extensive, and his memory so tenacious, that he is said to have been able to quote texts and authorities from the Bible, on all subjects, without any other assistance. He became prior of the convent of St. Eloi, at Paris, where he died, and was buried in 1362. Of his writings, which are voluminous, some are lost: the most important, however, remain, and are, 1. *Reductorium Morale utriusque Testamenti;* 2. *Repertorium Morale, seu Dictionarium Morale;* and 3. The *Gesta Romanorum.* He is also known to have been the translator of Levy, by order of John, king of France; and in that office to have invented and introduced various words, which are now of good authority in the French language. A MS. of this translation is preserved in the Sorbonne, at Paris.‡ The *Reductorim Morale* is divided into two parts; the *first* of which contains thirty-four books, and consists of allegorical expositions of different passages of Scripture, selected according to their order from the historical and prophetical books of the Old and New Testaments, and the Apocrypha. The following brief extract from the exposition of Genesis i, may give an idea of the work :—

* Cavei Hist. Lit., App., p. 22. † Montfaucon's Journey through Italy, p. 438.

‡ Le Long, Bibliotheca Sacra, tom. ii, p. 634. Warton's Hist. of English Poetry. vol. iii, Dissert. on the *Gesta Romanorum*, pp. i–vi. xxxvi. lxxxvii. Lempriere's Universal Biography. Lond., 1808, 4to.

"*In the beginning God created the heavens and the earth*, &c.—It appears, that as God exercised himself in the creation of the great world, so he continually exercises himself in the creation of the little world, man, and in the formation of the moral man, I say, therefore, that the light is faith, the firmament is hope. The waters above (the firmament) are troubles sent by God; the waters under (the firmament) are temptations arising from the carnal nature. The earth is the body; herbs and trees are good works; fruits and seeds are virtues and meritorious deeds. Lights signify discretion; the sun is divine wisdom, the moon worldly knowledge. Fishes, which are always in water, signify devotion; but birds, divine contemplation; cattle, the help and assistance of the poor; reptiles, compassion for the sufferings of others; beasts signify devils, and evil thoughts. Man, made in the image of God, designates the formation of the moral man, and the moral perfection of the mind. Paradise denotes final blessedness, and the consequent glory. This I say, therefore, that in the little world, that is, in the morally perfect man, the first thing necessary is the light of faith, to illuminate the mind, and to discover the truth; and to dissipate and confound error and darkness: hence it is said, Acts ix, 'There shined round about him a light from heaven.'"

The second part of the *Reductorium Morale* treats "Dererum proprietatibus," [Of the properties of things,] and is a curious compendium of pneumatology, natural history, &c. It is divided into twenty-four books, in which every subject is allegorized after the manner of the preceding exposition or commentary: the following is an example:—

"Of Britain."

"Britain, i. e., England, is a large island, surrounded by other islands. Near it is one called *Silura*,* the soil of which is so obnoxious to serpents, that it will kill any serpent introduced into it; and the inhabitants extraordinary, for they wholly discard money, and the use of it, bartering one thing for another, procuring necessaries rather by exchange than purchase, and revealing to men and women the knowledge of future events. By that island I understand religion, especially the Mendicant orders; by the soil which yields sustenance to them, the knowledge of the Scriptures, which opposes, kills, and destroys serpents, i. e., vices and temptations: they are also accustomed not to value money, but to seek necessaries by exchanging, that is, by begging, and to

* One of the Scilly isles.

think of nothing but futurity: Wisd. viii, 'She knoweth things of old, and conjectureth aright what is to come.'

"According to Solinus, there was formerly in Britain a temple dedicated to the goddess Minerva, where the perpetual fires never whitened into ashes, but, when suffered to go out, were transformed into globes of stone. Say, therefore, if you please, that the goddess Minerva is the Blessed Virgin, whose temple is the conscience of a righteous man, in which, without doubt, the fire of perpetual charity ought to burn, and never be lost in the ashes of sinners, but transform itself into the stone of perseverance."

The *Repertorium*, or *Dictionarium Morale*, is the most valuable of the works of Berchorius. It is a voluminous theological dictionary, in which all the words of the Vulgate version of the Bible are alphabetically arranged and explained; and discovers extensive theological knowledge, and uncommon acquaintance with the Scriptures. The following article, selected for its brevity, will serve as a specimen of the work:—

"*Proverbium.* (Proverb.) An enigma, or parable, i. e., an obscure speech, or a common saying, promulged as a law or rule. A proverb is used for

An allegorical proposition;
An authentic declaration;
A prophetic enunciation;
A scornful expression.

It is taken for an allegorical proposition, and is thus used John xv., where it is said, 'Now speakest thou plainly, and speakest no proverb.' Also, for an authentic declaration, and is so used 1 Sam. xxiv: 'As saith the proverb of the ancients: wickedness proceedeth from the wicked.' Again, for a prophetic enunciation, as Eccles. xxxix: 'He will seek out the secrets of grave sentences, (*Vulg.* Proverbiorum,) and be conversant in dark parables.' Also, for a scornful expression, and is thus used 1 Kings ix: 'Israel shall be a proverb, and a by-word among all nations.'"*

These works have been repeatedly printed; the edition from which the above translations have been made is in two ponderous folio volumes, printed at Cologne, 1620.

The *Gesta Romanorum* is a singular compilation of romances, apologues, and stories. It was one of the most favourite books of that period; and seems to have been "compiled from the obsolete Latin chronicles of the later Roman, or rather German story,

* Berchorii Opera, tom. i, pp. 1, 906; et tom. ii, p. 959. Colon. Agrip. 1620, fol.

heightened by romantic inventions, from legends of the saints, Oriental apologues, and many of the shorter fictitious narratives which came into Europe with the Arabian literature, and were familiar in the ages of ignorance and imagination. The classics are sometimes cited for authorities; but these are of the lower order, such as Valerius Maximus, Macrobius, Aulus Gellius, Seneca, Pliny, and Boethius. To every tale a *Moralization* is subjoined, reducing it into a Christian, or moral lesson. Most of the Oriental apologues are taken from the *Clericalis Disciplina*, or a Latin dialogue between an Arabian philosopher and Edric his son, never printed, written by Peter Alphonsus, a baptized Jew, at the beginning of the twelfth century, and collected from Arabian fables, apothegms, and examples. Some are also borrowed from an old Latin translation of the *Calilah u Damnah*, a celebrated set of Eastern fables, to which also Alphonsus was indebted." This popular work was one of the very early printed books, several editions having been published before A. D. 1500; and was translated into Dutch in 1484. Warton has prefixed a learned "Dissertation" on the *Gesta Romanorum* to his "History of English Poetry," vol. iii, from which the preceding remarks are taken.

In ITALY, classical learning began to revive, principally by the exertions of FRANCIS PETRARCH, who, as an elegant writer has said, "rescued his country's name from obscurity, and rendered it the admiration of Europe; who sought the society of learned foreigners, and was among the first to promote the cultivation of the Greek tongue; who, himself a philosopher, historian, orator, poet, and philologist, encouraged, by his example, every liberal pursuit."* And who, had he not disgraced his moral character by an infamous passion for Laura, the wife of Hugo de Sade, lord of Saumane, must have claimed the unreserved applause of every friend to literature and genius.

Yet, with all his ardour and enthusiasm for the cultivation of literature, Petrarch remained so ignorant of the Greek, that when a Greek Homer was sent him from Constantinople, he lamented his inability to taste its beauties. But his defective knowledge of that copious tongue was occasioned by the deplorable darkness of the age in which he lived, and not by his own indifference or neglect. For such was the lamentable indifference to the study of the Greek, that not one scholar versed in that language was to be found at Rome. It was reserved for his friend BOCCACIO, or

* Berington's Literary History of the Middle Ages, p. 410.

Boccace, to enjoy the pleasure, and obtain the honour, of introducing to public notice, and consequent remuneration, Leo, or Leontius Pilatus, the first Greek lecturer at Florence. This was about the year 1360. He had been detained at Florence, when on his way from the East to Avignon, by the advice and hospitality of Boccacio, who lodged the stranger in his house, and prevailed upon the magistrates to elect him a member of their academy, and to settle on him an annual stipend. The appearance of the lecturer was disgusting. He was clothed, says his disciple, (*De Geneal. Deorum.*, lib. xv, cap. vii,) in the mantle of a philosopher, or a Mendicant; his countenance was hideous; his face overshadowed with black hair; his beard long and uncombed; his deportment rustic; his temper gloomy and inconstant; nor could he grace his discourse with the ornaments, or even the perspicuity, of Latin elocution. But his mind was stored with a treasure of Greek learning; history and fable, philosophy and grammar, were alike at his command. The inconstancy of his disposition led him to return to Constantinople, after having filled the professor's chair only three years. Still unsettled, he determined to revisit the country he had left, and for that purpose embarked on board a vessel destined for Italy, but as they approached the shore the ship was assailed by a tempest, and our unfortunate teacher, who had lashed himself to the mast, was stricken dead by a flash of lightning.*

The theological writers in Italy, at this period, were few, and their writings in general unimportant. The chief of those who employed their pens on subjects of divinity attempted, by allegorical and mystical comments, to illustrate or explain the sacred writings; but nothing appears to have been published worthy of notice, unless, perhaps the Margarita Biblica of Guido de Pileo, a Dominican friar, bishop of Ferrara, who died in 1331; in which the author has endeavoured, in hexameter verses, to give an epitome and allegorical exposition of the Old and New Testaments. An edition of it, without place or date, was printed in the very infancy of the typographical art.†

In Germany, Joannes Rusbrochius, a native of Brabant, and prior of the monastery of the priory of Viridis Vallis, who died A. D. 1380, wrote a number of mystical works, among which was one in the German tongue, "On the Tabernacle of Moses," in which he, in his way, explains many parts of the books of Exodus,

* Berington's Literary History of the Middle Ages, b. vi, pp. 434–436.

† Le Long, tom. ii, p. 906.

Numbers, and Leviticus. The whole of his works have been twice printed at Cologne; first in 1552, in folio, and again in 1609, quarto. In these editions his German works are translated into Latin. About the year 1300 a prose version of the Scriptures was made into Dutch, but the author is not known.*

If we turn to the north of Europe, the chief occurrences that interest the Biblical scholar are private translations of the Scriptures into the vernacular language of Sweden and Poland, one of them executed at the request of a princess, whose name has been deservedly transmitted to succeeding ages; and the other translated by the no less illustrious princess whose name it bears. St. Birgit, or Bridget, was the daughter of Birger, or Birgines, a prince of the royal blood of Sweden, and of Ingeburgis, daughter to Sigridis, a lady descended from the kings of the Goths, and was born A. D. 1302. She married Ulpho, prince of Nericia, in Sweden, who died in 1344, in the monastery of Alvastre. After the death of her husband she founded a religious order, called from her the *order of the Brigittins*, or *Brigettins;* and built the great monastery of Wastein, in the diocess of Lincopen, in Sweden. At her request, Matthias, or Matthew of Sweden, her confessor, and canon of Lincopen, translated for her use, she being ignorant of Latin, the Bible into Swedish, accompanied with short learned annotations. The translator, who was also called *Matthew of Cracow*, in Poland, probably from being a native of that city, was afterward raised to the see of Worms, where he died in 1410.† He wrote on several theological subjects, such as the mass, eucharist, &c. Some of his MSS. are said to be still preserved in different libraries. St. Bridget died July 23d, 1373. Her pretended "Revelations" have been repeatedly printed, at Lubec in 1492, at Nuremberg, 1521, with cuts, much esteemed; at Rome, 1521, &c.‡ No copy of the translation of the Scriptures which she procured is now to be found; but in the library of the university of Leipsic there is a MS. in 12mo., containing the Latin Bible, fairly written, said to have been transcribed with her own hand.§

The Polish version is attributed to Hedwige, daughter of Louis,

* Cavei Hist. Lit., App., p. 57. Acta Eruditorum. An. 1733, p. 62, 4to.

† Messenius places his death about A. D. 1352; and says he was intimate with the Dominicans of Stockholm, among whom he breathed his last; but Butler professes to state the time of his death from his epitaph. See Messenii *Scondia Illustrata*, ii, tom. ix, cap. vi, p. 43. Stockholm, 1700, fol.

‡ Butler's Lives, vol. x, October 8, pp. 158–166.

§ Le Long, Biblioth. Sacra, tom. i, p. 240.

1

king of Hungary and Poland; or, according to some writers, daughter of Casimir the Great. She was chosen sovereign queen of Poland in 1384, and her panegyrists assure us that "she was eminent for her immense charities to the poor, her liberality to churches, monasteries, and universities; her humility, and aversion to pomp or gaudy apparel; her meekness, which was so wonderful, that in so exalted a station she was utterly a stranger to anger and envy;" and that "she read no books but such as treated of piety and devotion; the chief being the Holy Scriptures, Homilies of the Fathers, Acts of Martyrs, and other saints, and the Meditations of St. Bernard, &c."* In 1386 she married Jagello, a pagan duke of Lithuania, on condition that he should embrace the Christian faith, and establish it in his dominions. At his baptism he received the name of Vladislaus, and subsequently persuaded the subjects of his dutchy to make profession of the gospel. Hedwige died at Cracow in 1399.† Johannes Lasicius, in his work *De Gentis Franciscæ Gestis*, lib. i, professes to have seen an elegant MS. of this translation.‡

In the royal library at Copenhagen there is a MS. (No. 8 of the MSS., in folio, of the Thottian catalogue,) formerly in the possession of Count Thott, containing a Danish version of part of the Old Testament, supposed to have been made in the thirteenth, or, at the latest, in the beginning of the fourteenth century. The following account of it I owe to the kindness of the Rev. Dr. Ebenezer Henderson, who favoured me with a valuable MS. History of the Danish Versions, written by himself, and to which this work will be principally indebted for what relates to the Biblical history of Denmark.

The Danish MS. of the Old Testament, deposited in the royal library at Copenhagen, "forms an ordinary folio, and has been strongly bound in wooden boards, covered with skin. It has already suffered considerable damage by its exposure in a humid place, and is fast mouldering away at the ends. It is written on paper, in two parallel columns. Toward the beginning, the lines marking the space to be filled by the text have been drawn with ink, the colour of which is considerably paler than that with which the text itself is written; but the rest has been ruled with a leaden pen. The text forms one whole, no blank space being left either between the chapters or the books. The number of the chapter

* Butler's Lives, vo . x, October 17, p. 425, *note*.

† Mosheim's Eccles. Hist., vol. iii, p. 298.

‡ Le Long, Biblioth. Sacra, tom. i, p. 439.

is begun on the same line with the conclusion of the preceding, and is either longer or shorter, according to the space that was to be filled up. The title of the book is written at the top of the page, as far as the middle of the twelfth chapter of Exodus, from which to the end it is omitted. The initial letter of every chapter is roughly ornamented, and is written with a kind of red paint, which has something of a glossy surface, resembling wax. The same material is used in correcting what was improperly written, and in writing the titles of the books and chapters. It is also employed in punctuation, which consists of a stroke drawn transversely through the line, answering to the more common stops; and where any remarkable word or sentence begins, a red stroke is drawn through the first letter of the word. At the foot of the page are a number of prayers and pious effusions, through a considerable part of Genesis, but they are the work of a later hand. The first two leaves, and part of the third, have been devoured by the tooth of time; and the text now begins Genesis ii, 10. It is also defective from Genesis xxx, 36, to xxxi, 29, and ends with 2 Kings xxiii, 14."

"The version is done exactly according to the Vulgate, and faithfully adopts all its faults, nor can this be matter of surprise to those who know that it has been doubted, by those best acquainted with the ecclesiastical history of that country, whether at that period there were any of the clergy who so much as understood the Greek Testament in Denmark; and that many of the ecclesiastics themselves had not an opportunity of forming any acquaintance even with the Vulgate. The translator of the Danish version has not only in general servilely followed the Vulgate, but has at times attempted to express the derivation of the Latin words in his version, which could not fail, in many instances, to render it ridiculous. Thus the Almighty is introduced, Genesis xxvi, 5, as commending Abraham for making use of *wax candles* in the observance of his religious rites. The Vulgate has *ceremonias*, which this translation renders: 'Because Abraham obeyed my voice, and kept my charge and commandments, and kept feast-days with wax, that is, wax candles, and laws.' The same rendering occurs also in several other places. In Exodus xxviii, 4, the Latin terms used to describe the garments of the priests are explained by the sacerdotal apparel of the Romish Church. Great use is made of synonymes by way of explication, especially in those passages in which Latin words are introduced."

"Translations of the prefaces of Jerome are introduced at their proper places; and sometimes, though rarely, a passage is introduced from Peter Comestor's *Historia Scholastica.* Thus the story respecting the grave of Joseph is related after Exodus xiii, 19; a long account is given of the infancy and youth of Moses at the end of Numbers xii, and, at the end of 1 Samuel xxv, a comparison is drawn between Saul and the devil, and one between David and a spiritual man, which concludes, 'O St. David, pray for us.'"

A full account of this MS. is given by Dr. Wöldike, in the second volume of the Transactions of the Royal Society of Copenhagen, who concludes, from the size of the volume, that there may have originally been two more, comprising the whole Bible; but Dr. E. Henderson remarks, that "the abrupt manner in which this fragment ends, at the beginning of the first column on the last page, without regard to any division in the Bible, shows that its present size is merely accidental, and that either the original [from which this MS. appears to be a copy] has not extended further, or the transcriber has been prevented by death, or some other unavoidable cause, from prosecuting his labour."

Pontoppidan (Annales Eccles. Danicæ Diplom., tom. iv, p. 563) mentions his having found, in a MS. B. Bircherodii, a notice respecting an order issued 1671 by Christian V. to print a very ancient MS. of the Bible, which was preserved in the royal library, and which he supposes to have been the MS. just described; but the order appears never to have been put into execution, a circumstance that cannot but be lamented by the Biblical scholar, as the MS. is evidently in a state of decay.

Among the GREEKS of this century, Euthalius Johannes Cantacuzenus, and Simon Jatumæus, are most worthy of notice. CANTACUZENUS, born in Constantinople, was bred to letters and to arms, and admitted to the highest offices of the state. The emperor Andronicus loaded him with wealth and honours; and at his death, in 1341, left to him the care of the empire, and the guardianship of his son, John Paleologus, then only nine years of age, until his son should be capable of assuming the reins of government himself. This trust he discharged for some time with the utmost fidelity and diligence, till, the empress dowager and her faction having proclaimed him a traitor, he was led to listen to the entreaties of the army and nobles, and to assume the imperial purple. A civil war ensued, in which Cantacuzenus was victorious. At a suitable age he associated the young Paleologus with him in the empire, and confirmed the union by giving him his daughter in marriage. Jealousy and suspicion again gave rise to civil commotions, till, weary of the troubles of sovereignty, and unwilling to continue the contest, Cantacuzenus abdicated his share in the empire, assumed the habit of a monk, and, retiring into a monastery, adopted the name of Joasaph, or Josaphat, and devoted himself to the duties of religion and the pursuits of literature. In this relinquishment of worldly grandeur he was accompanied by his wife, who entered a nunnery, and changed her name from Irene to Eugenia. In his retirement he wrote a History of his own Times, of which a splendid edition, with a Latin translation, was published at Paris, in three volumes, folio, 1645;—an Apology for Christianity, against the Mohammedans, with four books in confutation of the Errors of Mohammed and the Alcoran, written in 1360, at the request of a Christian monk, who had been converted from Mohammedanism; and edited by Rudolph Gualter, who translated them into Latin, and published them with the Greek, at Basil, in 1543, folio, and afterward with the Alcoran, in 1555;—and a work against the Jews, designed to refute their errors. This latter work is also sometimes noted as "Nine Sermons" against the Jews. In his writings Cantacuzenus assumed the name of Christodulus. The time of his death is uncertain, though he is supposed to have lived many years in his retirement.*

Simon or James Jatumæus, a Dominican friar, a native of Constantinople, flourished about the close of this century. He was first, bishop of Geirace, in Calabria Ultra, in Italy, and afterward archbishop of Thebes, in Bœotia. His knowledge of the Greek, and Latin, and Hebrew languages, in which he was thoroughly versed, enabled him to form from the best and most correct Greek copies a regular series or Harmony of the whole of the New Testament, and to translate it into Hebrew and Latin. These versions, with the Greek, he placed in three parallel columns on each page, and with considerable labour and diligence, disposed them with so much exactness, that each version answered to the other, line for line, and sentence for sentence, both in sense and words. A copy of this curious Triglott Harmony was formerly kept in the library at Genoa.†

Euthalius Rhodius was a monk of the order of St. Basil, who, after the example of Cardinal Hugo's Latin work, compiled

* Cavei Hist. Lit., App., pp. 37, 38. Fabricii Delectus Argumentorum, &c., p. 124. Hamburg, 1725, 4to.

† Sixt. Senens. Bibliotheca Sanct., lib. iv, p. 378. Le Long, Bibliotheca Sacra tom. i, p. 61.

a Greek Concordance of the Bible. Nothing more is known of him, except that he lived at the commencement of this century;* nor is there any copy of his work known to exist at present.

Directing our views eastward, we find a PERSIAN translation of the four Gospels, made by order of the prince Ibn Sahm Addaula ibn Scirana. The following subscription at the end of a MS. of this version is characteristic of the age and country in which it was written:—

"These four glorious GOSPELS of Matthew, Mark, Luke, and John, were finished in the city of Caffa,† inhabited by Christians, (prayers being performed,) on the third day of the week, the ninth of the month Tamuz, in Latin called July, in the year of Christ the Messiah, 1341, by the hand of the weakest of the people of God, SIMON IBN JOSEPH IBN ABRAHAM AL TABRIZI. May the God of those that fear him (that is, of the Christians) by his grace and providence show mercy, that when they read or hear this (book of the) Gospels, they may say a Pater Noster and Ave Maria, for the poor writer, that, through the divine mercy he also may be forgiven. Amen. And this (book of the) Gospels was written by the command and counsel of his lord and king, (the glory of princes and merchants, and the honour of the people of Christ,) the friend

* Sixt. Senens Biblioth. Sanct., lib. iv, p. 286.

† CAFFA, or Cafa, is a city and port town of the Crimea. It was anciently called Theodosia, and since it came into the possession of the Russians, this name has been restored to it. It is at present chiefly inhabited by foreigners of different religious persuasions. In July, 1815, a Bible Society was established in that city, designed particularly to comprehend in the sphere of its operations the countries lying on the shores of the Black Sea. On that occasion his excellency Bronefsky, governor of the city, transmitted to the Russian Bible Society a communication written by himself, in which he says, "Abhazi, Mingrellia, and Anatolia, being in the closest commercial connection with Theodosia, present a wide field for the Bible Society proposed to be in that city. It is well known that in former times, the Abhazi were enlightened by the faith of Christ, and belonged to the Greek communion, possessed their own bishops, and were reckoned to the *Eparché* of Alanie, the seat of which see was Theodosia, and afterward Phanagaria. After the fall of the Greek empire, however, the nation of the Abhazi, like the Circassians, being deprived of preachers, and not possessing a written language, returned to their heathenish customs, and at last many of them embraced the Mohammedan religion. Monuments of Christianity exist to the present time among them, in the remains of churches, for which the people have still respect. Another proof of this is the veneration which they have for the form of the cross. Certain of the Abhazian tribes in the vicinity of Annapa, perform their religious service, which is greatly mixed with heathenism, before a cross, placed upon a tree, or they simply cut out the form of the cross on the bark of the tree, and pray and offer sacrifices before it." See the *Twelfth Report of the British and Foreign Bible Society*, App., No. viii, p. 13. Lond. 1816.

and brother of the pure church, the lord and prince IBN SAHM AD-DAULA IBN SCIRANA, surnamed of Teflis. God be gracious to him and his kindred. Amen."*

"This version," remarks Dr. A. Clarke, "was made most evidently by a Christian of the Roman Catholic persuasion, who acted under the most predominating influence of his own peculiar creed; for it is not only interpolated with readings from the Vulgate, but with readings from rituals and legends."† It was printed with the Latin translation of Dr. Samuel Clarke, in the fifth volume of the London Polyglott, from a MS. belonging to the learned Dr. Pocock. A much purer and more simple version of the four Gospels, but of uncertain date, was published, with a Latin translation, in 1657, fol. It was translated into Latin, and prepared for the press, by Mr. Abraham Wheeloc, professor of Arabic in the university of Cambridge, who actually began to print it in 1652; but dying shortly after, the work was patronized by Thomas Adams, lord mayor of London, and finished under the care of Mr. Pierson, at the press of J. Flesher. It seems that Mr. Wheeloc had designed to affix critical notes to each chapter; but as the regular comment appears to have been prepared no further than to the seventeenth chapter of Matthew, the notes which the continuator found after the close of that chapter are all printed at the conclusion of the work.‡ It is probable that the former version was made from the Syriac, the latter from the Latin Vulgate.

Another version of the Gospels in Persian is mentioned by Le Long. It was transcribed in the year 1388, but from an original of much older date; and was sent to the college at Rome, from Agrâ, in the East Indies, by Jeronymo Xavier, a Roman Catholic missionary, who died at Goa in 1617.§

Returning again to the West, a singular occurrence in Ireland claims our attention. About the year 1358, Richard Fitzralph, archbishop of Armagh, possessed a translation, probably made by himself, of the New Testament in Irish. According to the information of Bale, quoted by Archbishop Usher, this copy was concealed by him in a certain wall of his church,‖ with the following note:—"When this book is found, truth will be revealed to the

* Waltoni Proleg., xvi.

† Dr. A. Clarke's Comment. *Introduction to the Gospels and Acts of the Apostles*, p. 14.

‡ Dr. A. Clarke's Comment., *ubi sup.*

§ Le Long, Biblioth. Sacra, tom. i, p. 133.

‖ A curious MS. original of the New Testament, (one Gospel, *St. Mark*, wanting,) found *walled* in Loddington Church, in Northamptonshire, was in the possession of

world; or Christ shortly appear." This, observes the narrator, was written in the spirit of prophecy, for the book was found when the church of Armagh was repairing, about the year of Christ 1530.* No vestige of this translation is supposed to remain; though Fox, in his "Actes and Monumentes of the Church," vol. i, p. 511, printed in 1570, says, "I credibly heare of certayne old Irish Bibles translated long synce into the Irysh tong, which if it be true, it is not other lyke, but to be the doing of this Armachanus;" and adds that this was "testified by certayne Englishmen, which are yet alyve, and have sene it."

RICHARD FITZRALPH, or FITZRAF, "a man worthy, for his Christian zeal, of immortal commendation," was brought up at Oxford, under John Baconthorpe, who was called the Resolute Doctor. His abilities recommended him to King Edward III., by whom he was promoted, first to the archdeaconry of Lichfield, then to the chancellorship of Oxford, and afterward to the archbishopric of Armagh, in 1347. He was the severe and professed opponent of the Mendicant friars, who, by their arrogance and encroachments on the rights of the clergy, had created very general disgust. Being cited by them to appear before Pope Innocent IV., he defended himself in the presence of the pontiff, in an oration, the substance of which is preserved in Fox's "Actes and Monumentes," vol. i, pp. 505–510. In this discourse he observes, that the Mendicant friars entice and delude so many of the young scholars who are sent to the universities, to enter their order, that "laymen, seeing their children thus to be stolen from them, refuse to send them to their studies, rather willing to keep them at home to their occupation, or to follow the plough, than to be circumvented and defeated of their sons at the university, as by daily experience doth manifestly appear. For where as, in my time," saith he, "there were in the university of Oxford thirty thousand students, now are there not to be found six thousand." And thus notices the decay of learning occasioned by their monopoly of books:—"These begging friars, through their privileges obtained of the popes to preach, to hear confessions, and to bury; and through their charters of impropriations, grow thereby to such great riches and possessions by their begging, craving, and catching, and intermeddling in church matters, that no *book* can stir,

Bishop More, who had borrowed it from the Rev. George Tew, the rector, but never returned it; and is supposed to be now in the public library at Cambridge, among the collection of books purchased at the death of the bishop for £6,000, by King George I., and presented to that university.—*Nichols's Literary Anecdotes*, vol. ix, p. 612.

* Usserii Hist. Dogmat., p. 156.

of any science, either of divinity, law, or physic, but they are able and ready to buy it up. So that every convent having a great library full stuffed and furnished with all sorts of books, and there being so many convents within the realm, and in every convent so many friars increasing daily more and more, it thereby comes to pass, that very few books, or none at all, remain for other students:" of which he gives this instance, "that he himself sent forth to the university four of his own priests or chaplains, who sending him word again that they could neither find the Bible, nor any other good profitable book of divinity, meet for their study, therefore were minded to return home to their country;" and adds further, that "he was sure, one of them was by this time returned."

The opposition of the good archbishop to what he considered to be the reigning abuses of his day, brought much trouble and persecution upon him. Our martyrologist tells us, that in a certain confession or prayer, composed by Fitzralph, and of which he himself had a copy, he relates the particulars of his many providential deliverances out of the hand of his enemies, and almost the whole history of his life, especially "how the Lord taught him, and brought him out of the profound vanities of Aristotle's subtlety, to the study of the Scriptures of God." The beginning of the prayer in Latin, as given us by Fox, deserves to be translated. "To thee be praise and glory, and thanksgiving, O Jesus, most holy, most powerful, most amiable, who hast said, 'I am the way, the truth, and the life;'—a way without deviation,—truth without a cloud, and life without end. For thou hast shown me the way; thou hast taught me the truth; and thou hast promised me the life. Thou wast my way in exile; thou wast my truth in counsel; and thou wilt be my life in reward." After this quotation, every pious character will regret that the honest martyrologist did not execute the design he had formed of publishing the whole confession.

Fitzralph remained some time in banishment, and died at Avignon, about A. D. 1360; yet such was the character he had maintained, that, on hearing of his death, a certain cardinal openly declared, "A mighty pillar of Christ's church was fallen."*

In ENGLAND, one of the principal promoters of learning was RICHARD DE BURY, or AUNGERVILLE, bishop of Durham, who was born in 1281, and died in 1345. A man singularly learned, and so devoted to literature that he kept transcribers, binders, and illuminators in his palaces, and expended the whole of his ample

* Foxes Actes and Monumentes, vol. i, pp. 502–511. Lond., 1570, fol.

income in purchasing scarce and curious manuscripts, for which purpose he employed agents not only in England, but in Italy, France, and Germany. Besides the fixed libraries which he had formed in his several palaces, the floor of his common apartment was so covered with books, that those who entered were in danger of trampling on them. By the favour of Edward III. he gained access to the libraries of the principal monasteries, where he shook off the dust from various volumes, (all MSS., as must necessarily be the case at that period,) preserved in chests and presses, which had not been opened for many ages; and while chancellor and treasurer of England, instead of the usual presents and new years' gifts appendant to his office, he chose to receive those perquisites in books.* The account given of him by honest John Stow, in his *Annales*, is too interesting not to be transcribed in his own words:—"Richard Bury," says he, "is somewhat to bee remembred for example to other. He was borne neere Saint Edmundsbury. By his father, Sir Richard Angaruill, knight, and his uncle, Sir John Willowby, his gouernour, he was first set to grammer schoole, and after sent to Oxford, from whence hee was called to teach Ed. of Windlesore, then prince: afterward this Richard was made principall recieuer to Edwarde the second in Gascoigne, at such time as yoong Edward with his mother fledde to Paris, whose expenses beginning to faile, the said Richard came to them priuily with a great somme of money, for the which cause he was pursued to Paris, where hee lay hid in a steeple by the space of seuen dayes. After this hee was made cofferer to Edward the third, then treasurer of the wardrobe, then clarke to the priuie seale by the space of fiue yeeres, in the which time twise hee went to Pope John. In the sixe and fortieth yeere of his age he was consecrated bishoppe of Durham, then was hee made treasurer of England, and after chancellour, since the which time hee was sent thrise to the French king, to claim the kingdome of France, and after that, to Antwerpe and other places in Brabant, in embassage by the space of nine yeeres. He was greatly delighted in the company of clearkes, and hadde alwayes many of them in his family, among whom were Thomas Bradwardine, afterward archbishoppe of Canterbury, Richard Fitz Ralph, archbishoppe of Armacham, Walter Burley, John Manditt, Robert Holcot, Richard Kilwington, all of them doctors of diuinitie, Richard Wentworth, or Beniworth, byshoppe of London, and Walter Segraue, byshoppe of Chichester. Euery day at his table, hee was accustomed to

* Warton's Hist. of English Poetry, vol. i, diss. 2.

haue some reading: and after dinner daily hee would haue disputation with his priuate clearkes, and other of his house, except some vrgent cause hadde let him. At other times hee was occupied, either in seruice of God, or at his bookes. Weekely he bestowed for the reliefe of the poore, eight quarters of wheat made into bread, besides the ordinary fragments of his house. Moreouer, in coming or going from Newcastle to Durham, hee bestowed sometimes twelue markes in almes, from Durham to Stockton eight markes, from Durham to Aukland fiue markes, from Durham to Middleham an hundred shillings, &c. Hee was so delighted in bookes, that he hadde more (as was thought) then all the byshoppes of Englande besides. Hee bestowed many rich ornaments on the church of Durham. Hee builded an hall or house in Oxford, induing it with reuenues needefull for his schollers. And also prouided in a library great store of bookes,* for the vse of the whole vniversitie, as the said bishop writeth himselfe in his booke entituled 'PHILOBIBLOS,' and appoynted the maisters of the hall to assigne five scholers for keeping of the common library."†

Yet such was the influence of the general contempt in which the laity were held by the clergy, that, while this great man was lamenting the total ignorance of the Greek language among his clerical brethren, he did not scruple to affirm, "*Laici omnium librorum communione indigni sunt*—The laity are unworthy to be admitted to any commerce with books:" a sentiment which sufficiently discovers the profound ignorance which must have reigned among all ranks of society, the clergy excepted. With very different feelings will the reader of the present day peruse his opinion of books, when he says, "*Hi sunt magistri qui nos instruunt sine virgis et ferula, sine verbis et colera, sine pane et pecunia. Si accedis non dormiunt; inquiris non se abscondunt; non remurmurant si oberres; cachinnos nesciunt si ignores*—These are teachers who instruct us without rod or ferula, without severe expressions or anger, without food or money. When we come to them, they are not asleep; when we inquire for them, they do not secrete themselves; when we mistake them, they do not complain; if we are ignorant, they do not despise us." The treatise from which these passages are selected was written with reference to the library which he bequeathed to the university of Oxford. It is entitled PHILOBIBLOS, or PHILOBIBLION, is written in Latin, in

* See p. 403 of this volume.

† Stow's Annales, or Generall Chronicle of England, pp. 240, 241. London, 1615, folio.

a declamatory style, and is divided into twenty chapters. In this work he laments that good literature had entirely ceased in the university of Paris, which he calls the "Paradise of the World;" and says that he purchased there a variety of invaluable volumes in all sciences, which yet were neglected and perishing. This learned prelate died in 1345, at his palace at Auckland.*

In lieu of *books*, the laity appear to have been presented with paintings and theatrical entertainments. Henry III., who was a most munificent encourager of the fine arts, kept several painters constantly in his service. One chamber in the palace of Winchester was painted green, with stars of gold, and the whole History of the Old and New Testament. In one room in the palace of Westminster, and in another in the Tower of London, the history of the expedition of Richard I. into the Holy Land was painted. The coronation, wars, marriages, and funeral of Edward I. were painted on the walls of the great hall, in the episcopal palace in Lichfield, A. D. 1312, by order of Bishop Langton. The principal churches and chapels were furnished with representations of the Virgin Mary, the apostles, and other saints; and the walls of some of them almost covered with Scriptural, moral, and allegorical paintings. Friar Symeon, who wrote an "Itinerary" in 1322, thus describes a series of paintings in the royal palace at Westminster: "Near this monastery" (of Westminster) "stands the most famous royal palace of England, in which is that celebrated chamber, on whose walls all the warlike histories of the whole Bible are painted with inexpressible skill, and explained by a regular and complete series of texts, beautifully written in French over each battle, to the no small admiration of the beholder, and the increase of royal magnificence." And Falcondus, the old historian of Sicily, relates, that at an earlier period (about A. D. 1200) the chapel of the royal palace at Palermo had its walls decorated with the History of the Old and New Testament, executed in beautiful Mosaic work.†

The theatrical entertainments of this period, especially those intended to represent the miracles and mysteries of Scripture, have been already noticed; it is therefore unnecessary to add any thing more, except to remark, that even on such occasions as the triumphant entry of a king or queen into any celebrated city, the pageants were almost always Scriptural or religious exhibitions.

* Savage's Librarian, vol. iii, pp. 38–40. London, 1809, 8vo.

† Henry's Hist. of Great Britain, vol. viii, pp. 297–299. Warton's Hist of English Poetry, vol. ii, pp. 216, 217.

Under these circumstances Biblical studies were but seldom pursued, particularly during the former part of this century. Archbishop Usher, indeed, assigns a translation of the whole Bible into ENGLISH to the close of the preceding century, and supposes several copies of it to be preserved at Oxford. But others have regarded these copies either as genuine or corrected ones of Wicliff's version, or of that said to have been made by Trevisa. Dr. James, in his "Treatise of the Corruption of Scripture," conjectures that a version of the English Scriptures existed long before the time of Wicliff.* These, however, are mere suppositions; nor have we any decisive proof of any considerable portion of the Scriptures being translated into the modern English earlier than about the middle of this century, unless the old GLOSSED BIBLE which the Rev. Dr. Adam Clarke possesses, and of which he has given several specimens in the General Preface to his Commentary, should be considered of older date. Some translations, indeed, seem to have been made of the Psalter, the Church Lessons and Hymns, and of some of the books of the New Testament, but they do not appear to have been published, being in all probability made for the translators' own use, or that of their immediate connections. The date of these partial translations cannot be accurately ascertained, since, from the circumstance of being anonymous, the only way of judging of their age is from the writing and language, which must necessarily render precision impossible.† With respect to the copy in the possession of Dr. A. Clarke, the following important communication, with which I have been obligingly favoured, will afford ample information.

"Of my large MS. English Bible, about which you inquire, I can only say, that I have reason to believe it to be earlier than the time of Wicliff. I reason thus from the *language*, which is of an older cast, and likewise the *orthography* and *construction* of the sentences. In many respects, the New Testament in it is dissimilar from the copies I have seen ascribed to Wicliff. Whether these have been amended, corrected, and altered, in later times, and mine is one of those which has undergone no revisal, but is just as Wicliff originally made it, I cannot say. This is merely a possible case; and if the supposition be founded that mine is Wicliff's translation, it must necessarily follow that all those which I have seen, and which Lewis has collated, have been considerably

* See Usserii Hist. Dogmat., p. 157, and Whartoni Auctarium, p. 424. James's Corruption of Scripture, p. 74, and Baber's Account of English Versions, p. lxvi.

† Lewis's Hist. of the English translations of the Bible, p. 17.

altered; and that there is not so old a copy of Wicliff remaining as my own. I am led to think that some of those copies examined by Lewis are not Wicliff's; else those which he has principally followed are much altered from the original. My conclusion, however, is simply this. Either mine is before Wicliff's time, because it differs so much from the copies generally ascribed to Wicliff, and from the text published by Lewis in 1731; or that text, and these from which it is taken, have been revised and altered from Wicliff's original, and mine is one of those which has not undergone such a revision."

"In what year my MS. was written I cannot tell:—the writing and orthography are old enough for at least fourscore years before Wicliff, who began his translation in 1378; but that mine could not be written twenty years later than that, is absolutely evident from this circumstance, that it most evidently appears to have been illuminated for Thomas of Woodstock, brother of John of Gaunt and Edward the Black Prince, and youngest son of Edward III., as it bears his arms in a shield at the beginning of Proverbs; arms which appear on his monument in Westminster Abbey; the singular bordure of which was never, so far as I can find, worn by any after his time. Now this Thomas of Woodstock was smothered between two feather beds, at Calais, by Thomas Mawbray, earl marshal of England, September 8th, 1397, at the command of Richard II., this prince's nephew. How long before 1397 this book was written I cannot tell; but it must have been, in the nature of things, several years before this time."

"I am, yours truly,

"A. CLARKE."

The earliest translator of any part of the Scriptures into English, in the fourteenth century, with whose name we are acquainted, was RICHARD ROLLE, a hermit of the order of St. Augustine, who resided in or near Hampole, in Yorkshire, whence he is sometimes called Richard of Hampole, or Richard Hampole. He wrote several Latin theological tracts, both in prose and verse. His *Stimulus Conscientiæ*, or "Pricke of Conscience," was written first in Latin prose, and afterward translated into English rhyme. Warton (Hist. of English Poetry, vol. i, pp. 256–266) has given several specimens of this work, so celebrated in its day, but which, he remarks, "has no tincture of sentiment, imagination, or elegance." Rolle was also the author of Annotations, or Commentaries, on the Psalms; the Hymns of the Old Testament, used in the services of the church; part of the book of Job; the Song of Solomon; the Lamentations of Jeremiah; the Revelation; the Lord's Prayer; and the Athanasian and Apostles' Creeds; besides several other theological works.* Some of the annotations are more properly poetical paraphrases than commentaries. His principal work was an English version of the Psalms. To this he prefixed a prologue, in which he thus speaks of the nature of his undertaking: "In this werke I seek no straunge *Ynglys*, bot lightest and communest, and swilk that is most like unto the *Latyne*: so that thai that knawes noght the *Latyne* be the *Ynglys* may com to many *Latyne* wordis. In the translacione I felogh the letter als-mekille as I may, and thor I fyne no proper *Ynglys* I felogh the wit of the wordis, so that thai that shalle rede it them thar not drede errynge. In the expownyng I felogh holi doctors. For it may comen into sum envious mannes hond that knowys not what he suld says, at wille say that I wist not what I sayd, and so do harme tille hym and tille other."† The Rev. H. H. Baber, in his "Historical Account of the Saxon and English Versions of the Scriptures," prefixed to his edition of Wicliff's New Testament, has selected the twenty-third psalm as a specimen of this translation, from a MS. in the British Museum:—

"Our Lord gouerneth me, and nothyng to me shal wante: stede of pasture thar he me sette. In the water of the hetyng forth he me brougte: my soul he turnyde."

"He ladde me on the stretis of rygtwisnesse: for his name."

"For win gif I hadde goo in myddil of the shadewe of deeth: I shal not dreede yueles, for thou art with me."

"Thi geerde and thi staf: thei haue coumfortid me. Thou hast greythid in my sygt a bord: agens hem that angryn me."

"Thou fattide myn heud in oyle: and my chalys drunkenyng what is cleer."

"And thi mercy shal folewe me: in alle the dayes of my lyf."

"And that I wone in the hous of oure lord in the lengthe of dayes."

The Commentary on the Psalms, if we must judge of it from the following extract given by Lewis, was excessively dry and insipid:—Psalm ii, 1, "*Whi gnastide the folke? and the puple thoughte ydil thoughtis?* The prophete snybbyng hem that shulde turmente crist seith, *whi?* as hoo seith, what enchesun hadde thei? sotheli none but yuel wille for he contrariede her ivele lywing in

* Cavei Hist. Litt., App., p. 35. Le Long, vol ii, p. 932.

† Lewis's History of the English Translations of the Bible, p. 13.

werk and word. *the folke* thei were tha knyghtis of *rome*, that crucified crist, thei *gnastide* aghen hym as bestis wode without resoun: and *the puple* that was the iuwes. *thoughte in ydel* that is, in vayne was ther thoughte whan thei wend have holde crist evere deed that thei myghte not doo for thi in vayne thei trauelide as eche man doth that thoruh—pryde and ypocrisye weneth to hude cristis lawful ordenaunce."

The translation is evidently made from the Latin Vulgate; and the gloss, or comment, formed after the model of the mystical and allegorical expositions of that age.*

An extract, translated from his tract De Emendatione Peccatoris, will give a more favourable idea of his theological writings:—

"If you desire," says he, "to attain to the love of God, and to be influenced with the desire of heavenly joys, and to be brought to the contempt of earthly things, be not negligent in reading and meditating the Holy Scriptures, and especially those parts of them which inculcate morality, and teach us to beware of the snares of the devil; where they speak of the love of God, and of a contemplative life; but leave the more difficult passages to disputants and ingenious men, who have been long exercised in sacred doctrines."

"This method assists us greatly to improve in what is good. In these we ascertain our failings and our improvements; in what things we have offended, and in what we have not; what we should avoid, and what we should practise. They discover most skilfully the machinations of our enemies; they inflame us to love, and move us to tears; and thus prepare for us a delicious feast, if we delight in them as in all riches. But let us not be urged to a knowledge of the Scriptures by any desire of the honour or favour of men, but only by a design of pleasing God, that we may know how to love him, and that we may teach our neighbour the same, and not that we may be considered as learned by the people. Nay, we ought rather to conceal our learning than to exhibit it to our own praise, as says the psalmist: 'Thy word have I hid in my heart,' (that is, from vain exhibition,) 'that I might not sin against thee,' Psalm cxix, 11. Therefore let the cause of our speaking be the glory of God, and the edification of our neighbour, that we may fulfil that scripture, 'His praise shall be continually in my mouth,' Psalm xxxiv, 1, which is done when we do not seek our own praise, nor speak contrary to his glory."†

* Lewis, *ut sup.*

† Biblioth. Pat., tom. xxvi, cap. ix, p. 614.

The piety of the author caused him to be regarded as a saint; and on the termination of his mortal sufferings, in 1349, he was buried in the convent of Hampole. At a later period, Henry Parker, Lord Morley, a nobleman and poet, who died an old man in the latter end of the reign of Henry VIII., and who has been mentioned by Bishop Bale as the author of certain tragedies and comedies, by which was probably meant mysteries and moralities, gave a proof rather of his piety than taste, by presenting to the Princess Mary, as a new year's gift, Hampole's Commentary on the Seven Penitential Psalms. This MS., with his epistle prefixed, is still preserved among the royal MSS. in the British Museum.*

JOHN DE TREVISA, who flourished toward the close of this century, has also been enumerated among the first translators of the Bible into ENGLISH. He was born at Caradoc, in the county of Cornwall, and educated at Oxford. His learning and talents gained him the patronage of Earl Berkeley, who appointed him his chaplain, and presented him to the vicarage of Berkeley, in Gloucestershire. He was also canon of Westbury, in Wiltshire. Warton, in his History of English Poetry, vol. i, p. 343, speaks of him as having been a great traveller; and Ant. Wood (Antiq. Oxon.) says, "He was a man of extensive erudition, and of considerable eloquence; and one of the first who laboured to polish his native language, and rescue it from barbarism." At the request of his munificent patron, he engaged in the translation of several Latin works into English, particularly Higden's *Polychronicon;* Bartholomæus *De Proprietatibus Rerum;* Vegetius *De Arte Militari;* and Ægidius Romanus *De Regimine Principum;* besides some others of inferior note. The most complete collection of his writings is in a ponderous MS. folio volume, written upon vellum, and preserved among the Harleian MSS., No. 1900, in the British Museum. This volume contains several tracts, of which the following have been mentioned:—1. A Dialogue between a Soldier and a Clergyman, (viz., Lord Berkeley and the author Trevisa.) 2. A Translation of a Latin Sermon of Radulf, or Fitz-Rauf, archbishop of Armagh, November 8th, 1357, against Mendicant friars. 3. The Book of Methodius Patarensis, "of the begynnyng of the world and the Rewmes bitwixte, of Folkis, and the end of Worldes—which the noble man Syent Jerom ī his werkes prysed." 4, 5. Two alphabetical Indexes to the Polychro-

* Warton's History of English Poetry, vol. iii, p. 85.

nicon. 6. Dialogue on Translations. This dialogue, between a clergyman and his patron, (viz., Trevisa and Lord Berkeley,) discusses the utility of translations in general, and of that of the *Polychronicon*, to which it was first prefixed, in particular. The following extract from it will exhibit his mode of reasoning:—

"*The Clerke.* The latyn is bothe good and fayre; therfore it nedeth not to haue an Englysshe translacyon.

"*The Lorde.* A blere eyed man but he were all blynde of wytte myght se the solucyon of this reason. And though he were blynde he myght grope the solucyon. But yf his feelynge hym fayled. For yf this reason were ought worthe, by suche maner arguynge me myght proue that the threscore and thyne interpretours and Aquyla, Symachus, Theodocion, and Origines, were lewdli* occupyed whan they translated holy wryte out of hebrewe into grece, and also that Saynte Jherome was lewdly occupyed when he translated holy wryte out of hebrewe into latyn. For the hebrewe is both good and fayre and I wryte by inspyracyon of the holy goost. And all these for theyr translacyons ben hygely preysed of all holy chirche."

"Also holy wryte in latyn is bothe good and fayr. And yet for to make a sermon of holy wryte all in latyn to men that can Englysshe and noo latyn, it were a lewde dede, for they be neuer the wiser. For the latyn but it be tolde them in Englysshe what it is to mene. And it maye not be tolde in Englysshe what the latyn is to mene without translacyon out of latyn into Englysshe. Thenne it nedeth to haue an Englysshe translacyon, and for to kepe it in mynde that it be not forgeten it is better that suche a translacyon be made and wryten than sayd and not wryten and so this forsayde lewde reason shol demene no man that hath any wytte to leve the makyng of Englysshe translacyon."

* * * * * * * *

"Also at prayenge of King Charles Johan Scot translated denys bokes† out of greke into latyn, and then out of latyn into frensshe, then what hath Englysshe trespaced that it myght not be translated into Englysshe. Also kynge Alurede that founded the vnyuersyte of Oxonford translated the best lawes into Englysshe tongue. And a grete dele of the Psalter out of latyn into Englysshe. And caused Wyrefryth bysshop of Wyrcetre to translate saynt Gregoryes bokes the Dyalogues out of latyn into Saxons. Also Cedmon of Whytley was enspyred of the holy goost and made wonder

* *Lewd*, ignorant; hence, perhaps, *lewd-man*, a layman.

† Probably the works attributed to Dionysius the Areopagite.

Poysyes into Englysshe nyghe of all the storyes of holy wryte. Also the holy man Beda translated saynt Johan's gospell out of latyn into Englysshe. Also thou wotest wher the Apocalypsys is wryten in the walles and roof of chappell bothe in latyn and in frensshe. Also the gospell and prophecye and the ryght fayth of holy chyrche muste be taught and preched to englisshe men that can* noo latyn. Thenne the gospell and prophecye and the right fayth of holy chyrche must be told them in Englysshe, and that is not done but by Englysshe translacyon, for such Englysshe prechynge is very translacyon, and suche Englysshe preching is good and nedefull, thenn Englysshe translacyon is good and nedeful."

"*The Clerke.* Yf a translacyon were made that myght be amended in ony point. Some men it wolde blame."

"*The Lorde.* Yf men blame that is not worthy to be blamed thenne they by to blame. Clerkes knowe well ynoughe that noo synfull man dothe soo well that it ne myght do better, ne make so good a translacyon that he ne myght be better. Therfore Origines made two translacyons. And Jherom translated thryes the Psalter."†

On the subject of Trevisa's Translation of the BIBLE, writers are divided in their opinions. For while some have strenuously maintained that he was the author of a translation of the Bible, others have obstinately denied the claim, and have asserted that he did no more than translate certain sentences, which were painted on the chapel walls, in Berkeley Castle. The affirmative opinion was first taken up by Bale and Pits, from a loose assertion of Caxton, in the Proheme of his edition of the *Polychronicon;* but on what authority our printer asserted it, or if he *saw* such a translation, why he did not think it at least as deserving of publication as the *Polychronicon*, are questions which may be thought to press hard upon the probability of its existence. The learned Wanley, the compiler of the catalogue of the Harleian MSS. has the following pithy observations upon it: "As to the Bible's being wholly translated by our author Trevisa, I perceive it mentioned by Caxton, and from him by Bale and Pits, who give the beginning of the preface thereunto; from Bale, Primate Usher takes the notion; and at length Mr. Wharton believes it may still be extant. I shall say no more but this: I shall be very glad to see one of them." (*Harl. Cat. MSS.*, No. 1900.‡) The Rev. T. F. Dibdin, whose

* *Can*, know.

† Polychronicon, lib. i, Dyalogue Fo. ii.

‡ Dibdin's Typographical Antiquities, vol. i, *Account of books printed by W. Caxton*, p. 140. Lond., 1810, 4to.

extensive bibliographical researches are universally known and acknowledged, has given some novel and interesting information respecting Trevisa's translation, in his Typographical Antiquities, vol. i, p. 142.*

"It happened," says he, "on the second course of Lectures on Ancient English Literature, which I delivered at the Royal Institution, having occasion to examine the literary character of Trevisa, and being very solicitous to obtain the minutest information relating to this Bible, I wrote to my friend the Rev. Mr. Hughes, who was resident in the earl of Berkeley's family, at Berkeley Castle. His reply to my queries, with his permission, I lay before the reader; from a conviction that it may afford him some satisfaction on so interesting a subject.

"*Berkeley Castle, Nov. 7th,* 1805.

"I take the earliest opportunity of answering yours, having been here but a few days. I have made every inquiry and search respecting the information you want, and am sorry to say it is not in my power to remove the uncertainty you labour under respecting Trevisa's translation of the Bible; notwithstanding I have the strongest reason to suppose, from circumstances I have met with, that such a translation was made, and was even made in the English language, and that it existed in this family so late as the time of James II. The book translated by Trevisa was given, *as a very precious gift*, by the lord of Berkeley to the prince (I suppose) of Wales, and the prince's letter, thanking the lord of Berkeley for his gift, I have read: he does not say *positively* that it was the Bible, but as he hopes (as far as I recollect) to be able to make good use of so valuable a gift, there is reason to suspect that he meant the Bible. The letter is still extant among the archives of the castle. Lord Berkeley (of whom I have made inquiries in order to ascertain what you wanted, if possible) has informed me, that the book given by his ancestor, is at present, as he has reason to believe, in the Vatican at Rome: when he was there several persons had mentioned their seeing such a book written by Trevisa, but he had not an opportunity to go and examine it himself, therefore *cannot ascertain that it was the Bible*. The only vestige of Trevisa remaining here now, are a few fragments of board, with

* The writer of the present work cannot permit the opportunity to pass, without publicly acknowledging his obligations to the ingenious and laborious editor of the Typographical Antiquities; who, on the solicitation of a stranger, gave him, in the most handsome manner, permission to "avail himself of any portion of his works, which he was disposed to think might be of the least importance to his pursuits."

nearly obliterated words of Latin, not sufficient to make out what was meant: the roof of this chapel was said by him to have had the Apocalypse written upon it, and I suspect these fragments to be the remains of it. The beams and wall-plates of the chapel are still remaining, and after removing several coats of lamp-black, &c., four lines were discovered upon each, written in the old English character, which are alternately Norman-French, and Latin. By removing also several coats of whitewash from a part of the chapel wall, a great deal of writing in the old English character was discovered; it was in a great state of decay, but I could make out that part of it was in Norman-French, and part in Latin; this is also thought to be of Trevisa's day: but not one certain vestige of him remains here, nor is even his grave in the church known, though he is said to have been buried in the chancel. I suspect all his translations, both from French and Latin, were into English, but suspicions won't do for you. I wish it were in my power to give you more certain information.

"Yours very sincerely,

"JOHN HUGHES."

In reply also to what has been urged against Caxton's assertion of a translation having been made by Trevisa, it is sufficient to remark, that the danger attending the printing of an English Bible, in Caxton's time, was such, that it would have required the utmost religious intrepidity to have attempted it; and that it is therefore highly probable, that whatever preference our printer might have for the Scriptures, he would not place his life in jeopardy for its publication. Sir Thomas More (Dyaloges, fol. 49, col. 1, ed. 1529) thus defends the printers of that age:—"That on account of the penalties ordered by Archbishop Arundel's constitution, though the old translations that were before Wycliff's days remayned lawful and were in some folkys handys had and red, yet he thought no prynter would lyghtly be so hote to put any Byble in prent at hys owne charge, whereof the loss should lie wholly on his own necke, and then hange upon a doubtfull tryall whyther the fyrst copy of his translacyon was made before Wycliff's dayes or synnes. For yff yt were made synnys, yt must be approued byfore the pryntyng." But such an approbation, Sir Thomas intimates, was not then to be had.*

Trevisa finished his translation of the *Polychronicon* in 1387;

* Dibdin's Typographical Antiquities. *Life of Caxton*, p. cxii.

and is said to have died in the year 1412, at a very advanced age.

But whatever judgment may be formed as to the translation by Trevisa, all are agreed that WICLIFF, the Morning Star of the Reformation, engaged in a translation of the WHOLE BIBLE into English, which he completed A. D. 1380.

The opposition made by this great reformer to the tyranny of papacy, and the vices of the friars, drew down upon him the thunders of the papal hierarchy, and subjected him to all the virulence of irritated ecclesiastics. His protests against their domination were declared to be the consequence of disappointed ambition; and his sentiments respecting the eucharist were denounced as heretical. To combat the arguments of his adversaries, and to defend himself against the attacks of power, and learning, and interest, he flew to the Word of God, and found it "a strong hold in the day of trouble." Skilled in all the niceties of school divinity, in which he is said to have reigned without a rival, he was able to expose the sophistry of the subtlest of his enemies: but only the sacred Scriptures could furnish him with a system of truth, and with the plain and lucid arguments by which that truth is best defended. The more powerful that his opponents became, and the greater the difficulties which he had to encounter, the more precious became the Bible, the more diligently did he study it, and the more strenuously did he recommend it to general attention, and universal perusal.

Of the necessity that existed for an English translation of the Bible, arising from the ignorance of both clergy and laity, the writings of Wicliff afford ample proof. In his "Great Sentence of Curse expounded," he assures us, that in his time there were "many unable curates that kunnen not the Ten Commandments, ne read their Sauter, ne understond a verse of it." Nay, that it was then "notorious that too many of even the prelates were sinners, in their being ignorant of the Law of GOD, and that the freres supplied, for the bishops, the office of preaching, which they did in so false and sophistical a manner, that the church was deceyved instead of being edified." In his tract entitled "The Wickett," he says the clergy affirmed, "It is heresy to speake of the Holy Scripture in *English;* and so they woulde condempne the Holy Goste that gave it in tongues to the apostles of Christe, as it is written to speake the Worde of GOD, in all languages that were ordayned of GOD under heaven, as it is wrytten:" and again in "The Husbandman's Prayer and Complaint," he complains, "Thilk that have the key of conning have y lockt the truth of thy teaching under many wardes, and y hid fro thy children."*

The views which this great man entertained of the distinction between the canonical and apocryphal writings, and of the qualifications requisite for an expositor of Scripture, discover the correctness of his judgment, and prepare us for receiving him as a distinguished and intelligent translator of the sacred writings. "I think it absurd," says he, "to be warm in defence of the apocryphal books, when we have so many which are undeniably authentic. In order to distinguish canonical books from such as are apocryphal, use the following rules: 1. Look into the New Testament, and see what books of the Old Testament are threin cited and authenticated by the Holy Ghost. 2. Consider whether the like doctrine be delivered by the Holy Ghost elsewhere in the Scriptures." And speaking of an expositor of Scripture, he observes: "1. He should be able by collation of manuscripts to settle well the sacred text. 2. He should be conversant in logic. 3. He should be constantly engaged in comparing one part of Scripture with another. 4. The student should be a man of prayer, and his disposition should be upright. 5. He needs the internal instruction of the Primary Teacher:" remarking, in another part of his writings, that "some are enlightened from above that they may explain the proper, literal, and historical sense of Scripture, in which sense all things necessary in Scripture are contained."† Probably intending, by this last remark, to guard his readers against the fantastic and allegorical method of expounding the Scriptures, which had been so prevalent in the church since the time of Origen, whose ardent and sportive imagination had indulged itself without restraint in figurative and fanciful interpretations of the divine oracles. This anxiety, that expositors should give the just sense of Scripture, led him to urge the necessity of seeking illumination from the inspirer of the sacred word; hence the direction to the student to be "a man of prayer;" and hence also his observation, that "sanctity of life promotes this illumination so necessary for understanding the revealed word; to continue which in the church is the duty of theologians, who ought to remain within their proper limits, and not invent things foreign to the faith of Scripture."‡

Under the influence of these views of the nature and importance

* Lewis's Life of Wicliffe, pp. 38, 67.

† See Milner's Hist. of the Church of Christ, vol. iv, pp. 132–134.

‡ Milner, *ut sup.*

of a faithful and perspicuous translation of the Holy Scriptures into the vernacular language of the nation, our reformer entered upon the vast undertaking. In this work Wicliff appears to have been assisted by other learned men, whose religious opinions were similar to his own; though it is not now possible to say to what extent they rendered him assistance. The Rev. H. H. Baber, in his "Historical Account of Saxon and English Versions of the Scriptures," says, that in a MS. of Wicliff's Bible, in the valuable library of Mr. Douce, *explicit translacionem Nicholay de Herford*, is written at the end of a portion of the book of Baruch, (viz., the two first chapters, and part of the third,) and adds, that "this remarkable notice is subscribed by a different hand, and with a less durable ink, than that used by the transcriber of the MS., and, if not written by Herford himself, was probably done by one who had good authority for what he thus asserted by his pen." This Nicholas de Herford, or Hereford, was of Queen's College, Oxford, and a strenuous asserter of Wicliff's doctrines. On this account he was cited to appear, with John Aston, priest, and Philip Rampingdon, or Repingden, two of the reformer's disciples, before Archbishop Courtney, at his court held at the Preaching Friars, London, in 1382. The answers which he and Dr. Repingdon gave in writing to the court being adjudged insufficient, heretical, and deceitful, they were ordered to appear again eight days afterward; but not then appearing, they were declared contumacious, and excommunicated, with all their adherents. Afterward he recanted his principles, but did not escape persecution; for Archbishop Arundel, who was jealous of his principles, threw him into prison, and never afterward released him from imprisonment.*

The MSS. of Wicliff's version are numerous, and are to be found in most of the public libraries of the United Kingdom, and in some of the valuable libraries of private individuals. At the end of some of these copies are tables of the portions of Scripture appointed to be read, or selected, for the "Pistlis" and Gospels throughout the service of the year. Sometimes we find these lessons transcribed at length, and, in some instances, of a different translation from that to which they are annexed. An edition, consisting of only one hundred and forty copies, of Wicliff's New Testament, was published in 1731, in folio, by the Rev. John Lewis, minister of Margate, in the county of Kent, who prefixed a "History of the English Translations of the Bible:" printed sepa-

* Lewis's Life of Wicliffe, pp. 208-212.

rately, with additions, in octavo, in 1739. Another edition of this translation of the New Testament, accompanied with "Memoirs of the Life, &c., of John Wicliff, D.D.," an excellent "Historical Account of the Saxon and English Versions of the Scriptures, previous to the opening of the Fifteenth Century," and a portrait of our great reformer, was published by the Rev. Henry Hervey Baber, M. A., an assistant librarian of the British Museum, and an assistant preacher at Lincoln's Inn, in 1810, beautifully printed in quarto, by R. Edwards, London. These are the only editions yet published of any part of this translation, and we have still to lament that the larger portion, the Old Testament, of a work so interesting to the theologian and philologist, hitherto remains in MS. without a single printed edition, notwithstanding the last-mentioned editor, with a highly creditable zeal, thus expresses himself in the preface to his edition of the New Testament: "I would gladly have extended my labours, by giving to the world Wicliff's version of the Old as well as of the New Testament, (a work which no man hath yet had the courage to attempt,) and hence have wiped away a reproach which a learned foreigner* hath, with too much reason, cast upon England; but as my fortune is by no means commensurate with my zeal, I must, I fear, relinquish even the most distant hope of ever engaging in such an honourable employment."

This translation was made by Wicliff from the Latin Bibles then in common use, or which were at that time usually read in the church; the reason of which seems to have been, not that he thought the Latin the original, or of the same authority with the Hebrew and Greek text, but because he did not understand those languages sufficiently to translate from them; few at that time possessing an extensive or critical acquaintance with them. He also translated word for word, as had been done before in the Anglo-Saxon version, without always observing the idioms of the different languages, which renders this translation not very intelligible, in some places, to those who do not understand Latin. This was probably done, as is said in a prologue to the Psalter of this translation, that "they who knew not the Latin, by the English might come to many Latin words."†

No sooner had Wicliff completed his translation, and made it

* Fabricius, after mentioning Wicliff's version of the Bible, thus expresses himself: "Mirum vero est, Anglos eam [versionem] tam diu neglexisse, quum vel linguæ causa ipsis in pretio esse debeat."—*Bibl. Lat. et inf. ætatis*, tom. v, p. 321, edit. 1754.

† Lewis's History of English Translations, p. 19.

public, than he experienced the most violent opposition. The translation of the Scriptures into the vernacular tongue was accounted heresy, and regarded as a measure fraught with the direst ills. Henry de Knyghton, a canon of Leicester, and cotemporary with Wicliff, thus declaims against the translation, in his work *De Eventis Angliæ:* "Christ committed the gospel to the clergy and doctors of the church, that they might minister it to the laity and weaker persons, according to the exigency of times, and persons, and wants; but this Master John Wicliff translated it out of *Latin* into *English*, and by that means laid it more open to the laity, and to women who could read, than it used to be to the most learned of the clergy, and those of them who had the best understanding: and so the gospel pearl is cast abroad and trodden under foot of swine, and that which used to be precious to both clergy and laity is made, as it were, the common jest of both; and the jewel of the church is turned into the sport of the laity, and what was before the chief talent of the clergy and doctors of the church is made for ever common to the laity."* William Butler, a Franciscan friar, in a tract written against this translation, pursues the point so far as to assert that "the prelates ought not to suffer that every one at his pleasure should read the Scripture translated (even) into Latin; because, as is plain from experience, this has been many ways the occasion of falling into heresies and errors. It is not therefore politic that any one, wheresoever and whensoever he will, should give himself to the frequent study of the Scriptures."†

Wicliff himself, in a homily on Matthew xi, 23, thus complains of the severe usage he met with on account of translating the Holy Scriptures:—"He, Antecrist," says he, "hath turned hyse clerkes to covetyse and worldely love, and so blynded the peple and derked the law of *Crist*, that hys servauntes ben thikke and few ben on Cristes syde; and algates they dyspysen that men shulden knowe *Crystes* lyfe, for thenne priestes schulden schome of hyre lyves, and specially these hye prestes, for thei reversen *crist* both in worde and in dede. And herfore on gret byschop of *englelond*‡

* Lewis's Life of Wicliffe, p. 67. † Ibid., p. 71.

‡ By *one great bishop of England* is probably meant John Bokynham, or Bukkingham, at this time bishop of Lincoln, in whose diocess Wicliff was promoted, and by whom, it seems, he was summoned and prosecuted for translating the Scriptures into English. By *another priest*, he seems to intend Wylliam de Swyndurby, a priest of Leicester, in this diocess, and a favourer of the sentiments of Wicliff. Knyghton tells us, that "the common people called him William the Hermit, from having formerly

is yuel payed, that Godde's lawe is written in englysche to lewede men, and he pursueth a prest for he wryteth to men this englysche, and sompneth hym and traveleth hym that hyt is harde to hym to

adopted that mode of life, and that at his first coming to Leicester he conformed to the usual habits of life, and conversed with the people; but beginning to 'preach against the faults, and particularly the pride of women,' they were so incensed against him that they proposed to stone him out of the place, till he changed his subject, and preached against the rich, and against their pride, and vanity, and excessive love of this world. Afterward he directed his declamations against the clergy and the church, affirming that the clergy 'lived lewd lives, and did ill receive the goods of the church, and spend them worse;' and preaching that 'parishioners were not obliged to pay their tithes and offerings to the clergy, if they did not live chastely, and in all other respects as became the priests of God; or if they did not stay in their parishes, and spend the goods of the church where they received them; or if they were unskilled in, or not ready in speaking the language in which they were to preach, so that they could not duly or sufficiently instruct the people.'" "He preached likewise," adds Knyghton, "that men might, consistent with charity, ask those who owed them money for what they were indebted to them, but might by no means sue them, or imprison them for debt;" and that "no one who lived contrary to the law of God was a priest, notwithstanding he might have been ordained by the bishop." By these and similar doctrines, the same author informs us, Swyndurby captivated the affections of the people, so that they declared they had never seen nor heard any one who so well explained the truth to them, and "reverenced him as another god."

When Bishop Bukkyngham heard of his proceedings, he immediately suspended him from all preaching in any chapel, church, or church-yard, within the diocess of Lincoln; and inhibited the people that none of them should presume to hear him preach, nor favour the preacher, under the penalty of excommunication. Swyndurby, however, was not to be deterred; but, on hearing the interdict of the bishop, made himself a pulpit on two millstones, which stood in the High-street, near the chapel he had formerly occupied, where he called the people together, and preached to them many times, saying, "He could and would, in spite of the bishop's teeth, preach in the king's highway, so long as he had the good will of the people." Then you might see, says Knyghton, throngs of people from every part, as well from the town as country, double the number that there used to be when they might hear him preach much more lawfully, pressing to hear him preach after this inhibition and thundering out the sentence of excommunication, which had been denounced in the abbey and many other churches. The bishop therefore cited him to appear in the cathedral of Lincoln. Knyghton says, that being convicted, he abjured his errors, but afterward relapsed, and went to Coventry, where he was expelled the diocess, with shame and contempt, by the diocesan and clergy. This account, however, can scarcely be admitted; for it is not probable that, if he had been convicted of heresy and error, and had publicly adjured, and afterward relapsed, he would have been so gently dealt with. Walsingham's account is therefore more probable, who says, that "when the bishop of Lincoln had made preparations to correct this man, and to take away from him his license to preach, the mad multitude raged in such a manner as frightened the bishop, and deterred him from proceeding against him." What became of him afterward is unknown: Fox, in his "Actes and Monumentes," conjectures that he was burnt in the following reign. See Lewis's *Life of Wicliffe*, pp. 222–228.

route. And thus he pursueth another prest by the help of the pharyses, [that is, the friars,] for he precheth *criste's* gospel frely withouten fables. O men that ben of *criste's* half, helpe ye nowe ageyns Antecrist. For the perelouse tyme is comen that *crist* and *poule* [Paul] tolden byfore. But on coumfort is of knyghtes* that they saveren muche the gospel, and have wylle to rede in *englysche* the gospel of *crist's* lyf."†

But our reformer, who had long and zealously vindicated the propriety of a translation of the Bible into the English language, was only the more convinced, by the opposition of his enemies, and by the weakness of their arguments, of the importance and utility of such an undertaking. The following extracts will exhibit the manner in which this great man defended the right of the people to read the Scriptures, and to have a translation of them into their mother tongue. "The Scripture," he observes, "is the faith of the church, and the more it is known in an orthodox sense, the better: therefore, as secular men ought to know the faith, so it is to be taught them in whatever language is best known to them. Besides, since the truth of the faith is clearer and more exact in the Scripture than the priests know how to express it, and that, if one may say so, there are many prelates who are too ignorant of Scripture, and others who conceal what is contained in it; it seems useful that the faithful should themselves search out or discover the sense of the faith, by having the Scriptures in a language which they know and understand. Moreover, according to the apostle, (Hebrews xi,) the saints by faith overcame kingdoms, and chiefly by the motive of faith hastened to their own country: why, therefore, ought not the fountain of faith to be made known to the people by those means, that will enable a man to know it more clearly? He who hinders this, or murmurs against it, does his endeavour to cause the people to continue in a damnable and unbelieving state. So the laws which are made by prelates are not to be received as matters of faith; nor are we to believe their words or discourses, any further than they are founded on Scripture, for, according to the constant doctrine of Augustine, 'the Scripture is all the truth.' A translation of the Scriptures, therefore, would do this good, that it would render priests and

* "The soldiers, with the dukes and earls, were the chief adherents and favourers of this sect. They were their most strenuous promoters, and boldest combatants;—their most powerful defenders, and their invincible protectors."—*Knyghton, De Event.*, quoted by Lewis in his History of English Translations, p. 22, *note.*

† Lewis's Hist. of English Translations, pp. 21, 22.

prelates unsuspected as to the words of it, which they explain. Christ and his apostles converted men, by making known to them the Scripture in a language which was familiar to the people; and for this purpose the Holy Spirit gave the apostles the knowledge of tongues. Why, then, ought not the modern disciples of Christ to collect fragments from the same loaf; and, as they did, clearly and plainly open the Scriptures to the people, that they may know them? Besides, since, according to what the apostle teaches, all must stand before the judgment seat of Christ, and be answerable to him for all the goods with which he has intrusted them, it is necessary that all the faithful should know these goods and the use of them, that their answer may then be ready. For an answer by a prelate or an attorney will not *then* avail, but every one *must* answer in his *own* person."*

Our renowned reformer, JOHN DE WICLIF,† it is supposed, was born about the year 1324, in the parish of Wiclif, a village near Richmond, in Yorkshire. He was first a commoner of Queen's College, Oxford, then newly founded by Robert Eaglesfield, chaplain to Queen Philippina, consort of Edward III. From thence he was soon removed to Merton College, which was at that time esteemed one of the most famous seminaries of learning in Europe, where he was a probationer, and afterward fellow. Here Wiclif availed himself of the high advantages he enjoyed, and by the native vigour of his mind, united to uncommon application, rose to the first rank of literary eminence. He is said to have committed to memory the most intricate part of the writings of the *Stagyrite*, and to have been an unrivalled disputant in the theology of the schools. He was excellently versed in the knowledge of civil and canon law in general, and of our own municipal laws in particular. But the Holy Scriptures were his principal study and chief delight, which was probably what gained him the title of *Doctor Evangelicus*, the Evangelic Doctor. Next to the Scriptures, he esteemed and studied the works of Augustine, Jerome, Ambrose, and Gregory. He was also a great admirer of the writings of Bishop Grosseteste and of Archbishop Fitzralph.‡ His defence of the university against the encroachments of the Mendicant

* Lewis's Life of Wicliffe, ch. v, p. 69.

† This mode of spelling our reformer's name I have adopted from Baber, who remarks, that "it is so spelled in the oldest document in which his name is known to appear, viz., in the instrument which nominated him one of the embassy to meet the pope's delegates, in 1374."

‡ See p. 357 of this volume.

friars gained him very general approbation; and in 1361 he was advanced to the dignity of master of Baliol College, and four years afterward to that of warden of Canterbury Hall. From this office he was ejected in 1367, by Archbishop Langham, with circumstances of great injustice. Wiclif appealed to the pope, who for some years artfully suspended the decision, but in 1370 confirmed the ejection, owing, as has been conjectured, partly to the pope's partiality for the Mendicants, and partly to Wiclif's defence of King Edward III. against the homage demanded by the pope.

In 1372 Wiclif began to read public lectures on divinity, in the university. At first he gently and covertly attacked the reigning abuses of the friars, and the general corruptions of papacy; but finding he gained the attention of his hearers, he openly and boldly exposed whatever he deemed erroneous in the habits of the ecclesiastics or the doctrines of the church. His intrepidity increased his fame, and he was almost everywhere regarded as the great defender of liberty and truth, except by the minions of the pope, who never ceased to pursue the object of their hate with every species of malignant rage. In 1374 he was sent by the king, in conjunction with the bishop of Bangor and others, upon an embassy to the pope, to treat concerning the liberties of the Church of England; and in the same year was presented by Edward to the valuable rectory of Lutterworth, in Leicestershire. Afterward, in 1375, he was confirmed in the prebend of Auste, in the collegiate church of Westbury, in Gloucestershire; and is said to have been again employed in a diplomatic character, being delegated with several barons of the realm to the court of the duke of Milan.

The embassies in which our reformer was engaged, and the extensive opportunities he thus possessed of examining the haughty claims of the Romish pontiff, and of marking the universal degeneracy of the papal hierarchy, roused his indignation, and sharpened his invectives against those who palliated or defended the gross depravities of the monks and friars, or the shameless oppressions of the papal court. Stung by the keenness of his censures, the Romish clergy rallied their forces, selected from his works nineteen articles of complaint and accusation, and despatched them to the pope. Bull after bull was transmitted by his holiness to England, to demand the trial of the arch-heretic, and the condemnation of his writings. These the government and university long treated with contempt; and though the university of Oxford at last yielded to receive the papal mandate, they refused to lend the least active assistance against Wiclif. But the archbishop of

Canterbury and the bishop of London, the resolute advocates of the papacy, cited him to appear before them on the thirtieth day after the notice. Wiclif immediately placed himself under the protection of John of Gaunt, duke of Lancaster, who had long known and esteemed him. By the advice of this nobleman, who accompanied him in person, he obeyed the citation; where the haughty and insulting expressions of the bishop of London to Lord Percy so irritated the duke, that he treated the bishop with contumely and contempt; the court broke up in tumult and confusion; and Wiclif was dismissed with an admonition not to repeat his obnoxious doctrines, either in the schools or the pulpit.

The death of the duke of Lancaster imboldening the English prelates, they again cited the heretic to appear before them, in 1378, when he was again rescued by the populace, and the authority of the queen dowager, widow of the Black Prince. The same year their commission ceased, by the death of the pope, Gregory XI. A double election ensued, the rival popes assuming the respective names of Urban VI. and Clement VII., though Urban at last proved the successful candidate. This event was noticed by Wiclif, in a tract "Of the Schism of the Roman Pontiffs;" and shortly after he published another, "Of the Truth of the Scripture." In the latter he contends for the translation of the Scriptures into English; and affirms that God's will is plainly revealed in two Testaments; that Christ's law sufficeth by itself to rule Christ's church; that a Christian man, well understanding it, may thence gather sufficient knowledge during his pilgrimage here upon earth; and that, whereas all truth is contained in Holy Scripture, whatever disputation is not originally thence to be deduced is to be accounted profane.

The extraordinary exertions and the harassing persecutions which Wiclif underwent during the year 1378 occasioned a fit of sickness that brought him almost to the point of death. Immediately on hearing of it, the Mendicant friars selected four grave doctors from their four orders, and after certain instructions, sent them, with four respectable citizens, aldermen of the wards, to the afflicted reformer. These commissioners found him lying in his bed, and are said, first of all, to have wished him health and recovery from sickness. After some time, they reminded him of the many and great injuries he had done to the Mendicant friars, by his sermons and writings, and exhorted him, that as he was now near death, he would, as a true penitent, bewail and revoke, in their presence, whatever he had said to their disparagement.

But Wiclif, immediately recovering strength, called his servants, and ordered them to raise him a little on his pillows. This being done, he said, with a loud voice, "I SHALL NOT DIE, BUT LIVE, AND DECLARE THE EVIL DEEDS OF THE FRIARS." On hearing this, the doctors and their associates left him in great confusion; and the sick man soon recovered, according to his prediction.

The year after his recovery from this sickness, this defender of the truth seems to have completed and published his TRANSLATION OF THE BIBLE, A. D. 1380; and soon afterward commenced a public attack upon the doctrine of transubstantiation. This he did in the lectures which he delivered at Oxford, in the summer of 1381. Violent and various were the measures adopted against him, in consequence of this opposition to the favourite doctrine of the Church of Rome. The prelates again summoned him to appear before them; the parliament, to which he appealed, rejected his appeal, and, at the instigation of his great adversary Courtney, formerly bishop of London, but now archbishop of Canterbury, passed an act against his "Conclusions," or opinions on the subject; his patron, the duke of Lancaster, advised submission; and he was at length dismissed from the chair of the divinity professor, which he had, for so many years, filled with unequalled applause.

But although compelled to quit the university, and retire to the rectory of Lutterworth, he pursued his studies, and continued his endeavours to promote the reformation of the church. Among the writings which distinguished his retirement was a tract on the causes "Why pore priests have no benefices;" written in defence of his followers. The reasons he assigns for their being without benefices, or not accepting them, are, 1. The fear of simony: 2. The fear of misspending poor men's goods: 3. The fear of being prevented from better occupation, or greater usefulness to the church, by being restricted to a single cure or parish. In the chapter on simony he thus describes the nefarious practices which then existed:—"Some lords to colouren their symony wole not take for themselves, but kenerchiefs for the lady, or a palfray, or a tun of wine. And when some lords wolden present a good man, and able for love of GOD, and Christen souls, then some ladies ben means to have a dancer, or tripper on tapits, or hunter, or hawker, or a wild player of summers gamenes, for flattering and gifts going betwixe."

The contest between Pope Urban VI. and the French, who were the friends of his rival, occasioned the pontiff to determine upon war. With this view, and to enable him to raise an army of sufficient force, plenary indulgences and pardons were promised to all who would afford personal or pecuniary aid. A bull to this effect was sent to Henry le Spencer, bishop of Norwich, who readily entered into the views of the pope, and obtained numerous contributors; so that even women presented their jewels, necklaces, rings, dishes, plates, and spoons, hoping to obtain absolution for themselves and their friends. Wiclif was not a silent spectator of such a violation of the religion of peace: he severely censured the rival parties, and in one of his tracts pointedly inquired, "Why wole not the proud priest of Rome grant full pardon to all men, for to live in peace, and charity and patience, as he doth to all men to fight and slee Christen men?" The exasperated pontiff cited Wiclif to appear before him; but his feeble state of health was offered as an apology for not undertaking so long and perilous a journey. He had already had one attack of palsy, and his debilitated frame sunk under a second attack of the same disease, two years afterward. His last seizure was during the time of divine service, in the church of Lutterworth; which on the third day terminated the valuable life of this great and intrepid reformer, December 30th, 1384. His body was buried in the chancel of his church, and there lay till 1428, when his bones were disinterred and burnt, and his ashes thrown into the Swift, a neighbouring stream, at the command of Pope Martin V., by Richard Flemyng, bishop of Lincoln, according to a decree of the infamous council of Constance, passed in 1415.

The most elaborate Life of Wiclif is that by the Rev. John Lewis; but the most correct list of his Works, and one of the best written lives, will be found prefixed by the Rev. H. H. Baber to his excellent edition of Wiclif's New Testament.

The opposition which was raised against Wiclif's translation, proceeded so far, that in 1390 (13. Ric. II.*) a bill was brought into the House of Lords for the suppression of it. On this occasion, John of Gaunt, duke of Lancaster, and uncle to the king, defended a vernacular translation, saying, "We will not be the dregs of all men; seeing other nations have the law of God, which is the law of our faith, written in their own language." Declaring, at the same time, in the most solemn manner, "That he would

* A Latin Psalter, ornamented with the most beautiful miniatures, and richly illuminated, for the use of this monarch when a youth, is preserved in the Cottonian library. It has a calendar, and various tables, besides hymns, and the Athanasian Creed. The king is represented, in different places, on his knees, before the Virgin Mary, who has the infant Jesus in her arms.—*Le Long*, vol. iv, p. 245.

maintain our having this law in our own tongue against those, whoever they should be, who first brought in the bill." The duke was seconded by others, who said, that "if the Gospel, by its being translated into English, was the occasion of men's running into error, they might know, that there were more heretics to be found among the *Latins*, than among the people of any other language. For that the decretals reckoned no fewer than sixty-six Latin heretics, and so the Gospel must not be read in Latin, which yet the opposers of the English translation allowed." The consequence of this firmness in Wiclif's patron and friends, was, that the bill was thrown out.*

It was probably this event which encouraged some of Dr. Wiclif's followers to review his translation, or rather, to make another, not so strict and verbal, but more according to the sense. The MS. copies of this translation are more rare than the others, but are to be met with in the Bodleian and other public libraries. One of these is said to have belonged to Bishop Bonner, of persecuting memory; who, in his book "Of the Seven Sacraments," (A. D. 1555,) observes, that he had "a Bible in *Englyshe* translated out of Latyne in tyme of heresye, almost eightscore yeare before that tyme," (that is, about 1395,) "fayre and truly written in parchement."†

From a MS. copy of this translation, in the library of Trinity College, Dublin, being inscribed with the name "J. Pervey," it has been concluded that John Purvey, or Purney, was the author of it. Knyghton (*De Event. Angliæ*) says, "He was a chaplain or curate, having no benefice of his own;—of a grave aspect and behaviour, affecting an appearance of sanctity beyond the rest of his fellows. In his clothes and dress he went as an ordinary man; and little regarding his own ease, was unwearied in studying, by travelling up and down, to persuade the people, and to bring them over to his sect. Being an invincible disciple of his master John Wiclif, he conformed himself to his opinions, and fearlessly confirmed them in every respect like an able executor. For having boarded with his master when he was alive, and thus having drank more plentifully of his instructions, he had more abundantly imbibed them, and always, even to his dying day, as an inseparable companion followed him and his opinions and doctrines, being unwearied in his labours and endeavours to propagate them." After Dr. Wiclif's death he used to preach at Bristol, till he was appre-

* Lewis's Hist. of English Translations, p. 28. † Ibid., p. 25.

hended and imprisoned by Thomas Arundel, archbishop of Canterbury, in Saltwood Castle, in Kent, a seat belonging to the archbishop. Here he was dreadfully tortured, and at last consented to recant, which he did at Paul's Cross, A. D. 1396. He was afterward promoted by the archbishop to a benefice, as is said, about a mile from the castle, which seems to intimate as if it were St. Mary's Hythe, or perhaps the rectory of Ostinhanger. But wherever the place was, he did not long continue in it, but quitted his benefice, and embraced his former opinions. After Arundel's death, he was again imprisoned by Archbishop Chichley, A. D. 1521; after which it is uncertain what became of him; though it is not improbable that he died in prison. Thomas of Walden, a zealous writer against the Lollards, or followers of Wiclif, gives him this character, that "he was the library of the Lollards, and Wiclif's glosser; an eloquent divine, and famous for his skill in the Law," or a notable canonist.*

But whoever was the author of the translation in question, it was most probably made by the same person who wrote the *Elucidarium Bibliorum*, or Prologue to the translation of the Bible; a work frequently, but erroneously, attributed to Wiclif himself. The design of the Prologue, which is in English, is to give a summary of the books of the Bible, with certain declarations of their use and authority. It was printed by John Gowghe in 1536, in 12mo., under the title of "The Dore of Holy Scripture." Another edition, in 12mo., was published in 1550, by Robert Crowley. The title of it was, "The pathway to perfect knowledge, the true copye of a prologue, wrytten about two hundred yeares paste by John Wycklyffe (as maye justly be gathered bi that, that John Bale hath wrytten of him in his Boke entitled, the summarie of famouse writers of the Ile of Great Britaine) the original whereof is found written in an olde Englishe Bible betwixt the Olde Testament and the Newe. Which Bible remaineth now in the Kyng hys Maiesties chamber." In this Prologue, which Lewis (Hist. of English Translations) and Baber (Life of Dr. Wiclif) have incontrovertibly proved to have been written after the reformer's death, the author gives the following account of his own translation of the Bible into English: "He, with several others who assisted him, got together," he says, "all the old Latyn Bibles they could procure: these they diligently collated, and corrected what errors had

* Fox's Actes and Monumentes, vol. i, p. 649, fol. 1570. Lewis's Life of Wicliffe, pp. 218–221. Lewis's Hist. of English Translations, pp. 34, 35.

crept into them, in order to make one Latin Bible some deal true; since many Bibles in Latin were very false, especially those that were new. Then they collected the doctors and common glosses, especially Lyra, with which they studied the text anew, in order to make themselves masters of the sense and meaning of it. Next they consulted the old grammarians and ancient divines as to the hard words and sentences, how they might be best understood and translated; which having done, they set about the translation, which they resolved should not be a verbal one, but as clearly as they could to express the sense and meaning of the text; for," says he, "it is to know that the best translating out of Latin into English, is to translate after the sentence, and not only after the words. So that the sentence be as open (either opener) in English as in Latin, and go not far from the letter." He adds, that "where the Hebrew, by witness of Jerome, of Lyra, and of other expositors, discordeth from our Latin Bibles, he had set in the margin, in manner of a gloss, what the Hebrew hath, and how it is understood in some other place. And that he did this most in the Psalter, that of all of our books discorded most from the Hebrew. In translating equivocal words," he remarks, "there might be some danger, since, if they were not translated according to the sense and meaning of the author, it was an error. Lastly," he tells us, that, "to make this translation as compleat and perfect as he could, he resolved to have many good fellows, and kunnyng, to correct it."* A MS. copy of this work is in the British Museum, *Harl. MS.* 1666. It is imperfect at the end.

The uncertainty and obscurity in which the author of the translation before us is involved, is not peculiar to himself; in numerous other instances it will appear that translators of different versions of the sacred writings are unknown. This has probably arisen from different causes; sometimes from that humble and self-diffident disposition, which has led the pious mind to retire from public view, and to aim only at the approbation of Him who "searches the heart;" and sometimes from a fear of persecution and suffering. For, although many in our day will be disposed to regard the man who first produced a translation of the Scriptures into the language of his country, as her greatest benefactor, and entitled to eminent rank in the annals of her moral improvement, it must be acknowledged, that these have not been the views of past ages; nor has history, in general, been constructed or written

* Lewis's Hist. of English Translations, p. 37. Lewis's Life of Wicliffe, p. 70.

under the influence of such impressions. Unfortunately, these co-operating causes prevent the possibility of an authentic biographical work being written, which should embrace the lives of all original translators of the sacred volume ; all that can be done, is to collect, from various quarters, such intimations as remain, respecting these valuable men, and their important labours.

"The lives of such persons, it may be said, could not have furnished many remarkable incidents; but we cannot tell: for although they did not all meet with similar treatment, to some of them, at least, the following lines are but too appropriate :—

> 'They lived unknown,
> Till persecution dragg'd them into fame,
> And chased them up to heaven. Their ashes flew
> ——No marble tells us whither. With their names
> No bard embalms and sanctifies his song ;
> And history, so warm on meaner themes,
> Is cold on this.' "*

CHAPTER XIII.

FIFTEENTH CENTURY.

Lollards—Bishop Arundel's Canon against Translations—Value of Books—Episcopus Puerorum—Learned Englishmen—Libraries—Henry VI.—John Huss—Jerome of Prague—Hussites—Invention of Printing.

WICLIF's followers were called LOLLARDS, from a German term, signifying *to sing hymns to God;* and increased so rapidly, that a contemporary writer affirms, "A man could not meet two people on the road, but one of them was a disciple of Wiclif."†

The vehemence with which they declaimed against the vices of the clergy, and the constant appeals which they made to the Holy Scriptures in defence of their opinions, drew down upon them the anathemas of their mitred adversaries, and occasioned the most severe laws to be enacted against those who should embrace their sentiments, or dare to read the word of God without ecclesiastical permission. In 1396, Thomas Arundel, archbishop of York, was translated to the see of Canterbury, and soon discovered by his conduct that he designed to employ against the Lollards all the additional power he had acquired by his promotion to the primacy.

* See Anderson's Memorial on behalf of the Native Irish, pp. 12, 13.

† Knyghton. See Lewis's Life of Wicliffe, ch. x, p. 175.

No sooner had Henry IV. gained possession of the throne of England, than Arundel, who had supported him in his pretensions to the crown, applied, with his clergy, to the parliament that met at Westminster, to obtain the sanction of the legislature to his cruel and iniquitous measures. In this he was unfortunately successful, and a severe law was passed against the dangerous innovations, as they were called, of the Lollards. By this law, made A. D. 1400, the bishops were authorized to imprison all persons suspected of heresy, and to try them in the spiritual court; and, if they proved either obstinate or relapsed heretics, the spiritual judge was to call the sheriff of the county, or the chief magistrate of the town, to be present when the sentence of condemnation was pronounced, and immediately to deliver the condemned person to the secular magistrate, who was to cause him *to be burnt to death*, on some elevated place, in the sight of all the people. The first person who suffered under the writ *De hæretico comburendo* was Sir William Sawtre, rector of St. Oswyth, London. One of the charges brought against him was, "That he had said he would not worship the cross on which Christ suffered, but only Christ that suffered upon the cross." Another of the charges was, "That he had declared, that a priest was more bound to preach the word of God, than to recite particular services at certain canonical hours." For such, alas! was the genius of the reigning superstition, that to worship the cross, and attend to customary formalities, was regarded as of more importance than to worship the Saviour, or to preach his gospel!*

In 1408 the archbishop held a convocation of the whole of the clergy of his province, at Oxford, the object of which was to frame certain constitutions against the Lollards. By the fifth constitution published in this covocation, it was ordained that "No book or treatise composed by John Wiclif, or by any other in his time, or since, or hereafter to be composed, be henceforth read in the schools, halls, inns, or other places whatsoever, within the province aforesaid; and that none be taught according to such [book,] unless it have been first examined, and upon examination *unanimously approved*, by the university of Oxford, or Cambridge, or at least by twelve men chosen by the said universities, or by one of them, under the discretion of us, or our successors; and then afterward [the book be approved] expressly by us, or our successors, and delivered in the name, and by the authority, of the universities,

* Fox's Actes and Monumentes, vol. i, p. 615. Henry's History of Great Britain, vol. x, b. v, ch. ii, p. 2.

to be copied and sold to such as desire it, (after it has been faithfully collated,) at a just price, the original thenceforth remaining in some chest* of the university for ever. And if any one shall read any book or treatise of this sort in the schools, or elsewhere, contrary to the form above written, or shall teach according to it, let him be punished according as the quality of the fact shall require, as a sower of schism, and a fautor of heresy."

Another constitution of the convocation was formed expressly *against the translation of the Scriptures into English*:—"VII. It is a dangerous thing,† as the blessed Jerome testifieth, to translate the text of the Holy Scriptures out of one language into another, because it is not always easy to retain the sense of the original in a translation, as the same blessed Jerome confesseth that, although inspired,‡ he frequently erred: we therefore enact and ordain, that no one hereafter do, by his own authority, translate any text of Holy Scripture into English, or any other tongue, by way of book, libel, or treatise; and that no one read any such book, libel, or treatise, now lately set forth in the time of John Wiclif, or since, or hereafter to be composed, in public or in private, in whole or in part, under pain of the greater excommunication, until the said translation be approved by the diocesan of the place, or, if occasion require, by a provincial council. Let him that acteth contrary be punished as a fautor of error and heresy."§

In the second year of the reign of Henry V., A.D. 1415, a law was passed, by which, in addition to the former laws against heresy, all Lollards, or those who possessed or read any of Wiclif's books, or entertained his opinions, were declared to be guilty of treason, and their goods ordered to be confiscated.‖ This law was considered as particularly directed against those who read the New Testament in English of Wiclif's translation. Our old writers thus express themselves respecting it: "In the said parliament"

* The books in the public libraries were, at that period, all kept in chests.

† Jerome's words, to which the constitution refers, are to be found in his letter to Pope Damasus, who had desired him to determine which of the various readings in the Latin copies agreed most correctly with the Greek text; and to which he replies, that it was very hazardous to decide: "For who is there," says he, "whether he be learned or unlearned, when he takes the Bible into his hands, and sees that what he reads differs from what he has been used to, who will not immediately clamour against me, as a falsifier and sacrilegious person, for daring to add, alter, or correct, any thing in books so ancient." See Lewis's History of English Translations, p. 44.

‡ Jerome never pretended to inspiration.

§ Labbei S. S. Concilia, tom. xi, pt. ii, p. 2095. Paris, 1671, fol.

‖ Fox's Actes and Monumentes, vol. i, p. 678.

(held at Leicester) "the kinge made this most blasphemous and cruell acte, to be a law for euer, That whosoeuer they were that should rede the Scriptures in the mother tong, (which was then called Wicleu's lerning,) they should forfet land, catel, body, lif, and godes, from theyr heyres for euer, and so be condempned for heretykes to God, ennemies to the crowne, and most errant traytors to the lande. Besides this, it was inacted, that neuer a sanctuary nor priuiliged grounde within the realme shulde holde them, though they were still permitted to theues and murtherers. And if in case they wold not gyue ouer, or were after their pardon relapsed, they shulde suffer death in two manner of kindes; that is, they shulde first be hanged for treason against the kinge, and then be burned for heresy against God, and yet neither of both committed."*

But violent as were the measures pursued against those who read the Scriptures in English, there were some found who at every hazard sought wisdom from the book of God. These, to promote the more general circulation of the Scriptures, caused select portions of Wiclif's translation to be written in small volumes, that the poor might purchase them, printing being unknown, and writing tedious and expensive. Lewis, the author of the "History of the English Translations of the Bible," possessed one of these copies in 24mo., which contained St. John's Gospel, the Epistles of St. James, St. Peter, St. John, St. Jude, and the Apocalypse.† The bishops' registers often mention these little books, or *libels*, as they were called, and notice them as being prohibited. Persons who were detected reading them, or even having them in possession, were prosecuted, and sometimes were burnt with them hanging about their necks. In 1429, Nicholas Belward, of South Elmham, in Suffolk, was accused of having in his possession a New Testament, which he had bought in London for *four marks and forty pence*, £2 16*s*. 8*d*., a sum equivalent to more than £40 at present; an astonishing price to have been paid by a *labouring man*, for such Belward appears to have been: William Wright deposing that he "had wrought with him continually by the space of one year; and studied diligently upon the said New Testament." In the same year an accusation was brought also against Margery Backster, in which it was deposed that she had desired Joan, the wife of one Cliffland, and her maid, to "come *secretly in the night* to her chamber, and there she

* Complete Collection of State Trials, vol. i, p. 49. Lond., 1730, 2d edit., folio.

† Lewis, p. 39.

should hear her husband read the *law of Christ* to them; which law was written in a book that her husband was wont *to read to her by night;* and that her husband was well learned in the Christian verity." Many other depositions, of a similar nature, were made by the enemies of the Lollards, in consequence of which the followers of Wiclif were subjected to various penances and imprisonments. Against Richard Fletcher of Beccles it was alleged, "He is a most perfect doctor in that sect, and can very well and perfectly expound the Holy Scriptures, and hath a book of the *New Law* in *English*." Against Sir Hugh Pye, priest, it was deposed, that he had "bequeathed to Alice, servant to William White, a New Testament, which they then called the book of the *New Law*, and was in custody of Oswald Godfrey of Colchester." Even the ability to read was enumerated among the crimes of this sect by their violent persecutors; for it is remarked in the deposi tions, that "William Bate, tailor, of Sything, and his wife, and his son, which can *read English* very well, is of the same sect;" that "the daughter of Thomas Moone is partly of the same sect, and can *read English*;" and that "John Pert, late servant of Thomas Moone, is of the same sect, and can *read* well, and did read in the presence of William White."*

The disciples of Wiclif, however, were not satisfied with knowing the truth, and themselves only reading the Scriptures: they were animated by more generous principles, and laudably anxious to place the Bible in the hands of others, as a powerful means of enlightening the mind, and influencing the heart. In the prosecution of this pious design, these early reformers were materially assisted by the zealous co-operation of Sir John Oldcastle, Lord Cobham, who expended considerable sums in collecting, transcribing, and dispersing the works of Wiclif; and in maintaining a number of itinerant preachers, who were employed in spreading the doctrines of our English reformer in different parts of the country, particularly in the diocesses of Canterbury, London, Rochester, and Hereford. Bale says, that he caused all the works of Wiclif to be copied by desire of John Huss, and to be sent into France, Spain, Bohemia, and other foreign countries. The support afforded the Lollards by this nobleman, and his zeal in the diffusion of evangelical truth, rendered him the object of the most cruel persecution. He was accused of heresy, condemned and imprisoned in the tower of London, from whence he found means to escape, but being reta-

* Fox's Actes and Monumentes, vol. i, pp. 786–788.

ken, in 1417, by Lord Powis, was suspended alive in chains, upon a gallows, and burnt to death.*

The excessive dearness of books, prior to the invention of printing, is a sufficient proof that the Lollards must have been countenanced and assisted by persons of wealth and influence, in spreading extensively the works of Wiclif, especially his translation of the New Testament. Several instances of the exorbitant prices of books, about this period, have been already adduced; the following will render the evidence still more decisive. In 1424, two *Antiphonars*, books containing all the invitatories, responsories, verses, collects, and whatever was said or sung in the choir, except the lessons, cost the little monkery of Crabhouse, in Norfolk, *twenty-six marks;* and the common price for a Mass-book was *five marks*, equal to the yearly revenue of a vicar, or curate, which, about this period, was fixed at five marks, (£3 6*s*. 8*d*.,) or two marks and his board.† At an early period of this century, Pierre Plaoul, bishop of Senlis, bequeathed a large quarto BIBLE, fairly written on vellum, to the house of the Sorbonne, at Paris; on the last leaf of which there was a Latin note, to the following effect: "This book, the value of which is fifteen pounds of Paris, belongs to the poor masters of Sorbonne, bequeathed to them by the reverend father in Christ, Pierre Plaoul, formerly bishop of Senlis, and an eminent professor of Holy Scripture, of the society of the aforesaid house; who died April 11th, 1415, and was buried in the church of St. Marcellus, near to the famous and memorable master Peter Lombard, bishop of Paris. May his soul rest in peace!" "A similar *printed* Bible," says Chevillier, "would not have cost six francs." In 1491, Bernard's Homilies on the Canticles were pawned for twenty shillings; and a few years earlier, A. D. 1471, when Lewis XI. of France borrowed the works of the Arabian physician Rhasis, from the faculty of medicine at Paris, he not only deposited, by way of pledge, a quantity of valuable plate, but was obliged to procure a nobleman to join with him as surety in a deed by which he bound himself to return it, under a considerable forfeiture.‡ Henry V. of England possessed so scanty a library, that he borrowed several books, which were claimed by their owners, after his death. The countess of Westmoreland pre-

* Fox's Actes and Monumentes, vol. i, p. 664, &c. British Biography, vol. i, p. 138 Lond., 1773, 8vo.

† Johnson's Ecclesiastical Laws, &c., vol. ii, A. D. 1222, 1305, 1362.

‡ Warton's Hist. of English Poetry, vol. i, diss. 2. Chevillier, De l'Origine de l'Imprimerie de Paris, pt. iv, ch. v, p. 371. Paris, 1694, 4to.

sented a petition to the privy council, A. D. 1424, praying that an order might be given under the privy seal for the restoration of a book, borrowed of her by the late king, containing the Chronicles of Jerusalem, and the Expedition of Godfrey of Boulogne; which was granted with great formality. Another petition was presented by the prior of Christ Church, Canterbury, stating, that the late king had borrowed from the priory the works of St. Gregory, which by his testament he had directed to be restored, but which had been withheld by the prior of Shine. After serious deliberation, the council issued an order to the prior of Shine, either to deliver up the book, or to appear before the council, and assign the reasons of his refusal.* Nor will it perhaps be deemed impertinent to add, that literature in general, and sacred literature in particular, was still further discouraged, by the almost universal preference of entertainment to instruction. The minstrels were more amply remunerated than the clergy; and the feast of the *Episcopus Puerorum*, or boy-bishop, more numerously attended than the most solemn festivals of the church. During many of the years of the reign of Henry VI., particularly in the year 1430, at the annual feast of the holy cross, at Abingdon, a town in Berkshire, twelve priests each received four-pence for singing a dirge; and the same number of minstrels were each rewarded with two shillings and four-pence, besides diet and provender for their horses. In the same year, the prior *de Maxtock* gave six-pence for a sermon, to an itinerant doctor in theology, of one of the Mendicant orders, who went about preaching to the religious houses. In a very mutilated fragment of a *Computus*, or annual account roll of St. Swithen's cathedral priory, at Winchester, under the year 1441, a disbursement is made to the singing boys of the monastery, who, together with the choristers of St. Elizabeth's collegiate chapel, near that city, were dressed up like girls, and exhibited their sports before the abbess and nuns of St. Mary's abbey, at Winchester, in the public refectory of that convent, on Innocents' day. Another fragment, of an account of the cellarer of Hyde abbey, at Winchester, has the following entry, under the year 1490: "In larvis et aliis indumentis puerorum visentium dominum apud Wulsey, et constabularium castri Winton, in apparatu suo, nec non subinstrantium omnia monasteria civitatis Winton, in ffesto Nicholai." That is, "In furnishing masks and dresses for the boys of the convent, when they visited the bishop at Wulvesey palace, the con-

* Henry's Hist. of Great Britain, vol. x, b. v, ch. iv, pp. 115, 116.

stable of Winchester castle, and all the monasteries of the city of Winchester, on the festival of St. Nicholas."* In many churches it was a common practice to elect a boy on St. Nicholas's or Innocents' day, to assume the garb, and perform the functions of the bishop, who was therefore denominated *episcopus puerorum*, or boy-bishop, and sometimes the *chorister-bishop*. This was particularly the case in England, in the church of Sarum. The learned John Gregory, of Oxford, wrote a tract, published after his decease, expressly on this custom of the church of Sarum, the title of which is, "Episcopus Puerorum in die Innocentium: or a discovery of an ancient custom in the church of Sarum, making an anniversary-bishop among the choristers." In this work, it is said, "The *episcopus choristorum* was a chorister-bishop, chosen by his fellow-children, upon St. Nicholas's day. Upon this day rather than any other, because it is singularly noted of this bishop, (as Paul said of his Timothy,) that he had known the Scriptures of a child, and led a life *sanctissime ab ipsis incunabilis inchoatam*. The reason is yet more properly and expressly set down in the English Festival:"

"It is sayed that his fader hyght Epiphanius, and his moder Joanna, &c. And whan he was born, &c., they made him christen, and caled him *Nycolas*, that is a mannes name, but he kepeth the name of a child, for he chose to kepe vertues, meknes, and simplenes, and without malice: also we rede while he lay in his cradel, he fasted Wednesday and Friday: these dayes he would souke but ones of the day, and therwyth held him plesed: thus he lyued all his lyf in vertues with his childes name. And therefore, children don him worship before all other saints."—*Lib. Festivalis* in die *S. Nicolas.*, fol. 55.

"From this day till Innocents' day, at night, (it lasted longer at first,) the *episcopus puerorum* was to bear the name and to hold up the state of a *bishop*, answerably habited with a *crosier* or pastoral staff in his hand, and a *mitre* upon his head: and such a one too some had as was *multis episcoporum mitris sumptuosior*, (saith one,) very much richer than those of bishops indeed."

"The rest of his fellows from the same time being were to take upon them the style and counterfeit of prebends, yielding to their bishop (or else as if it were) no less than canonical obedience."

"And look what service the very bishop himself, with his dean and prebends, (had they been to officiate,) was to have performed,

* Warton's Hist. of English Poetry, vol, ii, pp. 105, 106; vol. iii, p. 324.

the mass excepted, the very same was done by the chorister-bishop and his canons, upon the eve and the holyday."

"In case the chorister-bishop died within the month, his exequies were solemnized with an answerable glorious pomp and sadness. He was buried (as all other bishops) in all his ornaments. In the cathedral of Sarum there lieth a monument, in stone, of a little boy habited all in episcopal robes, a mitre upon his head, a crosier in his hand, and the rest accordingly."

Our author adds, that all the ceremonies were performed "with that solemnity of celebration, and appetite of seeing, that the statute of Sarum was forced to provide. *Sub pœna majoris excommunicationis, nè quis pueros illos in præfata processione, vel aliàs in suo ministerio, premat aut impediat quoquo modo, quo minùs pacificè valeant facere et exequi quod illis imminet faciendum*, &c. That no person whatsoever, under pain of anathema, should interrupt or press upon these children, at the procession, or in any other part of their service, in any ways, but to suffer them quietly to perform and execute what it concerned them to do."*

As to the divine service being performed on these festivals by children, not only was it celebrated by boys, but also by girls; for there is an injunction given to the Benedictine nunnery of Godstowe, in Oxfordshire, by Archbishop Peckham, in the year 1278, that on Innocents' day the public prayers should not any more be said in the church of that monastery, *per parvulas*, that is, by little girls. And so far back may a similar custom be traced, that at the Constantinopolitan synod, held in the year 867, at which three hundred and seventy-three bishops were present, it was found to be a solemn custom in the courts of princes, on certain stated days, to dress some laymen in the episcopal apparel, who should exactly personate a bishop, both in his tonsure and ornaments; and also to create a burlesque patriarch, who might make sport for the company. This scandal to religion was anathematized by the good bishops, but without complete success, the temporary check serving only to alter its direction and increase its energy.† In 1274 the council of Saltzburg forbade any one to assume the office of boy-bishop who was more than sixteen years of age, great enormities having sometimes been committed in the churches by those who had engaged in those ludi, or plays.‡ And the council of

* Gregory's Works, *Posthuma*, pp. 95, 113–117. London, 1671, 4to.

† Warton's Hist. of English Poetry, vol. iii, p. 324.

‡ Du Cange, v. *Episcopus Puerorum*.

Basil, in 1435, condemned them, though they continued to be practised for centuries afterward.*

There flourished, however, at the conclusion of the former and commencement of this century, several illustrious characters, who, notwithstanding the superstition and bigotry of their church, deserve to be recorded among the promoters of sacred literature and knowledge. ADAM ESTON, or EASTON, an Englishman, educated at Oxford, became a Benedictine monk of Norwich, and successively filled the sees of Hereford and London. He was eminently skilled in Hebrew, Greek, and Latin, and appears to have been the *first* of the moderns who attempted a translation of the Old Testament *immediately from the Hebrew*. This work he is said to have completed, except the Psalms. Robert Wakefield (who died in 1538) says, in the tract which he wrote on the purity of the Hebrew text, that, for some time, he had the work in his possession, but that at length it was stolen. In the preface to his translation he defends the integrity of the Hebrew original against Nicholas de Lyra and others, who supposed it to have been corrupted by the Jews. He was created a cardinal by Urban VI., but was afterward thrown into prison, with five other cardinals, by the same pontiff, where he remained for five years; after his release he wrote an account of his imprisonment. He died at Rome, A. D. 1397.†

JOHN of WHETHAMSTEDE, abbot of St. Albans, in the reign of Henry VI., was an eminently studious and learned writer. A MS. life of him, in the Cottonian library, enumerates more than fourscore separate treatises given to the abbey, many of which were written by himself. He expended large sums in beautifying and enriching his monastery; among other things, he adorned the roof and walls of the Virgin Mary's chapel with pictures, at an expense of forty pounds, and gave an organ to the choir of the church. He built a library at Oxford, and enriched it with books. To familiarize the history of his patron saint to the monks of his convent, he employed Lydgate, then a monk of Bury, in Suffolk, to translate the Latin legend of his life into English rhymes. For the translation, the writing, and the illuminations he paid *one hundred shillings;* and expended on the binding, and other exterior ornaments of the MS., upward of *three pounds*. It was placed before the altar of the saint, in the abbey church, Whethamstede

* Du Tilliot, Memoires pour servir à l'Hist. de la Fete des Foux, pp. 58–73.

† Bibliotheca Sacra, edit. Masch, pt. ii, tom. iii, cap. iii, sec. i, p. 432. Hody, De Bibl. Text., lib. iii, pt. ii, p. 440.

having adorned the altar with much magnificence. During his abbacy a grand transcript of the *Postilla* of Nicholas de Lyra on the Bible was begun at his command, with the most splendid ornaments and hand-writing. The monk who records this important anecdote lived soon after him, and speaks of this great undertaking, then unfinished, as if it were some magnificent public edifice. "God grant," says he, "that this work in our days may receive a happy consummation!" Some of Whethamstede's tracts, MS. copies of which often occur in our libraries, are dedicated to Humphrey, duke of Gloucester, who was fond of visiting the abbey, and employed our abbot to collect valuable books for him. A fine copy of his *Granarium*, an immense work, was presented by the duke to the library then lately erected by himself, at Oxford. A beautiful MS. folio of Valerius Maximus, enriched with the most elegant decorations, with a curious table, or index, made by Whethamstede, is still preserved in the Bodleian library. He was the author of a Chronicle, embracing a period of twenty years, from 1441 to 1461, inclusive. It contains many original papers, and gives a very full account of some events, particularly respecting his own abbey. He was ordained a priest A. D. 1382, and died 1464, being above a hundred years of age, eighty-two of which he had been in priest's orders.*

John Capgrave, another learned Englishman, was born in the county of Kent. He entered into the monastery of Augustine monks, at Canterbury, and after he had taken his doctor's degree at Oxford, became provincial of his order. He was the confessor and intimate friend of Humphrey, duke of Gloucester. In the library of Oriel College, at Oxford, there is a MS. Commentary on Genesis, written by Capgrave, who was reputed eminent as a theologian. It is the author's autograph, and is dedicated to the duke. In the superb initial letter of the dedicatory epistle is a curious illumination of the author, humbly presenting his book to his patron, who is seated, and covered with a sort of hat. At the end is this entry, in the hand-writing of the duke himself: "*Ce livre est a moy Humphrey duc de Gloucestre du don de frere Jehan Capgrave, quy le me fit presenter a mon manoyr de Pensherst le . . . . jour de . . . . l'an* MCCCXXXVIII," [probably MCCCCXXXVIII:] that is, "This book belongs to me, Humphrey, duke of Gloucester, the gift of brother John Capgrave, who presented it to me at my manor of Penshurst, the . . . day of . . .

* Warton's Hist. of English Poetry, vol. ii, pp. 45–47, 53. Henry's Hist. of Great Britain, vol. x, b. v, p. 132.

in the year 1438." Besides this Commentary on Genesis, and others on Exodus and Kings, presented also by the duke to the library at Oxford, he was the author of commentaries on almost all the books of the Old and New Testaments; as well as of a Catalogue, or Legend of the English Saints, printed at London, by Caxton, 1516, folio; a Biography of illustrious Men, who flourished under the Henries of England; and many other works, chiefly historical. He was decided in his attachment to the Church of Rome, but opposed and thundered against the depraved practices of the ecclesiastics of his day. He died at Lynn, in Norfolk, August 12th, A. D. 1464; or, according to Pitts, A. D. 1484.*

But the most munificent patron of general literature was the *good* HUMPHREY, duke of Gloucester. To him the Bodleian library, as it has been since called, was indebted for an extensive and princely donation of books, containing six hundred volumes. These books are called *Novi Tractatus*, or new treatises, in the university Register. They were the most splendid and costly copies that could be procured, finely written on vellum, and elegantly embellished with miniatures and illuminations, one hundred and twenty of which were valued at more than £1000. The magnificent copy of Valerius Maximus, the index of which was made by Whethamstede, was one of them. As he patronised, in a particular manner, the abbey of St. Albans, many of the abbots paid their court to him by sending him presents of books beautifully executed, and adorned with the most exquisite paintings, which seem to have constituted a part of his gift to the library at Oxford.† Humphrey was brother to Henry V. and the duke of Bedford, and uncle to Henry VI., during whose minority he occasionally administered the affairs of the kingdom, as regent.

The library of Baliol College, Oxford, was also founded in the early part of the fifteenth century. It was originally built in two parts; the lower, or west part, in 1427, by Dr. Thomas Chace, and the upper, or east part, about the year 1477, by Mr. Robert Abdy, both some time masters. William Lambert, who was master in 1406, and Robert Thwaites, who attained the same honour in 1451, gave many valuable MSS.; and William Wilton, a fellow, and afterward chancellor of the university, was also a contributor of books in 1492. Grey, bishop of Ely, in 1454, proved a most noble benefactor, not only in money for the building, but in

* Cavei Hist. Lit., sæc. xv, Append., p. 132. Warton's Hist of English Poetry, vol. ii, p. 46.

† Warton, *ubi sup.*

adding to the collection about two hundred MSS., many of them richly illuminated, which he had purchased in England and Italy. In the latter country he employed transcribers and illuminators, as appears by some of his MSS. still in this library. The illuminations were chiefly executed by Antonius Marius, an "exquisite painter," of Florence, during the bishop's residence in that city. On most, if not all of the MSS., the donors' arms were fastened, painted on vellum, and covered with pieces of thin horn, to prevent their being torn off or defaced. "But, with great resentment let it be spoken," says A. Wood, "divers of them which smelled of superstition, or that treated of school divinity, or of geometry, or astronomy, were taken away in that ignorant time of Edward VI., wherein people, under pretence of reformation, pilfered, and made havoc of those things which posterity hath since much desired to see."*

The countenance which the study of the sacred Scriptures derived also from the devotional habits of two royal personages ought not to be forgotten. These were ANN OF BOHEMIA and HENRY VI. The former of these illustrious characters was the beloved queen of Richard II., daughter of the emperor Charles IV., and sister to Winceslaus, king of Bohemia, and emperor of Germany. She was married to King Richard, A. D. 1382. Wiclif, in his book "Of the threefold bond of love," thus speaks of her: "It is possible that the noble queen of England, the sister of Cesar, may have the Gospel written in *three* languages, Bohemian, German, and Latin, and to hereticate her on this account would be Luciferian folly." Archbishop Arundel, in his sermon preached at her funeral in 1394, highly commends her, that "although she was a stranger, yet she constantly studied the four Gospels in English, and explained by the expositions of the doctors; and that in the study of these, and reading godly books, she was more diligent than even the prelates themselves, though their office and business required it."†

Of the attachment of King Henry VI. to the Holy Scriptures, and his regular habits of piety, the following account has been left by John Blackman, a Carthusian monk, and an intimate friend of the monarch himself:—

"He was incessantly occupied either in prayers, or in reading

* Chalmers's History of the Colleges, &c., attached to the University of Oxford, vol. i, p. 55. Oxford, 1810, 8vo. Wood's History and Antiquities of Oxford, edit. Gutch., p. 89, 4to.

† Usserii Hist. Dogmat., p. 161 Lewis's Life of Wicliffe, pp. 197, 198.

the Holy Scriptures, or chronicles, from which he derived many passages for his own spiritual consolation, as well as that of others. He was also accustomed to send to certain clergymen hortatory epistles, full of heavenly mysteries and salutary admonitions, to the astonishment of many. On ordinary days he spent his time not less diligently, in treating of the affairs of his kingdom with his council, according to the exigency of the case; or else in reading writings or chronicles. Hence Richard Tunstall, formerly his faithful chamberlain, has given testimony concerning him, both verbally and in his writings, saying, 'His delight was in the law of the Lord both day and night.' In confirmation of the same thing, the king himself heavily complained to me in his palace at Eltham, when I was with him there alone, engaged with him in his holy books, and listening to his salutary admonitions, and the breathings of his profound devotion; for being interrupted by a knocking at the royal gate by a certain powerful duke of the realm, the king said, 'They so disturb me, that I can scarcely snatch time to refresh myself, either by day or night, with the reading of any sacred doctrines, without being interrupted by some noise or other.' Something of a similar kind once happened also in my presence at Windsor."* Yet such was the inconsistency of this monarch, that while he himself read the Scriptures constantly, and regarded them as an inestimable source of instruction and consolation, his subjects were persecuted, imprisoned, and burned alive, for reading, or hearing, or pursuing the dictates of those very Scriptures!

The opinions of Wiclif, which had continued to spread in England, were now extended to the continent, and found in Bohemia, in particular, many who advocated the doctrines of the reformer, and zealously endeavoured to give them publicity and establishment. The attendants of Ann of Bohemia, queen of Richard II., on their return to their own country, had carried with them some of Wiclif's writings, and communicated the knowledge of his sentiments to the circle of their acquaintance;† but the principal agent in introducing Wiclif's works was a young Bohemian nobleman, named Faulfisch. This gentleman had been a student at Oxford, where he had embraced the views of the English reformer, and had brought to Bohemia several of his works, among which were his books *De Realibus Universalibus; De diversis quæstionibus contra Clerum; Dialogus; Trialogus; Super Evangelia ser-*

* Usserii Hist. Dogmat., p. 171.

† Fox's Actes and Monumentes, vol. i, p. 701.

mones per circulum anni, &c.* These were read with avidity by the celebrated John Huss, a native of Bohemia, who, by his genius and industry, had risen from obscurity to the honourable office of rector of the university of Prague, which was then in a flourishing condition, and crowded with students from various parts of Germany. He had also been nominated, A. D. 1400, one of the two preachers of Bethlehem, a great church dedicated to Matthias and Matthæus, which had been erected and endowed by an opulent citizen of Prague, for the purpose of having the word of God taught to the people in the vulgar tongue, both on festivals and ordinary days. Huss was soon joined by many of the clergy, and several of the nobility; in particular by Jerome of Prague, a man of superior talents and address, who had visited England for the sake of his studies, and brought from thence various writings of Wiclif. The adherents of our reformer, however, met with a violent and bigoted opponent in Subinco, surnamed *Lepus*, archbishop of Prague, a prelate of illustrious extraction, but so illiterate, that he only acquired the knowledge of letters after his advancement to the archbishopric. This determined enemy of the Hussites, as they were called, commanded that all the books of Wiclif should be brought to him, in order to be publicly burnt. The episcopal mandate was partially obeyed, and more than two hundred volumes, finely written, and richly ornamented with costly covers and gold bosses, were committed to the flames.† But the rage of Subinco and his party was not to be assuaged by the mere destruction of what were deemed heretical works; the teachers were still more the objects of their direst enmity. John Huss was driven from Prague, and obliged to take refuge in the village from whence he derived his name. In this retreat "he spent his time," says a Catholic historian, "in translating certain books of the Old and New Testaments into the vulgar tongue; to which he added commentaries, and gave thereby to women and tradesmen means of disputing with the monks and clergy." The council of Constance being assembled in 1414, he was cited to appear before it, and, contrary to the expectations of his enemies, acted with that noble decision that marked his character, and fearlessly presented himself on the first day of its sitting, under the protection of the *safe-conduct*, or passport, of the emperor Sigismund, which required

* Æneæ Sylvii Historia Bohemica, cap. xxxv, p. 65. Francofurt, 1687, 12mo Lewis's Life of Wicliffe, ch. ix, p. 143.

† Æneæ Sylvii Historia Bohemica, cap. xxxv, pp. 66–69. Ridderi De Eruditione Historia, cap. i, p. 40. Rotterd., 1680.

all the subjects of the empire "to suffer him to pass and repass secure; and, for the honour of his imperial majesty, if need be, to provide him with good passports." But the *safe-conduct* was perfidiously violated, and Huss was condemned, and burnt at the stake, A. D. 1415. His friend, and fellow-sufferer, JEROME, followed him through the flames the ensuing year. Æneas Sylvius, a cotemporary cardinal, and afterward pope, under the name of Pius II., says, "They bore their sufferings with constancy, going to the stake as to a feast, and suffering no expression to escape which could indicate uneasiness of mind. As the fire kindled they began to sing hymns, which even the flames and crackling of the fire could scarcely interrupt."* Thus, by the death of these two upright and excellent men, eternal infamy was attached to a council which, while it professed to be assembled for the reformation of the church, decreed the martyrdom of those who dared to oppugn its superstitions and errors, violated the most solemn engagements, supported the Teutonic knights in their enormities, refused to punish the advocates of regicide, and amused itself with the buffooneries of the most ridiculous dramatic entertainments. (See page 332.)†

Irritated by the death of their teacher and his friend, the Hussites flew to arms, and, under the conduct of the intrepid Zisca, a Bohemian nobleman, commenced a fierce and bloody war, which terminated first in the death of Zisca, and then in the division of the Hussites into *Calixtines* and *Taborites;* the former contending for the use of the cup (*calix*) to the laity in the eucharist, and the latter, who derived their name from a mountain denominated Tabor, to which they had fled, insisting upon a more general reformation, and the establishment of a purer doctrine and discipline. During the thirteen years' war carried on by the Hussites, the most destructive measures were too frequently adopted; and it must ever be lamented, that those who seceded from the Romish Church, on account of its unscriptural doctrines and practices, were hurried by their violence to depredations unworthy the character they claimed. On one occasion they destroyed a church and monastery, adjoining the king's palace, the largest and most beautiful in all Bohemia, and the burying places of its sovereigns. The church was magnificent; the altar was decorated with gold and silver, the

* Æneæ Sylvii Historia Bohemica, cap. xxxvi, p. 73. Earberry's Pretended Reformers, p. 49.

† See Fox's Actes and Monumentes, vol. i, p. 701–756; Milner's History of the Church of Christ, vol. iv, p. 209; and Warton's Hist. of English Poetry, vol i, p. 242.

ecclesiastical robes were interwoven with pearls, and the windows were large, and *glazed*. The dormitory of the monastery was capable of containing eight hundred monks; the offices were magnificently constructed; the cloister enclosed an extensive garden; and on its lofty walls the whole of the Old and New Testaments was inscribed, in characters rendered sufficiently legible, by increasing in magnitude in proportion to their distance and height.*

The Calixtines, having obtained the use of the eucharistical cup by papal permission, soon began to persecute, in their turn, the Taborites; who in many points resembled the Waldenses, and who having laid aside their martial principles, were become more moderate, and more deeply pious. Various sorts of torture were inflicted on them, numbers were barbarously murdered, and many died in prison; the sick were thrown into the open fields, where many perished with cold and hunger; and others were expelled from the cities and villages, with the forfeiture of all their effects. Thus driven from their homes, they were obliged to hide themselves in mountains and woods; and to escape detection by the smoke, to kindle no fires, except in the night, when they met to pray, and read the Word of God. In 1480, they received a great increase of their numbers, from the accession of Waldensian refugees, who escaped out of Austria, where their bishop, Stephen, had been burnt alive, and where a dreadful persecution had been raised against them. From these Bohemian refugees, the *Moravians*, or United Brethren, are descended, deriving the former term from the country they inhabited, and the latter from their brotherly union in the plan of discipline, &c., formed in 1457, by Gregory, the founder of the unity.†

Such were the noble struggles for the truth, and for the Holy Scriptures, as the grand rule of faith and practice, made by these ancient worthies: but the papal authorities knew too well, that their deeds could not bear the light, and therefore sought their safety in darkness. A striking instance of this occurred in 1418, when Eric, of Pomerania, requested permission from Pope Martin V. to found a university at Copenhagen, and only obtained it, on the express condition, that the Holy Scriptures should neither be read nor explained in it, but that the lectures should be confined to profane literature!‡

* Æneæ Sylvii Historia Bohemica, cap. xxxvi, pp. 74, 75. Earberry's Pretended Reformers, b. ii, p. 10.

† Milner's Hist. of the Church of Christ, vol. iv, cent. xv, ch. iii, *passim*.

‡ Dr. Henderson's MS. Hist. of Danish Versions, in wich he refers to Pontoppidan's Annal. Eccles. Dan., vol. ii, p. 521.

Other difficulties, also, besides those arising from papal opposition, presented themselves to such as were desirous of reading the Scriptures; for copies of them were rare and expensive, and could seldom be obtained but by the wealthy; except when the indefatigable advocates of gospel purity happened to have the opportunity, possessed the ability, and submitted to the labour of transcribing. Even those who had acquired the important art of writing, obtained with difficulty the materials requisite for transcription or epistolary correspondence.*

Happily about this period the noble and important ART OF PRINTING was discovered, and the sources of knowledge soon became comparatively easy of access. Our honest martyrologist thus enumerates the advantages resulting from this incomparable invention: "Hereby tongues are known, knowledge groweth, judgment increaseth, books are dispersed, the Scripture is seen, the doctors be read, stories be opened, times compared, truth discerned, falsehood detected, and with finger pointed, and all through the benefit of printing. Wherefore, I suppose that either the pope must abolish printing, or he must seek a new world to reign over: or else, as this world standeth, printing doubtless will abolish him. Both the pope, and all his college of cardinals, must this understand, that through the light of printing the world beginneth now to have eyes to see, and heads to judge. He cannot walk so invisibly in a net, but he will be spied. And although, through might, he stopped the mouth of John Huss before, and of Jerome, that they might not preach, thinking to make his kingdom sure: yet, instead of John Huss, and others, God hath opened the PRESS to preach, whose voice the pope is never able to stop, with all the puissance of his triple crown. By this printing, as by the gift of tongues, and as by the singular organ of the Holy Ghost, the doctrine of the gospel soundeth to all nations and countries under heaven: and what God revealeth to one man is dispersed to many, and what is known in one nation is open to all."†

* Beckman's History of Inventions, vol. ii, p. 223.

† Fox's Actes and Monumentes, vol. i, p. 837.

PART III.

FROM THE INVENTION OF PRINTING.

CHAPTER I.

FIFTEENTH CENTURY CONTINUED.

Invention of Printing—Early Printers—First printed Bibles—Book Censors—Indices Expurgatorii—Licensers of the Press.

PRINTING appears to be indebted for its origin to the art of *engraving on wood*, which was probably borrowed from the Chinese, among whom it was in use from the remotest periods. The first attempts at block-printing, in Europe, were made about the commencement of the fifteenth century, by the manufacturers of playing cards, who, after having employed blocks, or wood-engravings for their cards, began to engrave on wood the images of the saints, which the clergy distributed on certain occasions to the people. Prints of this description, of the same size as the playing cards, representing different subjects of sacred history and devotion, with a text analogous to the subject, opposite to the figure, are preserved in the library of Wolfenbuttle. But that they also engraved images of a larger size is proved by the very curious wood-cut of St. Christopher, found by Baron Heinecken, in the convent of the Chartreux, at Buxheim, near Memmingen, and now in the superb collection of Earl Spencer; a fac-simile of which is given in Dibdin's splendid *Bibliotheca Spenceriana*. From the inscription engraved and printed at the foot of the print, it is proved to have been executed A. D. 1423.* To the images of the saints succeeded historical subjects, chiefly Biblical or devotional, generally denominated Books of Images, with a text or explanation engraven on the same tablet, the fullest account of which is given by Baron Heinecken, in his *Idée Generale d'une Collection complette d'Estampes, avec une dissertation sur l'origine de la Gravure, et sur les premiers Livres des Images. Leipsic et Vienne*, 1771, 8vo. A judicious abridgment of this work, so far as refers to Books of Images, with corrections and notices of recently discovered works of this description, is contained in the appendix to

* Heinecken, Idée Generale d'Estampes, pp. 246, 248–251.

Horne's "Introduction to the Study of Bibliography," and is accompanied with a fac-simile of the first plate of the *Speculum Humanæ Salvationis*, supposed to have been executed between the years 1440 and 1457; and another of the *Biblia Pauperum*, supposed to have been executed between A. D. 1420 and 1425. Several fac-similes of works of this nature are engraved from rare copies in the possession of Earl Spencer, in the *Bibliotheca Spenceriana*, with bibliographical descriptions by the ingenious editor.

Of all the xylographic works, that is, such as are printed from wooden tablets, the *Biblia Pauperum*, and the *Speculum Salvationis*, are the most celebrated. The BIBLIA PAUPERUM, which consists of forty plates of Biblical subjects, with analogous extracts and sentences, is unquestionably a very rare and ancient book. The few copies of it which are now extant, are, for the most part, either imperfect, or in a very bad condition; which ought not to excite surprise, when it is considered that this work was executed for the use of young persons and common people, (whence its name, the Bible of the Poor,) who were thus enabled to acquire at a low price a knowledge of some of the events recorded in the Scriptures. This will account for the destruction of almost every copy, by repeated use; for in those times, when the present art of printing was unknown, there were but few persons who could afford to give a hundred louis d'or for the manuscript of a complete Bible. A somewhat later edition has fifty instead of forty plates.

The SPECULUM HUMANÆ SALVATIONIS, or as it is frequently termed, *Speculum Salutis*, is confessedly, both in its design and execution, the most perfect of all the ancient Books of Images which preceded the invention of printing. This compilation, which is in small folio, is a collection of historical passages from the Scriptures, with a few from profane history, which allude to them; and is ascribed by Heinecken (and after him by Lambinet) to a Benedictine monk, named brother John, in the thirteenth or fourteenth century. So popular was this Mirror of Salvation, that it was translated into the German, Flemish, and other languages, and very frequently printed.* The preface is printed with fusile types.

These Books of Images, chiefly executed in Holland,† though generally regarded as the first attempts of printing, were neverthe-

* Horne's Introduction to Bibliography, vol. ii, App., pp. ii, x.

† It is probable that many of these Books of Images were printed at Haerlem, and that from hence arose the opinion, that LAWRENS COSTER of Haerlem was the *inventor* of printing. See Horne's *Introduction to Bibliography*, vol. i, pp. 145–154; and *Classical Journal*, vol. xxi, No. 41, pp. 117–137. Lond., 1820.

less a different art from the modern printing, which consists in the use of separate moveable types; which at first were cut in wood, afterward in metal, and the art at length completed by the invention of founding types in moulds or matrices. For the invention of moveable types we are indebted to John Guttenberg, of Mayence, or Mentz, a celebrated town in Germany.

HENNE GOENSFLEISCH de Sulgeloch, or Sorgenloch, commonly called JOHN GUTENBERG, was born at Mentz, of noble and wealthy parents, about the year 1400. In the year 1424 he took up his residence at Strasburg, as a merchant. The abbé Mauro Boni says, that "stimulated by his genius to discover something *new*," he travelled in his youth through various countries, where he learned several arts unknown to the Germans. In 1430 he returned to his native city, as is evident from a deed of accommodation between himself and the nobles and burghers of the city of Mentz. A document adduced by Schoepflin proves him to have been a wealthy man in 1434. Between that period and 1439 he had conceived, and perhaps made some few trials of the art of printing with moveable, and probably with metal types, though his first attempts are supposed to have been with moveable characters cut in wood.* In the year 1441–2 Gutenberg lived at Strasburg, where he continued till about 1443, when he returned again to Mentz, and toward the year 1450 appears to have opened his mind fully to FUST, a goldsmith, of the same place, and prevailed on him to advance large sums of money, in order to make further and more complete trials of the art. Between the years 1450 and 1455 the celebrated BIBLE of six hundred and thirty-seven leaves, the *first important specimen of printing with metal types*, was executed between Gutenberg and Fust.†

This Bible, the first ever printed, is an edition of the LATIN VULGATE. It forms two volumes, in folio, is printed in the large Gothic or German character, and is said to be "justly praised for the strength and beauty of the paper, the exactness of the register, the lustre of the ink, and the general beauty and magnificence of the volumes." It is without date, a circumstance which has occa

* Santander observes, that moveable wooden types could not have been used in printing any work, owing to their fragile and spongy nature, which rendered them liable to be easily broken, as well as constantly subject to contraction or dilation. See Santander, *Dict. Bibliographique*, tom. i, p. 80, *note* 47.

† Dibdin's Typographical Antiquities, vol. i, p. lxxxvii, *note*. Santander, Dictionnaire Bibliographique choisi du quinzieme siècle, tom. i, ch. i, pp. 10–107. Bruxelles et Paris, 1805, 8vo.

sioned considerable dispute as to its priority to other undated editions executed about the same time. It has been noticed as containing six hundred and thirty-seven leaves, to distinguish it more accurately from the other editions without date. C. G. Schwarz, an eminent bibliographer, says, in his *Primaria quædam Documenta de Orig. Typog. Altorfii*, 1740, 4to., part ii, p. 4, that "in the year 1728, in a Carthusian monastery, a little beyond the walls of Mentz, he saw a copy of an old Latin Bible, which was printed in a large character, similar to what is called the Missal type; and that, however a few of the end leaves were cut out, so that the date, place, and printer's name could not be ascertained, yet, in an ancient MS. catalogue of the same library, an entry, or memorandum, was made, that this Bible, with some other books, (the names of which he had forgotten,) was given to the monastery by Gutenberg."* Copies of this superb work of Gutenberg's are in his majesty's library, in the Bodleian library, and in those of Earl Spencer and Sir M. M. Sykes, bart.

There is also a magnificent copy of this Bible in the royal library at Berlin, printed upon vellum, and enriched with a profusion of ancient and elegant embellishments; and in the king's library at Paris there are two other copies of this most valuable edition, one upon vellum, in four volumes, and the other upon paper, in two volumes. The latter copy has a subscription in red ink at the end of each volume. That at the end of the first volume, of which a fac-simile is given in the Classical Journal, No. 8, p. 481, is

Et sic est finis prime partis biblie
seu veteris testamenti. Illuminata
seu rubricata et ligata p henricum.
Albch alius Cremer Anno dm̄ mcccc
lvi festo Bartholomei apli
Deo gracias - - - - - - - Alleluia.

TRANSLATION.

"Here ends the first part of the Bible or Old Testament. Illuminated, or rubricated, and bound, by Henry Albch or Cremer, on St. Bartholomew's day, April, A. D. 1456. Thanks be to God. Hallelujah."

At the end of the second volume the subscription is

Iste liber illuminatus ligatus et completus est p henricum Cremer vicariū ecclesie collegiate sancti Stephani maguntini sub anno dni millesimo qua-

* See Dibdin, On the Vulgate Bible of 1450–1455; inserted in Classical Journal, No. 8, pp. 471–484.

trīngentesimo quinquagesimo sexto, festo assumptionis gloriose virginis Marie. Deo Gracias. Alleluia.

TRANSLATION.

"This book, illuminated and bound by Henry Cremer, vicar of the collegiate church of St. Stephen, at Mentz, was completed on the feast of the assumption of the Blessed Virgin Mary, A.D. 1456. Thanks be to God. Hallelujah."*

The expenses incurred by this publication were so considerable, that Fust instituted a suit against Gutenberg; who was obliged to pay interest, and also part of the capital advanced. In consequence of this suit the partnership was dissolved; and the whole of Gutenberg's printing apparatus fell into the hands of Fust. But Gutenberg was not to be discouraged from following his pursuits: he established a new press, and continued to exercise his art until 1465, when, being admitted by the elector Adolphus, of Nassau, into his band of gentlemen pensioners, with a handsome salary, he relinquished an art which had caused him so much trouble and vexation.† Gutenberg died A.D. 1468.

After the separation between Gutenberg and Fust, which took place in 1455, Fust began to print on his own account, with the assistance of Peter Schoeffer, a calligraphist, of Gernsheim; an industrious young man, of inventive talents, to whom is ascribed the art of founding types in moulds, or matrices; or, what is more probable, the invention of punches for striking the matrices; for which Fust rewarded him, by giving him his only daughter, Christina, in marriage.

The first publication which is known to have issued from the press of Fust and Schoeffer was a beautiful edition of the Psalms, in Latin, finished August 14th, 1457, which, from the place where it was printed, is usually denominated the Mentz Psalter. It is the first book known to be extant which has the name of the place where it was printed, and that of the printers, together with the date of the year when it was executed. The most perfect copy known is that in the imperial library of Vienna. It was discovered in the year 1665, near Inspruck, in the castle of Ambras, where the archduke Francis Sigismund had collected a prodigious quantity of MSS. and printed books; taken, for the

* Beloe's Anecdotes of Literature, vol. v, p. 83.

† Horne's Introduction to Bibliography, vol. i, p. 159. See also Dibdin's Bibliographical Decameron, vol. i, Fourth Day, where the various points in dispute respecting Gutenberg's claims are examined at large.

most part, from the famous library of Matthias Corvinus, king of Hungary, from whence it was transported to Vienna. The book is printed in folio, on vellum, and of such extreme rarity, that not more than six or seven copies are known to be in existence, all of which, however, differ from each other in some respect or other. The Psalter occupies one hundred and thirty-five leaves, and the *recto* the one hundred and thirty-sixth; the remaining forty-one leaves are appropriated to the litany, prayers, responses, vigils, &c. The psalms are executed in larger characters than the hymns; the capital letters are cut on wood, with a degree of delicacy and boldness which is truly surprising: the largest of them, the initial letters of the psalms, which are black, red, and blue, must have passed three times through the press. A fac-simile of the first letter of this noble Psalter is given in Horne's "Introduction to the Study of Bibliography," vol. i, p. 251. It is also given, with a few sentences of the first psalm, in the *Bibliotheca Spenceriana*, vol. i, p. 107, coloured exactly after the original. Another edition of this Psalter was printed in 1459 by the same printers, containing, probably, the first printed text of the Athanasian Creed. It is said not to be equally beautiful with the former edition, though executed with the same types and capital letters, and also on vellum. The St. Alban's and Benedictine monks are supposed to have been at the expense of these editions of the Psalter.*

In 1462 Fust and Schoeffer published a Latin Bible, in two volumes, folio. This is the first edition with a date, and, like all the other early typographical productions, is of extreme rarity and value. The copies of this Bible on paper are even more rare than those on vellum, of which last, more, probably, were printed, that they might have the greater resemblance to MSS., which the first printers endeavoured to imitate as much as possible. M. Lambinet, in his *Recherches sur l'origine de l'imprimerie*, p. 155, says, "It is certain that, from the year 1463, Fust, Schoeffer, and their partners, sold or exchanged, in Germany, Italy, France, and the most celebrated universities, the great number of books which they had printed; and, whenever they could, *sold them as MSS.* As proofs of which, it may be remarked, 1st. That we know of no work that issued from their press, betwixt the Bible of 1462 and the first edition of *Cicero de Officiis*, in 1465. 2d. Gabriel Naudè

* Horne's Introduction to Bibliography, vol. i, p. 160; and vol. ii, App., p. lii. Dibdin's Bibliotheca Spenceriana, vol. i, pp. 107, 108, 117. Dibdin's Typographical Antiquities, vol. i, "Life of Caxton," pp. ci, cii. Santander, Dict. Bibliographique, tom. i, *ut sup.*

informs us, that Fust brought to Paris a considerable number of copies of the Bible of 1462. As they were on parchment, and the capital letters illuminated with blue, and purple, and gold, after the manner of the ancient MSS., he sold them as such at sixty crowns But those who first purchased copies, comparing them together, soon found that they exactly resembled each other: afterward, they learned that Fust had sold a great number of copies, and had lowered the price, first to forty, and then to twenty crowns. The fraud being thus discovered, he was pursued by the officers of justice, and forced to fly from Paris, and return to Mentz; but not finding himself safe, he again quitted Mentz, and withdrew to Strasburg, where he taught the art to Mentelin. The facility with which Fust thus supplied Bibles for sale is said to have caused him to be accounted a necromancer, and to have given rise to the well-known story of the Devil and Dr. Faustus. Others have called the truth of this in question, and have remarked that there was a Faustus living at the same period, who wrote a poem *De influentia Syderum*, which, with a number of other tracts, was printed at Paris, "per Guidonum Mercatorem, 1496." His proper name was Publius Faustus Andrelinus Foroliviencis, but he called himself, and his friends in their letters to him called him, *Faustus*.* A curious deed of sale, of this edition of the Bible, informs us that Herman de Stratten, agent of Fust and Schoeffer, sold a copy of it to William Tourneville, bishop of Angers, for forty golden crowns, in 1470. The MS. memorandum, in Latin, was found in one of the vellum copies of this Bible: the following is the sense:—"I Herman, a German, workman of the honest and discreet John Guymier, sworn bookseller of the university of Paris, acknowledge to have sold to the illustrious and learned Master William, of Tourneville, archbishop and canon of Angiers, my most respectable lord and master, a BIBLE AT MENTZ, printed upon vellum, in two volumes, for the price and sum of forty crowns, which I have absolutely received, which also I ratify by these presents, promising to abide by the same, and guaranteeing my lord, purchaser of the said Bible, against any one who would dispossess him. In ratification of which I have hereunto affixed my seal, this fifth day of the month of April, in the year of our Lord MCCCCLXX. Herman."†

In 1462 Fust also printed an edition of the GERMAN BIBLE, in

* Gentleman's Magazine, 1812, part ii, p. 523. Peignot, Essai sur Parchemin, pp. 70, 100, *notes*. Chevillier, L'Origine de l'Imprimerie de Paris, pt. i, ch. i, p. 16. Paris, 1694, 4to.

† Dibdin's Biblioth. Spencer., tom. i, p. 16, *note*.

two volumes folio, which is the first German Bible with a date; but the priority must be allowed to an edition without date, place, or printer's name, of which a copy is in Lord Spencer's library. There is also a copy of the latter in the electoral library at Munich, with two MS. observations, the one of the date of 1467, being that of the illuminator, at the end of the prophet Jeremiah; the other is at the end of the Apocalypse, and contains a notice of the genealogical respectability of one Hector Mulich, and a memorandum to this effect: "1466, 27th of June, this book was bought unbound for twelve guilders." Hector Mulich received a patent of nobility from the emperor Ferdinand that same year. The author of this translation is unknown; and Walchius remarks, that "there were several ancient versions all made from the Latin, but so obscure and barbarous as to be almost unintelligible."*

In the same year (1462) Mentz was taken by storm, by Adolphus, count of Nassau. In the confusion that followed, Fust and Schoeffer suffered materially, in common with their fellow-citizens; and being obliged to suspend their typographical labours till tranquillity was restored, their workmen dispersed themselves, and established printing in several other parts of Europe. The death of Fust happened at Paris, in 1466; after which Schoeffer carried on the business alone till his decease, in 1502 or 1503. He left three sons, printers, the elder of whom succeeded to his father's business, and exercised his art till 1533. During the period that Schoeffer conducted the business alone, he published an edition of the Latin Bible, and two editions of the Latin Psalter. The Bible was printed in 1471, two volumes folio, and the Psalter in 1490 and 1502, folio.† Many editions of the Latin Bible were, about the same period, executed by other printers in different places, most or all of whom had learned the art from the original inventors; and so indefatigable were these early printers, that nearly one hundred editions of the Latin Bible were printed before the end of the fifteenth century, sixteen of which were accompanied with the *Postilla* or Commentary of De Lyra. Besides these, there were upward of thirty editions of the Latin Psalter, many of them with commentaries; three editions of the Latin New Testament, with Lyra's Notes; and several editions of the Prophets, the Gospels, or other parts of the sacred volume.‡

* Walchii Biblioth. Theologica, tom. iv, cap. viii, p. 77. Ineæ, 1765, 8vo. Dibdin's Biblioth. Spencer., tom. i, pp. 42, 46.

† Horne's Introduction to Bibliography, vol. ii, App., No. vii.

‡ See Le Long, Biblioth. Sacra, edit. Masch, pt. ii, tom. iii, cap. ii, *passim*.

One of the most extensive and eminent printers of this century was ANTONY KOBURGER, or COBURGER. His office was at Nuremberg, where he died in 1513. He was styled the prince of booksellers and printers, and is said to have employed twenty-four presses and one hundred men, besides furnishing work for the printers of Basil, or Basle, Lyons, and other places. He had warehouses at Nuremberg, Paris, and Lyons. Almost all his books relate to the canon law and to theology, and are distinguished for the lustre and magnificence of their execution. Of thirty-seven editions printed by him, thirteen are of the Bible, namely, twelve in Latin and one in German, all in folio. Most of the Latin editions were accompanied with the Postills of De Lyra. But his most superb work was the edition of the German Bible, which he printed in 1483, folio. This is said to be the first German Bible printed at Nuremberg; and is pronounced by Lichtenberger to be the most splendid of all the ancient German Bibles. It is embellished with impressions from the very curious wood-cuts which had been previously used for the Cologne edition of the Bible, printed by Quentel, in 1480, and which were also employed in the Bible printed at Halberstadt, in the Low Saxon dialect, in 1522: and it is worthy of remark, that in one of the large wood-cuts employed by Koburger, the *pope* is introduced as being among the principal of the *fallen angels!* The paper, characters, press-work, —all concur to prove this Bible a master-piece of typographical excellence.*

GUNTHER ZAINER is considered as having introduced printing into Augsburg; unless that honour should be conceded to John Bemler, who is supposed to have been the printer of a Latin Bible in two volumes folio, in 1466. From De Murr we learn, that in an old book of entries of benefactors to the Carthusian monastery at Buxheim, there is one of the date of 1474, in which the name of "dns Gunther' imp̄sor ciuis auguste" occurs, as the printer and donor of certain works, and among others of "the BIBLE IN THE VULGAR TONGUE, [German,] in super-royal form." Another entry informs us of the death of Gunther Zainer in 1478—"impressor librorum, ciuis Augustensis benefactor huius domus," "printer of books, citizen of Augsburg, benefactor to this house."†

CONRAD SWEYNHEIM, and ARNOLD PANNARTZ, two Germans, introduced the art of printing into Rome, in the year 1466, in the

* Horne's Introduction to Bibliography, vol. ii, App., No. vii, vol. iii, p. lx. Dibdin's Bibliographical Decameron, vol. i, p. 163.

† Dibdin's Biblioth. Spencer., tom. i, p. 50.

second year of the pontificate of Paul II., under the patronage of John Andreas, bishop of Aleria, who was the pope's librarian, and justly famed for his learning and generosity. They had previously exercised the art in the monastery of Subbiaco, in the kingdom of Naples, to which they had been invited by the monks; and where they had printed, in 1465, an edition of Lactantius's works, in which the quotations from the Greek authors are printed in a neat but heavy Greek letter, of which a specimen is given in Horne's "Introduction to the Study of Bibliography," vol. i, p. 245. They also were the first to introduce what has since been called the *Roman* character, instead of the *Gothic*, or black letter. The paper and types made use of by these printers were both excellent, and their ink, it is observed, "may vie in blackness with the best of the present day." They were encouraged by all the men of letters and fortune at Rome, and even by the pope himself, who frequently visited their printing-house, and examined, with admiration, every branch of this new art. The bishop of Aleria, espe cially, not only furnished them with the most valuable MSS. out of the Vatican and other libraries, but also prepared the copy, corrected their proofs, and prefixed dedications and prefaces to their works, in order to recommend them the more to the learned world, and followed this laborious task with such application, that he scarcely allowed himself time for necessary relaxation. These printers settled in the house of the Maximis, brothers, and Roman knights, from whence their works are dated. In 1471 they published a Latin Bible in two volumes folio, with an Epistle of the bishop of Aleria to Pope Paul III., Aristeas's History of the Septuagint, and Jerome's Prefaces to the different books of the Old and New Testaments. As this edition varies in several places from former editions, it is probable the bishop of Aleria furnished the printers with a more correct MS. copy from the library of the pope, or from some other source, or at least corrected the Mentz edition by such MS. Of this edition they printed five hundred and fifty copies. In the same year they commenced an edition of the Postills of De Lyra, in five volumes folio, which they completed the following year. This ponderous work seems to have ruined these indefatigable artists, for in a Latin petition of the printers to the pope, Sixtus IV., written by the bishop of Aleria, and prefixed to the fifth volume of De Lyra's Postills, or Commentary, they state themselves to be reduced to poverty by the pressure of the times, and the vast expense of the works they had printed, of which great numbers remained unsold. In the course of seven years they had published twenty-eight different works, some of them very large; the impressions of which amounted to twelve thousand four hundred and seventy-five volumes—an immense number at that period! It is evident, however, that some method must have been taken to extricate them from their distress; for although Sweynheim published nothing after the year 1473, and for that reason is supposed by some to have died about that time, yet his partner, Pannartz, continued printing until about 1476, using a smaller type than what had been used by him during the former partnership. An extract from the Latin petition of the printers to the pope is given, with a list of their works, in Beloe's "Anecdotes of Literature and scarce Books," vol. iii, p. 266. There is also a short extract from it in Le Long's *Bibliotheca Sacra.**

Ulric Gering, a German, and a native of Constance, with Martin Crantz and Michael Friburger, his associates, commenced printing at Paris in 1470; and in 1476, or, according to Chevillier, in 1475, printed a Latin Bible, in two volumes folio. This celebrated edition attracted much curiosity and discussion, about the middle of the last century, in consequence of a fraud practised upon a copy of it, now in the public library at Cambridge. By an alteration and erasure in the colophon, it is ascribed to the year 1463 or 1464; the words *tribus undecimus lustris*, in the first line, referring to the reign of Louis XI., being altered into *semi undecimus lustrum*, and the two last lines being erased. A full account of the detection of this fraud, which for many years engaged the attention of bibliographers, may be found in two letters written by Dr. Taylor, preserved in Nichols's "Literary Anecdotes," vol. i, pp. 542–548.

Chevillier observes, that "this was the first time the Holy Bible had been printed at Paris, or in the whole kingdom of France."†

Albert Pfister, of Bamberg, appears to have been the first printer in Germany who introduced *wood-cuts* into his publications, in order to illustrate the sacred text, but of a character and execution inferior to the Block-books, or Books of Images, executed in the Low Countries. The Histories of Joseph, Daniel, Judith, and Esther, printed by Pfister, in 1462, in the German language,

* Lemoine's Typographical Antiquities, pp. 21–23. Le Long, edit. Masch, pt. ii, tom. iii, cap. ii, sec. 1, p. 103, and sec. 3, p. 360.

† Chevillier, L'Origine de l'Imprimerie de Paris, p. 74. Nichols's Lit. Anec. Eighteenth Century, vol. i, pp. 542, 548, No. vi. Greswell's Annals of Parisian Typography, p. 5. London, 1818, 8vo.

is said to be "the earliest printed book containing text and engravings illustrative of Scriptural subjects;" and it is probable that this partial impression of the sacred text, thus decorated, gave the idea of publishing the entire text of the Bible, with similar embellishments, and in the same language, at Augsburg, about the year 1473, and a similar one by Fyner, of Eslingen, between the years 1474 and 1477: a practice frequently adopted afterward, both in the editions of the German and other vernacular translations, and in various editions of the Latin Bible. He is also supposed to have published a Bible about A. D. 1460, described in the *Bibliotheca Spenceriana*, tom. i, p. 7.*

Besides being established in many other places on the continent, in addition to those already noticed, printing was, about the same period, introduced into England, by WILLIAM CAXTON, a merchant of London, who, after residing many years abroad, was appointed in 1464, by Edward IV., as his ambassador (in conjunction with Richard Whetenhall) to negotiate a treaty of commerce with the duke of Burgundy, Edward's brother-in-law. During his residence in these countries he acquired the knowledge of printing; and became acquainted with Raoul Le Fevre, chaplain to the duke, whose "*Le Recueil des Histoires de Troyes*" he began to translate in 1468, and afterward published his English version in 1471, at the request of his patroness Margaret, dutchess of Burgundy. The original of this work was the first book Caxton printed, A. D. 1464–7. Of the exact period when he returned to England, and introduced the art of printing into the metropolis, we have no correct information. Thus much, however, is certain, that, previously to the year 1477, he had quitted the Low Countries, where he had principally resided, and was living in the vicinity of Westminster Abbey. To the erection of Caxton's press near one of the chapels attached to the aisles of the abbey is to be attributed the technical application of the term *chapel* to the internal regulations of a printing office:—

"Each printer hence, howe'er unbless'd his walls,
E'en to this day his house a *chapel* calls."

Nor is it improbable that his printing office might supersede the use of the *Scriptorium* of the abbey.

The first specimen of English typography is generally allowed to have been the "Game of Chess," in 1474; but Mr. Dibdin suspects that work to have been printed abroad, and thinks it more

* Dibdin's Bibliographical Decameron, vol. i, pp. 160, 373.

probable that the "Romance of Jason" was the earliest production of his press after its establishment in the abbey. The last work which he printed was his edition of the *Vitas Patrum*, or "Lives of the Fathers," in 1495. By the colophon it appears that these Lives were translated by him out of French into English, and that "he finished them at the last day of his life." He might have chosen this work as his final literary effort, observes one of his biographers, from a consideration that, "from the examples of quiet and solemn retirement therein set forth, it might further serve to wean his mind from all worldly attachments, exalt it above the solicitudes of this life, and inure him to that repose and tranquillity with which he seems to have designed it."* It is, however, to be regretted, that while most of the continental printers published one or more editions of the Latin Bible, or of some vernacular version, Caxton printed no part of the sacred volume; for which the best, and perhaps the only true apology is, the danger that would have attended such an attempt.†

Caxton, though the earliest, was not the *only* printer in England during the period in which he flourished. John Lettou, William de Machlinia, Wynkyn de Worde, and others, printed in Westminster and London, both before and after his decease; as did several also at Oxford, Cambridge, and St. Albans.

In glancing at the rapid extension of the invaluable art of printing, it ought not to be forgotten, that *Jews*, as well as Christians, became at an early period convinced of its importance, and engaged in it with ardour. The Psalms in Hebrew, with the Commentary of Kimchi, were printed in 1477, in 4to., by Joseph and his son Chaim Mordecai, and Hezekiah Monro, who printed three hundred copies of them. The Pentateuch, with the Targum and the Commentary of R. Jarchi, was printed at Bologne in Italy, in 1482, fol. Ruth, Ecclesiastes, Song of Solomon, and Lamentations, with the Commentary of Jarchi; and Esther with the Commentary of R. Abenezra, were printed also at Bologne, in fol., in the same year. The former and latter Prophets were first printed in Hebrew, at Soncino, in 1486, fol., with the Commentary of R. Kimchi. The Hagiographa were printed at Naples, 1487, in small fol., accompanied with several Rabbinical Commentaries. The *first* edition of the *whole* of the Hebrew Bible was executed by Abra-

* Dibdin's Typographical Antiquities, vol. i. *Life of Caxton, and Account of Books printed by W. Caxton, passim.* Horne's Introduction to Bibliography, vol. i, pp. 187–192.

† See the quotation from More's *Dyaloges*, p. 440 of this volume.

ham ben Chaim, at Soncino, in 1488, fol., with points. An edition, in octavo, was printed at Brescia, in 1494, by Gerson Moses ben Moses Menzeln. This latter edition is the one made use of by Luther, in his German translation; and his own copy of it is still preserved in the royal library at Berlin. Besides these, there were published at Soncino, in 1494, a folio and a quarto edition, without points, and an octavo one, with small types and points.*

In the early stages of typography, the name of the printer, his place of residence, and the date of his performance, were generally inserted at the *end* of each book, and not unfrequently accompanied by some pious doxology or ejaculation, in prose, or verse. From the invention of the art, to the year 1480, or even 1485, printed books were, generally speaking, without title-pages; and when first introduced, a simple line, or a line and a half, or at most three or four lines, toward the top of the page, constituted the whole of the decoration, till about 1490, when ornamental title-pages came into use, the most common of which was the representation of the author or writer at his desk; but subsequently, other devices were invented, some of them of the character of vignettes, others displaying the monogram, &c., of the printer. The leaves were without running title, direction word, number of pages, or divisions into paragraphs. The words were not divided at the ends of lines by hyphens, but in order to compress as much as possible within a given compass, the printers made use of vowels with a mark of abbreviation, as for instance, *dn̄o* for *domino; c'* for *cum ; quib'* for *quibus ; argētoq;* for *argentoque*, &c. The vowels and consonants *u* and *v*, *i* and *j*, are confounded together, and used one for the other; the diphthongs *æ* and *œ* were generally supplied by the simple *e : c* was often used for *t*, as *nacio* for *natio ; f* for *ph*, as *fantasma* for *phantasma ; mihi* was sometimes spelled *michi ; somnum, sompnum ; quotidiana, cotidiana ;* the orthography was consequently various, and often arbitrary. Capital letters were not used to begin a sentence, or for proper names of men, or places: blank spaces were left for the places of titles, initial letters, and other ornaments, to be supplied by the ingenious hand of the illuminator. The points by which they distinguished their sentences, were the colon, and period, and an oblique stroke (/)

* Kennicott, Dissertatio Generalis, sec. 59. Cod. 255–260, pp. 25, 91, 92. Le Long, edit. Masch, pt. i, cap. i, sec. 2, pp. 141, 142; and sec. 1, pp. 5, 7. De Rossi, De ignotis antiquiss. editionibus, cap. i, p. 3. Erlang, 1782, 4to. Whitaker's Hist. and Crit. Enquiry, p. 22.

for the comma. The character first used was a rude old Gothic mixed with Secretary, designed to imitate the hand-writing of those times; afterward the Roman was adopted by Sweynheim and Pannartz; and in 1502 the Italic was invented by Aldus. Ed. Rowe Mores, in his "Dissertation upon English Typographical Founders and Founderies," adds, that "metal characters were first used for the Greek by the monks of Subiaco," (Sweynheim and Pannartz,) "in 1465; for the Arabic, by Porrus of Genoa, in 1516; for the Æthiopic, by Potken, in 1513; and that the Congregation at Rome for the Propagation of the Faith in the year 1636 had, besides those we have just now mentioned, types for the Samaritan, for the Syriac, both Fshito and Estrangelo, for the Coptic, for the Armenian, for the Rabbinic Hebrew, and for the Heraclean, or ancient language of the Chaldees."*

The first printers executed their different works at their own expense, and sold them themselves, or by their agents, at their own risk. It was therefore necessary to employ large capitals; paper and other materials, as well as labour, being exceedingly dear, and the purchasers being but few; partly from the high prices of the books themselves, and partly from the illiteracy which so generally prevailed. These causes reduced many of the early printers to poverty; until the printers relieved themselves by confining their attention solely to printing, and leaving the bookselling part of the business to others. This created a distinct profession of *booksellers*, who frequently caused the books sold to be printed at their own expense, and thus also became *publishers*. Sometimes rich people of all conditions, and particularly eminent merchants, engaged in this branch of the profession, and employed the printers to print the manuscripts which they had purchased from the authors, or possessors. Thus the learned Henry Stephen, at Paris, was printer to Ulric Fugger, at Augsburg, from whom he received a salary for printing the many manuscripts which he purchased. In some editions, from the year 1558 to 1567, he subscribes himself *Henricus Stephanus, illustris viri Hulderici Fuggeri typographus*. In like manner, in the beginning of the seventeenth century, a society of learned and rich citizens of Augsburg, at the head of whom was Marx Welser, the city steward, printed a great number of books, which had commonly at the end these words, *Ad insigne pinus*. In Germany, this branch of trade was

* Horne's Introduction to Bibliography, vol. i, ch. ii, sec. 7. Rowe Mores' Dissert. upon English Typographical Founders, p. 12. Lond., 1778. Dibdin's Bibliographical Decameron, vol. ii, pp. 297–316.

at first established chiefly at Frankfort on the Mayn; and afterward at Leipsic, where, at the time of the fairs, several large booksellers' shops were opened for the disposal of their literary wares. These marts are still continued; and to them we owe the origin of the sale catalogues of booksellers, the earliest of which was printed at Frankfort, in 1554.*

The multiplication of books, and the consequent diffusion of knowledge, by the invention of printing, soon met with violent opposition from the transcribers and illuminators, of whom there were in Paris and Orleans only, upward of *ten thousand;* who, perceiving that the newly discovered art was likely to supersede their respective employments, attempted to suppress it by calling in the aid of the civil authorities. When printing therefore was first established at Paris, the copyists presented a memorial of complaint to the parliament, which caused their books to be seized and confiscated. Louis XI., who, with all his bad qualities, was the friend and patron of letters, prohibited the parliament from taking any further cognizance of the affair, and restored their property to the printers.† But a much more formidable obstacle was presented to the general spread of literature, by the restrictions imposed upon the authors and venders of books, by the ecclesiastical and civil powers. So early as the time of our King Henry II., nearly two centuries prior to the invention of printing, the manner of publishing the works of their authors, was to have them read over for three days successively before the university, or other judges appointed by the public; and if they met with approbation, copies of them were permitted to be taken, which were usually done by monks, scribes, illuminators, and readers, brought or trained up to that purpose for their maintenance;—a method adopted, probably, by every other university in Europe, at that period. In the year 1272 the university of Paris instituted a plan, not only for approving books, but for determining the price of them; and in the year 1323 appointed four officers, called *Taxatores Librorum*, to regulate the price of all manuscript books. Chevillier tells us, that the greater part of the MSS. bequeathed to the library of the Sorbonne, shortly after it was founded, have a price marked upon each of them; and that from a catalogue made of them in the year 1292, this library contained more than a thousand priced volumes, which, from the sum total specified at the

* Beckmann's Hist. of Inventions, vol. iii, pp. 118–120.

† Horne's Introduction to Bibliography, vol. i, p. 164, *note*. Dibdin's Bibliographical Decameron, vol. i, p. cxxvii.

end of the inventory, amounted in the whole to £3892 10*s*. 8*d*.! A similar practice afterward obtained in the universities of our own country; and it may be worthy of remark, that the act of the twenty-fifth of Henry VIII., ch. xv, sec. 4, granting to the lord chancellor, the lord treasurer, and the two chief justices, the power of regulating the prices of books, when too exorbitant, was not repealed till the twelfth of George II. The prices affixed to books by the "taxatores," or other officers, were, after the invention of printing, frequently expressed in the colophon of the respective works. Chevillier, in his "Origine de l'Imprimerie de Paris," pp. 368–375, has given a variety of colophons respecting the sums at which printers professed to sell their publications; thus Colinæus was obliged to sell his Greek Testament for a sum not exceeding twelve sous; and a Hebrew Psalter of Robert Stephens was priced at seven sous. In England, the price affixed by the king's authority to the New Testament with notes, printed by Richard Jugg, in 1553, quarto, was twenty-two pence per copy, in sheets.*

Soon after the discovery of printing, laws were made for subjecting books to examination; and the establishment of book-censors and licensers of the press was strenuously supported by the Romish clergy, who feared the circulation of publications inimical to their religious views, or their ecclesiastical domination. The earliest instance of a book printed with a permission from government is commonly supposed to occur in the year 1480; but Professor Beckmann mentions two books printed almost a year sooner than 1479, with the approbation of the public censor. The first is, *Wilhelmi episcopi Lugdunensis Summa de Virtutibus:* the other is a Bible, with the following conclusion: "In the year of the incarnation of our Lord 1479, on the vigil of Matthew the apostle; when this notable work, of the Old and New Testament, with the canons of the Gospels, and their harmonies, to the praise and glory of the holy and undivided Trinity, and the immaculate Virgin Mary, was printed in the city of Cologne, by Conrad de Homborch; *allowed* and *approved* by the university of Cologne."†

The oldest mandate for appointing a book-censor, with which we are acquainted, is that issued by Berthold, archbishop of Mentz, in the year 1486, which the curious reader will not be displeased to see at full length, with the instructions given to the censors:—

* Dibdin's Typographical Antiquities, vol. i, pp. 8–11, *note*.

† Beckmann's History of Inventions, vol. iii, pp. 105, 107.

Penal Mandate, forbidding the translation into the vulgar tongue, &c., of Greek, Latin, and other books, without the previous approbation of the doctors, &c.

"BERTHOLD, by the grace of God, archbishop of the holy see of Mentz, arch-chancellor of Germany, and electoral prince of the holy Roman empire."

"ALTHOUGH, by a certain divine art of printing, abundant and easy access is obtained to books on every science necessary to the attainment of human learning; yet we have perceived that certain men, led by the desire of vain glory, or money, do abuse this art; and that what was given for the instruction of human life is perverted to purposes of mischief and calumny. For, to the dishonouring of religion, we have seen in the hands of the vulgar certain books of the divine offices, and writings* of our religion, translated from the Latin into the German tongue. And what shall we say of the sacred laws and canons, which, though they have been written in the most suitable and careful manner by men acquainted with law, and endowed with the greatest skill and eloquence, yet the science itself is so intricate, that the utmost extent of the life of the wisest and most eloquent man is scarcely equal to it? Some volumes on this subject certain rash and unlearned simpletons have dared to translate into the vulgar tongue, whose translation, many persons who have seen it, and those, too, learned men, have declared to be unintelligible, in consequence of the very great misapplication and abuse of words. Or what is to be said of works on the other sciences, with which they sometimes even intermingle things that are false; and which, in order the more readily to find purchasers for them, they inscribe with false titles, and attribute to notable authors what are merely their own productions?"

"Let such translators, whether they do this with a good or with a bad intention, let them, if they pay any regard to truth, say whether the German tongue be capable of expressing that which excellent writers, both Greek and Latin, have most accurately and argumentatively written on the sublime speculations of the Christian religion, and on the knowledge of things. They must acknowledge that the poverty of our idiom renders it insufficient; and that

* It is probable that by the terms "libros de divinis officiis et apicibus religionis nostre," the archbishop referred to the vernacular translations, not only of the service-books of the Romish Church, called the *divine offices*, but also of the Holy Scriptures; the word *apices* being generally used, in the middle ages, for writings, epistles, &c. See Du Cange, *sub voce*.

it will be necessary for them to invent, from their own minds, new terms for things; or that, supposing them to make use only of the old ones, they must corrupt the sense of the truth, which, from the greatness of the danger attendant upon it, in the sacred writings, we greatly dread; for who would leave it to ignorant and unlearned men, and to the female sex, into whose hands copies of the Holy Scriptures may have fallen, to find out the true meaning of them? For instance, let the text of the Holy Gospels, or of St. Paul's Epistles, be examined, and no one of any knowledge will deny that there is a necessity for many things to be supplied, or understood, from other writings."

"These things have occurred to our minds, because they are the most common. But, what shall we think of those which are pending in very sharp disputes among writers in the Catholic Church? Many other instances might be brought forward, but it is sufficient for our purpose to have named a few."

"But, since the beginning of this art arose *divinely* (to give it its proper appellation) in this our golden city of Mentz, and continues in it to this day in its most improved and perfect state, it is with the greatest justice that we defend the glory of the art, and it becomes our duty to preserve the unspotted purity of the divine writings. Wherefore, with a view of meeting and restraining, as with a bridle, the aforesaid errors, and the daring attempts of shameless or wicked men, as far as we are able by the will of God, whose cause is in question;—we do, by strictly charging the observance of these presents, command all and every the ecclesiastical and secular persons subject to our jurisdiction, or transacting business within its limits, of whatever degree, order, profession, dignity, or condition they may be, that they translate no works on any science, art, or knowledge whatsoever, from the Greek, Latin, or other language, into the vulgar German; nor, when translated, either dispose of, or obtain copies, publicly or privately, directly or indirectly, by any kind of barter, unless before their impression they shall have been admitted, by patent, to be sold, by the most noble and honourable our beloved doctors and masters of the university in our city of Mentz, John Bertram de Nuremberg, in theology; Alexander Diethrich, in law; Theodoric de Meschede, in medicine; and Alexander Eler, in arts;—the doctors and masters deputed for this purpose in the university of our city of Erfurt; or if in the town of Frankfort, the books exposed for sale shall have been seen and approved of by an honourable, devout, and beloved master in theology, belonging to the place, and one or two doctors and licentiates, annually paid for that purpose by the governor of the said town. And whoever shall treat with contempt this our provision, or shall lend his counsel, assistance, or favour, in any way, directly or indirectly, in opposition to this our mandate, let him know that he has by so doing incurred the sentence of excommunication; and, besides the loss of the books exposed for sale, a penalty of one hundred florins of gold, to be paid into our treasury; from which sentence none may absolve him without special authority."

"Given at the chancery of St. Martin, in our city of Mentz, under our seal, on the fourth day of the month January, MCCCCLXXXVI."

The following are the instructions issued to the censors, and accompanying the above mandate:—

"BERTHOLD, &c., to the honourable, most learned, and beloved in Christ, Jo. BERTRAM, doctor in theology; AL. DIETHRICH, doctor in law; TH. DE MESCHEDE, doctor in medicine; and AL. ELER, master of arts;—health, and attention to the things underwritten."

"Having found out several scandals and frauds, committed by certain translators of literary works and printers of books, and wishing to counteract them, and according to our power to block up their way, we command that no one in our diocess, or under our jurisdiction, translate any books into the German tongue, or print, or sell them when printed, unless, in our city of Mentz, such works or books have first, according to the form of the mandate above published, been by you seen, and as to their matter approved of, both for translation and for sale."

"We do, therefore, by the tenor of these presents, (having great confidence in your prudence and circumspection,) charge you, that if at any time, any works, or books, intended to be translated, printed, or sold, be brought to you, you shall weigh their matter, and, if they cannot be easily translated according to the true sense, but would rather beget errors and offences, or be injurious to modesty, you shall reject them; and whatever books you shall judge worthy to be allowed, two of you, at least, shall sign them, at the end, with your own hand, in order that it may more readily appear what books have been seen and allowed by you. In so doing you will perform an office pleasing to our God, and useful to the state."

"Given at the chancery of St. Martin, under our privy seal, the 10th of January, MCCCCLXXXVI."*

* See Beckmann's Hist. of Inventions, vol. iii, pp. 108–113, for the Latin; where also reference is given to Guden's *Codex Diplomaticus*, tom. vi.

In the year 1501 the infamous pope Alexander VI. published a bull relative to the censure of books, which forms an excellent companion to the above mandate of the archbishop of Mentz. After lamenting that Satan sows tares among the wheat of Christ's church, the papal pontiff proceeds thus: "Having been informed that, by means of the said art, [of printing,] many books and treatises, containing various errors and pernicious doctrines, even hostile to the holy Christian religion, have been printed, and are still printed, in various parts of the world, particularly in the provinces of Cologne, Mentz, Triers, and Magdeburg; and being desirous, without further delay, to put a stop to this detestable evil;—we, by these presents, and by the authority of the apostolic chamber, strictly forbid all printers, their servants, and those exercising the art of printing under them, in any manner whatsoever, in the above said provinces, under pain of excommunication, and a pecuniary fine, to be imposed and exacted by our venerable brethren, the archbishops of Cologne, Mentz, Triers, and Magdeburg, and their vicars general, or official in spirituals, according to the pleasure of each, in his own province, to print hereafter any books, treatises, or writings, until they have consulted on this subject the archbishops, vicars, or officials, above mentioned, and obtained their special and express license, to be granted free of all expense; whose consciences we charge, that before they grant any license of this kind, they will carefully examine, or cause to be examined, by able and Catholic persons, the works to be printed; and that they will take the utmost care that nothing may be printed wicked and scandalous, or contrary to the orthodox faith." The rest of the bull contains regulations to prevent works already printed from doing mischief. All catalogues, and books printed before that period, are ordered to be examined, and those that contain any thing prejudicial to the Catholic religion to be burnt.*

In the tenth session of the council of Lateran, held under Leo X. in 1515, it was decreed, under pain of excommunication, that for the future no book should be printed at Rome, nor in the other cities and dioceses; unless, if at Rome, it had been examined by the "vicar of his holiness," and the "master of the palace;" or, if elsewhere, by the bishop of the diocess, or a doctor appointed by him, and had received the signature of approbation.† Philip II.,

* Beckmann's Hist. of Inventions, vol. iii, pp. 106–108. See also, for the original bull, Raynaldi Annales Ecclesiastici ab anno quo desinit Baronius, tom. xix, p. 514. Colon. Agrip., 1691, fol.

† Dictionnaire Portatif des Conciles, p. 280. Paris, 1764, 8vo.

king of Spain, is said to have had a catalogue printed of books prohibited by the Spanish Inquisition; and Paul IV., the following year, 1559, ordered the holy office at Rome to publish a similar catalogue; and Peignot (*Livres condamnés*, tom. i, p. 256) mentions one printed at Venice as early as 1543.* But this inquisitorial practice assumed its most formidable form in the council of Trent. "And first," says Dr. James, "the council appointed certain learned men, of all nations and countries there assembled, to gather such a Catalogue, or Index, together, as might contain all such books as were justly to be forbidden, whether written by or against them. This work, thus wisely thought upon, was diligently performed, and the Index made and presented unto the council; who referred all matters back again unto the pope's holiness, which then was Pius IV.; who, by his briefs and bulls, caused the same Index, together with certain rules, first by him approved and ratified, to be published abroad, and sent into all countries. This bull beareth date the 24th of March, 1564, in the fifth year of his popedom. But (it seemeth) that books increasing, and with books certain disorders that could not be prevented; in the end, Pope Sixtus, the fifth of that name, revising both Index and rules, with advice of the best divines, added very much thereunto, both in regard of the rules and of the books: and more he would have done, but that he was untimely prevented by death. Which being wisely perceived by Clement VIII., (a pope no less happy for ending and perfecting than the other was for intending and purposing great matters,) he resumes the Index, and appoints seven or eight of the gravest cardinals, besides other learned men, to oversee both it and whatsoever did belong thereunto: and in the end, for the better speed and more prosperous success of the sacred inquisition, appointed for the care and office of both prohibiting and purging books, he approves the Index thus revised, and confirms the privileges formerly granted, first by Pius V. unto the master of the sacred palace, and then by Gregory XIII. and Sixtus V. unto the cardinals of the congregation, for the better enabling of them, unto the performance of this so necessary and weighty a business, which doth so nearly concern the safety of their church and commonwealth."† The same learned librarian of the Bodleian further informs us, speaking of his own times, "In the Vatican library there are certain men maintained only to transcribe acts of

* Curiosities of Literature, vol. iii, p. 181. Lond., 1817, 8vo.

† James's Treatise on the Corruption of Scripture, &c., part iv, pp. 10, 11. Lond., 1611, 4to.

the councils, or copies of the works of the fathers. These men," he adds, "appointed for this business, do, as I am credibly informed, in transcribing books, imitate the letter of the ancient copies, as near as can be expressed. And it is to be feared that, in copying out of books, they do add and take away, alter and change the words, according to the pleasure of their lord, the pope: and so these transcripts may, within a few years, by reason of their counterfeiting the ancient hands, be avouched for very old MSS., deluding the world with a show of antiquity."* In the second part of his Treatise on the Corruption of Scripture, Councils, and Fathers, Dr. James exemplifies the charges brought against the Church of Rome for corrupting the ancient writings, both sacred and ecclesiastical.

In Rome, the compilers of the Catalogues, or Indexes, of prohibited books, are still continued, and called the Congregation of the Index. The works noticed in the Indexes are divided into three classes, the first containing a list of condemned *authors*, the whole of whose writings are forbidden, except by express permission; the second enumerating works which are prohibited, till they have been purged of what the inquisitors deem erroneous; the third comprehending those anonymous publications which are either partially, or totally forbidden. The manner in which the Romish literary inquisitors formerly decided upon the works presented to them, was sometimes criminally careless, and the results sufficiently curious. Gregory Capuchin, a Neapolitan censor, informs us, that his practice was to burn such Bibles as were defective in the text; and that his mode of ascertaining the accuracy or inaccuracy of the Latin Bibles was, to examine the third chapter of Genesis, and "if I find," says he, "the words, 'in sudore vultus tui, vesceris pane tuo,' instead of 'in sudore vultus tui, vesceris pane donec,' (thus adding the word *tuo*,) I direct such copies not to be corrected, but to be committed to the flames." As the "Indexes" were formed in different countries, the opinions were sometimes diametrically opposite to each other, and what one censor, or inquisitor, allowed, another condemned; and even in some instances the censor of one country has his own works condemned in another. Thus the learned Arias Montanus, who was a chief inquisitor in the Netherlands, and concerned in the compilation of the *Antwerp* Index, had his own works placed in the Index of *Rome;* while the inquisitor of Naples was so displeased

* James's Treatise on the Corruption of Scripture, &c., Appendix to Advertisement, &c.

with the Index of *Spain*, as to persist in asserting, that it had never been printed at Madrid. This difference in judgment produced a doubtful and uncertain method of censure, and it became necessary for the inquisitors to subscribe their names to the Indexes, in the following manner: "I, N.—inquisitor for such a diocess, do say, that this present book, thus by me corrected, may be tolerated and read, until such time as it shall be thought worthy of some further correction." But these Prohibitory and Expurgatory Indexes were reserved only for the inquisitors, and when printed, delivered only into their hands, or those of their most trusty associates. Philip II. in his letters patent, for the printing of the first Spanish Index, acknowledges, that it was printed by the king's printer, and at his own expense, not for the public, but solely for the inquisitors, and certain ecclesiastics, *who were not to be permitted to communicate the contents of it, or give a copy of it to any one.* And Sandoval, archbishop of Toledo, in the edition of 1619, prohibits, under pain of the greater excommunication, *any one to print the Index, or cause it to be printed; or when printed, to send it out of the kingdom, without a special license.* So difficult, indeed, were they to be obtained, that it is said the Spanish and Portuguese Indexes were never known till the English took Cadiz; and the Index of Antwerp was accidentally discovered by Junius, who afterward reprinted it.*

Even after the Reformation, a regular establishment of licensers of the press appeared in England, under Charles I., procured by Archbishop Laud, to prevent the introduction or publication of any works by the Genevan party, and in particular the Geneva Bible. The decree is dated July 1st, 1637, and marks the violence and persecuting spirit of the ruling system. It orders, "That the master printers from thenceforth shall be reduced to a certain number; and that if any other shall secretly or openly pursue that trade, he shall be set in the pillory, or whipped through the streets, and suffer such other punishment as that court (viz., the star-chamber) shall inflict upon him, that none of the said master printers shall from thenceforth print any book or books of divinity, law, physic, philosophy, or poetry, till the said books, together with the titles, epistles, prefaces, tables, or commendatory verses, shall be lawfully licensed, either by the archbishop of Canterbury, or the bishop of London, for the time being, or by some of their

* James's Treatise, Advertisement, &c., pt. iv, pp. 13, 14, 15, &c. Lomeier, De Bibliothecis, pp. 382–387. Franci Disquisitio de Papistarum Indicibus lib. prohib. et expurg., sec. 182, pp. 196, 197. Lips., 1684, 4to.

chaplains, or by the chancellors, or vice-chancellors of either of the two universities, upon pain of losing the exercise of his art and being proceeded against in the star-chamber, or the high-commission court respectively; that no person or persons do hereafter reprint, or cause to be reprinted, any book or books whatsoever, though formerly printed with license, without being reviewed, and a new license obtained for the reprinting thereof; that every merchant, bookseller, or other person, who shall import any printed books from beyond the seas, shall present a true catalogue of them to the said archbishop or bishop for the time being, before they be delivered or exposed to sale, upon pain of suffering such punishment as by either of the said two courts respectively shall be thought fit; that none of the said merchants, booksellers, or others, shall, upon pain of the like punishment, deliver any of the books so imported, till the chaplains of the said archbishop or bishop, for the time being, or some other learned man by them appointed, together with the master and wardens of the *Company of Stationers*, or one of them, shall take a view of the same, with power to seize on all such books which they find to be schismatical and offensive, and bring them to the said archbishop or bishop, or to the *high-commission* office; and finally, that no merchant, bookseller, &c., shall print, or cause to be printed beyond the seas, any book or books, which either totally, or for the greatest part, were written in the English tongue, whether the said books have been here formerly printed, or not; nor shall willingly nor knowingly import any such books into this kingdom, upon pain of being proceeded against in either of the said two courts respectively, as before is said."*

In many instances these prohibitory mandates only served to increase the inquiry after the works that had been forbidden, and to give publicity to the very volumes intended to be suppressed: it was thus that a bookseller of Paris, by giving out that the Colloquies of Erasmus were prohibited, sold above twenty-four thousand of one impression!†

* Heylyn's Cyprianus Anglicus, pt. ii, lib. iv, p. 341. Lond., 1671, fol.

† Jortin's Life of Erasmus, vol. i, p. 274. Lond., 1808, 8vo.

CHAPTER II.

FIFTEENTH CENTURY CONTINUED.

Promotion of Literature by Pope Nicholas V.—Janotus Manetto—Italian Version—N. de Malermi—D. N. Mirabellius—Capture of Constantinople—Spanish Versions—Vincent Ferrer—Bonifacio Ferrer—Councils and Inquisition—Expulsion of Moors and Jews from Spain—Paul of Burgos—Jacobus Perez—French Version—Gospel of Nicodemus—State of Literature—Bohemian, Saxon, German, Dutch, and Polish Bibles—Mammotrectus—Biblical Scholars—Mattheo Corvini, King of Hungary—Celebrated Jews.

Resuming the occurrences of the fifteenth century, we remark, with peculiar satisfaction, the literary exertions of Pope Nicholas V., and those of his secretary, Janotus Manetto, who, at a period when literature was emerging from under the cloud by which it had been obscured for ages, spared neither labour nor expense to promote its rising interests among their countrymen.

Thomas da Sarzana, or, as he is sometimes called, Tomaso Calandrino, was the son of a poor physician of Sarzana, a town of Italy, in the Ligurian Republic. His industry and learning were so extraordinary, that while he ranked only in the lower order of the clergy, he was chosen by the celebrated Cosmo de Medici to assist him in the arrangement of the library of St. Marco, at Florence. By rapid degrees he rose from his humble situation to the highest preferment in the ecclesiastical state, and succeeded to the pontifical chair in 1447, when he assumed the name of Nicholas V. During the eight years that he enjoyed the supreme dignity in the church, he acquired a high reputation, not by enlarging his territory or enriching his dependants, but by providing the most efficacious means for the extirpation of ignorance, and the acquirement of knowledge. When the bigoted Spaniards had published laws, in 1449, excluding all Jewish and heathen converts, and their posterity, from all offices of rank and emolument; and when the dean of the cathedral of Toledo had publicly defended the intolerant edicts, Nicholas, with enlightened liberality, issued a bull against the decree, excommunicating all those who offered to exclude the converted Jews and heathens from political or ecclesiastical offices from the priesthood and government: and when he conceived the first bull to be neglected, issued a second to maintain the generous policy which he had adopted. He was equally decisive in promoting the general diffusion of science. No expense was spared in the purchase of books; and where the originals could not be procured, copies were directed tc be made. His transcribers were everywhere employed; and the most learned men were engaged in translating into Latin the most valuable and useful of the Greek fathers, and ecclesiastical writers, as well as the most elegant and important classical authors. He caused the sacred Scriptures to be transcribed, and richly ornamented with gold and silver. He also offered a reward of five thousand ducats for the discovery of a copy of the Hebrew original of St. Matthew's Gospel; which, though fruitless as to its first object, probably occasioned the translation of the Gospel into that language. The Vatican, or pontifical library, which had been nearly dispersed by the frequent change of its possessors, and its removal from Rome to Avignon, and from Avignon to Rome, according as the popes fixed their residence at one or other of those cities, he enriched with five thousand MS. volumes, procured at immense expense. Nicholas also established public rewards at Rome, for composition in the learned languages, appointed professors in humanity, and became the liberal patron of learning and learned men. He allowed Francis Philelphus a stipend, for translating Homer into Latin; and it was by means of his munificent support, that Cyriac of Anconia, who may be considered as the first antiquary in Europe, was enabled to introduce a taste for gems, medals, inscriptions, and other curious remains of classical antiquity, which he collected with indefatigable labour in various parts of Italy and Greece. While this mild and munificent patron of letters was thus "sedulously employed, and marking with satisfaction the progress of his labours, the news which astounded Europe arrived, that the capital of the Grecian empire was in the hands of the Turks! The melancholy event is said to have preyed upon the gentle spirit of Nicholas, and helped to terminate his days in the spring of the year 1455."*

Janotus Manetto, or, more properly, Gianozzo Manetti, was by birth a Florentine. He was originally designed for a commercial life; but the strong and early bias of his mind led him to devote himself to literary pursuits, and particularly to direct his attention to theology. "This study," he said, "as best adapted to the condition of man, should end only with life; and he reposed in the contemplation of the divine nature, and the moral truths of religion! Augustine was here his favourite author, some of whose books his memory was sufficiently retentive to repeat."

To his classical acquirements in the Latin, he added an intimate

* Berington's Literary Hist. of the Middle Ages, b. vi, p. 476. Roscoe's Life of Lorenzo de Medici, vol. i, ch. i, pp. 56, 57. Lond., 8vo. Basnage's Hist. of the Jews, b. vii, ch. xxi, p. 691.

1

acquaintance with the Greek and Hebrew languages, and with science in general. To render the language of the sacred records more familiar, he took a Jew into his house, and afterward engaged another master of the same nation, with whom he read the Holy Scriptures in the original, and some ponderous commentators, for five hours each day. Nor did this suffice; for we subsequently find him covenanting with two Greeks, and a Hebrew, to live with him, on condition that each should converse with him in his own tongue.

His exalted moral qualities, united to his extensive learning, raised him to the highest offices, and he was employed in several embassies to foreign princes. But his excellences could not prevent him from becoming an object of envy; and after being subjected to heavy pecuniary fines, he quitted Florence, and resided at Rome, where he became secretary to Pope Nicholas V., who justly appreciated his worth, and honoured him with his confidence and esteem. The three last years of his life were spent at the court of Alphonsus, king of Naples, where he was principally engaged in writing, and so completely gained the friendship of Alphonsus, that he was heard to say, that, "were he reduced to a single loaf, he would divide it with Manetti." He died at Naples, A. D. 1459.*

His works comprise a variety of subjects, moral, historical, biographical, and oratorical, besides versions from the Hebrew and Greek. From the Hebrew he translated the Psalms into Latin; and the New Testament from the Greek.†

About the same time an ITALIAN version of the whole Bible was made from the Vulgate, by Nicholas de Malermi, or Malherbi, a Benedictine monk of Venice, of the order of Camaldoli, abbot of St. Michael de Lemo. In his preface he informs us, "that the reason of his undertaking his translation was the very great incorrectness of those translations which were already in the hands of the people, and in which some things were introduced that were not to be found in the text of the Scriptures," by which he probably refers to translations made from the French version of the work of Peter Comestor. He also says, "That the mutilations and editions of those translations were such, that it became much easier to execute a new translation, than to correct the old ones; and that he therefore suspended every other employment to devote himself to so important a work, which, however, he accomplished in about

* Berington, *ut sup.*, pp. 486–488.

† Le Long, edit. Masch, pt. ii, vol. iii, cap. iii, sec. i, p. 436; and sec. ii, p. 568.

eight months!" If this were actually the case, he must have engaged the assistance of others, or his translation have been a very hasty and incompetent one; but F. Simon thinks, that after all his professions, he merely corrected the preceding versions. He, however, informs us, that "his intention was to be serviceable to those who had not applied themselves to learning in their youth;" adding that "the Holy Scriptures instruct the learned in true wisdom, and the ignorant in true religion." The translation is accompanied by an Epistle to Dr. Laurentius, a professor of theology, in which he requests him to revise and correct his work, as he distrusted his own ability, and feared lest in some difficult places he should have mistaken the sense of the inspired writers. The professor's reply is subjoined, containing an eulogium on the elegance of the translation. The translator has also inserted, in Italian, all the Prefaces which are found prefixed to most of the Latin MSS. of Jerome's Bible.*

An edition of this Bible was printed at Venice by V. de Spira, in 1471, in two volumes, fol., and before the close of the fifteenth century had been several times reprinted at Venice. There was also an edition of the Italian Bible printed at Rome, in 1471, in fol., which has by some been supposed to be a different translation from the former, because it varies from it in some parts of the Old Testament; while others suppose the variations to be nothing more than corrections of Malermi's version.†

F. Simon affirms, that at this time, translations of the Epistles and Gospels, which are read at mass during the course of the whole year, were common in the Italian tongue, being executed for the instruction of the people; and supplying the place of the interpreters mentioned by St. Paul in the First Epistle to the Corinthians, chapter xiv.‡

Among the Biblical scholars of this age who flourished in Italy, DOMINICUS NANUS MIRABELLIUS deserves to be noticed, as the author of a Harmony of the Gospels, entitled *Monotessaron Evangeliorum*, which he accompanied with a laborious selection from the works of Gentile philosophers, poets, and orators, of passages illustrative of the Gospels. Among the authors quoted are, Seneca, Ovid, the Sybilline Oracles, Hermes Trismegistus, Pythagoras, Anaxagoras, Empedocles, Zeno, Plato, Aristotle, Isocrates,

* Simon's Crit. Hist. of the Versions of the N. T., pt. ii, ch. xl, pp. 336–338.

† Le Long, Biblioth. Sacra, tom. i, p. 354. Paris, 1723, fol. Walchii Biblioth. Theolog., tom. iv, cap. viii, p. 127.

‡ Simon's Crit. Hist. of Versions of N. T., pt. ii, ch. ii, p. 14.

Homer, Terence, Virgil, Horace, Plautus, Juvenal, Persius, Cicero, Claudian, Lucan, Pliny, A. Gellius, Macrobius, Valerius Maximus, &c. The work, which appears never to have been printed, is said, by Sixtus Senensis, to be preserved in the library of the Dominicans, at Genoa. Mirabellius was arch-presbyter of the church of Savona, and flourished about A. D. 1470.*

Two anecdotes, related by the biographer of the celebrated Lorenzo de Medici, may serve to throw light upon the literary history of Italy at this period, a subject extensively illustrated by the elegant, but partial biographer of the Medici, in his lives of Lorenzo and Leo X. The first relates to a MS. copy of Livy, sent by Cosmo de Medici to Alfonso, or Alphonsus, king of Naples. For such was the high value set upon it by the king, that although he had previously been at variance with Cosmo, the present conciliated the breach between them; and notwithstanding an intimation from his physician, that the book was probably poisoned, he disregarded their suspicions, and began with pleasure the perusal of the work. The other refers to a singular visiter at Florence, in 1474. This was Christian, or Christiern, king of Denmark and Sweden, who was journeying for the purpose, as was alleged, of discharging a vow. Having surveyed the city and paid a ceremonial visit to the magistrates, who received their royal visiter with great splendour, he requested to be favoured with a sight of the valuable copy of the Greek Evangelists, which had been obtained some years before from Constantinople; and of the Pandects of Justinian, brought from Amalfi to Pisa, and thence to Florence. His laudable curiosity was readily gratified, and he expressed his satisfaction by declaring, "that these were the real treasures of princes."† It is also worthy of note, that while the Hebrew tongue was cultivated, and several editions of the Hebrew Bible were printed in Italy, the learned Reuchlin complained, that not a single printed copy of the Hebrew Scriptures had passed the Alps, owing to the war waged by the emperor Maximilian.‡

The taking of Constantinople, and conquest of the Eastern empire, by the Turks, with its fatal effect on Pope Nicholas V., has been already cursorily noticed; but this event, so tragical to the inhabitants of the imperial city, proved ultimately so beneficial to the interests of literature, in the West, by the retreat of the learned

* Sixt. Senens. Biblioth. Sanct., lib. iv, p. 279.

† Roscoe's Life of Lorenzo de Medici, vol. i, ch. i, p. 34; and ch. iii, p. 158. London, 1796, 4to.

‡ Hody, De Bib. Text. Orig., pt. ii, lib. iii, p. 449.

Greeks into Italy, that it claims our particular regard. Cardinal Isidore, who had been constituted the titular patriarch of Constantinople, by Nicholas V., and was a witness of the horrible scene which ensued at the capture of the city, has left a most pathetic description of the circumstances of it, in a Latin epistle, which may be found in the Appendix to the third volume of Dr. E. D. Clarke's Travels, p. 383. By it we are informed, that the Turks, under Mohammed II., on entering the city spared neither rank, nor age, nor sex; the aged men and women were slain, the virgins were violated even in the sanctuary itself; the nobles were degraded into slaves; the temples of God were polluted, the images of the Saviour, of the Virgin Mary, and of the saints, were treated with contumely, and dashed to pieces; "the Holy Gospels, the missals, and the rest of the books belonging to the churches, were torn to pieces, defiled, and burnt;" the vestments, and other ornaments of the priests, were rent, or appropriated for the clothing and ornamenting of the victors; the sacred vessels were melted down, or turned to profane uses; in a word, the conquerors, urged by cruelty, lust, revenge, and a love of booty, spared neither place nor person.* Trithemius, (*in Chron. Sponheim.*, tom ii, App., p. 368,) adds, that the Turkish emperor being resolved, if possible, to extirpate Christianity from his newly acquired dominions, commanded all the copies of the Scriptures, and of the works of the orthodox fathers, that could be found, to be put into perforated vessels, and thrown into the sea.†

During the general carnage and confusion that ensued on the entrance of the Turks into Constantinople, and while the cruel conquerors were employed in plundering the city, many of the inhabitants, among whom were several men of various and extensive learning, escaped to the vessels in the harbour, and arrived safe in Italy, where they promoted the study of the Greek tongue, and gave increased energy to those scientific and literary pursuits which had already begun to engage the attention of many intelligent and literary characters in the Western empire, and which were so successfully aided by the recent invention of printing. The learned Humphrey Hody wrote an account of the chief of these illustrious exiles, which was published after his death by Dr. Jebb, and entitled *Dissertationes de græcis illustribus linguæ græce litterarumque humanarum instauratoribus.* London, 1742, 8vo.

* Dr. E. D. Clarke's Travels, pt. ii, sec. i, vol. iii, ch. i, p. 2; and Appendix, p. 383.
† Franci Disquisitio de Papist. Indicibus, sec. 180, p. 195.

Constantinople was captured, and the emperor Constantine slain, on the 29th of May, in the year 1453. "On the day of the capture, the sultan entered the city in triumph; viewed its still remaining monuments; and proceeded to establish the forms of a new government, and the rites of the Moslem worship."*

From recording the fall of Byzantium, and the asylum afforded in Italy to the learned Greeks who fled from the fury of the Mohammedan conquerors, we proceed to inquire into the state of Biblical literature in SPAIN.

Early in this century, a translation was made of the Scriptures into the SPANISH, in the dialect of Valencia. This version, which received the permission of the inquisitors, was made by Boniface Ferrer, the brother of St. Vincent, by whom, probably, he was assisted. An edition of it was printed at Valencia, in 1478, a fragment of which is still preserved in the Carthusian monastery of Portaceli.† The best account of this version is given by Santander, who observes, "This version of the Bible, in the Limousin or Valencian tongue, is so rare, that no complete copy of it is known to exist. The only certain fragment that we have of this version consists in the four last leaves, which were discovered in 1645, among the archives of the church of Valencia, and which have the subscription. Father John Bapt. Civera, a monk of the Chartreuse of Portaceli, having obtained these four leaves, he inserted them in his work, intituled *Varones illustres del Monasterio de Porta-Cœli*. The following is the subscription:—

"'Acaba la biblia molt vera e catholica, treta de una biblia del noble mossen berenguer vives de boil cavaller: la qual fon arromanzada en lo monestir de portaceli de lengua latina en la nostra valenciana per lo molt reverend micer bonifaci ferrer doctor en cascun dret e en facultad de sacra theologia: e don de tota la cartoxa: germa del benaventurat sanct vicent ferrer del orde de predicadors: en la qual translacio foren altres singulars homens de sciencia. E ara derrerament aquesta es stada diligentment corregida vista e regonegnda per lo reverend mestre jaume borrell mestre en sacra theologia del ordre et predicadors: e inquisidor en regne de valencia. Es stada empremptada en la ciutat de valencia a despeses del magnifichen philip vizlant mercader de la vila de jsne de alta Alemanya: per mestre Alfonso Fernandez de Cordova del regne de castella, e per mestre lambert palomar alamany mestre en arts: comencada en lo mes de febrer del any mil

* Berington's Lit. Hist. of the Middle Ages, Append., vol. i, p. 638.

† Thomson and Orme's Historical Sketch, &c., p. 40.

quatrecens setanta set: e acabada lo mes de Març del any mil CCCCLXXVIII.' "*

From this subscription we learn that the translation was made from the Latin, by Boniface Ferrer, assisted by other learned men, in the monastery of Portaceli, and in the Valencian dialect; that it was corrected and revised by John Borrell, a Dominican and inquisitor; that it was printed at the expense of Philip Vizlant, a merchant of Jesi, in the March of Ancona, by Alfonso Fernandez, of Cordova, and Lambert Palmar, or Pelmart, a German; and that the printing of it was begun in February, 1477, and finished in March, 1478.

Don Rodriguez de Castro, librarian to the king of Spain, corroborates the preceding account of this rare version, concerning which the most discordant notices have been given by different bibliographers, in his *Bibliotcca Espanola*, tom. i, p. 444, accompanied by an extract from the work itself, taken from the Apocalypse, of which a fragment is all that now remains. His words are, "La mas antigua," &c. "The most ancient [Spanish version] is that of all the books of the Old and New Testament which the Rev. Father Bonifacio Ferrer, (brother of St. Vincent Ferrer,) doctor of sacred theology, and of sacred and civil law, and general of the Carthusians, made in Valencian, and printed in Valencia, in 1478, as is seen in the last page, which is preserved in the Carthusian monastery of Portaceli, in the kingdom of Valencia, from which Dr. Francisco Asensio made a faithful copy, inserted here [in the 'Biblioteca Espanola'] verbatim, and which establishes the antiquity of this translation."†

VINCENT FERRER was born at Valencia, in Spain, according to Antonio, in 1352, but according to Butler, in 1357. He was early distinguished for learning and charity; in his eighteenth year he voluntarily embraced the monastic life, and in 1374 entered a convent of the order of St. Dominic, in his native city. In a short time after his profession he was deputed to read lectures of philosophy; and, removing to Barcelona, not only continued his scholastic exercises, but became a zealous preacher of the word of God. From Barcelona he was sent to Lerida, the most famous university of Catalonia, where he received the degree of doctor

* Santander, Dictionnaire Bibliographique, pt. ii, pp. 197–199. Bruxelles, 1806, 8vo.

† For this extract and translation from the "Biblioteca Espanola," printed at the royal printing-office, Madrid, two volumes folio, I am obliged to the kindness of the Rev. W. A. Thomson, one of the authors of the "Historical Sketch of the Translation and Circulation of the Scriptures."

from Cardinal Peter de Luna, in 1384. At the request of the bishop, clergy, and people of Valencia, he was recalled to his own country, and pursued his lectures and preaching with extraordinary reputation and success. One of his biographers remarks, "His heart was always fixed on God, and he made his studies, labour, and all his other actions, a continued prayer." The advice he gives to students, in his "Treatise on a Spiritual Life," is agreeable to his own practice, and is well worthy of attention:—"Do you desire to study to advantage? Let devotion accompany all your studies. Consult God more than your books, and ask him, with humility, to make you understand what you read. Study fatigues and drains the mind and heart. Go, from time to time, to refresh them at the feet of Jesus. Interrupt your application by short, but fervent and ejaculatory prayers. Never begin nor end your study but by prayer. Science is a gift of the Father of lights; therefore do not consider it merely as the work of your own mind or industry."

Vincent had now resided six years at Valencia, assiduously pursuing his pious labours, when Cardinal Peter de Luna, being appointed legate of Clement VII. to Charles VI., king of France, obliged him to accompany him. In 1394, on the death of Clement, the cardinal was chosen pope, by the French and Spaniards, and took the name of Benedict XIII. Vincent was then commanded to repair to Avignon, where he was raised to the dignity of master of the sacred palace; but, at his own earnest and frequently repeated request, was appointed apostolical missionary, and entered upon that office before the end of the year 1398, and for about twenty years laboured with indefatigable zeal in various parts of Europe. He visited Spain, France, the Netherlands, Germany, and Italy. Henry IV. invited him to England, sent one of his ships to fetch him from the coast of France, and received him with the greatest honours. After preaching in the chief towns of England, Scotland, and Ireland, he returned and pursued his missionary labours in the different parts of France, Italy, and Spain. The ordinary subjects of his sermons, which were delivered with unusual energy, were sin, death, judgment, hell, and eternity. Numerous Jews and Mohammedans are said to have been converted by his ministry, and multitudes of immoral characters to have been reclaimed. The two last years of his life were spent in Brittany and Normandy, whither he had gone at the desire of Henry V. He died in the city of Vannes, in 1419, at the age of sixty-two, or, according to others, at sixty-seven. He was canonized by Pope Calixtus III. in 1455.*

In the list of his writings Nic. Antonio mentions the following Biblical work: "BIBLIA, seu PROMPTUARIUM, sc. locorum sacræ Scripturæ singulis diebus, sive de tempore, sive de sanctis usurpandorum." At the beginning of the copy to which Antonio refers a note is prefixed, intimating that it had been bequeathed as a legacy by the author: "Hanc Bibliam inspirante Domino mihi Fr. Antonio de aurea mihi reliquit beatissimus Fr. Vincentius."† The chief of his other works are, A Treatise on a Spiritual Life; Commentary, or Sermons, on the Lord's Prayer, printed at Lyons, 1523, 4to., and again 1573, 8vo.; and Epistles.‡

BONIFACIO, or BONIFACE FERRER, was the brother of Vincent. Intending to engage in secular concerns, he married; but, after the death of his wife, was persuaded by his brother to enter the Carthusian monastery of Portaceli, near Valencia. His industry and attention to every part of the severe discipline of his order gained him universal approbation, so that, in the short period of four years, he became prior general, an office which he executed with the utmost fidelity. But having been elected during the schism in the papacy, and the council of Pisa, held in 1409, having deposed the schismatical popes, and chosen Cardinal Peter Philargi pope, who styled himself Alexander V., he requested and obtained permission to surrender up his dignity; and Stephen de Sævis succeeded to the office. Butler, (Lives of the Saints, vol. iv,) however, says, he was general of the Carthusians at the time of his death.

In the year 1412, the states of Arragon, Catalonia, and Valencia, being divided about a successor to the crown of Arragon, they agreed to choose nine commissaries, three for each kingdom; when Boniface, his brother Vincent, and Don Peter Bertrand, were chosen for the kingdom of Valencia. They met at the castle of Caspé, in Arragon. Ferdinand of Castile was unanimously declared to be the lawful heir; and Vincent Ferrer, haranguing the foreign ambassadors and people present, the decision was received with acclamation. Boniface died April 29th, 1419.§

The exact period when Boniface's translation of the Bible was

* Butler's Lives of the Saints, vol. v, p. 44. Antonii Bibliotheca Hispana Vetus, tom. ii, p. 136. Romæ, 1696, folio.

† Antonii Bibl. Hisp. Vet., tom. ii, p. 137.

‡ Butler, *ubi sup.* Le Long, Biblioth. Sacra, tom. ii, p. 723; edit. Paris, 1723.

§ Antonii Bibl. Hisp. Vet., tom. ii, lib. x, cap. iii, p. 140. Butler, vol. v, *ubi sup.*

made cannot, perhaps, be ascertained; but as Vincent was recalled to Valencia by King John II. in 1410, by whose command the version is by some said to have been made, and as he continued there about two years, it was probably commenced, if not completed, at that time.

About the year 1450, Alphonsus V., king of Arragon, is supposed to have translated the Proverbs of Solomon into his native tongue. He is also said to have read the whole Bible fourteen times, with glosses and commentaries; and to have become so expert in the Scriptures, as not only to relate the substance of them, but to repeat many parts of them correctly, from memory.*

It is, nevertheless, to be deplored that the study of the Scriptures was far from being general; and that the most profound ignorance reigned among the major part, even of the clergy. Few of them, comparatively, were acquainted with the Latin, though constantly used in the offices of the church; while feasting and debauchery are declared to have been their ordinary occupations. This occasioned the councils of Madrid and Arenda, in 1473; and various decrees were passed in them, designed to remedy the disorders and ignorance of the ecclesiastics of all ranks. The bishops were forbidden to ordain or promote those who were ignorant of Latin; the Scriptures were ordered to be daily read at the tables of the prelates themselves; the clergy, in general, were forbidden to wear gay apparel, to be clothed in silk, to walk in white sandals, or red or green buskins, or to put on mourning; they were also commanded not to play at dice, or fight duels; and those who died of the wounds received in a duel were ordered to be deprived of ecclesiastical burial. Other canons were framed against simony, clandestine marriages, ecclesiastical concubinage, dramatic exhibitions in churches, &c.†

But these injunctions were not succeeded by the reformation so necessary to the religious welfare of the church; for in 1499 Pope Alexander VI. found it requisite to send an epistle to the Spanish bishops respecting the ignorance of the clergy; urging them to adopt measures for the promotion of study and discipline among them.‡

Some attempts, however, were made, notwithstanding the almost universal depravity and ignorance which prevailed, to communicate

* Usserii Hist. Dogmat., p. 172.

† D'Aguirre, Collectio Maxima Concil. Hisp., tom. iii, pp. 672–677. Romæ, 1693–94, folio. Dictionnaire Portatif des Conciles, pp. 39, 302, 479

‡ D'Aguirre, *ut sup.*, tom. iii, p. 689.

a knowledge of the sacred writings to those who were acquainted only with their mother tongue. Le Long mentions a version of the Bible, in the dialect of Catalonia, written in the year 1407, of which an imperfect copy was preserved in the Colbertine library; he also notices an edition of the Psalter, in the dialect of Castile, printed, as he supposed, before A. D. 1500.* Fred. Furius, who wrote a treatise on the sacred Scriptures, printed in 1556, says, that at the close of the fifteenth century the Scriptures had not only been translated into his native dialect of Valencia, but into almost all the other dialects of Spain.† These translations were prevented from being circulated, by the establishment and influence of the inquisition, and the edict of Ferdinand and Isabella, (called also Elizabeth,) which enacted, that "no one should translate the Scriptures into the vulgar tongue, or have them in their possession, under pain of the severest punishment."‡ Fred. Furius adds, that "this prohibition extended only to those who were originally Jews, and not to others." He further remarks, that the lessons from the Gospels read in the churches during the whole year had been faithfully and elegantly translated, and permitted to be printed; and that he had seen and read the Epistles of St. Paul, translated into Spanish verse, in the dialects of both Castile and Valencia.§ Conrad Gesner, another author who flourished in the sixteenth century, notices these vernacular versions, but remarks, that in his day nearly all the copies of them had been burnt.‖ In January, 1492, the Spaniards took Granada, and extinguished the empire of the Moors in Spain, where they had been settled more than seven hundred years. Ferdinand de Talavéra, a man of great learning and exemplary piety, was nominated archbishop of Granada. His disposition was mild, patient, and charitable, without ambition, and without jealousy. He therefore consented that the archbishop of Toledo, the celebrated Ximenes, should possess equal authority with himself in his diocess. The two archbishops concerted measures for the conversion of the Mohammedans, thus placed under their care; and mutually agreed that the safest and most successful plan would be to gain over the Alfaquis, or priests and doctors of that sect. With this design they convened an assembly of them in the palace, addressed them familiarly, and,

* Le Long, Biblioth. Sacra, tom. i, pp. 362, 369, edit. 1723.

† Ibid., tom. i, p. 362.

‡ Le Long, *ut sup.*, p. 361. Usserii Hist. Dogmat., p. 175.

§ Simon's Crit. Hist. of the Versions of the New Testament, part ii, ch. ii, p. 18; and ch. xli, p. 344. Usserius, *ut sup.*

‖ Le Long, tom. i, p. 362.

after having exhorted them to renounce their errors and receive baptism, presented some of them with pieces of silk, others with scarlet caps, which were held by them in great estimation; and sent them away, well pleased with the condescension of the prelates, and the presents they had received. By these means many of the priests were led to profess Christianity, and to persuade the people to a similar profession; and so great was the success of these measures, that on the 18th of December, 1499, four thousand Moors received baptism. The refractory Moors Ximenes endeavoured to conquer, sometimes by inquisitorial treatment, sometimes by gentler and milder usage. Having at length subdued the more intractable of his opponents, particularly Zegri, a noble and valiant Moor, and conciliated the Mohammedan doctors, he ordered all the copies of the Koran, and every book that contained its doctrines, to be brought to him, and consigned five thousand volumes publicly to the flames. Neither illuminations, nor rich bindings, nor other ornaments of gold and silver, were suffered as a plea for their preservation. The only works exempted from the common flame were some treatises on medicine, for which the Moors had been famous, and which were transmitted to the library of the college of Alcala.*

The Moors having professed Christianity, it became a subject of discussion between the archbishops which was the best method of instructing their new converts in the religion they had embraced. The dispositions of these prelates discovered itself in the difference of their views. Ferdinand de Talavéra, in order to direct their attention to the divine offices, had ordered the daily lessons of the Old and New Testaments to be recited in the vulgar tongue; and permitted the books of the mass, and especially the Epistles and Gospels, to be translated into Arabic, and printed. Ximenes entirely disapproved of this procedure, and urged the impropriety of placing the sacred oracles in the hands of these half converts, affirming that weak minds always revered most what was concealed and mysterious; and contending that, since the Old and New Testaments contained many passages that demanded much intelligence and attention to understand them, it was best to leave them in the Hebrew, Greek, and Latin, the three languages consecrated by the inscription placed over the head of the dying Saviour. But while he strenuously contended against the Scriptures being translated into the vulgar tongue, he allowed the pro-

* Flechier, Histoire du Cardinal Ximenes, tom. i, liv. i, pp. 136–143. Amsterdam, 1693, 12mo.

priety of distributing, in the language commonly spoken, catechisms, prayers, and edifying narratives, and other books of religious instruction. The archbishop of Granada reluctantly submitted to the unyielding temper of Ximenes, and the book of God was withheld from the people.*

The expulsion of the Jews speedily followed the conquest of the Moors; for in March of the same year (1492) Ferdinand and Isabella banished the Jews out of Spain; by which eight hundred thousand persons were forced to quit the kingdom, and seek asylums in more favoured regions. In the number of those who were exiled were several eminent rabbis, particularly R. Isaac Abrabanel, the author of valuable commentaries on several parts of the Old Testament, and other esteemed works; R. Meir, author of a commentary upon Job; and R. Abraham, the compiler of the chronological work called *Juchassin*.†

Through the instructions of Vincent Ferrer, the terrors of the inquisition, and the dread of poverty and exile, many Spanish Jews were induced to make profession of the Catholic religion, some few of them sincerely, but most of them deceptively. Among the sincere converts from Judaism, during this century, in Spain, SOLOMON DE LEVI holds the chief place. He was a native of Burgos, and embraced Christianity from reading the works of Thomas Aquinas, or Aquino. At his baptism he took the name of Paulus de Sancta Maria, or Paul of Burgos. After the death of his wife he embraced the ecclesiastical state, and by his merits obtained places of trust and honour. He was preceptor to John II., king of Castile; and was successively archdeacon of Trevigno, bishop of Carthagena, and then of Burgos, where he died August 29th, 1445, aged eighty-two. Some authors relate that he was patriarch of Aquileia. He wrote, 1. *Scrutinium Scripturarum*, printed at Mantua, 1474, in folio; Mentz, 1478; Paris, 1520; Burgos, 1591. 2. *Additiones ad Postillam Magistri Nicolai de Lyra super Biblias;* generally printed with the Postils of De Lyra. In this work the author freely censures and corrects the notes of De Lyra, particularly where he differs from Aquinas, whose defence Paul universally undertakes. In his emendations of De Lyra he is often successful in what relates to philosophy and Hebrew antiquities; but in his criticisms of the Greek he more frequently fails. He is also considered as paying too implicit deference to the fathers and the scholastic writers. 3. *Quæstiones XII. de*

* Flechier, Hist. du Card. Ximenes, tom. i, liv. i, pp. 154, 155.

† Basnage's Hist. of the Jews, b. vii, ch. xxi, pp. 692, 693.

Nomine Tetragrammato; published with notes, by J. Drusius, Franeker, 1604, 8vo.

His three sons were baptized at the same time with him, when he became a Christian convert; and all distinguished themselves by their merit. The eldest, Alphonso, who succeeded his father as bishop of Burgos, wrote an abridgment of Spanish history; the second, Gonsalvo, became bishop of Placentia; and the third, Alvarez, who married into an illustrious family, published a history of John II., king of Castile.*

Another learned Spaniard of this period was JACOBUS PEREZ, bishop of Christopolitanus. He was a native of Valencia; and became a hermit of the order of Augustine. He died in 1491. He was the author of various works, particulary of a commentary on the Psalms; and a treatise against the Jews, printed at Lyons, 1512. He is chiefly noted for his singular opinions respecting the invention of the Hebrew vowel points, and the compilation of the Talmud. He says, "That the rabbis perceiving that, after the conversion of Constantine the Great, multitudes of both Gentiles and Jews embraced Christianity, and that their influence and revenues were consequently lessened, they convened a general meeting at Cairo, in Egypt; where they, with as much secrecy as possible, falsified and corrupted the Scriptures; invented five or seven points to serve instead of vowels; and forged the Talmud. (*Prolog. in Psalmos Tract.* 6.†)

It may also be deemed interesting to observe, that *printing* was introduced into Spain at an early period after its invention. Valencia is conjectured to be the city where printing was first exercised in that kingdom; and where a press was established in 1474. The earliest work printed there, of which the date has been ascertained, was *Obres, o Trobes les quales tracten de las hors de la Sacratissima Verge Maria, &c.*, 1478, 4to. The number of books printed in Spain, during the fifteenth century, was three hundred and ten. These appeared chiefly at Barcelona, Burgos, Salamanca, Saragossa, Seville, Toledo, and Valencia; and were principally executed by Germans.‡

If from Spain we turn to FRANCE, we find but little that claims

* Lempriere's Universal Biography. Lond., 1808, 4to. Cavei Hist. Litt., sæc. xv, p. 92, Append. Le Long, Biblioth. Sacra, edit. Masch., pt. ii, tom. iii, cap. ii, sec 3, p. 363.

† Hody, De Bibl. Text. Orig., lib. iii, pt. ii, p. 442. Cavei Hist. Litt., sæc. xv, p. 149. Append.

‡ Horne's Introduction to Bibliography, vol. i, p. 475. Clarke's Bibliographical Miscellany, vol. ii, p. 127.

our attention, relative to Biblical literature. The establishment of the newly invented art of printing in several cities of France has been noticed already; and the editions of the Scriptures which were printed were chiefly those of Comestor, or Guiars des Moulins. The following are the principal ones:—

A French version of the Old and New Testaments, printed at Lyons, without date, but supposed, with considerable probability, to have been published in 1477. The editors were Julian Macho and Peter Farget. Santander says, this was the *first* French version; but Le Long speaks of it merely as a revised edition of the translation of Guiars des Moulins. The following is Santander's bibliographical account of this and another rare edition of the Scriptures. "The Old Testament, translated into French. *Lyons, printed by Barth. Buyer*, (*about the year* 1477,) *in fol.*"

"The exact conformity of the characters of this most rare edition, with those employed by Barth. Buyer, in the impression of the *New* Testament, noticed in the following article, proves, I think, that they were printed at the same press; and that Julian Macho and Peter Farget were also the editors and correctors."

"The work is printed in two columns, in Gothic letters, and without signatures. Five leaves, which contain the table of rubrics with this title, *Cy commencent les rubriches de ce present livre*, precede the text, at the end of which, on the reverse of the last leaf, are these words: "Cy finit ce present livre." A copy was sold at the sale of Gaignat, in 1769, for eighty livres, one sol; and at the sale of La Valliere, in 1783, for ninty-nine livres, nineteen sols."

"The New Testament revised and corrected by Julian Macho and Peter Farget. *Lyons, Bartholomew Buyer*, without date, (about the year 1477,) *in fol.*"

"An exceedingly rare edition, and the first translation of the New Testament into French. It is printed in the same Gothic characters as the Old Testament mentioned in the preceding article, and which it was probably designed to accompany." The pages of this volume are in two columns, without figures or signatures. It begins with a table which occupies twenty leaves, which ends thus: "Cy finist la table du nouueau testament ensemble la declaration diceluy faicte et compassêe p̲ uenerable persōne frere iulliā docteur en theologie de l'ordre saīnt Augustī demourant au couuēt de lyō sus le rosne. loue soit dieu Amen."

"Then follows the text, at the end of which, on the *recto* of the last leaf, is this subscription: 'Cy finist l'apocalypse et semblablement le nouueau ueu et corrige p̲ uenerables persõnes freres iullien macho et pierre farget docteurs en theologie de l'ordre des Augustins de lyõ sus le rosne Imprime en la dicte uille de lyon par Bartholomieu Buyer citoien du dit lion."

"There is also another impression of this book, by the same printer, in the same characters, with the same number of leaves, and the same subscription, differing only in being printed in long lines, and the sheets having signatures; it is, however, considered as being equally ancient, and is equally esteemed."

"At Gaignat's sale, the former edition sold for ninety livres, and that with long lines for two hundred and eleven livres: and at La Valliere's, the former edition sold for ninety-nine livres, nineteen sols; the edition with long lines for ninety livres."

JULIAN MACHO was an Augustine monk, and doctor in divinity, of the convent of Lyons. Besides the *French New Testament*, noticed above, he was joint editor with John Bathalier, of a French *Supplement to the Golden Legend*, printed at Lyons, by Barth. Buyer, 1477, in fol.

PETER (PIERRE) FARGET, sometimes erroneously called Falget, Ferget, and Sarget, was also a monk of the order of Augustine, and doctor in divinity, residing in the convent of the order, at Lyons. Besides the revision of the New Testament, Farget published, in 1482, a French translation of the *Speculum Humanæ Vitæ*, under the title of *Miroir de la vie humaine;* printed at Strasburg, with Gothic characters, in small folio. He also translated out of Latin into French a work entitled, "The Consolation of Poor Sinners," in the form of a dialogue between Belial and Jesus Christ; besides other works of minor importance.*

Le Long mentions an edition also in quarto, in the Gothic type, executed at Paris, about the year 1478, which he conjectures to have been corrected from the *Historia Scholastica* of Peter Comestor, by William Le Menand; and either this, or the one which will be subsequently noticed, is, probably, the translation of which John Lambert speaks, in his answer to the bishop's articles, A. D. 1538. Lambert's words are: "You [the bishops] ask, whether I believe that the heads, or rulers, by necessity of salvation, are bound to give unto the people Holy Scripture, in their mother language? I say, that I think they are bound to see that the people may truly know Holy Scripture, and I do not know how that may be done so

* Santander, Dict. Bibliographique, 2de partie, pp. 197–199. De Juvigny, Bibliotheques Françoises, tom. ii, pp. 277, 278.

well, as by giving it to them truly translated in the mother tongue, that they may have it by them at all times, to pass the time godly, whensoever they have leisure thereto; like as they have in France, under the French king's privilege, and also the privilege of the emperor, and so do I know they have had it these *fifty-four* years in France, at the least, and it was translated at the request of a king, called, I trow, Louis, as appeareth by the privilege put in the beginning of the book." The king here mentioned was Louis XI.*

Another French version of the Bible has been attributed to Jean de Rely, made by order of Charles VIII. M. de la Monnoye says, "This pretended translation of Jean de Rely is nothing more than that which was made by Guiars des Moulins, in 1294, from the *Historia Scholastica* of Peter Comestor, and which Jean de Rely, who was canon of Notre-Dame, and was made bishop of Angers in 1491, revised by order of Charles VIII. It was printed in 1495, and again in 1538, by Antoine Bonnemere." To this the editor of the *Bibliotheques Françoises* subjoins as a correction of the above: "The oldest edition of the French translation, by Jean de Rely, appears to be that cited in the Catalogue of the printed Books in the King's Library, tom. i, No. 156. 'La Bible Historiale, où sont les Histoires Scholastiques, ou les Livres Hystoriaulx de la Bible, translatés de Latin en François, en la maniere que les maîtres ont traduit ez Histoires Scholastiques de Pierre le Mangeur, par Guyart des Moulins, revue par Jean de Rely, Pretre et Chanoine de S. Pierre d'Aire, de l'Archevêché de Tresves, par le commandement de Charles VIII., roi de France; Paris, pour Antoine Verard, in fol., 2 vols., vers l'an 1487.' It was afterward reprinted in 4to. in 1515 and 1535; and again in folio in 1538. According to the same catalogue, in the edition of 1538 the editor, Antoine Bonnemere, says, 'that the first edition was printed in 1495, after having been corrected.'"†

England next claims our regard. Wiclif and his followers had detected many of the errors, and exposed many of the superstitious practices, of the Church of Rome at this period; but the clergy obstinately refused to abandon either their errors or superstitions, and persecuted with the most unrelenting cruelty all who attempted the smallest reformation. "In a word," says an accurate historian,

* Le Long, Biblioth. Sacra, tom. i, p. 325. Fox's Actes and Monumentes, tom. ii, p. 415. Lond., 1641, fol.

† De Juvigny, Bibliotheques Françoises, tom. iii, Du Verdier. Art. "Bibles," pp. 267–270.

"ignorance, vice, and superstition seemed to have gained ground; though the revival of learning, and the reformation of religion, were at no great distance."* A singular instance of incompetence in a clergyman is related by Warton, in his History of English Poetry. In 1448, Waynflete, bishop of Winchester, on the presentation of Merton Priory, in Surrey, instituted a rector to the parish of Sherfield, in Hampshire. The rector, however, previously took an oath before the bishop, that on account of his insufficiency in letters, and default of knowledge in the superintendence of souls, he would learn Latin for the two following years; and that at the end of the first year he would submit himself to be examined by the bishop concerning his progress in grammar; and that if, on a second examination, he should be found deficient, he would resign the benefice.† The introduction of men into the sacred office, through the influence of rank, who were destitute of competent abilities, is further exemplified by an anecdote related of Erasmus: "At this time, (A.D. 1496,) I suppose," says his biographer, "he refused a large pension, and larger promises, from a young illiterate Englishman, who was to be made a bishop, and who wanted to have him for a preceptor. This youth seems to have been James Stanley, son of the earl of Derby, and son-in-law to Margaret, the king's mother, and afterward made bishop of Ely by her interest. However, it appears that the young gentleman, though ignorant, had a desire to learn something, and to qualify himself, in some measure, for the station in which he was to be placed."‡

So far were the clergy in general from attempting to circulate the Scriptures, or instruct the people in the knowledge of their contents, that, except such portions of them as were recited in the offices of the church, there was scarcely a Latin Testament in any cathedral church in England, till the time of the learned John Colet, dean of St. Paul's, in London, though the Latin was the only authorized language for the Scriptures and service books. Instead of the Gospel of Christ, the spurious Gospel of Nicodemus was affixed to a pillar in the nave of the church; which Erasmus says he had himself seen with astonishment in the metropolitan church of Canterbury.§ It is remarkable that Theodoret, (*Hæret. Fab.*, lib. i, cap. xx,) in the *fifth* century, complained of a similar

* Henry's History of Great Britain, vol. x, p. 42.

† Warton's Hist. of English Poetry, vol. ii, p. 429, *note* Z.

‡ Jortin's Life of Erasmus, vol. i, p. 5. Lond., 1808, 8vo.

§ British Biography, vol. i, "Life of Dean Colet," p. 377.

practice existing in his day. Tatian, says he, "composed a gospel which is called *Dia Tessaron*, [Of the Four,] leaving out the genealogies, and every thing that shows the Lord to have been born of the seed of David according to the flesh: which has been used not only by those of his sect, but also by them who follow the apostolical doctrine; they not perceiving the fraud of the composition, but simply using it as a compendious book. I have also met with above *two hundred* of these books, which were in esteem in our churches: all which I took away, and laid aside in a parcel, and placed in their room the Gospels of the Four Evangelists."*

The GOSPEL OF NICODEMUS, or *Acts of Pilate*, above mentioned, is a work supposed to have been forged, toward the close of the third century, by Leucius Charinus. It treats chiefly of the crucifixion and resurrection of our Lord, and of his descent into hell. It contains many trifling, silly, and ludicrous relations, such as, the standards or colours bowing to Christ as he passed; Jesus appearing to Joseph of Arimathea, after his resurrection, wiping his face from the dew, kissing him, and commanding him to remain in his own house for forty days; and a supposititious narrative of the events attending Christ's descent into hell, by Lentius and Charinus, two saints raised from the dead at the resurrection of the Saviour. The following extracts from this impudent forgery will enable the reader to judge of the kind of instruction afforded by these substitutes for the Gospel of Christ. The relation of Christ's descent into hell is introduced by Joseph of Arimathea addressing Annas and Caiaphas, who were astonished to hear that Jesus was risen from the dead, and that others were risen with him: "We all," says he, "knew the blessed Simeon, the high-priest, who took Jesus, when an infant, into his arms, in the temple. This same Simeon had two sons of his own, and we were all present at their death and funeral. Go, therefore, and see their tombs, for these are open, and they are risen; and behold, they are in the city of Arimathea, spending their time together in offices of devotion Some, indeed, have heard the sound of their voices, [in prayer,] but they will not discourse with any one, but they continue as mute dead men. But come, let us go to them, and behave ourselves toward them with all due respect and caution. And if we can bring them to swear, perhaps they will tell us some of the mysteries of their resurrection." Annas, Caiaphas, Nicodemus,

* Lardner's Works, vol. ii, p. 138. Lond., 1788, 8vo.

and Gamaliel, proceed to Arimathea; they find Charinus and Lentius at their devotions, and, adjuring them by the Law to relate what they had seen, they tremble, look up to heaven, make the sign of the cross upon their tongues, and then calling for paper, write the account of what they profess to have seen. "When we were placed with our fathers in the depth of hell," say they, "in the blackness of darkness, on a sudden there appeared the colour of the sun like gold, and a substantial purple coloured light enlightening (the place.) Presently upon this, Adam, the father of all mankind, with all the patriarchs and prophets, rejoiced and said, 'That light is the Author of everlasting light, who hath promised to translate us to everlasting light.' And while we were all rejoicing, our father Simeon came among us, and, congratulating all the company, said, 'Glorify the Lord Jesus Christ . . . .' "Afterward there came forth one like a little hermit, and was asked by every one, 'Who art thou?' To which he replied, 'I am the voice of one crying in the wilderness John the Baptist.' . . . . But when the first man our father Adam heard these things, that Jesus was baptized in Jordan, he called out to his son Seth, and said, 'Declare to your sons, the patriarchs and prophets, all those things which thou didst hear from Michael the archangel, when I sent thee to the gates of paradise, to entreat God that he would anoint my head when I was sick.' Then Seth said, . . . 'I Seth, when I was praying to God at the gates of paradise, behold! the angel of the Lord, Michael, appeared unto me, saying, ... 'I tell thee, Seth, do not pray to God in tears, and entreat him for the oil of the tree of mercy, wherewith to anoint thy father Adam for his headache, because thou canst not by any means obtain it till the last day and times.'" A dialogue then ensues between Satan, the prince and captain of death, and Beelzebub, the prince of hell, in which they are interrupted by suddenly hearing a voice, "as of thunder and the rushing of winds, saying, 'Lift up your heads, O ye princes; and be ye lift up, O everlasting gates, and the King of glory shall come in.'"

This is succeeded by the appearance of the King of glory enlightening the regions of darkness, and throwing the devils into confusion. "Then the King of glory trampling upon death, seized the prince of hell, deprived him of all his power, and took our earthly father Adam with him to his glory." A quarrel takes place between Satan and Beelzebub, in which the prince of hell reproaches the prince of death with being the occasion of the ruin of his kingdom, by urging the Jews to the crucifixion of Christ.

Jesus then places Satan under the power of Beelzebub; and delivers the saints out of hell. On the entrance of the saints into paradise they meet Enoch and Elias, and after a conversation between the liberated saints and them, the narrative proceeds: "Behold there came another man in a miserable figure, carrying the sign of the cross upon his shoulders. And when all the saints saw him, they said to him, 'Who art thou? For thy countenance is like a thief's; and why dost thou carry a cross upon thy shoulders?' To which he answering, said, 'Ye say right, for I was a thief, who committed all sorts of wickedness upon earth. And the Jews crucified me with Jesus; and I observed the surprising things which happened in the creation at the crucifixion of the Lord Jesus, and I believed him to be the Creator of all things, and the Almighty King, and I prayed to him, saying, "Lord, remember me when thou comest into thy kingdom." He presently regarded my supplication, and said to me, 'Verily, I say unto thee, this day thou shalt be with me in paradise.' And he gave me this sign of the cross, saying, 'Carry this, and go to paradise; and if the angel who is the guard of paradise will not admit thee, show him the sign of the cross, and say unto him, Jesus Christ, who is now crucified, hath sent me hither to thee.' When I did this, and told the angel, he presently opened the gates, introduced me, and placed me on the right hand in paradise, saying, 'Stay here a little time, till Adam, the father of all mankind, shall enter in with all his sons, who are the holy and righteous [servants] of Jesus Christ, who is crucified.'" The relation concludes with the thanksgivings of the patriarchs; and Charinus and Lenthius, after professing to have revealed all they were permitted, each deliver in a separate account, written on "distinct pieces of paper," which, on examination, "are found perfectly to agree, the one not containing one letter more or less than the other." Charinus and Lenthius immediately change "into exceeding white forms," and are seen no more. Joseph and Nicodemus afterward relate the account to Pilate, who enters it in the public records, and going to the temple, summons all the rulers, and scribes, and doctors of the law, and says to them, "I have heard that ye have a certain large book in this temple; I desire you, therefore, that it may be brought before me." And when the great book, carried by four ministers, [of the temple,] and adorned with gold and precious stones, is brought, Pilate adjures them to declare whether the Scriptures testify of Christ. Annas and Caiaphas dismiss the rest, and then avow their conviction that "Jesus Christ is the Son of God, and true and Almighty God."* Such is the nature of a work which was deemed of sufficient merit and importance to be translated into various languages, to be one of the earliest specimens of typography, and to be placed in the churches for the edification of the people!

In the universities and cathedral churches it was, at this period, a general custom for the public lecturers to read upon any book rather than upon the Scriptures. "Their readings," says Dr. Knight, (Life of Colet,) "were ushered in with a text, or rather a sentence, of Scotus and Aquinas; and the explication was, not trying it by the word of God, but by the voice of scholastic interpreters, and the intricate terms of what they call logic; which was then nothing but the art of corrupting human reason and the Christian faith. It is true, divinity lectures had been read in Latin within many cathedral churches, for the benefit of the priests and clerks belonging to them. But the subject of them (as of all sermons *ad clerum* in the two universities, and in all ordinary visitations of the rural clergy) was commonly a question in scholastic theology, running into frivolous doubts, and elaborate resolutions out of the oracles of Scotus and his puzzling interpreters; not to edification, but to a confounding the thoughts of God and religion." On one occasion the learned Grocyn gave a singular instance of candour and ingenuousness. He read in St. Paul's cathedral a lecture upon the book of Dionysius Areopagita, commonly called *Hierarchia Ecclesiastica*. In the preface to his lecture he declaimed with great warmth against those who either denied or doubted of the authority of the book on which he was reading. But after he had continued to read on this book a few weeks, and had more thoroughly examined its authenticity, he entirely changed his views of it, and openly declared that he had been in an error; and that the said book, in his judgment, was spurious, and never written by that author who is, in the Acts of the Apostles, called "Dionysius the Areopagite."†

Occupied as the clergy were in scholastic disputations, and the nobility in pursuit of pleasure and martial honours, they were generally inattentive to the interests of literature and science. The Latin language declined in its classical purity; and the Greek was almost unknown. The mathematical sciences, though not entirely neglected, were chiefly studied by the pretenders to astrology:

* Jones's New and Full Method of settling the Canonical Authority of the New Testament, vol. ii, part iii, ch. xxviii, p. 262, &c. Oxford, 1798, 8vo.

† British Biography, vol. i, pp. 328, 372, 377.

and when we find learning at so low an ebb among those of high rank, and of the ecclesiastical profession, we may justly conclude that the common people would be almost totally illiterate. We accordingly learn that "it was not till the reign of Henry IV. that villeins,* farmers, and mechanics, were permitted by law to put their children to school; and long after that, they dared not to educate a son for the church without a license from their lord."†

CORNELIUS VITELLIUS, an Italian, was the first who taught Greek in the university of Oxford; and from him the famous Grocyn learned the first elements of it, which he afterward perfected in Italy under Demetrius Chalcondyles, a learned Greek, and Politian, an Italian, professor of Greek and Latin at Florence. In Cambridge, Erasmus was the first who publicly taught the Greek grammar; though even Erasmus himself, when he first came into England in 1497, had so incompetent an acquaintance with that language, that our countryman Linacre, who was just returned from Italy, perfected him in his knowledge of it.

Dr. THOMAS LINACRE, or LYNACER, above named, was an eminent and most learned English physician, by whose exertions the College of Physicians was founded and incorporated, of which he held the office of president. In the decline of life, he resolved to change his profession for that of divinity, entered into holy orders, and was collated on the 23d of October, 1509, to the rectory of Mersham; and obtained afterward several preferments. An anecdote is related of him, which proves, that however accurate and extensive his grammatical knowledge of Latin and Greek might be, his ignorance of the Scriptures was so great, as to render him totally unfit for the sacred functions he assumed. Being ordained priest, at an age when his constitution was broken by study and infirmity, he, for the first time, took the New Testament into his hand, and having read the fifth and sixth chapters of St. Matthew's Gospel, threw away the book, swearing, "Either this is not the Gospel, or we are not Christians!"‡ This, however, will appear the less extraordinary, when it is remarked, that the study and use of the Scriptures was at that time so low, even in the university of Oxford, "that the being admitted a bachelor of divinity gave only

* *Villeins* were those, under the feudal system, who were liable to be sold with the land they occupied; but differed from *slaves*, by paying a fixed rent for the farm to which they were attached.

† Henry's Hist. of Great Britain, vol. x, b. v, p. 128.

‡ British Biography, vol. i, pp. 326, 330, 332. Sir E. Brydge's Restituta, No. 3. p. 159.

liberty to read the master of the Sentences, (Peter Lombard;) and the highest degree, that of doctor of divinity, did not admit a man to the reading of the Scriptures."*

The newly invented art of printing, which, toward the close of this century, was established in this kingdom by Caxton and others, was chiefly employed in printing translations from the French, made by Earl Rivers and Caxton; and multiplying legends, and devotional works of a legendary nature. Two of these deserve particular notice, viz., the *Liber Festivalis*, or Directions for keeping Feasts all the Yere; and the *Quatuor Sermones;* both of them printed in folio, by William Caxton, and frequently bound together. Of the first, Hearne observes, that "it consists of a course of homilies, in which are many odd stories; that it goes by no other name than that of *Festivale*, among curious men, who are very inquisitive after copies of it." (Robert Gloc. Chron., vol. ii, p. 739.) Oldys adds, "that some of these 'odd stories' are such, that the papists are now ashamed of them." (Biog. Brit., vol. iii, p. 369, note O.) "The fact is," says Mr. Dibdin, "whatever be the nature of these stories, all 'curious' theological scholars may be well inquisitive after the *Liber Festivalis*, as it is the origin or substratum of the English Common Prayer Book." The prologue tells us, that "for the help of such clerks, this book was drawn to excuse them for default of books, and for simpleness of cunning, and to show unto the people what the holy saints suffered and did for God's sake, and for his love; so that they should have the more devotion in God's saints, and with the better will come to church to serve God, and pray the saints of their help." That it was principally taken from the *Legenda Aurea*, or Golden Legend, is proved by the prologue of an ancient edition, in which the writer states, "This treatise is drawn out of 'Legenda Aurea,' that he that list to study therein, he shall find ready therein of all the principal feasts of the year, on every one a short sermon, needful for him to teach, and for them to learn; and for that this treatise speaketh of all the feasts of the year, I will and pray that it be called FESTIVAL."

Then follow, says Lewis, sermons on nineteen Sundays and ferials, beginning with the first Sunday in Advent, and ending with Corpus Christi day. Next are discourses or sermons on forty three holydays. Then follows a sermon *De dedicatione Ecclesiæ*, or on the church holyday. The following extracts will afford an idea of the style and nature of the work:—

* British Biography, vol. i, *Life of Colet*, p. 372, *note.*

THE LORD'S PRAYER.

"Father our that art in heavens, hallowed be thy name: thy kingdom come to us: thy will be done in earth as in heaven: our every day's bread give us to-day; and forgive us our trespasses, as we forgive them that trespass against us; and lead us not into temptation, but deliver us from all evil sin, Amen."

The following specimen is from the "Festival of Saint Michael."

"DE FESTO SCTI MICHAELIS."

"Good friends, such a day ye shall have Saint Michael's day the archangel: that day all holy church maketh mind and mention of all angels for the great succour, comfort, and help, that mankind had of angels, and especially of St. Michael. And for iij prerogatives he be had: for he is wonderful in appearing; for as Saint Gregory saith, when Almighty God will work any wonderful deed then he sendeth for Michael his servant, as for his bannerer: for he beareth a shield or sign of his arms—wherefore he was sent with Moses and Aaron to Egypt to work marvels: for though the sign was in Moses, the working was done by Michael: for he departed the Red Sea, and kept the waters in ii parts, while the people of Israel went through, and so passed; and led them forth from Jordan, and kept the water like an hill on each side of them, while they passed safe and sound to the land of behest. Also Michael is keeper of paradise, and taketh the souls that be sent thither."*

The *Quatuor Sermones*, which was a translation from the Latin, was most probably the Roman Catholic formulary of the day, respecting the religious topics of which it treats, namely, "The Lord's Prayer," "Belief," "Ten Commandments," and "Articles of Faith." In the translation of the creed, which we have in the first sermon, the fourth article is thus expressed, "I byleve, that he suffered payne under Ponce Pilate, &c.," the translator understanding Pontius to be the name of some place where Pilate was either born, or lived, or governed. Accordingly the book contains this silly tale: "The emperor, by counsel of the Romans, sent Pilate into a country called Pounce, where the people of that country were so cursed, that they slew any that come to be their master over them. So when this Pilate come thither, he applied him to her manners; so what with wiles and subtilty he

* Dibdin's Typographical Antiquities, vol. i, pp, 161–167.

overcame them, and had the mastery, and gat his name, and was called Pilate of Pounce, and had great domination and power." According to this manner of writing, excepting sometimes Ponce for Pounce, was this article of the creed expressed in English, from the fourteenth century down to A. D. 1532, when in the Primer of Salisbury use, it was altered to Pontius Pilate, which was followed by Archbishop Cranmer, in his notes on the King's Book, 1538.*

Another celebrated production of Caxton's press was his translation, from the French, of the *Legenda Aurea*. Of this work, some mention has been already made.† Caxton's translation, under the title of the "Golden Legende," was printed at Westminster, in 1483, fol. A story from the English translation may entertain the reader. "There was a man that had borrowed of a Jew a sum of money, and sware upon the altar of Saint Nicholas, that he would render and pay it again as soon as he might, and gave none other pledge. And this man held this money so long that the Jew demanded and asked his money. And he said that he had paid him. Then the Jew made him to come before the law in judgment, and the oath was given to the debtor, and he brought with him an hollow staff, in which he had put the money in gold, and he leaned upon the staff. And when he should make his oath and swear, he delivered his staff to the Jew to keep and hold while he sware, and then sware that he had delivered to him more than he owed to him. And when he had made the oath he demanded his staff again of the Jew, and he nothing knowing of his malice delivered it to him. Then this deceiver went his way, and laid him in the way, and a cart with four wheels came with great force and slew him, and brake the staff with gold, that it spread abroad. And when the Jew heard this, he came thither sore moved, and saw the fraud. And many said to him that he should take to him the gold. And he refused, saying, but if he that was dead were not raised again to life by the merits of Saint Nicholas, he would not receive it. And if he came again to life ho would receive baptism and become a Christian. Then he that was dead arose, and the Jew was christened."‡

Caxton bequeathed thirteen copies of this work to the church of St. Margaret, Westminster; from which it appears probable, that parts of it, like those of the "Festival," were read as homilies in

* Dibdin's Typographical Antiquities, vol. i, pp. 170–172.

† See pages 316, 353, of this volume.

‡ Beloe's Anecdotes of Literature and Scarce Books, vol. ii, p. 447.

the churches; and the multiplicity of editions by subsequent printers seems to strengthen this conjecture. Herbert supposes, that if not used in this manner, "they might be only placed in some convenient part of the church, as Fox's Book of Martyrs was at the beginning of the Reformation."*

None of our English printers, during this century, attempted to print the Bible, either in the Latin, or the vernacular tongue. In the application of printing to the purposes of sacred literature, the palm must be yielded to GERMANY, which as it had the honour of the invention of printing, so it was the first to apply it to the diffusion of Biblical knowledge. For not only were numerous editions of the Latin Bible, and several of the German versions printed there, but editions also were published in the Saxon and Bohemian dialects.

The BOHEMIAN Bible was printed at Prague, in 1488, fol., and again at Kuttenberg, in 1489, fol.† Æneas Sylvius, afterward Pope Pius II., bore a noble testimony to the Scriptural knowledge of the Bohemians, in a work of his on the "Acts and Sayings of Alphonsus, King of Spain," in which he declared, "That it was a shame to the Italian priests, that many of *them* had never read the whole of the New Testament, while scarcely a *woman* could be found among the Bohemians, (or Taborites,) who could not answer any questions respecting either the Old or New Testament."‡ He died in 1464. A copy of the Bohemian Bible, printed in 1488, is preserved in the public library at Dresden.

Lambecius, in his *Comment. de Biblioth. Cæs. Vindob.*, notices a magnificent MS. copy of the German Old Testament, preserved in the imperial library at Vienna. It was executed about A. D. 1400, for Wenceslaus, emperor of the West, and king of Bohemia. It is in large folio, ornamented with numerous paintings, richly illuminated, of some of which Lambecius has given engravings. The most frequent of the marginal paintings is an ornamented W, in which Wenceslaus is represented in prison, and sometimes as attended by a woman, supposed to represent Susannah, the mistress of the bath, who aided his escape in a boat from the prison where he had been confined by his barons, and who afterward became his favourite concubine. His second wife, who possessed powers far superior to the emperor, was Sophia, the daughter of John,

* Dibdin's Typographical Antiquities, vol. i, p. 193.

† Walchii Biblioth. Theolog., tom. iv, p. 130. Clarke's Bibliographical Miscellany, vol. ii, p. 107.

‡ Usserii Hist. Dogmat., p. 170.

duke of Bavaria; the celebrated John Huss was her confessor.* Dibdin has copied several of the paintings in the Bible of Wenceslaus from the fac-similes of Lambecius, in his splendid "Bibliographical Decameron," vol. i.

A Bible was printed in the dialect of LOWER SAXONY, according to Walch, at Cologne, in 1490, fol.† Another edition was published at Lubeck in 1494, in two volumes folio. It is accompanied with notes, said to be those of De Lyra, but more probably composed, at least in part, by Hugo de St. Victor, and other early commentators. From Seelen's *Selecta Literaria*, pp. 241, 242, says Mr. Dibdin, "it would appear that the intrinsic value of this impression is very considerable. In former times the Low German language was the usual vehicle for a vernacular version of the Scriptures; so that the present text is no trivial help for the understanding of some of the earlier editions of Luther's Bible; and although some parts of the commentary may not bear the test of severe critical investigation, yet there are others not void of propriety and sound sense; and considering the age in which it was probably composed, it breathes a spirit of liberality not usual in the ancient times of papacy."‡ The purity of its text is said to be equal to the rarity and beauty of the work.

This edition, says Vogt, is in great estimation, as well on account of its rarity, as of its whimsical gloss or commentary. The following is given as an instance of its singularity. In the third chap. of Genesis, ver. 16, where Eve is told she shall be henceforth under the power of her husband, the commentator remarks: "not only under his control, but under his severe discipline: subject to be beaten and bruised by him!" An interpretation too absurd for refutation.§

About the year 1475 appeared the first separate edition of the New Testament in Latin, in a small quarto form, for the convenience of general readers. Prefixed to the epistle of St. Jerome, which precedes the sacred text, is a notice in Latin, by the printer, explaining the cause of the publication, of which the following is the substance:—"It is the general cry, that every believer who professes to have any knowledge of letters, is bound to have an acquaintance with the Holy Scriptures, and more particularly with that part of the Bible called the New Testament. It is certain,

* Lambecii Comment. de Bibl. Cæs. Vindob., lib. ii, cap. viii, pp. 749–756. Vindob., 1669, fol.

† Walchii Biblioth. Theolog., tom. iv, p. 96.

‡ Dibdin's Biblioth. Spencer., tom. , p. 57.

§ Ibid., *ubi sup.*

however, that but few persons have the means of procuring tne *whole* of the Bible, and that many, even of the rich, prefer portable volumes. Induced by these considerations, as well as by the influence of my superiors, professors of sacred theology; and overcome by the zeal of certain monks and secular clergy, I have attempted, I hope, under favourable auspices, to print the present convenient volume, containing the whole of the New Testament, with a view to the glory of God; and shall be satisfied, if it afford benefit to any one." It is printed in double columns, with a delicate Gothic type. To the New Testament is subjoined, "Liber haymo de christianarum rerum memoria prolog."* Haymo, the author, was the disciple of Alcuin, in the ninth century, a monk of Fulda, and afterward bishop of Halberstadt. The work itself is an abridgment of ecclesiastical history.†

In 1475 an edition of the Dutch Bible was printed at Cologne, in two volumes folio; at Delft, in 1477, two volumes folio, and also in 4to. Another at Goudo, in 1479. These translations are said to have been mixed with many fabulous narratives, and were probably made at an earlier period than that of their being printed. They are supposed to have been preceded by an edition of the four Gospels, printed in 1472.‡

Le Long also mentions a Polish version of the Scriptures, which, from the colophon of a MS. copy upon vellum, appears to have been made about the middle of this century: "This Bible was executed by the command and desire of the most serene Queen Sophia; translated by Andrew de Jassowitz; and transcribed by Peter de Casdoszitz, August 18th, 1455, during the widowhood of Queen Sophia, and the reign of her son Casimir Jagellon." This Sophia was queen of Uladislaus IV. Andrew de Jassowitz flourished about A. D. 1410.§

In the year 1470 a curious work was printed by Schoeffer at Mentz, and by Helyas Helye, *alias* de Louffen, at Beraum, in folio, entitled *Mammotrectus*. It contains, 1. An exposition of the phrases of the Bible, and of the Prologues of St. Jerome. 2. Two little treatises of orthography and of accents. 3. A short declaration of the months, festivals, &c., and of the Jewish priests. 4. An explanation of ancient words and terms, in responses, hymns, ho-

* Dibdin's Bibl. Spencer., tom. i, pp. 31, 32, *note*.

† Cavei Hist. Litt., sæc. ix, p. 530.

‡ Le Long, Biblioth. Sacra, tom. i, p. 409, folio, 1723. Gentleman's Magazine, January, 1814, p. 30.

§ Le Long, Biblioth. Sacra, tom. i, p. 439, et *Index Auctorum*, p. 563.

milies, &c. 5. A declaration of the rules of the minor friars. The author of the work is supposed to be John Marchesinus, a priest of the order of minor friars, or of St. Francis, and a native of Reggio; who composed it in 1466, for the use of the less instructed in his own profession. It was printed more than twenty times in the fifteenth century.*

During this century, and especially toward the close of it, Germany and the neighbouring states produced several eminent men, who endeavoured to create an attention to literature in general, and laboured to promote an acquaintance with the original languages of the sacred Scriptures. Among these, Matthias Doringk, or Thoringk, Wesselus, Regiomontanus, and Reuchlin, particularly merit our esteem.

Matthias Doringk, or Thoringk, the celebrated author of the "Replies" to Paul of Burgos's "Additions" to the Commentary of De Lyra, was born at Kiritz, in the marche of Brandenburgh, and when young became a monk of St. Francis. After studying philosophy and theology with distinguished success, he rose to eminence, not only as a preacher, but as a lecturer on the Scriptures, and professor of theology. While professor of theology at Magdeburg, he undertook the defence of De Lyra's Postills, or Commentaries, against the strictures and objections of Paul of Burgos. His defence is generally found appended to the printed editions of De Lyra's work, along with the "Additions" of Paul of Burgos. In 1431 he held the office of minister of his order in the province of Saxe, and received letters from the landgrave of Thuringia, requesting him to introduce some reform among the Franciscans of Eisenac. About the same time he was sent as one of the deputies to the council of Basil, (one object of which was the reformation of the church,) by that party of his order who adhered to that council. Either at that time, or afterward, he was raised to be general of the order. The close of his life was spent in retirement, in the monastery of Kiritz, where he wrote the greater part of his works. The time of his death is disputed, some placing it in 1494, others, with more probability, in 1464. Besides the work already mentioned, he was the author of others, and among them of a "Chronicle," in which he treated the characters of the popes and cardinals with such freedom, as has led to the supposition that he was the writer of the "Nuremberg Chronicle;"

* Dibdin's Biblioth. Spencer., tom. i, pp. 154, 157. Horne's Introduction to Bibliography, vol. ii. App., p. lvi.

which, however, appears to be a mistake, as his work remains in MS. in the library of the university of Leipsic.*

JOHN HERMAN WESSELUS, of Groningen, was born about the year 1419. He studied at Zwoll and Cologne, and afterward at Paris, and was so celebrated for his talents and attainments as to be denominated "The Light of the World." His extraordinary religious knowledge and truly Christian spirit were so indisputable, and his views of gospel doctrines so clear, that he has justly been called "The Forerunner of Luther." So astonished was that great reformer when he first met with some pieces written by Wesselus, that he wrote a preface to the Leipsic edition of his works, printed in 1522, in which he says: "It is very plain he was taught of God, as Isaiah prophesied that Christians should be: (Isa. liv, 13:) and as in my own case, so with him, it cannot be supposed that he received his doctrines from men. If I had read his works before, my enemies might have supposed that I had learned every thing from Wesselus, such a perfect coincidence there is in our opinions."

Wesselus not only studied the Greek language, by the help of the Dominican friars who about this time passed over to the West from Constantinople, after its subjection to the Mohammedan government, but obtained from certain learned Jews a knowledge of the Hebrew, Chaldee, and Arabic tongues. Having been early instructed in the scholastic disputes, and having by his industry acquired an uncommon share of Biblical learning, he taught philosophy and philology with great applause at Groningen, Paris, Cologne, Heidelberg, and especially at Basil, where he had the famous Reuchlin for a hearer. His opposition to the Romish errors, and the prevalent subtleties of scholastic disputations, subjected him to considerable danger, but his reputation for learning and piety was so great, and his protectors were so powerful, that he escaped uninjured by the storm.

On the advancement of Cardinal Francis de Rovere to the papal chair, under the name of Sixtus IV., he sent for him to Rome, and promised to grant him whatever he would ask. Wesselus answered, "Holy father and kind patron, I shall not press hard upon your holiness. You well know I never aimed at great things. But as you now sustain the character of the supreme pontiff and shepherd on earth, my request is, that you would so discharge the duties of your elevated station that your praise may correspond with your dignity, and that when the great Shepherd

* Chalmers' Gen. Biog. Dict., vol. xii, pp. 272–274. London, 1813.

shall appear, whose first minister you are, he may say, 'Well done, good and faithful servant, enter into the joy of thy Lord:' and moreover, that you may be able to say boldly, 'Lord, thou gavest me five talents, behold, I have gained five other talents.'" The pope replied, "That must be *my* care: but do you ask something for yourself." "Then," rejoined Wesselus, "I beg you to give me out of the Vatican library a Greek and a Hebrew Bible." "You shall have them," said Sixtus; "but, foolish man, why don't you ask for a bishopric, or something of that sort?" "For the best of reasons," said Wesselus; "because I do not want such things." The Hebrew Bible thus presented was long afterward preserved in his native city of Groningen. He died in 1489, aged seventy.

His works have been several times printed, but the most complete edition was published in 1614, 4to., with a short account of his life by Albert Hardenberg.*

JOHN MULLER, commonly called REGIOMONTANUS, from his native place, Mons Regius, or Konigsberg, a town in Franconia, was born in 1436, and became the greatest astronomer and mathematician of his time. Having first acquired grammatical learning in his own country, he was admitted, while yet a boy, into the academy at Leipsic; from whence he removed, at only fifteen years of age, to Vienna, to enjoy the superior advantages afforded to his pursuits by the learned professors in that university. After some years the cardinal Bessarion arrived at Vienna, and soon formed an acquaintance with the youthful astronomer, who, in order to perfect his knowledge of the Greek tongue, accompanied the cardinal to Rome, where he studied under Theodore Gaza, a learned Greek. In 1463 he went to Padua, where he became a member of the university. In 1464 he removed to Venice, to meet and attend his patron Bessarion.† He returned the same year with the cardinal to Rome, where he made some stay, to procure the most curious books: those he could not purchase he took the pains to transcribe, as he wrote with great facility and elegance; and others he got copied at a great expense; for as he was certain that none of these books could be had in Germany, he intended, on his return thither, to translate and publish some of the

* Milner's Hist. of the Church of Christ, vol. iv, pp. 295, 296, 302. Enfield's Hist. of Philosophy, b. vii, ch. iii, p. 383. Hody, De Bibl. Text. Orig., pt. ii, lib. iii, p. 446.

† Among other curiosities in the library of Louvain, there is a MS. Bible, given to the doctors of the university, by Cardinal Bessarion, in grateful acknowledgment of their hospitable treatment of him. Horne's Introd. to Bibliog., vol. ii, p. 594.

best of them. It was probably at this period that he transcribed, in the most beautiful manner, the whole of the New Testament with his own hand, a labour which he undertook from the ardour of his attachment to the divine volume, and which he is said to have rendered familiar to him by constant perusal.

Having procured a considerable number of MSS., he returned to Vienna, and for some time read lectures; after which he went to Buda, on the invitation of Matthias, or Mattheo, king of Hungary, the great patron of learned men. The breaking out of the war occasioned his withdrawing to Nuremberg, where he set up a printing house, and printed several astronomical works. In 1474 he was prevailed upon by Pope Sixtus IV. to return to Rome, to assist in reforming the calendar. He arrived at Rome in 1475, but died there a year after, at only forty years of age, not without suspicion of being poisoned.*

John Reuchlin, who assumed the name of Capnio, was born at Pforzheim, a town of Suabia, in the electorate of Baden, A. D. 1454. Being trained up among the choristers of the church of his native town, he was noticed by the margrave of Baden, who took him under his care, and afforded him the opportunity of acquiring a liberal education. He afterward studied at Paris and Basil, and in 1481 obtained the degree of doctor of law at Orleans. On his return to Germany he accompanied Eberhard, count of Wirtemberg, to Rome; and afterward was sent on embassies to the emperor Frederick III. and the papal court. His extraordinary attachment to the Hebrew language discovered itself on both these occasions: at Rome he engaged a Jew to perfect his knowledge of that tongue, for which he paid him the enormous sum of a piece of gold an hour; at the court of Frederick, instead of receiving the usual presents of richly caparisoned horses or golden cups, or other valuable gifts of a similar nature, he requested and obtained a very ancient Hebrew Bible.

Though eminently learned in the Latin and Greek languages, he appears to have been chiefly occupied with the Hebrew, of which he composed a grammar, the first that had been written of that tongue by a Christian. He was also the author of a Hebrew lexicon, and of several other works relative to that primeval language. He is justly regarded as the restorer of Hebrew and Greek learning in Germany; though his singular erudition, and active promotion of literature, subjected him at that time to the most viru-

* Chalmers' Gen. Biog. Dict., vol. xxii, p. 506. London, 1812, &c., 8vo. Hody, De Bibl. Text. Orig., pt. ii, lib. iii, p. 447.

lent opposition, from the superstitious and ignorant inquisitors and monks. One of the most formidable disputes in which he was involved, arose out of his extensive knowledge of the rabbinical writings. John Pfeffercorn, a famous converted Jew, had long petitioned the emperor Maximilian to burn all the Jewish books except the Bible, as tending only to encourage superstition and impiety, and prevent the conversion of the Jews to Christianity. The emperor, partially yielding to his petition, sent orders to Uriel, archbishop of Mentz, to nominate some university to which, along with the inquisitor James Hochstrat, and John Reuchlin, the decision of the question might be referred. Reuchlin, in reply to the inquiries of the archbishop, remarked, that the Jewish works might be divided into three classes, historical, medical, and talmudical, which, although mixed with many fabulous and ridiculous fictions, were useful in the refutation of their errors and antichristian opinions. This decision he sent sealed to the archbishop; but Pfeffercorn, learning the sentence, immediately published a work against Reuchlin, calling him the champion and patron of the Jews; this was followed by a similar publication from Hochstrat. The opinion of Reuchlin was also condemned by the universities of Paris and Cologne, and the book which he had written in defence of it publicly burnt. On the other hand, the archbishop of Spire approved of Reuchlin, and gave judgment in his favour, in the cause brought before him by Hochstrat and his advocates. The dispute was ultimately carried to Rome, where Hochstrat remained for three years, but finding the delegates appointed by Pope Leo X. favourable to Reuchlin, he returned to Germany, where he afterward became active in committing some of the early Lutherans to the flames, and where he died, at Cologne, about A. D. 1527.

Toward the close of life, Reuchlin devoted himself to teaching the Hebrew and Greek languages, in the university of Ingolstadt, till, being incapacitated by the jaundice, he retired to Stutgard, where he died in 1521, aged sixty-seven.

Besides the works already mentioned, he published several others on Hebrew literature; a Translation from Hebrew into Latin of the VII. Penitential Psalms, printed in Hebrew and Latin, at Tubingen, 1512, 8vo.; a treatise *De Arte Cabalistica*, dedicated to Leo X.; an Abridgment of the History of the Assyrians, Persians, Greeks, and Romans, &c.*

* Cavei Hist. Litt., sæc. xv. Append., p. 183. Sleidan's History of the Reformation, by Bohun, lib. ii, pp. 29, 30. Jortin's Life of Erasmus, vol. i, pp. 60, 61, 122, 379. Hody, De Bibl. Text. Orig., lib. iii, pt. ii, pp. 447, 448.

The munificent patronage afforded to literature by Mattheo Corvini, king of Hungary and Bohemia, who died of an apoplexy in 1490, also merits particular notice. He succeeded his father to the throne of Hungary in 1457, and extended his reputation as a soldier throughout Europe, by the captures of Vienna and Nieustadt. But his love of literature, and patronage of learning, have transmitted his name with more tranquil and delightful recollections to posterity, than any warlike feats could possibly have done. Animated by an ardent thirst for knowledge, he became a most diligent collector of books, and during the last thirty years of his life spared no expense in the acquisition of a library, which placed him among the most illustrious patrons and guardians of literature. He purchased innumerable volumes of Greek and Hebrew writers at Constantinople, and other Grecian cities, at the period of the conquest of the Eastern empire by the Turks; and as the operations of the typographical art were yet but slow and imperfect, and the number of books hitherto printed but few, he maintained four learned transcribers at Florence, to multiply the copies of such classics as he could not procure in Greece. He erected three libraries in the citadel of Buda, in which he placed thirty thousand, or, according to others, fifty thousand volumes. The principal one, in which the chief part of his magnificent collection was placed, was a sort of vaulted gallery, divided into three parts: a fourth part forming a kind of convenient appendage for the reception of visiters. In this fourth part were two stained glass windows, and two doors; one of the doors opening immediately into the library, the other leading to the monarch's private apartment. In these libraries he established thirty amanuenses, skilled in writing, illuminating, and painting, who, under the direction of Felix Ragusinus, a Dalmatian, consummately learned in the Greek, Chaldee, and Arabic languages, and an elegant designer and painter of ornaments on vellum, attended constantly to the business of transcription and decoration. The librarian was Bartholomew Fontius, a learned Florentine, the writer of several philological works, and a professor of Greek and oratory, at Florence. The books were placed upon shelves according to their classes; and in this manner were covered with silk curtains, or hangings, adorned with silver and gold, or brocaded. The lower recesses next to the floor were appropriated to something like cupboards, which contained MSS. too large for their proper places, or of a character not easily admitting of classification. The exterior of this lower division, or probably the cupboard doors were skilfully and curiously carved. The books were chiefly vellum MSS., bound in brocade, and protected by knobs and clasps of silver, or other precious metal; and were ornamented or marked with the device or insignia of the owner, which was that of a black crow with a ring in his mouth, in allusion to the etymon of his name, Corvus, a crow, or raven. The library was likewise celebrated for the magnificent celestial globe it contained, and for the silver and marble fountains which played in the adjoining gallery, or court. When Buda was captured by the Turks, under Solyman II. in 1526, Cardinal Bozmanni offered for this inestimable collection two hundred thousand pieces of the imperial money, but without effect, for the barbarous besiegers defaced or destroyed most of the books, for the sake of their splendid covers, and the silver bosses and clasps with which they were enriched. Those which escaped the rapacity of the Turkish soldiery were thrown into a sort of subterraneous vault, there to moulder or perish, as it might happen. In 1666, Lambecius, the learned librarian of the imperial library at Vienna, was sent to Buda for the purpose of recovering the remains of the Corvinian library. He found there, in a crypt of the citadel, barely lighted with one window, and ventilated with one door, about four hundred volumes in number, lying upon an earthen floor, and covered with dirt and filth. Three manuscript copies of the "Fathers" were all that he was permitted to carry away. But in the year 1686 Buda was captured by the Austrian arms, when the remainder, though comparatively of little value, were removed to Vienna. Some of the most valuable volumes formerly belonging to this library have been discovered in the imperial library at Vienna, in the Wolfenbuttel library, and in that of Morelli, the learned librarian of St. Mark's, at Venice. In the public library of Brussels there are two exquisitely finished MSS. which once graced the library of Corvinus. The first is a Latin *Evangelistarium*, written in letters of gold, upon the most beautiful vellum, and not inaptly called "The Golden Book." It had become the property of Philip II. of Spain, who kept it in the Escurial library, under lock and key; and is said to have been formerly shown to strangers with great ceremony, and by torch light! The other is a magnificent Missal, highly illuminated.

Alexander Brassicanus, who saw the library at Buda before it was dispersed, noticed, among an immense number of other valuable works, the whole of the writings of Hyperides, the Grecian orator, with valuable scholia; a large book of the apostolical canons; the commentary of Theodoret on the Psalms; the works of Chrysostom, Cyril, Nazianzen, Basil the Great, Gregory of Nyssa, Theophanus, &c.*

During this century flourished also R. ISAAC, or MORDECAI NATHAN, a celebrated Jew, and the *first* who engaged in the laborious work of compiling a Hebrew Concordance, which he began in 1438, and completed in 1448, after ten years' wearisome toil. His book was published at Venice, 1523, but with considerable defects, many words and places being wholly omitted. A second edition was printed at Basil, 1581, by Ambrose Froben, in which some of the faults of the Venice edition were corrected, but without altering the form, or supplying the defects. A splendid edition, by Marius de Calasio, a Franciscan friar, was published at Rome in 1621, in four volumes folio, to which were added, 1. A Latin translation of R. Nathan's explanation of the several roots, with the author's own enlargements; 2. The Rabbinical, Chaldee, Syriac, and Arabic words, derived from, or agreeing with, the Hebrew root in signification; 3. A literal version of the Hebrew text; 4. The variations of the Vulgate and Septuagint; 5. The proper names of men, rivers, mountains, &c. Afterward John Buxtorf, the indefatigable propagator of the Hebrew language, undertook to correct and reform the preceding editions, and happily succeeded, by casting it into an entirely new form. This was printed after his death, by his son, at Basil, in 1632, folio. The Rev. W. Romaine published an improved edition of Calasio's work, in 1747, at London, in four volumes folio. "But in point of usefulness this is vastly inferior to 'The Hebrew Concordance, adapted to the English Bible, disposed after the manner of Buxtorf, by John Taylor, D. D.,' London, 1754, two volumes folio, which may be justly styled the sixth edition of R. Nathan's Concordance, for it has been the groundwork of the whole." Dr. Taylor's "work was published under the patronage of all the English and Irish bishops, and is a monument to their honour, as well as to the learning and industry of the editor."† The time of R. Nathan's death is uncertain.

Besides the Oriental and Biblical scholars who have been already noticed, there were several who, toward the close of this century, prosecuted similar studies with success; among these may be

* Dibdin's Bibliographical Decameron, vol. ii, pp. 455–462. Warton's History of English Poetry, vol. ii, pp. 417, 418. Lomeier, De Bibliothecis, cap. ix, p. 204. Horne's Introduction to Bibliography, vol. ii, p. 595.

† Taylor's Hebrew Concordance, Preface, sec. i, vol. i. Clarke's Bibliographical Dictionary, vol. ii, p. 113.

enumerated Marcus Lypomannus; Laurentius Valla; Baptista Mantuanus; John Picus, earl of Mirandola; Rodolphus Agricola; and John Creston.

MARCUS LYPOMANNUS, a counsellor and patrician of the republic of Venice, eminently skilled in Hebrew, Greek, and Latin, flourished in the early part of this century.*

LAURENTIUS VALLA, a Roman patrician, doctor of divinity, and canon of St. John of Lateran, was one of the chief restorers of the beauty of the Latin language. His work, "On the elegance of the Latin language," has been frequently printed. He was also the author of "Annotations on the New Testament," edited by Erasmus, who wrote in defence of them. Valla had a design to translate the New Testament into Latin; but being forbidden by the pope, he could only write notes upon the Vulgate, censuring the bad Latinity and the inaccuracy of this version. F. Simon is, perhaps, too severe upon him as a critic, and says, that as he was a mere grammarian, his remarks are inconsiderable. His "Annotations" were favourably received by Pope Nicholas V., who recalled him from Naples, whither he had fled to avoid the persecution of the inquisition. He died in 1457, in the fifty-second year of his age.†

BAPTISTA MANTUANUS, a monk of Mantua, of the order of the Carmelites, after being chosen six times vicar-general, was constituted general of the order. To polite literature he added the knowledge of the Hebrew, as well as of the Greek and Latin languages. He wrote a tract entitled *De Causa Diversitatis inter Interpretes S. Scripturæ*, in which he defended the Vulgate version against the Jews. His works were printed at Antwerp in 1607, in four volumes octavo. He died in 1516.‡

JOHN FRANCIS PICUS, or PICO, earl of Mirandola, was born February 24th, 1463. He lost his father early, but he found in his mother a most attentive guardian; and the care which she took of his education was repaid by the most astonishing improvement. It is said, that when he was only eighteen years of age he understood twenty-two different languages. In 1491 he gave up his estates, and retired to one of his castles, that he might devote himself entirely to theological studies, and especially to the study of the Scriptures. In this retirement he died, in 1494, at the age of thirty-one. He wrote against judicial astrology, combating the

* Hody, De Bibl. Text. Orig., lib. iii, part ii, p. 440.

† Hody, *ut sup.* Jortin's Life of Erasmus, vol. i, p. 20.

‡ Hody, *ut sup.*, p. 443. Le Long, Biblioth. Sacra, tom. ii, p. 624. Paris, 1723

cabalistic opinions of the Jews; defended the Septuagint version of the Psalms; and was the author of an Exposition of the Lord's Prayer, and many other works.* After he had withdrawn from the pomp and ambition of the court, he thus expressed himself in a letter to a friend: "Many think it a man's greatest happiness in this life to enjoy dignity and power, and to live in the plenty and splendour of a court; but of these, you know, I have had a share: and .... I am persuaded the Cesars, if they could speak from their sepulchres, would declare Picus more happy in his solitude than they were in the government of the world: and if the dead could return, they would choose the pangs of a second death rather than risk their salvation a second time in public stations."†

Rodolphus Agricola was a learned German. Toward the close of life he devoted himself entirely to the study of the Scriptures, and of the Hebrew tongue, which he had only begun to learn at forty; but in which he made such improvement, that, with the assistance of his teacher, he made a translation of the Psalms. He died in 1485, aged forty-three.‡

John Creston was an Italian Carmelite monk and doctor, of Placentia. He published an edition of the Psalms, in Greek, with a Latin translation, or rather corrected edition of the Vulgate, printed at Milan, 1481, in small folio, or quarto, at the expense of Bonaccursius Pisanus.§

* Hody, pp. 445, 446. Clarke's Bibliographical Dictionary, vol. v, p. 215. Le Long, tom. ii, p. 905.

† Butler's Lives, vol. ix, p. 71.

‡ Hody, p. 446. Jortin's Life of Erasmus, vol. i, p. 76.

§ Hody, p. 446. Le Long, edit. Masch., part ii, tom. ii, sec. i, p. 311.

CHAPTER III.

SIXTEENTH CENTURY.

Encouragement of Literature in Italy—George of Ambasia—Leo X.—Profligacy of the Papal Court—Polyglotts—Aug. Justinian—Complutensian Polyglott—Cardinal Ximenes—Mozarabic Liturgy—Editors of the Complutensian Polyglott—Sanctes Pagninus—Learned Italians—Spanish Councils—Hebrew Literature—State of Biblical Literature in France and England—Persecutions in England—Biblical Scholars—Low state of Biblical Knowledge in Germany—Astonishing Ignorance of many of the Clergy—German Scholars—Erasmus.

THE commencement of the SIXTEENTH century was marked by a rapidly increasing ardour for classical pursuits, and by the publication of various important and magnificent Biblical works, which displayed both the erudition and munificence of those who projected and executed them. In ITALY, the court of Rome, with singular inconsistency, lavished its favours on men of learning and scientific acquirements, regardless of the moral turpitude of their character, and the infidel profligacy of their opinions and habits. Incredible pains were taken to collect books from every quarter, at immense expense; and the papal thunders were directed against any persons who should purloin or disperse the volumes belonging to the libraries attached to the various monastic institutions. A curious proof of this fact is afforded by an epistle, addressed by the cardinal legate, George of Ambasia, to the canons of Bruges, from whom he had borrowed Hilary on the Psalms:—

"GEORGE of AMBASIA, presbyter of Saint Sixtus, cardinal of Rouen, legate of the apostolic see, to his dear friends the venerable the fathers, the canons, and chapter, of the sacred chapel of Bruges, wisheth peace."

"HAVING been informed that in the library of your sacred chapel there was an ancient copy of Hilary of Poitiers upon the Psalms; and taking great delight in literary pursuits, especially those which regard our holy religion, so far as our weak abilities will permit; we requested from your paternal kindness the loan of that book for a few days, to which you courteously acceded, notwithstanding the pontifical bull, which forbade any books being taken away from the library under pain of excommunication."

"Wherefore, having read the book with considerable pleasure, we have resolved to have it copied; for which purpose it will be requisite to have it in our possession for some months, though we intend, after it has been transcribed, to return it uninjured to your paternal care. We, therefore, absolve you from whatever censures or punishments you might incur by lending the book; and, by the authority with which we are invested, do hereby pronounce and declare you absolved, notwithstanding any thing to the contrary contained in the aforesaid bull, or in any other."

"Given at Bruges, the third day of March, MDVII.

"GEORGE, cardinal-legate of Rouen."*

The election of the young cardinal John de Medici to the pontifical chair in 1513 proved favourable to the general interests of literature, but increased the licentiousness of the papal court, and spread a baneful influence over the whole of the Romish hierarchy. The celebrity of this pontiff, who assumed the title of LEO X., and the intimate connection of his pontificate with the Reformation by LUTHER, may justify us in detailing at some length the more prominent traits of his life and character.

JOHN, or GIOVANNI DE MEDICI, was a native of Florence, the second son of Lorenzo, styled the Magnificent, and grandson of Cosmo the Great. From his infancy he was destined to the church, and received an education suited to the high rank and ambitious views of his father, which produced a correspondent gravity of deportment at so very early an age, that his biographer says, "he seems never to have been a child."

At seven years of age he was admitted into holy orders, and about a year afterward was appointed abbot of Fonte Dolce by Louis XI. of France, who also conferred upon him the abbacy of the rich monastery of Pasignans. Yet we are assured that at this early period he "was not more distinguished from his youthful associates by the high promotions which he enjoyed, than he was by his attention to his studies, his strict performance of the duties enjoined him, and his inviolable regard to truth." He, however, bore "his blushing honours thick upon him," for when he was only thirteen years of age he received the dignity of a cardinal from Pope Innocent VIII., and Pope Julius II. employed him as legate. On the 11th of March, 1513, being then only thirty-seven years old, he was elected supreme head of the church, on the decease of Julius, and assumed the name of Leo X.

The commencement of his pontificate seemed to realize the high expectations which had been formed of it, particularly by a

* Voyages Litteraires de deux Religieux Benedictins, tom. i, p. 29.

general amnesty published at Florence, his native city, respecting those who had been the occasion of the violent civil commotions which had taken place in it; and by the recall of the banished citizens to their country. With considerable address and perseverance he surmounted the difficulties which had prevented the enjoyment of peace between Italy and France; and composed the troubles which the ambition of the surrounding sovereigns, or the misconduct of his predecessors, had occasioned. Unhappily, however, the hopes that were entertained respecting him and the excellence of his pontifical government were never realized; his ambitious projects being accomplished by his advancement to the tiara, he became indolent and voluptuous; his assumed gravity gave way to the lowest buffoonery; his munificence degenerated into prodigality; and his attachment to truth was lost in the insincerity of his political engagements: even in his literary pursuits, *profane* was generally preferred to *sacred* literature; and his disposal of ecclesiastical dignities was frequently regulated by the aid afforded to his pleasures. He conferred the archbishopric of Bari on Gabriel Merino, a Spaniard, whose chief merit consisted in the excellence of his voice and his knowledge of church music; and promoted another person named Francesco Paoloso, for similar qualifications, to the rank of an archdeacon. "It seems to have been his intention," says one of his biographers, "to pass his time cheerfully, and to secure himself against trouble and anxiety by all the means in his power. He therefore sought all opportunities of pleasure and hilarity, and indulged his leisure in amusement, jests, and singing."*

An elegant writer thus characterizes the court of Leo: "While Leo, with equal splendour and profusion, supported the character of a sovereign prince, he was too prone to forget the gravity of the pontiff. He delighted in exposing to public ridicule those characteristic infirmities of some of his courtiers which his own penetration easily discovered. But these were venial aberrations from decorum in comparison with those excesses which Leo's example sanctioned, or at which his indifference connived. The few who, amid this more than syren fascination, still retained any sense of decency, were constrained to blush on beholding ecclesiastics mingling, without reserve, in every species of pleasurable dissipation. The younger cardinals especially, many of whom were junior branches of royal or illustrious houses, exulted in the free

* Roscoe's Life of Leo X., vol. iv, p. 486; and Life of Lorenzo de Medici, vol. ii, pp. 178–196, 379–383. Lond., 1806, 8vo., and Lond., 1800.

participation of indulgences, to which the most sacred characters were no restraint. Rome frequently saw her court, with a multitude of attendants, and an immense apparatus, accompany the supreme pontiff to partake of the sports of the field. Under the direction of the ingenious cardinal Bibiena, whose versatile talents appeared to equal advantage on serious, festive, or ludicrous occasions, the spacious apartments of the Vatican were metamorphosed into theatres. The pontifical tables teemed with luxurious viands, that realized the refinements of Apicius: and particular seasons afforded a sanction to the freedoms and buffooneries of the ancient Saturnalia. Jovius acknowledges that Adrian, a man of a frugal character, could not examine, without shuddering, the particulars of those enormous disbursements which marked the domestic establishment of his predecessor."*

Leo has been accused of treating revelation with contempt, and of advancing principles of an atheistical tendency. Old Bishop Bale, in his "Pageant of Popes," (p. 179,) printed 1574, relates this anecdote: "On a time when Cardinal Bembus did move a question out of the Gospell, the pope gave him a very contemptuous answere, saying, '*All ages can testifye enough how profitable that fable of Christe hath ben to us, and our companie.*'"† The authenticity of this anecdote has been denied by a late biographer of this pontiff, who calls it, "a story which it has justly been remarked, has been repeated by three or four hundred different writers, without any authority whatsoever, except that of the author above referred to."‡ But that this assertion is incorrect, appears by a quotation, containing the same anecdote, made from an old Spanish writer, by Greswell, in his *Memoirs of Angelus Politianus, Actius Sincerus Sannazarius, Petrus Bembus, &c.*, p. 135, where, after observing that several circumstances are recorded by the earlier reformed writers, "which reflect much on Bembo's character, and that of Leo X. his master," he adds, in a note, "The following is the bold language of an old Spanish writer, with regard to Leo X.

"Fue un hombre atheista, que ni pensó aver cielo, ni infierno despues desta vida: y assi se murio sin recebir los sacramentos. Sanazaro dize que no los pudo recebir porque los avia vendido.§

* Greswell's Mem. of Angelus Politianus, &c., pp. 141–145. Manchester, 1801, 8vo.

† Roscoe's Life of Leo the Tenth, vol. iv, ch. xxiv, p. 479. ‡ Ibid., p. 480.

§ The following is the epigram alluded to above:—

"In Leonem X. Pont. Max.
Sacra sub extrema si forte requiritis hora
Cur Leo non potuit sumere,—*vendiderat.*"
[Greswell, *ut sup.*, p. 104.

Veesse tambien claramente su atheismo por la respuesta que dio al Cardenal Bembo, que le avia alegado cierto passo del Evangelio: al qual dissolutamente respondio Leon estas palabras: Todo el mundo sabe quanto provecho aya traydo á nosotros, y á nuestra compaiña aquella fabula de Christo, &c."

"*Dos Tratados: el prima es del Papa y de su autoridad; et el segundo es de la Missa.* 2nd. ed. 8vo. 1599. The preface dated 1588, and subscribed C. D. V."*

On the first day of August in every year Leo was accustomed to invite such of the cardinals as were among his more intimate friends to play at cards with him, when he distributed pieces of gold to the crowd of spectators who were permitted to be present at this entertainment. He was also a thorough proficient in the game of chess, though he is said to have always reproved the playing with dice.†

Other gratifications in which Leo indulged were of the lowest and most disgusting nature; such as his entertaining in his palace a Mendicant friar, called Father Martin, whose chief merit consisted in eating forty eggs, or twenty capons, at a meal, and such like feats of voracious gluttony; and the pleasure he derived from deceiving his guests by preparing dishes of crows and apes, and similar animals, and seeing the avidity with which the high seasoned food was devoured. Yet brutish as were these sources of diversion, they have found an apologist in a celebrated writer, who regards them, when associated with Leo's literary pleasures, as serving "to mark *that diversity and range of intellect* which distinguished not only Leo X., but also other individuals of this extraordinary family!"‡ It must however be acknowledged, that his own meals were generally of the most frugal nature.

The profuse expenditure of Leo involved him in embarrassments, which led to the adoption of expedients, to supply the deficiency of his income, which for a while effected their purpose, but in the end became the means of limiting the pontifical authority, and of producing an ecclesiastical revolution, infinitely serviceable to the interests of religion and truth. Among the schemes which he adopted, to drain the wealth of the credulous multitude, was the open sale of *dispensations* and *indulgences* for the most enormous and disgraceful crimes, under pretence of aiding the completion of the magnificent and expensive church of St. Peter, at Rome. In

* Greswell's Memoirs of Angelus Politianus, &c., p. 135.

† Roscoe's Life of Leo the Tenth, vol. iv, ch. 24, pp. 486, 487.

‡ Roscoe's Life of Leo the Tenth, vol. iv, p. 491.

Germany, the right of promulgating these indulgences was granted to Albert, elector of Metz and archbishop of Magdeburg, who employed a Dominican friar named Tetzel, as his chief agent for retailing them in Saxony; who, executing his commission with the most shameless effrontery, roused the indignation of Luther against such flagrant abuses of the papal authority, and created such a feeling against the infamous measure, as terminated, by the gracious control of divine Providence, in the glorious REFORMATION from popery.*

The most illustrious trait in the character of Leo was his munificent patronage of learning and the fine arts. He was himself well versed in the Latin language, and possessed a competent knowledge of the Greek, accompanied with singular proficiency in polite literature, and extensive acquaintance with history in general. In the attention paid by him to the collecting and preserving of ancient MSS. and other memorials of learning, he emulated the example of his father, and by his perseverance and liberality at length succeeded in restoring to its former splendour the celebrated Laurentian library, which had been commenced by Cosmo de Medici, but had been afterward dispersed by the troops of Charles VIII. of France, on the expulsion of the haughty Piero di Medici from Florence. It was removed by Leo to Rome, from whence it was re-transferred to Florence, by his cousin and successor Clement VIII.; who, by a bull, dated December 15, 1532, made provision for its future security. Among the learned who were patronized by Leo are enumerated, Teseo Ambrogio; Sante Pagnini; Agostino Giustiniani; Agacio Guidaccerio; and particularly Erasmus, between whom and the pontiff an epistolary correspondence occasionally subsisted, and who dedicated to Leo his edition of the Greek and Latin New Testament. But his patronage of Oriental and Biblical scholars was certainly very far inferior in its remunerations to that which was bestowed upon the cultivators of the fine arts and more modern literature.† The two celebrated historians of the council of Trent are agreed as to his preference of profane to sacred literature; Fra. Paolo (*Conc. di Trent.*, lib. i, p. 5) thinks he might have been deemed "a perfect pontiff," if to his other "accomplishments he had united some knowledge of religion, and a greater inclination to piety; to neither of which,"

* Roscoe's Life of Lorenzo de Medici. vol. ii, ch. x, pp. 383, 384. Robertson's Hist. of Charles V., vol. ii, b. ii, pp. 91–95.

† Roscoe's Life of Lorenzo de Medici, vol. ii, ch. x, pp. 387–390. Roscoe's Life of Leo the Tenth, vol. iv, ch. xxiv, pp. 474–476; and vol. ii, ch. xi, pp. 396–404.

says the historian, "he appeared to pay any great attention;" and Pallavacini, the opponent of Fra. Paolo, acknowledges (*Conc. di Trent.*, lib. i, cap. iii, p. 51) that this defect "was more apparent, when, being instituted at thirty seven years of age the president and chief of the Christian religion, he not only continued to devote himself to the curiosity of profane studies, but even called into the sanctuary of religion itself those who were better acquainted with the fables of Greece, and the delights of poetry, than with the history of the church, and the doctrines of the fathers."* His indifference to religion and religious duties is further confirmed by his conduct respecting the discourses delivered in his presence. "In the year 1514 he ordered his master of the palace, on pain of excommunication, to see that the sermon delivered before him did not exceed half an hour; and in the month of November, 1517, being wearied with a long discourse, he desired his master of the ceremonies to remind the master of the palace, that the council of the Lateran had decided that a sermon should not exceed a quarter of an hour at most. In consequence of which remonstrances there was no sermon on the first day of the year 1518, the master of the palace being fearful that the preacher would exceed the prescribed limits."†

This celebrated, but irreligious pontiff, died after a short illness, on December 1st, 1521; not without suspicion of having been poisoned; but most probably from a fever, brought on by excess of joy at the unexpected success of the papal armies against France.

The impression and publication of the Polyglott Psalter of Giustiniani, or Justinian, and the Complutensian Polyglott Bible of Cardinal Ximenes, which were respectively dedicated to Leo, eminently distinguished his pontificate. On this subject, the learned author of the "Succinct Account of Polyglott Bibles" has the following remarks: "The taste that prevailed early in the sixteenth century for the cultivation of literature was partly the cause of, and partly owing to, the publication of the sacred writings in different languages. Certain men, in whom were providentially united a taste for sound learning, together with ecclesiastical influence, and secular opulence, determined to publish, first, PARTS, and then the WHOLE of the sacred writings, in such languages as were esteemed the learned languages of the universe. These were

* Roscoe's Life of Leo the Tenth, vol. iv, pp. 468, 469. See also Jortin's Life of Erasmus, vol. i, pp. 237, 261. London, 1808, 8vo.

† Roscoe's Life of Leo the Tenth, vol. iv, ch. xxiv, p. 489, *note.*

principally, *Latin*, *Greek*, *Hebrew*, *Arabic*, *Chaldee*, and *Syriac*; others of less importance were added to them. Such publications attracted general attention, and became greatly studied. Hence the taste, not only for sacred literature, but universal science, became widely diffused; and the different nations of Europe seemed to vie with each other in the publication of those works which have since obtained the denomination of POLYGLOTTS, that is, 'books in *many languages*.'"*

The first in order of publication was the Polyglott Psalter of Giustiniani, or Justinian, bishop of Nebbio, or Nebio, in the island of Corsica. The title of his work was, *Psalterium, Hebraicum, Græcum, Arabicum, et Chaldeum, cum tribus Latinis Interpretationibus et Glossis*; and we learn from the colophon, that it was printed at Genoa, 1516, by Peter Paul Porrus, in the house of Nicolas Justinian Paul. It is in folio. A preface is prefixed, dated Genoa, Cal. Aug. 1516, addressed by Justinian to Leo X. It is divided into eight columns, of which, the first contains the Hebrew; the second, Justinian's Latin translation, answering word for word to the Hebrew; the third, the Latin Vulgate; the fourth, the Greek; the fifth, the Arabic; the sixth, the Chaldee Paraphrase in Hebrew characters; the seventh, Justinian's Latin translation of the Chaldee Paraphrase; the eighth, Latin scholia, or notes.†

On the nineteenth Psalm, ver. 4, "Their words are gone to the end of the world," Justinian has inserted, by way of commentary, a curious sketch of the life of Columbus, and an account of his discovery of America, with a very singular description of the inhabitants, particularly of the female native Americans; and in which he affirms, that Columbus frequently boasted himself to be the person appointed by God to fulfil this prophetic exclamation of David. But the account of Columbus, by Justinian, seems to have displeased the family of that great navigator, for in the Life of Columbus, written by his son, (see Churchill's Coll. of Voyages, &c., vol. ii, p. 560,) he is accused of falsehood and contradiction; and it is even added, "that considering the many mistakes and falsehoods found in his History and Psalter, the senate of Genoa has laid a penalty upon any person that shall read or keep *it*,‡ and has caused it to be carefully sought out in all places it has been sent to, that it may by public decree be destroyed, and utterly extin-

* Dr. A. Clarke's Succinct Account of Polyglott Bibles, *Introd.* Liverpool, 1802, 8vo.

† Le Long, Biblioth. Sacra, ed. Masch, pt. i, cap. iii, sec. 25, p. 400.

‡ Qu. The *History* or *Psalter*?

guished."* After all, the mistakes of Justinian most probably arose, not from design, but from incorrect information.

The *Arabic* in this Psalter was the first that ever was printed; and the Psalter itself the first part of the Bible that ever appeared in so many languages.

Justinian undertook this work with the expectation of considerable gain, hoping thereby to assist his indigent relatives, but was miserably disappointed. His original intention, he informs us, in the account of himself prefixed to his Annals of Genoa, was to give to the public a similar Polyglott edition of the whole Bible. "I had always imagined," says he, "that my work would be eagerly sought after, and that the wealthy prelates and princes would readily have afforded me every assistance necessary for printing the rest of the Bible, in such a diversity of languages. But I was mistaken; every one applauded the work, but suffered it to rest and sleep; for scarcely was a fourth part sold of the two thousand copies which I had printed, exclusive of fifty more copies printed upon vellum, which I had presented to all the kings in the world, whether Christian or pagan." He, nevertheless, completed the MS. of the New Testament, a great part of which he wrote with his own hand; Sixtus Senensis says he had seen the Polyglott MS. of the four Gospels thus written, and also decorated by himself. After completing the MS. of the whole of the New Testament, he engaged in a similar compilation of the text and versions of the Old Testament; conceiving, as he said, "that his time could not be better employed than in the study of the Holy Scriptures."†

Augustin Justinian, or, according to his Italian name, Agostino Giustiniani, was born at Genoa, 1470. He entered at an early age into the order of St. Dominic, and enjoyed the advantages of good masters, and an excellent library. For many years he devoted himself entirely to study, except what time was occupied in the duties of instruction, from which he obtained permission to retire, in 1514, that he might apply solely to the preparing of the Pentaglott Bible for the press, and to the studies necessarily connected with so important a design. He published his Pentaglott Psalter, as a specimen of the work, in 1516, but being disappointed in the patronage he had too ardently expected, relinquished the

* Beloe's Anecdotes of Literature and Scarce Books, vol. i, pp. 109–111; and vol. iii, pp. 69, 76, 77.

† Simon, Lettres Choisies, tom. iii, pp. 109, 111. Amsterd., 1730, 12mo. Fabricy, Titres Primitifs, tom. i, p. 194. Sixt. Senens. Biblioth. Sanct., lib. iv, p. 251.

project of *printing* the rest of the Bible. Leo X. promised him greater promotion than the bishopric of Nebbio, to which he had been previously raised, but never fulfilled the engagement. Happily, about the same time Francis I. king of France, to whom the bishop of Paris had recommended Justinian, as a man of learning and merit, invited him to Paris, and bestowed on him a pension of three hundred crowns, with the titles of counsellor and almoner. He remained five years at the court of Francis, and during that period published various works ; and visited England and Flanders, returning by way of Lorraine, where he was received, and liberally entertained, by the reigning duke Anthony, and his brother the cardinal.

While at Paris, he taught the Hebrew language, as professor; and also published a Latin translation of the *Moreh Nebochim* of Maimonides, which he dedicated to his friend and patron Stephen Poncher, bishop of Paris. A copy of this work is in the possession of the present writer. It is a beautiful thin folio, printed by Jodocus Badius Ascensius. The title-page is enclosed in a curious ornamented border, and decorated with the vignette device of the printing press of Ascensius. The running title is executed with a beautiful Gothic type; the text is in the Roman character; and the capital letters with which the chapters commence are fine specimens of the initial letters on dotted grounds, especially the large R and D with which Justinian's dedication, and Maimonides' preface, respectively begin. The dedication and colophon both bear date A. D. 1520. This translation has generally been considered as the work of Justinian himself; but F. Simon says, he merely edited an old version which had been long in existence, and to which Aquinas and Bradwardine have referred, and of which he himself had seen a copy, written in a neat hand.

From Paris, Justinian returned into Italy, to visit his diocess, but with the intention of revisiting France, the king having promised him a rich benefice. These hopes were, however, blasted by the war breaking out between Leo and Francis. After his return to Italy he compiled his *Annali di Genova*, or History of Genoa, in Italian, to which he prefixed the account of his life, particularly of his publication of the Pentaglott Psalter. He likewise, with the permission of the pope, presented his valuable library to the republic of his native city. This collection contained about a thousand volumes of the most valuable and rare works, obtained from the most distant foreign parts, forming, at that time, as he assures us, a library almost without a parallel in Europe. In the accumulation of these literary treasures, he had been greatly aided by the commercial facilities afforded by the maritime city of Genoa. Among the works thus presented to the republic, was included the MS. of his Polyglott New Testament, written with his own hand. From a letter addressed by the abbé Poch to Gabriel Fabricy, we learn that the MS. is probably still preserved.

This very learned Dominican perished in a storm at sea, together with the vessel which was conveying him from Genoa to Nebbio, in the year 1536.*

The famous Complutensian Polyglott, published subsequently to Justinian's Psalter, was commenced in 1502, under the auspices of Cardinal Ximenes, archbishop of Toledo, who spared no expense, either in procuring MSS., or in recompensing the editors for their trouble. Esprit Flechier, bishop of Nismes, in his *Histoire du Cardinal Ximenes*, gives the following account of this important edition of the Holy Scriptures :—

"The archbishop, seeing the great corruption of manners that reigned even among the chief ministers of the church, dreaded the attempts of enemies to spread false doctrines by captious interpretations of the Old and New Testament, which, while they dazzled the simple, might appear unanswerable to the learned. For this reason, he undertook a new edition of the Bible, containing, for the Old Testament, the Hebrew text, the Vulgate Latin, the Greek of the Septuagint version, with a Latin translation, and the Chaldee Paraphrase, with a similar Latin interpretation ;—for the New Testament, the Greek text and the Vulgate. To these was added a volume, explaining the meaning of Hebrew words and idioms, highly esteemed by those who are intimately acquainted with the language."

"This most difficult undertaking required the influence and perseverance of a patron like the cardinal. He immediately procured the assistance of the most eminent scholars, Demetrius of Crete, a Greek by birth, Anthony of Nebrissa, Lopez Stunica, and Ferdinand Pintian, professors of the Greek and Latin languages; Alphonsus, a physician of Alcala, Paul Coronel, and Alphonsus Zamora, noted for their skill in the Hebrew tongue, having formerly taught that language among the Jews, but who having renounced Judaism, and embraced Christianity, had given proof of extraordinary erudition and genuine piety. To these he explained his design, promised to bear the whole expense, and granted them liberal

* Simon, Lettres Choisies, tom. iii, pp. 107–111. Sixt. Senens. Biblioth. Sanct., lib. iv, p. 251. Fabricy, Titres Primitifs, tom. ii, p. 294.

pensions. He urged upon them the necessity of diligence; 'Hasten, my friends,' said he, 'lest I fail you, or you fail me, for you need a protection like mine, and I need assistance like yours.' By these, and similar exhortations, and by the liberal encouragement afforded them, they became assiduous in their labour, and incessantly applied to the work, till the whole was completed."

"He caused diligent inquiry to be made for manuscript copies of the Old Testament, in order that the faults of former editions might be corrected, corrupted passages be restored, and obscure and doubtful expressions be explained. Pope Leo X. favoured him with MSS. from the Vatican library, frequently praised his magnificence and generosity, and even consulted him in the most important occurrences of his pontificate. For fifteen years the work was continued without interruption; and it is equally astonishing, that neither the long and tedious application wearied the constancy of the learned editors, nor that the oppressive cares which devolved on Ximenes relaxed either his zeal or his affection for this undertaking."

"He obtained seven Hebrew MSS. which cost him four thousand crowns of gold, independent of the Greek MSS. sent him from Rome; or the Latin ones in Gothic characters, brought from foreign countries, or procured from the principal libraries of Spain, every one of which was at least eight hundred years old. The whole charge of the work, including the pensions of the editors, the wages of the transcribers, the price of books, the expense of journeys, and the cost of the impression, amounted, according to the calculations that were made, to more than fifty thousand crowns of gold."

"This great work, which had occasioned so much care and expense, being at length completed, Ximenes dedicated it to Leo X., either to testify his gratitude, or because all works which regard the explanation of Scripture are suitably inscribed to the sovereign pontiff. . . . . When the last volume was brought him he hastened to receive it, and suddenly raising his hands and eyes to heaven, exclaimed, 'I thank thee, my Saviour Jesus Christ, that before I die, I see the completion of what I most earnestly desired.' Then turning to some of his friends who were present, he said to them, 'God has favoured me with success in things which to you have appeared to be great, and which probably have contributed to the public good; but there is nothing on which you ought to congratulate me so much as this edition of the Bible, which opens those sacred sources from which a purer theology may be drawn, than from those rivulets from whence, in general, it is sought.' "*

This Bible is divided into six parts, and comprised in four volumes folio. The New Testament was printed in 1514, as appears from the following subscription at the end of the Revelation, transcribed from a copy in the Collegiate library at Manchester:—

"Ad perpetuam laudem et gloriam dei et domini nostri iesu christi hoc sacrosanctum opus novi testamenti et libri vite grecis latinisq; characteribus noviter impressum atq; studiosissime emendatum: felici fine absolutū est in hac præclarissime Cōplutensi vniversitate: demandato et sumptibus Reuerendissimi in christo patris et illustrissimi dñi fratris Francisci Ximenez de Cisneros tituli sancte Balbine sancte Romane ecclie presbyteri cardinalis hispanie Archiepi toletani et Hispaniar̄. primatis ac regnor. castelle archicancellarii: industria et solertia honorabilis viri Arnaldi gulielmi de Brocario artis impressorie magistri. Anno domini Millesimo quingentesimo decimo quarto. Mensis ianuarii die decimo."

This was succeeded in the month of May, in the same year, by a Hebrew and Chaldee Vocabulary, and other tracts designed for the assistance of the student in the Oriental tongues. The Old Testament was printed in four parts, and completed in 1517, but the cardinal dying soon after the work was finished, and doubts being started by the Church of Rome, whether it was proper to bring it into general circulation, it did not receive the permission of Leo X. for its publication until the 22d of March, 1520; and the copies were not distributed to the world at large before the year 1522.†

A small number, (it is thought not more than four,) were printed on vellum. One of these is said to be in the Vatican library; another in the Escurial; and a third was lately purchased at the sale of the Mac Carthy library, by Mr. G. Hibbert, for £640.‡ The rest of the copies, of which only six hundred were printed, were upon paper. The price affixed to the work by the bishop of Avila, by order of the pope, was two golden ducats and a half; or about forty livres of French money; a considerable sum at that period.§

Francis Ximenes de Cisneros, the munificent patron of the

* Flechier, Histoire du Cardinal Ximenes, tom. i, liv. i, pp. 175–179. Amsterdam, 1693, 12mo.

† Le Long, Biblioth. Sacra, edit. Masch, pt. i, cap. iii, pp. 337, 338. Marsh's Michaelis, vol. ii, pt. i, ch. xii, sec. i, p. 432.

‡ Dibdin's Bibliographical Decameron, vol. iii, p. 169.

§ Calmet, Dict. de la Bible, p. iv. Paris, 1722, fol.

Complutensian edition of the Bible, and the most celebrated statesman of his day, was born at Torrelaguna, an obscure town in Spain, in 1437. At his baptism he received the name of Gonsalez, but on entering the order of St. Francis, exchanged it for that of the founder of the order. He received the first rudiments of his education at Alcala, and afterward studied the civil and canon law at Salamanca, and made such proficiency in it, that in a short time he was able to support himself by teaching it to others. He did not, however, suffer his legal pursuits to interrupt his course of general study, but continued his application to science, and especially to sacred literature, till he had acquired the usual accom plishments of the students of that period. He then returned to his father; but to avoid being chargeable to his parents, resolved to visit Rome, and endeavour to obtain ecclesiastical promotion He was twice robbed by the way; and was detained by his mis fortunes at Aix, in Provence, where he exercised the office of consistorial advocate, by which means his great abilities became partially known, and his prospects brightened. Hearing, however, of the death of his father, and the consequent distress of his mother and family, he determined to return into Spain. Having secured the papal bull to take possession of the first vacant benefice, he returned home, and was scarcely arrived, before the archpriest of Uceda died, and he entered upon the living. But his right to the benefice was contested by the archbishop of Toledo, who, designing it for one of his almoners, threw Ximenes into prison. At length he was liberated, at the request of the countess of Büendia, and permitted to enjoy his ecclesiastical preferment; but unwilling to be under the influence of a prelate who had treated him with so much severity, he exchanged his present situation for one in the diocess of Siguenza. Cardinal Gonzales de Mendoza, the bishop, appointed him to the office of grand vicar, and distinguished him by the confidence he reposed in him. While at Siguenza, he gained universal approbation and respect; and by his influence with John Lopez de Medina, archdeacon of Almazan, persuaded him to found a university at Siguenza. Whatever time he could possibly spare from the claims of official engagements, he dedicated to literary occupation: he learned the Hebrew and Chaldee tongues; and diligently devoted himself to the study of the Scriptures. At this period he appears to have laid the foundation of that Biblical knowledge for which he was afterward so eminently distinguished; and so deep was the impression made upon him by the perusal of the inspired volume, that he lost all relish for the acquisition of other science, so much so, that he used to say to his friends, that he would willingly exchange all his learning in the law for the explanation of a *single* passage of Scripture.

The anxieties of office, and the embarrassments of secular affairs, becoming insupportable, he resolved to assume the monastic habit. This he did by entering among the Franciscans at Toledo. After passing through the usual course of exercises, he made a profession in 1483, in his forty-sixth year, and was admitted a member of the order. By the permission of his superiors, he withdrew to a small convent in the neighbourhood of Toledo, called Castagnar, from being situated in the midst of a grove of chestnut trees. Here he practised extraordinary austerities, and generally passed part of the day in the wood, studying the Scriptures, sometimes on his knees, and sometimes prostrate on the ground; at other times he spent several days together in a cabin, raised with his own hand, on the top of a mountain covered with trees. His devotion and talents attracted the attention of the most illustrious characters of his country, and, recommended by the cardinal de Mendoza, the queen, Isabella, chose him for her confessor, in the year 1492, and the fifty-fifth of his age, to which he reluctantly yielded, on condition of never removing with the court. By common consent the chapter of his order elected him provincial; and after refusing for six months, he, by order of the pope, occupied also the archbishopric of Toledo. On his elevation to this dignity, instead of displaying a love of pomp and grandeur, he continued the austere and simple habits of monastic economy, yet discovering such a knowledge of public affairs, and exercising such prudence and decision in the regulation of his extensive archiepiscopal government, as rendered the fame of his wisdom equal to that of his sanctity. He provided for the poor; visited the churches and hospitals; established parochial registers, in which were entered the names of all the children baptized, of their fathers and godfathers, of those who were present at the baptism, with the year, month, and day, on which the ceremony was performed; reformed abuses; degraded corrupt judges, and placed in their room persons distinguished by their probity and disinterestedness. He ordained, that on every Sunday and holyday each curate should, after high mass, explain the Gospel in a plain, instructive manner, and in the evening, after Complin, teach the principal articles of the Christian doctrine, providing them, for this purpose, with catechisms, and other helps for instruction.

With the design of promoting the religious education of youth, and of introducing into the church pious and well-disciplined characters, he founded the college of St. Ildefonsus, at Alcala de Henarez, (anciently called Complutum.) This academy, or university, erected about A.D. 1500, soon became famous; and the celebrated Complutensian Polyglott Bible, which issued from it, under the patronage and at the expense of the founder, has rendered its fame perpetual.

The expulsion of the Moors from Spain, and the endeavour to convert the Mohammedan inhabitants who remained, called forth the vigorous talents of the archbishop, who laboured with success to subject them in profession to the Church of Rome; though his refusal to permit vernacular translations of the Scriptures was undoubtedly a prejudice to the sincerity of their conversion.

During his residence at Toledo he repeatedly visited the library of his cathedral, in which many MSS. were deposited, venerable from their antiquity, and valuable from their contents. Among the number which he examined, in order to obtain assistance in his designs, he met with several ancient volumes, written in Gothic letters, which led him to re-establish the Gothic, or Mozarabic offices, or liturgy, which had formerly been held in the highest veneration in the kingdom of Castile.

He employed Dr. Ortiz, a canon of the church of Toledo, and two others of the same city, to publish an edition of the Mozarabic Breviaries and Missals, and distributed among the ecclesiastics and churches a vast number of copies, and even founded a magnificent chapel in the cathedral of Toledo, that the Mozarabic liturgy might be constantly used.*

* The history of this liturgy is curious. In the sixth century the Visigoths occupied almost all Spain, under the empire of Honorius. As they were Arians, they created confusion in the public worship of the kingdom, associating novel with ancient practices and forms. But this nation having abjured their heretical opinions, and embraced the orthodox faith, through the instructions of Leander, archbishop of Seville, it was ordained by the fourth council of Toledo, that all the churches should adopt the same forms of prayer, Missals, and public Psalters; and St. Isidore, the successor of Leander, was charged with the care of carrying the decree of the council into effect. This practice continued for about one hundred and twenty years, till the Moors, having ravaged the country, and defeated the Spanish army, became masters of the kingdom. In this general calamity the royal city fell into the hands of the barbarians, who permitted the Christians to retain their profession, and allowed them six churches for the maintenance of their public worship. Many of the Catholics fled from their native country, rather than submit to the yoke of foreign authority; but others of them remained, and were denominated, from being mixed with the Arabs or Moors, *Mistarabes*, or *Mozarabes*, from *Moza*, the name of the Moorish general. These continued the

In 1506 he was appointed regent of the kingdom of Castile; in 1507 Pope Julius II. created him cardinal of Spain, and soon afterward received the office of inquisitor-general, the inquisition having been established in the kingdom, in 1477, by F. Thomas de Torquemada, of the order of St. Dominic, and prior of the convent of Saint Croix, in Segovia. An excellent historian has hus drawn the character of Ximenes, as the regent of Castile: "His political conduct, remarkable for the boldness and originality of all his plans, flowed from his real character, and partook both of its virtues and its defects. His extensive genius suggested to him schemes vast and magnificent. Conscious of the integrity of his intentions, he pursued these with unremitting and undaunted firmness. Accustomed from his early youth to mortify his own passions, he showed little indulgence toward those of other men. Taught by his system of religion to check even his most innocent desires, he was the enemy of every thing to which he could affix the name of elegance or pleasure. Though free from any suspicion of cruelty, he discovered, in all his commerce with the world, a severe inflexibility of mind, and austerity of character, peculiar to the monastic profession, and which can hardly be conceived in a country where that is unknown."*

His political engagements did not, however, divert his mind from that which lay near his heart, the prosperity of the university of Alcala. He invited the most learned men from different parts

use of St. Isidore's offices for near four hundred years, not only in the royal city itself, but in other cities of the kingdoms of Toledo, Castile, and Leon.

Alphonsus VI. having, after a long siege, expelled the Moors from Toledo, ordered the Roman Missal to be adopted, instead of the ancient one of St. Isidore, in all the churches where the latter had been in use. This was opposed by the clergy, nobility, and people, who urged the antiquity of their liturgy, and the authority by which it had been established. The dispute became so warm that at last it was agreed, according to the genius of the age, to terminate the contest *by single combat!* The king chose one knight, as the champion of the *Roman* office; and the people and clergy another, as the defender of the *Toletan* Missal; the combatants met, and the latter proved victorious. But Alphonsus refused to submit to the decision, and another mode of divining the intention of Heaven was suggested. Fasts and public processions were appointed, a great fire was kindled, and while the king and people repeated their prayers, a copy of each of the Missals was thrown into the flames; the Toletan escaped, and the Roman was burnt! The king then yielded permission to use the Toletan Missal in those ancient parishes of the kingdom of Toledo where the inhabitants had preserved their attachment to Christianity under the government of the infidels, but forbade it in all others. See Flechier, *Histoire du Card. Ximenes*, tom. i, liv. i, pp. 182, 186.

* Robertson's History of Charles V., vol. ii, b. i, p. 30.

of Europe; appointed them as professors of different sciences; richly endowed the whole establishment; made ample provision for its future prosperity; provided for the education of poor scholars; repaired the church of Alcala; and founded an extensive hospital and infirmary; in a word, he omitted nothing that might conduce to the welfare of the students, or promote the interests of religion and sacred literature.

After exercising the high office of regent, with a vigour and capacity seldom or never equalled, for about twenty months, leaving it doubtful whether his sagacity in council, his prudence in conduct, or his boldness in execution, deserve the highest praise, he died, after a short and violent illness, at Bos Equillos, as he was hastening to meet the newly proclaimed king Charles, at Valladolid. His death occurred on Sunday, the 8th of November, 1517, in the eighty-first year of his age; but whether occasioned by poison, or the ingratitude of the young king, is disputed. His dying words were, "In thee, O Lord, have I trusted, let me never be confounded."*

After this outline of the life of the munificent patron of the Polyglott of Complutum, or Alcala, the reader may justly expect some notice of the learned editors of the work.

Demetrius Ducas was by birth a Greek, a native of Crete, and a teacher in the university of Alcala. He published an edition of the "Greek Liturgies of Chrysostom, Basil the Great, &c." Rome, 1526.†

Anthony of Nebrissa, (or Lebrixa,) a town of Spain, was born in 1444. After having laid the foundation of learning by the knowledge of grammar and dialectics, he studied mathematics, physics, and ethics, at Salamanca, where he continued for five years; from whence he passed into Italy, and acquired the knowledge of the Greek, Latin, and Hebrew languages. In 1473 he returned into Spain, and was patronized by Alphonsus Fonseca, bishop of Seville, under whose auspices he opened a school for the restoration of the purity of the Latin tongue, which for nearly a thousand years had been obscured, or corrupted, by the conquests of the Vandals and Moors. He resided in the family of his patron during the three years that he governed the school. On the death of the bishop he removed to Salamanca, and obtained a double

* Flechier, Hist. du Card. Ximenes, *passim*. Barrett's Life of Cardinal Ximenes, *passim*. Lond., 1813, 8vo.

† Le Long, Biblioth. Sacra, *Index*, tom. i. Clarke's Bibliographical Dictionary, vol. iv, p. 276.

stipend as lecturer on both grammar and poetry, being the first to introduce the rules of art in the composition of the vernacular poetry of Spain. While he was thus studiously endeavouring to raise the standard of the literary attainments of his countrymen, he met with violent opposition from the adherents to scholastic subtleties and barbarous modes of instruction; he therefore quitted Salamanca in 1488, irritated by disrespect, and wearied with the fatigues of a laborious profession, and accepted a proposal from John Stunica, the military prefect of Alcantara, to come and reside in his family. A handsome salary was allowed him; and during the period of his residence with the prefect, he employed his leisure in composing a Spanish and Latin Dictionary, and various grammatical works. In the mean time one of the professors of the university of Salamanca dying, Anthony was chosen to succeed him, almost without a competitor. In this situation he remained till 1504, when King Ferdinand, who highly esteemed him, sent for him to court, and employed him as the historiographer of his reign. He was afterward employed by Cardinal Ximenes in the correction and arrangement of his Polyglott Bible; and chosen as the first professor of the university of Alcala, where he resided till his death, which happened suddenly, by apoplexy, July 2d, 1522, in the seventy-eighth year of his age.

Besides the Spanish Dictionary, printed at Alcala, (or Complutum,) 1532, and frequently since, and the Memoirs of the Reign of Ferdinand and Isabella, printed at Granada, 1545, he was the author of several theological, critical, and grammatical works, most of which have been printed.*

James Lopez Stunica was a learned Spaniard, eminently skilled in the Hebrew, Greek, and Latin languages. On the publication of Erasmus's edition of the Greek Testament, accompanied with a Latin translation and notes, Stunica wrote violently against them, and strenuously defended the Vulgate, even its corruptions and barbarisms. As he began to write against Erasmus while Cardinal Ximenes was living, the cardinal wisely advised him to send his remarks first, in manuscript, to Erasmus, that he might suppress them if Erasmus gave him satisfactory answers. But Stunica was too vain and haughty to listen to the conciliatory counsel of his patron; and happening one day to find some person reading the New Testament of Erasmus, he said to him in the presence of the cardinal, that he wondered how he could throw

* Antonii Biblioth. Hispan., tom. i, pp. 104–109. Cavei Hist. Lit., sæc. xv., App., pp. 174, 175.

away his time upon such *trash*, and that the book was full of monstrous faults. The cardinal immediately replied: "Would to God that all authors wrote such trash! Either produce something better of your own, or give over prating against the labours of others." This rough, and probably unexpected answer, made Stunica suppress his work till after the death of the cardinal; when he published a book against the Annotations of Erasmus, who replied to it. Afterward he drew up another work, more severe and virulent than the former, which he called "The Blasphemies and Impieties of Erasmus." Leo X., to whom Erasmus had dedicated his New Testament, forbade Stunica to publish any thing defamatory and scurrilous against his antagonist; and after the death of Leo, the cardinals and Adrian VI. laid the same commands upon him. Yet the book was secretly printed, and then published. This also was answered by Erasmus. Some time after Stunica attacked him again, and Erasmus replied in 1529; and in 1530 Stunica died.

He also wrote against Jacques le Fevre, usually called Faber Stapulensis, who had published a Latin version of the Epistles of St. Paul, accusing him of mistranslations, and defending the Vulgate against his remarks and corrections.

Besides these works, he published an *Itinerarium*, or account of his journey to Rome from Alcala. He died at Naples.*

FERDINAND NONNIUS, or NUNNES DE GUSMAN PINTIAN, a learned Spaniard, noted for his skill in the Oriental languages, was professor of Greek and Latin in the university of Alcala, and a knight of the military order of St. James of Compostella. He died in 1552.†

Of ALPHONSUS, a physician of Alcala, all that is known is that he was a converted Jew, possessing an accurate and extensive knowledge of the Hebrew tongue.‡

PAUL CORONEL was a converted Jew of Segovia in Spain. Before he embraced Christianity he had taught Hebrew among those of his own nation, and was learned not only in the Oriental, but also in the Greek and Latin languages. His learning and abilities, united to his knowledge of Christian theology, recommended him to the notice of Cardinal Ximenes, who employed him in his celebrated Biblical work, and of which he is said to have written the

* Jortin's Life of Erasmus, vol. i, pp. 246, 247. Lempriere's Universal Biography, art. "Stunica."

† Le Long, Biblioth. Sacra, tom. i, p. 11; et *Index Auctor.*, p. 573.

‡ Le Long, *ut sup.*

Hebrew lexicon that accompanies it. He is also reputed to have written additions to Nic. de Lyra's book, *De differentiis translationem*, but which were never printed. Prior to his residence at the university of Alcala, he had filled the important situation of professor of the Holy Scriptures in the university of Salamanca. He died at Segovia, September 30th, 1534.*

ALPHONSUS ZAMORA was born at Zamora, of Jewish parents, and educated in the knowledge of every kind of Hebrew and rabbinical learning. Previous to the expulsion of the Jews from Spain by Ferdinand and Isabella, in 1492, he governed their public schools. After embracing the Roman Catholic system of Christianity, he was selected by Cardinal Ximenes as a suitable person to be employed in editing his celebrated Bible, who for this purpose granted him a handsome stipend. In this work he was employed during fifteen years. In the catalogue of works written by Alphonsus, Nic. Antonio mentions the following:—

Vocabularium Hebraicum atque Chaldaicum veteris Testamenti; to which are annexed, *Interpretationes Hebraicorum, Chaldeorum, Grecorumque nominum veteris ac novi Testamenti.*

Catalogus eorum, quæ in utroque Testamento aliter scripta sunt vitio scriptorum, quàm in Hebræo et Græco in quibusdam Bibliis antiquis.

Introductiones Artis Grammaticæ Hebraicæ

These form one of the volumes of the Complutensian Polyglott, and were the second volume that was printed. But Colomesius (Ital. et Hispan. Orient., p. 218) quotes a work of Stunica's against Erasmus, (in cap. vii, Ep. ad Hebræos,) in which he attributes the Vocabulary, or Lexicon, to Paul Coronel.

Alphonsus was also the author of several other erudite grammatical and philological works, particularly a shorter, easier, and more lucid *Hebrew Grammar* than the one annexed to the Polyglott, begun under Cardinal Ximenes, and completed under Alphonsus Fonseca, successor to the cardinal in the archiepiscopal see of Toledo. It was printed at Alcala, by Michael de Eguia, 1526, 4to., with the title, *Artis Grammaticæ Hebraicæ Introductiones.*

He translated into Latin the Chaldee Paraphrases of Onkelos on the Pentateuch; Jonathan on Joshua, Judges, Kings, Isaiah,

* Antonii Biblioth. Hispan., tom. ii, p. 127. Colomesii Italia et Hispania Orientalis, p. 218. Hamburg, 1730, 4to. Wolfii Biblioth. Heb., tom. i et iii, No. 1813. Hamb. et Lips., 1715, 1727, 4to.

Jeremiah, Ezekiel, and the twelve minor Prophets; and R. Joseph, the Blind, and others, on Job, Proverbs, Song of Solomon, Ecclesiastes, and Lamentations.

Le Long also mentions him as the author of a Hebrew version of the Epistle to the Hebrews, accompanied with a Latin translation; but Marsh remarks that it was only an epistle written by himself to the Jews, in Hebrew and Latin, to confute their sentiments, and to convince them of the truth of Christianity; which agrees with the list of the works written by Alphonsus, given by Nic. Antonio in the *Bibliotheca Hispana*, in which we find no notice of any translation of St. Paul's Epistle to the Hebrews, but only of a Hebrew and Latin Epistle to the Jews residing at Rome: "Epistola, quam misit ex Regno Hispaniæ ad Hebræos, qui sunt in Urbe Romana ad reprehendum eos in sua pertinacia, hebraicè olim scripta, hic tamen Hebraicis Latinâ interpretatione interlineari adjuncta." He died in 1530.*

Besides the editors already named, Alvarez Gomez, who wrote the life of Ximenes in 1560, says that JOHN DE VARGARA, a learned Spaniard, doctor of divinity and professor of philosophy in the university of Alcala, was engaged in preparing for the press the books termed *Libri Sapientiales*, viz., Proverbs, Ecclesiastes, Song of Solomon, Wisdom, and Ecclesiasticus." Vargara died in 1557.†

Such was the patron and such were the editors of the famous Complutensian edition of the Scriptures; a work which, if defective, from the imperfect state of sacred criticism at that period, deserves, nevertheless, the highest praise, as a noble attempt to create attention to the original texts of the divine oracles, and may justly be regarded as the parent of those more perfect and immense compilations which have been made since of the original texts and most important versions.

Another great and important work, sanctioned and patronised by Pope Leo X., was the Latin translation of the Bible, by Sanctes Pagninus. This was the first version of the Scriptures from the original texts, after the revival of literature in the West. Pagninus, in the preface to his Bible, informs us that Leo being made acquainted with his design of translating the Old and New Testaments from the Hebrew and Greek originals, he sent to him, and

* Antonii Biblioth. Hisp., tom. i, p. 45. Rom., 1672, folio. Le Long, Biblioth. Sacra, tom. i, pp. 83, 303, 304, 462, 465. Paris, folio, 1723. Ibid., edit. Masch, pt. ii, tom. i, sec. 1, p. 13.

† Le Long, Biblioth. Sacra, tom. ii, pp. 11, 310, et *Index Auctor.*

requested to be allowed the inspection of his work. After examining several sheets, he was so satisfied with it, that he immediately ordered that the whole should be transcribed at his own expense, and gave directions that materials should be provided for printing it. A part of it was accordingly executed, but the unexpected death of the pontiff retarded its completion. After the decease of Leo, he removed first to Avignon, and then to Lyons, where the work was first printed in 1528, in 4to., by Anthony du Ry, at the expense of his kinsmen, Franciscus Turchus and Dominicus Bertus, citizens of Lucca, and Jacobus de Giuntis, a bookseller of Florence. "This version was the work of twenty-five years, and has been greatly extolled both by Jews and Christians, particularly the Old Testament, as the best Latin version that ever was made from the Hebrew, that of Jerome not excepted;" yet some critics have considered the translation to be too literal, and chiefly useful as a grammatical glossary, and illustrative of the Hebrew idiom. In the translation of the New Testament he was less successful than in the Old, and has too generally adopted the Jewish modes of expression. Though finished in 1518, it was not printed, as we have seen, till 1528, when it was published with the approbation of the pope, and with the bulls of Adrian VI. and Clement VII. prefixed to it. To the translation of the Bible he added a table of the Hebrew, Syriac, and Greek names contained in the Scriptures, with their derivations and meanings. This was the first Latin Bible in which the verses of each chapter were distinguished and numbered.*

SANCTES PAGNINUS, or, according to the Italian, SANTE PAGNINI, was born at Lucca, in 1466, and afterward became an ecclesiastic of the order of St. Dominic. He was accurately skilled in the Latin, Greek, Arabic, Hebrew, and Chaldee tongues, yet was supposed to excel particularly in the Hebrew. He diligently applied himself to a comparison of the Vulgate Bible with the original texts, and believing it either not to be the translation of Jerome, or greatly corrupted, undertook to form a new version, which he effected with great credit, producing a translation which has been, in a great measure, the model of all succeeding Latin versions.

Besides the translation of the Bible, Pagninus was the author

* Hody, De Bibl. Text. Orig., lib. iii, pt. ii, pp. 473–480. Fabricy, Titres Primitifs, tom. ii, pp. 152–156. Geddes's Prospectus, pp. 74, 75. Whittaker's Historical and Critical Enquiry into the Interpretation of the Heb. Scriptures, p. 19. Camb., 1819, 8vo.

of several other valuable works: the following are particularly deserving notice:—

Thesaurus Linguæ Sanctæ, seu Lexicon Hebraicum, printed at Lyons, 1529, folio. *Institutiones Linguæ Hebraicæ;* Lyons, 1526, 8vo. *Isagoge ad mysticos S. Scripturæ sensus;* Lyons, folio, 1536. In this work he explains cabalistically the principal part of Job and Solomon's Song, and the whole of the seventh chapter of the first Epistle to the Corinthians. *Catenæ Argenteæ;* or commentaries compiled from the fathers and others, on the Pentateuch and Psalms.

He died at Lyons in 1541, (or, according to Le Long, in 1536,) and was buried there. A marble monument was raised to his memory in the choir of the church of the Dominicans.*

Sacred literature revived with the general cultivation of science and letters; the Oriental languages were more extensively known and studied; and the Holy Scriptures began to be regarded as the purest source of theology and ethics; and though profound ignorance and depravity of manners still reigned generally in the church, many of the clergy deemed it their duty to acquaint themselves with the original languages, and several rose to considerable eminence as Biblical critics and expositors. The pursuits of Oriental and sacred learning extended to the laity, and there were not wanting scholars among them whose extent of information and critical research placed them in the foremost rank of theological students and authors. To the names of learned ITALIANS already noticed we may add those of Cardinal Cajetan, Theseus Ambrosius, Felix Pratensis, and Aldus Manutius.

CARDINAL CAJETAN, whose proper name was Thomas de Vio, was born in 1469, at Cajeta, a town in the kingdom of Naples, from which he assumed the surname of Cajetan. Entering into the order of St. Dominic, he rose successively to be general of his order, archbishop of Palermo, and at length cardinal and legate. He was employed in various negociations with foreign powers, but is chiefly distinguished by his opposition to Luther, and by his translation of the principal part of the Bible. Sent by Leo X. to suppress the rising influence of Luther and his friends, he displayed all the subtlety and imperiousness of the Romish legate; so that even Erasmus described him as a furious, imperious, and insolent ecclesiastic. We are therefore not surprised to learn that his legatine authority proved utterly inadequate to silence the in-

* Sixt. Senens. Biblioth. Sanct., lib. iv, p. 375. Le Long, Biblioth. Sacra, tom. ii, pp. 890, 1178, 1188. Paris, 1723.

trepid reformer, or to stop the progress of the Reformation. But while we detest his unhallowed conduct as the legate of the pope, we regard him with respect when, as the minister of the sanctuary, we find him studying the sacred volume, and labouring to transfuse the invaluable truths of Scripture into a literal translation of the word of God. Of this version of the Scriptures into Latin, Dr. Geddes gives the following account: "The famous Cardinal de Vio Cajetan, who, amid a multiplicity of state affairs, found means to devote a part of every day to serious study, left behind him, among other laborious productions, a translation of a great part of the Bible. As he was totally ignorant of the Hebrew, he employed two learned persons, a Jew and a Christian, as his interpreters; and having a sound judgment and discerning taste, he succeeded much better than could be expected. But his version was formed on this erroneous principle, that a translation of the Scripture cannot be too literal, should it even for that reason be unintelligible. This prepossession made him judge unfavourably of the Vulgate, which he often censures without reason; for which cause some zealots have unjustly taxed him with heresy. His translation has much the same faults with that of Pagninus, and may be of much the same use to the Hebrew student. It was printed with his commentary, at Lyons, in the year 1639." The books of Scripture contained in this translation were those of the Pentateuch, Joshua, Judges, Kings, Chronicles, Ezra, Nehemiah, Job, the Psalms, Proverbs, and the first three chapters of Isaiah. These, with his commentary, form five volumes in folio. The Psalms were printed separately, at Venice, 1530, folio, accompanied with the Vulgate version. At the commencement he explains his mode of translation.

A list of the rest of his works may be found in Freher's *Theatrum Virorum Eruditione Clarorum*, pars i, pp. 27, 28, Noriberg. 1688, fol. He died August 10th, 1534.*

Theseus Ambrosius, or, according to his Italian name, Teseo Ambrogio, one of the first Oriental scholars of his day, and regular canon of the Lateran, was of the noble family of the Conti d'Albonese, and born at Pavia, in 1469. He visited Rome in the year 1512, at the opening of the fifth session of the Lateran council, which commenced under Julius II. and was continued under Leo X. till 1517. In the eighth session of this council, a decree was

* Freheri Theatrum, pt. i, pp. 27, 28. Geddes's Prospectus, p. 78. Jortin's Life of Erasmus, vol. i, p. 260. Le Long, edit. Masch, pt. ii, tom. iii, cap. iii, sec. i, pp. 490, 528.

passed against those who denied the immortality of the soul; and the fourth canon ordained, that "all those who were in holy orders, after the time employed in grammar and logic, should spend five years more in studying philosophy, without applying themselves to divinity, or canon law." In the tenth session it was decreed, that "for the future, no books should be printed at Rome, nor in any other city or diocess, under pain of excommunication, without being first examined; at Rome, by the vicar of his holiness, and the master of the sacred palace; and in the other cities, by the bishop of the diocess, or some doctor of divinity nominated by the bishop; and being signed by them as approved."

The great number of ecclesiastics from Syria, Ethiopia, and other parts of the East, who attended the council, afforded Ambrogio an opportunity of prosecuting his studies with peculiar advantage; and at the request of the cardinal, Santa Croce, he was employed as the person best qualified to translate from the Chaldee, or Syriac, into Latin, the liturgy of the Eastern clergy, previously to the use of it being expressly sanctioned by the pope. After having been employed by Leo X. for two years, in teaching Latin to the sub-deacon Elias, a legate from Syria, whom the pope wished to retain in his court, and from whom Ambrogio received, in return, instructions in the Syriac tongue, he was appointed by the pontiff to the chair of a professor in the university of Bologna, where he delivered instructions in the Syriac and Chaldee languages, for the first time that they had been publicly taught in Italy. He is said to have understood at least ten different languages, many of which he spoke with the ease and fluency of a native.

In the commotions which devastated Italy, after the death of Leo X., he was despoiled of the numerous and valuable Eastern MSS. which he had collected at great expense, and by the industry of many years, and also of the types and apparatus which he had prepared for an edition of the Psalter in the Chaldee, which he intended to have accompanied with a dissertation on that language. This, however, did not dispirit him so as to cause him to lay aside his studies, for in the year 1539 he published at Pavia an "Introduction to the Chaldee, Syriac, Armenian, and ten other tongues; with the alphabetical characters of forty different languages:" which is considered by the Italians themselves as the earliest attempt made in Italy toward a systematic acquaintance with the literature of the East. This work was printed with the types, and at the expense of Ambrogio, as appears from the title of the work: *Introductio in Chaldaicam linguam, Syriacam, atque Armenicam,* *et decem alias linguas. Characterum differentium Alphabeta circiter quadraginta, &c.*" 1539, 4to. "*Excudebat Papiæ, Joan. Maria Simonetta Cremon. in Canonica Sancti Petri in Cælo aureo, sumptibus et typis authoris libri.*"*

Felix Pratensis, a native of Prata, in Tuscany, was of Jewish extraction. After his conversion to Christianity he entered the order of Hermits of St. Augustine. For many years he was successfully employed in instructing and preaching to the Jews, which occasioned him to be denominated *the scourge of the Hebrews.* In 1515 he translated and edited an edition of the Psalter, from the Hebrew, published by the celebrated Dutch printer, Daniel Bomberg, printed at Venice, in 4to., and dedicated to Pope Leo X. From the preface to this Psalter we learn, that this work formed but a small portion of the design expressed to Leo by Felix, who meditated a translation of the whole of the Old Testament. But the design does not appear to have received the approbation of Leo, for whose inspection, and with whose consent, this portion was printed; it was, therefore, most probably dropped, though Wolfius says, he translated Job, and some other books of the Bible. The version of the Psalms he completed in only fifteen days.

He was also employed by Daniel Bomberg in editing the Rabbinical Bible, printed at Venice in 1518, fol. This Bible contained not only the Hebrew text, but also the commentaries of several of the most eminent Jewish rabbis, the Chaldee Paraphrases, the Masora, Tables of the Sections of the Law, &c., and tracts on the Various Readings, &c. This Bible was dedicated to Leo X. A more complete edition of the Rabbinical Commentaries was afterward given to the public by the same printer, but by another editor, R. Jacob ben Chaim.

Felix died at Rome, November 5th, 1539, at nearly a hundred years old, and was burried in the church of St. Augustine.†

The Aldi were a family of eminent printers, who flourished in Italy at the close of the fifteenth, and during the greatest part of the sixteenth century. Aldus Pius Manutius, frequently called the elder Aldus, (to distinguish him from his grandson of the same name, who was also a celebrated printer,) and the first of these illustrious printers, was born about the year 1447, at Bassiano, a

* Roscoe's Life of Leo the Tenth, vol. ii, ch. xi, pp. 396, 399. Dictionnaire Portatif des Conciles, pp. 275, 284. Colomesii Italia et Hispania Orientalis, pp. 37, 38.

† Colomesii Ital. et Hist. Orientalis, p. 19. Wolfii Biblioth. Heb., tom. i et iii, No. 1835. Hody, De Bibl. Text. Orig., p. 461. Le Long. edit. Masch, pt. i, ch. i, sec. ii, pp. 96–99.

small town in the duchy of Sermonetta, in the vicinity of the Pomptine Marshes. His youth appears to have been spent at Rome, where he studied under the most eminent professors; and acquired that extensive information which rendered him afterward so admired as a Greek critic and grammarian. About the year 1488 he settled at Venice, with the view of establishing a printing-office. He it was, who, observing the many inconveniences arising from the vast number of abbreviations, which were at that time in use among the generality of printers, first contrived an expedient whereby these abbreviations were entirely removed, and yet books thereby but little increased in bulk. This he performed by introducing what is now called the *Italic* letter, though formerly the *Aldine*, from the name of its inventor; and sometimes *Cursive*, from its form. The senate of Venice, and the popes Alexander VI., Julius II., and Leo X., granted him the exclusive use of his newly invented character for fifteen years; but the Lyonnese printers disgraced themselves by their endeavours to counterfeit his invention, and by the publication of pirated editions of the classics edited by him. "He combined the lights of the scholar with the industry of the mechanic," so that while he gave the most sedulous attention to his printing-office, he carried on a very extensive correspondence with the literati of Europe, explained the classics to a numerous auditory of students, and also found time to compose various works, which are characterized by profound learning and critical skill. Conscious that his single labours were inadequate to the diffusion of literature, he assembled round him a circle of the most learned men of the age, some of whom lived in his house, and were entirely supported by him. Among other works which he projected for the benefit of literature was that of a Polyglott Bible in Hebrew, Greek, and Latin; of which, however, he executed only one specimen page in folio, which is now preserved in the royal library at Paris. The first printed edition of any part of the Greek Testament was executed by him at Venice, in 1504. It contained the first six chapters of St. John's Gospel; and was appended to an edition of the "Poems of Gregory Nazianzen." He also procured MSS. and made preparations for an edition of the Old and New Testament in Greek, but was prevented from completing his design by his death, which happened in 1515 or 1516. It was afterward printed in 1518, in fol., *min.*, by his father-in-law and partner, Andrea Turresano d'Asola. He was succeeded by his third son, Paulus Manutius, born in 1512; whose younger son Aldus, born in 1547, carried on the business till his own death, in

1597; when the family of these learned printers terminated, after having been for more than a century the glory of literature and typography. To the elder Aldus alone the world is indebted for the *editiones principes*, or first printed editions, of twenty-eight Greek classics; besides which, there are few ancient authors of note, of whom he did not publish editions of acknowledged accuracy, and (as far as the means of the art, then in its infancy, permitted) of great beauty; yet his modesty was such as led him to say, that, far from regarding the flatteries of such as praised his works, he could not himself affirm, that he had published so much as one book with which he saw cause to be satisfied. To his zeal and taste in publishing the works of the best Greek authors must chiefly be attributed the preference which has long been shown to the study of Greek literature.*

Of the success of Biblical literature in Spain, at the commencement of this century, some notice has been already taken, in the account of the Polyglott Bible of Cardinal Ximenes. To what has been there stated, it may be added, that in 1512 the Epistles and Gospels for the whole year, as read in the churches, were published in Spanish, by Ambrose de Montesin, a Spanish Franciscan friar, bishop of Sardinia. They were reprinted at Antwerp, 1544, in 8vo.†

In the same year (1512) the archbishop of Seville, D. Didaco Deza, held a provincial council, or synod, in which it was ordained that "the parish priests should instruct their parishioners in the mysteries of the holy Catholic faith; and should place in each of their churches, tables containing the articles of the Christian belief, and the ten commandments." It was also further enjoined, that "they should persuade the people to practise the *seven* works of mercy; explain the dominical lessons; admonish their parishioners to acquaint themselves with the general confession, and the ecclesiastical prayers, as the Pater Noster, Credo, and Salve Regina; and enforce the repetition of those prayers in the church. And all ecclesiastical and secular persons were forbidden to instruct their scholars in other things, or to teach them to write, under pain of excommunication, unless they first knew the prayers and contents of the tables."‡

* Clarke's Bibliographical Dictionary, vol. i, p. 48. Horne's Introduction to Bibliography, vol. i, pp. 242–244, 249; and vol. ii, App., No. vii, p. lx–lxxx. Le Long, edit. Masch, tom. ii, pt. ii, sec. i, p. 265; and App. Supp. and Emend., p. 8.

† Le Long, tom. i, p. 363; et *Index Auctor.* 571. Paris, 1723.

‡ Collectio Maxima Conc. Hisp, tom. iv, p. 3.

The Constitutions of Cardinal Mendoza also decreed, that the care of transcribing Missals should be committed to the sacrist, and that five Missals should be written every year for the respective chapels, on account of the great deficiency which then existed of those liturgical works, and for which an annual stipend should be allowed to the sacrist under whose directions and at whose cost the Missals should be copied.*

Archbishop Deza, who summoned the synod, was a Spaniard by birth, and a friar of the order of St. Dominic. He was the author of a "Defence of St. Thomas [Aquinas] against the replications of Matthias Dorinck;" and of a *Monotessaron*, or Harmony of the Evangelists. He died in 1525.†

In 1513 the book of Job, with the "Morals" of Gregory the Great, were translated out of the Latin into Spanish by Alphonsus Alvarez, of Toledo.‡

The dreadful persecutions which had been raised against the Jews, and the edicts in 1492 and 1496, by which six hundred thousand persons were expelled from Spain and Portugal, drove many of the refugees to Constantinople, where they established a printing-office, from which several HEBREW works of importance afterward issued. In 1505 the Pentateuch was printed in Hebrew and Chaldee, accompanied with Rabbinical commentaries; and again in 1506, in folio or quarto. The Jews also established a press at Thessalonica, at which the book of Job in Hebrew, with a Syriac commentary written in 1506, was printed in 1517; as the Pentateuch and Targum with Rabbinical commentaries had been the preceding year. Other portions of the Hebrew Scriptures were likewise, in different years, printed at each of these places.§

Returning to examine the state of sacred literature in FRANCE at this period, the Biblical labours of JACOBUS FABER STAPULENSIS are particularly deserving of notice. This learned man published in 1509, in folio, a Quintuple Latin Psalter, containing, besides the four versions, called the Italic, Roman, Gallican, and Hebraic,‖ a fifth, or amended edition of the Gallican. This edition of the Psalter appears to have been a work of considerable attention and labour, since we find that for the old, or *Italic* version, he made use of a most valuable *MS.* copy written with gold and silver let-

* Collectio Maxima Conc. Hisp., tom. iv, p. 31.

† Le Long, tom. ii, p. 699. ‡ Le Long, tom. i, *Index Auctor.*, p. 542.

§ Le Long, Biblioth. Sacra, edit. Masch, pt. i, cap. i, sec. 2, p. 123; App. Supp., pp. 8, 10, 11. De Rossi, De Ignotis—Editionibus, cap. x, xi, xiii, &c., App. Erlang, 1782.

‖ See p. 292 of this volume.

ters upon purple parchment, in uncial characters, in folio; supposed to have been part of the spoils of the city of Toledo, obtained by Childebert I., king of the Franks, about A.D. 542, and afterward to have been made use of by St. Germanus, bishop of Paris, who died in 576.* Faber accompanied the Psalter with short notes, which, from the sentiments expressed in them, subjected him to the suspicion of being tainted with heretical pravity; and occasioned the Psalter, which was more than once reprinted, to be placed in the *Index Expurgatorius*, or list of prohibited books.† He is also supposed to have been the author of a French version of the Psalms, printed in 1525, in 8vo., at Paris, by Simon de Colines;‡ to which were subjoined the contents or Arguments, in which he is said to have introduced his peculiar views of religion, similar to those of the Reformation; and is further mentioned as the French translator of the Song of Solomon, though with less certainty. He likewise published Commentaries on the Four Gospels, and the Epistles of St. Paul. To the latter was prefixed an Apology, intended to prove that the Latin translation, everywhere read, was not that of Jerome. His Commentary on the Four Gospels was printed at Meaux in 1522, in folio. His method is to exhibit, first the Latin text of this edition, and then to explain it, correcting at the same time those passages which he believes to be incorrectly translated. As he principally takes the Greek for his guide, he has added asterisks and obelisks to mark what is redundant, or what is wanting, in the Latin, after the example of Origen in the Greek. His Commentary on the Epistles of St. Paul was written in the abbey of St. Germain des Prez, and printed in folio, 1512. The Vulgate being authorized throughout all the Western churches, he printed it with this commentary, but annexed a new translation from the Greek. A Commentary on the General Epistles was published by him in 1527, printed at Basil, in folio; and Frisius has noticed a Commentary by him on Ecclesiastes.§

But undoubtedly his greatest and most important work was the

* Le Long, tom. i, p. 243. Paris, 1723, fol.

† Le Long, edit. Masch, pt. ii, tom. iii, cap. i, sec. 9, p. 13.

‡ The following prices, affixed to works printed by this printer, may show the value of books at the time:—

> "Vetus Testamentum, minora formâ, 1525, 12mo.—24 sous.
> Novum Testamentum, min. form., 1525, 12mo.—6 sous."
>
> [Dibdin's Bibliog. Decameron, vol. ii, p. 79.

§ Le Long, tom. i, cap. iv, pp. 333, 335; et tom. ii, p. 719. Paris, fol. Simon's Critical History of the Versions of the New Testament, part ii, ch. xxi, p. 178.

translation into French of the whole of the New Testament, printed at Paris in 1523, in 8vo., by Simon de Colines; the Gospels in June; the Epistles of Paul, the Catholic, or General Epistles, and the Acts of the Apostles, in October; and the Revelation in November. The work was published without the translator's name; but with a prefatory epistle, defending the translation. Another edition was printed in two volumes 8vo. by Simon de Colines, in 1524; a third was published the same year, but without the name of the printer, or the place where it had been printed; a fourth in 1529, &c.*

The publication of the Psalter, and especially of the New Testament, caused a violent persecution to be raised against Faber by the doctors of the Sorbonne, so that, after having been expelled from the faculty of theology at Paris, he was obliged to fly from France; and for some time resided at Strasburg, under a feigned name. F. Simon says, that he was encouraged in the publication of his work by certain powerful friends at the court of Francis I.

The prefatory epistle was prefixed to the second volume, or part of the New Testament, under the title of *Epistre exhortatoire à tous les Chrestiens et Chrestiennes.* In this epistle he praises Jean de Rely, dean of St. Martin of Tours, and bishop of Angers, for his revision of Guiars des Moulins' translation of Comestor's *Historia Scholastica* in 1487; but complains that the French Bibles which had preceded his version of the New Testament were full of faults, and corrupted by additions and retrenchments. The following is a specimen of his reasoning in defence of his translation:—

"Who is there, therefore, but will esteem it proper, and conducive to salvation, to have the New Testament in the vulgar tongue? What is more necessary to life, whether temporal or spiritual? If, in the different religious orders, they ordain, that if any one be ignorant of Latin he shall have the rules of his order in the vulgar tongue, carry it about him, and commit it to memory; and in their respective chapters frequently explain their rules to them; with how much more reason ought the unlearned among Christians to possess the *word of God*, the Scripture full of grace and mercy, which is *their* rule, and which alone is necessary, for only one thing is needful? This Holy Scripture is the Testament (last Will) of Jesus Christ, the Testament of our Father confirmed by his death, and by the blood of our Redeemer; and who is he

* Le Long, tom. i, pp. 335, 336. Jortin's Life of Erasmus, vol. i, p. 90.

that shall forbid the children to have, and see, and read their father's will? It is, then, highly expedient to possess it, and read it, and hear it, not only once, but often, in the *chapters* of Jesus Christ, which are the churches, where all the people, unlearned and learned, ought to assemble, to hear and honour the word of God. And such is the intention of our gracious king, who in heart as well as name is Most Christian, in whose hand God has placed so noble and excellent a kingdom, to the glory of the Father of mercy, and of Jesus Christ his Son;—a design which ought to inspire all in the kingdom with courage to advance in true Christianity, by following, understanding, and believing, the quickening word of God. And blessed be the hour when it shall be accomplished; and blessed be all those, both male and female, who shall procure it to be carried into effect, not only in this kingdom, but through all the world."*

The great objection against Faber's translation was, that it promoted the reformation in France, which had been begun by Luther in Germany; and which was characterized by the partisans of popery with the epithet of "Novelties." "These *Novelties*," says F. Simon, "were agreeable to the taste of some lords and ladies of the court. J. le Fevre, (Faber,) who edified the world by his exemplary life, gave great influence to these Novelties. His erudition was very great for the time in which he lived; and his amiable manners gained him the esteem and love of every one. Almost the only enemies he had were his own confraternity, the doctors of Paris. The famous Noel Beda, the sworn enemy of the belles lettres, openly declared himself against him and Erasmus; and the faculty of theology at Paris was at that time so opposed to vernacular translations of the Bible, that in the same year (1523) they censured this proposition, 'Omnes Christiani, et maxime clerici sunt inducendi ad studium Scripturæ sanctæ, quia aliæ doctrinæ sunt humanæ, et parum fructuosæ'—'All Christians, but especially the clergy, ought to be persuaded to study the Holy Scriptures, because other learning is human, and productive of but little good.' This permission, said this faculty, would renew the errors of the poor men of Lyons, [Waldenses,] which had been already condemned. The following are the express terms of the censure, taken from the registers of the Sorbonne: "Hæc propositio secundum primam partem, laicos quoscumque ad studium sacræ Scripturæ et difficultatum ejusdem esse inducendos sicut et

* Simon, Lettres Choisies, tom. iv, let. xv, p. 95.

clericos, ex errore pauperum Lugdunensium deducetur." This decree was afterward authorized by an edict of parliament in 1525, confirming a censure of these theologians, against a French version of the "Office of the Holy Virgin." In this edict it is expressly affirmed, that *it is neither expedient nor useful for the Christian public that any translations of the Bible should be permitted to be printed; but that they ought rather to be suppressed as injurious, considering the times.* The terms in which the faculty of theology expressed the censure were these: "Post maturam omnium magistrorum deliberationem, fuit unanimi consensu dictum et conclusum, quod in sequendo conclusiones dudum per ipsam factas, neque expediens est neque utile reipublicæ Christianæ, imo visâ hujus temporis conditione potius perniciosum, non solum translationem Horarum, sed etiam alias translationes Biblicæ, aut partium ejus, prout jam passim fieri videntur, admitti, et quod illæ quæ jam emissæ sunt supprimi magis deberent." These doctors designed this censure to be retrospective, and to extend to those versions of the Scriptures which had been previously published; and as no French version had yet been published by the French Calvinists, these different edicts, when speaking of the unhappiness of the times, can only refer to what was regarded as the heresy of Luther. On this very account the parliament of Paris, in a decree against the doctrine of Luther, made in 1525, subjoins these words: "The said court has ordained, and does ordain, that it shall be enjoined by the king's authority, that all persons who have in their possession the books of the Song of Solomon, the Psalms, the Revelation, the Gospels, the Epistles of St. Paul, and other books in the Old and New Testament contained in the Holy Bible, which have been lately translated out of Latin into French, and printed; and also a printed book, containing the Gospels and Epistles for Sundays, and other solemnities for the whole year, with certain Exhortations in French; shall bring them and deliver them up within eight days from the publication of this decree." This last work was supposed to be the production of Faber and his disciples; and the Exhortations were everywhere filled with declamations against any thing being preached to the people but the Gospel. The work was designed for the use of the churches at Meaux.*

The exile of Faber, which had been occasioned by the persecution of the doctors of the Sorbonne, did not continue long; for although Francis I. was captive in Spain, he was informed by his

* Simon, Lettres Choisies, tom. iv, let. xv, pp. 95–107.

sister Margaret of the treatment which Faber had received, and wrote in his favour to the parliament of Paris, by which means he was enabled shortly after to return again to France.*

This great man, who is usually called JACOBUS FABER STAPULENSIS, latinizing his name and the place of his birth, Jacques le Fevre of Estaples, was born about A. D. 1435. He travelled into foreign countries in quest of knowledge, and is said to have "seen not only Europe, but also Asia, and a part of Africa." Being chosen professor of the belles lettres and philosophy, in the university of Paris, he endeavoured, with some success, to introduce into the schools something more solid than the trifling studies of the scholastic doctors, especially an acquaintance with the learned languages. In 1517 he had a dispute with Erasmus, respecting the quotation from the second Psalm, in Hebrews ii, 7, which Erasmus had translated, "Thou hast made him for a little time lower than the angels;" but which Le Fevre contended ought to be translated, according to the Hebrew, "Thou hast made him a little lower than God." As they were friends, the debate was carried on with some civility, and soon dropped, leaving their friendship undiminished. In 1523 he left Paris and went to Meaux, where William Briçonet, the bishop, a patron of learning and of learned men, chose him for his grand vicar. This prelate being suspected of favouring Lutheranism, and persecuted on that account, Le Fevre was obliged to quit his service, for fear of being involved in the same calamity. After having spent some time in Germany, he returned to Paris, and became preceptor to Charles, duke of Orleans, the third son of Francis I. Margaret, queen of Navarre, sister to Francis I., honoured him with her protection, and invited him to Nerac in 1530, where he died in 1537.

Like Erasmus and some others, he continued in communion with the Church of Rome, while he seriously disapproved of her doctrines and practices. He is even said to have taken a journey to Strasburg by the queen of Navarre's order, to confer with Bucer and Capito concerning the doctrines of the reformers. Some remarkable circumstances relative to his death, which have been told by Catholic historians and others, ought not to be omitted. On the day of his death, being apparently as well as usual, while dining with the queen and some learned men whom this princess frequently invited to spend the day with her, Le Fevre appeared pensive and melancholy, and was observed to shed tears. The

* Sleidan's Hist. of the Reformation, b. v, p. 98. London, 1689, fol.

queen desired to know what was the cause of his sadness; he answered, "I am distressed because of the enormity of my crimes. I am now a hundred and one years of age; and though I have lived a chaste life, and have been preserved from those excesses into which many are hurried by the violence of their passions, yet I have been guilty of this heinous offence—I have known the TRUTH, and have taught it to many who have sealed it with their blood, and yet I have had the weakness to hide myself in those places where the crowns of martyrs are never distributed." Having said this, he dictated his will *vivâ voce*, went and lay down on his bed, and died in a few hours!*

The translation of the New Testament into French, by Le Fevre, (Faber,) was made from the Latin, and was the first Catholic French translation in which the sacred text was purely given, former ones being generally made, not from the text, even of the Vulgate, but from Comestor's legendary *Historia Scholastica*. Le Fevre's translation was several times reprinted, and from the opposition of the Catholic doctors, was sometimes printed without either the author's or printer's name. Le Long supposes that the anonymous translations placed in the *Index Librorum prohibitorum* of 1551 were Le Fevre's. The titles are thus given under the head of French books, *ab incertis auctoribus*:—

"Les saintes Evangiles de Jesus Christ;—et au commencement une Epistre exhortatoire qui sent la doctrine de Luther.

"Les saintes Evangiles de Jesus Christ;—au commencement il y a une Epistre Lutherienne."

Both his French Psalter and New Testament were prohibited so early as 1528, by the provincial synod of Beziers, in France, in the following terms:—

"Moreover, this synod decrees, that no books of the Lutheran heresy, or sectaries, nor any of the books of Scripture which have been translated out of Latin into the vernacular tongue, either of late or eight (or rather five) years ago, shall be sold or bought, except they have been examined by the ordinary of the place, under pain of being punished as offenders."† Such were the efforts of the Gallican clergy to prevent the circulation of the word of God, in the language of their countrymen; and such has been the general policy of the Romish hierarchy and such is still its practice,

* Clarke's Bibliog. Dict., vol. iii, pp. 226–228. Jorton's Life of Erasmus, vol. i, pp. 90, 391; and vol ii, p. 240.

† Le Long, Biblioth. Sacra, tom. i, cap. iv, p. 335. Paris, 1723.

While truths on which eternal things depend,
Find not, or hardly find, a single friend.

At this dark and melancholy period, ENGLAND presents a picture equally dreary with that of France. In a catalogue of the books belonging to Leicester Abbey in 1492, and which included what was, for that day, an extensive library, the following are the only copies of the Scripture which are noticed :—

"BIBLIE, defect' et usit'.
Each book of the Old Testament glossed.
Evangelia glossata.
Historiæ de Bibliâ in Gallico.
5 Psalteria abbreviata.
Psalterium."

On this scanty list, the learned and indefatigable historian of Leicester excellently remarks, that "from this catalogue it seems rather doubtful, whether in the library of this religious house there might be any one complete collection of all the Holy Scriptures. Supposing *Biblie*, in the first article, to have included both the Old and the New Testaments, it was a tome defective and worn. The second consisted of each book of the Old Testament only; and the third of the Gospels, without any mention of the Acts of the Apostles, of the Epistles, or of the Apocalypse. There is, howeveer, a separate mention of 'Actus Aplor' gloss', Apocalyps' gloss', Eple Pauli* gloss', Eple Canonice,' and among the last occurs the 'Canticus Canticorum.' Perhaps there might be some of those Augustine monks, to whom the divine oracles in the learned languages would have been of little use; and yet to these was not indulged a translation, there being in the consistorial acts at Rochester the minutes of a rigid process against the precentor of the priory of that cathedral, for retaining an English Testament, in disobedience to the general injunction of Cardinal Wolsey, to deliver up these prohibited books to the bishops of the respective diocesses."

"A. 1528, Jan. 15. In palatio Roffens', coram ipso reverendo patre, comparuit personaliter Dr. Will. Mafelde, monachus et precentor in eccles' Castr' Roffens' notatus, quod, post publicationem factam in civitate predictâ quod unusquisque sancta Dei Evangelia in idioma nostrum translata apud se servand' eidem reverendo patri inferrent, et traderent, sub pœnis in literis reverendi patris cardinalis contentis, idem Willūs hujusmodi libros post tempus per eundē rev' patrē limitat' apud se servavit et retinuit, &c."†

* "No other of the Epistles of the New Testament occur, save those of St. Paul."
† Nichols' Hist. & Ant. of the County of Leicester, vol. i, App., No. xvii, pp. 101–108.

In the dioceses of London and Lincoln many persons suffered on account of their attachment to the Scriptures, and to the cause of truth. At Amersham, in Buckinghamshire, in the year 1606, thirty persons were burnt in the right cheek, and made to bear fagots by way of penance. "The cause was, that they would talk against superstition and idolatry; and were desirous to hear and read the Holy Scriptures."* The register of the London diocess, during the episcopate of Richard Fitzjames, furnishes many other instances of persecution against those who were called Lollards, or followers of Wiclif. In 1511, Thomas Austy, Joan Austy his wife, Thomas Grant, John Carter, Christopher Ravius, Dionysia his sister, and Thomas Vincent, Lewis John, Joan John his wife, and John Web, were brought before the bishop, and accused of having "read and used certain English books, repugning the faith of the Romish Church; as the four Evangelists; Wiclif's Wicket; a book of the Ten Commandments of Almighty God; the Revelation of St. John; the Epistles of Paul and James, with other like." The persons thus accused were imprisoned, and through fear were led to abjure what were deemed their errors. In the same year, and by the same bishop, William Sweeting, and James Brewster, were burnt in Smithfield, in one fire, as relapsed heretics, having been formerly accused and abjured: the first charge in the examination of William Sweeting was, that he had had "much conference with one William Man, of Boxted, in a book which was called Matthew;" and James Brewster was charged with "having a certain little book of Scripture, in English, of an old writing almost worne for age, whose name is not there expressed;" and also with having "been five times with William Sweeting, in the fields, keeping beasts, hearing him read many good things out of a certain book. At which reading were also present, at one time, Woodroofe, or Woodbinde, a net maker, with his wife: also, a brother-in-law of William Sweeting: and another time Thomas Goodred, who heard, likewise, the said William Sweeting read." As James Brewster "could neither read nor write," his possessing a book of Scripture, that others might read to him out of it, was no small proof of his love to the word of God, when it was prohibited under pain of such dreadful punishment.†

A still more atrocious act of villainous cruelty was exercised against Richard Hume, a merchant-tailor, of London, in 1514.

* Fox's Actes and Monumentes, vol. i, p. 918.

† Ibid., vol. ii, pp. 10, 30. Lond., 1641, fol.

Being brought before Bishop Fitzjames, he was examined on the charge of heresy, when among other articles of accusation, it was urged against him, that he had "in his keeping divers English books, prohibited and damned by the law; as the Apocalypse, in English; Epistles and Gospels, in English; Wiclif's *damnable* Works; and other books containing infinite errors, in the which he hath been long accustomed to read, teach, and study daily." After his examination he was remanded to the prison called the Lollard's tower; where, two days afterward, he was found hanging, having been murdered by the chancellor, the sompner, or summoner, and the bell-ringer, as was fully proved before the coroner. But, to prevent, if possible, the discovery of the murder, and to blacken the character of the deceased, certain articles were selected from the Prologue to his Bible, and ordered by the bishop to be read at Paul's cross; the last of which was, that in the Prologue, "he defendeth the translation of the Bible and Holy Scripture into the English tongue, which is prohibited by the laws of our most holy church." After which a process was instituted against him, though already dead, in the bishop's court; and a definitive sentence of heresy given sixteen days after his death, by which his body was ordered to be burned, which was accordingly done, in Smithfield, on the 20th day of December, that same year.*

Persecution continuing to rage against those who read the Scriptures in English, and opposed the superstitions of the Church of Rome, several were burned at the stake; others confined to monasteries, and condemned to live upon bread and water; and many sentenced to bear a fagot at the market cross, to be burned in the cheek, to repeat every Sunday and Friday what was called "Our Lady's Psalter," and "every one of them to fast, bread and ale only every Friday, during their life; and every Even of *Corpus Christi*, every one of them to fast, bread and water during their life, unless sickness unfeigned let the same." The honest martyrologist, Fox, who was indefatigable in his endeavours to obtain authentic information relative to these sufferers for the sake of the gospel, has given a long list of the names of persons accused before John Longland, bishop of Lincoln, in 1521, with the charges brought against them, extracted from the bishop's register. An enumeration of a few of the charges will exhibit their nature.

* Fox, vol. ii, pp. 13–25.

Parties accused.	*Crimes objected against them.*
"Agnes Well, detected by her brother."	"For learning the Epistle of St. James, in English, of Thurstan Littlepage."
"J. Jennings, servant to James Morden; George, servant of T. Tochel; Thomas Grey, servant of Roger Bennet."	"These were detected for carrying about certain books, in English."
"Agnes Ashford, of Chesham, detected by James Morden."	"The cause laid to this Agnes was, for teaching this James the words following: 'We be the salt of the earth; if it be putrified and vanished away it is nothing worth. A city set upon an hill may not be hid. Ye teend not a candle and put it under a bushell, but set it on a candlestick, that it may give a light to all in the house. So shine your light before men, as they may see your works, and glorify the Father which is in heaven. No tittle nor letter of the law shall pass over till all things be done.' And five times he went to the foresaid Agnes, to learn this lesson: *Item.* that the said Agnes did teach him to say this lesson: 'Jesus seeing his people, as he went up to a hill, was set, and his disciples came to him; he opened his mouth, and taught them, saying: Blessed be the poor men in spirit, for the kingdom of heaven is theirs. Blessed be mild men, for they shall weld the earth.'* And twice he came to her to learn this lesson."
"Henry Milner."	"Counted for a great heretic, and learned in the Scripture."

* These quotations are evidently made from Wiclif's translation, notwithstanding some trifling variations. See Baber's edition of Wiclif's *New Testament,* ch v.

Parties accused.	*Crimes objected against them.*
"The wife of Bennet Ward and her daughter."	"For saying that Thos. Pope was the devoutest man that ever came in their house, for he would sit reading in his book to midnight, many times."
"John Phip."	"He was very ripe in the Scripture."
"John Phip."	"He was a reader, or rehearser, to the other."
"John Butler," (impeached by his own brother.)	"For reading to him," (his brother,) "in a certain book of the Scripture, and persuading him to hearken to the same."
"John Barret, goldsmith of London, Joan Barret his wife, Joan his servant."	"Because he was heard in his own house, before his wife, and maid, there present, to recite the Epistle of St. James: which Epistle, with many other things, he had perfectly without book." "Also because Joan, his wife, had lent to John Scrivener the Gospel of St. Matthew and Mark: which book he (Scrivener) gave to Bishop Smith."
"Durdant, by Stanes; Old Durdant; Isabel, wife of T. Harding; Harrop, of Windsor; Joan Barret, wife of John Barret, of London; Henry Miller, Stilman, tailor."	"All these were accused, because at the marriage of Durdant's daughter, they assembled together in a barn, and heard a certain Epistle of St. Paul read: which reading they well liked, but especially Durdant, and commended the same."
"John Littlepage, Alice, wife of Thurstan Littlepage."	"Because he was said to have learned the Ten Commandments in English, of Alice, Thurstan's wife, in his father's house."

Parties accused.	*Crimes objected against them.*
"Robert Collins, and his wife; John Collins, and his wife."	"For buying a Bible, of Stacey, for *twenty shillings!*"*
"The father of Robert Collins."	"This father Collins had been of this doctrine from the year of our Lord 1480."
"Alice Collins, wife of Richard Collins."	"This Alice, likewise, was a famous woman among them, and had a good memory, and could recite much of the *Scriptures*, and other good books: and therefore when any conventicle of these men did meet at Burford, commonly she was sent for, to recite unto them the declaration of the Ten Commandments, and the Epistles of Peter and James." (Also,) "For teaching Joan Steventon, in Lent, the Ten Commandments." "Item, for teaching her the first chapter of St. John's Gospel."
"John Heron."	"For having a book of the Exposition of the Gospels, fair written in English."†

These are but a few of the many instances adduced by Fox, from the register of Bishop Longland, of persons accused and suffering, either in one way or other, for possessing, or reading, or hearing the book of God; and for whose accusation husbands had been suborned against their wives, wives against their husbands; children against their parents, and parents against their children; brothers against sisters, and sisters against brothers. "But the fervent zeal of those Christian days," remarks the honest writer,

* We may form some judgment of the price of this Bible, by observing, that in 1514 the daily wages of a master carpenter, mason, bricklayer, tyler, or plumber, were 6d. per day, without diet, from Easter to Michaelmas: other labourers 4d. per day. In 1513 oats were 2s. 4d. per quarter. In 1533 beef was $\frac{1}{2}$d. per lb.; mutton $\frac{3}{4}$d. per lb.; fat oxen were sold for 26s. 8d. each; a fat lamb for 1s.—*Chronic Precios.*, pp. 116, 117, 162, 164.

† Fox, vol. ii, pp. 33–51.

"seemed much superior to these our days and times, as manifestly may appear by their sitting up all night, in reading and hearing; also by their expenses and charges in buying of books in English, of whom, some gave *five marks*,* some more, some less, for a book; and some gave a *load of hay* for a few chapters of St. James, or of St. Paul, in English."

Besides these worthies, who embraced the sentiments of Wiclif, there were many learned men who continued in strict communion with the Church of Rome, who, by their strenuous exertions in the cause of literature, and their preference of the inspired writings to the works of the scholastic writers, laid a foundation for the subsequent diffusion of sacred truth, among the higher and more erudite classes of society. Three of these, William Grocyn, William Latimer, and especially John Colet, deserve particular notice.

William Grocyn was born at Bristol, in the year 1442. He was educated in grammar learning at Winchester, and made perpetual fellow of New College in 1467. In 1479 he was presented by the warden and fellows of that college to the rectory of Newton-Longville, in Buckinghamshire. But as he still resided chiefly at Oxford, the society of Magdalen College made him their divinity reader. In 1485 he was made a prebendary of Lincoln; and in 1488 quitted his reader's place at Magdalen College, in order to travel into foreign countries. He was stimulated to this by the low state of learning in this kingdom, and by an ardent desire of higher attainments. In pursuance of this design he visited Italy, where he perfected himself in the Greek and Latin languages, under Demetrius Chalcondyles, a native of Athens, and Angelo Politian, professor of the Greek and Latin tongues, at Florence.

Grocyn having completed his studies abroad, returned to England, and fixed himself at Exeter College, Oxford, in 1491, where he took the degree of bachelor in divinity. He was professor, or public teacher of Greek, at Oxford, about the time when Erasmus was there. Soon after he removed to London, and then to the college of Maidstone, in Kent, where he was master. Erasmus owns great obligations to this man, who, by his generosity to his friends, reduced himself to straits, and was forced to pawn his plate to Dr. Young, master of the rolls; but the doctor returned it to him again, by his will, without taking either principal or interest. Erasmus represents him as one of the best divines and scholars of

* The *mark* is an old English coin valued at 13s. 4d. sterling, being a little more than three dollars of our money.—AMERICAN EDITOR.

the English nation; and in several of his epistles speaks of him in a manner that proves he cherished the most sincere regard for him, and entertained the highest opinion of his abilities, learning, and integrity.

An instance has been given, in a preceding chapter, of his candour and ingenuousness, in avowing the spuriousness of the *Hierarchia Ecclesiastica*, attributed to Dionysius, the Areopagite. Afterward, when Dean Colet had introduced the custom of reading lectures at his cathedral upon some part or other of the Scriptures, he engaged Grocyn, as one of the most learned and able men he could meet with, to carry his design into effect.

He died at Maidstone in the beginning of the year 1522, aged eighty, of a stroke of the palsy. He was buried in the choir of the church at Maidstone. Dr. Linacre was the executor of his will, and residuary legatee; and his godson, William Lily, the grammarian, had bequeathed by it a legacy of *five shillings!**

William Latimer became fellow of All Soul's College, at Oxford, in the year 1489. Afterward he travelled into Italy, and settled for a time at Padua, where he greatly improved himself, particularly in the Greek tongue. Returning to England, he was incorporated master of arts at Oxford in 1513; and soon after had for his pupil Reginald Pole, who became cardinal, and archbishop; and by whose interest he is said to have obtained the rectories of Saintbury and Weston-under-edge, in Gloucestershire, and a prebendary of Salisbury.

When Erasmus was at Oxford, Latimer was serviceable to him in the study of the Greek tongue; and when he was preparing the second edition of his Greek Testament for the press, he begged his assistance, knowing him to be accurate in the language.

We have nothing extant of this learned man, he being, as we have his character by Erasmus, a man of more than virgin modesty, under which was veiled the greatest worth. He died very aged, and was buried in the chancel of the church of Saintbury. He was considered as one of the greatest men of that age; a master of all sacred and profane learning. Leland celebrates also his eloquence, judgment, piety, and generosity.†

John Colet, the great and excellent dean of St. Paul's, and whose history is intimately connected with that of sacred literature, was born in London, in the year 1466. He was the eldest son of Sir Henry Colet, knight, who was twice lord mayor. His mother

* British Biography, vol. i, pp. 326–329. Jortin's Life of Erasmus, vol. i, p. 6, &c.

† British Biography, vol. i, pp. 328, 329. Jortin's Life of Erasmus, vol. i, pp. 6, 9.

was a woman of great worth and exemplary piety. "I knew in England," says Erasmus, "the mother of John Colet, a matron of singular piety. She had by the same husband eleven sons and eleven daughters; all of whom were torn away from her by death, except her eldest son; and she lost her husband far advanced in years. She herself, though arrived at her ninetieth year, looked so smooth, and was so cheerful, that you would have thought she had never shed a tear, nor brought a child into the world; and, if I mistake not, she survived her son, Dean Colet. Now that which supplied a woman with such a degree of fortitude was not learning, but *piety toward God.*" To her instructions and example her son, probably, was indebted for those religious impressions which gave an early bias to his mind in favour of a devout and holy life.

In 1483 our student was sent to the university of Oxford, where he spent seven years in the study of logic and philosophy, and then took his degrees in arts. He was well acquainted with the writings of Cicero; and read with great diligence the Latin translations of the works of Plato and Plotinus, the Greek not being at that time taught in any of our grammar schools; he also made considerable progress in the mathematics.

Having resolved to enter the church, he was presented, when but nineteen years of age, and only in the order of an acolythe, with the rectory of Denington, in Suffolk, by Sir William Knevit, knight, and his lady. He was also instituted to the rectory of Thyrning, in Huntingdonshire, on the presentation of his father, in 1490; which he resigned before the end of the year 1493.

In order to acquire a knowledge of the Greek language, and to improve and extend his acquaintance with the languages and sciences which he had already studied, as well as to enlarge the circle of his literary friends, he visited France and Italy. At Paris he associated with the celebrated Budæus, and with Deloine, and Robert Gaguinus, the historian. In Italy he contracted an intimacy with several learned foreigners and several of his own countrymen, particularly Grocyn, Linacre, William Latimer, and William Lily. He was also, during the time of his travels, presented to the prebend of Botevant, in the cathedral church of York; to this were added a canonry in the church of Saint Martin's Le Grand, London, and the prebend of Good Easter, in the same church.

He appears to have returned from his travels in 1497; and on the 17th of December the same year was ordained deacon, and priest a short time afterward. He did not long continue with his friends in London, before he withdrew to Oxford, in order to prosecute his studies with greater success. In this situation, however, he was neither inactive nor useless. He gratuitously read public lectures in the university, by way of exposition on the Epistles of St. Paul: and although he had not taken any degree in divinity, yet there was not, we are told, a doctor in divinity or law, nor abbot, nor any other dignitary in the church, but came gladly to hear him, and brought their books along with them. Others followed the example; and Dr. Knight assures us, that about this time it became "almost a custom for men of distinguished parts and learning in that university to set up voluntary lectures, by way of exposition and comment on some celebrated writer: to which the students would repair, more or less, according to the opinion they had of the men and their performances. Among others, we are certain Mr. Thomas More read upon St. Austin's book *De Civitate Dei*, while a very young man, to a very great auditory. This exercise was also set on foot at Cambridge. We are told by a learned author, that Dr. Warner, afterward rector of Winterton, in Norfolk, and who assisted Bilney at the stake, read there publicly. George Stafford read also a lecture in the same place upon St. Paul's Epistle to the Romans; being probably induced thereto by the example more especially of Dr. Colet."

About this time Erasmus visited England, with whom Colet soon formed an intimate friendship; which he endeavoured to improve to a more accurate and critical knowledge of the Scriptures. With this design he proposed to Erasmus some doubts and queries relative to certain obscure and difficult passages in the Epistles of St. Paul; but Erasmus, with that timid caution which so strongly marked his character, replied, "Since it is dangerous to dispute openly of these matters, I had rather reserve them for our private conversation, as fitter for word of mouth than writing." Colet also informed Erasmus, that it was his determination to banish, if possible, the wrangling of the scholastic divines, and restore those theological studies which were founded upon the Scriptures and the primitive fathers; and that for this end he had in Oxford publicly expounded the Epistles of St. Paul; and earnestly pressed him to undertake a similar public exposition of some part of the Old Testament, while he himself was employed in the New. Erasmus, however, declined the undertaking, but exhorted Colet to persevere in his laudable design, assuring him, that when he was conscious to himself of a sufficient degree of strength and ability, he would readily lend him assistance. This friendship was maintained to the close of life, and the correspondence of these two great men served to animate them in the pursuit of Biblical learning, in which they met with frequent and violent opposition, especially from the scholastic doctors, who were so enraged at any attempts to promote the study of the Greek tongue, that they could not forbear uttering invectives against it from the pulpit; and strove to suppress it by the cry of "Heresy." Hence the proverb, *Cave a Græcis, ne fias Hæreticus; Fuge literas Hebræas, ne fias Judæorum similis*—"Take care of Greek, lest you become a heretic: avoid Hebrew, lest you become like Jews." Standish, bishop of St. Asaph, and provincial of the Franciscans, in a declamation against Erasmus, styled him GRÆCULUS ISTE; which became for a long time afterward the phrase for a heretic, or one suspected of "heretical pravity."

This aversion to the study of every thing that tended to lessen the authority of the schoolmen, or to spread an acquaintance with the original Scriptures, obtained during the whole of the reign of Henry VII. and the beginning of the reign of Henry VIII. About the latter period, a preacher at Oxford declared openly, at St. Mary's, against the pernicious innovation of the Greek tongue; and raised such a ferment about it among the students, that the king, who was then at Woodstock, having been correctly informed by Mr. (afterward Sir) Thomas More, and the learned Richard Pace, of the true cause of the commotion, sent his royal letters to the university, to allow and encourage that study among the young men. Not long after this, a divine, who was preaching at court, declaimed and railed violently against Greek learning and new interpretations of the Scripture. Richard Pace (who afterward succeeded Colet as dean of St. Paul's) was then present, and cast his eyes upon the king, to observe how he was affected with the discourse; and the king smiled upon Pace, in contempt of the invectives of the preacher. After sermon Henry sent for the divine who had preached, and appointed a solemn disputation, at which he himself proposed to be present, for the purpose of debating the matter between the preacher opposing, and Mr. Thomas More defending, the use of the Greek tongue. When the appointed time came, More began with an eloquent apology in favour of that copious and ancient language. But the divine, instead of replying to the arguments of More, fell upon his knees, and implored pardon of the king for the offence he had given in the pulpit, endeavouring to excuse himself by saying, that "what he had done was by the impulse of the Spirit." "Not of the Spirit of Christ," rejoined

Henry, "but of the spirit of infatuation." The king then asked him, whether he had read the writings of Erasmus, against which he had declaimed? To this he answered in the negative. "Why then," said the king, "you are a very foolish fellow, to censure what you have never read." "I have read," said he, "something they call MORIA," (*Moriæ Encomium*, the Praise of Folly.) "Yes," replied Pace, "may it please your highness, such a subject is fit for such a reader." At last the preacher, to bring himself off, declared that he was now better reconciled to the Greek tongue, because it was derived from the Hebrew. Upon which the king, who was amazed at the ignorance of the man, dismissed him; but with an express charge that he should never again preach at court.

In 1502 Colet was made prebendary of Durnesford, in the church of Sarum; and on the 20th of January, 1503–4, he resigned his prebend of Good Easter. In 1504 he took the degree of doctor in divinity. On the 5th of May, 1505, he was instituted to the prebend of Mora, in the cathedral church of St. Paul; and in the same year, and in the same month, without the least solicitation of his own, was raised to the dignity of dean of St. Paul's, on which occasion he resigned the vicarage of Stepney.

Dr. Colet soon began to distinguish himself in the important station to which he was now advanced. He restored and reformed the decayed discipline of his cathedral church, and commenced what was there a novel practice, by preaching himself upon Sundays and solemn festivals. In this course of preaching he did not restrict himself to single texts from the Gospel or Epistle for the day, but selected more general subjects, as the Gospel of St. Matthew, the Lord's Prayer, the Apostles' Creed, and continued a series of discourses upon them till he had completed the discussion of the doctrines they maintained. His audience was usually crowded, and among his hearers were the principal courtiers and citizens. He also called in to his assistance other divines of learning and talents, among whom was William Grocyn, and John Sowle, a Carmelite friar of an unblamable life, and a great admirer and preacher of the writings of St. Paul.

The frequent preaching of Dean Colet, in his own cathedral, stimulated some others to follow his example, particularly Dr. Collingwood, at Litchfield, who introduced the practice of preaching every Sunday, being the first and only preacher among all the deans of that cathedral. Before Dr. Colet reformed the practice, it had been usual, both in the universities and in the cathedral churches, for the public lecturers to read upon any other book than the Scriptures; but after he had himself read lectures upon St. Paul's Epistles, both in the university of Oxford and in St. Paul's cathedral, and retained several learned men, successively, to read these theological lectures in his church, for which he made them a generous allowance, he at last procured a settlement at St. Paul's for a similar lecture to be constantly read there, three days in every week.

These divinity lectures, and Dr. Colet's method of expounding the Scriptures, raised among the people an inquiry after the sacred writings, sunk into neglect by the metaphysical disputants, and the superstitious and ignorant clergy. This, together with the contempt which the dean expressed for the religious houses or monasteries, and the display which he made of their abuses, doubtless contributed to prepare the minds of the people for the Reformation, which, by the gracious providence of God, soon afterward took place. It is therefore no wonder that the bigots to popery considered him as an enemy, and attempted to stir up persecution against him. The ecclesiastics were stung to revenge, and a prosecution was commenced against him for heresy, in which Dr. Fitzjames, bishop of London, was the principal agent. The main charges exhibited against him to Archbishop Warham were three; the *first* of which was, that he had taught that images were not to be worshipped; the *second*, that he had preached against the temporal possessions of the bishops; and the *third*, that he had preached against the cold and unaffected manner in which some men read their sermons, which was understood to reflect upon the bishop himself. But the archbishop, who knew and valued the integrity and worth of Colet, became his advocate and patron, and dismissed him without giving him the trouble of a formal answer. Tyndal, in his reply to More, adds, that the bishop of London would have made Colet a heretic, for translating the Pater Noster into English, had not the archbishop of Canterbury defended him: and Bishop Latimer, who was at the time a young student at Cambridge, remembered the noise occasioned by the prosecution of Colet for heresy, and says expressly, that "he was not only in trouble, but should have been burnt, if God had not turned the king's heart to the contrary."

The enemies of the dean were not easily repulsed. Disappointed in their accusation of heresy, they attempted to fix upon him a suspicion of sedition, or treason. In this they were equally foiled; for the young king (Henry VIII.) sent for him, and in private advised him to go on, reproving and reforming a corrupt and dissolute age, nor suffer his light to be extinguished in times so densely dark; assuring him that he was sensible of the good effect of his excellent preaching and life, and promising that no one should injure him with impunity. The dean thanked the king for his royal protection, but begged that no one might suffer on his account, for he would rather, he said, resign his deanery, and live in privacy. Another attack was made upon the dean, of a similar nature, but which was equally unsuccessful; the king dismissing him with marks of affection and promises of favour. After this the dean continued his constant course of preaching, though he seems never to have recovered his character for *orthodoxy* with the bigots of his church.

In the mean time, his father, Sir Henry Colet, dying, in 1510, he succeeded to a very considerable estate. He therefore delivered his church revenues to his steward, to be expended in housekeeping and hospitality; and employed the annual produce of his paternal estate in acts of piety, beneficence, and generosity. Having no very near or poor relations, he founded the Grammar School of St. Paul's, in London, which he endowed with lands and tenements for the support of a head master, a second master, or usher, and a chaplain, for the instruction of one hundred and fifty-three boys in the Greek and Latin languages, and placed it under the care of the company of mercers. The dean also appointed WILLIAM LILY to be first head master of his school.*

* The celebrated grammarian, WILLIAM LILY, or LILYE, was born at Oldham, in Hampshire, about 1466. At the age of eighteen he was admitted a demy-commoner of Magdalen College, Oxford. Having taken the degree of bachelor of arts, he left the university and travelled to Jerusalem. On his return he resided a considerable time in the island of Rhodes, where he studied the Greek under the learned men who had fled thither for protection, after the taking of Constantinople. From thence he proceeded to Rome, where he further improved himself in the Latin and Greek languages, under John Sulpitius and Pomponius Sabinus. On his arrival in England, in 1509, he settled in London, and taught grammar, poetry, and rhetoric, with good success, and is said to have been the first who taught Greek in that city. When Dr. Colet founded St. Paul's school, he was appointed head master. He had been twelve years in that laborious and useful situation when he was seized with the plague and died, in 1522. He was a married man at the time of his appointment to the school. His two sons, George and Peter, were both learned men. The eldest of them published the first exact map that was ever drawn of this island. Mr. Lily had also a daughter named Dionysia, who was married to John Ritwyse, usher, and afterward successor to him in the mastership of St. Paul's school.

Lily had the character of an excellent grammarian, and a successful teacher of the learned languages. He published several small Latin pieces, principally poems and

In 1511, at the opening of the convocation of the province of Canterbury, Archbishop Warham appointed Dean Colet to preach the Latin sermon on that occasion. In this sermon, which is still extant, he attacked the corruptions of the church and clergy in the most warm and spirited manner. His text was from St. Paul's Epistle to the Romans, ch. xii, ver. 2: "Be not conformed to this world, but be ye transformed," &c. In treating of conformity to the world, he explained what was meant under four heads;—devilish pride, carnal lusts, worldly covetousness, and secular business. "These," said the dean, "are in the world, as St. John witnesseth, who says, that all that is in the world is either 'the lust of the flesh, the lust of the eye, or the pride of life.' And these same things do now so reign in the church, and among ecclesiastical persons, that we may, in a manner, truly say, all that is in the church is either the lust of the flesh, the lust of the eye, or the pride of life." He then proceeded to discuss, in the most bold and spirited manner, the different topics he had proposed; and concluded by a pointed address to the bishops, pressing the necessity of reformation, and of an immediate and firm exercise of discipline, agreeably to the canons of the church, which he proposed should be read in that convocation.

His honesty and zeal against the corruptions of the clergy increased the number of his enemies, but, protected by the king, he escaped that degradation and martyrdom which, with a less powerful patron, he would probably have suffered; and, under the sanction of royalty, succeeded to other preferments besides those which have already been mentioned. He was rector of the fraternity or gild of Jesus, in St. Paul's church, for which he procured new statutes: and also chaplain and preacher in ordinary to King Henry, and, if Erasmus were not mistaken, one of his privy council. About his fiftieth year he formed a resolution to withdraw from active life, and spend the rest of his days in retirement; but

orations. His principal work, or at least that by which he is best known, is *Brevissima Institutio, seu ratio grammatices cognoscendæ*; London, 1513; commonly called "Lily's Latin Grammar." This was a very excellent work for its time. Bishop Wettenhall's Grammar, the Eton Grammar, and multitudes of others, are but abridgments of it. The English rudiments of it were written by Dr. Colet; the preface by Cardinal Wolsey; the syntax chiefly by Erasmus; and the other parts by other hands; so that, although it bears Lily's name, he probably had not the largest share in the work, and therefore, during his life, modestly refused the honour of having it ascribed to him. It has since been greatly improved, and has passed through innumerable editions. See *Brit. Biog.*, vol. i, pp. 384, 385: and Clarke's *Bibliog. Dict.*, vol. iv, p. 19.

he was prevented by death: for being seized with the sweating sickness, "he retired to the lodgings he had built in the monastery of the Carthusians at Sheen, near Richmond, in Surry; when, having spent the little remainder of his days in devotion, he surrendered up his last breath to Him that first gave it, on the 16th of September, 1519." His body was afterward carried to London, and buried in the cathedral church of St. Paul, with an humble monument, that he had several years before appointed and prepared, with only this inscription on it, JOANNES COLETUS.

The dean, as to his person, was tall and comely, and his mien and carriage graceful. His learning was considerable, and his piety exemplary. As a preacher, he was eloquent and nervous. In his goods, furniture, entertainment, apparel, and books, he was neat and clean, but despised all state and magnificence: and while the higher clergy were generally clothed in purple, his dress was always black, and plain. Frugal at his meals, it was his custom for many years to eat but one meal, that of dinner. As soon as grace before meat was said, some boy, with a good voice, read distinctly a chapter out of one of St. Paul's Epistles, or out of the Proverbs of Solomon; and from thence the dean took occasion to introduce grave and improving conversation, by which means his guests were refreshed in mind as well as body. At other times, when he had no agreeable companion, one of his servants read some part of the Holy Scriptures. "In his journeys he would sometimes make me," says Erasmus, "his companion, when no one could be more pleasant; yet he always carried a book with him, and his conversation was all about CHRIST." He loved little children, and compared them, like Jesus, to angels, for innocence and simplicity. To glorify God, and to be useful to men, appeared to be the great aim of his life; which occasioned Erasmus to say, when he heard of his death, "I know his state is happy; he is now delivered from a troublesome and wicked world, and enjoys the presence of his Redeemer JESUS, whom he loved so affectionately in his life."*

Such was Dean Colet, a man who, amid the darkness of the age, shone as a light in a benighted land; and who deserves to be ranked among those who were essentially serviceable in the spread of Scriptural knowledge; an honour to his country, a blessing to posterity.

An increasing attention began now to be paid to the Greek

* British Biography, vol. i, pp. 361–402. Jortin's Life of Erasmus, vol. iii, App., No. ii, pp. 14–25.

tongue, as the original language of the New Testament; and such was the veneration of some persons for it on this account, that although they did not understand the language itself, yet because it was the original text, they caused it to be interlined in their copies of the Vulgate. Dr. Hody mentions a MS. of this kind, preserved in the library of Corpus Christi College, Oxford, executed in the most beautiful manner, on parchment, in two volumes in folio. The Latin was written with black, and the Greek with red ink.*

Thus was divine Providence preparing the way for the reformation of his church, and for the revival of sacred literature from that state of profound ignorance into which it had been sunk for ages. Many instances of that general disuse of the Holy Scriptures among the clergy and members of the Church of Rome which preceded the age of Luther, and of the necessity of some powerful interposition to break the fetters of the most slavish superstition, and to rescue the sacred volume from the bondage in which it was detained, have been already adduced; and if we again pass to the CONTINENT, and examine the state of those countries where the great deliverance was first effected, it must add to our gratitude, for the gracious and energetic interposition of that God whose word is TRUTH.

Several of the German monasteries had no public library for the use of the monks; and in some of them not a single copy of the Scriptures could be found. Prior to the publication of the Greek Testament by Erasmus, not a copy could be procured in all Germany; so that Conrad Pellican was obliged to obtain one from Italy. In some churches Aristotle's Ethics and similar works were read instead of sermons, a practice which in some places had subsisted from the time of Charlemagne; in others, the works of Aquinas were explained; and in some, lectures on the heathen poets were delivered, where the word of God ought to have been preached. The original languages of the Scriptures were not only generally neglected, but the study of them was despised. Conrad Heresbachius relates that he heard a monk declaiming in a church, who affirmed, "A new language is discovered, called Greek, and is the parent of all heresy. A book written in that language is everywhere got into the hands of persons, and is called the *New Testament.* It is a book full of daggers and poison. Another language has also sprung up, called the Hebrew, and those who

* Hody, De Bibl. Text. Orig., lib. iii, pt. ii, cap. xii, p. 458.

learn it become Jews." Even *Latin*, the common language of their religious services, was so little understood by the monkish clergy, that the most ridiculous mistakes were made by them, both in the performance of their offices and in their writings: an instance is related of one, who, instead of the usual form in baptism, was accustomed to say, "Baptizo te in nomine Patria, et Filia, et Spiritus Sancti;" of another, who, when he had received letters of recommendation for orders, couched in these terms, "Otto Dei gratia, rogat vestram clementiam, ut velitis istum clericum conducere ad vestrum Diaconum;" and was ordered to read the epistle, which was considerably abbreviated in the writing, was so totally ignorant of the Latin as to form the abbreviations into the following unmeaning words: "Otto Dei gram, rogat vestram clam, ut velit istum clincum clancum, convertere in vivum Diabolum;" and of a third, who for "famulus Dei," constantly repeated "mulus Dei."*

The grossest ignorance of the Scriptures prevailed, not only among the laity, but also among many of the clergy. Degrees in divinity were conferred upon those who had scarcely ever read the Bible; and numbers of divines were far advanced in life before they had even seen one! In the year 1510 the university of Wittemberg registered in its acts, Andrew Carolostad, afterward one of the reformers, as being *sufficientissimus*, fully qualified for the degree of doctor, which he then received; though he afterward acknowledged, that he never began to read the Bible till eight years after he had received his academical honours. Albert, archbishop and elector of Mentz, having accidently found a Bible lying on a table, in 1530, opened it, and having read some pages, exclaimed, "Indeed, I do not know what this book is; but this I see, that every thing in it is against us." Gerard Listrius, in his note on the *Moriæ Encomium* of Erasmus, says, "I have known many doctors in divinity, as they were called, who have candidly acknowledged that they were fifty years of age before they had read the Epistles of St. Paul:" and Musculus affirms, (*Loc. Com.*,) that prior to the Reformation, "many priests and pastors had not so much as *seen* a Bible." Those who devoted themselves to the study of the Scriptures were objects of derision, and treated as heretical; while the advocates of the Aristotelian philosophy were regarded as the oracles of wisdom, and the only true theologians.

* Lomeier, De Bibliothecis, cap. viii, pp. 155, 180. Hody, De Bibl. Text. Orig., pt. ii, lib. iii, pp. 464, 465. Hottingeri Analecta Historico-Theologica: diss. i, *De Necessitate Reformationis*, pp. 12, 52. Tigurin, 1652, 12mo.

The divines of Cologne published one work, entitled *De Salute Aristotelis*, "Aristotle on Salvation;" and another, illustrated with theological notes, bearing the title of *De vita et morte Aristotelis*, "Aristotle on Life and Death;" and concluding with this sentence, "Aristotle was the forerunner of Christ in the kingdom of nature, as John the Baptist was in the kingdom of grace." Even the Bible itself was disregarded, or contemptuously noticed. John Faber, canon of Leutkirch, and suffragan of Constance, and afterward bishop of Vienna, impiously declared that men "might live peaceably and amicably together, without the Gospel;" and Cardinal Hosius daringly affirmed, that "it would have been better for the church (of Rome,) if the Gospel had never been written."*

This view of the degraded state of sacred literature, previous to the Reformation, is further confirmed by the following extract from the learned historian of The Helvetic Confederacy:—

"The generality of the priesthood did not scruple to acknowledge their deficiency in the most elementary parts of learning. The canons of the collegiate church of Zuric having to notify an election to the bishop of Constance, confessed that they transmitted it in the handwriting of their notary, because several of them could not write. In the examination for holy orders, it was deemed amply sufficient that the candidate could read, and tolerably comprehend what he read:† even after the Reformation had made some progress, the people firmly believed, and the priests confirmed them in the persuasion, that the bells travelled every passion week to Rome to receive fresh baptism; and that the exorcisms of priests could effectually dispel swarms of locusts, and all manner of insects. When, at an assembly of the clergy in the Valais, mention was made of the Bible, only one of the priests had ever heard of such a book: and several, on other occasions, did not scruple to declare, that it would be an advantage to religion if no Gospel were extant; and that the study of the Greek and Hebrew languages greatly savoured of heresy."

"Had the clergy, however, in this unpardonable state of ignorance," continues the writer, "maintained a decorum in their conversation and manners, they might still have preserved a degree of respect and influence, which would probably have somewhat re-

* Hotingeri Analecta, diss. 1, pp. 1–82. Lomeier, De Bibliothecis, cap. viii, pp. 166, 167. Hody, *ut sup.*

† "The report of the examination of Leonard Brun for priest's orders, not long before the Reformation, was, 'Bene legit, competenter exponit et sententiat, computum ignorat, male cantat—Fiat admissio.'"

tarded the progress of the Reformation. But the profligacy even of the heads of the church had arrived at a pitch which it was no longer possible to tolerate, or palliate. Without dwelling on the many flagrant instances of depravation, which are not disguised even by the ecclesiastical writers of the Romish Church, all men must feel a painful conviction when they learn, from the charges that were brought by the citizens of Lausanne, againt their clergy, that the priests used often, even in the churches, and in the midst of divine service, to strike the persons to whom they bore ill-will, some of whom had actually died of their wounds; that they walked the streets at night, disguised in military dresses, brandishing naked swords, and insulting the peaceable inhabitants; and that the frequent rapes, violences, and insults they committed, were never punished, or even restrained. The following are the words of the eighteenth article:—'We have also to complain of the canons, that they reduce the profits of our town brothel, several of them carrying on the traffic of prostitution in their own houses, which they throw open to new comers of all descriptions.'* It is no small corroboration of the merited clamours raised against the clergy, that their own zealous advocate and protector, Charles V., publicly declared to them, that if their lives had been less reproachable, they would never have had to contend with a Martin Luther."†

From such an awful detail of depravity, the consequence, principally, of that universal ignorance of the word of God which had been studiously induced by the inhibitory mandates of the papal power, and the restrictive measures of the Romish clergy, we turn with satisfaction to notice a few instances of a very different and more enlightened nature. For amid the general gloom some characters were found whose pursuits and studies threw rays of sacred light across "the palpable obscure." Jacobus Faber, of Daventer; Joannes Frobenius, the celebrated printer; but especially Desiderius Erasmus, deserve to be remarked for their promotion of Biblical learning.

Jacobus Faber, of Daventer, was born in the year 1472. His preceptor was Alexander Hegius, who was also the instructer of Erasmus. In 1499 he published an heroic poem. Afterward he became the reader of the second class of Daventer, and edited the works of his master; part of which he dedicated to Erasmus, in

* "These charges consist of twenty-three articles, and are given at length in Ruchat's Hist. de la Reform. de la Suisse, tom. i, p. xxxii. They are of the year 1533."

† Planta's History of the Helvetic Confederacy, vol. ii, b. ii, ch. vi, pp. 358–363. London, 1807, 8vo.

1503. In the year 1511 he edited "Cato's Distichs," with additions. About the same time Jacobus Faber Stapulensis (Jacques Le Fevre, of Estaples) presented him with a copy of his Quintuple Psalter, printed in 1509. Many MSS. in the handwriting of Jacobus Faber of Daventer are still extant in the library of that city, among which are Latin translations of the Greek canons and menology. He appears to have been an indefatigable transcriber of Biblical MSS., for on the first page of a MS. formerly belonging to Faber, J. C. Wolfius, of Hamburg, has made the following note: "I have a Hebrew MS. of Genesis and Exodus, with Faber's name written at the beginning and end." The same learned person possessed also a MS. of the Greek New Testament, transcribed by Faber, which was afterward purchased by Wetstein, out of Wolfius's library, and collated for his Greek Testament. It contains the following books of the New Testament, in this order: John, Luke, Matthew, Mark; the Epistles of St. Paul; the Acts; and the Catholic (or General) Epistles: the Epistle of Jude is written twice, and from two different copies. Jacobus Faber copied it from a MS. written at Mount Athos, in 1293, by Theodore, the writer also of a Greek MS. of the four Gospels, preserved in the library of Christ Church, in Oxford. The ancient MS. which Faber copied, or with which he collated his transcript, was one which had been presented from the Vatican library to John Herman Wesselus, of Groningen, by Pope Sixtus IV.* Faber's copy is on paper, in two volumes, 4to. At the beginning is a note, of which the following is the purport: "I have collated the four Gospels more than once, with great care and labour, with an ancient MS. on vellum, formerly belonging to J. Wesselus, of Groningen. The labour it has occasioned me I cannot easily tell, as I have met with no one to assist me in the collation." He was living in 1517. The time of his decease is uncertain.†

John Frobenius, or Froben, was one of the most celebrated printers of his day. He was a native of Hammelburg, in Franconia. He received his education at Basil; and after having made great progress in literature, commenced the business of a printer in that city. He selected the works of the best authors for publication; and spared no expense to obtain perfect MSS. He employed persons of the highest literary merit, as the editors and correctors of the press, in proof of which it is sufficient to name

* See page 531 of this volume.

† Jorton's Life of Erasmus, vol. i, p. 104, *note*. Marsh's Michaelis, vol. ii, pt. i, ch. viii, p. 360.

Sigismund Gelenius, the learned author of a "Greek, Latin, German, and Slavonian lexicon;" and John Œcolampadius, or Hawksheim, one of the principal reformers, and author of several Latin translations of the Greek fathers.

The respectability of Froben's character, and his constant care of never printing any thing offensive to morals and religion, procured him both celebrity and opulence. In the publication of the works of the fathers, particularly of Jerome, he was joined by John Amerbach, a pious and wealthy printer, who had educated his three sons in the study of the Greek, and Hebrew, and Latin tongues, to qualify them for editing the works of this his favourite author.

In 1514 he contracted an intimate friendship for Erasmus, who came to reside at Basil, principally with the design of publishing the works of Jerome, for which he had made considerable preparations, where he found Froben and Amerbach engaged in a similar undertaking, who committed to him the direction of the work.

But what gave the greatest celebrity to Froben was his printing the Greek New Testament, which was edited by Erasmus. This was the first published edition of the Greek Testament after the invention of printing; for although the Complutensian edition was first printed, it was not published till 1522, whereas this was published in 1516. The design of publishing this edition originated with Froben, who engaged Erasmus as the editor; for Beatus Rhenanus, who was for some time one of the correctors of Froben's press, in a letter addressed to Erasmus, dated April 17th, 1515, makes the proposal in the following terms:—"Petit Frobenius abs te Novum Testamentum, pro quo tantum se daturum pollicetur, quantum alias quisquam"—"Froben requests you to undertake the New Testament, for which he promises to give you as much as any other person." During the time he was employed upon it, Erasmus lodged in the house of Froben, as appears from the subscription at the end of the first edition, which is, "Basiliæ, in ædibus Johannis Frobenii Hammelburgensis, Mense Februario, anno MDXVI."

Froben also commenced an edition of the works of Augustine, in ten volumes; and had formed the design of printing the works of all the Greek fathers, when his life was terminated by a universal palsy, supposed to be the consequence of a dreadful fall, some years before. He died, universally lamented by all who knew him, at Basil, in 1527.*

* Jorton's Life of Erasmus, vol. i, pp. 58, 393. Marsh's Michaelis, vol. ii, pt. i, ch. xii, p. 443; and pt. ii, p. 854.

Erasmus, who occasionally assumed the prænomen of Desiderius, was born at Rotterdam, about A. D. 1467; and received the early part of his education at an illustrious school, at Daventer, where Alexander Hegius was his master, and Adrianus Florentius, afterward Pope Adrian IV., was his school-fellow. At the age of thirteen he lost his parents; his mother by the plague, and his father by grief for her death. The three guardians to whose care he was left by his father proved dishonourable and base; and in order to rob him of his patrimony, determined to make him a monk, for which purpose they forced him into a convent of friars, at Balduc, in Brabant; from whence he was removed to another, at Sion, near Delft, and thence to a third, at Stein, near Torgau. His aversion to the monastic state induced him to resist their attempts for some years; but at length, overcome by their unwearied endeavours, he entered among the regular canons, and made his profession in 1486.

He did not, however, remain long in the monastery, for in 1490 he was received into the family of Henry à Bergis, archbishop of Cambray; and subsequently obtained leave from Julius II., and then from Leo X., to lay aside the habit of the order, and to quit the monastic profession.

From the time that Erasmus quitted his convent to the period when he published his New Testament, he resided chiefly in England and France, and occasionally visiting Italy. In every country he indefatigably pursued his studies, obtaining a precarious subsistence from the generosity of his literary friends, the emoluments of instruction, and the publication of several of his minor productions. For several years his mind was occupied with a design of publishing the works of Jerome, but especially of printing an edition of the Greek Testament, with notes. Early in 1515 he received proposals from Froben, the celebrated printer of Basil, to reside in that city, and become the editor of a Greek Testament. The proposal according with his own previous intention, he removed to Basil, and edited both the Greek Testament and the works of Jerome, which respectively appeared in the year 1516.

This edition of the Greek Testament Erasmus accompanied with a Latin Version; and Various Readings, selected from several MSS., the works of the fathers, and the Vulgate. It was printed in folio, in two columns, with the notes at the end; and reprinted in 1519, 1522, 1527, and 1535. The publication of the New Testament raised a host of enemies against Erasmus, some of whom censured his temerity, while others laboured to affix the stigma of inaccuracy and heresy upon him; and one of the colleges at Cambridge forbade it to be brought within its walls! Many of his adversaries strove to have it placed among the prohibited works, but the dedication to Leo X., with the approbation of it expressed by that pontiff, and especially his brief annexed to the later editions, prevented for a time the accomplishment of the malicious intentions of the Spanish, and other monkish divines. His edition of Jerome, and several of his other works, met with a severer fate, and were not only placed in the *Indices Expurgatorii*, as works to be corrected and *purged*, but, in some instances, were condemned to the flames.

The liberal and enlightened manner in which Erasmus, in the prefatory discourses prefixed to his New Testament, recommended and defended vernacular translations, and the universal perusal of the sacred volume, placed him among the warmest advocates for the circulation of the Scriptures. His Preface, Paraclesis, and Apologia, deserve to be read and studied by every lover of the Bible, and probably greatly aided the Reformation, and subsequent diffusion of Scriptural truth. The following brief extracts will give an idea of his manner of reasoning:—

"I differ exceedingly from those who object to the Scriptures being translated into the vernacular tongues, and read by the illiterate: as if Christ had taught so obscurely, that none could understand him but a few theologians: or as if the Christian religion depended upon being kept secret. The mysteries of kings ought, perhaps, to be concealed, but the mystery of Christ strenuously urges publication. I would have even the meanest of women to read the Gospels, and Epistles of St. Paul; and I wish that the Scriptures might be translated into all languages, that they might be known and read, not only by the Irish and Scots, but also by Saracens and Turks. Assuredly, the first step is to make them known. For this very purpose, though many might ridicule, and others might frown, I wish the husbandman might repeat them at his plough, the weaver sing them at his loom, the traveller beguile the tediousness of the way by the entertainment of their stories, and the general discourse of all Christians be concerning them, since what we are in ourselves, such we almost constantly are in our common conversation."

"Letters, written by those we love and esteem, are preserved, and prized, and carried about with us, and read again and again; and yet there are thousands of Christians who, although otherwise learned, never once, in the whole of their life, read the books containing the Gospels and Epistles. Mohammedans violently defend their opinions; and Jews, from their infancy, learn the precepts of Moses; but why are we not equally decisive in favour of Christ? They who profess the institute of Benedict, adopt, and learn, and follow a rule written by a man nearly illiterate. They who are of the order of Augustine, are well versed in the rule of its author. The Franciscans adore the traditions of Francis, possess themselves of them, and carry them with them to every part of the world, nor ever think themselves safe but when they have the book in their bosom. And why should they attribute more to rules written by *men*, than Christians in general to RULES which *Christ* has delivered to all; and into which all have been equally initiated by baptism."*

Soon after the publication of his Greek Testament, Erasmus commenced a series of paraphrases on the New Testament, forming an extensive supplement to the notes accompanying the Greek. His Paraphrase of St. Paul's Epistle to the Romans was dedicated to Cardinal Dominic Grimani, who was himself a man of erudition, and translated into Italian a treatise of St. Chrysostom: his library, next to that of the pope, was at that time the most considerable in Rome; and contained eight thousand volumes. The dedication is dated A. 1517. In 1519 he dedicated his Paraphrase of St. Paul's Epistles to the Corinthians to the prince Cardinal de Marca. In the same year he dedicated his Paraphrase of St. Paul's Epistles to the Ephesians, Philippians, Colossians, and Thessalonians, to Cardinal Campegius; and his Paraphrase of St. Paul's Epistles to Timothy, to Titus, and to Philemon, to Philip of Burgundy, archbishop of Utrecht. His Paraphrase of the Epistles of St. James and St. John, and of the Epistle to the Hebrews, he dedicated, in 1520, to Cardinal Matthew, who had exhorted him to undertake the paraphrase of these Epistles. In 1522 he dedicated his Paraphrase of St. Matthew to Charles V., and closed his dedication with an excellent admonition to this young emperor, in which he reminds him, that "all wars, however justly undertaken, or however moderately conducted, are always followed by a train of calamities and sufferings." In his preface to this paraphrase, he exhorts the laity and the common people to read and study the Scriptures, which ought, as he says, to lie open to all well-disposed people, and to be translated into all modern languages.

In 1523 Erasmus dedicated his Paraphrase of St. Luke to Henry VIII., king of England. He tells the king, that Charles V.

* Erasmi Nov. Test., *Paraclesis.* Basil, 1516, fol.

and Ferdinand, and Christiern of Denmark, and Queen Catharine, were readers of the Holy Scriptures. He also draws an argument for the truth of Christianity from its successful propagation, and its salutary effects.

The Paraphrase of St. John was dedicated to Ferdinand, brother of the emperor Charles V. In the dedication Erasmus gives Ferdinand a great character; and exhorts him to persevere in his good dispositions, and offers him excellent advice. At the end of the paraphrase is an epistle to the reader, recommending to him piety, and dissuading him from superstition. The Paraphrase of the Acts of the Apostles, Erasmus dedicated to Pope Clement VII. in 1524. The Paraphrase of St. Mark, which, in 1521, he had inscribed to Cardinal Matthew, he dedicated in 1533 to Francis I., king of France. In his dedication he exhorts Christian princes to peace, and pacific dispositions; and observes, with pleasure, what a demand there was for the New Testament, and *how many thousand copies were sold every year*. The Paraphrase of the Epistles of St. Peter and of St. Jude he dedicated to Cardinal Wolsey; and after complimenting the cardinal, informs him that he has no favours to solicit, besides the cardinal's countenance and approbation. The Paraphrase of St. Paul's Epistles to the Galatians appears to have been published without any particular dedication. Erasmus published no paraphrase of the Revelation. These paraphrases were afterward collected, and published, together with his other works. The best edition is that by Le Clerc, printed at Leyden, 1703, eleven vols. fol. Besides the paraphrase of the New Testament, he also published paraphrases, or discourses, on some of the Psalms. His discourse on the first Psalm was dedicated by him, in 1515, to Beatus Rhenanus, a learned and pacific man, one of the correctors of Froben's press. In the dedication he exhorts all persons to read the Scriptures, which (as he afterward affirmed in his other writings) ought to be translated into vulgar tongues, and put into the hands of the vulgar: he also exhorts the common people not to have an implicit faith in their teachers, nor to suffer themselves to be led by the nose like bears.

The bold and satirical manner in which Erasmus attacked the corruptions of the Romish Church and clergy, not only in his Biblical works, but in his numerous other writings, exposed him to the hatred and malicious machinations of a host of enemies, who regarded him as one of the most dangerous and powerful opponents of the Roman Catholic hierarchy and doctrines. His works were exclaimed against as disseminating heretical opinions, and placed in the *Indices Expurgatorii* as dangerous to be read; and himself only escaped the punishment of heretical pravity, by the influence of his friends, and the cowardly dissimulation of some parts of his conduct. For though possessed of an enlightened mind, a correct judgment, and uncommon learning, he unfortunately had neither piety nor firmness enough to become a martyr to the truth; nor to meet the fiery zeal of his adversaries with the intrepidity of a reformer. It was this fear of suffering which most probably occasioned his opposition to Luther, with whom the monks ranked him, for "Erasmus," said they, "laid the egg, and Luther hatched it."

Erasmus continued writing and publishing to the very close of his life, occasionally satirizing the monks, exposing the absurdities of many of the doctrines of his church, and defending the advocates of reformation and truth. In the last year of his life he published his discourse, or commentary, on the fourteenth Psalm, which he entitled, "Of the Purity of the Christian Church," consisting of allegorical interpretations, and moral reflections upon the text. He also republished his letters, adding several received from the emperor, and other princes, and from men in the highest stations; and remarks, that while revising them, he had found that within the space of ten years many of his best friends and old correspondents were dead, which caused him to meditate on the shortness and uncertainty of human life. He intended to have revised and printed the "Works of Origen," adding a few short notes; but before it was completed he was called away by death; and the work was published after his decease, with a preface, by Beatus Rhenanus.

About a month before his death he was seized with a dysentery, which his feeble frame, already weakened by disease, was unable to sustain, and which proved mortal on the 12th of July, 1536. The last of his days were spent in constantly imploring the mercy of Almighty God, and of Jesus Christ, without speaking of those Catholic ceremonies which he had so frequently blamed in the monks. He was buried in the cathedral church of Basil, or, as it is generally called, Bâsle.

In his person he was low of stature, well shaped, of a fair complexion, cheerful countenance, low voice, and agreeable elocution; neat and decent in his apparel; and a pleasant companion.*

The unprecedented circulation of the anti-monastic writings of Erasmus, and the repeated editions of his New Testament, created

* Jortin's Life of Erasmus, *passim*.

universal interest, and essentially aided the progress of truth, by exposing the vices of the monks, and causing the vast superstructure of superstition to tremble to its foundation; but the far more difficult labour of establishing the doctrines of the Gospel on an immoveable basis was reserved for the intrepid and illustrious LUTHER, who, with a fearless independence of spirit, embraced, defended, and propagated those evangelical and important doctrines, which, by the gracious providence of God, induced and confirmed the happy event of the ever-memorable REFORMATION.

1

END OF VOLUME ONE.

CATALOGUE OF BOOKS

PUBLISHED BY CARLTON & PHILLIPS.

I.

Biblical Literature.

Barr's Bible Index and Dictionary.

A Complete Index and Concise Dictionary of the Holy Bible: in which the various Persons, Places, and Subjects mentioned in it are accurately referred to; and difficult Words briefly explained,—designed to facilitate the Study of the Sacred Scriptures. Revised from the third Glasgow edition. By the Rev. JOHN BARR. To which is added, a Chronology of the Holy Bible, or an Account of the most Remarkable Passages in the Books of the Old and New Testaments pointing to the time wherein they happened, and to the Places of Scripture wherein they are recorded.

12mo., pp. 210. Sheep $0 45

This work is intended not only to assist unlearned readers in understanding the language of the Bible, but chiefly in readily turning to the places where every topic of information comprised in it occurs.

Truly a choice companion for the Biblical student. No one who has ever read it will readily consent to dispense with it.—*Chr. Adv. and Journal.*

Benson's Commentary.

A Commentary on the Old and New Testaments. According to the Present authorized Version. With Critical, Explanatory, and Practical Notes: the Marginal Readings of the most approved printed Copies of the Scriptures, with such others as appear to be countenanced by the Hebrew and Greek Originals; a copious collection of Parallel Texts; summaries of each Book and Chapter; and the Date of every Transaction and Event recorded in the Sacred Oracles, agreeably to the Calculations of the most correct Chronologers. By Rev. JOSEPH BENSON, M. A.

Imperial 8vo., 5 vols., pp. 4872.	**Sheep, plain $13 50**
———————	**Plain calf 16 50**
———————	**Calf gift 18 00**
———————	**Calf extra 22 00**

Also in twenty numbers, at 45 cents each.

This is a work of great labour, and justly characterized by the Wesleyan Conference, in their vote of thanks to Mr. Benson, as marked by "solid learning, soundness of theological opinion, and an edifying attention to experimental and practical religion."—DR. BUNTING.

An elaborate and very useful Commentary on the sacred Scriptures, which, independently of its practical tendency, possesses the merit of compressing into a comparatively small compass the substance of what the piety and learning of former ages have advanced, in order to facilitate the study of the Bible. Its late author was distinguished for his critical and exact acquaintance with the Greek Testament.—T. HARTWELL HORNE.

A work replete with sound theological and critical learning, and which will at once perpetuate his name and extend his usefulness.—R. TREFFRY.

Townley's Illustrations of Biblical Literature.

Illustrations of Biblical Literature: exhibiting the History and Fate of the Sacred Writings from the earliest Period to the present Century; including Biographical Notices of Translators and other eminent Biblical Scholars. By JAMES TOWNLEY, D. D.

8vo., 2 vols., pp. 1206. Sheep.. $3 00

This work forms part of the course of study adopted by the last General Conference.

These ample volumes comprise a rich fund of instructive and pleasing information on the subject of sacred biography. They have been compiled from a great variety of publications, many of them inaccessible to the generality of readers, and some of them of extreme rarity. . . . The industry and accuracy of Dr. Townley will entitle his volumes to the approbation of the critic and the patronage of the public. They afford a more comprehensive view of the progress of Biblical translations, and of the literary and ecclesiastical history of the Holy Scriptures, than is to be found in any other work.—*(London) Eclectic Review.*

It is a subject of heartfelt gratification to every American patriot, that erudite works of such intrinsic value, and of such a costly character, are reissued in our country at so low a price. Dr. Townley's Illustrations, when first published in London, about twenty years ago, were reviewed by one of the most learned British scholars of his generation. As his judgment is perfectly correct, we transcribe it: "These volumes present a connected view of the history of Biblical translations from the earliest date to the present century, and are enriched by most copious and interesting biographical notices of the most eminent scholars and critics, with occasional sketches of the history of the manners of the darker ages."

Some idea may be formed of the vast diversity of matter which these two volumes contain, when one fact only is remembered,—the Index fills nearly *twenty-four pages* of double columns in a small type. The work contains several engravings of antique languages, elucidating the historical notices with which they are connected.

The whole work is divided into three parts, of which we present merely the general summary:—

Part I. From the giving of the law to the birth of Christ, in two chapters.

Part II. From the birth of Christ to the invention of the art of printing, in thirteen chapters, exhibiting the historical details in progression by the successive centuries.

Part III. From the invention of printing until the present time, in twelve chapters.

Dr. Townley's Illustrations are essential to every good library; and to all persons who are desirous to attain an adequate and a correct acquaintance with the literature and the learned men of times gone by.—*Christian Intelligencer.*

Watson's Conversations.

Conversations for the Young, designed to promote the profitable Reading of the Holy Scriptures. By RICHARD WATSON.

12mo., pp. 300. Muslin or sheep.................................... $0 60

Though this work is designed for the benefit of young people, there are few adults who may not derive instruction from a serious perusal of it. It is worthy of a place in every Christian family and in every Sunday-School in the land.

The plan of the work is new, and is attended with many advantages. A young person is introduced, who has some knowledge of the contents of the Bible, whose disposition is serious and inquisitive, and who proposes questions for his own satisfaction on the principal facts and doctrines of Scripture. These call forth corresponding replies, and give the work a very interesting and miscellaneous character.

The sacred books are noticed in order. Difficulties are proposed and solved; the objections of unbelievers are stated, and refuted; an immense number of inquiries relating to the chronology, antiquities, phraseology, prophecies, and miracles of Scripture, are proposed and answered; and the whole has a direct bearing on the momentous subject of personal religion.

The design of this little work is most admirable; namely, the furnishing young persons with *general views* on Scriptural subjects, by the aid of which the words of eternal life may be so grafted in the hearts and minds of readers as to "guard them against fatal errors, and open to them that scheme of Christianity, in experience and practice, to which every part of Divine Revelation is made subservient, from which it derives its only value." In the masterly treatment of this subject, Mr. Watson has bequeathed to the Christian world an enduring legacy, and conferred a lasting obligation on the readers and students of Biblical Literature and Theology.

Clarke's Sacred Literature.

A Concise View of the Succession of Sacred Literature, in a Chronological Arrangement of Authors and their Works, from the Invention of Alphabetical Characters to A. D. 395. By ADAM CLARKE, LL. D.

12mo., pp. 420. Muslin or sheep **$0 70**

The work commences with the giving of the law on Mount Sinai. It contains the date and argument of every book of Scripture, and of all the writings of the Jews and Christian Fathers that are extant, down to the year 395; and in some instances the analysis of the different works is copious and extensive.

This work contains much important information relative to Biblical and ecclesiastical literature.—T. HARTWELL HORNE.

We know not in what manner we could render a more valuable service to the student who is directing his attention to this branch of knowledge, than to recommend him to avail himself of the guidance which the interesting work before us supplies.—*Eclectic Review.*

Coles's Concordance.

A New Concordance of the Holy Scriptures of the Old and New Testaments. By Rev. GEORGE COLES.

24mo., pp. 960. Sheep **$1 00**
———— **Calf neat** **1 25**
———— **Morocco extra** **2 00**

The preparation of such a book is necessarily a work of vast labour, but, when completed, the work is of great value.

Cruden's has been considered the best Concordance hitherto known. Several others have been in use, but they have been incomplete, and inadequate to the wants of a Bible student. The chief objections to Cruden's Concordance have been its unwieldy size and high price. That work, moreover, is about a hundred years old, and if not defective in its arrangement, certainly admits of manifest improvement, as is proved by the volume before us.

Coles's Concordance, although containing all the references of Mr. Cruden's, and many new ones, is so compactly printed as hardly to exceed the size of a pocket Bible, and is sold at the low price of one dollar. It contains no less than 960 pages, and is destined to remain to future generations a monument of the careful research and the untiring perseverance of its author. The greatest possible care has been taken to have every reference correct.

This, to say the least that can be said, is, in almost every respect, the very best Concordance now extant. It is really an improvement on all the older works, being both more copious and more correct. What more can we say? We have used it considerably since it was laid upon our table, and shall continue to use it in preference to any and every other within our reach.—*Ladies' Repository.*

Right glad are we that so valuable a contribution to Biblical literature has been furnished by a Methodist preacher. We are pleased that the author has confined himself strictly to the work which he undertook, without invading the province of the lexicographer or the theologian. We do not hesitate to recommend it heartily to all students of the Bible.—*Southern Christian Advocate.*

Every Bible student has known the value of a good Concordance. Very little progress could be made in the doctrinal study of the Scriptures without one. To Sabbath-school teachers and members of Bible classes a Concordance is indispensable. The one named at the head of this notice is said by good judges to be superior to all its predecessors.—*Rhode Island Pledge.*

Covel's Bible Dictionary.

A Concise Dictionary of the Holy Bible. Designed for the Use of Sunday Schools and Families, with Maps and Engravings. By Rev. JAMES COVEL, JR.

18mo. pp. 536. Sheep **$0 60**

This is a convenient and valuable book of reference, compiled from the best authorities. A good Bible Dictionary is an almost indispensable requisite to every teacher and student of the word of God. There are many larger and more expensive works than this, but few, if any, cheaper, and better adapted to practical use

Blatch's Confirmation of Scripture.

The Historical Confirmation of Scripture; with special Reference to Jewish and Ancient Heathen Testimony. By WILLIAM BLATCH.

18mo., pp. 144. Muslin or sheep $0 25

These Lectures arose from a conviction in the mind of the author of the importance of furnishing the mass of Christian professors with a cheap and digested manual of the direct historical evidence to the facts narrated in Scripture.—*Preface.*

Clarke's Ancient Israelites.

Manners of the Ancient Israelites: containing an Account of their peculiar Customs, Ceremonies, Laws, Polity, Religion, Sects, Arts, Trades, Divisions of Time, Wars, Captivities, &c.; with a short Account of the Ancient and Modern Samaritans. Written originally in French, by CLAUDE FLEURY. The whole much enlarged from the principal Writers. By ADAM CLARKE, LL.D. From the second London edition.

18mo., pp. 386. Muslin or sheep $0 40

This book is an excellent introduction to the reading of the Old Testament, and should be put into the hands of every young person.—BISHOP HORNE.

Clarke's Commentary.

The Holy Bible, containing the Old and New Testaments. The Text carefully printed from the most correct Copies of the present authorized Translation, including the Marginal Readings and Parallel Texts: with a Commentary and Critical Notes; designed as a help to a better understanding of the Sacred Writings. A new edition, with the Author's final Corrections. By ADAM CLARKE, LL.D.

Imperial 8vo., 6 vols., pp. 5528.	**Sheep**	**$16 00**
———	**In plain calf**	**20 00**
———	**Calf gilt**	**21 50**
———	**Calf extra**	**25 00**

Also in twenty-four numbers, at 45 cents each.

Upon this valuable Commentary the learned and industrious author spent forty years of his life, twenty-five in preparing it for press, and fifteen in carrying it through. In it "the most difficult words are analyzed and explained; the most important readings in the collections of Kennicott and De Rossi on the Old Testament, and in those of Mill, Wetstein, and Griesbach, on the New, are noticed; the date of every transaction, as far as it has been ascertained by the best chronologers, is marked; the peculiar customs of the Jews and neighbouring nations, as frequently alluded to by the prophets, evangelists, and apostles, are explained from the best Asiatic authorities; the great doctrines of the law and gospel of God are defined, illustrated, and defended; and the whole is employed in the important purposes of practical Christianity." The work concludes with a copious index, and a selection of important various readings of the New Testament from ten ancient manuscripts.

The literary world in general, and Biblical students in particular, are greatly indebted to Dr. Clarke for the light he has thrown on many very difficult passages.—T. HARTWELL HORNE.

Dr. Clarke's chief work, that on which he spent a laborious life, and on which his name will descend to posterity with the greatest lustre, is his Commentary on the Holy Scriptures. —REV. S. DUNN.

Our libraries needed to be enriched with expositions of Scripture, agreeing with our own views of truth,—a want which has been supplied in the varied excellences of a Benson, a Clarke, and a Watson. There are passages in Dr. Clarke's Commentary upon the Holy Scriptures which may be justly classed among the choicest productions of modern theology.—*Wes. Mag.*

This invaluable Commentary ought to be in the possession of every minister and student of theology.—*N. Y. Com. Adv.*

Dr. Clarke often succeeds to admiration in expressing the sense of Scripture.—*Columbian Star*, (Baptist.)

Watson's Dictionary.

A Biblical and Theological Dictionary: explanatory of the History, Manners, and Customs of the Jews and neighbouring Nations. With an Account of the most remarkable Places and Persons mentioned in Scripture; an Exposition of the principal Doctrines of Christianity; and Notices of Jewish and Christian Sects and Heresies. By RICHARD WATSON. With five Maps.

8vo., pp. 1007.	Sheep	$2 75
————	Plain calf	3 25
————	Calf gilt	3 50
————	Calf extra	4 00

This Dictionary is Biblical, Theological, and Ecclesiastical. It is fair in its statements, judicious in its selections, and sufficiently comprehensive in its scope. It is indeed a more complete body of divinity than are many works which have been published under that name.

Watson's Exposition.

An Exposition of the Gospels of Matthew and Mark, and of some other detached Parts of the Holy Scriptures. By RICHARD WATSON.

8vo., pp. 538.	Plain sheep	$1 75
————	Plain calf	2 00
————	Calf gilt	2 25
————	Calf extra	2 50

The sole object of this learned and original work is the elucidation of the Scriptures. The author has aimed to afford help to the attentive general reader, whenever he should come to a term, phrase, or a whole passage, the meaning of which is not obvious, and to exhibit the true Theology of the sacred volume. The notes, therefore, are brief upon the plainer passages, and most copious where explication appeared necessary. *No real difficulty has been evaded.*—T. HARTWELL HORNE.

The spirit of pure and elevated devotion with which the author's warm heart was so richly imbued, is plentifully diffused through these notes. Their direct tendency is to lead the soul to God. The work is complete as far as it extends, and it remains an affecting monument of its author's industry, piety, and Christian purposes.—*Wesleyan Magazine.*

Wesley's Notes on the New Testament.

Explanatory Notes on the New Testament. By Rev. JOHN WESLEY, A. M.

8vo., pp. 734.	Plain sheep	$1 80
————	Plain calf	2 20
————	Calf gilt	2 40
————	Calf extra	2 60

——— Pearl edition.

18mo., pp. 446.	Sheep	$1 00
————	Sheep extra	1 13
————	Morocco tucks, gilt edges	2 25

This work forms part of the course of study adopted by the last General Conference.

For a brief exposition of the sacred text, we have long considered the Notes of Mr. Wesley as the best extant; the sense is given in as few words as possible. We see that the commentator is a profound Biblical scholar, and that he gives us the results of the best efforts of both ancient and modern times for the illustration of the inspired writings of the New Testament. We have long wished Wesley's Notes more generally diffused among our people, and particularly that our young preachers might always have them at hand. We hope the present small and cheap edition (Pearl edition) will secure this desirable object. The work is beautifully got up. The type, though necessarily small, is exceedingly clear and readable. We earnestly recommend this edition of Wesley's Notes to our people, especially to the young of both sexes. But no *young preacher* should be without it.—*Methodist Quarterly Review.*

Though short, they are always judicious, accurate, spiritual, terse, and impressive, and possess the happy and rare excellence of leading the reader immediately to God and his own heart.—DR. A. CLARKE.

* *Wickens' Fulfilment of Scripture Prophecy.*

Fulfilment of Prophecy, as exhibited in Ancient History and Modern Travels. By STEPHEN B. WICKENS.

18mo., pp. 352. Muslin or sheep $0 45

Seldom have we read a volume of more real merit with such modest pretensions as this. The subject is universally interesting, but has generally been presented in too scholastic a form for the mass of readers. The present author has redeemed it from this objection, and by condensing the Biblical arguments, and interspersing throughout the volume a large amount of sacred geography and general history, has so enlivened his pages that the volume is rendered peculiarly interesting to the general reader. He has spared no labour in his researches, and has added to former expositions of prophecy information gleaned from every modern traveller of note.—*New-York Spectator.*

The author presents to the reader, within a small compass, and in an interesting form, the most satisfactory evidence that holy men of God spake as they were moved by the Holy Ghost.—*Presbyterian.*

This excellent compilation brings together into one view the results of the researches of modern travellers as they bear upon and illustrate the most important prophecies of Scripture.—*So. Chr. Advocate.*

This book may be read with advantage by all who love the study of prophecy.—*Baptist Christian Watchman.*

It goes over nearly the same ground as Keith, but is written in a more popular style, and is improved by extracts from some modern works, which Keith does not appear to have used.—*Baptist Advocate.*

The compiler has prepared an epitome of the fulfilment of Scripture prophecy, which elevates our views of the inspired volume, and will have a powerful tendency to convince the infidel of, and confirm the Christian's belief in, its truth.—*Canada Christian Guardian*

www.ingramcontent.com/pod-product-compliance
Lightning Source LLC
LaVergne TN
LVHW021105110826
845150LV00001B/179

9781425564957